D

Rediscover Shanghai on the Yangzi Delta:

A Historical Dictionary of China's Most Important City, from A to Z

Text & Photos by Eric N. Danielson

2019 Preface

This new book is based on the text from two previous books I wrote about this city, *Discover Shanghai* (2010), and *Shanghai and the Yangzi Delta* (2004), both issued by the same publisher in Singapore.   This current project started in October 2017 when I finally received the legal return of the copyright from the publisher of the two previous volumes.   It was originally intended to be simply a reprint or reissue of the previous volumes without any changes, but instead evolved into a year-long complete update and revision of the text that lasted throughout all of 2018 and on into the Spring Festival of 2019.

The new text has been completely updated and revised, and is now fully bilingual with both phonetic pinyin and Chinese characters provided for Chinese names of people and places, whereas the previous two volumes did not include any Chinese characters, and in some cases contained faulty translations that have since been corrected.

The text still begins with an introductory historical narrative in chronological order, but after that the contents are presented in alphabetical order from A to Z, as they were in *Discover Shanghai* (2010), but in stark contrast to the geographical organization of *Shanghai and the Yangzi Delta* (2004), which some people found confusing.

The Appendix includes a list of Shanghai's mayors and a historical street index which can be used to match the present-day street names with the names they had before 1949.

In the new appendix there are also four essays I've written on Shanghai since 2010, covering the topics of Shanghai's Lost Foreign Cemeteries, Jiangwan Town (Jiangwan Zhen) [江湾镇], the Bund (Waitan) [外滩], and Chongming Island.

This book contains all new photos that have never been published before.   None of them are the same as those previously published in my two prior volumes in 2010 and 2004.   The photos of the Bund (Waitan) [外滩] were taken in the Fall of 2010, those of Jiangwan Town (Jiangwan Zhen) [江湾镇] in February 2015, and the rest of them are all new shots taken in 2018. The photo on the front cover has also been changed from the two prior volumes. However, the text has become so long that most of the photos will need to be in Volume II.

There is an appendix containing a collection of historic maps of Shanghai, and the alphabetical sight entries do include the exact bilingual street address for each one.

The change Shanghai has experienced since I published *Discover Shanghai* (2010) are indeed remarkable, and even more so since I wrote my first book on the city, *Shanghai and the Yangzi Delta* (2004).   Much like the lyrics to Mike Monroe's song, *"Ballad of the Lower East Side,"* over the past 14 years Shanghai has experienced both capitalist economic gentrification, and a return of a more conservative social order, that together have made it almost too expensive for residents to live here, and in some ways has spoiled the charming local color that the city once had.   The wealth of historic architecture the city once had has continued to suffer from the twin demons of destruction to make way for the construction of new, modern buildings, and misguided preservation projects that often leave old buildings looking as if they were brand new.

Still, despite all these changes, I wouldn't choose to live anywhere else.   After nearly 20 years since I received my first job offer in Shanghai back in January 1998, I'm still living and working here.   It's my second hometown.

Eric N. Danielson
Shanghai, China
Spring Festival, February 2019

Table of Contents

Libraries
Longhua Airport
Longhua Buddhist Temple & Pagoda
Longhua Guomindang Military Garrison
Longhua Revolutionary Martyr's Cemetery
Lu Xun's Former House
Lu Xun Park
Maglev Line
Marble Hall
Marshall House
Mid-Lake Pavilion Tea House
Moganshan Lu Artists Colony
Moller Mansion
Morris Garden
Mosques
Museums
Nanjing East Road
Nanjing West Road
Nanxiang Dumplings
The Old Shanghai County Town
Pagodas
Park Hotel
People's Park
People's Square
Pudong New Area
Qingpu Town & District
Race Club Building
Shanghai Concert Hall
Shanghai Municipal Council Building
Sheshan Hill
Sheshan Observatory
Sheshan Roman Catholic Cathedral
Song Family Compound
Songjiang Ancient Mosque
Songjiang Town & District
Song Jiaoren's Tomb
Song Qingling's Former House
Song Qingling's Tomb
St. John's University
Stone Gate Houses
Subway System
Sun Yat-Sen's Former House
Suzhou Creek
Swire Mansion
Taoist Temples
Theaters
Tianma Shan Hill
Urban Planning Exhibition Center
West Bund
World Expo 2010

Xintiandi
Xujiahui French Catholic Community
Xujiahui Library
Yangzi River Waterfront
Yuanming Buddhist Lecture Hall
Yu Yuan Garden
Zhenru Buddhist Temple
Zhujiajiao Ancient Water Town

Appendix

XI. Photos
Note: These had to be put in a separate Volume II for reasons of space.

A Brief History of Shanghai

Shanghai's Early History: 713 A.D.-1842 A.D.

The development of Shanghai [上海] over time as an important urban center has throughout its history been inextricably linked with the changes in geography along China's three main inland waterways, the Yangzi River (Changjiang) [长江], the Hangzhou-Beijing Grand Canal (Jinghang Da Yunhe) [京杭大运河], and the Yellow River (Huang He) [黄河].   Likewise, the changing water-borne trade policies of various dynasties and regimes has alternately benefited and damaged Shanghai's economic growth and urban development.   A brief review of the history of this ever evolving geographic landscape and changes in government trade policy will help the reader to understand how, why and when Shanghai developed into the city we know today.

The land area of the modern day Shanghai Municipality (Shanghai Shi) [上海市] and surrounding Yangzi Delta has a very recent geological history, having been formed through the gradual eastward movement of the coastline over the past 2,000 years.   In the Eighth Century, the East China Sea coastline probably followed the present day course of the Huangpu River (Huangpu Jiang) [黄浦江].   During the **Xuanzong** [玄宗] reign (712-756) of the **Tang Dynasty** [唐代] (618-907) a dike was built along the western shore of the Huangpu River in 713 A.D. in order to protect the Shanghai area from the sea.   Prior to that time, much of the Yangzi Delta region was still under water or at best marshlands barely emerging from the sea.   The Yangzi Delta of the 8th Century has been described by Professor **Mark Elvin** as being a, "shifting landscape," and "a maze of canals."   Indeed, during the Taiping Rebellion (Taiping Tianguo) [太平天国](1850-1864) when Shanghai was attacked in three major offensives between 1860 and 1863, armies and troops traveled along the network of canals as far inland as the city's modern-day districts of Jiading [嘉定], Qingpu [青浦], and Songjiang [松江], with armed steamships playing a central role, and many crucial battles taking place in the city moats around the walled towns.   Even as late as 1932 **E.S. Wilkinson** was able to devote an entire book, _Shanghai Country Walks_, to primarily documenting and mapping the network of dozens of streams and canals which then still criss-crossed the greater Shanghai area and the dozens of wooden and stone foot bridges that crossed them.

In the **Tang Dynasty** [唐代] (618-907), Shanghai was a small fishing village known as **Hudu** [沪渎].   This village was located West of the Huangpu River [黄浦江], and South of what was then called the Song River (Song Jiang) [松江].   The Song River later changed its name to the Wusong River (Wusong Jiang) [吴淞江], and finally it became known in the past century as the Suzhou River (Suzhou He) [苏州河].   The Huangpu River [黄浦江] was originally considered to be a tributary of the Song or Wusong River, the reverse of what anyone would think today, which explains why the confluence of the Huangpu and Yangzi Rivers is still today known as Wusong Mouth (Wusong Kou) [吴淞口], rather than the seemingly more logical Huangpu Kou [黄浦口].   The Wusong River [吴淞江] originally flowed eastward from Lake Tai (Tai Hu) [太湖] directly to the East China Sea coastline, where it flowed into the Pacific Ocean (Taiping Yang) south of the mouth of the Yangzi River. Thus Shanghai in the Tang Dynasty was literally on the sea, which explains its name.   "Hai" means sea, and "shang" means above.   In fact, at that time the eastern section of today's city would have still been underwater.

In the middle of the Tang Dynasty [唐代] (618-907) Shanghai became part of a new county called **Huating** (Huating Xian) [华亭县], which was a part of Suzhou Prefecture (Suzhou Fu) [苏州府].   The main urban center of Huating County was the town of Songjiang.

The village of Hudu [沪渎] evolved into the town of Shanghai during the **Northern Song** (Bei Song) [北宋] (960-1126) and **Southern Song** (Nan Song) [南宋] (1127-1279) dynasties. Shanghai was officially upgraded in rank from a village (cun) to a market town (zhen) in **1074**. More important for the area's future development was the construction of a second sea dike in **1172**.   This **Song** Dynasty dike was located east of the earlier Tang Dynasty dike, thus pushing the seacoast further away from the area of settlement, and extending the Yangzi Delta lands into areas that had previously been submerged under water.

During the **Yuan Dynasty** [元朝] (1279-1368), 200 years after becoming a market town, Shanghai was upgraded in status again to the level of a county (xian) [县] in 1292, or by some accounts 1298.   Shanghai County (Shanghai Xian) [上海县] was created out of the northern parts of Huating County (Huating Xian) [华亭县], and headed by a County Magistrate (Zhixian) [知县], but was made part of the recently established Songjiang Prefecture (Songjiang Fu) [松江府], which was no longer subordinate to Suzhou, and was headed by a Prefectural Magistrate (Zhifu) [知府].   Songjiang Prefecture [松江府] had its capital at the old town of Huating [华亭], now renamed Songjiang Town.   The counties included in Songjiang prefecture were Huating [华亭县], Qingpu [青浦县], Nanhui [南汇县], Baoshan [宝山县], and Shanghai [上海县].   Huating County [华亭县] was then roughly equivalent to today's Songjiang District [松江区]. Thus, one can see that the territory of Songjiang Prefecture (Songjiang Fu) [松江府] in the 13th Century was almost identical to the area encompassed by the Shanghai Municipality (Shanghai Shi) [上海市] today, with some notable exceptions such as Jiading [嘉定] and Chongming [崇明], which were not yet included.   Shanghai's administrative status as a county attached to Songjiang Prefecture (Songjiang Fu) [松江府] would continue for over 600 years until the end of the Qing Dynasty [清朝] in 1911.

Although at this stage the city's growth seemed to be following an upward trend, Shanghai's economic and urban development suffered a series of three nearly fatal blows during the Ming Dynasty [明代] (1368-1644).

First of all, Ming Dynasty founder Zhu Yuanzhang [朱元璋] (1328-1398), who reigned as Emperor **Hongwu** [洪武] (1368-1398), decided to have coastal shipping shifted away from Shanghai to the Yangzi River port of Liuhe Kou [浏河口], the modern day port of **Taicang** [太仓] in Jiangsu Province.   Liuhe Kou [浏河口] was located on the Liu Stream (Liu He) [浏河], which was a small tributary of the Yangzi River.   This was likely the same river port later used by the fleets of Admiral **Zheng He** [郑和] (1371-1433) when they sailed to and from the East China Sea on seven voyages during the reign of the third Ming Dynasty Emperor **Yongle** [永乐] (1403-1424).   Nowadays, Taicang Port is a major oil shipment center, where oil tankers belonging to Exxon Mobil, BP, and Shell anchor at docks extending far out into the Yangzi River.

Next, Zhu Di [朱棣] (1360-1424), who reigned as the third Ming Emperor Yongle [永乐] (1403-1424) decided to restore the Hangzhou-Beijing **Grand Canal** (Jinghang Da Yunhe) [京杭大运河], which had not functioned since the end of the Southern Song Dynasty (1127-1279).   Reconstruction began in 1411 and the section between the Yangzi River (Changjiang) [长江] and the Yellow River (Huang He) [黄河] was finally opened to traffic in July 1415.   As a result, coastal ships stopped carrying the annual grain tribute from the South to the northern capital in Beijing, and instead barges began taking the shipments up the inland canal system.   Since the Grand Canal traveled through Zhejiang and Southern Jiangsu provinces (the Jiangnan region) from Hangzhou to Suzhou, and then crossed the Yangzi River at Zhenjiang where it traveled through Northern Jiangsu (Jiangbei) via Yangzhou and on northward to Xuzhou, where it crossed into Shandong Province, this meant that Shanghai was now being entirely bypassed by this important aspect of maritime trade.

The third fatal blow to Shanghai's earlier prosperity was the gradual change in maritime trade policy during the century after the death of Zhu Zhanji [朱瞻基] (1398-1435), who reigned as Emperor Xuande [宣德] (1426-1435).   Although during the reigns of the two emperors Yongle [永乐](1403-1424) and Xuande [宣德] (1426-1435), the admiral **Zheng He** [郑和] (1371-1433) had sailed seven voyages around the world, using Nanjing as his base, the successors who reigned after Xuande [宣德] (1426-1435) halted any further construction of ocean-going vessels in a major change of policy.   In 1477 the written records of Zheng He's seven voyages were actually removed from the government archives and apparently destroyed.   By 1500, two-masted ships were the largest permitted to be built.   Ships of this size were only suitable for inland waterways, and were too small for ocean voyages. Finally, in 1525 an imperial edict ordered the destruction of all existing ocean-going ships and the arrest of any merchants caught sailing them.

Professor Linda Cooke Johnson has concluded that these three changes in Ming Dynasty maritime trade policy ushered in "a three hundred year decline" for Shanghai, during which the town actually shrank in both size and population.   Nonetheless, at leas two other positive developments occurred for Shanghai during the Ming Dynasty.

The first positive development came in 1404 when local authorities changed the main channel of what is now known as the Suzhou River (Suzhou He) [苏州河], but was then known as either the Song River (Song Jiang) [松江] or Wusong River (Wusong Jiang) [吴淞江], so that rather than flowing east to the sea as it had until then, it would instead turn north at Shanghai and flow towards a confluence with the Yangzi River, at a spot still known today as Wusong Mouth (Wusong Kou) [吴淞口].   Although the other changes in Ming Dynasty maritime trade policy prevented Shanghai from immediately reaping any benefits from this rerouting of the Wusong River, the long-term effects were immense.   Later in the Qing Dynasty when maritime trade policy was changed again, Shanghai would be ideally connected to the Yangzi River trade route in a way it never had been before.

Secondly, in 1554 local residents finally succeeded in petitioning the Ming Dynasty to build a town wall (chengchiang) [城墙] and moat (huchenghe) [护城河] around the Shanghai county town (Shanghai xiancheng) [上海县城] in an area that was once known variously as **Nanshi** [南市区] or **Nantao** (Nandao) [南岛].   The Shanghai county town (xiancheng) [上海县城] had never had a defensive wall before this time, and the fortifications gave it much added security against the repeated lootings it had previously suffered from Japanese pirates (woko) [倭寇].   However, this wall was not very high or very long, compared to other city walls such as those in Nanjing.   It was roughly ten meters in height and five kilometers in circumference.   A city map from the Tongzhi [同治] (1861-1875) reign of the Qing Dynasty shows that the town wall then had seven land gates (chengmen) [城门], four water gates (shuiguan) [水关], and four watch towers (genglou) [更楼].   The circular pattern of the former wall and surrounding moat can still be seen in the location of **Renmin Lu** [人民路] and **Zhonghua Lu** [中华路], which were built in their place in 1912 after the wall was torn down and the moat filled in.

Thus, by the late Ming Dynasty, the Shanghai county town (xiancheng) [上海县城] was fully protected by a surrounding wall (chengqiang) [城墙] and moat (huchenghe) [护城河], but it was smaller than it had been in the Song and Yuan dynasties, and it had lost the economic benefits of its previous role in coastal maritime trade.   Nonetheless, it was still an important enough town to have its existing **City God Temple** (Chenghuang Miao)[城隍庙] rebuilt in 1602 during the reign of Ming Emperor **Wanli** [万历] (1573-1620). This same temple still stands today in the Yu Yuan Bazaar) (Yuyuan Shangcheng) [豫园商城] area of the former Nanshi District (Nanshi Qu) [南市区].

During the middle of the Qing Dynasty (1644-1911), **Shanghai County** (Shanghai Xian) [上海县] experienced a number of events that gradually revived its economy and urban development.   Qing Emperor **Kangxi** [康熙] (1661-1722) reversed the previous Ming Dynasty prohibitions on ocean-going vessels in **1684**, thus giving Shanghai the opportunity to resume its previous role as an important coastal port.   As part of the resumption of maritime trade, Emperor **Kangxi** [康熙] in **1688** established a network of new customs stations for the four southern coastal provinces of Jiangsu, Zhejiang, Fujian and Guangdong. The main customs' collection station for Jiangsu province was initially located at Songjiang Town, the capital of **Songjiang Prefecture** (Songjiang Fu) [松江府], to which **Shanghai County** (Shanghai Xian) [上海县] still belonged.   Shanghai was just one of 22 smaller branches under the administration of the Jiangsu provincial customs office headquartered in Songjiang.   As such, administratively it was considered on the same level as other provincial customs house branches at Taicang [太仓] and Zhenjiang [镇江].

Thus, in the 17th Century **Shanghai County** (Shanghai Xian) [上海县] was still at the bottom of the ladder in terms of both political and economic institutions.   Politically it was a county (xian) [县] on the same level as Qingpu, headed by a County Magistrate (Zhixian) [知县], and under the direction of the Songjiang prefecture (Songjiang Fu) [松江府] government, headed by a Prefectural Magistrate (Zhifu) [知府].   Economically its role in maritime trade was the same as that of **Taicang** [太仓], then known as Liuhe Kou [浏河口].

However, in the early 18th century two important government policy changes made by the Qing Dynasty Emperor Yongzheng [雍正] (1722-1735) revived the city's political and economic development once and for all.

The first change came in September 1724, the second year of the Yongzheng reign, when Shanghai's political role was given a boost with the establishment of an office of Circuit Intendant (Daotai) [道台] in Shanghai to oversee the Suzhou-Songjiang-Taicang Circuit. The Circuit Intendant (Daotai) [道台] was appointed directly by the Emperor and was responsible for military defense and customs tariffs in his circuit (taidao) [太道]. He ranked above both the Shanghai County Magistrate (Zhixian) [知县], and the Songjiang Prefectural Magistrate (Zhifu) [知府].

For roughly 186 years, from 1725 until 1911, Suzhou and Songjiang prefectures were jointly governed as part of an administrative division known as the Susong Taidao [苏松太道], which was attached to Jiangsu Province [江苏省]. It was headed by a government official known as the Daotai [道台] whose government office (yamen) [衙门] was located in Shanghai County [上海县], inside the Big East Gate (Da Dong Men) of the walled county town, which was part of Songjiang Prefecture (Songjiang Fu). As a result, the official was sometimes also known as the Shanghai Daotai [上海道台]. The available existing records of 55 officials who were appointed as the Shanghai Doatai during this time period show that they were never natives of Shanghai or Jiangsu, but instead always came from other parts of China, The ethnic Han Chinese appointed to the post came from Zhejiang (12), Hunan (9), Guangdong (5), Anhui (5), Shandong (3), Jiangxi (3), Henan (3), Shanxi (2), Hubei (1), Guangxi (1), and Sichuan (1) provinces. At least eight of the 55 Shanghai Daotai were ethnic Manchus (Manzu) [满族] whose ancestors hailed from Liaoning Province up in Northeastern China. The native place of two Shanghai Daotai is unknown. The Daotai position was frequently rotated to new appointees, often changing once a year and sometimes even twice in one year. Although there were a couple who managed to survive for five or six years, most officials were lucky if they could keep the post for three to four years. However, there is no record available for the first five years from 1725 to 1730, and a long gap in recorded appointments from 1749 to 1837.

More important for Shanghai's economic development was the second change made by the Qing Emperor **Yongzheng** [雍正] (1722-1735), when in 1732 **he** decided to move the headquarters for the Jiangsu provincial customs from the prefectural capital in Songjiang to the Shanghai county town (Shanghai xiancheng) [上海县城]. Furthermore, Shanghai county town (Shanghai xiancheng) [上海县城] was made the exclusive customs station for all the foreign trade of Jiangsu province.

As a result of the policy changes instituted by the Qing emperors Kangxi [康熙] and Yongzheng [雍正], Professor Linda Cooke Johnson has concluded that, "By **1735** Shanghai had become the major port of entry and exit for the produce and coastal traffic of the whole lower Yangzi region," even though, "In its official role as a county seat for Shanghai Xian it was on the lowest level in the governing hierarchy of county, prefecture, and province."

In the **1820**s the Hangzhou-Beijing Grand Canal (Jinghang Da Yunhe) [京杭大运河] once again began to become unnavigable in its northern section due to flooding on the Yellow River (Huang He)[黄河], which had started changing its course in a new direction.   As a result, in **1824** shipment of the annual grain tribute north to Beijing was transferred from inland canal barges to ocean-going vessels operated out of Shanghai.   This of course gave Shanghai's maritime trade-based economy another huge boost.

However, none of these benefits of maritime trade which came Shanghai's way during the mid-**Qing** Dynasty would have ever occurred if the Wusong River had continued to flow directly into the East China sea, instead of having been rerouted during the Ming Dynasty to flow North into the Yangzi River at Wusong Port (Wusong Kou) [吴淞口].   In fact, during the Qing Dynasty the main body of water flowing from Shanghai to Wusong Kou [吴淞口] was known as the Wusong River (Wusong Jiang) [吴淞江], and was not called the Huangpu River (Huangpu Jiang) [黄浦江] as it is today, which explains why the confluence of the Huangpu and Yangzi Rivers is still called Wusong Kou [吴淞口] instead of Huangpu Kou [黄浦口].   Two of the first European visitors to Shanghai, Hugh Hamilton Lindsay and Karl Friedrich August Gutzlaff, recorded after their brief visit on the ship HMS Lord Amherst in **1832** that the waterway between present-day downtown Shanghai and the Yangzi River was still called the Wusong River (Wusong Jiang) [吴淞江] by local inhabitants.

Thus, prior to its opening to foreign trade as a Treaty Port in **1842**, Shanghai county town (Shanghai xiancheng) [上海县城] had already been an important economic center for about 100 years.   However, its economic strength was never matched by an equal political importance.   In fact, it was not even considered a city by the Qing Dynasty government, but instead was attached as a suburban satellite county to Songjiang prefecture (Songjiang Fu) [松江府], the capital of which was then still considered a much more important urban center. As late as the mid-19th century, two of present-day Shanghai's outlying suburban districts, **Songjiang** [松江] and **Jiading** [嘉定], both had more temples, gardens, scholar-officials, and other traditional signs of wealth than the area we now know as downtown Shanghai. Thanks to more recent economic development in the city center, it is the outlying suburban districts that today offer the most well-preserved, pre-colonial era historic sights to see.

Establishment of The Foreign Concessions: 1842-1863

After having begun down in Guangzhou in 1839, the First Opium War between Britain and China moved north in the Spring of 1842 when a massive armada of approximately 75 warships assembled at the mouth of the Yangzi River under the joint command of Admiral Sir William Parker, General Sir Hugh Gough and diplomatic plenipotentiary Colonel Sir Henry Pottinger.   The British fleet sailed 30 miles up the Yangzi River to attack the Wusong Forts (Wusong Paotai) [吴淞炮台] where the Huangpu River flows into the Yangzi River in present-day Baoshan District (Boashan Qu) [宝山区].   During a four-and-a-half hour naval bombardment on the morning of June 16, 1842, the leader of the Chinese defense, Chen Huacheng was blown to smithereens, and the next day the Wusong Forts (Wusong Paotai) [吴淞炮台] were occupied by landing parties from the 9,000 British troops commanded by General Gough.   On June 19, 1842 the British fleet sailed 15 miles up the Huangpu River and anchored outside of the walled county town of Shanghai (Shanghai xiancheng) [上海县城], which surrendered without a fight.

Shanghai made a favorable impression on the British, who except for the 1832 Lord Amherst expedition were the first foreign visitors to see the town since the expulsion of the Jesuits in the early 18th century. Captain Arthur Cunynghame described the town as a "great entrepot of commerce," and "a place of considerable wealth and active trade." After Pottinger and Gough had enjoyed five days of residence in the town's Yu Garden (Yu Yuan) [豫园], the British fleet departed and sailed back up the Huangpu River to Wusong Kou [吴淞口], and then proceeded westward up the Yangzi River. After capturing the town of **Zhenjiang** [镇江] in a fierce battle on July 21, the British fleet anchored outside the city walls of **Nanjing** [南京] on August 5, 1842.

Shanghai's history was forever changed by the resulting August 29, 1842 **Treaty of Nanking** (Zhongying Nanjing Tiaoyue) [中英南京條約] between Britain and China, which ended the First Opium War. This treaty not only ceded Hong Kong to Britain as an outright colony, but gave British citizens certain extraterritorial rights to live in China free from Chinese law or governance in five treaty ports, including Shanghai, Guangzhou, Xiamen, Fuzhou and Ningbo. The Americans and the French soon followed the British example by signing similar treaties with China. The Sino-American **Treaty of Wangxia** negotiated by Caleb Cushing and Peter Parker signed on July 3, 1844, and the Sino-French **Treaty of Whampoa** signed on October 24, 1844, both gave their citizens similar extraterritorial rights to live in China within the five designated treaty ports.

Three foreign settlements were set up in Shanghai shortly thereafter. The British, the Americans and the French all staked out their respective concessions on the West side of the Huangpu River (Puxi) [浦西], in the area that comprises the center of downtown Shanghai today. The Sino-British Land Regulations of 1845 set the initial boundaries and rights of the **British Settlement** (Shanghai Ying Zujie) [上海英租界]. The French concluded an agreement with local Chinese authorities for the establishment of their **French Concession** (Shanghai Fa Zujie) [上海法租界] on April 6, 1849. The **American Settlement** (Shanghai Mei Zujie) [上海美租界] was established in February 1854 by the first U.S. Consul in what was then called Hongkou [虹口], or Yangzi Pu, but what is today known as Yangpu [杨浦].

In July 1854 the three foreign settlements tried to come together to establish a unified governing body known as the **Shanghai Municipal Council**, but the French dropped out of the arrangement in 1862.

The British and American concessions were later merged into the International Settlement (Shanghai Gonggong Zujie) [上海公共租界] in **1863**, but the French resisted efforts to merge their concession, leaving Shanghai with two separate foreign controlled settlements located side by side.

After their establishment, the British-American International Settlement and the French Concession both functioned as self-governing entities with their own municipal governments, court systems, educational institutions, police forces, militia, and public utilities. They taxed their foreign and Chinese residents alike, built expansive public works including networks of roads, bridges, and public parks, and defended their territory against outside invasion.

13

The Small Sword and Taiping Rebellions

The occupation of the old walled city of Nanshi by the **Small Sword Society** (Xiaodao Hui) [小刀会] in September 1853 posed the first serious threat to the foreign concessions and resulted in the creation of the first voluntary military force comprised of foreign residents. The **Shanghai Volunteer Corps (SVC)** had its origins in the celebrated April 4, 1854 **Battle of Muddy Flat**, when 300 British and American volunteers defeated a Chinese force of 10,000 troops that was threatening the western frontier of the foreign concessions, then a line known as Defence Creek which roughly followed present-day Tibet Midddle Road (Xizang Zhong Lu), just East of People's Square (Renmin Guangchang) [人民广场]. Ironically, in this battle the foreigners' SVC was allied with the Small Sword Society (Xiaodao Hui) [小刀会] against Qing Dynasty troops.   The evacuation of the old walled town by the Small Sword Society (Xiaodao Hui) [小刀会] in February 1855 did not mean the end to the immediate threat to the concessions security as there was still the Taiping rebellion to contend with.   Nonetheless, the SVC did not become an official permanent fighting force until 1870 when the Shanghai Municipal Council took over responsibility for funding, equipping and housing it.   During its 78 years of existence the SVC would be mobilized 25 times to deal with various domestic disturbances, social unrest and emergencies in the city.

The **Taiping Rebellion** (Taiping Tianguo) [太平天国] (1850-1864), during which Shanghai was attacked three times between 1860 and 1862, caused the creation of several other volunteer foreign military units to defend the concessions.   In these cases the foreign units aided the Qing Dynasty troops against the Taiping rebels, making important contributions to the recapture of the towns of Songjiang and Suzhou from the rebels.   The American General **Frederick Townsend Ward** and his successor the British General **Charles George Gordon** were able to make themselves world famous with their exploits in the defense of the Shanghai area.   Ward ended up being buried like an emperor with a Chinese-style temple dedicated to him in Songjiang Town (Ward's memorial temple no longer exists), while Gordon and the other foreign volunteers were collectively memorialized with a monument in the Public Gardens on the Bund (Gordon's monument was destroyed after 1949).   These contributions to the defense of Shanghai gave the resident foreign community even more a sense of ownership over their concessions.

The Taipings' First Shanghai Offensive: June 1860-August 1860

At a May 2, 1860 council of Taiping leaders in Nanjing, the decision was made to target Shanghai with a new offensive to try to break out of the encirclement of their capital city by Qing forces under the command of Zeng Guofan.   The man put in charge of capturing Shanghai was **Li Xiucheng**, the **Loyal King** (Zhong Wang),, who would spend the next three years absorbed in this effort.   When the Taipings did break out of the Nanjing siege in the spring of 1860 and headed East towards Shanghai, the Qing commander Zeng Guofan was focusing on Taiping strongholds to the West of Nanjing, such as the Yangzi River town of Anqing, and there was no effective Qing army to defend China's eastern coastal region.

After capturing Suzhou on June 2, 1860, the Taiping army commanded by the Zhong Wang approached Shanghai from the West and Northwest between June 17 and June 22, 1860, capturing the northwestern towns of Taicang and **Jiading**.   Ward's newly founded corps of foreign mercenaries joined Qing troops in recapturing both towns on June 26, 1860.

However, soon after the town of **Songjiang** fell to the Taipings for the first time. Songjiang Town was then surrounded by a wide moat and a city wall four miles in circumference with double gates in the Ming Dynasty style. Ward's first attempt to recapture Songjiang town at the end of June 1860 was unsuccessful.

In mid-July 1860 Ward's corps made a second attempt to recapture **Songjiang** Town from the Taipings, who had already succeeded in capturing most of the towns around the present-day city center of Shanghai. On July 16, 1860 Ward's corps advanced on **Songjiang** Town for a second attempt at recapturing it from the Taipings. He left his base camp at **Guangfulin** [广富林] (near Sheshan Hill), and approached the city at night using river steamships to sail up the network of canals, enter the city moat, and thereby reach the city gates. The interior of the walled city was bombarded by six pieces of Taiping artillery, which Ward had captured and turned around. Ward established his headquarters near the Songjiang Confucius Temple. After the July 16-17, 1860 third battle for Songjiang, the Taipings retreated to the nearby town of **Sijing**, which nowadays is located in Songjiang District.

At the end of July 1860 the Ward Corps began planning to recapture the town of **Qingpu** from the Taipings. Qingpu Town, located at an important intersection of inland waterways, was then surrounded by a circular wall and moat. In the unsuccessful attack of August 2, 1860, Ward was wounded five times and lost half of his men in attempting to seize the South Gate (Nan Men) of the **Qingpu** city wall. On August 9, 1860 Ward's corps returned to besiege **Qingpu** once again, but failed a second time and was forced to retreat to Songjiang town.

On August 18, 1860 the Taipings captured **Xujiahui** [徐家汇], a center of French Catholic missionary activity in the 19th and early 20th centuries, but nowadays a popular shopping area on the western fringes of the Shanghai city center, and it was probably then when Longhua Temple (Longhua Si) [龙华寺] was destroyed. Soon after capturing Xujiahui the Taipings reached the city wall protecting the Shanghai County Town (xiancheng) in Nanshi, but the gates were defended by a combined force of Qing, British, American, and French troops, who were well armed with modern weapons. By August 20, 1860 the Taipings were encamped just "half a mile" from the British Settlement's horse racing course, which is today occupied by People's Park (Renmin Gongyuan) [人民公园] and People's Square (Renmin Guangchang) [人民广场]. However, on August 24, 1860 the Zhong Wang gave up his first attempt to capture Shanghai and withdrew all Taiping troops away from the city center. Nonetheless, most of the towns in the countryside surrounding Shanghai were still occupied by Taiping garrisons.

<u>Shanghai's Quiet Interlude: Sept. 1860-December 1861</u>

In October 1860 Admiral Sir James Hope arrived in Shanghai to take command of British military forces in the area.   On February 12, 1861 Hope sailed up the Yangzi River with a fleet of ten British warships.

Admiral Hope entered into successful negotiations with the Taipings in their capital city of **Nanjing**, whereby the British pledged to remain neutral in the Chinese civil war between the Taipings and the Qing Dynasty.   In exchange, the Taipings agreed to allow the British to established three new consulates in cities under their control, including Hankou, and guaranteed the security of British maritime trade on the Yangzi River.   Most importantly for the history of Shanghai was the Taipings' promise not to attack the city for a period of one year, with Admiral Hope declaring he would defend a thirty-mile radius around the city center.

The Taipings launched a new offensive in Eastern China with the capture of the treaty port of Ningbo in present-day Zhejiang province in the beginning of December 1861.   The Taipings' capture of Ningbo seemed to threaten the year-long truce they had agreed to in respect to Shanghai, so in late December Admiral Hope made a second journey up the Yangzi River to Nanjing.   However, this time he failed to get a renewal of the earlier February 1861 agreement.

<u>The Taipings' Second Shanghai Offensive: January 1862-May 1862</u>

By January 1862 **Li Xiucheng** [李秀成] (1823-1864), the Taipings' Loyal King (Zhong Wang) [忠王], was marching towards Shanghai with an estimated force of 100,000 men.   At the time, Shanghai's foreign garrison amounted to only 600 British and not more than 500 French troops.   By early January 1862 the Taipings had reached **Wusong Kou** [吴淞口], but the town was successfully defended by the Ward Corps among others.   However, the town of **Gaoqiao** across the Huangpu River from Wusong Kou in Pudong was captured by the Taipings.

The Taipings once again controlled all of **Qingpu** County, as well as parts of Songjiang County, such as Tianma Shan Hill and Guangfulin.   However on February 5, 1862 the Ward Corps recaptured the small hill of Tianma Shan from the Taipings.   It may have been during this fighting that the Huzhu Ta Pagoda on Tianma Shan Hill was damaged, as it still bears a giant hole in one side today.   In February 1862 **Songjiang Town**, 25 miles southwest of the Shanghai city center, was under siege by 20,000 Taipings with the Ward Corps trapped inside.   On February 20, 1862 a mixed force of British, French and Ward Corps troops attacked and recaptured the town of **Gaoqiao** in Pudong, where a monument still marks the site today.   In March 1862 the Taipings were still in control of all of **Qingpu** County and had besieged the Qing garrison at Sijing Town in Songjiang District.   On March 14, 1862 the Ward Corps broke the siege of **Sijing** Town and rescued the Qing garrison that had been trapped inside.

During the spring of 1862 the anti-Taiping coalition of military forces around Shanghai experienced three key changes in leadership, with the arrival of British General Sir Charles Staveley; Li Hongzhang [李鸿章] (1823-1901), the new Qing commander of the Huai Army (Huai Jun) [淮军]; and British adventurer Charles Gordon.   All together these three events combined to make 1862 a turning point in the defense of Shanghai against the Taiping rebels.

In late March 1862, General Sir Charles Staveley arrived in Shanghai to take command of British troops, who now numbered 2,500 men.   On April 22, 1862 the British and French military commanders in Shanghai agreed that they should clear the Taipings from a 30-mile radius around the city center.   They specifically targeted the surrounding county towns of Jiading, Qingpu and Songjiang as being necessary for them to keep out of Taiping hands. Of the three towns, Qingpu and Jiading were then occupied by the Taipings.

Li Hongzhang [李鸿章] (1823-1901) was formally appointed Governor of Jiangsu Province (which then included all of present-day Shanghai) on April 25, 1862.   This appointment had taken nearly two years to get approved, since Zeng Guofan [曾国藩] (1811-1872) as Imperial Commissioner for Jiangnan had first proposed it in August 1860.   Even before his appointment had been formally approved, Li Hongzhang [李鸿章] (1823-1901) had arrived at Zeng Guofan's headquarters in Anqing, Anhui with 8,000 men of his newly formed Huai Army (Huai Jun) [淮军] of recruits from northern Anhui and Jiangsu provinces north of the Yangzi River.

On April 25, 1862 a Qing army successfully attacked the Taiping garrison at the town of **Nanxiang** in Jiading County.   The capture of Nanxiang opened the way for an advance on the Taiping stronghold of Jiading Town.   The occupation of Nanxiang was followed on April 30, 1862 by the convergence of about 6,400 Qing, British, French and Ward Corps troops outside the walls of **Jiading** Town.   On May 1, 1862 the allied force successfully assaulted **Jiading** Town's city walls, which were three miles in circumference, and defended by 6,000 Taipings.   500 of Ward's Corps garrisoned **Jiading Town**, while the rest returned to Songjiang Town by steamship and gunboat.

Charles George Gordon, then an Engineer in active British military service, was transferred from Tianjin to Shanghai, where he arrived on May 3, 1862.   Gordon arrived just in time to take part in the next recapture of the Taipings' stronghold of Qingpu Town.

Ward planned another assault on the Taipings at **Qingpu** Town for the second week of May 1862.   An allied force of about 4,600 Qing, British and Ward Corps troops arrived at the Taiping stronghold of **Qingpu** Town on May 10, 1862 after sailing from Songjiang in a fleet of steamships and gunboats.   On May 10, 1862 Gordon reconnoitered the Taiping's **Qingpu** Town defenses by taking a small boat up a canal and sheltering under a "small pagoda" (possibly the Wanshou Ta).   He estimated that the moat around the town was 90 feet wide, and the town walls 20 feet high.   **Qingpu** Town was captured by the British force after naval guns blew a breach in the wall. On May 12, 1862 **Qingpu** Town was successfully recaptured from the Taipings and garrisoned by 1,500 Ward Corps troops under Edward Forester.   At this point in mid-May 1862 all three key county towns of Songjiang, Qingpu, and Jiading had been recaptured from the Taipings.

The Taipings' Third Shanghai Offensive: May 1862-October 1862

However, the defeat of a Qing force at Taicang on May 17, 1862 led to a Taiping counter-attack all along Shanghai's 30-mile radius defensive perimeter. The three key county towns of Jiading, Qingpu and Songjiang were all besieged, lines of communications cut, and Guangfulin in Songjiang County was reoccupied. On May 26, 1862 the British garrison evacuated **Jiading** Town, which they had held since May 1st, and it was then reoccupied by the Taipings once again. The county towns of **Songjiang** and **Qingpu** were both garrisoned by the Ward Corps and subjected to lengthy sieges. Breaches previously made in the city walls by artillery during earlier battles had not yet been repaired.

On June 1, 1862 Ward, in command of the garrison at **Songjiang** Town, decided to burn down the suburbs outside the city wall as a defense tactic. Ward's ships were still able to enter and leave the walled city through the water gates (shui men).

Ward and Admiral Hope succeeded in reaching **Qingpu** Town by ship from Songjiang Town on June 10, 1862 and rescued the Ward Corps garrison, which had been trapped there under siege by the Taipings since mid-May. However, Ward made no attempt to hold onto Qingpu Town this time, and instead had the town burned down before retreating back to Songjiang town.

By the end of June 1862 the only places in Songjiang Prefecture not occupied by the Taiping forces of the Loyal King (Zhong Wang) were the walled fortresses of the **Shanghai** county town (xiancheng) and **Songjiang** Town. Every other important town within the 30-mile radius around the present-day Shanghai city center was held by the Taiping rebels. In the summer of 1862 **Li Hongzhang** [李鸿章] (1823-1901), the new Governor of Jiangsu Province, took charge of the military campaign against the Taipings in the Shanghai area, under the oversight of Zeng Guofan [曾国藩] (1811-1872), the Viceroy of the three Liang Jiang provinces of Jiangsu, Anhui and Jiangxi. Li's arrival, along with his so-called **Huai Army** (Huai Jun) [淮军], eventually resulted in greater Chinese leadership of the local struggle against the Taipings and a diminished freedom of action for the various foreign armies and freebooters who had until then acted largely independent of Chinese authority.

In July 1862 a new strategy focused on first evicting the Taipings from territory East of the Huangpu River in an area now known as the Pudong New District (Pudong Xinqu). On July 7, 1862 Li Hongzhang's Huai Army succeeded in recapturing **Fengxian** County and then advanced on Jinshan County. On July 17 a combined Qing-Ward Corps forced recaptured **Jinshan** County from the Taipings.

On August 5, 1862 a combined Huai Army-Ward Corps force assembled outside the city walls of **Qingpu** Town, which had been held by the Taipings since June 10. The battle for **Qingpu** Town began on August 7, 1862, but despite the use of artillery and ship's guns it took four whole days until enough breaches were made in the city walls that the South Gate (Nan Men) could be entered and the town recaptured on August 10 for the second time in four months. However, much of the Taiping garrison had escaped through the North and West gates, and in mid-August **Qingpu** Town was once again besieged by a force of 20,000 Taipings. The Qing-Ward Corps garrison successfully resisted the siege of Qingpu town for several days, but soon after this victory **Ward** suffered a fatal injury during a battle outside of Ningbo, in Zhejiang province, on September 20, 1862. The command of his force fell temporarily to his fellow American H.A. Burgevine.

Although the Taipings had lost Songjiang and Qingpu county towns, **Jiading** Town was still held by the Taipings until the fall of 1862.   **Jiading** Town was the last major stronghold still held by the Taipings in the Shanghai area when it was attacked again on October 23, 1862 by an allied military force including British land troops under General Staveley, British naval forces under Admiral Hope, and units of the EVA under Ward's immediate successor Henry A. Burgevine, and **Gordon**.   Success was achieved on October 24, 1862 when artillery breached holes in the town wall and the attackers crossed the town moat across bridges of boats tied together.   This was the third time that Jiading had changed hands in four months.   Jiading was thus the first town in the present-day Shanghai metropolitan area to be captured by the Taipings in the summer of 1860 and the last one they finally abandoned in the fall of 1862.

After this the greater Shanghai area was never seriously threatened by the Taiping rebels again, and the battles Gordon was involved in with the other Qing forces under Li Hongzhang [李鸿章] (1823-1901) moved on to first Taicang, then Suzhou, and finally Nanjing itself.

Eventually, Major **Gordon** was recommended as a replacement for Burgevine by General Staveley on January 17, 1863.   However, **Gordon** himself apparently did not know of his own appointment until March 24, 1863.   In his diary entry for March 27, 1863, the Jiangsu Provincial Governor **Li Hongzhang** [李鸿章] (1823-1901), who had detested both Ward and Burgevine, praised **Gordon**'s appointment as "a direct blessing from Heaven." *
* Quoted from J.W. Foster, "*Memoirs of Li Hung Chang*."

The International Settlement (Shanghai Gonggong Zujie) [上海公共租界]

As previously noted, the Shanghai Municipal Council had been established in July 1854, but it was not until 1863 when the International Settlement (Shanghai Gonggong Zujie) [上海公共租界] was created out of the merger of the former British Settlement (Shanghai Ying Zujie) [上海英租界] and American Settlement (Shanghai Mei Zujie) [上海美租界].   It occupied most of the **Bund** (Waitan) [外滩] waterfront along the Huangpu River, as well as parts of what are now Hongkou and Yangpu districts north of the Suzhou River.   The main street of the International Settlement was **Nanking Road**, today's Nanjing East Road (Nanjing Dong Lu) [南京东路], which at its intersection with **Tibet Road** (Xizang Lu) changed its name to **Bubbling Well Road** (Nanjing Xi Lu).   It was in this settlement that most business and commerce took place.   The northern limits were clearly marked by **Suzhou Creek** west of Xizang Zhong Lu and the appropriately named **Boundary Road** (Tianmu Lu) in the Zhabei district.   Shanghai's North Train Station sat just across the Settlement's northern boundary, in the same place where the modern station stands today.   The Settlement's eastern limit was the **Huangpu River**, and the southern limit the boundary with the French Concession along what was originally a canal known as the **Yangjingbang** but later became Yanan Dong Lu and Yanan Xi Lu.   In 1853 the western boundary of the British Concession had been considered to follow the North-South line of **Defence Creek**, where present day Xizang Zhong Lu (Tibet Middle Road) runs, but since this boundary had not actually been clearly marked in the original agreements with Chinese authorities, over time the International Settlement was able to continue expanding in a westward direction.

One method of covert expansion was an aggressive road building program, which consistently extended far outside the settlement's established boundaries. Once a new road was built, the Settlement authorities would insist that all residents and businesses located along it must pay taxes to the Shanghai Municipal Council. In turn, as taxpayers they were then entitled to Settlement police, fire and militia protection. The Settlement authorities would then appeal to the Chinese government that these taxpayers and roads outside the concession boundaries should be brought inside by extending the boundary to include them. Use of this method over time resulted in extending the Settlement's official western boundary as far as the Buddhist temple **Jingan Si** on Bubbling Well Road (Nanjing Xi Lu), near the latter's convergence with Yanan Xi Lu.

However, there was a very large western area of Shanghai known as the **Outside Roads Area** (Yuejie Zhulu) [越界筑路], which was never formally annexed into the Settlement, although repeated attempts were made to do so. Nonetheless, this Outside Roads Area had municipal streets and parks which were built, maintained and policed by the Shanghai Municipal Council, and foreign residents who paid taxes to the Settlement authorities.

The concentrated area of foreign settlement in western Shanghai extended as far West as the north-south line followed by **Keswick Road** (Kaixuan Lu), which still runs parallel to the modern day Zhongshan Lu ring road. In fact, the first 13 kilometer-long Zhongshan ring road was originally built by the local Chinese municipal government on the site of the present one in 1928 in an attempt to restrict the expansion of the foreign settlements. **Jessfield Park**, now known as Zhongshan Park (Zhongshan Gongyuan) [中山公园], was owned and operated by the International Settlement in this Outside Roads Area, and the American missionary run **St. John's University** (Shanghai Sheng Yuehan Daxue) [上海圣约翰大学], founded in 1879, was located right across the street from the rear entrance to the park. The **McTyeire Girls School**, founded in 1890 and attended by the famous Soong sisters, was also located in this Western Outside Roads Area on Edinburgh Road (Jiangsu Lu), which ran from Avenue Haig (Huashan Lu) in the south to Brennan Road (Changning Lu) in the north.

Although the **Western Outside Roads Area** (Huxi Yuejie Zhulu) [沪西越界筑路] largely stopped at Keswick Road (Kaixuan Lu), there were a few Outside Roads built by the Shanghai Municipal Council which extended as far west as the north-south line of the aptly named **Rubicon Road** (Hami Lu). These longer western extension roads included **Hungjao Road** (Hongqiao Lu), the **Great Western Road** (Yanan Xi Lu), **Lincoln Road** (Tianshan Lu) and **Brenan Road** (Changning Lu).

In addition to the Western Outside Roads Area, there was a similar **Northern Outside Roads Area** (Hubei Yuejie Zhulu) [沪北越界筑路] controlled by the International Settlement authorities in Hongkou District north of the formal settlement border on **Boundary Road** (Tianmu Lu). This Northern Outside Roads Area was centered around **Hongkew Park** (present-day Lu Xun Park), which was owned and operated by the Shanghai Municipal Council, and extended as far North as modern day Dalian Xi Lu. Settlement roads in this area included **Szechuen North Road** (Sichuan Bei Lu), **Dixwell Road** (Liyang Lu), **Darroch Road** (Duolun Lu), and **Scott Road** (Shanyin Lu).

In conjunction with the Outside Roads strategy, a series of four diplomatic agreements gradually enlarged the official boundaries of the International Settlement. Starting with an area of only 138 acres in **1846**, the British concession had already grown to 470 acres in **1848**. The merger of the British and American concessions in **1863** gave the newly established International Settlement a total area of 1,779 acres. As part of their expansion policy, in the 1880s the Shanghai Volunteer Corps began holding military maneuvers as far West as Jingan Temple (Jingan Si) on **Bubbling Well Road** (Nanjing Xi Lu), and in 1884 the Shanghai Municipal Police began patrolling this area on a daily basis. In May **1899** the Shanghai Municipal Council concluded successful negotiations with the Chinese authorities that extended the Settlement boundaries to its farthest limits, including almost all the roads previously built outside the boundaries. This 1899 extension added 1,896 acres North of the Suzhou River and 1,908 acres to the West of the existing Settlement. At its maximum size after the 1899 extension, the International Settlement covered 8.3 square miles of what is now downtown Shanghai, including 31,000 feet of prime waterfront along the Huangpu River. Its western boundary was now just past Jingan Si, and roughly followed the north-south line of today's Yanping Lu, just west of Jiaozhou Lu, from the intersection of Huashan Lu and Changshu Lu in the south to Suzhou Creek in the north.

The outside road building strategy had been such a success in gaining boundary extensions that the Settlement continued this policy until in **1925** they had built 48 miles of roads outside their boundaries. However, despite repeated attempts at negotiations, the 1899 extension proved to be their last. Discouragement at the failure of the lengthy extension negotiations and increasing Chinese nationalism caused the Settlement to largely halt its outside roads building program after 1925. Nonetheless, the 10,332 foreign residents still living on the existing outside roads in **1935** continued to pay taxes to the Shanghai Municipal Council and in return received the protection of Settlement police and the comforts offered by the Settlement public utilities, such as gas, telephone, water, and electricity.

The International Settlement was governed by the Shanghai Municipal Council which elected a chairman once every one or two years. In the beginning terms were for one year, but later two years became more common, and in a few rare cases lasted even longer. John Purdon managed to serve two separate two year terms, for a total of four years, while Stirling Fessenden holds the record of six continuous years in office from 1923 to 1929. Members of the council were elected by ratepayers, but rather than one man one vote, each ratepayer had a number of votes equal to the amount of property and income tax they paid to the settlement government, thus giving the wealthy residents a far greater say than the average person. Four members of the Keswick family associated with Jardine Matheson held the position of Chairman, as did two members of the Dent family. The Keswick and Dent families were so powerful that they each had a road in Shanghai named after them. From 1854 to 1943 there were 56 chairmen, of whom 43 were British (77%), 12 were American (21%), and 1 was Japanese. With the exception of the final one, all the Chairmen were either of British or American nationality.

The Shanghai Municipal Council of the Interantional Settlement passed its own laws, and operated its own municipal police force, courts, jails, public works department, fire department, public parks, postal service and postage stamps, and a paramilitary militia known as the Shanghai Volunteer Corps (SVC). It even had its own flag, seal, and motto: "Omnia Juncta in Uno," (All Joined Into One). In later years it operated all the public utilities within the settlement, including water, electricity, natural gas, telecommunications, and public transporation such as tramways.

The French Concession (Shanghai Fa Zujie) [上海法租界]

The French Concession (Shanghai Fa Zujie) [上海法租界] started in the East with a very narrow mouth along the Huangpu River, wedged in between the International Settlement to the North and the Chinese walled city of the Shanghai county town in Nanshi district to the South.   This bottleneck only had three streets, Avenue Edward VII (Yanan Dong Lu), Rue Du Consulat (Jingling Dong Lu) and Avenue Deux Republiques (Renmin Lu).   This bottleneck was characterized by urban commercial buildings, many of which can still be seen.   **Rue Du Consulat** (Jingling Dong Lu) was named after the French Consulate, which stood at the intersection of this street and the Bund.   It still has its distinct buildings, which hang over the covered sidewalks running past them.   **Avenue Edward VII** (Yanan Dong Lu) marked the northern boundary with the International Settlement.   It was shaped like a snake because it followed the course of the former **Yangjingbang Creek**, which was filled in when the road was built.   **Avenue des Deux Republiques** (Minguo Lu/Renmin Lu) marked the concession's southern boundary and wound around the circular pattern of the Shanghai county town wall in Nanshi.   A narrow stretch of French territory known as the **Quai de France** did extend along the Huangpu River as far south as **Fangbang Dong Lu**, but this was less than one block wide due to the existence of the Shanghai county town's city wall directly behind it.

However, once past the obstacle of the Shanghai county town's circular wall, the French Concession at its peak expanded much more widely to the South, West and North. **Avenue Edward VII** (Yanan Zhong Lu) continued to be the border with the International Settlement, but the way the road veered far to the North at a diagonal angle gave the French room to expand in this direction as well.   Where Avenue Edward VII (Yanan Zhong Lu) became the **Great Western Road** (Yanan Xi Lu), the French Concession's western boundary followed **Avenue Haig** (Huashan Lu) to Xujiahui.   The furthest western limits of French control extended as far as the Roman Catholic missionary community at **Xujiahui**. The southern limit was **Route de Zikawei** (Xujiahui Lu and Zhaojiabang Lu), which followed the course of **Siccawei Creek**, then large enough for sailing houseboats out to Mount Sheshan in Songjiang district.   Veering North from Siccawei Creek and following the winding **Rue de Captaine Rabier**, part of which lay on what is now a southern section of Xizang Nan Lu, the French Concession's southern border connected with the western side of the Shanghai county town's wall at the intersection of **Rue Millot** (Fangbang Xi Lu) on the French side and **Fangbang Zhong Lu** on the Chinese side.   The French concession was largely a residential area of leafy, tree-lined suburbs dotted with impressive mansions.   Its main business street was **Avenue Joffre** (Huaihai Lu).

The French used a similar road building strategy as the British and Americans in order to expand their concession's boundaries, and in the end they were even more successful at it. The French started out with just 3,800 feet of waterfront along the Huangpu River. However, in **1861** they won a small extension of 23 acres of waterfront along the Huangpu River, south of their original area and east of the Shanghai county town's wall.   On January 27, **1900** the French received a larger extension of 171 acres to the west of their original concession.   Finally, on July 31, **1914** the French received their third and last extension of 2,167 acres of new territory to the west of their existing concession.   This extension of 1914 took their western boundary all the way to **Xujiahui** and **Avenue Haig** (Huashan Lu).   At its height after 1914 the French Concession covered 3.9 square miles of present day downtown Shanghai.

Shanghai's Unique Architecture: 1870-1937

The frequent social upheavals and political instability in the rest of China during the late 19th century and early 20th century caused Shanghai to experience a huge growth in population, as well as a corresponding boom in construction to build housing for all the new immigrants. Prior to 1860, the foreign concessions had not permitted Chinese residents to live within their boundaries, but during the uprising of the **Small Swords Society** (Xiaodao Hui) [小刀会] from September 1853 to February 1855, and the **Taiping Rebellion** (Taiping Tianguo) (1850-1864) during which Shanghai was attacked three times between 1860 and1862, an estimated 110,000 Chinese refugees were allowed in who later elected to stay. During the warlord era of 1911 to 1927, compared to the rest of the country, Shanghai offered relative security of investment for the Chinese middle and upper classes, as well as a safe haven for political leaders of various factions and parties.

Although they were at first reluctant to accept Chinese as permanent residents of the concessions, foreign residents soon realized there was money to be made in selling and renting housing to these new residents. Once the temporary refugees became permanent residents, more substantial housing for them had to be constructed. It was this real estate market that later created the wealth of such landlord tycoons as Silas A. Hardoon and the Sassoon family. With the birth of Shanghai's real estate market came the creation of whole new neighborhoods of stone gate houses (shikumen) [石库门], which are unique to this city. These are rows of two-story wood, brick and cement houses, which are connected together and face inward towards a common courtyard or lane (known as a lilong [里弄] or a longtang [弄堂]) that is entered from the main street via a stone gate inscribed with the name of the lane. As late as 1949 three-quarters of the residential housing in Shanghai still consisted of lane houses of various types such as lilong [里弄], longtang [弄堂], and shikumen [石库门].

The presence of foreign control over Shanghai's downtown area in the guise of the International Settlement also encouraged foreign investors from all over the world to come here and construct residences and commercial buildings in the architectural style of their various home countries.

Thanks to this influx of influences, and Shanghai's later history that served to preserve them, the city now has examples of an eclectic array of architecture from around the world, some of which can no longer be found in their countries of origin. Styles that can be found here in plentiful supply include Art Deco, Greco-Roman, Oxford-Cambridge, Baroque, Beaux-Arts, Gothic, Tudor, Corbusier, Frank Lloyd Wright, and American colonial.

After 1927 further urban development was sparked by the new Guomindang central government in Nanjing, which launched a nationwide campaign of urban renewal in all the cities under its control. Shanghai's share in this campaign was a new metropolitan government center in **Jiangwan** Town.

At the same time, a new Chinese style of modern architecture emerged out of local designers' attempts to modernize traditional designs by adding some Western influences, while still preserving some Chinese characteristics as well. This merger of Chinese and Western styles resulted in a kind of neo-classical Chinese architectural renaissance, which is still a trademark of the Republican (Minguo) time period (1911-1949).

Much of this amazingly eclectic assortment of architecture still remained until the economic development begun in 1990 started to replace it with new modern structures. Shanghai's cityscape changed very little between 1937 and 1990, although the lives of its residents certainly did go through some wild gyrations with the ebb and flow of various political storms.

The Growth of Economic Shanghai: 1843-1937

It could be said that economics has always dominated politics in Shanghai throughout its history. Even in the Ming and Qing Dynasties, political power always resided elsewhere. Not only has it never once been the capital of a dynasty or national regime, it has never held a rank higher than a city, and until 1927 was a mere county seat governed from the prefectural capital in Songjiang town. Despite its unimportance politically, Shanghai had been the regional economic powerhouse for at least one hundred years before the arrival of the first Westerners in 1843.

Nonetheless, it was during the period of Western influence from 1843 to 1937 that Shanghai experienced a scale of economic growth that was then unparalleled in its history. British merchants established the Shanghai Electric Co. in 1882, which provided the first electric lighting in the city. This was followed shortly by the establishment on August 1, 1900 of the Shanghai Mutual Telephone Company, which provided the first phone service in the city to its 93 subscribers.

The city's population doubled between 1910 and 1927 from 1.3 million to 2.6 million. This growth in the number of residents helped fuel the boom in residential construction that resulted in the creation of Shanghai's unique architecture and class of real estate magnates discussed earlier. The SMC issued 81,903 building permits in the International Settlement alone between 1910 and 1925. Industrial construction took a huge leap as well, with a total of 816 new factories built in Shanghai between 1910 and 1925.

However, it was in the fields of finance, shipping and insurance that Shanghai truly became one of the four most important cities in the entire world economy. The mural still painted on the ceiling of the old Hong Kong and Shanghai Bank (Xianggang Shanghai Huifeng Yinhang) [香港上海汇丰银行] building on the Bund (Waitan) records the fact that when the building was built in 1923 Shanghai was ranked along side Tokyo, London and New York in economic importance.

Foreign banks rushed to set up branches in Shanghai and provided the capital needed by Chinese and foreign merchants, industrialists and developers, as well as loaning money to the Chinese government itself. The **Chartered Bank of India, Australia and China**, was a British-owned bank established in 1853, which opened its first Shanghai branch in 1857 and constructed its own building on the Bund in 1922. The **Hong Kong and Shanghai Banking Corporation** (Xianggang Shanghai Huifeng Yinhang) [香港上海汇丰银行] opened its first Shanghai office in 1865 and completed its building on the Bund in 1923. The Japanese-owned **Yokohoma Specie Bank**, Ltd., opened its first branch in Shanghai in 1892 and finished construction on its building on the Bund in 1924. The **Russo-Chinese Bank** opened its first branch in Shanghai in 1892 and constructed its building on the Bund in 1903, after which its name was changed to the St. Petersburg **Russo-Asiatic Bank** (Hua E Daosheng Yinhang) [华俄道胜银行] in 1905. The Shanghai branch of the French-owned **Banque de l'Indochine** opened its first Shanghai branch in 1899 and built its own building on the Bund in 1911.

In 1895 **HSBC** began financing the Chinese imperial government with a series of three loans issued in 1896, 1898 and 1905 for indemnity payments to Japan resulting from the 1895 Treaty of Shiminoseki ending the First Sino-Japanese War, and the Boxer Indemnity resulting from the 1900 Boxer Rebellion. It was these loans that began the practice of China's customs revenue being deposited in equal amounts with the creditor foreign banks, giving them an enormous amount of constant cash flow.

In 1898 **HSBC** established the British and Chinese Corporation, Ltd. (BCC) to finance railway construction in China. Later, in 1905, HSBC and the Banque de l'Indochine jointly established the Chinese Central Railways Company, Ltd. (CCR) for the same purpose. The CCR's Hu Guang railway loan of 1911, amounting to 10 million British Pounds, set off the nationalist railway recovery movement that helped spark the Wuchang Uprising of October 1911 leading to the overthrow of the Qing Dynasty.

In 1913 a Consortium of five foreign banks with branches in Shanghai was formed, including **HSBC**, Yokohoma Specie Bank, Banque de l'Indochine, and the Russo Asiatic Bank. Together these foreign banks in Shanghai financed the Beijing regime of Yuan Shi Kai with the 1913 Reorganization Loan of 25 million British Pounds. It was this money which allowed Yuan Shi Kai to crush the abortive 1913 Second Revolution launched by the supporters of Sun Zhongshan.

In 1914 the **Bank of Taiwan** entered the Shanghai market, and in 1915 it led a consortium of Japanese banks in loaning the Beijing regime of Yuan Shi Kai approximately 120 million Yen in unsecured loans, which were apparently intended to further the Japanese government's political aims in China.

Foreign banks continued to dominate China's finances until 1928. After this, competition from Chinese banks increased when the new Guomindang government began to sponsor three Chinese commercial banks, the Bank of China, the Bank of Communications, and the Agricultural Bank. A new **Central Bank of China** (Zhongyang Yinhang) [中央銀行] was also established with its head office in the national capital of Nanjing, the government's Minister of Finance serving concurrently as the Governor of the central bank.

Foreign shipping companies operated vast fleets of cargo ships along China's inland and coastal waterways from headquarters in Shanghai. The American-owned Russell and Co. formed the **Shanghai Steam Navigation Company** on March 27, 1862. By 1864 more than ten foreign firms had one or more steamers on the Yangzi River. The British Dent Co. had one, the British Jardine Matheson Co. had two, and Russell Co. had a fleet of five Yangzi River steamships, by far the largest. By June 1866 Russell had increased the size of their fleet to six steamers, Dent had doubled theirs from one to two, but Jardine Matheson still had only two. Between 1867 and 1872 Russell's increased their fleet of China coast and Yangzi River steamers from 12 ships to 19 ships, with seven of these sailing the Yangzi River route in 1867 and nine by 1872.

The British partnership of Richard Shackleton Butterfield and John Samuel Swire, known as Butterfield & Swire for short, or Taikoo (Taigu) [太古] in Chinese, opened their Shanghai office in the Fletcher Building on the Bund (Waitan) on January 1, 1867. They were the Shanghai agents for the British trans-oceanic steamship service commonly known as the Blue Funnel Line, although it was officially named the **Ocean Steamship Co.**, which was actually owned by Alfred Holt. The Blue Funnel Line had been founded in 1866 and initially operated a fleet of three steamships between Britain and China. To augment this ocean steamship service, Butterfield and Swire formed the **China Navigation Co**. in London on January 1, 1872, with the stated purpose of competing for the Yangzi River transport trade. The capital was entirely British, and the chief owner was John Samuel Swire himself, although Alfred Holt held a small stake.

The 1870s were a time of fierce rivalry between various shipping companies seeking to dominate transportation on the Yangzi River. Jardine Matheson had purchased the **China Coast Steam Navigation Co**. in 1872 and established the **Yangtze Steam Navigation Co**. in 1879. In 1872 the Chinese themselves also decided to get involved in competition for the Yangzi transport trade, and in that year the reform-minded scholar-official Li Hongzhang [李鸿章] (1823-1901) formed the **China Merchants' Steam Navigation Co**., which eventually managed to put two steamships on the Yangzi River two years later.

In 1873 Shanghai had three major foreign steamship companies operating a total of 27 ships on river and coastal routes. Russell & Co. had 17 ships, Jardine Matheson six ships, and B&S four ships. By the end of 1873 B&S had already succeeded in capturing at least half of the Yangzi River transport trade, which had previously been monopolized by Russell's. By March 1874 B&S' **China Navigation Co**. had a fleet of five steamships on the Yangzi River, in comparison to Russell's six ships.

Maps show that in 1874 the steamship wharves were all located in either the Yangpu section of the Huangpu, or the French Bund, with none of them being along the Huangpu Bund of the International Settlement between the Suzhou River and the Yangjingbang canal.

In the 1920s foreign steamship passenger lines, such as the **Robert Dollar Line**, began taking some of the first leisure tourists through the Three Gorges (San Xia) and as far up the Yangzi River as Chongqing. The Japanese shipping company Nishin Kisen Kabushiki Kaisha (NKKK) had been formed in 1907 and by 1929 had a fleet of 26 steamships sailing between China's coastal cities and Yangzi River ports. Butterfield & Swire's **China Navigation Co**. had a fleet of 87 ships sailing China's inland and coastal waters by 1929, making it by far the largest in China. B&S also continued to manage the China business of the **Ocean Steamship Co**., informally known as "the Blue Funnel Line," which sailed between Europe and China.

Western insurance companies arrived to underwrite cargo vessels and shipments of trade goods against damage or loss. **Yangtsze Insurance Association**, Ltd., a British company first established in 1862, built its offices on the Bund in 1926. Two American insurance companies, American Asiatic Underwriters and the Asia Life Insurance Co., were both founded in Shanghai, in 1919 and 1921 respectively, and later merged into the **American International Assurance Co**. (AIA) in Shanghai in 1931. Another British insurance company, **Union Insurance Society of Canton**, Ltd., set up its Bund office building in 1922.

Oil companies such as the Standard Oil Co. of New York and Asiatic Petroleum set up huge tank farms in Pudong and operated fleets of vessels to carry kerosene oil for the lamps and cooking stoves of China up the Yangzi River. The British-owned **Asiatic Petroleum Co**. constructed their own building on the Shanghai Bund in 1916, and by 1929 they had a fleet of nine vessels sailing the Yangzi River. The American-owned **Standard Oil Co. of New York** (Socony) also had its own fleet of ships sailing the Yangzi, but by 1929 size of their fleet had reached 11 ships, surpassing that of their rival APC.

Economically, Shanghai hit its peak in 1924, becoming the fourth busiest shipping port in the world, and the entry/exit point for half of China's foreign trade.   In 1931 fifty-two per cent of the foreign investment in China was centered in Shanghai, and by 1936 half of China's total foreign trade was shipped in or out of Shanghai.   As a result the Chinese central government at that time earned between 40 and 50 percent of its tax revenue from import and export duties collected by the Shanghai Customs House (Shanghai Jiang Hai Guan).

With the prominent position held by large foreign firms before the 1949 revolution, it's often overlooked that between 1842 and 1949 a large indigenous class of Chinese businessmen also developed.   M.J. Levy documented the birth and growth of this social group just as it was about to die a premature death in his 1949 study, _The Rise of the Modern Chinese Business Class_.   More recently Marie Claire Bergere and Parks Coble have revisited this topic in their publications.

Although Shanghai had long had a large network of traditional merchant associations known as trade guilds or provincial guilds (huiguan) [会馆], the rise of the city's new class of modern Chinese entrepreneurs was illustrated by the creation of new merchant organizations. The **Shanghai General Chamber of Commerce** (Shanghai Zong Shanghui) [上海总商会] was formed in 1911, with its original 21 directors, increased to 35 by 1918.   The **Chinese Cotton Mill Owners' Association** was formed in 1918.

In 1920 the Chinese shipping magnate **Yu Qiaqing** [虞洽卿](1867-1945), owner of the Ningbo-Shaoxing Steamship Line (Ning Shao Luchuan Gongsi) [宁绍轮船公司], the Siming Bank (Siming Yinhang) [四明银行], and the Sanbei Company (Sanbei Gongsi) [三北公司], became Director General (lishi zhang) [理事长] of the first **Shanghai Stock Exchange** (Shanghai Zhengquan Wupin Jiaoyisuo) [上海证券物品交易所].   In 1923 Yu Qiaqing [虞洽卿](1867-1945) became President (Huizhang) [会长] of the **Shanghai General Chamber of Commerce** (Shanghai Zong Shanghui) [上海总商会], but when he was defeated for re-election in 1925 he formed the new **Shanghai Business Federation** (Shanghai Shangjie Lianhe Hui)[上海商界联合会].   That same year he also became Superintendent of the Shanghai Commercial Port Municipal Administration (Songhu Shangbu Shizheng Duban) [淞沪商埠市政督办].

The **Shanghai Bankers Association** (Shanghai Yinhang Gonghui) [上海银行公会] had held its inaugural meeting on July 8, 1918 with twelve local Chinese banks represented, but by 1925 the number of member Chinese banks belonging to the association had doubled to 24. There were also **Chinese Ratepayers Associations** in both the International Settlement and French Concession, representing those Chinese property owners who paid taxes there.

In 1928 **Yu Qiaqing** [虞洽卿](1867-1945) was the Chairman (Zhuxi) [主席] of the International Settlement's Chinese Rate Payers Association (Gonggong Zujie Nashui Huaren Hui) [公共租界纳税华人会].   From 1929 to 1940, Yu Qiaqing [虞洽卿](1867-1945) served continuous successive terms on the **Shanghai Municipal Council** of the International Settlement (Shanghai Gonggong Zujie Gongbu Ju) [上海公共租界工部局], as well as the Greater Shanghai Municipal Council.   In 1936 the Shanghai Municipal Council renamed a section of Yanan East Road (Yanan Dong Lu) [延安东路] near its intersection with Tibet Middle Road (Xizang Zhong Lu) [西藏中路] in honor of Yu Qiaqing [虞洽卿]

(1867-1945) as Yu Qiaqing Road (Yu Qiaqing Lu) [虞洽卿路].   When the Second Sino-Japanese War broke out in 1937, Yu Qiaqing [虞洽卿](1867-1945) became Director General (lishi zhang) [理事长] of the Shanghai Refugee Emergency Relief Association (Shanghai Nanmin Jiuji Hui)[上海难民救济会] established by the Shanghai Municipal Council.   In the Fall of 1940 Yu Qiaqing [虞洽卿](1867-1945) went to Chongqing, where the Guomindang had established their temporary national capital, and thus he avoided the Japanese occupation of Shanghai's foreign settlements from 1941 to 1945.

Shi Liangcai [史量才] (1880-1934) was the owner of the newspapers Shen Bao [申报], Xinwen Bao [新闻报], and the China Press, and in the early 1930s headed the **Shanghai Civic Association**, which served as a forum for local Chinese businessmen.

All of this foreign investment and local economic development in turn helped create a domestic middle class of Chinese businessmen and their educated youth who both financed and participated in the bourgeois revolutions and mass movements which shook Shanghai and the rest of China during the early 20th Century.   But it also created a new proletarian class of disatisfied industrial workers who pushed these movements to a farther extreme than the middle class had ever wished to go.

Revolutions and Wars: 1911-1949

Despite Shanghai's relative economic stability and prosperity, the political scene from 1911 onward until the revolution of 1949 was characterized by successive demonstrations, labor strikes, public protests, riots, attempted revolutions, massacres of civilians, and foreign invasions.   The two foreign concessions offered a safe haven to Chinese revolutionaries of various political persuasions, with the result that nearly every Chinese warlord, revolutionary and political leader had a house in either the International Settlement or the French Concession.   However, at the same time these concessions were targets for protests and demonstrations as symbols of foreign imperialism in a time of growing Chinese nationalism.   Some of the same Chinese who benefited from the safe sanctuary offered by the concessions, ironically also criticized their existence and called for their abolition.

As China's wealthiest and most economically developed city, it was also considered a prize catch by all of China's warring internal factions, as well as foreign invaders.   Thus the primacy of economics and the making of money that probably motivated most of Shanghai's foreign and Chinese citizens was during this time repeatedly intruded upon and interrupted by political events, with only brief periods in between where economic stability and normality could resume.

1911 Republican Revolution (Xinhai Geming) [辛亥革命]

The 1911 Revolution (Xinhai Geming) [辛亥革命] which overthrew the Qing Dynasty was largely played out in Wuhan, where it started on October 10, and in Nanjing, where the first republican government was established on January 1, 1912.   Action in Shanghai was limited to a successful attack on the Jiangnan Arsenal led by **Chen Qimei** [陈其美] (1878-1916) and his lieutenant Chiang Kai-shek (Jiang Jieshi) [蒋介石] (1887-1975) in November 1911.   Chen ended up becoming the military governor of Shanghai for the next year, while Jiang had taken the first step in what would prove to be a very long military and political career.   Both Chen and Jiang owed their ideological allegiance to Sun Yat-sen

(**Sun Zhongshan**) [孙中山] (1866-1925), who passed through Shanghai on December 25, 1911 on his way to his January 1, 1912 inauguration as the first president of the Chinese Republic in Nanjing.

After resigning the presidency in favor of Yuan Shikai [袁世凯] (1859-1916) in April 1912, Sun later instigated the abortive **Second Revolution** (Erci Geming) [二次革命] against Yuan in mid-July 1913, with the immediate causus belli being Yuan's assassination of the Guomindang's parliamentary leader **Song Jiaoren** [宋教仁] (1882-1913) at the Shanghai Railway Station on March 20, 1913.   Since Yuan's regime was based in Beijing, most of the fighting occurred in provinces South of the Yangzi River, such as Jiangxi, Jiangsu and Guangdong, where Sun had his power base.   Although once again Nanjing was the center of action, this time there was significant fighting in the Shanghai area, unlike in 1911.   The fighting in Shanghai was centered around the revolutionaries' attempts to capture the forts at Wusong Kou and the Jiangnan Arsenal near the Longhua Garrison.   Just as in 1911, these attempts were led by Sun's lieutenants, Chen Qimei [陈其美] (1878-1916) and Chiang Kai-shek (Jiang Jieshi) [蒋介石] (1887-1975), and were financed by the famous family of **Charlie Soong** (Song Jiashu) [宋嘉树](1864-1918).   However, the Second Revolution failed to be a repeat performance of the first, and by early September Yuan had restored order.

After the failure of the 1913 Second Revolution (Erci Geming) [二次革命], Sun was forced into exile in Japan, along with his lieutenants and the Song family, until he returned to Shanghai in 1916.   Sun moved into a house in Shanghai's French Concession with his second wife, **Song Qingling** [宋庆龄] (1893-1981), in 1918.   They lived in this house, which can still be visited today, off and on at various times between 1918 and his death in 1925. The Shanghai house served as a safe refuge for Sun during his repeated periods of political exile from his power base in Guangzhou (Canton), where he served as the president of three successive regimes in opposition to the officially recognized government in Beijing.

However, by 1918 Sun had become out of touch with the popular nationalist movements emerging spontaneously amongst China's young intellectuals and educated middle class. Oddly enough, he played absolutely no role at all in China's first real popular movement, the May Fourth Movement (Wusi Yundong) [五四运动] of 1919, although this was centered in Shanghai and he was living in the city at the time.

1919 May 4th Movement (Wusi Yundong) [五四运动]

The May Fourth Movement (Wusi Yundong) [五四运动] started in Beijing, but quickly spread to Shanghai, which became the new center of activity.   The movement began on May 4, 1919 when students of Peking University (Bei Da) [北大] were arrested by Chinese police for demonstrating against the terms of the Treaty of Versailles ending World War I, which was then being negotiated at the Paris Peace Conference.   Although China had joined the Allied Powers in declaring war against Germany and Austria-Hungary, Chinese were shocked to find the proposed terms of the treaty called for the surrender of Germany's former colonies in Shandong Province to Japan.   China's delegation in Paris, which included Jiading native and St. John's graduate Wellington Koo (Gu Weijun) [顾维钧] (1888-1985), had not yet signed the treaty, and the protestors hoped their actions could prevent this from happening.

News of the events in Beijing was not reported in Shanghai's newspapers until May 6th. The first to react were the students of Fudan University, led by Professor Shao Lizu, who was also the editor of the newspaper Minguo Ribao. With these college students taking the lead, a boycott of Japanese goods was organized by Chinese merchants in the Nanshi district on May 9th. Eventually the boycott spread to even the large Wing On and Sincere department stores on Nanking Road in the International Settlement. Chinese depositors of Japanese banks withdrew all the funds from their accounts.

Further organization of the student movement took place on May 11th, when the Shanghai Students Union was formed by representatives of 12,000 students from 61 schools. On May 26th all university students in Shanghai went on strike, and began to hold a succession of mass rallies, public demonstrations and parades through the city streets. Students from not only Fudan, but also St. John's, Tongji, and Nanyang universities took part. Disruption of normal campus life was so great at St. John's that the school administration decided to end the academic year early without holding final exams, and simply closed the university down until the fall. When the administration of Aurora University in the French Concession refused permission for its students to join the strike, an estimated 165 of them chose to drop out of the school on May 28th.

By June 5, 1919 the student strike and boycott movements had evolved into a general strike of all Chinese shops, merchants, and businesses organized by the Shanghai Chamber of Commerce. Although it started in Nanshi District, by the end of the first day it had spread to all Chinese shops in the French Concession and International Settlement as well. According to the account of Joseph T. Chen, this general strike was so successful that it even included the prostitutes of Shanghai's red light districts, as well as the underworld Green Gang (Qing Bang) [青帮] then led by Huang Jinrong [黄金荣](1868-1953), who ordered his followers to temporarily cease their criminal activities as a patriotic gesture. As a result the 1919 general strike saw the lowest crime rate in years.

The May Fourth Movement in Shanghai was almost exclusively a middle-class phenomenon led by university students and merchants. Peasants played no role in it at all, and industrial workers in the factories of Zhabei, Yangpu and Pudong were quite slow to join, only going on strike when the events were near their end.

The strike reached a climax on June 8th when twelve Chinese banks decided to close their doors in support, bringing finance in the city to a standstill. Even worse from the standpoint of the city's foreign residents was the strike by their chauffeurs, which started the same day. These events sparked several crucial responses from the local Chinese authorities and the government of the International Settlement. The military governor of Shangha, Lu Yongxiang [卢永祥] (1867-1933), sent a telegram to the central government in Beijing begging them to give in to the protestors' demands, while at the same time he declared martial law in the Chinese parts of the city. The main English language newspaper of the city, the North China Herald, accused the protestors of being "Bolsheviks," and the Shanghai Municipal Council reacted by banning any further street demonstrations in the International Settlement and mobilizing the Shanghai Volunteer Corps.

News arrived from Beijing on June 11th that the central government was about to concede to the protestors' demands, and this caused the Chinese banks to reopen and some striking employees went back to work. The next day, June 12, was declared victory day and was marked by celebratory parades through the streets of both the French Concession and

International Settlement, as well as the Chinese districts of the city. One unfortunate incident which marred the celebrations was the injury of nine marchers and death of one other when Shanghai Municipal Police opened fire on a crowd that had gathered at the appropriately named Shandong Road. Remarkably, there was no mass protest in response as there would be when a similar incident occurred on May 30, 1925. Throughout the May Fourth Movement in Shanghai, none of the protests were directed at the imperialism of Western countries such as the U.S., Britain, and France, but rather they exclusively targeted the Japanese.

An estimated 100,000 participants joined in the final protest against the Treaty of Versailles on July 1st, but ironically it was not until the next day, July 2nd, that news finally arrived in Shanghai confirming that China's delegation in Paris had refused to sign the treaty.

In June 1921 the **Chinese Communist Party** (Gongchandang) [共产党] was founded in the French Concession. Both the house where the meetings were held, and the girl's school where the delegates slept, can still be visited today. The First national congress of the party was attended by 12 Chinese delegates, including Mao Zedong [毛泽东] (1893-1976), and the Dutch Comintern representative H. Sneevliet, alias G. Maring. Neither of the party's two real founders were there, as Chen Duxiu [陈独秀] (1879-1942) was then in Guangzhou, and Li Dazhao [李大钊] (1889-1927) in Beijing. On July 31 the congress moved to a boat in the middle of the South Lake (Nan Hu) in the nearby Zhejiang province town of Jiaxing.

Nonetheless, the French Concession and International Settlement offered a safe haven for the first four national congresses of the Chinese Communist Party, which only stopped using this haven in 1927. Without the safety offered by Shanghai's foreign concessions during the Communist Party's first six years of existence, its history may have been considerably different or even aborted.

Despite Shanghai's relative economic prosperity, for many of the Chinese laborers working in Shanghai's numerous factories and mills life was less than perfect. Although according to Li Lisan [李立三] (1899-1967), one of the party leaders of the time, there were fewer than 10 Communist Party members in Shanghai when he arrived there in the fall of 1924, grievances over working conditions led to the organization of Communist influenced labor unions and an increasing number of strikes in early 1925. The events leading up to the **May 30th Incident** of 1925 (Wusa Yundong) [五卅运动] started when Japanese-owned textile mills in Shanghai began laying off and locking out Chinese workers in January of that year. The February 1925 strike in the Japanese cotton mills led to the formation of the Communist-influenced Shanghai General Labor Union (Shanghai Zonggong Hui) [上海总工会]. The following weeks of worker and student demonstrations started out as anti-Japanese but snowballed into including a host of grievances against the foreign concessions.

After British Sikh police arrested some protesters on May 30, 1925 and took them to the Louza (Laozha) Police Station, the station was besieged by an estimated 2,000 demonstrators at the intersection of Kweichow Road and Nanking Road demanding the prisoners' release. The nervous policemen inside decided to open fire on the crowd, killing and injuring a large number of people. It's worth noting that the Sikh police kept their families housed inside the station, and they may have had their safety in mind. As news spread throughout Shanghai and around China, what had started as a single protest against the Japanese quickly became a nationwide anti-British movement. A general strike of all workers and students occurred in Shanghai starting on June 3 and lasting until July, although continuing social unrest continued until September. The **Shanghai Volunteer Corps** was mobilized for a record three months to handle the crisis until finally being demobilized on August 28th.

As in 1919, student participation in the May 30th Movement protests was once again so great that both the University of Shanghai (Hujiang Daxue) [沪江大学] and St. John's University (Shanghai Sheng Yuehan Daxue) [上海圣约翰大学] were forced to shut down before the normal end of the academic year. St. John's President, H.L. Hawks Pott argued so violently with the demonstrating students of his university that at least half those enrolled withdrew from the school and later founded a new rival institution known as Guanghua University [光华大学].

In response to the events in Shanghai, similar incidents took place in most of China's major cities. A similar massacre occurred in Guangzhou when foreign troops defending the concessions on the island of **Shameen Dao** opened fire on a mob of protesters across the narrow canal separating the island from the rest of the city. Riots occurred all up and down the Yangzi River, including the towns of Zhenjiang, Jiujiang, Hankou, and Chongqing. It could be said that this marked the beginning of a new wave of Chinese nationalism that lasted for the next several years.

The Guomindang's 1926-1927 **Northern Expedition** (Bei Fa) [北伐] from its base in Guangzhou had the objective of re-unifying China under their rule, after the years of regional warlord rule since the 1911 Revolution. At this time, as part of the first United Front started by Sun Yat-sen [孙中山] (1866-1925) in 1924, the Guomindang included members of the Chinese Communist Party as well as a non-Communist left wing. The party had a much broader and varied membership base at that time, and its members were full of youthful idealism. Even men such as Lu Xun [鲁迅] (1881-1936) and Mao Dun [茅盾] (1896-1961), now considered left-wing heroes, then served as Guomindang officials in Guangzhou.

However, by March 1927 the party had split into two factions, the left-wing at Wuhan and the right-wing under Chiang Kai-shek (Jiang Jieshi) [蒋介石] (1887-1975) in Nanchang. Jiang was expelled from the Chairmanship of the Guomindang's Central Executive Committee by the Wuhan regime at a meeting of the CEC held from March 10 to 17, 1927. Nonetheless, he still commanded the loyalties of most Guomindang military commanders in eastern China, and had powerful allies in Shanghai among both the Chinese capitalist class and the Chinese organized crime leaders of the Green Gang (Qing Bang) [青帮].
.

By March 20, 1927, the eastern column of the Guomindang's Northern Expedition under the command of General Bai Chongxi [白崇禧] (1893-1966) was on the outskirts of Shanghai. However, before Bai's army could occupy the city, the Communist-led **Shanghai General Labor Union** (Shanghai Zonggong Hui) [上海总工会] launched a general strike on March 21 involving between 500,000 and 800,000 workers. A simultaneous armed workers uprising succeeded in seizing control of Shanghai's Chinese districts within 48 hours.

Although Bai Chongxi's troops succeeded in occupying the **Longhua Garrison** by March 22, they felt outnumbered against the half million armed workers in control of the city, and their nearest reinforcements were the 10,000 troops under General He Yingqin [何应钦] (1890-1987) in Hangzhou. The weakness of Bai's position was made even more apparent when the armed workers chose to ignore his March 30 declaration of martial law, which had required them to disarm. As a result, Bai's commander-in-chief, Chiang Kai-shek (Jiang Jieshi) [蒋介石] (1887-1975), turned to Shanghai's Chinese capitalists and the Green Gang (Qing Bang) [青帮] for help in securing control of the city.

In the Spring of 1927 the Chinese businessman Yu Qiaqing [虞洽卿](1867-1945) headed a merchant group known as the **Shanghai Federation of Commerce and Industry** (Shanghai Shangye Lianhe Hui) [上海商业联合会], which loaned Chiang Kai-shek (Jiang Jieshi) [蒋介石] (1887-1975) $3 million U.S. Dollars (15 million Chinese dollars) on March 26, 1927, money which probably financed the April 12, 1927 Guomindang right wing coup d'etat in Shanghai. According to Brian Martin, 500,000 Chinese dollars were given to the Green Gang (Qing Bang) [青帮] by Jiang in early April 1927 in order for them to purchase weapons. Furthermore, the Green Gang (Qing Bang) [青帮] had already received a large quantity of weapons from the French Concession authorities in late February.

On the evening of April 11, 1927 at a meeting between Du Yuesheng [杜月笙] (1888-1951) and SMC Chairman Stirling Fessenden at the former's home, the latter agreed to allow Green Gang paramilitary militia to cross the territory of the International Settlement in order for them to travel from their base in the French Concession to the strikers strongholds in the Chinese Zhabei District. The Green Gang's armed offensive against the worker's militia started early on the morning of April 12, and by the next day all the armed workers had surrendered or been defeated. The SLGU called another general strike of 100,000 workers on April 13, but this ended without achieving any successful results on April 15, 1927.

The first United Front between the Communists and the Guomindang ended with the April 1927 Shanghai coup. As a result, Shanghai ceased to be the safe haven that it had been for Communist activities since the party's founding six years previously. **Chen Duxiu** [陈独秀] (1879-1942), who had supported the United Front with the Guomindang, was blamed for the disaster and forced to resign at a meeting held in Wuhan on August 7, 1927, in favor of a new leadership dominated by Li Lisan [李立三] (1899-1967). Later Chen was even expelled from the party in 1929. After the April 1927 coup in Shanghai and the September 1927 collapse of the Left-Guomindang regime in Wuhan, the Communist party no longer had a safe refuge for its meetings anywhere in China's main cities. The Chinese Communists sixth party congress of July 1928 actually had to be held in Moscow, since no safe place was available in China. Some Communist leaders chose to flee overseas, while others such as Mao Zedong [毛泽东] (1893-1976) gave up on the cities entirely and turned instead to China's countryside. By January 1928 three small bands of Communist guerrillas led by Mao, Zhu De [朱德] (1886-1976), Chen Yi [陈毅] (1901-1972), and Peng Dehuai [彭德怀] (1898-1974) had taken refuge in the Jinggang Shan Mountains of Jiangxi province.

The establishment of the Guomindang's new national government in Nanjing was soon followed by the creation for the first time ever of a Shanghai municipal government. Established on July 14, 1927, this municipal government included a mayor (shizhang) [市长] appointed by the Nanjing central government, and a municipal council that was in turn appointed by the mayor.   Although the foreign concessions were still outside of its boundaries, the **Municipality of Greater Shanghai** covered an area of 320 square miles, completely surrounding those enclaves and including the districts of Zhabei [闸北], Nanshi [南市], and Pudong [浦东].   One of the new municipality's first projects was to begin construction of a new civic center in the town of **Jiangwan** (Jiangwan Zhen) [江湾镇], just north of the Hongkou District controlled by the International Settlement.   This new Jiangwan city center eventually included a museum, library, stadium, and city hall, all of which were designed by the Chinese architect **Dong Dayou** [董大酉](1899-1973).

The Shanghai Municipality had two mayors within its first three months of existence.   The first Mayor of Shanghai was **Huang Fu** [黄郛] (1880-1936), who only served for about five weeks from July 7, 1927-August 14, 1927.   Huang had become a member of the Tongmenghui [同盟会], predecessor to the Guomindang , in the early 1900s while in Japan, where he first met Chiang Kai-shek and Zhang Qun while they were students at the same Japanese military academy.   He later participated in the 1911 Revolution in Shanghai along with Chiang Kai-shek (Jiang Jieshi) [蒋介石] (1887-1975) and Chen Qimei [陈其美] (1878-1916), and briefly served as Acting President of China for less than a month in Novemer 1924. Huang Fu [黄郛] was followed as Shanghai Mayor by Wu Zhenxiu [吴震修] (1883-1966), who barely survived in the post for one month from August 15, 1927-September 16, 1927.

The first Mayor to survive for more than a month was Zhang Dingfan [张定璠] (1891-1945), who managed to stay in office for a year-and-a-half from September 17, 1927-March 31, 1929.

Zhang Qun [张群] (1889-1990) was appointed as the fourth Mayor of Shanghai on April 1, 1929 and served for almost three years until January 1932.

The years of nationalist demonstrations and protests since 1925 began to pay dividends in 1928 when Shanghai's foreign concessions started to dismantle some of the more discriminatory policies towards their Chinese population.   In the International Settlement all the public parks were open to Chinese visitors for the first time, including Jessfield Park (Zhongshan Gongyuan) [中山公园], Hongkew Park (Lu Xun Gongyuan) [鲁迅公园], and the infamous Public Gardens on the Bund (Waitan) [外滩].   The first three Chinese members were invited to join the Shanghai Municipal Council in 1928.   By 1930 their number had been increased by two for a total of five, the same number of members held by the British. Two Japanese members had already been allowed to join the S.M.C. back in 1902, meaning that it was increasingly becoming a truly international body.   A Chinese Company had already been added to the Shanghai Volunteer Corps in 1907, meaning that by 1928 the Chinese population of the International Settlement now had nearly equal rights to participate in the concession's politics, recreational facilities, and military defense.   A similar trend was occurring in the French Concession, which added three Chinese members to its Municipal Council in 1927.

Shocked by the excesses of the Guomindang right-wing in their crack down on all forms of dissenting ideas, in 1930 the **League of Leftist Writers** [左翼作家联盟] was formed in Shanghai by a group of Chinese intellectuals who included Mao Dun [茅盾] (1896-1961), Ding Ling [丁玲] (1904-1986), and Lu Xun [鲁迅] (1881-1936).   Once again the foreign concessions provided a safe haven for a meeting which could not have then been held in Chinese territory, as the League held its inaugural session in a French mansion on a lane just off the Settlement's Darroch Road (Duolun Lu) [多伦路].   Today the Duolun Lu neighborhood has been revived as a memorial dedicated to these intellectuals of the 1930s.

The 1932 Shanghai War

Trouble began simmering in Shanghai soon after news arrived of the Japanese occupation of Manchuria in September 1931. The strength of nationalist feeling then running in Shanghai can still be seen in the form of the **Missing Corner Pavilion** erected at that time in Nanxiang town's Guyi Yuan [古漪园] Garden.   The pavilion's roof is decorated with clenched fists raised in defiance at each corner except for the northeastern one representing Manchuria.

The first Japanese troops arrived in Shanghai in September when 500 Japanese marines were landed in Hongkou, supposedly to protect the large resident Japanese population there. An anti-Japanese boycott begun on September 27 was extremely effective in inflicting punishment on all the local Japanese-owned factories and shops.   The boycott of Japanese goods and services lasted for the next four months.

Rising tensions between China and Japan in 1932 coincided with the resignations of both the local leader Shanghai mayor Zhang Qun [张群] on December 10, and the national leader Chiang Kai-shek (Jiang Jieshi) [蒋介石] (1887-1975) on December 22, 1932, leaving a power vacuum at the top of both the Guomindang central and local governments.   This volatile situation was completed by the coincidence that 19th Route Army of 33,500 Chinese troops led by General Cai Tingkai [蔡廷锴] (1892-1968) happened to be in Shanghai in December 1932.

On January 6, 1932 Wu Tiecheng [吴铁城] (1888-1953) was sworn into office as Shanghai's new Mayor (Shizhang) [市长], as well as simultaneously Commanding Officer of the Song Hu Garrison.   Wu was born in Jiujiang, Jiangxi Province, although his ancestral home was Xiangshan in Guangzhou, Guangdong Province.   He had had an illustrious career with the Guomindang ever since the 1911 Revolution that overthrew the Qing Dynasty.   He represented Jiangxi Province at the 1912 National Assembly held in Nanjing to elect Sun Yat-sen (Sun Zhongshan) [孙中山] (1866-1925) as the first president of China.   After the failure of the Second Revolution in 1913, he went into exile in Japan with Sun, returning to China with him in 1916.   Wu later served in various important posts with the early Guomindang regimes in Guangdong from 1920 to 1928, including Police Commissioner and Garrison Commander of Guangzhou, as well as Sun Zhongshan's personal adjutant. Since 1929 he had been a member of the Guomindang's top two political bodies, the Central Executive Committee and Central Political Council.

Shortly after Wu's inauguration as Mayor of Shanghai, he received his first ultimatum from the local Japanese Consul on January 23, 1932. At that time, a fleet of 13 Japanese warships was already anchored in the Huangpu River and 13 more were on their way. The sudden resignation on January 25, 1932 of the Guomindang's acting head of state, Sun Ke, put further pressure on Mayor Wu to handle the dangerous situation in Shanghai all alone without aid from the central government. On January 27, 1932 the Japanese Consul General repeated his ultimatum to Mayor Wu, who finally felt compelled to formally accept all of the Japanese demands on January 28, 1932, just in time to meet the deadline they had set for that day.

Nonetheless, at 8:30 p.m. on the evening of January 28, the Admiral in command of the Japanese fleet ordered the Chinese army to evacuate Zhabei district. At 11:25 p.m. he issued another order that the Chinese troops withdraw from Zhabei.

On the morning of January 29, 1932 a Japanese aerial bombardment of Zhabei began, carried out by planes based on an aircraft carrier in the Huangpu. Despite their tremendous superiority in air and naval forces, at this time the Japanese ground forces amounted to only 1,833 marines who were up against the Chinese 19th Route Army's 33,000 troops under the command of General Cai Tingkai occupying Zhabei District and the strategic North Railroad Station. Until reinforcements arrived on February 15, 1932, the Japanese did not have more than 3,000 troops in Shanghai, although a fleet of 34 Japanese warships including an aircraft carrier, cruisers, and destroyers lay anchored in the Huangpu and Yangzi Rivers. However, on Feb. 14-15th 17 Japanese troop transports landed 21,000 reinforcements, with their total number soon rising to over 50,000 men.

As a result, a military stalemate ensued, and five weeks after the hostilities had begun the Chinese were still in control of Zhabei District and the North Train Station. Mayor Wu held daily press conferences to mobilize public opinion at home and abroad. However, despite the courageous stand by China's local military forces and political leaders, 230,000 Chinese civilian refugees chose to flee into the foreign concessions south of the Suzhou River. The SMC police also withdrew from those parts of the International Settlement that were north of the Suzhou River, leaving Hongkou and Yangpu districts to the Japanese.

From Feb. 20th the Japanese offensive concentrated on Jiangwan town, with the Jiangwan Race Course falling the same day. After this the Japanese commander made his headquarters at Fudan University. Finally, on February 26th the Chinese defenders withdrew from Jiangwan town, although they continued to hold Zhabei district.

After the fall of Jiangwan, the Japanese refocused their attention on capturing the Wusong Forts at the confluence of the Huangpu and Yangzi Rivers. On the morning of March 1st, 15,000 Japanese troops were landed at the Yangzi River port of Liuhe, just west of the strategic Wusong Forts. By this time the entire Japanese expeditionary force in Shanghai had increased to 90,000 troops. The Japanese advanced from Liuhe eastward towards the rear of the Wusong Forts and southward towards the town of Jiading. With the Japanese now behind the Chinese front line of defense running from Zhabei district to Wusong, on March 2nd the Chinese command gave the order for a withdrawal of all their troops from the Zhabei, Baoshan and Wusong areas westward to the town of Kunshan. With that decision the first Sino-Japanese battle for Shanghai was effectively over.

Sensing that they had achieved as much of a victory as possible, the Japanese declared a unilateral cease-fire the next day, on March 3, 1932. The military stalemate had lasted for 35 days, and ended without a clear victory by either side. The Chinese had demonstrated that they could stall a Japanese offensive for five weeks, but lost 14,000 casualties. The Japanese eventually occupied Zhabei and the North Train Station, but they had lost 4,000 casualties and suffered the humiliation of a protracted battle rather than the overnight coup they had expected.

On March 5 both sides accepted the proposal to hold truce talks, and negotiations eventually began in Shanghai on March 24, shifted to Geneva in April, and then came back to Shanghai where the final agreement was signed on May 5, 1932. Although the Chinese defeated a Japanese proposal to demilitarize Pudong, they had to accept a demilitarized zone around the rest of Shanghai in which no Chinese troops would be allowed, order to be maintained by a police unit known as the Peace Preservation Corps (Bao'an Dui).

By the time Chinese police returned to Zhabei District in May 1932 after the signing of the Sino-Japanese truce, the area was in ruins caused by the fighting. Buildings destroyed during the 1932 battle for Shanghai included 12,000 residences; 4,000 stores; 600 factories; and 240 schools. In addition, 540,000 refugees had fled from their homes in the battle zone. An estimated 85 per cent of Zhabei's residents had fled during the battle, and by June 1932 the population was still 43 per cent less than it had been before the fighting started in January 1932.

The most important result of the battle was that the Japanese military retained de-facto control over the Hongkou and Yangpu Districts of the International Settlement, including the Northern Outside Roads Area around Hongkew Park (Lu Xun Gongyuan), although they refrained from formally declaring it a Japanese concession. The Suzhou River became the de-facto northern boundary of the International Settlement, as far as British-American control was concerned. From January 1932 onward, a Japanese Naval Landing Party was permanently stationed at a military camp south of **Hongkew Park** (Lu Xun Park), and Japanese marines regularly patrolled the streets of the Hongkou and Yangpu districts.

By 1937 Shanghai had become a truly international city. According to the 1935 census for the International Settlement and 1936 figures for the French Concession, the 20,679 Japanese residents formed the largest group of any single foreign nationality. In second place came the Russian community of 14,845, most of whom lived in the French Concession. Both the Japanese and the Russians far outnumbered the 9,603 British residents and 3,808 Americans.

However, since the French Consul governed the French Concession like a dictator, and voting in the International Settlement was based on property ownership, the Japanese and Russians continued to be largely shut out of local politics. Reforms made to the apportionment of seats on the Municipal Council had resulted in a more multinational body, but still one that represented property owners rather than demographics. The council elected for the year 1937 included five Britsh, five Chinese, two Americans, and two Japanese.

Meanwhile, **Wu Tiecheng** [吴铁城] (1888-1953) continued to serve as Shanghai's mayor until April 1937, only a few months before the Japanese invasion of August 1937. Although the foreign concessions were of course outside his domain, Mayor Wu governed a Greater Shanghai that covered 494 square kilometers and had a population of 1,655,070. During his four-year term in office he oversaw the rebuilding of areas damaged by the 1932 Shanghai War, and the development of the new Jiangwan town civic center. He also attempted to establish a more representative local government by founding the first ever Municipal Council for Shanghai's Chinese districts in October 1932. After giving his annual New Year's Address to the people of Shanghai, reviewing the progress made towards construction of a model municipality, Wu was replaced as mayor in April 1937 by O.K. Yui (Yu Hongjun) [俞鸿钧] (1898-1960) who only remained in office for eight months until November 1937, once the Japanese conquest of the Chinese administered parts of the city were complete.

The Solitary Island (Gu Dao) [孤岛] 1937-1941

Five years of relative peace were broken when the Japanese attacked Shanghai a second time in August 1937. On August 9, 1937 an incident at Hongqiao Aiport resulted in the deaths of two Japanese sailors and one Chinese police man (bao'an). This in turn caused the Japanese Naval Landing Party to begin receiving reinforcements on August 11.

The International Committee for Enforcement of the Peace Agreement of 1932 met on August 12, but an outbreak of war seemed imminent. On the same day the Chinese 87th and 88th Divisions took up positions in the Zhabei and Jiangwan areas of the Chinese municipality north of Suzhou Creek, outside the northern boundaries of the International Settlement.

Fighting finally erupted between Japanese and Chinese troops in Zhabei district and Jiangwan town on August 13. The most severe clashes occured around the Shanghai North Railway Station and the Japanese Naval Landing Party barracks.

Two incidents on Saturday, August 14 caused severe civilian casualties in the center of the supposedly neutral International Settlement. In the first incident, Chinese warplanes trying to bomb Japanese naval vessels anchored in the Huangpu mistakenly dropped bombs at the intersection of Nanking Road, today's Nanjing East Road (Nanjing Dong Lu) [南京东路] and the Bund (Waitan), damaging the **Cathay Hotel** (Peace Hotel) and **Palace Hotel**. At least 1,590 Chinese and foreign civilians were reportedly wounded and killed in this incident. Photos of the aftermath show Nanking Road littered with building debris, burned out wreckage of vehicles, and dead bodies. Later the same day another Chinese warplane accidentally dropped its bombs on the intersection of Thibet Road (Xizang Zhong Lu) and Avenue Edward VII (Yanan Dong Lu) [延安东路], wounding and killing numerous Chinese and foreign civilians immediately outside the **Great World Amusement Center** (Dashijie) [大世界]. The total number of civilian casualties from this second incident was estimated at 2,017. More civilians were injured and killed in the International Settlement on August 23, 1937 when both the Sincere Co. and Wing On department stores at the intersection of Nanking Road, today's Nanjing East Road (Nanjing Dong Lu) [南京东路], and Zhejiang Lu were hit by two airplane bombs, causing 773 civilian casualties.

By August 23rd Japanese forces had landed at Wusong Kou, and their total numbers had reached an estimated 50,000 men.   From their Wusong Kou beach head, the Japanese tried to advance in two directions, northwest to Luodian, and southwest to Yangpu.

On August 30 the American Robert Dollar passenger liner SS President Hoover was hit by a bomb from a Chinese airplane as it lay anchored off Wusong Kou.

On September 6, 1937 Chinese troops began to withdraw from the Yangzi River port towns of Baoshan and Wusong Kou.   This was followed by a withdrawal from the Jiangwan civic center on September 12.   By September 13th the Chinese army had taken up new positions along a defensive line running from Zhabei district northward through the Baoshan district towns of Liuhang and Luodian to the Yangzi River port of Liuhe.   After changing hands several times, the village of Luodian finally fell to the Japanese on September 18th.   By October 3rd the Chinese defenders in Baoshan district had withdrawn west of the Luodian-Liuhang highway, but continued to hold a line from Zhabei through the town of Nanxiang to the port of Liuhe.   The center of the fighting in Zhabei was the North Railway Station, which finally collapsed after receiving numerous direct hits from Japanese artillery and bombers on October 19th.

After 75 days of successful resistance to the Japanese invasion, the Chinese army was finally compelled to withdraw from Zhabei district on October 27, 1937.   Crossing over to the south bank of Suzhou Creek, the Chinese defenders followed a scorched earth rear guard defense of setting all Zhabei ablaze on their way out.

In a heroic but suicidal act of defiance, a single Chinese military unit of 500 men led by Guomindang **General Xie Jinyuan** [谢晋元] (1905-1941) refused to retreat from Zhabei during the general withdrawal of October 27th.   Capturing the attention of all the local news media, this unit was dubbed the "Lone Battalion."   Encamped inside a large warehouse on the north bank of Suzhou Creek at the intersection of North Thibet Road (Xizang Bei Lu) and North Suzhou Road (Bei Suzhou Lu) [北苏州路], the "Lone Battalion" of only 500 men bravely held out against the entire Japanese army of 50,000 soldiers for five days until they were finally ordered to retreat southward across the Thibet Road Bridge (Xizang Bei Lu Qiao) into the safety of the neutral International Settlement early on the morning of October 31st. [The current Xizang Zhong Lu-Bei Lu Bridge is an impressive masonry structure built in Min Guo style with an elegant arch and four towers, but it is difficult to tell whether it is a true historic relic or a more modern imitation.]

The Number Four Company Warehouse (Sihang Cangku) [四行仓库] still stands at No. 1 Guangfu Lu, on the west side of the northern approach to the Xizang Bei Lu-Zhong Lu Bridge over the Suzhou Creek (Suzhou He).   The massive masonry structure building is six stories high and almost an entire city block long, forming a solid wall along the river. Although the front of the building facing the riverside Guangfu Lu is flat, the rear side facing Guoqing Lu has a convex half oval shape.   Similarly, the front façade seems to have been restored and looks modern, whereas the rear side appears more authentic and unrestored. At any rate, the building itself, despite having been built in 1935, is no architectural gem and would not normally catch the eye were it not for its immense size and historical significance. A small plaque in the exterior wall outside the main entrance on Guangfu Lu simply notes the date of construction.

Inside the ground floor lobby visitors are greeted first by a bronze statue of Guomindang General **Xie Jinyuan** [谢晋元] (1905-1941), while to the right on the wall hangs an oil portrait of the same general.   Oddly, neither the statue nor the portrait display any Guomindang symbols on General Xie's uniform.   The simple five pointed star that appears on his hat in both images gives the false impression that he was a Communist rather than a Guomindang military officer.   Attendants seated beside the elevator note that there is a further historical exhibit on the top floor of the building, but disagree whether that is the sixth or seventh floor. From the outside one can see that a partial seventh floor has been tacked on top of the original roof.

The Chinese new defensive line of Suzhou Creek held until the morning of November 9th when Japanese troops finally managed to cross to the south bank of the river over the **Jessfield Bridge** in northwestern Shanghai, near **Jessfield Park** (Zhongshan Gongyuan). From here the Japanese advanced around the western limits of the International Settlement and French Concession, moving through the Hongqiao and Xujiahui areas to encircle the final group of Chinese defenders in the Nanshi district of southern Shanghai.   With the evacuation of the last Chinese troops from Nanshi on November 11th, and the occupation of the district by the Japanese the next day, the battle for Shanghai was effectively over, almost exactly three months after it had started in mid-August.

The impact of the fighting on the city's infrastructure included the almost total destruction of the newly built Jiangwan Museum (recently restored), and the North Railway Station, as well as considerable damage to the Jiangwan City Hall, which nonetheless managed to survive.

The Japanese Occupation Begins

Although the average person had little choice, the Chinese political and economic upper class were faced with a difficult choice to either flee Shanghai and join the Guomindang national government in internal exile in Chongqing or remain in Shanghai and try to cooperate with the Japanese.   Some businessmen such as Huang Jinrong stayed to protect their assets, while others such as Du Yuesheng fled to Chongqing.   Some Chinese politicians saw the occupation as an opportunity.   For example, Wang Jingwei chose to collaborate with the Japanese as head of their puppet Chinese national government in Nanjing because he had been defeated in his contest with Jiang Jieshi over leadership of the Guomindang and saw no other way to ever achieve the leading role he wanted.   Similarly, there were five Chinese politicians who served as Mayor of Shanghai during the 1937-1945 Japanese occupation of the city.   Su Xiwen [苏锡文] (1889-1945), who served as Shanghai Mayor from December 5, 1937 to October 15, 1938, and again briefly for about one month from October 11 to November 19, 1940, died of illness in 1945.   Fu Xiaoan [傅筱庵] (1872-1940), who served as Shanghai Mayor from October 16, 1938 to October 10, 1940, was assassinated while in office.   His three successors in the position all survived the war but were captured, imprisoned, and put on trial by the Guomindang afterward.
Although Shanghai's foreign residents had until now seen themselves as neutral bystanders in the Sino-Japanese War, their lives began to be immediately affected by the new Japanese occupation.   On November 26 the Japanese took over control of all public communications, including postal services, radio stations, and telegraph, in both the International Settlement and French Concession.   By January 6, 1938 Japanese censorship of all communications in both foreign settlements was in place.

On December 3rd a Japanese victory parade was held in which 6,000 of their fully armed troops marched all the way from Yuyuan Lu down Nanking Road, today's Nanjing East Road (Nanjing Dong Lu) [南京东路], the main street of the International Settlement, to the Bund (Waitan).   Accounts differ about what happened the next day when Japanese troops attempted a similar victory parade through the French Concession.   By all accounts they were initially stopped at the boundary of the French Bund (Falanxi Waitan) [法兰西外滩] by French authorities aided by a blockading line of armored cars, and then eventually allowed to proceed.   This much is confirmed by photos of the incident, but the terms of the agreement they reached seem debatable.   According to some the Japanese were first disarmed, while others simply say they were escorted by French police.   At any rate, the neutrality of both foreign settlements was definitely violated in a way that showed Shanghai's foreign residents who the new masters of their fate were.

After December 1937 Shanghai became a solitary island (gu dao) [孤岛] surrounded for the next four years by Japanese occupied territory and cut off from the inland Yangzi River ports that had previously been the source of its imports and the destination for its exports by the battles being waged upriver between the Japanese and Guomindang armies.   The December 12, 1937 **Panay Incident** in which an American naval vessel and a fleet of Standard Oil tankers sailing on the Yangzi River above Nanjing were sunk by a Japanese air raid, resulted in foreign gunboats and commercial shipping being bottled up in the ports of Shanghai and Chongqing.   Inland commerce came to a standstill, the local economy stagnated, and construction of new buildings essentially came to a halt.

Nonetheless, the Shanghai Municipal Council continued to function and a semblance of independence was maintained by both foreign concessions.   The Japanese took full possession of the northern half of the International Settlement across the Suzhou River, but the Garden Bridge (Waibaidu Qiao) [外白渡桥] and other bridges across the Suzhou River were sandbagged and patrolled by the Shanghai Volunteer Corps as the crossing points into hostile territory.   Both the Astor House and Broadway Mansions hotels on the North side of the Suzhou River were taken over and occupied by the Japanese.

Ironically, the existing real estate owned by E.D. Sassoon and other landlords in the concessions actually increased in value after the Japanese occupation of the surrounding Chinese districts.   People were desperate to move into the relative safety of the International Settlement and French Concession, and willing to pay any price for it, much as they had been during the Taiping rebellion eighty years before in the 1860s.   E.D. Sassoon's property in the Settlement was alone valued in early 1938 as being worth 8,750,000 British pounds.   The prosperity of the real estate market lasted long enough for the Shanghai Times to publish a 415-page guide in 1939 on how to get rich by investing in Shanghai property, _The Profitable Path of Shanghai Realty_.   However, the 1941 Japanese occupation, followed by the Guomindang hyperinflation and the Communists' seizure of private property would soon make these investments worthless.

The End of Empire

Even before Pearl Harbor, Japanese frusration at their perceived under-representation on the Municipal Council of the International Settlement had resulted in the attempted assassination of the British council chairman W.J. "Tony" Keswick by a Japanese gunman at the annual ratepayers meeting held at the **Shanghai Race Club** (Paoma Zonghui) [跑马总会] on January 26, 1941. Although Keswick survived the attack, it did result in a new apportionment of council seats in which Japanese membership was increased from two to three, British membership was decreased from five to three, Chinese membership was decreased from five to four, and American membership was increased from two to three. In addition, Germany, Holland, and Switzerland were each given one seat, for a total membership of 16.

The **Shanghai Volunteer Corps** had been mobilized 25 times before, but was not called out to defend the city when Japanese troops finally marched in on December 8, 1941, and the city was occupied without a single shot being fired in its defense. The one exception was the small British naval vessel HMS Petrel, which was blown up and sunk in the Huangpu River just off the Bund. This absence of a battle at least had the affect of preserving the city center from any more war damage besides that already done in 1937. Although some of Shanghai's resident foreigners had evacuated the city before the final Japanese occupation, many had mistakenly chose to stay, refusing to believe that this was really the end of the Western imperial era, and later wound up in Japanese concentration camps.

Victor Sassoon was lucky enough to be in Bombay when the Japanese occupied the Settlement on December 8, 1941, so he escaped being interned in a Japanese prisoner of war camp. As an avid public supporter of the British war effort, he would undoubtedly have been treated badly by the Japanese. Others were not so lucky, including Sir Frederick Maze, the Inspector General of the Maritime Customs Service. The fate of those who were interned has been aptly portrayed by Hugh Collar in his book, _Captive in Shanghai_, as well as J.G. Ballard in his memoir, _Empire of the Sun_, later adapted into a movie of the same name by Stephen Spielberg. Wealthy upper class elites accustomed to luxurious lives of opulence attended by servants and chauffeurs found themselves living in squalid barracks fighting over an insufficient amount of boiled potatoes and dying of dysentery.

After the 1941 occupation it was some time before the first foreign residents of the city were interned in Japanese concentration camps in 1942. The first batch of internees included only those who were citizens of the Allied Powers and who were considered to be community leaders. The majority continued to remain free until January 1943, when the remaining Allied citizens were rounded up. Citizens of the Axis Powers such as Germany and Vichy France, and neutral countries such as Sweden and Switzerland, were not affected by the Japanese occupation and continued to live freely in the city from 1941 to 1945.

Although the North China Daily News stopped publishing on December 7, 1941, the American-owned Shanghai Evening Post and Mercury, and the British-owned Shanghai Times both continued publishing after the Japanese occupied the city.

The SMC decided on December 8, 1941 to continue functioning, in compliance with Japanese request, and although a Japanese (Katsuo Okazaki) became chairman for the first time, replacing John Hellyer Liddell on January 5, 1941, the Allied members of the council remarkably continued to serve in office for over one year of Japanese occupation until late

January 1943, when the American and British members were finally forced to resign. During the same time period Allied nationals also continued to serve in the SMC bureaucracy, particularly the finance and public works departments.

On Sept. 2, 1942 the Shanghai Volunteer Corps was finally formally dissolved, having survived the first 10 months of Japanese occupation. The Russian Detachment was transferred to the SMC police. One of the ironies of the Japanese occupation was that the former upper class of British and Americans suffered the most, while the Russians who had been looked down upon as low class remained free and even prospered.

In September 1942 all Allied nationals were required to begin wearing identifying arm bands in public, and in November 1942 the first select Allied nationals began to be rounded up. Internment of Allied nationals became wholesale in January 1943 with approximately 8,000 Allied nationals being interned in seven internment camps in the Shanghai area.

In the end, the International Settlement and French Concession managed to exist for a period of about 100 years. The International Settlement was abolished by the Allied powers in 1943, along with the other unequal treaties. The French Concession continued to exist under the administration of the collaborationist Vichy government until 1945. Although their history was fairly short, it was during these years that Shanghai saw its greatest development prior to the second building boom that started in 1990.

During the 1937-1945 Japanese occupation, there were five Chinese Mayors of Shanghai who chose to collaborate with the Japanese. Su Xiwen [苏锡文] (1889-1945) served two terms, first from December 5, 1937 to October 15, 1938, and then again from October 11 to November 19, 1940. In between Su's two terms, Fu Xiaoan [傅筱庵] (1872-1940) was Mayor from October 16, 1938 to October 10, 1940, when he was assassinated while still in office. Chen Gongbo [陈公博] (1892-1946) was the longest serving of the five collaborationist Shanghai Mayors, being in office for four years from November 20, 1940 to November 11, 1944. Wu Songgao [吴颂皋] (1898-1953) was Shanghai Mayor from November 12, 1944 to January 14, 1945. Zhou Fohai [周佛海] (1897-1948) was Shanghai Mayor from January 15, 1945 to September 12, 1945, including a month after the Japanese surrender, during which he continued in office at the request of Chiang Kai-shek (Jiang Jieshi) [蒋介石] (1887-1975.

The Guomindang Interlude: 1945-1949.

After the August 15, 1945 surrender of Japan declared by Emperor Hirohito, there was an almost month-long gap before the Guomindang could assert their control over Shanghai. Guomindang troops and government officials had to be air-lifted into Shanghai from their wartime capital of Chongqing by the U.S. Air Force. In the meantime, Zhou Fohai [周佛海] (1897-1948), the last of the wartime mayors to collaborate with the Japanese, was asked by Chiang Kai-shek to continue in office and maintain order with the help of Japanese troops who had not yet been disarmed.

By the middle of September 1945 the Guomindang authorities had regained control of Shanghai. Qian Dajun [錢大鈞] (1893-1982), initially became the first post-victory Mayor of Shanghai from September 12, 1945 until April 19, 1946, when he was replaced by K.C. Wu (Wu Guozhen) [吴国桢] (1903-1984). In the three years and nine months after the war during which the Guomindang controlled the city, life never really returned its pre-war state of normality.

The post-war victory over Japan and the end of the foreign concessions was celebrated by moving the Chinese municipality's government offices from their previous location in Jiangwan Town to the former **Shanghai Municipal Council** headquarters on Jiangxi Lu, and the changing of many Shanghai street names to honor Guomindang party officials.

Former Guomindang President **Lin Sen** [林森] (1868-1943) had his name affixed to the former Avenue Foche of the French Concession, which then became known as Lin Sen Road (Lin Sen Lu) [林森路], but is now known as Huaihai Road (Huaihai Lu).   Boulevard des Deux Republiques was briefly renamed Republic of China Road (Minguo Lu) [民国路] from 1946 to 1949, and then renamed again as People's Road (Renmin Lu) [人民路] after 1949. American General Albert C. Wedemeyer even had a road named after him, Weidemai Lu [魏德迈路], now known as Handan Lu [邯郸路].

Not content with having only one road named after himself, Guomindang leader Chiang Kai-shek (Jiang Jieshi) [蒋介石] (1887-1975) had no less than seven roads in both the former International Settlement and Fench Concession named after his nickname, Zhongzheng [中正], including Avenue Edward VII, the present day Yanan East Road (Yanan Dong Lu) [延安东路]; Avenue Foch West, the present day Yanan Middle Road (Yanan Zhong Lu) [延安中路]; the Great Western Road, present day Yanan West Road (Yanan Xi Lu) [延安西路]; Yates Road present day Shimen Yi Lu [石门一路]; Carter Road, present day Shimen Er Lu [石门二路]; Route des Soeurs, present day Ruijin Yi Lu [瑞金一路]; and Route Pere Robert, present day Ruijin Er Lu [瑞金二路].

However, those who had spent the eight years of the 1937-1945 Sino-Japanese war in exile in Sichuan looked upon those who had remained in Shanghai as collaborators with the Japanese puppet regime and treated them accordingly as a conquered people rather than liberated brothers.

Of the five Shanghai Mayors who served during the 1937-1945 Japanese occupation, two had already died while in office, one from natural causes and another by assassination. The three surviving collaborationist Shanghai Mayors were all captured by the Guomindang, imprisoned, and put on trial.   None of them escaped punishment.   Chen Gongbo [陈公博] (1892-1946) was convicted of treason in a court room trial held in Suzhou in April 1946, sentenced to the death penalty, and executed on June 3, 1946.   Wu Songgao [吴颂皋] (1898-1953) was sentenced to life in prison, where he finally died in 1953.   Zhou Fohai [周佛海] (1897-1948) was sentenced to the death penalty on November 7, 1946, despite having cooperated with the Guomindang during the month-long transition from Japanese occupation, but later died of a heart attack in a Nanjing prison on February 28, 1948.

Outside of politics, the most notable accusations of wartime collaboration were aimed at two Chinese university presidents who had remained in Shanghai during the war and kept their colleges open for classes; William Z.L. Sung (Shen Siliang) [沈嗣良] (1896-1967) President of St. John's University (Shanghai Sheng Yuehan Daxue) [上海圣约翰大学] from 1941 to 1946, and T.K. Van (Fan Zhengkang) [樊正康] (d.1972) President of the University of Shanghai (Hujiang Daxue) [沪江大学] from 1938 to 1946.   Keeping these two protestant missionary university's open in Shanghai during the war was controversial because the staff and students of the other ten protestant colleges in Japanese occupied China had retreated to Sichuan Province along with the Guomindang until the war was over.

Fan was replaced in 1946 by Henry H. Lin (Ling Xianyang) [凌宪扬] (1905-1958), simply because Lin had spent the war in the Guomindang capital of Chongqing while Van had been in Japanese occupied Shanghai.   Oddly, Fan's replacement Henry Lin ultimately suffered a worse fate than he did.

William Z.L. Sung (Shen Siliang) [沈嗣良] (1896-1967) suffered a much worse fate, being tried for collaboration by the Jiangsu High Court and imprisoned for two years starting in 1946 until he was finally acquitted of all charges and released in 1948.   He left China in 1949 and moved to the U.S.

After the end of the Sino-Japanese War in August 1945, the city was flooded with U.S. military personnel who occupied several key buildings in the downtown city center, as well as the **Jiangwan Airport** in Yangpu District.   Several hundred members of the U.S. Military Assistance Group in China occupied the Broadway Mansions, along with the Foreign Correspondents Club.   U.S. General **Albert C. Wedemeyer** lived in Victor Sassoon's private suite at the Cathay Hotel (Peace Hotel), only leaving sometime in 1946.   U.S. General **George C. Marshall** spent the whole year of 1946 in Shanghai trying to negotiate a peace settlement between the Guomindang and the Chinese Communist Party, but by January 1947 he had given up and the Chinese Civil War had resumed once again.   While he was here he lived in a mansion that is still referred to as the **Marshall House**, aka Taiyuan Villa (Taiyuan Bieshu) [太原别墅], which was later occupied by Mao's fourth wife Jiang Qing, and now serves as a branch of the Rujin Hotel.   The normal economy and society were disrupted by all these U.S. military personnel spending hard currency, while surplus U.S. military supplies and UNRAA aid often ended up on the black market.

On April 20, 1946 **K.C. Wu** (Wu Guozhen) [吴国桢] (1903-1984), assumed the position of Shanghai Mayor, a post he would hold for exactly three years until he fled to Taiwan with his family on April 30, 1949.   Wu was a native of Hubei province who had graduated from the Nankai Middle School in Tianjin, the Qinghua School in Beijing, and in 1926 he earned a Ph.D. from Princeton University in the U.S.   He served as Mayor of Hankou from 1932 to 1938, then Mayor of Chonqing from 1939 to 1942, during a time when it was the temporary national capital.   From 1943 to 1945 he was a deputy chief of the Foreign Affairs Ministry. In 1945 he became head of the publicity department of the Guomindang party central committee.   During his three years as Shanghai mayor Wu lived in a mansion that still stands today at 201 Anfu Lu in the area of the former French Concession.   The walled garden compound features an enormous lawn and a water fountain decorated with four Greco-Roman statues that were smashed into pieces during the Cultural Revolution, but later pieced back together again.

Wu was a very well educated man with a lot of professional experience running the administration of other large cities, but he still proved unable to successfully manage the extraordinary social and economic problems faced by post-war Shanghai.   Hyperinflation raged out of control. In January 1947 100 Yuan of Guomindang currency was equal to one U.S. dollar, but one year later it took 2,370 Yuan to equal one dollar in January 1948, and six months after that the rate of exchange had increased to 51,851 Yuan to the dollar by June 1948. Prices increased an average of 33.7 per cent per month from August 1945 to July

1948, and then skyrocketed to 300 per cent per month form August 1948 to April 1949. As a result, it required bundles of notes tied together in packets to make even the smallest purchase. Prices were rising so fast that the cost of living index had to be calculated every week, and in turn employee wages were paid weekly, four times a month.

Despite the victory over Japan, the economic and military situations remained dangerously unstable. Many Chinese and foreign businessmen could sense the wind's direction and decided early on to liquidate their assets and move overseas permanently. For example, Victor Sassoon was already planning the move of his business from China to the Bahamas, where he set up his new headquarters in Nassau. His assistant Ovadia returned to Shanghai in 1946 with the primary task of liquidating all of Sassoon's fixed assets in Shanghai, which were then valued at 7.5 million British pounds, with the Sassoon House building alone worth 1 million pounds, but it was hard to find buyers. In 1948 he paid his last visit to Shanghai and then left for the last time before the end of the year. One result of the lack of economic confidence was that virtually no new buildings were constructed during this time, with the result that when the Communists captured the city in May 1949 the skyline was basically the same as it had been when the Japanese surrounded Shanghai in the Fall of 1937. Between 1945 and 1949 only one new building was constructed on the Bund, the city's prime waterfront real estate beside the Huangpu River, the Bank of Communications Building (Jiaotong Yinhang Da Lou) [交通银行大楼] at 14 Zhongshan Dong Yi Lu [中山东一路 14 号].

In response to the financial and economic emergency within their territory, a new currency reform (bizhi gaige) [币制改革] aka (huobi gaige) [货币] was announced by the Guomindang central government in Nanjing on August 19, 1948, according to which Chinese citizens were forbidden to own gold, silver, or foreign currency and were required to surrender all their gold, silver, and foreign exchange in return for a new paper currency known as the Gold Yuan (Jin Yuan) [金圆]. Violators who were caught could have these assets seized by the government. The old Guomindang Yuan bank notes were exchanged at a rate of three million old Yuan to one new Gold Yuan (Jin Yuan) [金圆]. Added to this was another policy was another that froze all commodity prices, in order to stop hyperinflation.

Since it was the country's financial and economic center, Guomindang leader Chiang Kai-shek (Jiang Jieshi) [蒋介石] (1887-1975) sent his own son **Chiang Ching-kuo** (Jiang Jingguo) [蒋经国] (1910-1988) to Shanghai to implement the new finance and economic reforms there himself as head of the Shanghai Economic Control Committee (Shanghai Jingji Guanzhi Weiyuanhui) [上海经济管制委员会]. Over the next few months, the city's finances & economy were taken out of the hands of the mayor, **K.C. Wu** (Wu Guozhen) [吴国桢] (1903-1984). Jiang had been educated in the Soviet Union during a long stay there, and in many ways he was seen as hostile towards the bourgeois capitalist class. The price controls forced merchants to either sell goods at a loss, hoard goods in warehouses until prices went up later, or resort to selling on the black market. Chiang's draconian measures to enforce the government's economic policies included the arrest of prominent members of the upper class, such as Du Weibing [杜维屏], son of crime boss Du Yuesheng [杜月笙] (1888-1951), and Kong Lingkan [孔令侃] (1916-1992), son of former finance minister H.H. Kung (Kong Xiangxi) [孔祥熙] (1880-1967), which only earned him more resentment from the very social strata that should have been supporting the Guomindang regime. First lady Song Meiling was forced to intervene to secure the release from prison of many members of the upper class.   His brief but fierce strangle-hold over the Shanghai economy formally came to an end on November 1, 1948 when the Guomindang central government abolished the Shanghai Economic Control Committee (Shanghai Jingji Guanzhi Weiyuanhui) [上海经济管制委员会], and Chiang Ching-kuo's position along with it.

In addition to the economic collapse which was only made worse by the Gold Yuan (Jin Yuan) [金圆] fiasco and caused the Guomindang to lose any remaining public support it may have once had from the urban middle & upper classes, the military debacle of the November 1948-January 1949 **Battle of Huaihai** (Huaihai Zhanyi) [淮海战役] proved to be the decisive turning point in the Civil War.   After this defeat, Chiang Kai-shek (Jiang Jieshi) [蒋介石] (1887-1975) formally resigned as Guomindang President and was replaced by his Vice-President **Li Zongren** [李宗仁] (1891-1969), who attempted to negotiate a peaceful end to the civil war with the Communists while the Guomindang still controlled the half of the country south of the Yangzi River.   Although an honorable man who was much respected for having led the only Guomindang military victory over the Japanese at Taierzhuang [台儿庄] in March-April 1938, Li was powerless because behind the scenes Chiang Kai-shek continued to secretly control the government financial resources and maintained the loyalty of those Guomindang military officers who had graduated from the Whampoa Academy in Guangzhou (Huangpu Junxiao) [黄埔军校].

As of December 1948 the Central Bank of China (Zhongyang Yinhang) [中央銀行] housed in the former Yokohoma Specie Bank, Ltd. (Zhengjin Yinhang) [正金银行] on the Bund (Waitan) still held nearly 5 million taels (115 tons) of gold that had essentially been confiscated from Chinese citizens in August 1948 through the Gold Yuan scheme.   In a series of at least three or four separate operations, all this gold was shipped from Shanghai to Taiwan, along with all the silver and foreign currency.   On December 2, 1948 a British journalist named George Vine witnessed what he believed to be the first shipment of an estimated 2 million taels of gold being loaded onto ships and sent to Taiwan.   In a second incident in January 1949 an estimated 920,000 taels of gold (24 tons), large quantities of silver, and all of the foreign currency was shipped from Shanghai to Taiwan.   Later in February 1949 a fleet of nine C-46 aircraft were reportedly used by the Guomindang to fly more of the gold reserves from Shanghai to Taiwan.   According to some sources there was a fourth and final shipment of assets on May 18th.   Due to the extreme secrecy of the operations, and the fact that some knowledgeable witnesses were supposedly assassinated, exact dates and figures are hard to confirm, and sources often disagree about exactly how much money was taken, when, and how it was transported.   The Guomindang government official in charge of the shipments, Wu Songqing [吴嵩庆], never talked about it to anyone, but kept a diary that was later discovered by his son after his death.

The "Liberation" of Shanghai, May 1949

The Liberation (Jiefang) [解放] of Shanghai from the Guomindang by the Red Army on May 27, 1949 came a little less than a month after the earlier fall of the Guomindang national capital in Nanjing on April 23rd and was the last real battle of the Chinese Civil War, although Chengdu, the capital city of Sichuan province, would hold out until the end of December 1949. The neighboring cities of Suzhou and Hangzhou had also already fallen by the end of April, meaning that Shanghai was encircled on all sides except for the eastern seaboard. The Red Army advanced from Hangzhou to the southwest, taking Jiaxing on the Zhejiang-Shanghai border on May 12, 1949. This was the same approach that had been taken by the Taiping rebels in 1860-1862; Chiang Kai-shek (Jiang Jieshi) and Chen Qimei in 1911; Bai Chongxi in 1927; and the Japanese in 1937.

A defensive line of 5,000 concrete bunkers that had been constructed from Qibao Town in Minhang District to the Shanghai-Nanjing railway line was intended to safeguard Shanghai's western and southwestern frontier. Some of these fortifications can still be seen today, standing abandoned and forlorn in the middle of farmers' fields, including one on the north side of Caobao Road in Qibao Town. Trained by German military advisors in such methods in the 1930s, this kind of block-house strategy had succeeded in driving the Communists out of the Jiangxi Soviet area in 1934, but failed to defend Shanghai in May 1949.

With the battle for Shanghai proper starting on May 12, 1949, by May 14th the southwestern districts of Songjiang, Qingpu, and Jiading had all fallen to the Red Army, as had parts of Pudong including Jinshan, Fengxian, Nanhui, and Chuansha. However, the Guomindang tried to hold onto the Gaoqiao area as their last foothold in Pudong, even transferring troops there from the city center, because this was adjacent to the Wusong Kou passage where the Huanpgu and Yangzi rivers met, providing an essential maritime escape route from the city.

Since it was surrounded by hostile forces on all its land borders, access to the sea was seen as the only possible lifeline for the Guomindang defenders. Therefore, on May 18th the Guomindang commander General **Tang Enbo** [汤恩伯] (1899-1954) chose to make his decisive last stand at Wusong Kou, where the Huangpu flows into the Yangzi River. The waterway at the confluence remained under the control of the Guomindang navy, upon one of whose ships Tang Enbo had already taken refuge. Many members of the Chinese middle and upper classes, as well as many foreigners, chose to evacuate the city over the next few days, either flying out from the three airports that still remained opened or sailing on one of the last ships in port, which included an American destroyer.

By May 19th the Jiangwan Airport was within range of the Red Army's guns and being hit by incoming fire, and by May 23rd the Guomindang navy had been forced to withdraw from the Shanghai area by the coastal artillery fire of the Red Army. By May 24, 1949, the Red Army had occupied Hongqiao and Longhua towns, including both airports located there, as well as most of the downtown area south of Suzhou Creek and most of Pudong. The capture of Wusong and Gaoqiao by the Red Army on the night of May 25th cemented their control of the Wusong Kou area, preventing any hostile ships from entering or leaving the confluence of the Huangpu and Yangzi rivers. With the previous capture of all three airports several days earlier this cut off the last remaining possible avenue of escape.

The last remaining areas of Shanghai under Guomindang control were actually north of Suzhou creek in Zhabei, Yangpu, Hongkou, Boashan, and Chongming districts.   From May 25-27, 1949 there was the so-called "Battle of Broadway Mansions," during which 1,000 diehards of the Guomindang army occupied a line along the north side of Suzhou Creek, including the Post Office Building and the Broadway Mansions Building, from which their snipers were able to prevent the Red Army from crossing the Garden Bridge.   On May 26th, the deputy commander of the Songhu Garrison, General Liu Changyi [刘昌义] surrendered. Once the Red Flag was raised atop the Broadway Mansions building on May 27th, 1949, the "Liberation" of Shanghai was officially completed, although the occupation of Chongming Island was not finished until June 2, 1949.   Despite frequently found comments that this was a bloodless occupation, and widely varying statistics, there were at least 15,000 casualties on the Guomindang side and approximately 8,000 casualties among the Red Army, for a combined total of 23,000 casualties, not a small number.

Although it would be wrong to say that most of Shanghai's residents welcomed the Communists with enthusiasm, it would be correct to say that most probably welcomed the departure of the Guomindang, with its inflationary economic policies and iron-fisted police enforcement.   In fact, city residents reportedly intervened in the final days of the battle to prevent the Guomindang from carrying out a scorched earth strategy in which they had planned to destroy the city on their way out.   The city's residents definitely wanted a change, the Guomindang had definitely lost the mandate of heaven, but the residents were given only one choice as a new alternative, and after a brief interlude of fairly moderate polices under the administration of Shanghai's first post-Liberation mayor **Chen Yi** [陈毅] (1901-1972) that lasted until the 1957 Anti-Rightist Campaign (Fanyou Yundong) [反右运动], that alternative turned out to be just as arbitrary and iron-fisted as its predecessor.   The real tragedy of the Chinese Revolution, as first pointed out by **Harold Isaacs**, was that there was no moderate third force organized enough to take the middle way that probably most people would have wanted the country to pursue.

Cosmopolitan Shanghai 1843-1949

Until May 1949 Shanghai was an incredibly cosmopolitan city, with nationalities from all over the world represented amongst its resident population. Even the Shanghai Volunteer Corps, normally viewed as simply a tool of British imperialism, reflected the multinational nature of the population. At various times in its history the SVC included Phillipino, German, Austro-Hungarian, Portuguese, American, Japanese, Chinese, Russian and even Jewish military units.

Shanghai's Russian Community

Swelled by White Russian refugees from the Russian Civil War, Shanghai's Russian community was large enough to support the construction of several Russian Orthodox Churches (Dongzhen Jiaotang)[东正教堂], two of which still exist today but have been converted into trendy restaurants, as well as a monument to the Russian writer Pushkin, which also still stands today. The Russian detachment of the Shanghai Volunteer Corps (SVC) was by far its largest military unit and its costs accounted for more than half of the SVC's annual budget. Many of the books published about Shanghai in the 1920s and 1930s were written by resident Russian authors, such as A. M. Kotenev and I.I. Kounin. Illustrations for locally published books and newspapers were provided by Russian artists such as A. Yaron and George Sapojnikov (Sapajou). Having escaped from Communism in their home country, few if any Russians chose to stay in Shanghai after it was captured by the Chinese Communists in May 1949.

In 1917 the Russian population of Shanghai was only 700-800, but thanks to the 1917 Russian Revolution, by 1920 the resident Russian population of Shanghai had already grown to 2,000-3,000. Shanghai's Russian community experienced its greatest growth during the seven years from 1922 to 1929 when the annual waves of immigrants averaged 1,500 new Russian arrivals each year. By 1929 the Russian community of Shanghai had grown to a total of more than 13,000 persons.

Over 3,000 White Russian refugees who fled from Vladivostok when the Russian Civil War finally ended in December 1922 eventually ended up in Shanghai. The first White Russian fleet of fifteen ships commanded by Admiral I.K. Stark anchored at Wusong Kou with 1,688 passengers. Later a second White Russian fleet of three ships commanded by Lt. General F.L. Glebov arrived in Shanghai in September 1923 with 1,000 armed Cossack officers, soldiers, and sailors. Finally another Russian ship arrived with 700 former White Russian soldiers on board.

When in 1925 the Soviet Union took over control of the Chinese Eastern Railway, 2,000 more White Russians departed Harbin for Shanghai in search of work. This coincided fortuitously with the June-August 1925 Shanghai general strike, during which White Russians began taking the place of striking Chinese workers. By 1927 the Russian refugee population of Shanghai had reached over 8,000.

In January 1927 100 of General Glebov's men formed the first Russian detachment of the International Settlement's Shanghai Volunteer Corps (SVC). By 1928 the Russian Detachment consisted of 250 officers and men in two companies. They were the only full-time paid troops of the SVC.

By January 1932 Shanghai's Russians numbered 15,768 persons and were the second largest group of non-Chinese residents after the Japanese. The Russian detachment of the SVC had by then grown to three companies totaling 435 enlisted men and 19 officers. Later a fourth Russian company was added to make up the Russian Battalion. When in March 1935 the Soviet Union sold the Chinese Eastern Railway to Japan, it created yet another exodus of Russians from Manchuria to Shanghai.

Russians formed 60 per cent of the Shanghai Municipal Orchestra. Aleksandr Pushkin's birthday was celebrated by the local Russian community every June 6th. There were six Russian daily newspapers in Shanghai, of which the leading Russian newspaper was *Shankhaiskaia Zaria,* as well as a Russian radio station.

The Russian Orthodox Cathedral (Dongzhen Jiaotang)[东正教堂] on Rue Paul Henri, now known as Xinle Lu [新乐路] began construction in 1932. A second Russian Orthodox Church (Dongzhen Jiaotang)[东正教堂], The St. Nicholas Church on Rue Corneille, now known as Gaolan Lu [皋兰路], was built in 1932 as a memorial to Tsar Nicholas II and was frequented by White Russian army officers and their families.

At the time of the Japanese December 8, 1941occupation of the city, Shanghai had 30,000 Russian refugees and an additional 6-8,000 Russian Jews. Shanghai's Slavic community apparently did not suffer the same persecutions during the Japanese occupation as did the city's Western inhabitants, and at the end of the war in 1945 the Russian community was still largely intact. However during the Guomindang interlude of 1945-1949 they began to leave. 4,000 White Russians returned to the Soviet Union between August 1947 and March 1948 under a general amnesty program.

Shanghai's Jewish Community

Some of Shanghai's wealthiest businessmen were Jewish, including the Sassoon, Kadoorie and Hardoon families. Many of the fabulous mansions they lived in and the commercial enterprises they built can still be seen today. This group of Jewish residents was the first wave to arrive in the 19th Century and uniformly belonged to the Sephardim or Baghdadi Jewish community originating in the Middle East rather than the Ashkenazim of Russia and Eastern Europe.

David Sassoon & Sons had first set up a branch of its import-export business in Shanghai in 1845. They also had an office in Hankou. Later, Sir **Victor Sassoon** (1881-1961) headed the new rival family firm of E.D. Sassoon and Co. from 1920. **Silas A. Hardoon** worked for both of the two rival Sassoon family companies, and is most famous for the garden he built in Shanghai in 1909, the Hardoon Garden (Hatong Hua Yuan) [哈同花园], which was demolished in 1954. Sir **Elly Kadoorie** (1867-1944) was a Sephardic (Baghdadi) Jew who served as the President of the Shanghai Zionist Association from 1915 to 1928. The Kadoorie's famous residence, the so-called Marble Hall, was built in 1924 and continued to serve as the Kadoorie family home until 1949.

At the beginning of the 20th Century there were between 800 and 1,000 Sephardic (Baghdadi) Jews in Shanghai. In 1924 Shanghai's Jewish population had reached 3,000, including the 19th Sephardic immigrants and the Ashkenazim who had arrived from Russia since 1900. By the middle of the 1930s the Shanghai Jewish community had risen to 5,000.

More than 50 Jewish newspapers and magazines were published in Shanghai from 1903-1949, and more than 30 newspapers were published by Jewish refugees in Shanghai. The most influential of them all, *Israel's Messenger,* published its first issue on April 22, 1904. **N.E.B. Ezra** was one of its three founders and served as the Chief Editor from 1904 to 1936. During the same time he acted as Secretary of the Shanghai Zionist Association.

Shanghai's Jewish population supported the construction of a number of synagogues, two of which still stand today, but neither of which are used as houses of worship now. When the Communists occupied Shanghai in May 1949, the city had four main synagogues. The Sephardic **Ohel Rachel Synagogue** on Seymour Road (Shanxi Bei Lu) was founded by Sir Jacob Sassoon in 1920. The **Ohel Moshe Synagogue** on Ward Road (Changyang Lu) was founded by Russian Jews in 1907, and later moved to its present site in 1927. The **Beth Aharon Synagogue** on Museum Road (Huqiu Lu) [虎丘路] was established by Silas A. Hardoon in 1927, and housed the Mir Yeshiva during the 1937-1945 Japanese occupation, but was "demolished" in 1985. The so-called **New Synagogue** was built on Rue de la Tour (Xiangyang Nan Lu) by Russian Ashkenazim in 1941. After 1953 it was the only functioning synagogue still in operation. Services continued until 1956, making it not only the last built before the 1949 revolution, but also the last to be closed down by the new Communist regime. After its closure over 4,000 Jewish books were shipped from Shanghai to Israel. In 1993 the New Synagogue was "demolished."

Other Jewish community institutions included a school and a social club. The **Shanghai Jewish School** on Seymour Road (Shanxi Bei Lu), which opened in 1932 and operated until 1949. It is a two-story, rectangular, red brick building, near the Ohel Rachel Synagogue. The **Shanghai Jewish Club** on Route Pichon (Fenyang Lu) looks like a two-story French residential mansion with a carport, and is now apparently surrounded by an asphalt playground of a school. The **Shanghai Jewish Club** held an annual ball every year from 1920 to 1949, and in 1947 laid the foundation stone for a new expansion of the building.

The Jewish unit of the Shanghai Volunteer Corps may have been the first Jewish fighting force of modern times. In September 1932 the first Jewish platoon of the SVC was formed. A second platoon was added a few months later. On May 26, 1933 a completely Jewish company of SVC was formed.

Shanghai was the only city in the world that welcomed Jewish refugees from Germany with open arms during the 1930s, accepting an estimated 20,000 to 30,000 Jewish refugees from Europe before 1941. By Pan Guang's estimate, at the end of 1941 the city contained a total of 25,000 Jewish refugees. Although Victor Sassoon was never a practicing Jew, he aided the Jewish refugees who settled in the Hongkou ghetto area reserved for them by the Japanese.

On February 18, 1943 the Japanese proclaimed what was officially known as the "Designated Area for Stateless Refugees," but was unofficially called the Hongkou Jewish ghetto. According to the Japanese proclamation, the boundaries of the area were to follow a line connecting Muirhead Road with Dent Road in the West, the International Settlement's northern boundary in the North, Yangpu Creek in the East, and a line connecting Wayside Road (now Huoshan Lu) [霍山路] with East Seward Road in the south. According to a map in Pan Guang's study, the Jewish ghetto was apparently bordered by Yangpu Lu to the south, with Point Road (now Dinghai Lu) [定海路] marking the northern limit, Chow Foong

Road the western limit, and King Chow Road the eastern limit.   Its central area included Ward Road (now Changyang Lu) [长阳路], Wayside Road (now Huoshan Lu) [霍山路], and Tang Shan Road.   Since the names of these rather obscure streets have all since changed, it's fortunate that a memorial in Huoshan Park (Huoshan Gongyuan) [霍山公园] states that the Designated Area for Stateless Refugees was bounded by Gongping Lu in the West, Tongbei Lu in the East, Huiming Lu in the South, and Zhoujiazui Lu on the North.   By 1956 the Jewish refugees had all left Shanghai.

The Koreans

A large Korean population lived here before the Japanese occupations of 1937 and 1941, having sought to escape the brutal Japanese occupation of their home country, which had been annexed by Japan in 1910.   After the Japanese occupations of 1937 and 1941 these refugee Koreans were once again enslaved by the Japanese.   A monument to this now vanished population has been erected in Lu Xun Park.

The Japanese

As discussed in the section on the 1932 Shanghai war, the Hongkou and Yangpu Districts had so many Japanese residents that the area was often referred to as the "Japanese Concession," although no such concession formally existed, and the area was in fact officially still part of the British dominated International Settlement.   After the end of World War II in August 1945, the entire Japanese population was deported back to Japan.

Intellectual Shanghai: 1918-1949

The history of Intellectual Shanghai before 1949 is closely connected with that of Revolutionary Shanghai.   In fact, they had common origins in the person of a single man, **Chen Duxiu** [陈独秀] (1879-1942).   Chen was not only the founder of the Chinese Communist Party in 1921, but also the founder of the crucial literary magazine, *New Youth (Xin Qingnian)* [新青年], published in Shanghai starting in 1915.   It was this magazine which first published such budding new authors as **Hu Shi** [胡适](1891-1962) and **Lu Xun** [鲁迅] (1881-1936).   Later, in March 1930, the Chinese Communist Party inspired the creation of the era's most influential literary organization, the **League of Leftist Writers** (Zuoyi Zuojia Lianmeng) [左翼作家联盟].   This group came to include all the intellectual celebrities of the day, such as **Ding Ling** [丁玲] (1904-1986), **Mao Dun** [茅盾] (1896-1981), **Ba Jin** [巴金] (1904-2005), **Guo Moruo** [郭沫若] (1892-1978), and **Lu Xun** [鲁迅] (1881-1936).   Today there are many sights of interest in Shanghai's Hongkou District related to these pre-revolutionary intellectuals, so an understanding of who they were would be quite useful for a visitor.

Lu Xun [鲁迅] (1881-1936)

The most famous of these writers, both then and now, was undoubtedly **Lu Xun** [鲁迅] (1881-1936.   Lu Xun [鲁迅] (1881-1936) was born as Zhou Shuren [周树人] in the city of Shaoxing in Zhejiang Province on September 25, 1881.   His first higher education was at a Naval College in Nanjing, which still stands there today on Zhongshan North Road (Zhongshan Bei Lu).   Finally he went to Japan to study for several years.   He first focused on medicine at the Sendai Medical College, and then later moved to Tokyo to study literature.   In 1910 he returned to China and worked as a teacher and headmaster, first at the Hangzhou Normal School and then at the Shaoxing Normal School.   After the 1911 Revolution he worked briefly for the new Republican Ministry of Education in both Nanjing and Beijing.   He ended up living in Beijing from 1912 to 1919, staying at the Shaoxing Guild House there, and it was there that he wrote his first stories.

When China's so-called "Literary Revolution" began, Lu Xun adopted his famous pseudonym and began publishing his first short stories in the magazine, *New Youth* (*Xin Qingnian)* [新青年], *known* also by its French name *La Jeunesse*, which had been founded three years earlier in 1915 by Chen Duxiu [陈独秀] (1879-1942), who was later one of the founders of the Chinese Communist Party in 1921.   **Hu Shi** [胡适](1891-1962) had earlier published an essay in *New Youth* (Xin Qingnian) [新青年] in January 1917 calling for a reform of Chinese literature through use of the vernacular **Baihua** [白话] language used by the everyday man on the street, rather than the much more formal literary language which had dominated Chinese writing until then.   Lu Xun's important new contribution to Chinese literature was to be the first writer to take up Hu Shi's suggestion and compose short stories in this Baihua [白话] vernacular.   In addition, he developed a satirical style of writing known as **Zawen** [杂文], in which he indirectly criticized targets of his wrath in the current Chinese society, often by using the allegory of disguising his real opponents in the cloak of historical figures from the past.   In 1918 Lu Xun's first short story, "*Diary of a Madman,*" appeared in *New Youth (Xin Qingnian)* [新青年], and this was followed shortly thereafter by "*Kong Yiji*" [孔乙己], published the same year.   These first two short stories initiated what was probably his peak period of writing.   Over the next eight years he published "*The True Story* of Ah-Q," (1921-22), "*A Call to Arms*," 1923, and "*Wandering*," 1926.   After this he became more involved in, and victimized by, the politics of his time.

In 1926 he became the Dean of Zhongshan University in Guangzhou, then the political and military base of the Guomindang.   In the same year he wrote one autobiographical piece about his hometown of Shaoxing, "*From Hundred Plant Garden to Three Flavor Study*," (1926).   While in Guangzhou he supported the Guomindang's **Northern Expedition** (Bei Fa) [北伐] (1926-1928) to re-unite China under their rule, and even gave lectures at the Guomindang's military officer training academy on Whampoa Island.   However, after the April 12, 1927 **Shanghai Massacre** of leftists (Siyier Canan) [四一二惨案] perpetrated by the right-wing of the party led by Chiang Kai-shek (Jiang Jieshi) [蒋介石] (1887-1975), Lu Xun broke with the Guomindang and began gradually cooperating more with the Communist Party.   After this his published works were banned by the Guomindang in all areas under their control, and he moved to Shanghai in search of the relative safety from political persecution offered by the International Settlement.   During this time he experimented with prose poems in two works, "*Wild Grass*," (1927) and "*Dawn Blossoms Plucked at Dusk*,"(1928).   His last major work, "*Old Stories Retold*," came out just before his death on October 19, 1936 and was actually a collection of stories he had been working on since 1922.

Although he had joined the League of Leftist Writers [左翼作家联盟] in 1930, he never fully agreed with the Communist Party's policy that all writing should serve the political goals of the revolution.   In one notable quote, he criticized those who thought "that literature should be used to propagandize, to advance, to incite, to help carry out the revolution," and instead argued that, "good writing has never been produced under orders from other people; good writing is free..."   During the last ten years of his life, Lu Xun was in fact caught in between the political agendas of both the Guomindang on the right and the Communist Party on the left.

He spent the last months of his life locked in a violent debate with official Communist party policy.   After the **League of Leftist Writers** (Zuoyi Zuojia Lianmeng) [左翼作家联盟] was dissolved in early 1936, a new Communist-sponsored writers association had been formed, and a new policy line laid out by the party that all writers should now support the United Front with the Guomindang.   Lu Xun not only refused to join the new writers' association but in a June 1936 manifesto signed by 66 supporters he publicly rejected the party line, partly out of opposition to its content and partly on the principle that writers should never be told what they should or shouldn't write by any party or government, right or left.   Arrayed against him in support of the party line were **Guo Moruo** [郭沫若] (1892-1978), Zhou Yang, and Xu Maoyong, most of whom prospered under the new regime after 1949.

At the May 1942 Yanan Forum on Literature and Art, Mao Zedong [毛泽东] (1893-1976) directly criticized those writers such as **Ding Ling** [丁玲] (1904-1986) who had continued to use Lu Xun's now forbidden satirical Zawen [杂文] style of writing.   Mao's comments were later republished in 1967 as "*On Literature and Art*."   It is therefore most ironic that the 1956 version of Lu Xun's tomb now bears an inscription from Mao Zedong.   Furthermore, Lu Xun's writer friends who had supported him in the 1936 debate all paid the price later, most being purged between 1955 and 1957, including **Ba Jin** [巴金] (1904-2005), Feng Xuefeng, Hu Feng, and Huang Yuan, with only **Mao Dun** [茅盾] (1896-1981) surviving in his post as Minister of Culture until he too was purged in 1965.   Some of Lu Xun's biographers in the

West, such as T.A. Hsia and Harold Isaacs, have speculated that if he had lived longer Lu Xun himself would probably have also been purged sometime after 1949. During the Cultural Revolution Lu Xun's former home, which had been turned into a museum, was closed to the public, and his former wife's home was searched, during which her collection of his private correspondence was seized, causing her to suffer a fatal heart attack in 1968.

Mao Dun [茅盾] (1896-1981)

Like Lu Xun, **Mao Dun** [茅盾] (1896-1981) was a Guomindang official in Guangzhou in 1926. However, during the Guomindang's Northern Expedition to unify China under their rule, he sided with the left-wing of the party that had set up a separate regime in Wuhan, where he served as the editor of its official newspaper, the Minguo Ribao. After the Guomindang right-wing seized power under the leadership of Jiang Jieshi, Mao Dun escaped to the safety of Japan for several years, returning to Shanghai just in time to join in the founding of the League of Leftist Writers (Zuoyi Zuojia Lianmeng) [左翼作家联盟] in 1930. During the 1930s he published his two most famous works, "*Midnight*," and "*Spring Silkworms.*"

After the 1949 revolution he was initially rewarded for his loyalty to the party by being appointed as Minister of Culture and having his previous works republished. However, in 1965 he was suddenly purged from his post and disappeared from view for the duration of the Cultural Revolution, as did his published works, which vanished from the shelves. As late as 1978 it was still impossible to buy a copy of "*Midnight*" in China, this despite the fact that this work more than any other exposed the worst evils of the pre-1949 social order which the revolution was supposedly intended to solve.

When Mao Dun [茅盾] (1896-1981) suddenly reappeared in 1977 it turned out that he had spent the previous twelve years under house arrest, a fairly light sentence compared to others, but his worst punishment had been that he was prohibited from writing all that time. After being out of print since 1957, Mao Dun's classic work, "*Midnight*," was finally reissued in 1979, along with another volume of collected works, "*Spring Silkworms and Other Stories.*" However, he died on April 5, 1981 without having been able to publish any additional new works.

Ding Ling [丁玲] (1904-1986)

The woman writer **Ding Ling** [丁玲] (1904-1986) suffered a similar fate of dual persecution by both regimes before and after the 1949 revolution. Her writing career had started with the 1928 story, "*The Diary of Miss Sophie*," which was followed several years later by, "*Shanghai In the Spring of 1930.*" After joining the League of Leftist Writers (Zuoyi Zuojia Lianmeng) [左翼作家联盟] in 1932, she was kidnapped by the Guomindang police in 1933 and imprisoned at the regime's capital in Nanjing. Public pressure finally forced her release three years later in 1936, after which she immediately fled to the Communist redoubt in Yanan and joined the party's leadership there.

Once in Yanan she came into conflict with the Communist Party over two controversial essays she published there. "*We Need the Zawen*," published on October 23, 1941 in Jiefang Ribao, was a defense of the satirical style of writing Lu Xun had used to expose the failings in others. "*Thoughts on March 8*," which criticized the unequal treatment of women in Communist controlled territory was published in Jiefang Ribao on March 9, 1942, the day after International Women's Day.   As a result, in May 1942 she came under heavy direct fire from Mao Zedong himself at the Yanan Forum on Literature and Art, after which she was silenced during several years of forced Marxist re-education.

Although later she won the 1951 Stalin Prize for Literature, her continued demands for freedom of speech caused her to repeatedly fall afoul of the party line.   She was purged from all her positions during the 1957 Anti-Rightist Campaign, much earlier than those who began to suffer at the start of the Cultural Revolution nine years later.   After being expelled from the party, Ding Ling [丁玲] (1904-1986) disappeared from public view until her rehabilitation in 1975.   By the time of her release she had spent 22 years in Communist prisons and labor camps.   During that time all of her published works were banned.   Only in 1985, the year before she died, was she finally allowed by the Communist Party to publish a volume of nine of her collected works, *Miss Sophie's Diary and Other Stories.*

Higher Education

Under the heading of intellectual Shanghai we could also include the fate of the pre-Liberation universities and their leadership.   Among the 13 Protestant Colleges in China that had been set up by Christian missionaries, two were located in Shanghai, **St. John's University** (Shanghai Sheng Yuehan Daxue) [上海圣约翰大学] founded in 1879 in present day Changning District, and the **University of Shanghai** (Hujiang Daxue) [沪江大学] founded in 1906 in present day Yangpu District.   Both controversially continued to operate during the Japanese occupation of 1937-1945, which caused their wartime presidents to be arrested after the war was over.   By September 1952 both had been shut down and taken over by the new Shanghai municipal government, only to reopen later under new names and administrators or merged into other educational institutions.

Both campuses continue to function as educational institutions to this day.   The St. John's University campus is by far the better preserved with nearly all of its previous historic buildings still intact, whereas the University of Shanghai campus stood right in the pathway of numerous military invasions of Shanghai coming from Wusong Kou towards the city center, including in the 1911 Revolution, the 1932 Japanese invasion, the 1937 Japanese invasion, and the 1949 liberation of the city by the Red Army, as a result of which most of its historic buildings were destroyed.

In September 1952 the campus and buildings of **St. John's University** (Shanghai Sheng Yuehan Daxue) [上海圣约翰大学] in between Zhongshan Park (Zhongshan Gongyuan) [中山公园]and the Suzhou River at 1575 Wanhangdu Lu in Changning District [长宁区万航渡路 1575 号] were occupied by the Politics & Law School (Zhengfa Xueyuan) of East China Normal University (Huadong Shifan Daxue), now known as **East China Politics & Law University** (Huadong Zhengfa Daxue) [华东政法大学].

In 1952 the **University of Shanghai** (Hujiang Daxue) [沪江大学] Yanpgu District campus and its buildings beside the Huangpu River were occupied by the predecessors of the present-day **Shanghai University of Science & Technology** (Shanghai Ligong Daxue) [上海理工大学] located at 470 Jungong Lu [軍工路].

Henry H. Lin (Ling Xianyang) [凌宪扬] (1905-1958), the last President of the University of Shanghai (Hujiang Daxue) [沪江大学] was arrested in 1951, held for six years until he was briefly released in 1957, then re-arrested again the same year and sentenced to ten years in prison.   He died in September 1958 in a prison labor camp at the age of 53.   Twenty one years later, in 1979 his widow succeeded in getting his 1957 conviction reversed and he was posthumously rehabilitated.

Criminal Shanghai: 1843-1949

The Opium Trade

Criminal Shanghai had its roots in the 19th century opium trade.   As the name of the 1839-1842 Opium War implies, the British practice of importing and selling opium in China was at least one of the issues involved.   It's an unfortunate fact that many of the early British and American trading companies in China imported opium in order to finance their exports of Chinese products abroad.   The opium trade soon moved from Canton (Guangzhou) to Shanghai after it was opened as a treaty port in 1843.   By 1845 Shanghai had become a major opium entrepot.   As a result of the 1858 Treaty of Tientsin (Tianjin), the opium trade was legalized in the British Concession, which began issuing licenses to dealers.   However, the tide of moral indignation began to turn against the opium trade in 1909 with the establishment of the International Opium Commission.   This was followed soon after by the 1911-12 Hague Conference, which succeeded in forcing the International Concession to outlaw opium.   Although this caused otherwise reputable foreign companies to abandon the trade, the resulting vacuum only created an opportunity for new organized crime figures to seize control of it, not unlike the prohibition of alcohol in the U.S. during the 1920s.

The Green Gang (Qing Bang) [青帮]

The most notorious of the Chinese crime organizations to emerge was the Green Gang (Qing Bang) [青帮] led by the triumvirate of Huang Jinrong [黄金荣](1868-1953), Zhang Xiaolin [张啸林] (1877-1940) and Du Yuesheng [杜月笙] (1888-1951), who were sometimes colloquially referred to as "Shanghai's Three Big Shots" (Shanghai San Daheng) [上海三大亨].   The crucial role the Green Gang played during the political events of 1927 has already been described.   In the beginning, Huang and Zhang were the more senior partners, and Du was merely their young apprentice.

Huang Jinrong [黄金荣](1868-1953) had joined the French Concession police force in 1892 at the age of 24.   He later became a Detective, then Inspector and finally in 1919 Chief Superintendent, before retiring from the police force in 1925 to devote himself full-time to his criminal activities.   Two sights in Shanghai related to him that can still be seen today include the Great World Amusement Center (Dashijie) [大世界], which he acquired in 1931, and the traditional Chinese garden where he once lived, Huangjia Huayuan [黄家花园], now known as Guilin Park (Guilin Gongyuan) [桂林公园]. Huang chose to stay in Shanghai both after it was captured by the Japanese in December 1941 and again after the Communist's Red Army liberated the city in May 1949, even while both of those times his business partner Du Yuesheng fled to Hong Kong.   On May 7, 1951 Huang submitted to the new authorities a completed written confession of his crimes, which is still held in the Shanghai Municipal Archives.   As part of his political re-education, or punishment for his sins, in 1951 he was forced to use a broom to sweep the sidewalk and street in front his own former building, the Great World Amusement Center (Dashijie) [大世界], while photographers took pictures of him that were later published in the local Shanghai newspapers. He finally died in Shanghai in June 1953 at the ripe old age of 85.

Du Yuesheng [杜月笙] (1888-1951) was originally an uneducated peasant from the backwoods village of Gaoqiao in Pudong. His name was first mentioned in the local Shanghai media in late 1924 when a letter to the editor of the North China Herald accused him of being "an opium and arms smuggler." The opium trade provided the foundation of Du's career. Du Yuesheng had reached an agreement with French Concession authorities in 1925, which gave Du what Brian Martin calls "an official monopoly" on opium trade in the concession and allowed him to sell it on "an open basis," and this was reaffirmed in a second agreement of February 1927. A similar agreement had been reached between Du and SMC Chairman Stirling Fessenden for "non-operation of the opium laws" in the International Settlement. Du also reached an agreement with the Guomindang central government in 1932 that maintained his opium monopoly in the Chinese districts of Shanghai. In July 1935 Du was ironically made one of the three standing committee members of the Shanghai Municipal Opium Suppression Committee, which simply allowed him to protect his own opium business.

However, it was Du's ability to build on the financial success of his opium business and develop a career as a local politician that truly set him aside from his fellow Green Gang leaders. When the French Concession Chinese Ratepayers Association was established in January 1927 Du was among its leaders. In July 1929 he was actually appointed by the French Consul to the Provisional Commission, the French Concessions' equivalent to a Municipal Council. When in November 1930 the French Consul agreed to allow the Chinese Ratepayers Association to elect the Chinese members of the Provisional Commission, this effectively gave Du control over the commission's Chinese membership, since he already controlled the association.

Du's political career in the French Concession suffered a setback when he was forced to resign from the Provisional Commission on February 15, 1932. Shortly thereafter, in mid-February 1932, one of the most notorious events of Du's life occurred when the entire leadership of the French Concession succumbed to fatal or near fatal illnesses immediately after having dinner together at Du's house. The victims included the French Consul General Koechlin; the commander of French military forces, Colonel A. Marcaire; and the French Chief of Police, Etienne Fiori. Fiori later recovered, but among the other fatal victims of Du's dinner party was M. du Pac de Marsoulies, the first owner of the **Marshall House**, which still stands today and is now known as the Taiyuan Villa (Taiyuan Bieshu) [太原别墅].

In the 1930s Du's political career expanded out of the French Concession and into the Chinese administered municipality of Greater Shanghai (Shanghai Shi). Du took over chairmanship of the Shanghai Civic Association in November 1934, and in July 1936 Du was elected to the five-man standing committee of the Shanghai Chamber of Commerce (Shanghai Shi Zong Shanghui) [上海市总商会].

In addition to his career as a local politician, Du's transformation from opium dealer was remarkable for his entry into legitimate fields of respectable business, most notably banking. Du was either a founder or later joined the Board of Directors of at least six commercial banks in Shanghai. He was involved in the 1928 establishment of the Pudong Commercial Bank, of which he later became Chairman; established the Zhonghui Bank in March 1929 and served as its Chairman of the Board; joined the Board of Directors of the Commercial Bank of China in June 1932, and later became its Chairman of the Board; founded the Minfu Union Commercial Bank in 1933; helped establish the Bank of Asia in 1934; was one of the founders of the China Investment Bank in 1935; and acquired the Jiangsu-Zhejiang Commercial and Savings Bank In 1936. His two greatest achievements in the banking industry came in 1935 when he was appointed by the Guomindang central government to the Board of Directors of both the Bank of China (Zhongguo Yinhang) and the Central Bank of China (Zhongyang Yinghang) [中央銀行].

The main historic sights related to Du's life that can still be seen today include several former mansions now belonging to the Donghu Hotel, as well as another building currently occupied by the Mansion Hotel. See the the entry for Du Yuesheng's Da Gong Guan [杜月笙大公馆] under the letter D in the alphabetical section of this book for more details.

Prostitution and Sexuality

In addition to opium, Shanghai's other main vice was undoubtedly prostitution. Prostitution was so common in pre-1949 Shanghai that many travel guidebooks for visitors included directions to the main red light districts, which included Fuzhou Lu and Sichuan Bei Lu.

Brothels were always legal and licensed in the French Concession, but the International Settlement went through a continuing series of changing polices towards it, fluctuating between toleration, regulation, and unsuccessful attempts at abolition. A 1920 Shanghai Municipal Council plan called for the licensing of prostitutes and the gradual abolition of prostitution within five years. By December 31, 1924 the last licensed brothel in the International Settlement was closed, but the "license and eliminate scheme" ultimately failed to work owing to several reasons; upper class prostitutes known as courtesans or sing song girls escaped through a legal loophole that licensed them separately; lower class call girls simply moved into hotels as their base of operations; and many brothels simply moved into the French Concession, Extra-Settlement Outside Area Roads, or Chinese-administered parts of the city where prostitution was still legal.

The various Chinese governments of Shanghai also found themselves unable to eliminate prostitution and instead turned to licensing and regulation. In 1928 the Guomindang outlawed prostitution in the provinces of Jiangsu, Zhejiang and Anhui, but this simply resulted in a mass migration of prostitutes into the foreign concessions of Shanghai. During the Guomindang interlude in Shanghai from 1945 to 1949, prostitutes and brothels were licensed, while their successors The PRC also continued to license prostitutes for the first two years of their regime.

Attempts at accurately estimating the numbers of prostitutes at any given time are thwarted by the various methods and motives involved in counting them, as well as the continuing growing phenomenon of so-called "unlicensed" prostitutes who worked part-time under the disguise of outwardly legitimate occupations such as dancers in dance halls, massage girls in massage parlors, waitresses, and tour guides.

Available statistics counting the officially licensed full-time Chinese prostitutes working out of easily visible brothels begin with a health official's count in 1871 of 1,632 in the International Settlement and 2,600 in the French Concession. The 1871 survey would seem to imply that the phenomenon of widespread prostitution in Shanghai preceded the arrival of significant foreigners in the city, and the root causes of it thus may lie in Chinese society itself. In fact, Sing Song Girls (Xian Sheng) and "official prostitutes" (Guan Ji) were common during the Yuan and Ming Dynasties. A survey conducted by the Shanghai Municipal Council in 1915 counted 7,791 prostitutes; while a 1920 vice report counted 4,522 prostitutes in the International Settlement alone. In addition to the Chinese prostitutes counted in these numbers, in the 1930s it was estimated there were another 8,000 Russian prostitutes. At the time the Sino-Japanese War ended in 1945, there were 902 licensed brothels and 4,982 Chinese prostitutes recorded.

Estimates which included both official full-time and amateur part-time Chinese prostitutes ranged from 60,000 in 1920; 120,000 in 1927; 100,000 in 1935 (1 in every 13 Chinese women); and 25,000 in the International Settlement alone in 1937. After 1945 it was estimated there were 50,000 full-timers and an equal number of part-timers (1 in every 15 Chinese women).

In the 1930s young girls described as so-called "floating rafts" wandered public places in search of dates with strange men, hotels attracted mobile massage girls who went door to door, and performances by strippers and nude girls were openly advertised in the media. Gail Hershatter has concluded in her book *Dangerous Pleasures* that there was a "popularization" of prostitution in Shanghai during this time. Hershatter describes this widespread trend towards greater and greater public openness towards sexuality as the, "sexualizing of Shanghai life," which she says "blurred the boundaries between prostitutes and other women." This assessment of pre-1949 Shanghai social morals could just as easily describe the Shanghai of the economic boom years from 1990 to 2013.

When the Communists occupied Shanghai In early 1949 there were 518 licensed brothels and 1,897 licensed prostitutes. By mid-1950 prostitution was still officially legal, but the numbers had been reduced down to only 158 licensed brothels and 662 licensed prostitutes. By November 1951 this had been further reduced to 72 licensed brothels and 180 licensed prostitutes. The final crackdown came on November 25, 1951 when 324 brothel owners were arrested and 501 prostitutes were rounded up for re-education camps. In 1958 the Communist regime officially declared that prostitution no longer existed in China.

The Departure of the Foreigners, 1949-1955

Many of the foreigners residing in Shanghai fled for their lives as soon as it became clear that the Red Army would occupy the city in May 1949.   In April 1949 there were 2,000 Americans living in Shanghai, but by May 27th, 1949, the official date of Shanghai's "Liberation" by the Red Army, that number had already been reduced down to 1,200, meaning that 800 Americans had fled in the month leading up to the city's capture. However, some who had deep roots in the city, such as businessmen who ran companies there, faculty who taught at the universities, missionaries who worked at the churches, and of course those who had actually been born there during the previous century of colonial rule, elected to stay for as long as possible.   Thus, a significant foreign community remained until the spring of 1951, with a handful of holdouts lasting until 1954 or even 1955.

On April 25, 1950, the U.S. Consulate General in Shanghai closed its doors.

Two days later, on April 27, 1950, a special train evacuated 1,000 Americans and other foreigners from Shanghai to Tianjin where they boarded a waiting passenger liner for onward travel to San Francisco.   The mouth of the Yangzi River had been mined by the retreating Guomindang, and it was still closed to ships.

In December 1950 the central government in Bejing seized the assets of all Americans in China, including property and bank accounts.

The Shanghai American Chamber of Commerce closed its offices in the American Club building at the end of 1950, and the American Club itself seems to have closed at the same time.

All the foreign missionaries were expelled from Shanghai, and the rest of China, in April 1951, including those who had been working as faculty at the 13 Protestant Christian Colleges in China, as well as the clergy at the many churches and cathedrals.

Nonetheless, even after April 1951 there were still enough foreign businessmen and diplomats left in the city to keep two foreign clubs operating.   The French Club remained open until January 1, 1954, and the Dome Club in the HSBC building until April 1955.

By 1961 there were only 24 foreigners left living in Shanghai, a city that had once had hundreds of thousands of them.

The Slow Death of Economic Shanghai: 1949-1957

Under the administration of Chen Yi [陈毅] (1901-1972), who served as Shanghai Mayor from May 28, 1949 until November 1958, it could be said that five important facets of pre-1949 Shanghai society discussed in this essay died as a direct result of the 1949 revolution, including criminal Shanghai, cosmopolitan Shanghai, intellectual Shanghai, religious Shanghai, and economic Shanghai.   While the demise of organized crime was undoubtedly a blessing, the city was just as certainly a bleaker and less vibrant place after the loss of its cosmopolitan, sexual, intellectual and religious qualities, and a much poorer place for all concerned after the destruction of its existing market economy.

However, economic Shanghai did not immediately die in May 1949, as has so often been presumed.   Rather it was slowly strangled to death by increasingly vindictive government policies over the next six years, until by 1956 all remnants of the previous economic system had been virtually eliminated.   Many foreign businessmen, multinational companies and Chinese entrepreneurs elected to stay in Shanghai after May 1949, or even returned after having briefly fled, taking an optimistic attitude that they could still do business with the new regime.   Unfortunately, for nearly all of them their willingness to cooperate with the new authorities earned them no benefits and simply resulted in the loss of all their assets and even in some cases their very lives.

A vivid picture of what life was like for the foreign businessmen in Shanghai during the 1950s has been left for us in the memoirs of Lucian Taire, *Shanghai Episode*, and the vast archives of the Hong Kong and Shanghai Bank Corporation, organized into a four volume history by Frank H.H. King between 1987 and 1991, as well as in Aron Shai's 1996 monograph, *The Fate of British and Chinese Firms in China, 1949-1954:   Imperialism Imprisoned*.   These accounts depict the almost impossible conditions they tried to work under.   Punitive tax rates were calculated not only on current revenue but retroactively for years back into the past, and seemed intended to equal the exact amount of the firm's assets, forcing them to sign deeds for all their property over to the new government.   Despite the sharp decline in the amount of actual business conducted, companies were not allowed to lay off excess employees without government permission, which was never given.   In fact, government permission was now required to open or close a business, and to hire or fire any employee, as well to raise or decrease wages and benefits.   All employees were organized into labor unions which occupied nearly half of each work day in meetings with their managers demanding more and more increases in wages and benefits. Partial sales of assets to generate the revenue needed to pay staff salaries and expenses also required government permission, which was never given.

Furthermore, even those firms who wanted to close up shop and leave the country found it difficult to do so until they had satisfied all the government's demands by paying off the huge amounts calculated as owed in back taxes, staff wages and benefits, etc.   Foreign staff were held hostage in China by the new government which refused to issue them the necessary exit permits unless another foreign replacement was sent first.

Life for these foreign hostages was quite difficult.   Chinese employees were encouraged to spy on their foreign managers, office files were ransacked at night, packages and correspondence sent through the mail were censored.   Based on supposedly suspicious information collected from their employees, office files or mail, foreign staff were often called in for questioning by the police and quite a number served time in jail.   By 1954 all the foreign recreational clubs had been closed down, leaving those foreign residents still at liberty nowhere to go but the office and home.   The last to close was the former **French Club**, the Cercle Sportif Francais, which held a bittersweet New Year's Eve party on December 31, 1953, just hours before Communist party officials occupied the premises the next morning.   After that only the so-called **Dome Club** in the Hong Kong and Shanghai Bank remained until that building was signed over to the Chinese government in April 1955.

Foreign hostages were held until all the government's demands on the companies were met. Final resolution of these conflicts usually involved a combination of shipping in a large amount of foreign exchange and finally signing over all their assets in China to the government in the form of a Deed of Transfer. After this was done the company's foreign staff would be allowed to leave the country. As late as June 1954 the British government was still negotiating for exit visas to be given to several British businessmen who had been trapped in Shanghai since 1949.

If conditions for foreign firms and their foreign employees in China were bad during the 1950s, they were even worse for those Chinese businessmen who had mistakenly chosen to stay. The currency devaluations associated with the introduction of the so-called old Renminbi in May 1949 and the new Renminbi in March 1955 erased the value of even the largest pre-1949 bank deposits and cash assets that had been denominated in currencies issued by the Guomindang. After the May 28, 1949 currency reform, 100,000 of the Guomindang's Gold Yuan currency issued less than a year earlier in August 1948 became worth only 1 Renminbi. Then, following the March 1, 1955 currency reform 10,000 of the old Renminbi issued in 1949 became worth only 1 of the new Renminbi.

In addition to this financial strangulation, Chinese businessmen and anyone at all related to the former Guomindang regime were automatically looked upon with suspicion as potential political enemies of the new regime and subjected to countless interrogations, self-criticism sessions, and forced public confessions of supposed crimes, after which many were executed or imprisoned. Chinese businessmen were paraded through the streets with self-deprecating sign boards around their necks and forced to publicly apologize for the fact that they had been businessmen.

Once they knew they were under investigation, many people chose to take matters into their own hands rather than await an inevitable fate. Lucian Taire has estimated that during the first six years of the PRC 4,000 Chinese businessmen committed suicide in Shanghai alone, often quite publicly where everyone could see them, such as jumping off a downtown building, apparently as a final public protest against the regime's persecution of the Chinese middle class. One of the most dramatic suicides was by a man who reportedly jumped off the roof of the Hong Kong and Shanghai Bank building on the Bund and crashed through the Bank Hall's glass skylight.

In 1956 those privately-owned Chinese businesses that had somehow managed to survive until then were all nationalized under various schemes including joint private-state ownership, collectives, and cooperatives. A giant meeting was held at Longhua Temple in 1956 to celebrate the state's seizure of all remaining private Chinese companies and their conversion into joint private-state enterprises. By this time the Economic Shanghai of the pre-1949 era was definitely dead.

In 1957 the **Anti-Rightist Campaign** (Fanyou Yundong) [反右运动] rounded up anyone considered politically untrustworthy, including the so-called "red capitalists," Chinese businessmen and managers who had tried to cooperate with the state in the new socialist economy. Contrary to the popular perception that purges did not occur until the Cultural Revolution started nine years later, many previously loyal supporters of the Communist revolution were deprived of their positions and imprisoned at this time. Left-wing writers such as **Ding Ling** [丁玲] (1904-1986) were punished for their continuing efforts to preserve some freedom of speech. Even the later Prime Minister of the country, **Zhu Rongji** [朱镕基]

(1928-present), was persecuted during this campaign for not being sufficiently leftist politically.

This intolerance toward moderate voices within culture and society was followed by the ultra-leftist economic policies of Collectivization and the 1958 **Great Leap Forward** (Dayuejin) [大跃进].   The result was famine and mass starvation in the rural countryside, as vividly described by Yang Jisheng [杨继绳] (b.1940) in his heartbreaking memoir and evidence-based study "Tombstone" (2012) first published in Chinese in Hong Kong in 2008 as "Mubei" [墓碑], as well as increasing criticism of Mao Zedong's leadership from within the Communist Party leadership in Beijing.

At the August 1959 **Lushan Conference** (Lushan Huiyi) [庐山会议] of the Chinese Communist Party Central Committee (Zhongguo Gongchandang Zhongyang Weiyuanhui) [中国共产党中央委员会], moderates led by **Liu Shaoqi** [刘少奇] (1898-1969), Deng Xiaoping [邓小平] (1904-1997) and Peng Zhen [彭真] (1902-1997) scored a major victory against Mao Zedong's ultra leftist economic policies and cultural intolerance.   Liu Shaoqi [刘少奇] (1898-1969) had overseen the drafting of the 1954 Constitution (Xianfa) [宪法] as Chairman of the National People's Congress (Quanguo Renmin Daibiao Dahui) [全国人民代表大会], had been First Vice Chairman (Diyi Fu Zhuxi) [第一副主席] of the Party Central Committee since 1956, and in April 1959 had replaced Mao as Chairman (Zhuxi) [主席] of the national government and Head of State (Guojia Yuanshou) [国家元首], effectively making him President of China, although Mao remained Chairman of the Chinese Communist Party (Dang Zhuxi) [党主席].   At the Lushan Conference, Liu publicly blamed Mao for the "man-made problems" of the 1958 Great Leap Forward (Dayuejin) [大跃进] (1958-1960).   Mao was forced to publicly accept the blame for his mistakes, and after the conference was over he went into early retirement as an honorary but largely powerless figurehead, spending his time at his various villas and retreats around the country. Although Mao scored one small victory by having the moderate Defense Minister Peng Dehuai [彭德怀](1898-1974) replaced with his ally Lin Biao [林彪] (1908-1971), the 1959 Lushan Conference ushered in a five year period of relative stability and moderation in all fields, including culture as well as economics.

Controls on Traditional Culture, 1949-1966

For the first seven or eight years after Shanghai's "Liberation" (Jiefang) [解放] by the Red Army in May 1949, public expressions of traditional Chinese culture in the form of temples and religious practices continued to be permitted by the new regime, albeit under the supervision of a newly established government bureaucracy of religious associations set up for each of the five officially state recognized religions.   The **Buddhist Association of China** (Zhongguo Fojiao Xiehui) [中国佛教协会] was established in Beijing in May 1953, with a local branch organization in Shanghai (Shanghai Shi Fojiao Xiehui) [上海市佛教协会]. In the same month, the **Islamic Association of China** (Zhongguo Yisilan Jiao Xiehui) [中国伊斯兰教协会] was also established in Beijing, with a local organization branch organization in Shanghai (Shanghai Shi Yisilan Jiao Xiehui) [上海市伊斯兰教协会].   This was followed in August 1954 by the establishment of the **China Protestant Patriotic Three-Self Movement Committee** (Zhongguo Jidujiao Sanzi Aiguo Yundong Weiyuanhui) [中国基督教三自爱国运动委员会] or simply (Sanzi Jiaohui) [三自教会] for short, with a local branch organization in Shanghai (Shanghai Shi Jiedu Jiao Sanzi Aiguo Yundong Weiyuanhui) [上海市基督教三自爱国运动委员会].   All protestant denominations were grouped together under this one organization, with no distinction being made between Methodist, Presbyterian, Baptist, Episcopalian, Anglican, etc.   Next, the **China Taoist Association** (Zhongguo Daojiao Xiehui) [中国道教协会] was established in Beijing in April 1957.   Finally, the **China Catholic Patriotic Association** (Zhongguo Tianzhu Jiao Aiguo Hui) [中国天主教爱国会], with local organization Shanghai Shi Tianzhu Jiao Aiguo Hui [上海市天主教爱国会].

These religious associations have played a dual role of ensuring religious groups follow government policies, but have at times also channeled government funding and resources to support the facilities and staff of these religious groups.   They have also worked to eliminate and prevent any foreign interference in China's religious institutions, ensuring that they are "patriotic" Chinese run organizations.   This started with the expulsion of all the foreign missionaries in April 1951.   Of course this also had an impact on education, as foreign missionaries had previously established 13 Protestant colleges all across China, and these were now taken by Chinese administrators and faculty.

Note that neither Judaism nor Eastern Orthodox Christianity were included among the five officially government recognized religions after 1949, meaning that Jewish synagogues and White Russian churches have never had any protected status since then and were considered fair game for government take-over from early on.   Also, one might argue that Christianity and Islam were not part of traditional Chinese culture, but there had been a significant Chinese Christian population in China since the Ming Dynasty and a large ethnic Han Chinese Muslim population, the so-called Huimin, since the Song Dynasty.   Some evidence even suggests that there was an ethnic Han Chinese Jewish population in Kaifeng during the Song Dynasty, but by 1949 that one unique community of Chinese Jews had largely died out and disappeared.

The first wave of mass closures of Buddhist temples in Shanghai actually did not occur until 1958.   This was in line with other changes in the economy and society at that time, as the elimination of the Chinese middle class and upper class during the 1957 **Anti-Rightist Campaign** (Fanyou Yundong) [反右运动] and nationalization of industry, and 1958 collectivization of agriculture as part of the **Great Leap Forward** (Dayuejin) [大跃进], also had the effect of eliminating a major source of financial support for Buddhist temples and their population of monks as these middle and upper classes were the people who normally would have donated money to temples and paid monks for the performance of religious ceremonies.   Buddhist temples in urban areas were especially hard hit as they had no farm land to grow their own food to feed the resident monks.   On the other hand, those Buddhist temples located in rural areas had their normal economics disrupted by the 1950 **Land Reform** (Tudi Gaige) [土地改革], which took away temple estates that had been used to either grow crops to feed the resident monks or had been rented out to tenant farmers.

After the 1959 **Lushan Conference** described above, the pendulum swang back the other way again as official policy under President **Liu Shaoqi** [刘少奇] (1898-1969) shifted into reverse and allowed a brief revival of traditional Chinese culture for about five years, with much greater toleration shown for Buddhism, Taoism and Confucianism.   The classics of traditional Chinese literature were reintroduced to public education.   Celebrations were held to commemorate the anniversary of Confucius' death.   Traditional Peking Opera performances were sponsored once again.   Political opponents who had previously fled abroad were welcomed back to the mainland, including the last Guomindang President **Li Zongren** [李宗仁] (1891-1969), who returned to China in July 1965.   It finally looked as if the regime had successfully found the middle ground that most people had desired back in 1949, when the regime had come to power ten years earlier.

The most complete set of data on the history of Buddhist temples in Shanghai after 1949 is available for Jingan District, thanks to the details compiled in the 1995 Jingan Quzhi [静安区志].   According to this official source, there were 34 Buddhist temples in Jingan District alone when the Communists occupied Shanghai in May 1949.

26 of these 34 temples belonged to the Zen meditation sect (Chan Zong), four of them were associated with Tibetan Buddhism, while only two belonged to the Pure Land sect (Jingtu Zong), and several belonged to obscure Buddhist sects that no longer exist in Mainland China, such as the Mi Zong, Caodong Zong, and Tiantai Zong.

27 of these 34 temples had been established during the Republic of China (Minguo) period (1911-1949), testifying to what Holmes Welch has called a "Buddhist Revival" during that time.   Only 3 had been established during the Qing Dynasty (1644-1911), 1 supposedly in the Three Kingdoms, and the establishment date for 1 was unknown.

With only one exception, most of these 34 Buddhist temples in Jingan District seem to have remained open during the first seven or eight years of the People's Republic of China, but in 1958 the first wave of 17 Buddhist temples in Jingan District were closed, for a total of 18 of 34 closed by then.   Still, 16, or nearly half, remained open.   However, another 6 Buddhist temples in Jingan District were closed in 1960, for 24 total closed by then, leaving only 10 still open after 1960.

The two waves of mass closures of temples in 1958 and 1960 was followed by a four-year pause in mass closures of temples until 1964 when four more Buddhist temples in Jingan District were closed. This corresponds to the more moderate national government policies implemented by President Liu Xiaoqi and Prime Minister Deng Xiaoping during that time.

By the end of 1964, 29 of 34 Buddhist temples in Jingan District had been closed, while five still remained open. However, one more temple was closed in 1965.

Thus, by 1966, on the eve of the Cultural Revolution, which is usually blamed as the culprit for the destruction of traditional Chinese culture, 30 of the 34 Buddhist temples that had existed in Jingan District in May 1949 had already been closed, leaving only four surviving Buddhist temples to be closed when the Cultural Revolution started in 1966.

The Cultural Revolution (Wenhua Da Geming) [文化大革命] (1966-1976)

In a desperate attempt to seize power once again and break out of his enforced early retirement, in the Summer of 1965 **Mao Zedong** [毛泽东] (1893-1976) secretly fled from the national capital in Beijing, which was controlled by the party moderates, such as President Liu Shaoqi and Peng Zhen [彭真] (1902-1997), who had been the Beijing Party Secretary since 1948 and Mayor of Beijing since 1951, to Shanghai where he used the local print media controlled by his fourth wife **Jiang Qing** [江青] (1914-1991) to fire the opening shots of what became known as the Cultural Revolution.

In the November 10, 1965 issue of the Shanghai newspaper *Literary Currents (Wenhui Bao) [文汇报]*, Yao Wenyuan [姚文元] (1931-2005), one of the future members of the Gang of Four who later led the Cultural Revolution from their base in Shanghai, published an article criticizing a popular Peking Opera called *"Hai Rui Dismissed from Office" (Hai Rui Ba Guan) [海瑞罢官])*, which had been written by historian and Beijing Vice-Mayor Wu Han [吴晗] (1909-1969). In the article, *"A Criticism of the New Historical Drama Hai Rui Dismissed from Office" (Ping Xinbian Lishiju Hai Rui Ba Guan) [评新编历史剧海瑞罢官]*, the author Yao Wenyuan [姚文元] (1931-2005) complained that although the events described in the play took place in the 16th Century during the Ming Dynasty, it was actually meant as an allegory for current events in which the dismissed Ming Dynasty official Hai Rui [海瑞] (1514-1587) represented former Defense Minister Peng Dehuai, who had been dismissed from office at the 1959 Lushan Conference because he dared to criticize Mao Zedong for the Great Leap Forward, while the Ming Dynasty Emperor Jiajing, who fired Hai Rui [海瑞] because of his 1565 memorial to the throne criticizing the emperor and sentenced him to death in 1566, represented Mao Zedong himself. The opera had first been performed in 1961 and had become popular without attracting any criticism during the five years of relatively moderate central government policies towards traditional Chinese culture in the first half of the decade. However, this was a trap intentionally set by Mao for the moderate party leaders in Beijing who swiftly fell into it just as he had planned when Beijing Mayor Peng Zhen [彭真] (1902-1997) defended his Vice-Mayor Wu Han [吴晗] (1909-1969).

On April 18, 1966 the Shanghai edition of _Liberation Army Daily (Jiefang Jun Bao)_ [解放军报] declared the official start of what it called, "the Great Socialist Cultural Revolution." In May 1966 Peng Zhen [彭真] (1902-1997), who had basically run Beijing for the previous 18 years, was removed from his positions as Beijing Party Secretary and Mayor of Beijing, and also lost his seat on the Politburo. By June 1, 1966 the moderates of Beijing had disappeared, and Mao's leftist faction had seized control of the Beijing municipal party committee, and editorial control over the national newspaper, _The People's Daily (Renmin Ribao)_ [人民日报]. Control of the national capital and news media, as well as the support of Defense Minister **Lin Biao** [林彪] (1908-1971), gave Mao the power base he needed to truly launch the nationwide Cultural Revolution.

Mao Zedong returned to Beijing in triumph on July 18, 1966 and by August had demoted President **Liu Shaoqi** [刘少奇] (1898-1969) and begun forming the **Red Guards** (Hongweibing) [红卫兵] militia units. The normal party institutions, such as the party congress, central committee and politburo, were circumvented on November 22, 1966 with the creation of a new Cultural Revolutionary Central Committee led by his wife **Jiang Qing** [江青], with local branches of revolutionary committees set up throughout the country soon after. By April 1967 the official head of state, President Liu Shaoqi [刘少奇] (1898-1969), who was still Chairman of the national government and a senior member of the Politburo, had been placed under house arrest and later disappeared, never to be seen in public again.

For the next decade the 1966-1976 Cultural Revolution was largely directed from Shanghai by the **Gang of Four** (Siren Bang) [四人帮], led by Mao's wife Jiang Qing [江青] (1914-1991). Gang of Four member Zhang Chunqiao [张春桥] (1917-2005) acted as the Shanghai Revolutionary Committee Chairman (Shanghai Shi Geming Weiyuanhui Zhuren) [上海市革命委员会主任], a position roughly equivalent to the previous posts of city mayor and city party secretary, both of which were abolished, for almost ten years from February 24, 1967 until October 6, 1976. The other two members of the gang were Yao Wenyuan [姚文元] (1931-2005), and Wang Hongwen [王洪文] (1935-1992). Although they publicly championed the cause of the workers and peasants, the Gang of Four hypocritically lived lavish lives of luxury within the walled garden compounds of many of Shanghai's choicest old colonial mansions, including the **Marshall House**, aka Taiyuan Villa (Taiyuan Bieshu) [太原别墅], the **Da Gong Guan** [大公馆] of former Green Gang boss Du Yuesheng [杜月笙] (1888-1951), the Morris Garden (now the Ruijin Hotel), and the former **French Club** (now the Garden Hotel).

All universities were closed, with their students and professors shipped off to the countryside to learn from the peasants, along with other educated urban residents. Some university buildings were taken over for the purpose of providing political indoctrination to workers and peasants, giving rise to claims by some that they remained open, but all normal college degree programs stopped functioning for a decade.

Anyone considered even remotely capitalist was hounded to the verge of suicide or imprisoned.   This even included such high ranking moderate Communist Party leaders such as President **Liu Shaoqi** [刘少奇] (1898-1969), the official head of state as Chairman of the national government and a senior member of the Politburo; **Deng Xiaoping** [邓小平] (1904-1997), the General Secretary of the party; **Chen Yi** [陈毅] (1901-1972), the Foreign Minister and former Mayor of Shanghai; **Zhu De** [朱德] (1886-1976), the founder of the Red Army and hero of the 1934 Long March; and **Peng Zhen** [彭真] (1902-1997), who had been Party Secretary of Beijing since 1948, Mayor of Beijing since 1951, and a Politburo member.

During this ten-year period all temples and churches in Shanghai were closed to the public, most had their contents looted and destroyed, the priests and monks "sent home," while those buildings that weren't destroyed were occupied for secular uses, typically by factories, workshops, or warehouses.   Red Guards (Hongweibing) [红卫兵] ravaged China's cultural heritage by destroying hundreds of Buddhist, Taoist and Confucian temples all across the country, including the **Confucius Temple** (Wen Miao) [文庙] in downtown Shanghai's former Nanshi District (Nanshi Qu) [南市区].   Temple buildings which were left standing, such as Shanghai's **Longhua Buddhist Temple** (Longhua Si) [龙华寺], and the **City God Temple** (Chenghuang Miao) [城隍庙], had their entire contents looted and were occupied by factories or used as commercial warehouses.   The Songjiang Ancient Mosque (Songjiang Qingzhen Gu Si) in Songjiang Town was closed and did not reopen again until 1987.   Many tombs of famous Chinese celebrities and previous foreing residents were destroyed by the Red Guards (Hongweibing) [红卫兵], including those at Shanghai's Inernational Cemetery (Wanguo Gongmu) [万国公墓], such as those of Song Qingling's parents, and that of Ming Dynasty scientist Paul Hsu (Xu Guangqi) [徐光启] (1562-1633) in Xujiahui [徐家汇].
A 1975 English language guide book to Shanghai published by the China International Travel Service (CITS), the first since 1949, contained not a single mention of any of the many temples in Shanghai, neither in the text nor on the accompanying map of the city.   All Buddhist, Taoist, Confucian, and City God temples were ignored by this guide book as if they did not exist, including even famous tourist sights such as the **Jade Buddha Temple** (Yufo Si) [玉佛寺], Jingan Si [静安寺], and Longhua Si [龙华寺] Buddhist temples, and the Shanghai **City God Temple** (Chenghuang Miao) [城隍庙].   This is further evidence that all these religious establishments were at that time still closed to the public.   The 1975 travel guide is humorous for its attempt to begin promoting foreign tourism for the first time since 1949, while at the same time being full of Communist propaganda such as repeated promotion of the *"movement to criticize Lin Piao* and Confucius."*   It seems especially odd now that the Chinese central government promotes and funds a worldwide network of Confucius Institutes, and has allowed a revival of neo-Confucianism.

* Lin Biao [林彪] (1908-1971)

Recovery From the Cultural Revolution, 1976-1979.

Although the official starting and ending dates of the Cultural Revolution are always given as 1966 and 1976 respectively, much damage to China's traditional culture and normal economic institutions had begun long before that, and required years afterwards to repair. By 1976, China had no class of educated economic managers left.   Universities were reopened after having been closed for a decade, but it would take some time to train a new generation of economic leaders.

Shanghai continued to be governed by the same unusual local government institutions established during the Cultural Revoluiton, a Revolutionary Committee headed by a Chairman, rather than by a city mayor or party secretary, for more than three years from the official end of the Cultural Revolution in October 1976 until December 1979.   The city mayor structure of government was not restored until December 1979, and even then the person holding the post continued to be Peng Chong [彭冲] (1915-2010), the same one who had been the Chairman of the Revolutionary Committee, until March 1981.

In fact, it could be said that the Cultural Revolution did not formally end until the middle of 1981, when the new party leadership finally condemned it and the man who had started it. The central committee meeting of June 27-29, 1981 replaced Mao's designated successor **Hua Guofeng** with **Hu Yaobang** as the new central committee chairman, and appointed Hu's ally Deng Xiaoping [邓小平] (1904-1997) as chairman of the military control commission. This new leadership adopted a lengthy resolution on party history that condemned both Mao and the Cultural Revolution.   Hu Yaobang in his speech of July 1, 1981 given on the 60th anniversary of the party's founding went even further by praising former party leaders whose lives or reputations had suffered under Mao, including Liu Shaoqi [刘少奇] (1898-1969), Zhu De [朱德] (1886-1976), Peng Dehuai [彭德怀](1898-1974), Li Dazhao [李大钊] (1889-1927), and even Li Lisan [李立三] (1899-1967).

Religious institutions in Shanghai such as Christian churches, Islamic mosques, Buddhist and Taoist temples, some of which had actually been closed in the 1950s, did not begin to reopen until the 1980s.   **Longhua Buddhist Temple** (Longhua Si) was one of the first to reopen in September 1982, but others took much longer.   The Yuan Dynasty **Songjiang Ancient Mosque** in Songjiang Town did not reopen for religious services until 1987, after a massive four-year restoration project that lasted from 1981 to 1985, implying that it had suffered extensive damage.   **Jingan Buddhist Temple** (Jingan Si) did not reopen until 1990, after six years of reconstruction that had started in 1984.   The Chenxiang Ge [沉香阁] Buddhist Temple reopened on February 14, 1994 after years of repairs.   Shanghai's **City God Temple** [城隍庙] remained closed until January 1995.   The Shanghai **Confucius Temple** (Wen Miao) [文庙] had to be completely rebuilt from scratch in 1999 on a vacant lot where it had once previously stood.   A few notable ones, such as the **Holy Trinity Cathedral** (Sheng Sanyi Tang) [圣三一堂], were still being occupied for non-religious purposes until very recently.

The most noticeable fact at the time reforms really started in 1980 was how little the city's skyline had changed since 1937, a period which due to the various wars and revolutions had seen virtually no new construction.   The **Park Hotel** (Guoji Fandian) [国际饭店] on Nanjing West Road (Nanjing Xi Lu) [南京西路] built in 1934 was in 1980, nearly 50 years later, still the tallest building in all of China.   When **Harold Isaacs**, the American writer and former resident of 1930s Shanghai, returned to the city in 1981 after an absence of 45 years, he was startled to find it looking almost the same as before.   This caused him to title the description of his visit a "Journey in a time capsule."   Indeed the city was even for some time after that a kind of living museum.

The First Era of Economic Reform and Development: 1979-2002

In retrospect, few people now remember that Shanghai was far from the first city to feel the effects of economic reforms.   First of all, the economic reforms of the 1980s started out with the agricultural sector first, and only later moved on to gradually giving industrial managers more and more autonomy from the central economic planners.   When it finally came time for new urban development, Shanghai was left out of the scheme to establish Special Economic Zones (SEZ) designed to attract foreign investment.   Instead, five much smaller towns were chosen to become SEZ's.   In fact, during the 1980s Shanghai's economy continued to slumber, not only held back by the lack of foreign investment, but burdened by the requirement to pass on nearly all its tax revenue to the central government in Beijing.

It was not until 1990 that Shanghai's economy began to see the first sparks of reignition. Some of the earliest changes included allowing the city to keep most of its own tax revenue, the establishment of the Pudong New Area, and the creation of China's first post-revolutionary stock exchange, which was initially housed in the ballroom of the old **Astor House** Hotel (Pujiang Fandian) [浦江饭店].   These changes were no doubt helped along by the presence of two former Shanghai politicians at the national government level. Jiang Zemin had been the Mayor of Shanghai from 1985 to 1987 and then Shanghai Party Secretary since 1987 when he was chosen by Deng Xiaoping in June 1989 to replace Zhao Ziyang as General Secretary of the Chinese Communist Party.   Zhu Rongji had been the Mayor of Shanghai since he replaced Jiang Zemin in 1987 when he was advanced to the post of Vice-Premier of China's central government in 1991.   Furthermore, during his famous inspection tour of China's provinces South of the Yangzi River in 1992, Deng Xiaoping admitted that the biggest mistake he had ever made was leaving Shanghai out of the economic reforms of the 1980s.   Later that same year, the 14th Party Congress of the Chinese Communist Party resolved to, "build Shanghai into one of the world economic, financial and trade centers as fast as possible..."   By 1997 Shanghai had 40 per cent of the world's total number of construction cranes.

Major events in the city's trajectory towards renewed global prominence since that important 1992 decision have included the hosting of the September 1999 **Fortune 500 Forum** and the October 2001 **APEC** Conference.   By December 2002 Shanghai had become the fourth busiest container shipping port in the world, surpassing both Kaohsiung in Taiwan, and Rotterdam in the Netherlands, and falling just behind Pusan in South Korea.   This puts the city full circle back to the position it had in world trade in 1924, when it was previously listed as the world's fourth busiest shipping port.   Common social talk of local inhabitants now revolves around not whether but when Shanghai will replace Hong Kong as the dominant regional economic center of East Asia.   During the same month the city's new claim to fame was further boosted by its winning of the right to host the 2010 **World Expo** and the announcement of plans to open a new **Universal Studios** theme park by 2007.   However, by October 2014 Universal Studios had instead announced plans to built a theme park in Beijing, and their planned them park in Shanghai never materialized.   Nonetheless, **Shanghai Disneyland** opened in the Pudong New Area of Shanghai on June 2016, after a decade of planning and construction, at a cost of $5.5 billion USD.

Although the last official census was conducted in 2010, since the year 2016 the Shanghai municipal government has estimated the city's total population to be over 24.15 million people, including an estimated 9.72 million (40%) Chinese who have migrated to Shanghai from other provinces, usually for economic reasons, and who are not counted as permanent residents.   In fact, Chinese migrants have accounted for nearly all of the city's population growth, as the natural birth rate among permanent Chinese residents has been almost zero, with only 96,200 babies born to them in the year 2015.

The city's population of permanent Chinese residents and long-term migrants who have lived there for more than six months is swelled by another 300 million foreign and domestic tourists who visit each year.   The city government estimates that 8,543,700 foreign tourists visited Shanghai in 2016.   There are also at least 170,000 foreign expatriates who were estimated to be working here in 2015, although other sources estimated that to be 209,000 expatriates as of October 2018.   As a result, on any given day the actual number of people living or staying in the city and jamming its transportation network and public conveniences may be millions more than the official population statistics state.

City officials have had to admit that their previous estimate that Shanghai's population would reach 17 million by the year 2020 was a serious underestimate.   In December 2017 it was announced that the city government intended to limit Shanghai's population growth to a total of 25 million people by the year 2035, but experts were extremely skeptical as to how this goal would be achieved.   For example, in the decade between the year 2000 and the year 2010 the city's population grew at a rate of more than 40%.

Shanghai's urban city center within the Outer Ring Road covers an area of 667 square km., but the entire area within the Shanghai Municipality (Shanghai Shi) totals 6,340 square km (2,400 square miles).   The Shanghai municipal region comprises much of the Yangzi Delta, and is roughly equivalent in territory to that previously included in the old Songjiang Prefecture (Songjiang Fu) from the Yuan to the Qing dynasties.   As of November 2018, the Shanghai municipality was divided up into 16 districts, after half a dozen administrative changes in the past 18 years that included the elimination and merger of some previous districts, and the upgrading of all counties to district status.

The downtown urban core within the Zhongshan Inner Ring Road is comprised of the four districts of Jingan (including the former Zhabei District since 2017), Huangpu (including the former Nanshi District since the year 2000, and the former Luwan District since 2011), Xuhui, and Changning, with five more outlying districts of Minhang, Putuo, Yangpu, Hongkou, and Baoshan also being heavily developed urban areas.   Parts of the formerly rural Pudong New Area on the east side of the Huangpu, such as Lujiazui, now have to be considered as forming part of the downtown core, which was previously exclusively located on the West side of the river (Puxi).

In addition to these ten heavily urbanized central districts, Shanghai includes six rural districts and one island county, which are seldom visited by foreigners.   Due to the cheaper land, some factories and industrial parks have been built in these outlying areas by multinational companies in recent years.   Nonetheless, they still possess many traditional small towns, open farmland, and villages typical of Jiangnan culture.   These rural areas of the Shanghai municipality include the six districts of Songjiang, Qingpu, Jiading, Jinshan, Fengxian, and Chongming.   Chongming Island (Chongming Dao) in the Yangzi River estuary, along with the two smaller islands of Changxing and Hengsha, was a county belonging to Shanghai from 1958 to 2017, but in January 2017 it was raised from the status of a county to that of a district. The former Nanhui District is also largely a rural area, with the exception of its former district capital of Huinan Town, but was mered into the Pudong New Area in 2009.

In order to relieve overcrowding within the city center, urban planners have designed a comprehensive development plan for the whole municipality that calls for the movement of population and industries to the outlying areas, which are still largely open countryside at the moment. This "muli-centric" approach calls for the creation of 11 medium-sized New Towns. Most of these New Towns are actually the existing district seats of Shanghai's suburban and rural districts, including Baoshan, Jiading, Songjiang, Jinshan, Minhang, and Qingpu. These towns won't need to be built so much as rebuilt and redeveloped as new urban centers. Since several of these district seats have also been designated as Historic Towns deserving preservation, it will be interesting to see how well urban development and historic preservation can be balanced in these cases.

The most important role for **Luchaogang Harbor** [芦潮港] had been to serve as the departure and arrival point for passenger ships traveling between Shanghai and the island of Putuoshan in Zhejiang. However, Luchaogang [芦潮港] is now the coastal anchor point for the **East China Sea Bridge** (Donghai Daqiao) [东海大桥], which was completed in December 2005 and runs 32.5 km (20.2 miles), connecting the mainland of the Pudong New Area with **Yangshan Deep Water Port** (Yangshan Shenshui Gang)[洋山深水港] on a small island out in Hangzhou Bay that technically belongs to Zhejiang Province.

Most interesting of all is the plans to further utilize the enormous amount of open space currently available out on the under populated but isolated Chongming Island in the Yangzi Estuary, ranked as China's third largest island after Taiwan and Hainan. Up until a few years ago, the island was only connected to the rest of Shanghai by ferry boat service, hence limiting the number of people and industries that would want to locate there.

However, the combined **Shanghai Yangzi River Tunnel** and **Shanghai Yangzi River Bridge** opened on October 31, 2009 and now connect Chongming Island with the Shanghai mainland to the south in Pudong New District. To the north, Chongming Island is also now connected with Qidong [启东市] in northern Jiangsu Province by the **Chongqi Bridge**, and the **Chonghai Bridge** connecting western Chongming Island with Haimen in northern Jiangsu is also under construction.

The **Shanghai Yangzi River Tunnel** starts on the south bank of the Yangtze at Wuhaogou, Pudong and ends in the south of Changxing Island. It is 8.9 kilometres (5.5 mi) in length, and has two stacked levels. The upper level is for a motorway, and has three lanes in each direction, with a designed speed of 80 kilometres per hour (50 mph). The lower level is reserved for a future Shanghai subway line to Chongming Island.

The **Shanghai Yangzi River Bridge** starts at the tunnel exit, crosses Changxing Island at ground level, then crosses to Chongming Island, ending at Chenjia Town. It consists of two long viaducts with a higher cable-stayed section in the middle to allow the passage of ships. The total length is 16.63 kilometres (10.33 mi), of which 6.66 kilometres (4.14 mi) is road and 9.97 kilometres (6.20 mi) bridge. The overall shape of the bridge is slightly S-shaped.

The length of the central span is about 730 metres (2,395 ft).   The bridge has six lanes, three in each direction, with space on the shoulders reserved for the future construction of the planned Line 19 of the Shanghai subway system to Chongming Island.

Line 19 of the Shanghai subway system will link Rongqiao Road station on Line 9 in Pudong New District to Chongming Island via Changxing Island, with a branch from the latter to Hengsha Island. The line will use the Shanghai Yangzi River Tunnel and Bridge, which were designed to take its tracks. The first phase of the line from Rongqiao Road to Changxing Island is scheduled to open by 2020.

The Chongming-Qidong Yangzi River Bridge (Chongqi Daqiao) [崇启大桥] opened to traffic on Christmas Eve 2011, while the Chongming-Haimen Bridge (Chonghai Daqiao) [崇海大桥] is still under construction.

Despite all the added overland transportation routes, some ferry boat routes continue to operate between the three islands in Chongming District. Hengsha Island can still only be reached by taking a ferry boat. On Chongming Island, Chengqiao's Nanmen Port offers service to the Shidongkou and Baoyang Road ports in Baoshan District and to Liuhegang in southern Jiangsu Province; Xinhai's Niupeng Harbor to Qinglonggang in Haimen; and other ports offer connections with Wusong and Chongming District's two other islands.

A Tale of Two Cities

If Mao Dun were still alive, he might have revisited the theme of his classic story, "*Midnight*," and written a new novel exposing the sharp contrast between rich and poor residents within the same municipality.   The gap between the two extremes of wealth and poverty had become quite noticeable by 2003, and even the Chinese central government was admitting that that the gap between rich and poor Chinese was growing wider rather than closing.

Shanghai was rated as having the 5th highest cost of living of any city in the world in 2002. The districts in the urban core of Puxi and Pudong within the Inner Ring Road were already inhabited by a new white collar middle class, who lived in apartments that then cost on average $1,000 USD (8,000 Rmb) per square meter to buy or in other words a 100 square meter apartment cost on average $100,000 (800,000 Rmb) to purchase, with prices for some apartments rising even higher to $1,500 USD (13,000 Rmb) per square meter.   A coterie of nouveau riche were paying $1,000 to $2,000 USD per month just to rent apartments or buy villas in Qingpu for $1,000 USD per square meter.

By 2003 a new Chinese middle class had arisen, as evidenced by some hard statistics as well as some casual observations.   In January 2003, 51.2 per cent of Shanghai's population had a home computer, 4.2 million people had some form of Internet access, 6.72 million people had a fixed-line home phone, and 9.12 million people owned a mobile phone.   Using ownership of information technology devices as our measuring stick, we could say that roughly half the population of 16 million is participating in the city's new prosperity, but on the other hand this also means that half of the people are not.   The glass may be half full, but it is also half empty.   Casual observations note that in 1999 nearly all the motor vehicles on the roads seemed to be taxi cabs, while today streets are choked with privately owned cars. Anyone who has lived in a Chinese apartment building knows the delights of being woken up at 7:00 a.m. each and every day by the relaxing drone of jackhammers, pneumatic drills, buzz saws, and hammers.   But these irritating sounds are themselves evidence of a new prosperity, as people only redecorate homes that they have purchased.

Characteristics of the 2003 middle class included owning a Buick Sedan produced by Shanghai General Motors at their plant in Pudong, which was then operating at full capacity producing 100,000 cars per year, having a maid (ayi) to cook and clean for them, taking winter vacations overseas or at worst on China's tropical Hainan Island, playing golf at newly established courses in Pudong and Qingpu, going indoor skiing at facilities that generate artificial snow, dancing in the Hengshan Lu [衡山路] discos till dawn, wearing the latest and most fashionable imported designer clothes bought from stores on Huaihai Middle Road (Huaihai Zhong Lu) [淮海中路], buying diamond jewelry from Cartier and silk scarves from Hermes at stores on Nanjing Xi Lu, recklessly throwing money at Shanghai's unstable stock market headquartered in Lujiazui, drinking cappuccino every day at one of the 26 Starbucks outlets then in the downtown area, and eating out at Italian and Japanese sushi restaurants.

Fashion.

Since 1990 life in Shanghai has been increasingly like the plot of Kurt Vonnegut's novel, *Time Quake*, in which people suddenly recover their free will to make their own choices and decisions after years of military regimentation.   The Mao Suit is dead.   The so-called Mao Suit (Zhongshan Zhuang) [中山装], an article of clothing actually first designed by Sun Yat-sen (Sun Zhongshan) [孙中山] (1866-1925) and originally worn by Guomindang officials as well as Communists became inextricably associated with the reign of Mao Zedong when it was the required uniform for the whole country.   As late as the early 1980s urban gatherings were a sea of identical colors and styles.   Nowadays you have to search long and hard to find even one person wearing a Mao suit.   Even construction workers swing their sledge hammers while wearing the best Western style suits they can afford.   Not even the lowliest peasant wants to be caught dead wearing a Mao suit.

It's hard to believe that in 1973 bell-bottom pants were banned by the government as symbols of decadent Western imperialism.   Nowadays the Chinese youth seen strolling down Huaihai Lu are often dressed in such bizarre and risqué fashions as to even cause a Westerner to blush red in the face with shock.   Currently popular styles include dangerously sharp pointy shoes and boots, faux leopard, zebra and tiger skin furry jackets, and black leather pants.

Many women's fashions focus on exposing certain strategic parts of their body, with unusually placed holes revealing arms, legs, tummies, and waists.   Extremely short shorts revealing half their buttocks, ultra min-skirts hiked up to the crotch, and hip exposing low waist jeans worn without any belt are standard wear for Shanghai girls in the summer months.

Fashion shows and beauty contests are now becoming quite common events.   Ms. Zhuo Ling of Shanghai was the fourth runner up in the 2002 Miss Universe contest.   Visits to the city by world famous fashion experts such as Vivienne Westwood are becoming more frequent, and at least one fashion design school, the Lasalle College of Donghua Daxue, is churning out young fashion designers every year.   Shanghai hosted a three-week-long International Fashion Festival in March 2003, complete with risqué swimsuit and lingerie shows that were unbelievably televised on CCTV.   Sidewalk news stands are well stocked with Chinese translations of Western fashion magazines, such as *Elle, Cosmopolitan* and

Harper's Bazaar.   In short, Shanghai is an extremely fashion-conscious, or even obsessed, city.

However, along with attempts to modernize their appearance come the fashion victims who seem unaware of how embarrassingly ridiculous they look.   Some young men dress so wildly that they would be mistaken for pimps in most American cities, complete with their floor-length bright pink and orange tiger skin pattern felt overcoats and matching felt zebra pattern cowboy hats.   Dying their normally uniform black hair in all shades of outrageously bright orange, yellow, red, blue, and pink colors is now all the rage with both young men and women.   Three-piece orange plaid polyester suits can be seen being worn by some on downtown streets.   Next to the newly arrived skateboarding craze, the most annoying sight is probably the young Chinese teenagers dressed and acting like wannabe black rap stars, complete with tight fitting nylon skull caps and extremely baggy pants.

The Primacy of Economics over Politics.

Since 1990 Shanghai has in many ways seemed to return to its pre-1949 primacy of economics above all else.   Nonetheless, politics still occasionally reasserts itself when one least expects it.

While Shanghai's economic predominance was guaranteed by the presence of Jiang Zemin [江泽民] (1926-present) and Zhu Rongji [朱镕基] (1928-present) in Beijing, Chen Liangyu [陈良宇] (1946-present) became the most powerful local official in Shanghai for about five years after his two mentors were promoted to the central government.   As Huangpu District Head (Qu Zhang) [区长] from February 1987 to October 1992 Chen was in charge of running the city's downtown urban center.   From October 1992 to December 2002 Chen was Deputy Party Secretary (Fu Shuji) [副书记], and from 1996 was also a Deputy Mayor (Fu Shizhang) [副市长].   In 1997 he became an alternate member of the Party Central Committee.   After the demise of Xu Kuangdi, Chen temporarily also became acting Mayor [市长] of Shanghai for nearly 15 months from December 7, 2001-February 21, 2003.   In October 2002 Chen was promoted from Deputy Secretary to Party Secretary (Shuji) [书记] of Shanghai and the following month, November 2002, he was elected to the Polituburo of the Central Committee. He continued to serve as both Shanghai Party Secretary and City Mayor during the roughly five month period from October 2002 until February 2003.   After Han Zheng became City Mayor in February 2003, Chen continued to be Shanghai Party Secretary, as well as a member of the Central Committee and the Politburo, until he was dismissed on September 24, 2006.

Under China's present system of government, each city has both a Mayor and a Party Secretary, both of whom head parallel bureaucracies, but it is the Party Secretary who reigns supreme.   This fact was well illustrated by the sudden overnight disappearance of Shanghai's previous mayor Xu Kuangdi [徐匡迪] (1937-present) during an otherwise quiet weekend in December 2001.   Xu had been Mayor of Shanghai since February 1995 and was extremely popular both at home and abroad.   He was lionized in the foreign media as "the Rudy Guiliani of China."   Although appointed by the Party, he probably could have been elected by a popular vote.

The only brief official notice was issued to the news media during a weekend and stated that he had been transferred to a small academic institute in Beijing, the Chinese Academy of Engineering.   This move to Beijing was clearly not a promotion, as it had previously been for the earlier Shanghai municipal leaders Jiang Zemin [江泽民] (1926-present) and Zhu Rongji [朱镕基] (1928-present).

The unofficial explanation was that Xu's high profile had irritated Chen Liangyu [陈良宇] (1946-present), the Shanghai Communist Party Deputy Secretary and Deputy Mayor, who felt that Xu was getting too much of the credit for Shanghai's rapid economic development. In a classic power struggle between state and party, the Communist Party reasserted its dominance of local political power.   The only good news for Xu was that he was not accused of having committed any crimes while in office, as has often happened with the sudden demise of local political leaders in China.

Xu reappeared publicly in Shanghai for the first time in three years when the Shanghai Daily on November 3, 2004 reported his attendance at the World Engineers Convention being held in the city.   Although Xu's role at the convention was as President of the Chinese Academy of Engineering, local news media actually referred to him as the "former mayor of Shanghai" and published his photo.

After Xu's sudden departure, Chen temporarily took over the post of both Mayor and City Party Secretary, until a suitable replacement for Xu could be found.   Even after Xu was permanently replaced as Mayor by Han Zheng [韩正] (1954-present) in February 2003, it was clear that Han cowered in the shadow of Chen, while Chen created a sort of cult of personality around himself.   Han was rarely allowed to make major public speeches or take policy initiatives on his own, nor was he publicly given the credit for any major accomplishments.

Meanwhile, local press reports made it seem that Chen was everywhere doing everything, single handedly solving every city problem.   It was rare for a day to go by without his name being mentioned in the newspaper in connection with some latest wonderous achievement towards the city's further development.   Han's name rarely appeared in the local news media without Chen, and Chen's name was always prominently mentioned at the very beginning of news stories, whereas Han's name appeared much later as an after thought. The third floor of the Shanghai Municipal Archives exhibition hall opened on the Bund in 2004 was dedicated largely to showing Chen Liangyu as the mastermind of Shanghai's modernization.

On Tuesday September 26, 2006 local newspapers suddenly announced Chen Liangyu's fall from power.   China Daily proclaimed, "Shanghai leader stripped of power," while Shanghai Daily trumpeted, "City party head fired."   The next day the public assault against Chen continued in the local media.   The front page of Shanghai Daily cried, "Full weight of justice awaits Chen," while China Daily claimed, "Chen's ouster wins wide public support." The way in which the local news media suddenly turned against Chen overnight, with front page stories on September 26   branding him as a criminal, was truly Orwellian, and only serves to illustrate how mainland journalists still lack any true independence and still print whatever the powers that be tell them to write.

Over the previous two years, Chen had reportedly had open clashes during Politburo meetings with Prime Minister Wen Jiabao over new central government policies meant to bring down real estate property prices. Chen viewed these new policies as bad for Shanghai's economy, and wanted to continue to let property markets operate without new restrictions. In fact, after the new property market policies were implemented by the central government in mid-2005 real estate prices and sales of new housing in Shanghai dropped sharply in a temporary setback, costing many small and large investors a lot of money in lost profits. Quite a few local property developers and real estate agencies were expected to go bankrupt by the end of this year. Many newly built homes sat empty and unsold at that time. Those who had purchased new homes just before the summer 2005 change in policy found that they had paid more than the buildings were worth after the new policy caused the market correction. Chen's resistance against these central governmment economic policies was only one more reason for his downfall.

The official reasons given for Chen's downfall was the misuse of the city's social security pension fund. 3 billion Renminbi ($375 million USD) was found missing from the fund. This money was apparently loaned to a dozen property developers to construct real estate projects in the city. Half of the total was loaned to the Hong Kong developer Shui On Land Ltd., which has constructed a number of real estate projects in Shanghai, including the infamous Xintiandi complex. In the central government's view this was corruption, whereas in the local government's view it may have seemed like a good investment that would help the local economy as well as earn a profit for the pension fund. Shui On admitted to participating in the scheme and agreed to immediately repay their share of the money. Chen was also investigated for his close ties to two local businessmen, Wu Minglie, the founder of the New Huangpu (Xin Huangpu) real estate development company, and Wang Chengming, former chairman of the Shanghai Electric Group, both of whom lost their seat on the Shanghai People's Congress during the week after Chen's dismissal.

However, other motives for Chen's removal were undoubtedly the central government's desire to recentralize its control over local governments throughout the country; eliminate the influence of the Jiang Zemin [江泽民] (1926-present) faction within the party; and begin a new more equitable redistribution of wealth throughout the nation, in pursuit of Hu's more harmonious society. Rumors had circulated that Chen would be dismissed at the annual Central Committee meeting held on October 8, 2005 in Beijing. Nonetheless, Chen survived that meeting, reportedly due to the backing of former President Jiang Zemin [江泽民] (1926-present). One year later the Central Committee meeting held on October 8, 2006 confirmed Chen's dismissal from both the Politburo and the Central Committee, as well as his loss of the post of Shanghai Party Secretary.

The end result of this whole process of change may be that Shanghai will have to compete more against other cities in China for domestic and foreign investment. A new foreign exchange regime that was to be tested in Shanghai was instead shifted to Tianjin. There may be fewer grandiose infrastructure projects built here. In a culture where many business deals depend on personal relationships in a system known as "guanxi," businessmen and local officials may now be too afraid to talk to each other for fear of being caught in the anti-corruption net. More local revenue may have to be sent to Beijing. Plans are already under foot to centralize control over local pension funds, and municipal governments will no longer be allowed to keep funds from the sale of land development rights.

The Return of the Foreigners

Despite more than 100 years as a cosmopolitan multinational city, soon after May 1949 Shanghai became a city with an entirely homogenous population for the first time since 1843. By the time foreigners began returning in the 1980s they were considered a curious and unusual sight. The Shanghai American Chamberof Commerce reopened in 1987, 37 years after closing its doors in 1950.

Since the latter half of the 1990s, the official Shanghai city government policy has been to welcome foreigners. In 2001 it was estimated that 55,000 expatriates were living in Shanghai, although this is surely an underestimate, based only on officially registered residents and not counting those here on business consultant or tourist visas. A new Residence Card for foreigners, similar to a Green Card in the U.S., was unveiled in the summer of 2002. The government actually set the goal of having a foreign resident population of 10 to 15 per cent, which it believes is necessary for Shanghai to recover its lost cosmopolitan aura. English language road signs began to appear for the first time since 1949 during the year 2002. Restrictions on where foreigners could rent and buy housing were removed. Still, foreigners living in Shanghai may occasionally feel the brunt of official restrictions or unofficial harassment in their daily lives. Sudden night time crack downs by Shanghai police occasionally shut down a whole strip of bars and nightclubs along Maoming South Road (Maoming Nan Lu) that were popular with Shanghai's resident foreign community. The official explanation has been that all of them were coincidentally guilty of violating the city's fire code. American restaurant-owner Kathleen Lau has been forced to relocate her restaurants several times due to sudden demands by the local government to reclaim the property, as happened first with her Kathleen's Five restaurant on top of the former Shanghai Race Club building and again with her restaurant on the Bund. And there are still the periodic dawn police raids on foreigners' apartments to check if they have registered their residential address with the police, as is still required by law.

China's admission into the WTO in the Fall of 2001 set off a gold rush of ambitious foreigners heading East with dreams of striking it rich. Unfortunately, many of them learned the hard way that the golden time to come had been four or five years earlier, before much of the economy was localized and foreign expat business managers began their continuing slow exit. Nonetheless, the air in the foreign expat community continued to buzz with talk of business deals and rumors of deals, in a cloak and dagger atmosphere not unlike Casablanca during World War II. Every foreigner in town, it seemed, had a business plan in search of investors and/or gullible employees willing to work for free in some kind of profit sharing/stock option scam. 5% of zero profit is still zero. All too often the talk was nothing more than hot air, and the slick business partner's investors turned out to have been none other than his parents, who finally decided to cut him off the dole. The economic sector most affected by this unstable pattern of foreign business investment was of course the English training industry. Between 2002 and 2008 the Boulevard of Broken Dreams was paved with the tears of laid off employees of foreign owned and managed English training companies such as Boston Training Technologies (BTT), Linguaphone, Kai En, Informatics, and ALTEC. In some cases teachers and local office staff went to work at the training center one morning only to find that the doors were padlocked and all the foreign managers/owners had run away without saying goodbye, never to be seen again, leaving staff unpaid for their final month's work. In 2008 it was up to the larger Chinese-owned and managed education companies such as Web International English to function as a lifeboat to rescue all the suddenly unemployed foreign teachers who had nowhere else to go.

Shanghai Ladies then and now

Despite previous government attempts to present a clean image of Shanghai to the world, until a few years ago, anyone who spent more than a week here could see the only slightly veiled signs of prostitutions resurgence, a phenomenon that seemed to go hand in hand with the rapid economic development of the 1990s and early 2000s.   Although in most cases the girls didn't walk the streets openly, their touts or pimps did, especially along Nanjing Road, Hengshan Road [衡山路], and outside five star hotels such as the Okura Garden Hotel, located on the site of the former French Club.   They would openly call out in English to passing foreigners, and sometimes even grab them by the arm.   The girls themselves usually hid inside one of several types of front establishments: the once ubiquitous hair salons which despite their trademark red and white barber poles outside didn't provide hair cuts and yet stayed open all night long; hotel hair salons providing door to door 'massage' services in guests rooms; and KTV (karaoke) bars that had private rooms for 'singing' songs with a girl.   Any man who spent a night in a Chinese hotel then would undoubtedly experience the unsolicited nocturnal phone calls from anonymous female strangers offering to come to his room and provide an "anmo," which technically speaking meant a massage, but in reality meant whatever service you were willing to pay for.   Printed advertising cards bearing photos of attractive women with their phone numbers and the message "Call me!" would be anonymously slid under your hotel room door. To be fair, conditions in Shanghai only reflected what had become a nationwide phenomenon.   Since 2013 a new crack down campaign by the Shanghai city government has had remarkable success in changing this situation, apparently for the long-term.

Just as Gail Hershatter has documented In her study of pre-1949 sexuality in Shanghai, in the 1990s it once again became difficult to distinguish who was a prostitute and who was not. Many young women survived by finding relatively rich older men to act as their boyfriends or sugar daddies, and didn't seem to mind if the man was already married, as long as he supported them financially.   Walking down any major street in Shanghai, one could readily see the Sugar Daddy phenomenon without even trying to find it.   Incredibly attractive young female bombshells in tight ultra-short mini skirts walked arm in arm with fat, balding men with greasy comb overs who were twice their age and were old enough to be their fathers, but weren't.   The other phenomenon of the second wife (Er Nai) was also extremely common, particularly amongst married businessmen from Hong Kong and Taiwan who spent half their time living in places like Shanghai, Beijing and Shenzhen.   Just as before 1949, many outwardly legitimate jobs commonly functioned as covers for more lucrative work as part-time prostitutes, such as KTV singing girl, bar hostess, barber shop masseuse, hotel masseuse, etc.

As mainland magazines and changes in women's fashionable dress clearly showed, there was simply a growing revival of sexuality in general.   Much like the human behavior described in Kurt Vonnegut's novel "Timequake," you could say this new assertion of sexual freedom was in reaction against the previous prudish morality of the 1949-1979 period. Local news stands in the 1990s began openly selling magazines featuring photo collections of nude Chinese models, and the first public exhibition of nude Chinese female photos was shown in Shanghai, ironically at the Workers' Cultural Palace [上海市工人文化宫].   Graphic public displayal of affection also became rampant among young Chinese couples who unashamedly groped and fondled each other on crowded subway trains and buses.

Virgins became in such short supply that in the spring of 2003 a millionaire Chinese businessman actually took the drastic step of placing ads in nearly 20 newspapers nationwide looking for a virgin Chinese girl to be his wife.   Despite the man's wealth, few girls responded, apparently because they couldn't meet his main requirement, with Shanghai providing the fewest number of respondents from any one city.

Locally televised Shanghai fashion shows routinely included Chinese models wearing incredibly revealing lingerie and thong swimsuits that left little if anything to the imagination. Entertainment television programs and outdoor promotional events at shopping centers routinely included scantily clad young women bumping and grinding in dance moves with devastating pelvic thrusting and frantic hip swinging.   In short, sex was back out of the closet and into the open, and both commercial advertisers and television producers had realized that sex sells.

On August 12, 2006 the China Daily national newspaper trumpeted, "Sex no longer a taboo as adult products show spices up Shanghai."   Complete with a photo of a young, large breasted Chinese woman in a very skimpy bikini, the story reported on the holding of the third annual adult toy and sexual health exhibition in Shanghai.   By contrast, the event went unreported by the local Shanghai Daily newspaper.

However, since 2013 the party has largely been over, as new local and central government crackdowns successfully reinformace the type of puritanical morality that existed from 1949 to 1979.   New dress codes restrict how actors can dress on television, exhibition models have been covered up from head to toe like Catholic nuns, no more all-night barber shops that don't give haircuts, no more in-house hotel massage services, acres of empty retail space once occupied by massage parlors has been taken over by real estate agencies, there are no more "happy endings."

Urban Development Vs. Historic Preservation

With the economic revival of the 1990s came the city's first building boom since 1937, with its resulting forest of gleaming new skyscrapers, and the increasing loss of whole neighborhoods of historic homes and commercial buildings.   Finding the right balance between economic development and historic preservation has been difficult for the city, although it has tried to grapple with this issue.   There are 11 areas in the city center which the Shanghai development plan has designated as "historic conservation areas," including Nanjing Road, Hengshan Road [衡山路], Maoming Road, Sinan Road, the Bund (Waitan), Shanyin Road, Longhua Town, and Jiangwan Town.   Also included is the so-called "Old Inner City," the former walled town of Nanshi, which has seen an unprecedented amount of development in the past several years, with the result that the Yu Garden (Yu Yuan) [豫园] is now well on its way to becoming an island surrounded by a forest of skyscrapers.   In fact, the centuries-old Nanshi District was formally abolished as a separate administrative unit in the year 2000 in order to better facilitate urban development in that area of the city.   As part of this massive urban development, 80,000 familes have to be relocated every year from their former homes to new residences elsewhere.

Despite a public policy in favor of preservation of key historic sites in the city, there have been numerous cases of seemingly wanton destruction that could have been avoided. Probably the most egregious case was that of the historic boyhood home of world famous Chinese architect **I. M Pei**, which despite worldwide appeals was demolished in the year 2001 to make way for a patch of grass. Historic preservation here often means developing a sight into a shopping mall, such as Xintiandi, where the original environment is in fact entirely altered to suit modern purposes and only an outer shell of a facade remains along the lines of a Potempkin Village with a false front and a hollow inside.

Outside the city center an additional four rural villages have been designated as "famous historic towns," including Zhujiajiao, Songjiang, Jiading and Nanxiang. However, preservation of these towns often means tearing down the authentic historic structures and rebuilding Disneyland-type copies. In addition three of the four historic towns will have to co-exist with the development of so-called New Towns right beside them. Furthermore, absent from this preservation list were the equally historic towns of Qingpu [青浦城区] and Jinze [金泽镇], the latter in particular rivaling Zhujiajiao in its number of historic sites and unspoiled authenticity. The fate of rural towns not designated on the official preservation list can only be speculated.

In January 2005 new public signs began to appear labeling historic buildings. These "Heritage Architecture" signs are bilingual, and include basic information such as the date of construction, and occasionally the architect and original owner. They are in addition to the previous generic "Municipal Preserved Building" signs that marked the 300-400 historic buildings on the city's protected list.

That Sinking Feeling

This new urban development has caused city planners to recall Shanghai's geological history as land originally reclaimed from the sea back in the Eighth Century, since the weight of all the new structures is causing the city to slowly sink back underwater again. Even before the construction boom of the 1990s, the city was sinking at a rate of 10 centimeters per year back in the 1960s. Experts have estimated that if that rate had continued, the city would have already been submerged below sea level by 1999. However, thanks to a complicated system of pumping millions of tons of water in and out of the ground, the rate of subsidence has now been slowed down to only 10 millimeters per year.

Nonetheless, an incident on July 1, 2003 showed what could happen to the whole waterfront along the Huangpu River, when an eight-story building in the Dongjiadu [董家渡] neighborhood on Zhongshan Nan Lu suddenly collapsed due to sinking soil beneath its foundation. In a chain reaction, the section of the Huangpu River flood wall just across the street also collapsed, threatening to flood the entire neighborhood, the street began to buckle, and at least three other buildings nearby had to be torn down on purpose over the next few days because they were leaning at dangerous angles. The Metro Four subway tunnel under construction beneath the building also collapsed.

The government's own Labor and Social Security Bureau, which issues work permits to foreigners, had to evacuate all of its files and abandon its offices in the 25-story Linjiang Huayuan office building on the riverfront side of Zhongshan Nan Lu because it too was in danger of collapsing from subsidence of the soil beneath its foundation.

On September 29, 2006 Shanghai Daily reported that the city's elevated highways (gaojia), such as Yanan Lu, the Inner Ring Road, and the South-North Road, were all suffering from sinking supporting pillars caused by land subsidence. An estimated 1 billion yuan investment was estimated as necessary to complete a proposed three-year renovation project to shore up the elevated highways' supporting pillars.

From Past to Future

New arrivals from abroad still speak of wanting to see Shanghai before it changes too much, but the fact is that the city is already an entirely different one than it was just five years ago. Whole historic neighborhoods in the city center have disappeared, while new towns are emerging out in the suburbs where previously there was nothing but farmer's fields. The **Nanshi District** (Nanshi Qu), previously home to the remains of the old Chinese walled city, was actually abolished by decree, while plans are afoot to create whole new satellite cities out in the formerly rural counties of Songjiang, Qingpu, and Jiading. What this city will look like in another five-year's time is anyone's guess. In addition to the practical information useful for a traveler, this book is meant primarily to be a guide to the historic sights from Shanghai's past which still remain to be seen, as well as a window into what the city may look like in the near future.

An Abbreviated History of Shanghai

The historic origins of the present-day modern metropolis of Shanghai [上海] can be traced back to two small ancient communities that once existed in the Tang Dynasty [唐代] (618-907).   One was a small fishing village known as **Hudu** [沪渎], located at the confluence of the Huangpu River (Huangpu Jiang) [黄浦江] and the Wusong River (Wusong Jiang) [吴淞江], now more commonly known as Suzhou Creek (Suzhou He) [苏州河].   The Chinese character for "Hu" [沪] still appears on Shanghai car license plates, and all long-distance highways are named as if they were leading to or coming from "Hu," such as the Shanghai-Nanjing Expressway (Hu-Ning Gaosu Gonglu) [沪宁高速公路].

The other ancient community was **Green Dragon Town** (Qinglong Zhen) [青龙镇], once a busy shipping port on the Wusong River (Wusong Jiang) [吴淞江], the former site of which is now located in Green Dragon Village (Qinglong Cun) [青龙村] of White Crane Town (Baihe Zhen) [白鹤镇] in Shanghai's Qingpu District (Qingpu Qu) [青浦区].   Although archeological excavations have dug up buried artificats, and the history of the site is testified to in written records, today the only visible remnant is the Qinglong Pagoda (Qinglong Ta) [青龙塔], with the recently rebuilt walled compound of the Qinglong Buddhist Temple (Qinglong Si) [青龙寺] standing nearby.   The Qinglong Pagoda is considered to be the oldest existing one in Shanghai today, as it was reportedly first built over 1300 years ago in 743 A.D., the same year as the adjoining Buddhist temple, during the Tianbao [天宝] reign of the Tang Dynasty [唐代] (618-907).

In the middle of the Tang Dynasty [唐代] (618-907) , the area that is now the Shanghai city center became part of **Huating County** [华亭县], which had its urban center in present-day Songjiang Town [松江镇], the capital of Shanghai's suburban Songjiang District [松江区].   In the 8th Century A.D., the East China Sea coastline probably followed the present day course of the Huangpu River.   Since Shanghai in the Tang Dynasty was literally on the sea, this explains its present name.   "Hai" [海] means sea, and "shang" [上] means above.

During the Northern Song Dynasty (Bei Song) [北宋] (960-1127) Shanghai had its official status upgraded from a village to a town in 1074.   Towards the end of the Southern Song Dynasty (Nan Song) [南宋] (1127-1279), Huating County (Huating Xian) [华亭县] was upgraded to Huating Prefecture (Huating Fu) [华亭府] in 1277, but in 1278 the name was changed to Songjiang Prefecture (Songjiang Fu) [松江府].   During the early Yuan Dynasty [元朝] (1279-1368) Shanghai was upgraded again to the level of a county (Shanghai Xian) [上海县] in 1292, but was still part of Songjiang Prefecture (Songjiang Fu) [松江府], which had its capital at the old town of Huating [华亭], now renamed Songjiang Town (Songjiang Zhen) [松江镇].   By the time of the Yongzheng [雍正] reign (1722-1735) of the Qing Dynasty (1644-1911), the territory of Songjiang Prefecture (Songjiang Fu) [松江府] was almost identical to the area now encompassed by the Shanghai Municipality [上海市], with the exception of Jiading District [嘉定区] in the city's northwest corner and Boashan District [宝山区] in the north, both of which belonged to Suzhou Prefecture.   In 1720 the territory of Songjiang Prefecture included the counties of Huating [华亭], Shanghai [上海], Qingpu [青浦], Fengxian [奉贤], Jinshan [金山], and Nanhui [南汇], with Chuansha [川沙] being added in 1805.

The August 29, 1842 **Treaty of Nanking** (Zhongying Nanjing Tiaoyue) [中英南京條約] between Britain and China which ended the First Opium War (1839-1842) designated Shanghai as one of five treaty ports, and opened the city to foreign trade for the first time. However, prior to 1842 Shanghai had already been an important economic center for about 100 years, although its economic strength was never matched by an equal political importance. Soon after Shanghai's forcible opening up to the outside world, British, American, and French foreign settlements were established there. The British Settlement (Shanghai Ying Zujie) [上海英租界] was created in 1845, the Shanghai American Settlement (Shanghai Mei Zujie) [上海美租界] in 1847, and Shanghai French Settlement (Shanghai Fa Zujie) [上海法租界] in 1849. From 1854 to 1862 the three foreign settlements cooperated under one municipal government headed by the Shanghai Municipal Council (Shanghai Gongbu Ju) [上海工部局] established in 1854, but after the French dropped out of this arrangement in 1862, the British & American settlements merged into the unified International Settlement (Shanghai Gonggong Zujie) [上海公共租界] in 1863.

The Shanghai foreign settlements functioned as self-governing entities with their own municipal governments, court systems, educational institutions, police forces, volunteer militia, public utilities, and network of public roads. They taxed their foreign and Chinese residents alike, built expansive public works including networks of roads, bridges, and public parks, and defended their territory against outside invasion.

During the time of their existence, the settlements territory continued to expand, partly due to additional agreements with Chinese authorities, but largely due to an aggressive road building strategy in which municipal roads would be constructed beyond the official territorial limits into the Outside Roads Areas (Yuejie Zhulu) [越界筑路], after which municipal utilities, police, and public works services would be extended along those roads, and to pay for these services residents living along the roads would then be taxed by the settlement authorities, creating a population of taxpayers living outside the formal boundaries, until finally the boundaries would be extended either dejure or defacto. This road building expansion strategy was not unlike the more recent Israeli strategy of expanding illegal Jewish settlements in the West Bank.

The era of Shanghai's dominance by the Europeans and Americans lasted for about 100 years, until the unequal treaties were abolished by the Allied powers in 1943 during World War II, although since Vichy France was an Axis power, the Shanghai French Concession technically continued to exist throughout the Japanese occupation until after the end of the war in 1945 when a new Sino-French treaty was signed in February 1946.

Foreign control over Shanghai's downtown area encouraged foreign investors from all over the world to come here and construct residences and commercial buildings in the architectural style of their various home countries. As a result, the city still has examples of an eclectic array of architecture from around the world, some of which can no longer be found in their countries of origin. Styles that can be found here in plentiful supply include Art Deco, Greco-Roman, Oxford-Cambridge, Baroque, Beaux-Arts, Gothic, Tudor, Corbusier, Frank Lloyd Wright, and American colonial.

The International Settlement (Shanghai Gonggong Zujie) [上海公共租界]

From 1854 to 1862 the three foreign settlements cooperated under one municipal government headed by the Shanghai Municipal Council (Shanghai Gongbu Ju) [上海工部局] established in 1854, but after the French dropped out of this arrangement in 1862, the British & American settlements merged into the unified International Settlement (Shanghai Gonggong Zujie) [上海公共租界] in 1863.

In the beginning, the International Settlement (Shanghai Gonggong Zujie) [上海公共租界] occupied most of the **Bund** (Waitan) [外滩] waterfront along the Huangpu River, as well as parts of what are now Hongkou [虹口] and Yangpu [杨浦] districts north of the Suzhou River. The main street of the International Settlement was **Nanking** Road, now Nanjing East Road (Nanjing Dong Lu) [南京东路], which at its intersection with **Tibet Road** (Xizang Lu) [西藏路] changed its name to **Bubbling Well Road** (Nanjing Xi Lu).   It was in this settlement that most business and commerce took place.   The northern limits were clearly marked by **Suzhou Creek** west of Xizang Zhong Lu [西藏中路] and the appropriately named **Boundary Road** (Tianmu Lu) in the Zhabei district.   Shanghai's North Train Station sat just across the Settlement's northern boundary, in the same place where the modern station stands today. The Settlement's eastern limit was the **Huangpu River**, and the southern limit the boundary with the French Concession along what was originally a canal known as the **Yangjingbang** but later became Yanan Dong Lu [延安东路] and Yanan Xi Lu [延安西路].   In 1853 the western boundary of the British Settlement had been considered to follow the North-South line of **Defence Creek**, where present day Tibet Middle Road (Xizang Zhong Lu) [西藏中路] runs, but since this boundary had not actually been clearly marked in the original agreements with Chinese authorities, over time the International Settlement was able to continue expanding in a westward direction.

One method of covert expansion was an aggressive road building program known as the Outside Roads Areas (Yuejie Zhulu) [越界筑路], in which new road construction consistently extended far outside the settlement's established boundaries.   Once a new road was built, the International Settlement authorities would insist that all residents and businesses located along it must pay taxes to the Shanghai Municipal Council.   In turn, as taxpayers they were then entitled to Settlement police, fire and militia protection.   The International Settlement authorities would then appeal to the Chinese government that these taxpayers and roads outside the concession boundaries should be brought inside by extending the boundary to include them.   Use of this method over time resulted in extending the International Settlement's official western boundary as far as the Buddhist temple **Jingan Si** [静安寺] on Bubbling Well Road (Nanjing Xi Lu), near the latter's convergence with Yanan Xi Lu.

However, there was a very large western area of Shanghai known as the **Western Outside Roads Area** (Huxi Yuejie Zhulu) [沪西越界筑路], which was never formally annexed into the Settlement, although repeated attempts were made to do so.   Nonetheless, this Outside Roads Area had municipal streets and parks which were built, maintained and policed by the Shanghai Municipal Council, and foreign residents who paid taxes to the Settlement authorities.

The concentrated area of foreign settlement in western Shanghai extended as far West as the north-south line followed by **Keswick Road** (Kaixuan Lu) [凯旋路], which still runs parallel to the modern day Zhongshan Lu inner ring road.   In fact, the first 13 kilometer-long Zhongshan Lu ring road was originally built by the local Chinese municipal government on the site of the present one in 1928 in an attempt to restrict the expansion of the foreign settlements.   **Jessfield Park** (Zhongshan Gongyuan) [中山公园] was owned and operated by the International Settlement in this Outside Roads Area, and the American missionary run college **St. John's University** (Shanghai Sheng Yuehan Daxue) [上海圣约翰大学] was right across the street from the park.   The **McTyeire Girls School**, founded in 1890 and attended by the famous Soong sisters, was also located in this **Western Outside Roads Area** (Huxi Yuejie Zhulu) [沪西越界筑路] on Edinburgh Road (Jiangsu Lu), which ran from Avenue Haig in the south to Brennan Road in the north.   Although the Western Outside Roads Area largely stopped at Keswick Road (Kaixuan Lu) [凯旋路], there were a few Outside Roads built by the Shanghai Municipal Council which extended as far west as the north-south line of the aptly named **Rubicon Road** (Hami Lu) [哈密路].   These longer western extension roads included **Hungjao Road** (Hongqiao Lu), the **Great Western Road** (Yanan Xi Lu) [延安西路], **Lincoln Road** (Tianshan Lu) and **Brenan Road** (Changning Lu).

In addition to the **Western Outside Roads Area** (Huxi Yuejie Zhulu) [沪西越界筑路], there was a similar **Northern Outside Roads Area** (Hubei Yuejie Zhulu) [沪北越界筑路] controlled by the International Settlement authorities in Hongkou District north of the formal settlement border on **Boundary Road** (Tianmu Lu).   This Northern Outside Roads Area was centered around **Hongkew Park** (Lu Xun Park), which was owned and operated by the Shanghai Municipal Council, and extended as far North as modern day Dalian Xi Lu. International Settlement roads in this area included **Szechuen North Road** (Sichuan Bei Lu), **Dixwell Road** (Liyang Lu), **Darroch Road** (Duolun Lu), and **Scott Road** (Shanyin Lu).

In conjunction with the Outside Roads strategy, a series of four diplomatic agreements gradually enlarged the official boundaries of the International Settlement.   Starting with an area of only 138 acres in **1846**, the British concession had already grown to 470 acres in **1848**.   The merger of the British and American concessions in **1863** gave the newly established International Settlement a total area of 1,779 acres.   As part of their expansion policy, in the 1880s the Shanghai Volunteer Corps began holding maneuvers as far West as Jingan Temple (Jingan Si) on **Bubbling Well Road**, today's Nanjing West Road (Nanjing Xi Lu) [南京西路], and in 1884 the Shanghai Municipal Police began patrolling this area on a daily basis.   In May **1899** the Shanghai Municipal Council concluded successful negotiations with the Chinese authorities that extended the Settlement boundaries to its farthest limits, including almost all the roads previously built outside the boundaries.   This 1899 extension added 1,896 acres North of the Suzhou River and 1,908 acres to the West of the existing Settlement.   At its maximum size after the 1899 extension, the International Settlement covered 8.3 square miles of what is now downtown Shanghai, including 31,000 feet of prime waterfront along the Huangpu River.   Its western boundary was now just past Jingan Buddhist Temple (Jingan Si) [静安寺] , and roughly followed the north-south line of today's Yanping Lu, just west of Jiaozhou Lu, from the intersection of Huashan Lu and Changshu Lu in the south to Suzhou Creek in the north.

The outside road building strategy had been such a success in gaining boundary extensions that the Settlement continued this policy until in **1925** they had built 48 miles of roads outside their boundaries. However, despite repeated attempts at negotiations, the 1899 extension proved to be their last. Discouragement at the failure of the lengthy extension negotiations and increasing Chinese nationalism caused the Settlement to largely halt its outside roads building program after 1925. Nonetheless, the 10,332 foreign residents still living on the existing outside roads in **1935** continued to pay taxes to the Shanghai Municipal Council and in return received the protection of Settlement police and the comforts offered by the Settlement public utilities, such as gas, telephone, water, and electricity.

The French Concession (Shanghai Fa Zujie) [上海法租界]

The French Concession (Shanghai Fa Zujie) [上海法租界] started in the East with a very narrow mouth along the Huangpu River, wedged in between the International Settlement (Shanghai Gonggong Zujie) [上海公共租界] to the North and the Chinese walled city of Nanshi District [南市区] to the South. This bottleneck only had three streets, Avenue Edward VII (Yanan Dong Lu) [延安东路], Rue Du Consulat (Jingling Dong Lu) and Avenue Deux Republiques (Minguo Lu/Renmin Lu). This bottleneck was characterized by urban commercial buildings, many of which can still be seen. **Rue Du Consulat** (Jingling Dong Lu) [金陵东路] was named after the French Consulate, which stood at the intersection of this street and the Bund [外滩]. It still has its distinct buildings, which hang over the covered sidewalks running past them. **Avenue Edward VII** (Yanan Dong Lu) [延安东路] marked the northern boundary with the International Settlement. It was shaped like a snake because it followed the course of a former creek known as the **Yangjing Bang** [洋泾浜], which was filled in 1914-15 when the road was built. **Avenue des Deux Republiques** (Minguo Lu/Renmin Lu) marked the concession's southern boundary and wound around the circular pattern of the Nanshi [南市] town wall. A narrow stretch of French territory known as the **Quai de France** did extend along the Huangpu River waterfront as far south as **Fangbang Dong Lu** [方浜东路], a road that was named aftern another former creek, but this was less than one block wide due to the existence of the Chinese walled city directly behind it.

However, once past the obstacle of the Nanshi district's walled town, the French Concession at its peak expanded much more widely to the South, West and North. **Avenue Edward VII** (Yanan Zhong Lu) continued to be the border with the International Settlement, but the way the road veered far to the North at a diagonal angle gave the French room to expand in this direction as well. Where Avenue Edward VII (Yanan Zhong Lu) became the **Great Western Road** (Yanan Xi Lu), the French Concession's western boundary followed **Avenue Haig** (Huashan Lu) to Xujiahui [徐家汇]. The furthest western limits of French control extended as far as the Roman Catholic community at **Xujiahui** [徐家汇]. The southern limit was **Route de Zikawei** (Xujiahui Lu [徐家汇路] and Zhaojiabang Lu [肇嘉浜路]), which followed the course of **Siccawei Creek**, then large enough for sailing houseboats out to Sheshan Mountain in Songjiang District. Veering North from Siccawei Creek and following the winding **Rue de Captaine Rabier**, part of which lay on what is now a southern section of Xizang Nan Lu [西藏南路], the French Concession's southern border connected with the western side of the Chinese walled city at the intersection of **Rue Millot** (Fangbang Xi Lu) on the French side and **Fangbang Zhong Lu** on the Chinese side. The French concession was largely a residential area of leafy, tree-lined suburbs dotted with impressive mansions. Its main business street was **Avenue Joffre** (Huaihai Zhong Lu) [淮海中路].

The French used a similar road building strategy as the British and Americans in order to expand their concession's boundaries, and in the end they were even more successful at it. The French started out with just 3,800 feet of waterfront along the Huangpu River. However, in **1861** they won a small extension of 23 acres of riverfront along the Huangpu, South of their original area and east of the Chinese walled town. On January 27, **1900** the French received a larger extension of 171 acres to the West of their original Concession. Finally, on July 31, **1914** the French received their third and last extension of 2,167 acres of new territory to the West of their existing concession. This extension of 1914 took their western boundary all the way to **Xujiahui** [徐家汇] and **Avenue Haig** (Huashan Lu). At its height after 1914 the French Concession covered 3.9 square miles of present day downtown Shanghai.

The Chinese City Government

In 1927 the national government in Nanjing officially designated the parts of Shanghai under Chinese control as a city for the first time in its history. A municipal government was established, complete with a mayor and a municipal council. Although the foreign concessions were still outside of its boundaries, the **Municipality of Greater Shanghai** covered an area of 320 square miles, including the districts of Zhabei, Nanshi, and Pudong. The municipal government constructed a new civic center in **Jiangwan** Town of Yangpu District (Yangpu Qu) [杨浦区] that eventually included a museum, library, stadium, and city hall.

Shanghai's development was interrupted by two Japanese military offensives, the first in January 1932, and the second in August 1937. The International Settlement and French Concession remained unoccupied by the Japanese until 1941. However, after December 1937 Shanghai became a solitary island (gu dao) surrounded for the next four years by Japanese occupied territory. The local economy stagnated, and construction of new buildings essentially came to a halt. The period of full scale Japanese occupation of the whole city from 1941 to 1945 saw the European and American residents rounded up and held in prisoner of war camps.

By September 1945 Guomindang authorities had regained control of Shanghai, but in the three years and nine months after the end of the Sino-Japanese War during which the Guomindang controlled the city, life never really returned its pre-war state of normality. The May 24, 1949 Communist takeover of Shanghai came one month after the April 23rd fall of the Guomindang capital in Nanjing and was the last real battle of the Chinese Civil War.

In 1956 those privately-owned Chinese businesses that had somehow managed to survive until then were all nationalized under various schemes including joint private-state ownership, collectives, and cooperatives. A giant meeting was held at Longhua Temple in 1956 to celebrate the state's seizure of all remaining private Chinese companies and their conversion into joint private-state enterprises. This was followed by the 1957 Anti-Rightist Campaign which rounded up and imprisoned the remnants of the businessmen and other members of the educated middle class.

The **Cultural Revolution** (Wenhua Da Geming) [文化大革命] (1966-1976) began in Shanghai, and its leaders, known as the **Gang of Four** (Siren Bang) [四人帮], made the city their headquarters.   Although they publicly championed the cause of the workers and peasants, the Gang of Four (Siren Bang) [四人帮] hypocritically lived lavish lives of luxury within the walled garden compounds of many of Shanghai's choicest old colonial mansions. During this decade, all universities in Shanghai were closed, as were all the temples and churches in the city.   Red Guards (Hongweiping) destroyed a number of Shanghai's historic sites, including the Confucius Temple (Wen Miao) [文庙] in Nanshi District, the tomb of Xu Guangqi (aka Paul Hsu) in Xujiahui, and the Foreigner's Cemetery (Wanguo Gongmu) [万国公墓] located in the present day Song Qingling Mu Yuan. Shanghai's Longhua Buddhist Temple (Longhua Si) and the City God Temple (Chenghuang Miao) had their entire contents looted and were occupied by factories or used as commercial warehouses.

Churches and temples did not begin to reopen until the early 1980s.   Some, such as Shanghai's City God Temple, remained closed even until the mid-1990s.   A few notable ones, such as the Holy Trinity Cathedral (Sheng Sanyi Tang) [圣三一堂], were still being occupied for non-religious purposes until recently.

The most noticeable fact at the time economic reforms started in 1980 was how little the city's skyline had changed since 1937.   The Park Hotel (Guoji Fandian) [国际饭店] on Nanjing West Road (Nanjing Xi Lu) [南京西路] built in 1934 was still the tallest building in China in 1980.   When American writer **Harold Isaacs** returned to the city in 1981 after an absence of 45 years, he was startled to find it looking almost the same as before.   He described his visit as a "Journey in a time capsule."   Indeed the city continued to be a kind of living museum throughout the 1980s, and was largely unaffected by the economic reforms of that decade.

It was not until 1990 that Shanghai's economy began to see the first sparks of reignition with the creation of the Pudong New Area and a new stock exchange.   In 1992 Deng Xiaoping [邓小平] (1904-1997) admitted that the biggest mistake he had ever made was leaving Shanghai out of the economic reforms of the 1980s.   Later that same year, the 14th Party Congress of the Chinese Communist Party resolved to, "build Shanghai into one of the world economic, financial and trade centers as fast as possible..."

Major events in the city's trajectory towards renewed global prominence since that important 1992 decision have included the hosting of the September 1999 **Fortune 500 Forum** and the October 2001 **APEC** Conference.   By December 2002 Shanghai had become the fourth busiest container shipping port in the world, surpassing both Kaohsiung in Taiwan, and Rotterdam in the Netherlands, and falling just behind Pusan in South Korea.   This puts the city full circle back to the position it had in world trade in 1924, when it was previously listed as the world's fourth busiest shipping port.   Common social talk of local inhabitants now revolves around not whether but when Shanghai will replace Hong Kong as the dominant regional economic center of East Asia.   During the same month the city's new claim to fame was further boosted by its winning of the right to host the 2010 **World Expo** and the announcement of plans to open a new **Universal Studios** theme park by 2007.   However, by October 2014 Universal Studios had instead announced plans to built a theme park in Beijing, and their planned them park in Shanghai never materialized.   Nonetheless, **Shanghai Disneyland** opened in the Pudong New Area of Shanghai on June 2016, after a decade of planning and construction, at a cost of $5.5 billion USD.

Although the last official census was conducted in 2010, since the year 2016 the Shanghai municipal government has estimated the city's total population to be over 24.15 million people, including an estimated 9.72 million (40%) Chinese who have migrated to Shanghai from other provinces, usually for economic reasons, and who are not counted as permanent residents.   In fact, Chinese migrants have accounted for nearly all of the city's population growth, as the natural birth rate among permanent Chinese residents has been almost zero, with only 96,200 babies born to them in the year 2015.

The city's population of permanent Chinese residents and long-term migrants who have lived there for more than six months is swelled by another 300 million foreign and domestic tourists who visit each year.   The city government estimates that 8,543,700 foreign tourists visited Shanghai in 2016.   There are also at least 170,000 foreign expatriates who were estimated to be working here in 2015, although other sources estimated that to be 209,000 expatriates as of October 2018.   As a result, on any given day the actual number of people living or staying in the city and jamming its transportation network and public conveniences may be millions more than the official population statistics state.

City officials have had to admit that their previous estimate that Shanghai's population would reach 17 million by the year 2020 was a serious underestimate.   In December 2017 it was announced that the city government intended to limit Shanghai's population growth to a total of 25 million people by the year 2035, but experts were extremely skeptical as to how this goal would be achieved.   For example, in the decade between the year 2000 and the year 2010 the city's population grew at a rate of more than 40%.

Shanghai's urban city center within the Outer Ring Road covers an area of 667 square km., but the entire area within the Shanghai Municipality (Shanghai Shi) totals 6,340 square km (2,400 square miles).   The Shanghai municipal region comprises much of the Yangzi Delta, and is roughly equivalent in territory to that previously included in the old Songjiang Prefecture (Songjiang Fu) from the Yuan to the Qing dynasties.   As of November 2018, the Shanghai municipality was divided up into 16 districts, after half a dozen administrative changes in the past 18 years that included the elimination and merger of some previous districts, and the upgrading of all counties to district status.

The downtown urban core within the Zhongshan Inner Ring Road is comprised of the four districts of Jingan (including the former Zhabei District since 2017), Huangpu (including the former Nanshi District since the year 2000, and the former Luwan District since 2011), Xuhui, and Changning, with five more outlying districts of Minhang, Putuo, Yangpu, Hongkou, and Baoshan also being heavily developed urban areas.   Parts of the formerly rural Pudong New Area on the east side of the Huangpu, such as Lujiazui, now have to be considered as forming part of the downtown core, which was previously exclusively located on the West side of the river (Puxi).

In addition to these ten heavily urbanized central districts, Shanghai includes six rural districts and one island county, which are seldom visited by foreigners.   Due to the cheaper land, some factories and industrial parks have been built in these outlying areas by multinational companies in recent years.   Nonetheless, they still possess many traditional small towns, open farmland, and villages typical of Jiangnan culture.   These rural areas of the Shanghai municipality include the six districts of Songjiang, Qingpu, Jiading, Jinshan, Fengxian, and Chongming.   Chongming Island (Chongming Dao) in the Yangzi River estuary, along with the two smaller islands of Changxing and Hengsha, was a county belonging to Shanghai from 1958 to 2017, but in January 2017 it was raised from the status of a county to that of a district.   The former Nanhui District is also largely a rural area, with the exception of its former district capital of Huinan Town, but was mered into the Pudong New Area in 2009.

In order to relieve overcrowding within the city center, urban planners have designed a comprehensive development plan for the whole municipality that calls for the movement of population and industries to the outlying areas, which are still largely open countryside at the moment.   This "muli-centric" approach calls for the creation of 11 medium-sized New Towns.   Most of these New Towns are actually the existing district seats of Shanghai's suburban and rural districts, including Baoshan, Jiading, Songjiang, Jinshan, Minhang, and Qingpu.   These towns won't need to be built so much as rebuilt and redeveloped as new urban centers.   Since several of these district seats have also been designated as Historic Towns deserving preservation, it will be interesting to see how well urban development and historic preservation can be balanced in these cases.

The most important role for **Luchaogang Harbor** [芦潮港] had been to serve as the departure and arrival point for passenger ships traveling between Shanghai and the island of Putuoshan in Zhejiang.   However, Luchaogang [芦潮港] is now the coastal anchor point for the **East China Sea Bridge** (Donghai Daqiao) [东海大桥], which was completed in December 2005 and runs 32.5 km (20.2 miles), connecting the mainland of the Pudong New Area with **Yangshan Deep Water Port** (Yangshan Shenshui Gang)[洋山深水港] on a small island out in Hangzhou Bay that technically belongs to Zhejiang Province.

Most interesting of all is the plans to further utilize the enormous amount of open space currently available out on the under populated but isolated Chongming Island in the Yangzi Estuary, ranked as China's third largest island after Taiwan and Hainan.   Up until a few years ago, the island was only connected to the rest of Shanghai by ferry boat service, hence limiting the number of people and industries that would want to locate there.

However, the combined **Shanghai Yangzi River Tunnel** and **Shanghai Yangzi River Bridge** opened on October 31, 2009 and now connect Chongming Island with the Shanghai mainland to the south in Pudong New District.   To the north, Chongming Island is also now connected with Qidong [启东市] in northern Jiangsu Province by the **Chongqi Bridge**, and the **Chonghai Bridge** connecting western Chongming Island with Haimen in northern Jiangsu is also under construction.

The **Shanghai Yangzi River Tunnel** starts on the south bank of the Yangtze at Wuhaogou, Pudong and ends in the south of Changxing Island. It is 8.9 kilometres (5.5 mi) in length, and has two stacked levels. The upper level is for a motorway, and has three lanes in each direction, with a designed speed of 80 kilometres per hour (50 mph). The lower level is reserved for a future Shanghai subway line to Chongming Island.

The **Shanghai Yangzi River Bridge** starts at the tunnel exit, crosses Changxing Island at ground level, then crosses to Chongming Island, ending at Chenjia Town. It consists of two long viaducts with a higher cable-stayed section in the middle to allow the passage of ships. The total length is 16.63 kilometres (10.33 mi), of which 6.66 kilometres (4.14 mi) is road and 9.97 kilometres (6.20 mi) bridge. The overall shape of the bridge is slightly S-shaped.

The length of the central span is about 730 metres (2,395 ft). The bridge has six lanes, three in each direction, with space on the shoulders reserved for the future construction of the planned Line 19 of the Shanghai subway system to Chongming Island.

Line 19 of the Shanghai subway system will link Rongqiao Road station on Line 9 in Pudong New District to Chongming Island via Changxing Island, with a branch from the latter to Hengsha Island. The line will use the Shanghai Yangzi River Tunnel and Bridge, which were designed to take its tracks. The first phase of the line from Rongqiao Road to Changxing Island is scheduled to open by 2020.

The Chongming-Qidong Yangzi River Bridge (Chongqi Daqiao) [崇启大桥] opened to traffic on Christmas Eve 2011, while the Chongming-Haimen Bridge (Chonghai Daqiao) [崇海大桥] is still under construction.

Despite all the added overland transportation routes, some ferry boat routes continue to operate between the three islands in Chongming District. Hengsha Island can still only be reached by taking a ferry boat. On Chongming Island, Chengqiao's Nanmen Port offers service to the Shidongkou and Baoyang Road ports in Baoshan District and to Liuhegang in southern Jiangsu Province; Xinhai's Niupeng Harbor to Qinglonggang in Haimen; and other ports offer connections with Wusong and Chongming District's two other islands.

Recent social changes have included the disappearance of the pimps, hookers, jaywalkers, smokers, sidewalk vendors, outdoor street markets, and "happy ending" massage parlors that used to make it a more colorful place. Sidewalk newsstands that once stood in every neighborhood have disappeared, along with the print publications they used to sell. Itinerant salesman no longer approach pedestrians offering to sell them a wrist watch.

Dongtai Lu, the 200-meter-long antique street that opened in the early 1980s and featured at least 125 shops, was the last of the previously many outdoor street markets to be forcibly shut down and demolished in May 2015, following in the wake of the Xiangyang Lu Street Market, the Huating Lu Street Market, the Jiangyin Lu Bird & Flower Market, and many others now long-gone. The Huating Lu Street Market once had 400 stalls along a 732-meter-long walking street, but was the first to be closed down in the year 2000 after having been open for about 20 years since the early 1980s; while it's successor the Xiangyang Lu Market opened in October 2000, had 900 vendors at its peak, and was closed down approximately six years later in June 2006. The Jiangyin Lu street market stretched for 200 meters and had 100 stalls.

These street markets first opened up in Shanghai in the early 1980s and gave budding new entrepreneurs the chance to run their own business during the first years of China's capitalist market economy reforms. Although the street markets were criticized by some for offering counterfeit copies of famous brand name products, the quality was usually good, and there was something much more enjoyable about the whole experience than shopping inside a normal department store or indoor shopping mall. There was a sense of adventure and discovery in looking for and finding that special item. Prices were never fixed, and it was expected by both parties that the exchange of goods would involve heated haggling back and forth over the price. This bargaining was always the fun part, as each party tried to get the best deal for themselves. For foreigners it meant a good chance to practice your Chinese language skills as well, or else use the unique Chinese sign language for numbers. You would walk away either feeling victorious at having won yourself a real bargain or feeling cheated at having paid too much. Either way, this was an experience you could never get at a regular indoor store where prices were fixed and staff had no authority to negotiate.

A campaign to enforce a ban on smoking indoors has forced smokers outdoors into the blazing hot sun or wind and rain. Posters inside the lobby of every building say "No Smoking" in huge letters and even advise those witnessing violations to call a hotline and report the offender. Many retail convenience stores have even stopped offering tobacco products for sale.

Due to new regulations that are actually being enforced, in Shanghai you no longer hear the constant explosion of firecrackers and fireworks during the lunar New Year known as the Spring Festival. Instead there is a deafening silence that is quite eerie to anyone who has experienced the way it was before.

On some main roads, as many as five layers of metal barricades now prevent pedestrians from crossing the street at anywhere but the designated crosswalks. Cops who used to spend all day hiding in the comfortable confines of their police stations now for the first time walk beats on the sidewalks, lining the city's main streets like sentries, spread only a few feet apart within sight of each other.

The once ubiquitous massage parlors with their storefront windows advertising their wares that once made parts of the city resemble Amsterdam have now all been closed down, white stripes of paper with messages from the police written on them wheat-pasted in an X pattern sealing their doors shut, leaving lots of vacant retail space on some streets. Maybe they were massaging more than feet, contrary to their signs outside.

Urban development has continued with the expansion of the city's enormous subway system to be reputedly the longest in the world, including at least 4,000 trains, 675 kilometers (420 miles), more than 367 stations, and currently 16 fully operational lines that reach as far out from the downtown city center as Huinan Town in the east, Jiading town in the west, Wusongkou in the north, and Songjiang Town in the south, but for some reason still stop at Xujing Town in Shanghai's southwest Qingpu District. Qingpu Town is probably the only district capital that still can't be reached by subway. By the end of 2018 it is expected that the number of lines will have grown to 18. When I first arrived in Shanghai in early 1999, there was only one subway line, which ran between the downtown city center and suburban Xinzhuang Town in Minhang District. The college where I first worked in 1999, and the dormitory next door where we used to live, have both been torn down to make way for a new subway station.

In December 2002 Shanghai was the world's fourth busiest shipping container port, having regained the position it had previously held in 1924, but 12 years later it had risen to first place by 2014, according to Forbes magazine, surpassing Singapore, Hong Kong, and Busan.

Although the last official census was conducted in 2010, and there have been no new official statistics released since 2015, the city's population is estimated to have grown to over 25 million in 2017, more than double what it was 32 years earlier in 1982, making it the third most populous city in the world after Tokyo and New Delhi, and larger than the size of the total population of Australia. 9 million people, or nearly 40% of the city's residents, are internal migrants from other parts of China, what native Shanghainese call the "Outside Place People" (Waidiren).   In fact, it's this internal migration that has continued to fuel the city's population growth, not the natural birth rate, as fertility rates among native inhabitants have been declining since 1993. However, many of the new social and economic policies may have the intentional or unintentional effect of driving the Waidiren out of the city.   An official target has been set to limit the population to a maximum of 25 million.   The number of foreigners officially registered as temporary residents of Shanghai has more than tripled from 55,000 in 2001 to over 160,000 in 2017, with Japanese being the largest nationality, followed by Americans and Koreans.

While the city's total territory has remained the same, the number of districts has shrunk from 20 administrative divisions when I first arrived here in 1999 down to only 16 today,   as Huangpu, Jingan, and Pudong districts have continued to expand in a series of mergers. Nanhui District was swallowed by the Pudong New District in May 2009, while Luwan District was absorbed by Huangpu District in June 2011, Nanshi District already having been eaten up by Huangpu District in June 2000, and Zhabei District was merged into Jingan District in November 2015.   This loss of four districts since 1999 would have reduced the total number down to 15 districts, except that Chongming County, which comprised several islands in the Yangzi River Estuary, was raised to the status of a district in June 2016, giving Shanghai a total of 16 administrative districts.   Thus the last county within the boundaries of the Shanghai municipality was eliminated, the culmination of a trend since the early 1990s in which Shanghai's counties were upgraded to district status.

Housing costs have skyrocketed to undreamed of heights, which some analysts keep predicting might be a bubble ready to burst, creating a situation similar to the U.S. financial crisis of 2008.   In March 2003 I wrote that it cost on average 8,000 Rmb (then $100 USD) per square meter to purchase an apartment in the Shanghai city center, but by May 2017 Shanghai Daily was reporting that it now cost over 50,000 Rmb ($7,222 USD) per square meter to buy an apartment in the city, an increase of 525% within 14 years.   Housing rental costs have seen a similar trend.   A one-bedroom apartment in Minhang District now costs 10,000 Rmb ($1,500 USD) per month to rent, whereas five years ago it cost half that. Foreign teachers can only afford to rent a single room in a multi-room apartment, often shared with total strangers, whereas before they could afford a two-bedroom apartment of their own.   Some residents have resorted to living in hotel rooms, with older hotels partially being converted into long-term low-cost rental housing, after all the electricity, running water, and Internet are all included for free.   In June 2017 rare public protests broke out on the streets of Jingan District demonstrating against the city's housing policies, but were quickly suppressed.

In 2003 I wrote that out of a then total population of 16 million people, 51.2 per cent of Shanghai's population had a home computer, 4.2 million people had some form of Internet access, and 9.12 million people owned a mobile phone.   Today smart phones equipped with wireless Internet (WiFi) are ubiquitous, with many people doing most of their communicating and shopping via the Wechat mobile phone application. While this new technology is convenient, it also means constantly bumping into people on the street who walk while staring down at the smart phone held in their hand, without looking where they are going.   Taxi drivers even use digital maps on their cell phones to determine which route they will take to get you to your destination.

Several historic buildings in the city that had long been closed to the public have finally had lengthy restoration projects completed after years of delays that made it seem as if they would never be completed, including the **Holy Trinity Cathedral** (Sheng Sanyi Tang) [圣三一堂], the **Great World Amusement Center** (Dashijie) [大世界], and the former **Shanghai Municipal Library** (Shanghai Shili Tushuguan) [上海市立图书馆] in Jiangwan Town [江湾镇]. Unfortunately, in some cases over zealous clean up efforts have left the old buildings looking as if they were brand new.   In some ways I preferred the living museum of architecture that I found when I first arrived in Shanghai in early 1999.   The dust, dirt, and grime on the original wooden handrails and wooden doors of buildings dating from the Republic of China (Minguo) time period (1911-1949) or even the Qing Dynasty (1644-1911) made you feel as if you were really walking in the footsteps of the previous occupants from a bygone era.   You could almost see their fingerprints and smell the musty aroma they had left behind.   On the other hand, it's nice to see the ongoing trend of historic structures that had been occupied by the new government after 1949 finally being appreciated for their architectural heritage, rather than just their office space, and opened up to the public for the first time in decades, or in some cases for the first time ever.

Politically the city had experienced great stability under the leadership of Han Zheng [韩正], who started out as the head of Luwan District in 1992, became a vice-mayor in 1998, mayor in 2003, and then city party secretary in 2012.   Somehow he survived the fall of two predecessors, mayor Xu Kuangdi [徐匡迪] in 2001, and former Shanghai party secretary Chen Liangyu [陈良宇] in September 2006, and hasn't been implicated in the nation-wide anti-corruption campaign of the past five years that has caused government and party leaders in other provinces to drop like flies. However, his promotion to the politburo standing committee in October 2017 means that his long tenure of running Shanghai's municipal administration for the past 25 years is finally coming to an end, as he will now have to move to Beijing.

Shanghai From A to Z: Alphabetical Subject Index

A   American Club
     Archives

B   Buddhist Temples
     The Bund (Waitan)
     The Bund Waitan Yuan Area: R.A.S. Building, etc.

C   Canidrome
     Cathedrals and Churches (Jiaotang)
     Chenxiang Pavilion Buddhist Temple
     Chinese Communist Party's First Congress Hall
     Chongming Island (Chongming Dao)
     City God Temples (Chenghuang Miao)
     City Wall (Chengqiang)
     Confucius Temples (Wen Miao)
     Customs Libary

D   Dajing Pavilion (Dajing Ge)
     Duolun Lu Culture Street
     Du Yuesheng's Da Gong Guan

F   French Club
     French Concession
     French Municipal Council Director's Home

G   Gardens (Yuanlin)
     Great World Amusement Center (Dashijie)
     The Green Gang (Qing Bang)
     Grosvenor House
     Guilin Park (Guilin Gongyuan)

H   Hengshan Road (Hengshan Lu)
     Huaihai Road (Huaihai Lu)
     Huangpu River (Huangpu Jiang)

I   Interneational Cemetery
     International Settlement

J   Jade Buddha Temple (Yufo Chan Si)
     Jewish Monuments
     Jiading City God Temple (Jiading Chenghuang Miao)
     Jiading Confucius Temple (Jiading Kong Miao)
     Jiading Town
     Jiangnan Arsenal
     Jiangwan Town (Jiangwan Zhen)
     Jingan Buddhist Temple (Jingan Si)
     Jinze Ancient Town (Jinze Gu Zhen)

L   Libraries
     Longhua Airport
     Longhua Buddhist Temple & Pagoda
     Longhua Guomindang Military Garrison
     Longhua Revolutionary Martyr's Cemetery (Longhua Lieshi Lingyuan)
     Lu Xun's Former House (Lu Xun Guju)
     Lu Xun Park (Lu Xun Gongyuan)

M   Maglev Line
     Marble Hall
     Marshall House (Taiyuan Villa)
     Mid-Lake Pavilion Tea House (Huxing Ting Chalou)
     Moganshan Lu Artists Colony
     Moller Mansion
     Morris Garden
     Mosques (Qingzhen Si)
     Museums (Bowuguan)

N   Nanjing East Road (Nanjing Dong Lu)
     Nanjing West Road (Nanjing Xi Lu)
     Nanxiang Dumplings

O   The Old Shanghai County Town

P   Pagodas (Baota)
     Park Hotel (Guoji Dajiudian)
     People's Park (Renmin Gongyuan)
     People's Square (Renmin Guangchang)
     Pudong New Area (Pudong Xinqu)

Q   Qingpu Town & District

R   Race Club Building

S   Shanghai Concert Hall
     Shanghai Municipal Council Building
     Sheshan Hill
     Sheshan Observatory (Sheshan Tianwentai)
     Sheshan Roman Catholic Cathedral (Sheshan Tianzhu Jiaotang)
     Song Family Compound
     Songjiang Ancient Mosque (Songjiang Gu Qingzhen Si)
     Songjiang Town & District
     Song Jiaoren's Tomb (Song Jiaoren Mu)
     Song Qingling's Former House (Song Qingling Guju)
     Song Qingling's Tomb (Song Qingling Mu)
     St. John's University (Sheng Yuehan Daxue)
     Stone Gate Houses (Shikumen)
     Subway System (Shanghai Ditie)
     Sun Yat-Sen's Former House (Sun Zhongshan Guju)
     Suzhou Creek (Suhou He)

Swire Mansion

T Taoist Temples
   Theaters
   Tianma Shan Hill

U Urban Planning Exhibition Center

W West Bund
   World Expo 2010
   Wusong Kou

X Xintiandi
   Xujiahui French Catholic Community
   Xujiahui Library (Xujiahui Cangshulou)

Y Yangzi River Waterfront
   Yuanming Buddhist Lecture Hall
   Yu Garden (Yu Yuan)

Z Zhenru Buddhist Temple (Zhenru Si)
   Zhujiajiao Ancient Town (Zhujiajiao Guzhen)

The American Club (Huaqi Zonghui) [花旗总会]

The Shanghai American Club (Huaqi Zonghui) [花旗总会] was founded on July 4, 1917 when there were about 1,500 Americans resident in Shanghai. It was originally housed in a space inside a bank building located at 33 Nanjing Road, near its intersection with Henan Road, until that became too small for their growing membership. Some English sources mistakenly state that the club's Chinese name was Meiguo Zonghui [美国总会], when actually it was Huaqi Zonghui, Huaqi meaning literally "the Stars & Stripes," or Amerian flag, in the same way that China's red flag is known as the Hongqi. So, a literal translation of its Chinese name would actually be the Stars & Stripes Club or American Flag Club.

The land for a new building was purchased in 1922 at the present-day address of 209 Fuzhou Road (Fuzhou Lu 209 hao) [福州路 209 号] in Huangpu District [黄浦区]. The International Settlement's Central Police Station and Shanghai Municipal Coucil Headquarters building were both conveniently located nearby.

The Amrican architectural firm of R.A. Curry was contracted to design the structure, while most of the design work was actually done by Hungarian architect Laszlo Hudec, who chose an American Colonial Georgian Revival style for it. Many of the construction materials were imported from the U.S., including the red bricks for the exterior façade as well as the wood used for the floors and paneling, but the marble for double staircase on the ground floor was imported from Italy. The ground breaking occurred in May 1923, and the corner stone of the American Club building was laid on January 10th 1924 by Jacob Gould Schurman, the American Ambassador to China. The formal opening of the red brick, six-story building was held in April 1925. Visitors were greeted by the Italian marbel double stair case in the lobby and modern elevators that could take them upstairs or downstairs. The basement featured a bowling alley, barber shop, and Turkish baths; while the lower floors had a bar, library, lounge, card rooms, and billiards room; there were 50 guest rooms on the second, third, and fourth floors; a large dining room on the fifth floor, as well as several smaller private dining rooms, that supposedly served "American-style cuisine;" a ballroom, staff quarters on the sixth floor; and a roof garden on top.

Initially club membership was limited to white, male, U.S. citizens, with all women, African Americans and Chinese excluded. However, in July 1937 the club was opened to white female U.S. citizens, and in later years some upper class Chinese were reportedly admitted, especially those who were businessmen and returned students who had studied in America.

At some point the Shanghai American Chamber of Commerce (Zhong Mei Shang Hui) [中美商会], which had been founded in 1915, moved their offices from the Dollar Building (Dalai Dalou) [大来大楼] at 51 Canton Road (Guangdong Lu 51 hao) [广东路 51 号], which had been built in 1921 by the U.S. Robert Dollar Steamship Line Dalai Lunchuan Gongsi) [大来轮船公司], and into the Shanghai American Club building. It's possible that this happened when the Dollar Line went bankrupt in 1938.

From December 1941 to August 1945 the building was occupied by Japanese military intelligence, but after the Victory over Japan the building was returned to the Shanghai American Club.

Dates for the existence of the Shanghai American Club are usually given as being from 1917 to 1949. However, the present-day Shanghai Chamber of Commerce claims that its predecessor organization occupied space in the Shanghai American Club building until possibly as late as the end of 1950. Assuming that is correct, the building may not have been seized by the new authorities until the end of that year.

From 1953 to 1991 the building was occupied by the Shanghai High Court (Shanghai Shi Gaojji Renmin Fayuan) [上海市高级人民法院] , as well as the Shanghai Intermediate Court (Shanghai Shi Zhongji Fayuan) [上海市中级法院], and was known as the High Court Building (Gaoji Dalou) [高法大楼].

After the court moved out in 1991 the building sat empty, despite being designated as a municipal protected historical building in 1994, until July 2018 when the building suddenly underwent a major restoration of its interior and was re-occupied by the newly established Shanghai Financial Court (Shanghai Jinrong Fayuan) [上海金融法院] on August 20, 2018. The original interior decorations have been remarkably well preserved thanks to it having been occupied by a government institution during the Cultural Revolution, which prevented it from being damaged by the Red Guards. However, as a functioning law court, public access for visitors who want to see it may now be limited.

Address: 209 Fuzhou Road (Fuzhou Lu 209 hao) [福州路 209 号] Huangpu District [黄浦区]

Archives (Dangan Guan) [档案馆]

The Shanghai Municipal Archives (Shanghai Shi Dangan Guan) [上海市档案馆] is considered by many Western researchers to be the most open and helpful archives in China. Unlike others which provide readers a hand-written catalogue which can only be utilized on site, the Shanghai Archives sells a series of brochures which list all files open to the public. Readers also can buy a guide book entitled, "*Concise Instruction To Shanghai Municipal Archives*," which furnishes detailed information on all documents held by the Archives. In addition, the Archives has a computer system which readers can use to find all files related to their research. Unlike other Chinese archives which have many restrictions on making photocopies and taking notes, in the Shanghai Archives readers can request a photocopy of almost any documents they are allowed to read. The only exception is for those books which are too old to copy because they might be damaged. The public catalogue of the Shanghai Municipal Archives had previously excluded all documents related to any political issues. However, recently there have been moves toward even greater openness.

On July 10, 2004 Shanghai Daily reported that the Shanghai Municipal Archives had opened up 26,838 previously closed files to the public for the first time. These files are apparently all foreign language documents of the two foreign concessions former governments dating from the 1849 to 1943 period. The newly opened files constitute approximately half of the 60,000 volumes of foreign language files the archives has from this time period. A bilingual index of the open files is now available online from the Shanghai Archives web site at http://www.archives.sh.cn.

The earliest files dating from the middle of the 19th century include those on the Shanghai Arsenal from 1851 to 1933, the Municipal Council of the International Settlement from 1849 to 1943, the French Concession from 1849 to 1946, and the Zikawei Observatory from 1873 to 1950.

The history of private education in Shanghai before 1949 is well documented with files from Shanghai University (1906 – 1952), St. John's University (1879 – 1952), Aurora University (?-1952), and the Soochow University Law School (1915 – 1952).

The city's political history is represented by thousands of files on revolutionary activities dating back to 1911, including records of the Shanghai General Labor Union from its founding in 1924, as well as records of the 1927-1949 Guomindang regime's party, government, military and police offices in the city, such as those from the Songhu Garrison Commander's Headquarters from 1928 to 1949, the Shanghai Municipal Government from 1927 to 1949, and files from law courts and prisons, and all municipal district police stations up to 1949.

Economic history is represented by records of the Bank of China dating from 1915 to 1949, and the Central Bank of China's records from 1908 to 1953, the Shanghai Chamber of Commerce from 1916 to 1951, as well as many other private banks.   Records illustrate how virtually all private banks were shut down by 1951-1952, although a handful survived until 1955.   Commercial retail history is represented by files on the three famous Nanking Road department stores of Wing On (1918-1954), Sun Sun (1928 -1956), and Sincere (1917-1966?).   Files on over 400 different industry associations of private enterprises and traditional trade guilds show how they slowly disappeared from 1955 to 1958, with not a single one left in existence by 1959.

The local Shanghai news media is represented by copies of the Xinmin Evening News dating back to 1929, and the Wenhui Daily to 1938, as well as issues of Miller's Review from 1917 to 1953.

Post-1949 Revolution files include ones on sensitive topics such as those from the land reform of 1950 to 1954, the Religious Affairs Bureau for 1950 to 1966, a surprising number of files from the Shanghai Revolution Committee and Shanghai Militia that ran the city during the Cultural Revolution (Wenhua Da Geming) of 1966-1976, as well as several thousand files from the lengthy investigation into the Gang of Four from 1976 to 1984, and the reversal of false accusations against "wrongly designated rightists" from 1978 to 1980.

Shanghai Municipal Archives (Shanghai Shi Dangan Guan) [上海市档案馆]
Address: 326 Xianxia Lu, Shanghai, 200335
Telephone: (021) 6295-3167 Fax: (021) 6295-1562
Web Site: http://www.archives.sh.cn.

Shanghai Archives, Bund Branch

In 2004 the Shanghai Archives opened up a new branch in a modern building on the former French Bund, located between Jingling Dong Lu and Yanan Dong Lu.   However, this branch seems more dedicated to being a kind of museum than a place of actual research. By purchasing a 10 Rmb ticket you can gain access to the second and third floors where an impressive array of exhibits of genuine historic artifacts.   The collection of relics on display here was in fact of much better quality than the mainly fake replicas displayed at the official Shanghai History Museum now located in the Oriental Pearl T.V. Tower in Pudong. Exhibits here at the Archives Bund Branch include old maps of Shanghai's round walled city, maps of the foreign concessions, the Shanghai Municipal Council Flag, the Shanghai Volunteer Corps book, a copy of the St. John's University flag, the St. John's University yearbook, and a host of excellent high quality black and white photos, including an early shot of Fudan University from 1920, and the October 2, 1949 raising of the red flag over the old Shanghai Municipal Council Headquarters.   Surprisingly, no one seems to mind if you take photos of the exhibits. The third floor is dedicated to Shanghai's revolutionary history from 1949 to the present, and used to end with exhibits dedicated to the genius of former city party secretary Chen Liangyu, who considered himself to be the mastermind of Shanghai's modernization before his sudden fall from power in 2006.

Actual archives can be accessed here in a reading room on the 5th floor (x 1515).   A Chinese language brochure describing the facility is available at the ground floor reception desk.   There is a useful book shop on the ground floor offering historical publications produced by the Archives staff, most of which are in Chinese.   One exception is the bilingual publication, "*Selected Archival Treasures of Shanghai*," Orient Publishing Center, 1996 (120 Rmb).

Open from 9:00 a.m.-5:00 p.m.
Address: #9 Zhongshan Dong Er Lu [中山东二路 9 号]
Phone: (021) 6333-6633

B

Buddhist Temples in Shanghai

According to Pan Mingquan [潘明权] (b.1947) of Shanghai Finance and Economics University in his encyclopedic work, _Shanghai Buddhist & Taoist Temples_ (_Shanghai Fosi Daoguan)_ [上海佛寺道观]," (2003), there were 64 Buddhist temples within the Shanghai municipality at that time, with the top ranked seven being in order of importance the Jade Buddha Temple (Yufo Chan Si) [玉佛禅寺], Longhua Si [龙华寺], Jingan Si [静安寺], Yuanming Buddhist Lecture Hall (Yuanming Jiangtang) [圆明讲堂], Chenxiang Ge [沉香阁], Zhenru Si [真如寺], and Fazang Jiang Si [法藏讲寺], all of which are located in the urban city center.   You can find each of these seven most important Shanghai Buddhist temples listed in my book in alphabetical order with their own separate entries.

Zhou Fuchang [周富长], ed. _Shanghai Zongjiao Zhilu_ [上海宗教之旅] (2004) agrees with Pan Mingquan on the ranking of the top five Buddhist temples, but omits Fazang Jiang Si and Zhenru Si from the top list.   It lists a total of 71 Buddhist temples in Shanghai, categorized by district.   According to this list, not counting the top 5 Buddhist temples in the city, there were then 11 in Chongming, 8 in Qingpu, 6 in Songjiang, 6 in Nanhui, 5 in Jinshan, 5 in Fengxian, 5 Buddhist temples in Pudong, 4 in Jiading, 4 in Baoshan, 3 in Minhang, 2 in Hongkou, 1 in Changning, 1 in Putuo (Zhenru Si), 1 in Zhabei, 1 in Luwan (Fazang Jiang Si), 1 in Jing An (not including Jingan Si), 1 in Yangpu, and 1 in Huangpu.   Of course this was before the district boundaries were changed later.   Since 2004 Huangpu District was expanded to included Nanshi District, Zhabei and Luwan districts were eliminated, and Pudong District was expanded to include Nanhui District.

Regardless of the discrepancy between Pan Mingquan's total of 64 Buddhist temples in 2003 and Zongjiao Zhilu's total of 71 Buddhist temples in 2004, both of these probably represent a sharp decline from the pre-1949 total, since accoding to the 1995 _Jingan District Annals_ (_Jingan Quzhi_) [静安区志], there were 34 Buddhist temples in Jingan District alone when the Communists occupied Shanghai in May 1949.

The Bund (Waitan) [外滩]

The Bund (Waitan) [外滩] is the historic waterfront area along the west side of the Huangpu River (Puxi) between Yanan Dong Lu in the south and the Suzhou River to the north.   A walking tour of the Bund should start at its south end with the **Gutzlaff Signal Tower**, which stands where the Bund intersects with Yanan Dong Lu, at a spot once occupied by the winged goddess Victory Monument, and head north to the **Garden Bridge** (Waibaidu Qiao) [外白渡桥] over the Suzhou River.   In this 1.5 km. section of the waterfront there are 26 significant pre-revolutionary colonial buildings constructed in various types of European architectural styles.   Their exteriors are still largely intact, having survived numerous wars and revolutions.   These buildings were once the headquarters of European and American banks, insurance companies and shipping lines, including Jardine Matheson and the Glen Line Steamship Co.   In many cases the biggest changes are the red flags flying from flag poles atop each and every one of these former bastions of capitalism and colonialism. Although it is usually referred to as the Bund (Waitan) [外滩], the official name of the waterfront road is Zhongshan Dong Yi Lu [中山东一路] and Zhongshan Dong Er Lu.

Previously a half dozen colonial era monuments erected by Shanghai's foreign residents lined the Bund, but these have all disappeared without a trace.   A memorial to those foreigners who died defending the city from the Taiping rebels once stood in the original Public Gardens; while a bronze statues of British Consul and Minister to China **Sir Harry Parkes** (1854-1931) stood at the foot of Nanking Road; another statue of the Imperial Customs Commissioner **Sir Robert Hart** (1835-1911) stood across the street from the Customs House; and the winged goddess **Victory Monument** dedicated to the Allied martyrs in World War I stood at the foot of Yanan East Road (Yanan Dong Lu), right at the border between the International Settlement and the French Concession.   By far the largest of these was the winged goddess statue, officially known to foreigners as the Allied War Memorial, but known to Chinese as the European War Victory Memorial (Ouzhan Shengli Jinianbei) [欧战胜利纪念碑] or more commonly called the Angel of Peace (Heping Nushen Xiang) [和平女神像].   It was erected in February 1924 to commemorate the 200 foreign residents of Shanghai who died in WWI (1914-1918), and often featured prominently in the foreground of panoramic photos taken of the Bund from its south end, including one I used to keep framed on the wall of my apartment, and which had been once been given to me by a local Chinese restaurant.   It was the scene of annual Armistice Day ceremonies held every year on November 11th.   The statue of Sir Robert Hart was erected in May 1914 and originally stood at the foot of Jiujiang Road before it was moved in 1927 to stand directly in front of the Shanghai Customs House.   For years the fate of these monuments was a mystery, but fairly recent research published in 2014 in a series of articles by **Robert Bickers** has shown that they were all removed by the Japanese in September 1943 and most likely later melted down as scrap metal.   However, the enormous pedestal upon which the winged goddess statue had stood was not removed until August 1960.

The old Public Gardens created by the British in 1866, and infamous for their 'No Dogs or Chinese Allowed' prohibition against Chinese visitors until those restrictions were lifted in 1928, were replaced with an enormous concrete breakwater and elevated promenade constructed between 1989 and 1992. This was followed in 1994 by the erection of the massive concrete tripod **People's Heroes Monument** (Shanghai Shi Renmin Yingxiong Jinian Ta) [上海市人民英雄纪念塔] inside Huangpu Park at the confluence of Suzhou Creek and the Huangpu River, directly across the street from the former British Consulate.

A subterranean **Bund Museum** is hidden deep inside the foundation of the People's Heroes Monument.   Admission is free and the exhibits are surprisingly impressive.   The collections of this northern Bund Museum include not only a wide assortment of black and white photographs, but also some rare relics not seen elsewhere.   Relics include two genuine iron boundary markers, inscribed in English and Chinese, which once marked the borders of the International Settlement.   You can also see the official coat of arms seals of the International Settlement, the Shanghai Volunteer Corps, and the French Concession. One item not seen in any other Shanghai museum is the actual flag of the International Settlement.   In addition, there is a collection of rare documents and books not even found in the Shanghai Library, including the bound annual reports of the International Settlement.

On February 14, 2008 it was announced that a 3.3 kilometer-long highway tunnel would be built under the Bund (Waitan) and beneath Suzhou Creek (Suzhou He) in order to better connect Hongkou and Huangpu districts.   As part of this project the 100-year-old **Garden Bridge** (Waibaidu Qiao) [外白渡桥] built over Suzhou Creek in 1907 was temporarily dismantled and then reassembled approximately a year later in March 2009, while the **Wusong Road Water Gate Bridge** (Wusong Lu Zha Qiao) [吴淞路闸桥] just upstream from it was completely demolished in 2009.   In addition, the eastern end of the Yanan East Road Expressway (Yanan Dong Lu Gaojia) was torn down.   The Bund (Waitan) traffic tunnel construction project was completed in 2010.

A number of the historic buildings have been occupied by new upscale tenants over the past several years.   In October 2002 the former St. Petersburg Russo-Asiatic Bank built in 1905 at No. 15 the Bund became the home of the newly established **Shanghai Gold Exchange**, the first gold trading center allowed in China since 1949.   In 2003 a **Giorgio Armani** designer clothing store moved into the former Union Insurance Building constructed in 1916. The building's original address was No. 4 the Bund, but four is considered unlucky by Chinese because it sounds the same as their word for death, so the developers renamed it **Three on the Bund**.   The famous restaurant **M on the Bund** occupies the upper floors of the former Nishin Navigation Company building erected between 1921 and 1925 at No. 5 the Bund (although the restaurant's entrance is at #20 Guangdong Lu).   The former Chartered Bank of India, Australia and China, completed in 1922, was renovated in January 2003 and turned into the upscale **Bund 18** development.   In addition, the first new building on the Bund since 1937, the **Peninsula Hotel**, was scheduled for completion in late 2009 on a spot right beside the former British Consulate at #32 Zhongshan Dong Yi Lu [中山东一路].

Since 2003 bilingual historical plaques have been placed on most of the historic buildings along the Bund providing visitors with basic information about when the structures were built and who their original occupants were.

The nine most significant historic buildings along the Bund include the following in order from south to north: the Gutzlaff Signal Tower, the Shanghai Club, the Hongkong and Shanghai Bank, the Custom House, the North China Daily News, the Palace Hotel, the Peace Hotel, the Bank of China, and the British Consulate.

Palmer & Turner Architects

By my count, 10 of the 26 historic buildings on the Bund were designed by the architectural firm of Palmer & Turner, a partnership founded in 1891 by Clement Palmer (1857-1952) and Arthur Turner (b.1858), who had met while working for the firm of British architect William Salway (1844–1902), which was founded in Hong Kong in 1868.   In 1912 Palmer & established a branch office in Shanghai that was managed by George Leopold "Tug" Wilson (1881–1967).

1. The Union Insurance Building (Youli Da Lou) [有利大楼] built in 1916, aka Three on the Bund, but actually located at No. 4 Zhongshan Dong Yi Lu.

2. The Hong Kong and Shanghai Bank (Xianggang Shanghai Huifeng Yinhang) [香港上海汇丰银行] completed in 1923.

3. The Custom House (Jiang Haiguan) [江海关] completed in 1927.

4. The Chartered Bank Building (Maijiali Yinhang Da Lou) [麦加利银行大楼] completed in 1922, renovated in January 2003 and turned into the upscale Bund 18 development.

5. The Yokohama Specie Bank (Zhengjin Yinhang Da Lou) [正金银行大楼] constructed between 1923 and 1924.

6. Peace Hotel (Heping Fandian) [和平饭店], aka Sassoon House (Shasun Dasha) [沙逊大厦] completed in 1929.

7. Bank of China Building (Zhongguo Yinhang Da Lou) [中国银行大楼] completed in 1937.

8. The Yangtsze Insurance Building (Yangzi Da Lou) [扬子大楼] completed in 1920.

9. The Glen Line Building (Gelin Youchuan Da Lou) [格林邮船大楼] completed in 1922.

10. Broadway Mansions (Bailaohui Dasha) [百老汇大厦] completed in 1934.

Nearest Metro Station: Nanjing East Road (Nanjing Dong Lu) [南京东路] Station on Line 2.

The **Gutzlaff Signal Tower** (Xinhaotai) [信号台]

A walking tour of the Bund (Waitan) [外滩] should begin at its southern end at the **Gutzlaff Signal Tower** (Xinhaotai) [信号台], built by the French in 1865 and named after Karl Friedrich August Gutzlaff (1803-1851), who was one of the earliest European visitors to Shanghai.   It was originally located at the foot of Avenue Edward VII (Yanan Dong Lu) in the part of the Huangpu River waterfront known as the **French Bund** (Falanxi Waitan) [法兰西外滩] because it belonged to the French Concession.   It was rebuilt in 1884 and 1907. The French used the Signal Tower to transmit weather reports from the Jesuit-run Zikawei Observatory at Xujiahui to ships at sea.   It continued to serve this function until 1956. The signal tower was moved 22.4 meters to its current location in 1993, and in 1999 it underwent a full restoration, after which it was reopened as a museum and café.   Although the museum is interesting, the café is astronomically expensive.   However, you can enjoy the museum's photos and ascend a circular staircase inside the tower to a birds-eye view of the present-day Bund.   English language booklets are available.

Address: 1 Zhongshan Dong Er Lu [中山东二路 1 号].

Twenty Six Historic Buildings on the Bund

1.   The Asiatic Petroleum Building (Yaxiya Da Lou) [亚细亚大楼]

This seven story building located at #1 on the Bund was constructed in 1916 by Mr. George McBain, and thus was first known as the **McBain Building**, but in 1917 it was acquired by the **Asiatic Petroleum Company**, a British-owned subsidiary of the Royal Dutch Shell oil company, which had extensive shipping and tank farm facilities over in Pudong on the east side of the Huanpgu River.   Asiatic Petroleum ran their own fleet of steamships up and down the Yangzi River.   In 1929 this fleet numbered nine vessels.

Most, if not all, the staff of Asiatic Petroleum left Shanghai after its May 1949 Liberation by the Red Army, their building on the Bund was occupied by the East China Petroleum Company in 1950, and according to a Reuters news report at the time, "China Grabs Oil Company," Asiatic Petroleum's operations in China were completely nationalized on May 1, 1951 in a decree by Prime Minister Zhou Enlai, who cited "national security" reasons. However, according to some sources, Asiatic Petroleum continued to maintain at least a residual token presence in the building until as late as 1966, when their last remaining staff were withdrawn. Since Britian did recognize the PRC in 1950 and maintained limited diplomatic relations with Beijing, including keeping a consulate open in Shanghai until 1967, this seems at least plausible.

Since 1996 the building has been home to the headquarters of the **China Pacific Insurance Co**.   In recent years it has also housed secondary offices for **AIA Insurance**, which has its headquarters at No. 17 on the Bund a few blocks further to the north, as well as a branch of the Bank of Shanghai.   Although the exterior of the building is still impressive, the entire interior has been gutted and redecorated, leaving none of the original interior.   Even the entrance doors and steel gates are new replacements of the originals.

Address: No. 1 Zhongshan Dong Yi Lu [中山东一路 1 号], intersection with Yanan Dong Lu.

2. The **Shanghai Club Building (Shanghai Zonghui)** [上海总会]

One of the most legendary buildings on the waterfront is the old Shanghai Club (Shanghai Zonghui) [上海总会] with its famous Long Bar, which at 110 feet in length was reputed to be the longest in the world.   Built in 1910 to replace an earlier club house that had stood there since 1864, this was such a bastion of upper class members only privilege that according to legen when the Japanese attacked in 1937 bar stool occupants inside supposedly let helpless victims be machine-gunned outside on the club's front steps rather than allow non-members to come inside.   Today the building is still there.   Its twin bell towers and six Greco-Roman columns make its exterior stand out, even amongst its equally impressive neighbors.   However, after completing its role as the decidedly down market **East Wind Hotel** (Dongfeng Fandian) [东风饭店], and the location of the very first Kentucky Fried Chicken restaurant in Shanghai, its interior was closed to the for 12 years from 1998 to 2010. During its days as the East Wind Hotel (Dongfeng Fandian) [东风饭店], the legendary Long Bar was inexplicably sawn up into three separate pieces.

In its heyday before 1949, the Shanghai Club (Shanghai Zonghui) [上海总会] offered many forms of recreation and entertainment to its members, including a bowling alley in the basement, a library, book store, reading rooms, card rooms, billiard rooms, a dining room, and the famous long bar.   Seats at the bar were designated according to one's social position, with those holding the highest positions getting the seats closest to the window facing the Bund, and junior members getting the seats furthest away at the opposite end. Passing through the iron gates at the entrance and ascending a flight of steps, one entered the Grand Hall, an open atrium rising up to the second floor mezzanine.   The upper floors held bedrooms where guests could spend the night, with the servants' quarters and kitchen being on the top floor.

Looking up at the facade of the building, one last trace of its former role is the initials "S.C.," standing for Shanghai Club, which could still be seen on the iron drain spouts.   Right above the canopy over the front entrance were the original inscribed dates, 1864 on the left side, and 1910 on the right side, commemmorating the completion of the first and second buildings.   The view of these dates from the sidewalk below is unfortunately obscured by the canopy.

The original iron gates decorated with their decorative boughs of leaves have for years stood guard over the entrance with its original wooden doors, but they were padlocked shut for 12 years.   In mid-May 2001 the old Shanghai Club was suddenly given a new coat of bright white paint, and later an English language sign over the front door reading "Shanghai Club" was added, but this was apparently only for the filming of a movie, and it continued to remain closed to the public.   Oddly, this was also the only building on the Bund that had not yet been given a bilingual historical plaque by the city government.

As of May 2009 the building's exterior had been painted white yet again, its top floor was covered in scaffolding, and workers seemed to be redecorating the interior, but I was still not allowed to go inside.   Not until September 15, 2010 did it finally reopen to the public as the new Waldorf-Astoria Hotel, after having been closed for 12 years since 1998.

Address: No. 2 Zhongshan Dong Yi Lu [中山东一路 2 号]

3. The Union Insurance Building (Youli Da Lou) [有利大楼]

Designed by Palmer & Turner architects and completed in 1916, this six-story building with a bell tower balanced on top of its northeast corner was the Shanghai offices of the **Union Insurance Society of Canton**, Ltd., a British company that had its headquarters in Hong Kong, where it was established in 1835.   Like the other Western insurance companies with offices along the Bund, they specialized in providing marine insurance to the ships that sailed the Yangzi River, as well as those engaged in the transpacific trade.   Starting in 1918 the Union Insurance Building also held the Shanghai offices of the American architect **Henry K. Murphy** and his partner Richard Henry Dana.   In January 2003 this building was vacant and closed, but showed signs of interior and exterior renovation in progress, with a wall of scaffolding erected on the building's South side.   It reopened in December 2003 as a combination of insanely expensive foreign managed restaurants, bars & clothing shops, including a Georgio Armani designer clothing store.   Because the building's true address is considered unlucky by Chinese because it sounds the same as the word for death, the developers have insisted on naming it "Three on the Bund," although actually it is No. 4.   Also, although the bulding faces the Bund and the Huangpu River, its main etrance has always been on the side street of Guangdong Lu.

Address: No. 4 Zhongshan Dong Yi Lu [中山东一路 4 号]

4. Nisshin Navigation Company (Riqing Da Lou) [日清大楼]

Construction on this building started in 1921 and was completed in 1925.   It originally housed the offices of the Japanese steamship line Nisshin Kisen Kabushiki Kaisha (Riqing Qichuan Zhushi Huishi) [日清汽船株式会社].   NKKK had been formed in 1907 from the merger of four previously independent Japanese shipping lines. In 1929 they had a fleet of 26 steamships sailing between China's coastal cities and Yangzi River ports.   Many of the company's ships were named after Yangzi River ports, including the Fuling Maru, the Yunyang Maru, and the Lushan Maru.

After the Japanese surrender of August 1945, NKKK vacated the building and the China Merchants Steam Navigation Co. moved in.   After the Liberation of Shanghai by the Red Army in May 1949, the building was taken over by the Shanghai Maritime Bureau, which occupied it into the 1990s.

By January 2003 this building had become a branch of the Huaxia Bank.   Although it is open to the public, the entire inside has been gutted and redecorated, leaving none of the original interior.   Even the entrance doors and steel gates are new replacements.

However, within the same building is the now famous roof top restaurant, **"M on the Bund,"** host to an annual literary festival, which is actually entered from a side door at #20 Guangdong Lu.   This side entrance does have an impressive pair of original iron gates decorated with the golden numbers, "1921," the year construction of the building began.

Address: No. 5 Zhongshan Dong Yi Lu [中山东一路 5 号]

5. The China Merchants Bank (Zhongguo Tongshang Yinhang Da Lou) [中国通商银行大楼]

China Merchants Bank (Zhongguo Tongshang Yinhang) [中国通商银行] was founded in 1897 as the first Chinese-owned commercial bank. In 1906 they constructed this four-story Gothic style building.

This building is sometimes incorrectly attributed to Russell & Company (Qíchang Yanghang) [旗昌洋行], which went bankrupt in 1891, fifteen years before the building was constructed.

Later, after the 1911 Revolution overthrowing the Qing Dynasty, it served for a time as the **Shanghai Municipal Council** offices, until the new SMC headquarters on Jiangxi Lu was completed in November 1922. The architecture of the building is English Gothic style.

In the 1980s it served as the offices of the Changjiang Shipping Co., which decorated the outer fence with images of ships' anchors, and replaced the original revolving doors with new metal ones. However, as of January 2003 the building was completely empty and boarded up, the metal gates covering the front entrance locked, and no signs of life inside except for a watchman sitting in the dark. In 2009 it was turned into a Dolce & Gabbana high end fashion retail store and martini bar.

Address: No. 6 Zhongshan Dong Yi Lu [中山东一路 6 号]

6. Great Northern Telegraph Company (Dabei Dianbao Gongsi Da Lou) [大北电报公司大楼]

The **Great Northern Telegraph Co.** had occupied this site on the Bund since 1881. In 1908 they completed construction on the building that currently stands there now. In 1921 the Great Northern Telegraph Co. moved out of this building.

In 1945, the **China Merchants Bank** (Zhongguo Tongshang Yinhang) [中国通商银行] moved from next door at #6 to here at #7. Later the Changjiang Shipping Co. also moved in.

Since 1995 it has been serving the Thai-owned **Bangkok Bank** (Pangu Yinhang) [盤谷銀行]. Other Thai institutions were also located here until 2008, including the Royal Thai Consulate General on the third floor, and the Thai Trade Center on the second floor. The entire inside has been redecorated, leaving none of the original interior.

Address: No. 7 Zhongshan Dong Yi Lu [中山东一路 7 号]

7. Russell & Company Building (Qíchang Yanghang Da Lou) [旗昌洋行大楼]

The American-owned Russell and Co. (Qíchang Yanghang) [旗昌洋行] moved their headquarters to this location in 1846.

Although previously they had focused on the opium and tea trade, on March 27, 1862 Russell & Co. formed the **Shanghai Steam Navigation Company** (Qichang Lunchuan Gongsi) [旗昌轮船公司].   By 1864 Russell & Co. had a fleet of five Yangzi River steamships, by far the largest.   By June 1866 Russell had increased the size of their fleet to six steamers.   Between 1867 and 1872 Russell's increased their fleet of China coast and Yangzi River steamers from 12 ships to 19 ships, with seven of these sailing the Yangzi River route in 1867 and nine by 1872.

Nonetheless, starting in 1873 Russell & Co. started to face increased competition from Butterfield & Swire (Taigu Yanghang) [太古洋行] as well as the new **China Merchants Steamship Company** (Lunchuan Zhaoshang Ju) [轮船招商局] founded that year in Shanghai by Chinese government official Li Hongzhang. In 1877 the China Merchants Steamship Company purchased all the ships of the Shanghai Steam Navigation Company from Russell & Co.   Finally, in 1891 Russell & Company went bankrupt.

In 1901 the previous Russell & Co. building was torn down (chaichu) [拆除] by its new owners, the **China Merchants Steamship Company** (Lunchuan Zhaoshang Ju) [轮船招商局], and the currently existing structure was built as a brand new three-story building in the same location.   In 1930 the **China Merchants Steamship Company** (Lunchuan Zhaoshang Ju) [轮船招商局] was taken over by the Guomindang national government. After the Liberation of Shanghai in May 1949, this building was occupied by the Shanghai Harbor Affairs Inspection Bureau (Shanghai Gangwu Jiandu Ju) [上海港务监督局].   As a result it is sometimes also known as the Harbor Supervision Building (Gang Jian Da Lou) [港监大楼].   It was also occupied by the Ministry of Transportation Shanghai Maritime Search & Rescue Center (Jiaotong Bu Haishang Soujiu Zhongxin) [交通部上海海上搜救中心], as well as the People's Steamship Company (Renmin Lunchuan Gongsi) [人民轮船公司].

When I first came to Shanghai in 1999, the building was in such a shabby condition that I neglected to even include it in my previous lists of buildings on the Bund published in my prior books on Shanghai in 2003 and 2010.   Somehow it looked as if it didn't even belong there.   However, it has now been renovated to give it a much more attractive image, making it harder to miss.   A Chinese inscription now clearly visible over the front entrance reads "**China Merchants Steamship Company Headquarters** (Lunchuan Zhaoshang Zongu) [轮船招商总局] 1901."   The ground floor is now occupied by a high end retail store selling fashionable designer clothes.

Address: No. 9 Zhongshan Dong Yi Lu [中山东一路的 9 号]

8. The **Hong Kong and Shanghai Bank**
(Xianggang Shanghai Huifeng Yinhang) [香港上海汇丰银行]

The first Shanghai branch of the Hong Kong and Shanghai Bank (HSBC), known in Chinese simply as "Wayfoong" or "Huifeng" [汇丰], was opened in 1865, the same year that the bank was established in Hong Kong. They acquired a piece of property on the Bund in 1873, but it was not until October 1919 that the architectural firm of Palmer & Turner was selected to design the existing building. Construction started in 1920 and was completed in time for a grand opening ceremony on June 23, 1923. The gala event was attended by a host of diplomatic and military celebrities. The plaque recording the event is still embedded in the North wall of the building's portico.

The whole structure was balanced on what was called a "floating foundation" or "concrete raft," a new innovation made necessary by the unstable soil of silt and mud found all along the Bund. Even so, the ground floor started out six feet up in the air and later settled down to sidewalk level once the whole building was completed. Another innovation was a complicated central heating and air-conditioning system composed of air ducts, streams of cool and hot water, fans, and pumps installed beneath the floors and roof. The whole system required a team of engineers to operate. Other relatively new modern conveniences included a fleet of six electric elevators.

The front of the Greco-Roman style building facing the Bund had a granite facade, penetrated at the ground floor level by a three-arched entrance into the Banking Hall. On either side of this entrance were a pair of bronze lions, one depicted as roaring, the other at rest. Before reaching the Banking Hall, visitors passed through an octagonal Entrance Hall covered with its own small dome, the inside of which was decorated with a colorful mosaic depicting what were then the eight banking centers of the world. This included not only Paris, London, and New York, but also Shanghai. Each city depicted in the mosaic was represented by a symbolic image, and in Shanghai's case it was none other the HSBC's building on the Bund, joined by the old Customs House next door. The 150 foot high dome over the Entrance Hall was supported by eight marble columns imported from Italy. The Banking Hall itself was illuminated by natural sunlight pouring through a long glass skylight in the ceiling. At either end of the hall were four massive columns of Italian marble, and the floor itself was also marble.

After the Liberation of Shanghai in May 1949, the HSBC Shanghai branch remained open until April 1955 when HSBC was forced to sign a settlement with the Chinese government that forced it to move out of its beautiful 1923 building on the Bund (Waitan).

After HSBC's April 1955 eviction, their former Bund headquarters building became the offices of the Shanghai Municipal People's Government and remained so into the early 1990s. It was here that Zhu Rongji [朱镕基] (1928-present) had his office when he served as Mayor of Shanghai from 1988 to 1991, before being promoted to Vice Premier in Beijing. Finally, in 1994 the Municipal Government moved out of the old HSBC building and into their present building across the street from Peoples Square. Then the building was taken over by a branch of the Pudong Development Bank (Shanghai Pudong Fazhan Yinhang) [上海浦东发展银行], which continues to occupy it today.

Address: No. 12 Zhongshan Dong Yi Lu [中山东一路 12 号]

9. The Custom House (Jiang Haiguan) [江海关]

From 1927 to 1949 this was the national headquarters for the **China Maritime Customs Service**, which was responsible for collecting import and export duties on all external and internal shipping, including that along the Yangzi River, and which was largely staffed by foreigners. When the original Chinese-run customs house was burned down during the **Small Sword Society** (Xiaodao Hui) [小刀会] rebellion in September 1853, customs collection stopped until a new foreign-run customs house was opened on the Bund of the International Settlement in February 1854. This initiated foreign control of China's customs collection, which was at first limited to Shanghai but was expanded to all of China in 1861 in the form of the newly established Imperial Maritime Customs Service. This foreign-run service continued even after the 1911 Revolution and lasted until the 1949 Revolution. Although in later years its staff included increasing numbers of Chinese, the top post of Inspector General of Customs was always held by a British citizen, as were most of the Customs Commissioner posts in the various coastal and Yangzi River ports.

The present day Custom House had two predecessors that stood on the same spot. The first was a small three-story wooden structure built in the style of a Chinese temple in 1857. The second was a more modern three-story Western style building erected in 1893. It had a tall clock tower that stood in between the building's North and South wings, and in some ways resembled an Oxford University campus building. In 1925 this building was torn down and construction started on the present day Custom House, designed by Palmer & Turner architects, which was finally completed in December 1927.

Its architecture still makes it stand out as one of the three most noticeable structures on the Bund, along with the near by Hong Kong and Shanghai Bank and Peace Hotel. Four huge granite Roman columns mark the front entrance. After having been reset to play the song, "The East is Red," during the Cultural Revolution, the clock tower with its four faces now once again chimes its bells loudly precisely on the hour, so accurately that you can set your watch to it. Iron gates at front entrance still bear the inscription, "Custom House." Inside the first floor lobby you can still see the original octagonal blue, green, and gold mosaic mural painted on the lobby's ceiling, with eight panels depicting traditional Chinese sailing ships.

The interior of the building had not yet been renovated, which still gave it some of the musty air of days gone by, but uniformed guards would stop you from proceeding further inside than the lobby.

Address: No. 13 Zhongshan Dong Yi Lu [中山东一路 13 号]

10. The Bank of Communications Building (Jiaotong Yinhang Da Lou) [交通银行大楼].

This had originally been the site of the German-owned **Deutsche-Asiatic Bank** since the 1880s, but after World War I the Germans lost all of their assets in China, and this property was then taken over by the Chinese-owned Bank of Communications (Jiaotong Yinhang) [交通银行].

The original **Bank of Communications** (Jiaotong Yinhang) [交通银行] was a Chinese-owned institution established in December 1907 under a charter from the Qing government with the goal of financing steamship lines, railways, telegraphs, and postal services. It administered the funds of the Board of Posts and Communications. It received a new charter from the Republican government in 1914, but after being plundered as his personal piggy bank by President **Yuan Shikai** [袁世凯] (1859-1916) it was almost driven into bankruptcy. Later it was reorganized by the new Guomindang regime in Nanjing as a national bank in November 1928.

The bank's Shanghai headquarters building was designed in Art-Deco style and constructed between 1947 and 1948, during the short interregnum of Guomindang post-war administration of the city. This was the last building constructed on the Bund before the May 1949 Liberation of Shanghai by the Red Army. After Liberation it was occupied by the **Shanghai Municipal General Trade Union** (Shanghai Shi Zong Gong Hui) [上海市总工会].

In December 2002 the upper floors of the building were undergoing a complete interior restoration, while the ground floor had been occupied by a branch of the **Bank of Shanghai**. The original revolving door has been removed, but the exterior has been given a fresh coat of paint.

Address: No. 14 Zhongshan Dong Yi Lu [中山东一路 14 号]

11. The St. Petersburg Russo-Asiatic Bank (Hua E Daosheng Yinhang Da Lou) [华俄道胜银行大楼]

The original **Russo-Chinese Bank** was formed in 1892 to finance construction of the Russian-owned Chinese Eastern Railway in Manchuria.   In 1899 it acquired this plot of land on the Bund that had previously been owned by Dent & Co., which had gone bankrupt.   The bank's new building on the Bund was completed in 1903.   In 1905 the bank was renamed the St. Petersburg **Russo-Asiatic Bank** (Hua E Daosheng Yinhang) [华俄道胜银行]. After the 1917 Russian Revolution, the Russo-Asiatic Bank was reorganized in Paris under French law.   The Russian bank somehow managed to continue operating in Shanghai for another nine years, thanks partly to the funds of the formerly Russian-owned Chinese Eastern Railway which were deposited with it, as well as its share of the Chinese Customs revenue deposited as payment towards loans previously made to the Chinese imperial government.   However, the Russo-Asiatic Bank was finally liquidated once and for all in January 1926.

After this the bank's former headquarters was used as office space by a variety of foreign companies for several years.   **Thomas Cook & Son** Ltd. had its Shanghai office located here, specializing in providing railway and steamship tickets for passage into the interior of China.

In 1928 it became the headquarters of the Guomindang's new **Central Bank of China** (Zhongyang Yinhang) [中央銀行] and as such the building started to become known as the Central Bank Building [中央银行大楼].   Later, from 1945 to 1949 this role was replaced by the former Yokohoma Specie Bank, Ltd. (Zhengjin Yinhang) [正金银行] up the Bund further to the north.

Since 1994 the building has been known as the **Foreign Exchange Trade System Center** (Zhongguo Waihui Jiaoyi Zhongxin) [中国外汇交易中心].   In October 2002 it became the home of the newly established **Shanghai Gold Exchange**, the first gold trading center allowed in China since 1949, and still the only one in the country.   Although the August 1948 Gold Yuan fiasco had resulted in the Guomindang regime absorbing most privately owned gold, the Shanghai Gold Exchange was still functioning when the Communists occupied the city in May 1949.   However, one month later the exchange was suddenly closed down in June 1949.   All remaining privately owed gold and foreign currency were confiscated and those individuals involved in the operation of the gold exchange were imprisoned.   Fifty-two years later, in 2001 Chinese citizens were once again permitted to buy gold in the form of the newly minted one-ounce Panda gold coin series, and in December 2002 citizens were finally allowed to buy gold bullion as well.   However, restrictions still prevent individuals from selling gold, even though they can buy it and own it. Therefore, trading on the Gold Exchange is currently limited to banks and companies. However, this restriction is expected to be lifted in 2003.   Nonetheless, as of January 2003 uniformed guards were still preventing private individuals from entering the building.

Address: No. 15 Zhongshan Dong Yi Lu [中山东一路 15 号]

12. The Bank of Taiwan Building (Taiwan Yinhang Da Lou) [台湾银行大楼]

The Japanese-owned Bank of Taiwan (Taiwan Yinhang) [台湾银行] was established in Taipei in 1899 at a time when Taiwan was a Japanese colony following the terms of the 1895 Treaty of Shimonoseki which ended the First Sino-Japanese war. In 1914 the **Bank of Taiwan** entered the Shanghai market, and in 1915 it led a consortium of Japanese banks in loaning the Beijing regime of Yuan Shi Kai approximately 120 million Yen in unsecured loans, which were apparently intended to further the Japanese government's political aims in China.

Construction started on the bank's new Shanghai branch on the Bund in 1924 and was completed in 1926.   This is a quite narrow building, with four massive granite columns out front, and only four stories in height, designed in Greek temple style.   As of January 2003, the building had become a branch of the China Merchants Bank (Zhaoshang Yinhang) [招商银行].   At one time this was one of the few Chinese banks besides the Bank of China that could exchange foreign currency into Renminbi.   As a result, this attracted swarms of black market money changers who publicly camped out on the sidewalk outside shouting, "Change money, change money!"   Foreign pedestrians were particularly targeted, so it paid to be careful when walking this stretch of the waterfront.   However, those more colorful days are now long gone under the new law and order regime.

Address: No. 16 Zhongshan Dong Yi Lu [中山东一路 16 号]

13. The North China Daily News Building (Zilin Da Lou) [字林大楼]

Construction of this building began in 1921 and was completed in 1924.   It was designed by Henry E. Morris Jr. to be the headquarters of Shanghai's leading English language newspaper, the **North China Daily News**, but it also served as the offices of the predecessor to the American insurance company **AIA**.   During the Cultural Revolution statues of naked Herculean gods holding up the top floors were covered up, and remained hidden until as late as 1996.   However, they have recently been uncovered once again to reveal their rippling muscles.   An English inscription on a frieze in the front facade still says, "Journalism, Art, Science, Literature, Commerce, Truth, Printing."   The arched entrance portals on the ground floor are in remarkably good shape, and still bear their original gold leaf black and gold mosaic decorations.   However, two statues of naked goddesses that once guarded both sides of the main entrance were removed during the Cultural Revolution (Wenhua Da Geming) [文化大革命] (1966-1976).   Although modern offices now occupy the main rooms, the hallways have been kept in their authentic condition, including the tile floors and decorative motifs along the walls.   Incredible views of the Bund can be had from the building's roof garden and its windows facing south.   I was fortunate enough to work in the building as a consultant for six months during the first half of 2004, and often enjoyed the view from the roof, from where I took many photographs of the Bund.

The **North China Herald** was the first English language newspaper in Shanghai, and published its first issue on August 3, 1850.   For the first 14 years it was issued as a weekly periodical, but in June 1864 it switched to daily publication and the name was accordingly changed to the **North China Daily News** (Zilin Xibao) [字林西报].

Henry E. Morris Sr. purchased the newspaper in 1901.   In 1920 ownership of the newspaper was inherited by his son, **Henry E. Morris Jr.**, who in addition to constructing the newspaper's new building on the Bund also built a compound of villas now known as the Shanghai Intercontinental **Ruijin Hotel** (Shanghai Rujin Zhouji Jiudian) [上海瑞金洲际酒店]. He was also owner of the **Canidrome** dog racing stadium (Yiyuan Paogouchang) [逸园跑狗场], which later after 1949 became known as Shanghai Culture Square (Shanghai Wenhua Guangchang) [上海文化广场].

China Daily News continued publishing until March 31, 1951, over 100 years since its founding.   Somehow it had managed to survive for almost two years after the May 1949 Liberation of Shanghai by the Red Army.   Nonetheless there has been no talk of reviving the newspaper nor of returning part of its original building to the descendants of the paper's former owners, unlike the case of the building's other former occupant, AIA.   The **Shanghai Library** (Shanghai Tushuguan) [上海图书馆] possesses the only complete set of original copies of the North China Herald and Daily News in China.

The **American International Assurance Co**. (AIA) (Meiguo Youbang Baoxian Youxian Gongsi) [美国友邦保险有限公司] was founded in Shanghai in 1931, with the merger of American Asiatic Underwriters and the Asia Life Insurance Co., founded in 1919 and 1921 respectively.   After 1949 AIA moved its headquarters to New York City, in the U.S., and changed its name to AIG, but the company never forgot its Shanghai roots.   AIA returned to China in September 1992 when it became the first foreign insurance company approved to operate in the PRC since 1949.   Finally, in May 1998 AIA became the first foreign company to have its original building on the Bund returned to it, when the company's Shanghai branch resumed occupancy of No. 17.   As of May 2009 AIA was still the only foreign company to have returned to its original quarters.   As a result, nowadays it is more commonly known as the AIA Building (Youbang Dasha) [友邦大厦].

Address: No. 17 Zhongshan Dong Yi Lu [中山东一路 17 号]

14. The Chartered Bank Building (Maijiali Yinhang Da Lou) [麦加利银行大楼]

Before 1949 this was the Shanghai branch of the **Chartered Bank of India, Australia and China**, a British bank with headquarters in London, which was first, established in England in 1853.   The **Chartered Bank** of India, Australia and China established its first Shanghai branch in 1857, and also had an office in the Hankou British Concession in Wuhan.

The Chartered Bank's new branch on the Bund was designed by the Shanghai architectural firm of Palmer & Turner and completed in 1922.   The facade of this building is dominated by two enormous stone Greco-Roman columns.   In January 2003 this building became vacant and its entrance was sealed off, apparently in preparation for restoration of the interior. Gazing through the street level windows one could see that the original interior was still intact at that time.   After its 2003 restoration it turned into the upscale **Bund 18** (Waitan Shiba Hao) [外滩十八号] development.

Address: No. 18 Zhongshan Dong Yi Lu [中山东一路 18 号]
Web Site: http://www.bund18.com

15. The Palace Hotel (Huizhong Fandian Da Lou) [汇中饭店大楼]

This six-story Victorian structure once known as the Palace Hotel (Huizhong Fandian) [汇中饭店] was completed in 1906 but did not officially open for business until 1908. It was constructed on the site of the previous Central Hotel (Zhongyang Fandian) [中央飯店] built here in 1850. **Sun Yat-sen** (Sun Zhongshan) [孙中山] (1866-1925) stayed here in December 1911 after he returned to China from America and was on his way to Nanjing to take up his new post as the first President of the Republic of China. The Shanghai **American Chamber of Commerce** (Zhong Mei Shang Hui) [中美商会] was founded here at a meeting of 45 American businessmen held on June 9, 1915. In 1927 **Chiang Kai-shek** (Jiang Jieshi) [蒋介石] (1887-1975) and **Song Meiling** [宋美龄] (1898-2003) held their engagement ceremony in the hotel lobby here. From 1956 to 2007 it was known as the **South Building of the Peace Hotel** (Heping Fandian Nan Lou) [和平饭店南楼].

Until 2007, the Palace Hotel had somehow maintained its original gorgeous interior decorations without succumbing to either the fates of destructive Chinese-style "restoration" or rotting decay. Its first floor lobby and dining room were particularly impressive. Passing through the original single wood and glass revolving door, visitors were greeted by a lobby with crystal chandeliers hanging from a gilded plaster ceiling supported by white marble columns, with dark wood paneling on the walls. To your left was the entrance to the **Palace Hall** restaurant, which also featured an impressively authentic Victorian interior with windows providing a view of the street life out on Nanjing East Road (Nanjing Dong Lu) [南京东路]. Because customers eating here could be seen by passers by on the street outside, this was once the most impressive place to show off your wealth. Taking the flight of wooden steps up from the ground floor to the first floor, one reached the Shanghai Bund Restaurant. On its sixth floor the Palace Hotel featured the Harbor Roof Garden, including private tea rooms inside both of its cupolas facing the Huangpu River.

On April 17, 2007 the Palace Hotel's owner, the Jinjiang International Hotel Management Co., announced the South Wing of the Peace Hotel (Heping Fandian Nan Lou) [和平饭店南楼] would shut down for a two year restoration project. It was expected to reopen in spring 2010 as the Shanghai Swatch Art Hotel, managed by a joint venture between Jinjiang and the Swatch Group AG of Switzerland. It's now officially known as the Swatch Peace Hotel (Siwoqi Heping Fandian) [斯沃琪和平飯店]. Although the official address is on the Bund, the actual entrance is at 23 Nanjing East Road (Nanjing Dong Lu) [南京东路].

Address: No. 19 Zhongshan Dong Yi Lu [中山东一路 19 号]

16. The Peace Hotel (Heping Fandian) [和平饭店]

This historic hotel was designed by Palmer & Turner architects and constructed by **Sir Victor Sassoon** (1881-1961) between 1926 and 1929 and was originally named the **Cathay Hotel**, or sometimes known as the **Sassoon House** (Shasun Dasha) [沙逊大厦].   The building held its grand opening in March 1930.

This 12 story building was designed by the American architecture firm of Palmer and Turner, and features a triangular base with a tower at the end facing the river, which rises to an enormous pyramid on top.   When the **Bank of China** (Zhongguo Yinhang) [中国银行] building was completed next door in 1937 the two became rivals for the claim to being the tallest building on the Bund.

When the Chinese government seized control of the hotel from Victor Sassoon in 1954 the Cathay's name was changed to today's Peace Hotel.   Since 1956 the Cathay Hotel has been known as the **North Building of the Peace Hotel** (Heping Fandian Bei Lou) [和平饭店北楼].   The Peace Hotel was purchased by the **Jinjiang Group** in 2001.

In April 2007 the Peace Hotel closed for a three-year restoration project under the direction of design consultants HBA/Hirsch Bedner Associates.   Its grand reopening was scheduled for March 2010, just in time for the World Expo.   Although it would continue to be owned by Jinjiang International Hotels Group, it would be managed by Fairmont Hotels & Resorts, so plans called for it to be renamed as the Fairmont Peace Hotel.

The building's many fascinating features included its stone walls, its cast iron ornaments, and its original wooden revolving doors.   Also notable were the **Nine Nations Suites** designed to conform to the style of different nationalities, including Chinese, British, Indian, American, French, Japanese, Italian, German and Spanish.   These were to be preserved in their original designs and be available for rent.

You could still catch a glimpse of the famous octogenarian **Jazz Band** playing the hits from the 1920s in the ground floor Jazz Bar.   Since the current version of the band was formed in 1980, six quite elderly gentlemen have continued to play a rousing rendition of "When the Saints go Marching In" to full houses of applauding foreigners.

Most of the restaurants were previously on the 8th floor, including the Dragon-Phoenix Room, the Peace Grill, and the Peace Hall, although the Nine Heaven Hall was on the 9th floor.

On the 10th floor is the famous **Sassoon Room** where Victor Sassoon once lived.   This was also where **U.S. General Albert C. Wedemeyer** stayed during the 1945-1946 period when the U.S. military occupied the hotel.   This room had been turned into a banquet hall, but plans called for it to be the new **Presidential Suite**.   It faces the Huangpu River, and from the outside you can see it is the only room with a stone balcony.   Just above the stone balcony is the trademark Sassoon symbol of two dogs with their heads turned to face each other.

From the 11th floor you could access the rooftop garden bar.   On the same floor was the **Bankers' Hall**, with a bird's eye view of the Huangpu River.

In previous years the main entrance to the hotel had faced Nanjing East Road (Nanjing Dong Lu) [南京东路], the two massive iron gates protecting the entrance facing the Bund being kept locked.   However, plans called for four revolving door entrances to be opened, one in each direction.   Other changes to the ground floor have included a restored octagonal stained glass rotunda over the atrium and a reopened mezzanine that had been covered up.

Restoration plans called for 270 guestrooms, 39 suites, eight restaurants, the famous Jazz Bar, and a restored Peace Hall with a sprung wooden dance floor.

Address: No. 20 Zhongshan Dong Yi Lu) [中山东一路 20 号]
Phone: (021) 6321-6888 Fax: (021) 6329-0300
Website: http://www.fairmont.com/peace-hotel-shanghai/

17. The Bank of China Building (Zhongguo Yinhang Da Lou) [中国银行大楼]

This building designed by Palmer & Turner architects replaced the earlier German Club structure that had previously been built on the same site back in 1907.   After the First World War, when the Germans lost all their treaty privileges in China, the German Club had become the Bank of China's headquarters.   When the new Bank of China headquarters was completed in 1937 it became the tallest building on the Bund, towering above the Cathay Hotel, its next door rival for the title.   Unlike the present-day Bank of China, which is a purely commercial bank, the Bank of China established in 1912 served many functions of the government's central bank until the 1949 revolution, although officially there was a separate Central Bank located next door in the former Yokohoma Specie Bank, Ltd. (Zhengjin Yinhang) [正金银行] building from 1945 to 1949.   **T.V. Song** (Song Ziwen) had an office here when he was Governor of the Bank of China.   Its architectural style is noteworthy for the traditional blue tiled Chinese roof with upturned eaves, which tops the modern granite structure below.   This is one of the few buildings on the Bund still serving its original purpose and occupied by the original tenants.   In 2009 the building still had its original single brass and glass revolving door leading into a marble lined lobby.   A flight of steps lead up from the ground floor lobby to the vaulted banking hall, the roof of which was supported by eight black marble columns on either side, for a total of 16.   The interior seemed little changed, the lobby area itself still showing the authentic signs of decades of wear and tear.

Address: No. 23 Zhongshan Dong Yi Lu [中山东一路 23 号]

18. The Yokohama Specie Bank (Zhengjin Yinhang Da Lou) [正金银行大楼]

Designed by Palmer & Turner architects, and constructed between 1923 and 1924. This was the Shanghai branch of the Japanese-owned Yokohoma Specie Bank, Ltd. (Zhengjin Yinhang) [正金银行]. The bank had been established in Yokohoma, Japan in 1880, and opened its first Shanghai branch in 1892. They also had a branch in the Hankou foreign concessions district in Wuhan.

After the end of the Sino-Japanese War in 1945, the Shanghai branch of the Yokohama Specie Bank was closed and all their assets liquidated, as were all Japanese businesses in China, immediately. The building was then taken over by the Chinese government and used as the headquarters of the Central Bank of China (Zhongyang Yinhang) [中央银行] from 1945 to 1949. During that time the building was known as the Central Bank Building (Zhongyang Da Lou) [中央大楼]. Oddly enough, during the Republic of China period (1911-1949) this central bank was never located in the national capitals of Beijing and Nanjing, but rather here in the financial center of Shanghai. The most famous story about this building are the accounts by observers who on January 10, 1949 saw Chiang Kai-shek and his son Chiang Ching-kuo looting China's entire gold and silver reserves and loading them onto ships bound for Taiwan, four months before the Red Army occupied the city in May 1949. After the Liberation of Shanghai by the Red Army in May 1949 it became the Peoples Bank of China East China District Office Building (Zhongguo Renmin Yinhang Huadong Qu Hang Banggong Lou) [中国人民银行华东区行办公楼]. From 1956 until the 1990s, the building was occupied by the Shanghai Municipal Spinning & Weaving Management Office (Shanghai Shi Fangzhi Guanli Ju Da Lou) [上海市纺织管理局大楼]. Since 2003 it has returned to its original function as a bank, as a branch of the Industrial and Commercial Bank of China (ICBC) (Zhongguo Gongshang Yinhang) [中国工商银行].

The building has two massive granite columns, which seem to once have had stone sculptures at the top that have since been broken off. The second floor stone balconies are supported by stone sculptures which look like American Indian heads, which have had their noses broken off. A pair of iron gates and a single new revolving door lead inside. The interior seems almost entirely new, having been gutted and then redecorated, but has been redone in semi-authentic reproduction of its original. A long rectangular central skylight hangs over the main banking hall. Inside the lobby area there are several modern reproductions of the original Indian head sculptures on the outside of the building. It's not clear why the Yokohoma bank would have used this symbol. Unfortunately there is no foundation stone, nor any original inscriptions visible.

Address: No. 24 Zhongshan Dong Yi Lu [中山东一路 24 号]

19. The Yangtsze Insurance Building (Yangzi Da Lou) [扬子大楼]

Construction of this seven-story building designed by Palmer & Turner architects started in 1917 and was completed in 1920.　It was originally the headquarters of the **Yangtsze Insurance Association**, Ltd., a British company first established in 1862.　As such it was known as the Yangtsze Insurance Building (Yangzi Boaxian Da Lou) [扬子保险大楼].　At that time the Pinyin phonetic system did not yet exist and the phonetic spelling of Yangzi River had not yet been standardized, hence the company's spelling of Yangzi as Yangtsze, which seems odd to us today.　According to their own advertisements, they specialized in offering marine insurance and protection against floods, typhoons, and riots, all of which were in plentiful supply up and down the Yangzi River in those days.

The original stone coat of arms has obviously been removed from over the 2nd floor center window.　The two entrance doors are new reproductions replacing the original ones.　No foundation stone is visible, and the interior of the bank itself seems to have been entirely gutted and redecorated.

However, if you look inside the southern of the two front entrances, you discover the former main lobby with its original interior still largely intact.　The white marble walls are accented by stained glass windows.　The marble coat of arms over the lobby elevator has had its letters removed, but the shadows are still legible, revealing the building's former name, "Yangtsze Insurance Building."

In the 1990s this was known as the Municipal Provisions Import & Export Company Building (Shi Shipin Jinchukou Gongsi Da Lou) [市食品进出口公司大楼], but since 2003 the building has served as branch of the Agricultural Bank of China (Zhongguo Nongye Yinhang) [中国农业银行].

Address:　No. 26 Zhongshan Dong Yi Lu [中山东一路 26 号]

20. The Jardine Matheson Building (Yihe Yanghang Da Lou) [怡和洋行大楼]

Construction of this building started in 1920 and was completed in November 1922 as the new Shanghai headquarters for the British trading and shipping company Jardine Matheson, sometimes known by its Chinese name "Ewo Hong" (Yihe Yanghang) [怡和洋行].　It was originally only a six-story building, but in 1983 two extra floors were added on top to make it an eight-story building.

Jardine Matheson was one of the earliest and largest British firms involved in the China trade back when it was restricted to Canton (Guangzhou).　In fact, the company played a leading role in starting the First Opium War in 1839.　After the war was ended by the 1842 Treaty of Nanking, Jardine Matheson was also the first British company to acquire land and build a permanent facility in Hong Kong.　They first acquired this plot of land on the Shanghai Bund in 1843, and constructed an earlier building on this site in 1851.

Jardine Matheson became heavily involved in the Yangzi River trade, and operated their own fleet of ships, which sailed regularly between Shanghai and the Hankou foreign concessions upriver in Wuhan.　Jardine Matheson purchased the **China Coast Steam Navigation Co**. in 1872 and established the **Yangtze Steam Navigation Co**. in 1879.

They were a very powerful force in local Shanghai politics and had a seat permanently reserved for one of their representatives on the Shanghai Municipal Council, the governing body of the International Settlement. Members of the Keswick family, who were managing partners in the firm, served as Chairman of the Shanghai Municipal Council on four separate occasions. After the 1949 revolution, several of Jardine Matheson's top foreign managers in China were imprisoned and held hostage by the new Communist regime.

The building has four round stone columns on its front facade. The original Jardine's stone coat of arms over the entrance has obviously been completely chiseled off. In 2003 a step inside still revealed a happy sight for the historian, an interior that had not yet been renovated, which in China usually means complete demolition of any original artifacts. The ground floor lobby and staircase seemed to have been left much as they were before, with 50 years of dust having accumulated since. A friendly watchman at the front desk didn't seem to mind visitors snooping around. Unfortunately, the revolutionary censors had done a good job of removing any symbols or inscriptions betraying the identity of the original owners. No signs of the Ewo name were to be found.

Since 1955 Jardine's former headquarters has been known as the Shanghai Foreign Trade Building (Waimao Da Lou) [外贸大楼]. Over the main entrance is a Chinese language sign that reads, "Wai Mao Da Lou" [外贸大楼].

In 2003 a Japanese restaurant occupied the ground floor. Later in 2008 the building was acquired by the Roosevelt China Investment Corporation, whose Chairman Tweed Roosevelt is a descendant of two U.S. presidents, Teddy Roosevelt and Franklin D. Roosevelt. After that the building was renamed the House of Roosevelt, which now houses a collection of upscale restaurants and bars, including one on the roof, a wine cellar, a private membership only club, and a Rolex store on the ground floor.

Address: No. 27 Zhongshan Dong Yi Lu [中山东一路 27 号]

21. The Glen Line Building (Gelin Youchuan Da Lou) [格林邮船大楼]

Designed by Palmer & Turner architects, this seven-story building was completed in March 1922. It served as the headquarters for the steamship company known as the **Glen Line** (Gelin Youchuan) [格林邮船].

Two small columns mark the entrance, over which the original stone coat of arms has obviously been covered up with cement. Inside the interior has been completely gutted and redecorated.

In the 1990s this was known as the Municipal People's Radio Station Building (Shi Renmin Diantai Da Lou) [市人民电台大楼], but since 2003 the building has served as a branch of the China Everbright Bank (Zhongguo Guangda Yinhang) [中国光大银行].

Address: No. 28 Zhongshan Dong Yi Lu [中山东一路 28 号], or No. 2 Beijing Dong Lu [北京东路 2 号]

22. Bank of Indo-China (Donfang Huili Yinhang Da Lou) [东方汇理银行大楼]

Built between 1910 and 1911, the interior was later redesigned in 1930.   This was the offices of the Shanghai branch of the **Banque de l'Indochine** (Donfang Huili Yinhang) [东方汇理银行], a French bank with its headquarters in Paris that was first established in 1875.   The bank opened its first branch in Shanghai in 1899, and also had a branch in the Hankou foreign concessions district of Wuhan.   The bank's name is a reminder that most of Southeast Asia was then a French colony known as Indo-China.

Two small columns mark the entrance, over which stands a stone urn.   Two round coat of arms have obviously been covered up with wet cement.   The exterior door is a new steel replacement, but the interior wooden double door and frame leading into the lobby seem to be the originals.   Inside the interior has been restored, but is nonetheless impressive and semi-authentic in style.   A central skylight hangs over the main banking hall.

In the 1990s this was known as the Oriental Building (Dongfang Da Lou) [东方大楼], but since 2003 it has also been a branch of the China Everbright Bank (Zhongguo Guangda Yinhang) [中国光大银行].

Address: No. 29 Zhongshan Dong Yi Lu [中山东一路 29 号]

23. The Former British Consulate (Yingguo Lingshiguan Jiuzhi) [英国领事馆旧址]

Sometimes known as the Shanghai British Consulate General (Yingguo Zhu Shanghai Zonglingshiguan) [英国驻上海总领事馆], other times known simply as the Former Site of the British Consulate (Yingguo Lingshiguan Jiuzhi) [英国领事馆旧], and more recently referred to as 33 Waitan Yuan [外滩源 33 号], this prime piece of real estate at the confluence of Suzhou Creek (Suzhou He) [苏州河] and the Huangpu River (Huangpu Jiang) [黄浦江] was first acquired by the British in November 1843, and was the site of the first British Consulate building completed here in July 1849.   The 1849 structure burned down in a fire in December 1870 on Christmas Eve.   Reconstruction started two years later in 1872.   The present structures in the former British Consulate compound were completed between 1872 and 1884 on the same site as the previous consulate constructed there in 1849.   In the meantime, the Consulate's status had been upgraded to that of a Consulate General in 1880.   These are the oldest existing buildings on the Bund.   This was once the center of British power in Shanghai during the 100 years of the two foreign concessions.   The complex of buildings included not only the existing British Consulate Building completed in 1873 but also the **British Supreme Court for China** completed in 1871 and extended in 1913, the **British Consul's Residence** completed in 1884, a separate house for the **British Vice Consul's Residence**, and the **British Naval Office**.   The British Supreme Court for China was established in 1865 and abolished in 1943 along with all the previous unequal treaties and extraterritoriality. During its existence, the court always had two full-time British judges, who had jurisdiction over all British citizens in China, Japan, and Korea.

During the Japanese occupation from December 1941 to August 1945 the British Consulate was closed for almost four years, but reopened again after the Japanese surrender.

The British abandoned this compound after the May 1949 Liberation of Shanghai by the Red Army, but in 1950 Britain recognized the People's Republic of China as the new government, allowing for the partial restoration of diplomatic relations, which would not be fully restored until the exchange of ambassadors in 1972.   After an absence of five years, in September 1954 the first of a series of 8 post-Liberation British Consuls returned to this same site on the Bund, each one staying for a period of two years, until finally in May 1967 the last British Consul to occupy this historic compound was forcibly driven out by an angry mob in the midst of the Cultural Revolution.   Technically, for diplomatic reasons, they were not allowed to be called Consuls or Consul Generals, and instead were referred to as Commissioners or Assistant Directors.   Full diplomatic relations were re-established between the PRC and the U.K. in 1972, but the British Consulate General in Shanghai was not re-established until February 1985, and at a different location than before, at 244 Yongfu Lu [永福路 244 号], their historic compound on the Bund having been lost forever after the May 1967 incident.

Meanwhile, the former British Consulate was taken over by the Shanghai Municipal Government and used as their No. 2 Office Building.   For decades after 1967 this compound surrounded by an iron fence was not open to the public.   Visitors were usually sent away by the uniformed guards at the front gate.   Back in 2003, I was able to secretly sneak inside the compound with a camera through the back door of a dress shop that used to be next door.   I wandered around long enough to photograph the main building inside and out, as well as the exterior of the former Consul's Residence behind it, before someone caught me and chased me away.   I managed to escape through the same dress shop back door that had fortunately remained wide open.   If the dress shop had closed their back door I would have been trapped inside the compound and caught by the guards.   One of my photographs of the interior, showing the central staircase, appeared in my 2003 book Shanghai and the Yangzi Delta, but unfortunately the editor mislabeled the caption as being the Pujiang Hotel (Pujiang Fandian) [浦江饭店].

When I explored the site in 2003, there were eight historic buildings located within the compound.   The main consulate building still sat on an expansive estate of green lawns. Viewed from the lawn, the long rectangular consulate building still looked impressive, and for its age the actual structure was still fairly solid.   However, from up close you could see that the exterior's paint had faded, and the interior had been allowed to deteriorate into an extremely shabby state.   Many of its windows were broken.   Just behind the main consulate building stood the former British **Consul's Residence**, a two-story house with a covered carport driveway that was connected to the main consulate building via a covered pedestrian walkway.   A third original building was a much smaller two-story house behind the consulate that had served as the **Vice Consul's Residence**.   No relics of British imperialism seemed to have survived, with the possible exception of an old iron canon that sat in a small children's playground in the parking lot beside the main building.

When the Bund Origin (Waitan Yuan) [外滩源] urban redevelopment project began in early 2007 the former British Consulate compound was evacuated by its municipal government tenants and abandoned.   It sat abandoned for several years until restoration started in May 2009.   The consulate compound's historic buildings had survived intact until its 2009 restoration, albeit in somewhat dilapidated condition.   However, after the 2009 renovations only three historic buildings were left standing, the main **Consulate Building** facing the Huanpgu River, the **Consul's Residence** behind it in a hidden corner of the compound, and the **British Supreme Court for China** facing Yuanmingyuan Road in the back of the compound.   The Vice Consul's Residence, the Naval Office, and other buildings had all been torn down.

By September 2010 it had been reoccupied by the management of the new **Penninsula Hotel** (Bandao Dajiudian) [半岛大酒店] next door, the first new building constructed on the Bund since 1948.   The compound is now officially known as 33 Waitan Yuan [外滩源 33 号]. While doing field research for my 2010 book *Discover Shanghai*, I attempted to revisit the former British Consulate Building, but was met at the front door by a quite unfriendly woman who refused to allow me to enter the building with the excuse that, "This is private property." The scene was rich with irony, indeed.   An e-mail to the Peninsula Hotel about the incident went unanswered.

Unobstructed views of the front of the former British Consulate compound used to be hard to come by as the low-rise structures lay hidden behind a fence and obstructed by the cement pillars and ramps of the elevated approaches leading up to the Wusong Road Water Gate Bridge across Suzhou Creek, which has since been torn down.   The best view available from outside the compound was to look down on it from the 17th floor of the Broadway Mansions (Bailaohui Dasha) [百老汇大厦] on the north side of Suzhou Creek (Suzhou He) [苏州河].   The razing of a row of shacks that once stood behind the consulate has now provided a better view of the back side of the site from Yuanmingyuan Lu, from which there is now also a back entrance gate to the fenced compound that previously only had one front gate facing the Bund.
Address: No. 33 Zhongshan Dong Yi Lu [中山东一路 33 号]

24. The Russian Consulate

Built in 1917 by the Russian imperial government, which was overthrown that same year, this consulate continued to be occupied by the Tsar's diplomatic representative until 1920, when it was closed down.   Unlike the British Consulate just across the Suzhou River (Suzhou He) [苏州河], the Russian Consulate was recently returned to its original owners and now flys the flag of the double eagle once again.
Address: No. 20 Huangpu Lu [黄浦路 20 号]

25. The Astor House Hotel (Pujiang Fandian) [浦江饭店]

The Pujiang Hotel (Pujiang Fandian) [浦江饭店] started out its roller coaster career as the most luxurious hotel in Shanghai, descended down to becoming the cheapest place in town to stay, and has now experienced yet another reversal of fortune thanks to a major overhaul of its interior.   Built in 1910 as The Astor House, this Victorian style structure was the first in all of China to have electric lights and telephones installed.   Located on the north side of the Garden Bridge (Waibaidu Qiao) [外白渡桥] crossing the Suzhou River (Suzhou He) [苏州河], the hotel had a panoramic view of the Bund (Waitan) [外滩] until 1917 when the construction of the Russian Consulate across the street blocked its view.   The hotel's ballroom used to feature weekly Saturday night dances that became one of the regular social events of Shanghai.   Before 1949 the Astor House was the temporary home of such celebrities as Charlie Chaplin, Albert Einstein, George Bernard Shaw, and Chiang Kai-shek (Jiang Jieshi) [蒋介石] (1887-1975).   In 1959 the name of the hotel was changed to the Pujiang. Shanghai's first post-Liberation   stock exchange was opened in the old ballroom of the Astor House in 1991, but it has since moved to a new modern facility of its own in Pudong.

The Pujiang had become a two-star youth hostel with dormitories full of bunk beds inhabited by teenage backpackers who paid as little as 55 Rmb per night. Its impressive exterior architecture and history were all that remained of its former glory. However, after a massive restoration of its original interior, the Pujiang has reopened under the old Astor House name and is now targeting a higher class of clientele once again.

Address:　No. 15 Huangpu Lu [黄浦路 15 号]

26. Broadway Mansions (Bailaohui Dasha) [百老汇大厦]

This hulking red brick behemoth stands on the Hongkou side of the steel frame **Garden Bridge** (Waibaidu Qiao) [外白渡桥], which was constructed across the **Suzhou River** (Suzhou He) [苏州河] in 1907, and looks down on the Waitan (Bund) below. Designed by Palmer & Turner architects and completed in 1934 by Sir Victor Sassoon as an eighteen-story luxury residential building, its rooftop restaurant provided foreign war correspondents with a bird's eye view of the Japanese invasion of Shanghai in August 1937 and the Communist takeover of May 1949.

In mid-August 1937 the building was taken over by the Japanese military, who forced all non-Japanese occupants to leave, raised the Japanese flag from the roof top, and used it as their headquarters until the foreign concessions across the Suzhou River were finally occupied on December 8, 1941. In March 1939 it was sold to a Japanese company. Later the Nanjing puppet regim of Wang Jingwei had a Foreign Affairs Bureau office in the building.

After the Japanese surrender in August 1945, the building was occupied mainly by the U.S. Military Assistance Group to China, and houses several hundred U.S. military personnel. It also became the home of the Foreign Correspondents Club of China, and housed some foreign news reporters until the Liberation of Shanghai by the Red Army in May 1949. It was the scene of the last significant battle of the Chinese Civil War as Guomindang snipers used its heights to slow down the Red Army's crossing of the Garden Bridge over the Suzhou River for two days from May 25-27, 1949. By the end of June 1949 the last remaining foreign residents had been evicted by the new regime.

It was originally called the Broadway Mansions (Bailaohui Dasha) [百老汇大厦], named after the main street running past it, which is now called Daming Dong Lu, but was then known as Broadway (Bailaohui)[百老汇]. However, on May 1, 1951 the name was changed to the less bourgeois **Shanghai Mansions** (Shanghai Dasha) [上海大厦]. Finally, on August 5, 2000 it was again rechristened under its former name of Broadway Mansions (Bailaohui Dasha) [百老汇大厦] and reopened as a relatively expensive four-star hotel. It's now popular with visiting foreign tourists.

Although the 18th floor **River Viewing Balcony** is open by appointment only, the 17th floor restaurant offers great panoramic views of the Waitan from its row of private banquet rooms. This same 17th floor housed the bar where members of the Foreign Correspondents Club of China held their parties from August 1945 to May 1949.

Address:　20 North Suzhou Road (20 Bei Suzhou Lu) [北苏州路 20 号]
Web Site:　http://www.broadwaymansions.com

The Bund's Waitan Yuan Area [外滩源]

Museum Road (Huqiu Lu) [虎丘路] and the parallel street known as **Yuanmingyuan Lu** [圆明园路] once formed the culture district for European and American residents of pre-1949 Shanghai. This is where libraries, museums, architects and other cultural organizations had their offices. The area is bounded by South Suzhou Road (Nan Suzhou Lu) to the North, Dianchi Lu to the South, Sichuan Bei Lu to the West and the Bund (Waitan) to the East. Yuanmingyuan Lu is notable for having buildings only on its West side, the East side being the boundary wall of the former British Consulate's grounds. Yuanmingyuan Lu and Huqiu Lu are the only streets running from north to south between Sichuan Bei Lu and the Bund. In early 2007 residents and companies were evacuated from most of the buildings on these two streets in preparation for their wholesale renovation as part of the city's **Waitan Yuan** [外滩源] project to redevelop this northern corner of the Bund. The 25-story Wenhui Mansion office building that once stood on the south side of the British Consulate compound was torn down in April 2006. In its place construction of a new 15-story **Peninsula Hotel** at 32 Zhongshan Dong Yi Lu [中山东一路 32] began in October 2006 and opened in late 2009, just in time for the 2010 World Expo. The hotel is owned by Hong Kong and Shanghai Hotels, Ltd., a company that is still controlled by the famous Kadoorie family, and which used to own four historic hotels in Shanghai before 1949, including the Palace Hotel, Astor House, and the Majestic Hotel.

Historic sights along Museum Road (Huqiu Lu) [虎丘路] include at #20 the former building of the **Royal Asiatic Society North China Branch** (Yazhou Wenhui Bei Zhongguo Zhihui) [亚洲文会北中国支会]. The six-story Art-Deco building was designed by Palmer and Turner and completed in 1933. At #128 stands the **Christian Literature Society** building, designed by Hungarian architect Laszlo Hudec, and completed in 1933. It's a ten-story red brick structure with a granite block tower in the center. The former **YMCA National Headquarters** building built between 1919 and 1924 is located at #131. The **Capitol Theater** (Guanglu Da Xiyuan) [光陆大戏院] stands at #146 Huqiu Lu [虎丘路 146] on the corner with South Suzhou Road (Nan Suzhou Lu) [南苏州路]. It's an eight-story building with a small three-story tower on top. It was designed in Art-Deco style and completed in 1928. Until early 2007 it still bore a giant Broadway-style neon marquee billing itself as, "New York, New York," the name of a former nightclub located here in the early 1990s.

Historic buildings on Yuanmingyuan Lu [圆明园路] include the former **YWCA Building** (Nu Qingnian Hui Da Lou) [女青年会大楼] at #133. Completed in 1933, it was designed in Art-Deco style with some curious Chinese ornamentation decorating the red brick facade. The stone doorway is designed to look like a traditional Chinese wooden pai lou gate, and still bears a 13 character Chinese inscription over the top that reads from right to left as was the custom before 1949. In the left corner of the front façade an original inscribed corner stone can still be found. The **Lyceum Building** (Lanxin Da Lou) [兰心大楼] at #185 was completed in 1927. It was originally a six-story brick building dominated by a seven story square tower in the center, but in recent years two additional floors were added on top. In 2009 the original iron gate guarding the front entrance still bore the number 24, denoting its original address. The **China Baptist Publications Building** (Zhenguang Da Lou) at #209 was completed in 1930 and is another one of the many in Shanghai designed by Hungarian architect Laszlo Hudec. It features a telescoping tower in the center similar to that of the Park Hotel (Guoji Fandian) [国际饭店], also designed by Hudec.

C

The Canidrome (Yiyuan Paogouchang) [逸园跑狗场]

The Canidrome (Yiyuan Paogouchang) [逸园跑狗场] was built in 1928 by Henry E. Morris, Jr. (Xiao Malisi) [小马立斯], owner of the North China Daily News and the lovely garden estate now known as the Shanghai Intercontinental Ruijin Hotel (Shanghai Rujin Zhouji Jiudian) [上海瑞金洲际酒店] located on the other side of Maoming South Road (Maoming Nan Lu), for the primary purpose of hosting dog racing events, on which gamblers could place bets just like they would at a horse race.   It was located on the former Rue Lafayette of the French Concession, taking up nearly a city block of land. In addition to its racetrack and a stadium with grandstands that could seat 50,000 spectators, the Canidrome also had a hotel and was known for its ballroom (wuting) [舞厅], which offered nightly dinner dances with live music provided by big bands that often featured African American musicians from the U.S. The five-story main building had a tower in the center of the façade facing the street, while the backside featured a large grandstand of seats facing the oval race track, in the center of which was a large grass playing field suitable for playing other types of team sports.

Dog racing went into a decline with the start of the Second Sino-Japanese War in August 1937, after which many of the wealthier patrons fled the city, then was completely halted with the Japanese occupation of downtown Shanghai in December 1941 and never again resumed, not even after the Guomindang occupied the city in 1945.   However, besides dog racing the venue also hosted other sporting events, such as boxing, jaialai, soccer, rugby games, and at least one American football game between U.S. Army and Navy teams on December 1, 1945 that was billed as "the China Bowl."   Somewhat bizarrely, the event started with the U.S. national anthem being performed by U.S. military bands, who during the half-time peformed a set of half a dozen other patriotic Americans songs, including "Anchor's Away," and the U.S. Marines Hymn.

After May 1949 the site of the Canidrome became a public facility renamed as **Culture Square** (Shanghai Wenhua Guangchang) [上海文化广场].   For the first several years immediately after the Liberation it was used for holding large political rallies, and according to contemporaneous reports in Time magazine, even mass executions of poltical prisoners. The whole site was dramatically altered in a reconstruction that lasted for two years from April 1952 to 1954.   A large stage was constructed in the middle of the former playing field, while most of the race track and field were covered up with an enormous flat roof that stretched from the grandstand to the new stage and was supported by a newly erected steel frame structure.   Many more additional rows of seats were installed facing the stage.   The completed new structure was a fan-shaped extension off of the original main building into the former race course.   Once completed this reconstruction and extension project converted it into the city's largest indoor meeting hall (da huichang) where government conferences and party congresses were convened.

During the Cultural Revolution the Gang of Four used this venue for public denunciations and executions of rival party leaders and intellectuals.   In December 1969 a large fire broke out that seriously damaged the stage area, meeting hall, and part of the exhibition hall, as well as causing nearly 400 casualties, but the destroyed buildings had all been rebuilt by September 1970, now with a 19 meter high stage, and became known as the New Culture Square (Xin Wenhua Guangchang).

134

From 1976 to 1996 the former ballroom was used as an auditorium that hosted large conferences and meetings.   It also occasionally hosted musical performances and art exhibitions.   From 1997 until October 10, 2005 the site was home to the Shanghai Xianhua Wholesale Flower Market (Shanghai Xianhua Pifa Shichang) [上海鲜花批发市场], the largest one in all of East China, covering 15,000 square meters and serving 300 retail flower shops.

On November 30 2005 the Canidrome's former five-story main building covering 3,400 square maters was actually blown up in a demolition explosioin in order to make way for construction of a new theater that was not completed until 2011, when it opened under the name of SAIC Shanghai Culture Square (Shangqi Shanghai Wenhua Guangchang) [上汽上海文化广场], SAIC being the abbreviation for the Shanghai Automotive Industry Corporation, a large domestic car manufacturer.   Inside there is an exhibition on the site's history.

Although on maps you can still see the teardrop oval shape of the former race course, the site now occupies almost all the land in between the rectangular city block of Maoming South Road (Maoming Nan Lu) to the East, Shanxi South Road (Shanxi Nan Lu) to the West, Fuxing Middle Road (Fuxing Zhong Lu) to the North, and Yongjia Road (Yongjia Lu) to the South.

Address: The main entrance to the former site of the Canidrome is located at 597 Fuxing Middle Road (Fuxing Zhong Lu 597 hao) [复兴中路 597 号].

Cathedrals and Churches (Jiaotang) [教堂]

Christian missionaries have left behind a massive amount of historical religious architecture built before 1949. According to Zhou Fuchang [周富长], ed. *Shanghai Zongjiao Zhilu* [*上海宗教之旅*] (2004), there were then 74 Roman Catholic churches & cathedrals (Tianzhujiao Jiaotang) [天主教教堂], and 106 Protestant churches (Jidujiao Jiaotang) [基督教教堂], for a total of 180 Christian churches in Shanghai, not counting the two former Russian Orthodox ones. This is more than double the combined number of approximately 84 Buddhist and Taoist temples in Shanghai.

Zhou Fuchang [周富长] lists three of the most important Roman Catholic churches as 1) the Xujiahui Cathedral, 2) the Sheshan Cathedral, and 3) Dongjiadu Cathedral. Then he breaks down the number of Catholic churches according to each district of the city. At that time there were 12 Roman Catholic churches in Pudong, 8 in Songjiang (including the Sheshan Cathedral), 7 in Chongming, 7 in Fengxian, 6 in Jiading, 6 in Qingpu, 5 in Nanhui, 4 in Baoshan, 4 in Jinshan, 3 in Minhang, 2 in Changning, 1 in Putuo, 1 in Zhabei, 1 in Hongkou, 1 in Yangpu, 1 in Huangpu, 1 in Luwan, 1 in Jingan. Except for the Xujiahui Cathedral, no mention is made of Xuhui District. Counting both the Dongjiadu Cathedral and the St. Joseph's Cathedral together there would have been two in Huangpu District.

The section on Protestant churches in Zhou Fuchang [周富长] (2004) is peculiar because there is no mention at all of the **Holy Trinity Cathedral** (Sheng Sanyi Tang) [圣三一堂] at 219 Jiujiang Lu [九江路] in Huangpu district, which should have been listed as the most important one. Instead, **Moore Memorial Methodist Church** (Mu'en Tang) [沐恩堂] at #316 Tibet Middle Road (Xizang Zhong Lu) and the **Community Church** (Guoji Libai Tang) [国际礼拜堂] at #53 Hengshan Road [衡山路] are listed as the top two ranking Protestant churches in Shanghai. After this comes a break down of Protestant churches in Shanghai by district. At tha time there were 22 Protestant churches in Fengxian, 11 in Qingpu, 10 in Baoshan, 9 in Pudong, 9 in Jinshan, 8 in Chongming, 7 in Nanhui, 7 in Minhang, 6 in Jiading, 5 in Songjiang, 2 in Luwan, 2 in Putuo, 1 in Changning, 1 in Zhabei, and 1 in Yangpu. Except for the Moore there was no mention of Protestant churches in Huangpu District, and except for the Community Church there was no mention of ones in Xuhui District.

Possibly the first church built in Shanghai, and currently one of the oldest buildings in the city, is the Jingyi Church (Jingyi Tang) [敬一堂], sometimes also called simply the Old Catholic Church (Lao Tianzhu Tang) [老天主堂], which started out in the Ming Dynasty as the Ever-Spring Hall (Shi Chun Tang) [世春堂], which was built in 1553 as a house by Pan Yunduan [潘允端] (1526–1601) and later was converted into a Roman Catholic church in 1640 by descendants of Xu Guangqi [徐光启] (1562-1633), who had been converted to Christianity when he met the Jesuit Matteo Ricci. The house was built in 1553 on Anren Li, the same road where the first Chenxiang Ge [沉香阁] Pavilion was also built by Pan Yunduan. Pan Yunduan's descendant Pan Guoguang later sold the house to Xu Guangqi's granddaughter, who converted it into a Catholic church (Tianzhu Tang) in 1640. The church was later seized by the government in 1730 during the Qing Dynasty as part of a crack down on Catholocisim by the Yongzheng emperor. In 1861, during the Xianfeng reign, the building was returned to the Catholic Church. After 1949 the church was turned into the gymnasium of the Wutong Road Elementary School (Wutong Lu Xiaoxue), which it still belongs to now.

During the century that Shanghai was dominated by foreigners from 1843 to 1943 many Christian churches of various denominations were built here by Americans, British, French and Russians.

Protestant churches of note include the **Community Church** (Guoji Libai Tang) [国际礼拜堂] at #53 Hengshan Road [衡山路] built by Americans in 1924, and the **Moore Memorial Methodist Church** (Mu'en Tang) [沐恩堂] at #316 Tibet Middle Road (Xizang Zhong Lu), which was designed by Hungarian architect Laszlo Hudec and completed in 1931.

The main Anglican church in Shanghai, the **Holy Trinity Cathedral** (Sheng Sanyi Tang) [圣三一堂] at 219 Jiujiang Lu [九江路] in Huangpu district, was designed by Sir Gilbert Scott and built between 1866 and 1869 on the site of an earlier church built there in 1847. The cathedral's tower was added in 1893. Chinese movie star **Hu Die** [胡蝶] (1908-1989), aka "Butterfly Wu," but whose real name was Hu Ruihua [胡瑞华], held her gala wedding ceremony here on November 23, 1935.

The church was taken over in the early 1950s by the government-sponsored China Protestant Patriotic Three-Self Movement Committee (Zhongguo Jiedu Jiao Sanzi Aiguo Yundong Weiyuanhui) [中国基督教三自爱国运动委员会] or simply (Sanzi Jiaohui) [三自教会] for short. It was apparently operated as a Protestant Church into the 1960s, then was heavily damaged during the Cultural Revolution (1966-1976), and finally occupied by the Huangpu District government which used it as office space and an auditorium for large meetings starting in the early 1980s.

In June 2004 the building was officially returned to China's protestant church, but announcements that it would "be reopened soon" proved premature. Feasibility studies and fundraising for the building's renovation lasted for another three years, while the estimated costs spiraled out of control from "several million yuan" to 49 million yuan, before reconstruction work finally started in mid-2007. The clock tower, which had been added to the church in 1893, was entirely destroyed during the Cultural Revolution and had to be completely rebuilt, all of the wooden pews had been removed and were replaced with new ones, and a new organ was installed to replace the original which had gone missing, but due to cost constraints it proved impossible to replace all of the destroyed stained glass windows. By May 2009 the long-delayed restoration project was still in progress and was expected to take another three months, after which the cathedral would once again be opened to the public for the first time since 1949.

The cathedral finally reopened to the public for the first time in decades in 2014 after nearly ten years of restoration. However, when I tried to visit the church on Christmas Eve 2017 I found the metal gates locked, and no guard in sight. You can still view the front exterior of the restored church by walking around its fenced perimeter through a small public park next door on the east side, and the backside can be viewed from the garden of the former church bishop's residence on the west side, which is open to the public as a restaurant now separate from the church itself. The graves of 110 foreigners' who were buried on the church grounds between 1937 and 1952 have all completely disappeared.

The former cathedral boys' school next door, where author **J.G. Ballard** was once a student, has been occupied by the national headquarters of the China Protestant Patriotic Three-Self Movement Committee (Zhongguo Jidujiao Sanzi Aiguo Yundong Weiyuanhui) [中国基督教三自爱国运动委员会] or simply (Sanzi Jiaohui) [三自教会] for short.

Between 1847 and 1935 French Roman Catholics constructed four impressive cathedrals that still stand today. The **Dongjiadu Roman Catholic Cathedral** (Dongjiadu Tianzhu Tang) [董家渡天主堂] at #175 Dongjiadu Lu was built between 1847 and 1853, and was originally named after St. Francis Xavier, the earliest Jesuit missionary to come to China. This was the first church to be erected in Shanghai after the city was opened to foreign settlement by the 1842 Treaty of Nanking, making it the oldest one in the city. **St. Joseph's Roman Catholic Cathedral** (Sheng Ruose Tang) [圣若瑟堂] at #36 Sichuan Nan Lu was built between 1860 and 1862. It has at times also been known as the Yangjingbang Cathedral (Yangjingbang Tianzhutang) or simply the Sichuan Nan Lu Cathedral (Sichuan Nan Lu Tianzhutang). **St. Ignatius Cathedral** in Xujiahui (Xujiahui Tianzhutang) [徐家汇天主堂] was completed in 1910, and the **Sheshan Roman Catholic Cathedral**, once known as the Basilica Minor of St. Mary (Sheshan Shengmu Tianzhutang) [佘山圣母天主堂], was constructed over a ten-year period of time, from April 1925 to November 1935, on top of Shanghai's highest mountain in Songjiang district. Usually a protestant church is simply called a Jiaotang in Chinese, while a Roman Catholic Church is called a Tianzhu Jiaotang.

There were also several Russian Orthodox churches (Dongzhen Jiaotang)[东正教堂] built here. The **Xinle Lu Russian Orthodox Church** (Xinle Lu Dongzhen Jiaotang) [新乐路东正教堂] at #55 Xinle Lu [新乐路], formerly Rue Paul Henri of the French Concession, was built between 1932 and 1934 and has five impressive onion domes. In 2002 it was turned into a restaurant known as The Dome. The **St. Nicholas II Russian Orthodox Church** (Gaolan Lu Dongzhen Jiaotang) [皋兰路东正教堂] at #16 Gaolan Lu [皋兰路], formerly Rue Corneille of the French Concession, was built by White Russian military officers between 1932 and 1933 in memory of the last Russian Tsar. Later it became a French restaurant known as the Ashanti Dome. Both of these former Orthodox churches are currently vacant.

Chenxiang Ge Buddhist Temple (Chenxiang Ge) [沉香阁]

The Chenxiang Ge Pavilion [沉香阁] was originally a single small structure housing a wooden statue of the Goddess of Mercy (Guanyin), and was later expanded into a full scale Buddhist temple.   It was first built by Pan Yunduan [潘允端] (1526–1601), the same person who built the famous Yu Yuan Garden, in 1600, the 28th year of the Wanli reign of the Ming Dynasty, but at a different location nearby on Anren Lane (Anren Li).   The original pavilion collapsed at the end of the Ming Dynasty.   In 1801, the 6th year of the Jiaqing reign of the Qing Dynasty, the Chenxiang Ge Pavilion was rebuilt at its current location.   The Front Hall was built four years later in 1805.   In 1814, the 19th year of the Jiaqing reign, the Da Xiong Bao Dian was built.   Throughout the Daoguang reign the temple was repaired and expanded many times.   During this time a Heavenly Kings Hall (Tian Wang Dian) was added.   In the Tongzhi reign, due to the temple's great expansion from what was originally only one building, the temple's name was changed from Chenxiang Pavilion to Compassionate Cloud Zen Courtyard (Ciyun Chanyuan) [慈云禅院].

All the statues and other religious contents of the buildings were destroyed during the Cultural Revolution, but the empty structures themselves survived and were occupied by a factory workshop.   In 1983 religious use resumed of some of the buildings that had been partly repaired, but it was not until 1994 that the whole temple was renovated. The Chenxiang Ge Buddhist Temple fully reopened on February 14, 1994 after years of repairs. There are three courtyards, and in the third stands the temple's namesake Guanyin Pavilion (Chenxiang Guanyin Ge) [沉香观音阁] containing a wooden statue of Guanyin made from Chenxiang wood.   In 1996 the temple was made a national-level protected cultural relic.

A functioning Buddhist nunnery Coverig an area of 2,378 sq. meters, it includes three main halls on a central axis,.

Entering the orange walled compound through the Mountain Gate (Shan Men), a three-portal gateway with its roof of upturned eaves, there are three courtyards separating the three main buildings on the south-north axis.   The first building you enter is the Heavenly Kings Hall (Tian Wang Dian) [天王殿].   On either side stand the Bell Tower (Zhong Lou) [钟楼] and Drum Tower (Gu Lou) [鼓楼].   Next, in the second courtyard comes the Hall of the Great Hero (Da Xiong Bao Dian) [大雄宝殿].   On either side of this courtyard stand the Guest Hall (Ke Tang) [客堂] and the Ancestor Hall (Zu Tang) [祖堂]. Finally, in the third courtyard is the two-story Goddess of Mercy Pavilion (Chenxiang Guanyin Ge) [沉香观音阁], with the ground floor sometimes referred to separately as the Ciyun Tang [慈云堂], while the Guanyin statue is housed upstairs on the second floor.   Along the sides of the third courtyard are found two more halls, the Dining Hall (Zhai Tang) [斋堂] and the Achievements Hall (Gongde Tang) [功德堂].

Many resident Buddhist nuns now live here, and can be seen walking around the Yu Yuan Bazaar area.   Although near the more famous Taoist City God Temple (Chenghuang Miao), its hidden location down a narrow side alley off of the main street makes it less overrun by tourist hordes.

Address: 29 Chenxiang Lu [香阁路 29 号], formerly Nanshi District, now Huangpu Qu.
Phone: (021) 6320-3431

The Chinese Communist Party's First Congress Hall (Zhongguo Gongchandang Diyici Quanguo Daibiao Dahui Huizhi) [中国共产党第一次全国代表大会会址]

The Chinese Communist Party (Gongchandang) [共产党] secretly held its first national party congress in this simple two-story red brick stone gate house (shikumen) from July 23-30, 1921.   This location on the former Rue Wantz of the French Concession was considered a safer place for the congress than anywhere else in Chinese-controlled territory. Nonetheless, the final day of the meeting had to be held on board a boat in the middle of the South Lake (Nan Hu) in the nearby Zhejiang province town of Jiaxing on July 31st.   The First national congress of the party was attended by 12 Chinese delegates, including **Mao Zedong** [毛泽东] (1893-1976), as well as the Dutch Comintern representative H. Sneevliet, alias G. Maring. Neither of the party's two real founders were there, as **Chen Duxiu** [陈独秀] (1879-1942) was then in Guangzhou, and **Li Dazhao** [李大钊](1889-1927) in Beijing.

The site now covers four two-story shikumen buildings, the first of which has had its interior entirely gutted and converted into a modern museum facility.   Exhibits on the second floor contain an amazing collection of real relics related to Shanghai's modern history, including many related to the former foreign concessions.   There is an enormous bronze plaque that once served as a boundary marker for the International Settlement, with a bi-lingual inscription dated May 8, 1899, as well as a genuine flag once flown by the settlement's Shanghai Volunteer Corps, and police billy clubs and uniforms once used by the settlement's police force.   Most amazing of all is the leather padded wooden armchair where once sat the chairman of the settlement's Shanghai Municipal Council, complete with the SMC's bronze seal embedded in the wooden back rest.   The seal bears the same crest as the SVC flag, with the Latin slogan, "Omnia Juncta In Uno."

The actual site of the meeting is in one of the other lilong shikumen houses on the site. This house was built in 1920 and at the time of the congress belonged to Li Shucheng, the brother of delegate Li Hanjun.   Inside there is a dinner table with 13 place settings for the delegates.

Admission to the site is now free, but when you enter you have to pass through a metal detector similar to that at an airport.

Although the full name of the site is (Zhongguo Gongchandang Diyici Quanguo Daibiao Dahui Huizhi) [中国共产党第一次全国代表大会会址], it is usually abbreviated as (Zhonggong Yidahui Zhi) [中共一大会址].

Address: 76 Xingye Lu [兴业路76], Huangpu District [黄浦区]
Phone: (021) 5383-2171
Fax: (021) 6311-0136
Nearest Metro Station: Huangpi Nan Lu [黄陂南路] on Line 1.

Chongming Island (Chongming Dao) [崇明島]

Chongming is the third largest island in China, after Hainan and Taiwan, but only had a population of 730,000 people as of the 2010 census, making this a delightful piece of rural countryside sitting in the middle of the Yangzi River's mouth. The island is currently 80 km long from East to West, and 18 km wide at its broadest point, but it used to be much smaller. Formed from the silt flowing down the Yangzi River, at its current size of 1,200 sq. km. it is the world's largest alluvial island, and is still growing at a rate of 500 additional hectares per year. The first recorded founding of a town on Chongming Island occurred in 705 A.D. during the Tang Dynasty when a town named Chongming was established. In 1277 during the Yuan Dynasty a Chongming Prefecture was created. Later, in 1396, during the second year of the Hongwu reign of the Ming Dynasty, Chongming's status was downgraded from a prefecture to a county, an administrative level that it would maintain until 2017. Over the centuries Chongming was bounced back and forth between various jurisdictions, at various times being placed under the administration of Nantong, Yangzhou, Suzhou, Taicang, and Songjiang. In 1958 Chongming Island was made a county within the Shanghai municipality, and in January 2017 it was upgraded to the status of a district within the Shanghai municipality. The whole Chongming District also includes the two other Yangzi River islands of Changxing and Hengsha. Chongmng Island sits only 10 km away from the heavily industrialized Baoshan District, but the environment is light years away from the urban center, with most of the island consisting of wide open farmland. Several national forest parks and wildlife preserves are located there. There are also historic sights dating back to the Song, Yuan, Ming and Qing dynasties.

Golden Turtle Hill (Jin Ao Shan) [金鳌山] in Chengqiao Town [城桥镇] has been the site of temples and pagodas since the late Yuan Dynasty (1279-1368). At the foot of the hill is the Memorial Hall (Jinian Guan) [纪念馆] and Tomb (Mu) of **Tang Yicen** [唐一岑], a county magistrate who died defending the island against an attack by Japanes pirates (woko) [倭寇] in 1554.

On top of Golden Turtle Hill (Jin Ao Shan) [金鳌山] stands the **Guard the Sea Tower** (Zhenhai Ta) [镇海塔], which was first built in 1893 and later restored in 1986. It is a nine-story, windowless, octagonal pagoda with plaster walls painted red. Its appearance is quite similar to the Homeward Looking Tower on Ming Shan in Fengdu. The top floor contains a lighthouse (deng ta) [灯塔] for giving directions to passing ships at night. Nearby stand the Qingyuan Hall, Guanyin Pavilion and Deyue Bridge.

The **Study Palace** (Xue Gong) [学宫] located at 696 Ao Shan Lu in Chengqiao Town [城桥镇] was originally built in 1327 during the Yuan Dynasty. It features a stone footbridge over a pool leading to the **Da Cheng Hall** devoted to the worship of Confucius. The whole area is surrounded by trees. This is one of only three Confucius temples left standing in Shanghai today, the other two being located in Jiading Town and on Wen Miao Lu [文庙路] in the Old West Gate (Lao Xi Men) [老西门] area of Shanghai's former Nanshi District. It has served as the **Chongming County Museum** (Chongming Xian Bowuguan) since 1999. The most interesting part of the museum is the **Ancient Ships Exhibition Hall**, although it also has other exhibits devoted to the formation and development of Chongming Island. Across the steet is the waterfront riverside park known as Yingzhou Gongyuan [瀛洲公园].

Shou An Buddhist Temple (Shou An Si) [寿安寺] occupies a large walled compound in between **Jin Ao Shan Park** and the main road of Ao Shan Lu is the oldest temple on Chongming Island. It was set up during the Song Dynast in the year 1241. After being damaged later, the present temple was reconstructed in 1983. Inside the temple are the Grand Hall (Da Dian), the Heavenly Kings Hall (Tian Wang Dian) and 16 Arhat statues (Shiliu Luohan). On the 2nd floor of the west wing-room is a 6-meter-long **Reclining Jade Buddha** (Yu Wo Fo) that weighs 13 tons and is the biggest one in Shanghai.

Han Shan Buddhist Temple (Han Shan Si) [寒山寺] located at 21 Dong Men Lu covers an area of 7,000 sq. meters with 32 rooms, and has a history of about 400 years. In the Ming Dynasty a woman surnamed Zhu came to Chongming by boat where she had her head shaved and became a nun named Dian Xiu. She built Han Shan Temple with statues of the two famous Buddhist monks Han Shan and Shi De, who are also associated with the origins of the more famous Han Shan Si in Suzhou.

Dongping National Forest Park (Dongping Guojia Senlin Gongyuan) [东平国家森林公园] is a man-made forest of straight rows of trees covering 353 hectares, established in 1959. Many of the trees were planted by youth sent from the cities to the countryside during the Cultural Revolution (1966-1976.) The park features bicycling, horse-drawn carriages, horse back riding, rock climbing, boating on a lake, fishing in a stocked pond, and bird watching.

The Dongtan National Bird Sanctuary (Chongming Dongtan Niaolei Guojia Ziran Baohu Qu) [崇明东滩鸟类国家级自然保护区] is the seasonal home of many migratory birds that fly a route between Siberia and Australia. Established in 1998, it covers an area of 242 square miles on the eastern tip of the island. More than 290 species of birds have been spotted there, and over 300,000 birds stay there for at least part of every year. It is an important winter habitat for migratory birds, such as cranes, swans, ducks, and heron. As such, it is considered the top bird-watching spot in China. Unfortunately, in recent years the sanctuary has faced challenges from invasive plant species and poachers. A visitors' center was erected in 2010 in a part of the sanctuary that is open to the public.

Chongming Transportation:

On September 25, 2006 work started on a project to build an 8.9 km. long tunnel from Pudong to Changxing Island, and a companion 10.3 km. long bridge from Changxing to Chongming Island, the tunnel, the bridge, and the connecting highway across Changxing Island making a 25 km. route from Pudong to Chongming. The combined **Shanghai Yangzi River Tunnel** and **Shanghai Yangzi River Bridge** (Shanghai Changjiang Suiqiao) [上海长江隧桥] opened on October 31, 2009 and now connect Chongming Island with the Shanghai mainland to the south in Pudong New District. To the north, Chongming Island is also now connected with Qidong [启东市] in northern Jiangsu Province by the **Chongqi Bridge**, and the **Chonghai Bridge** connecting western Chongming Island with Haimen in northern Jiangsu is also under construction.

The **Shanghai Yangzi River Tunnel** starts on the south bank of the Yangtze at Wuhaogou, Pudong and ends in the south of Changxing Island. It is 8.9 kilometres (5.5 mi) in length, and has two stacked levels. The upper level is for a motorway, and has three lanes in each direction, with a designed speed of 80 kilometres per hour (50 mph). The lower level is reserved for a future Shanghai subway line to Chongming Island.

The **Shanghai Yangzi River Bridge** starts at the tunnel exit, crosses Changxing Island at ground level, then crosses to Chongming Island, ending at Chenjia Town. It consists of two long viaducts with a higher cable-stayed section in the middle to allow the passage of ships. The total length is 16.63 kilometres (10.33 mi), of which 6.66 kilometres (4.14 mi) is road and 9.97 kilometres (6.20 mi) bridge. The overall shape of the bridge is slightly S-shaped. The length of the central span is about 730 metres (2,395 ft).   The bridge has six lanes, three in each direction, with space on the shoulders reserved for the future construction of the planned Line 19 of the Shanghai subway system to Chongming Island.

Line 19 of the Shanghai subway system will link Rongqiao Road station on Line 9 in Pudong New District to Chongming Island via Changxing Island, with a branch from the latter to Hengsha Island. The line will use the Shanghai Yangzi River Tunnel and Bridge, which were designed to take its tracks. The first phase of the line from Rongqiao Road to Changxing Island is scheduled to open by 2020.

The Chongming-Qidong Yangzi River Bridge (Chongqi Daqiao) [崇启大桥] opened to traffic on Christmas Eve 2011, while the Chongming-Haimen Bridge (Chonghai Daqiao) [崇海大桥] is still under construction.

Despite all the added overland transportation routes, some ferry boat routes continue to operate between the three islands in Chongming District. Hengsha Island can still only be reached by taking a ferry boat. On Chongming Island, Chengqiao's Nanmen Port offers service to the Shidongkou and Baoyang Road ports in Baoshan District and to Liuhegang in southern Jiangsu Province; Xinhai's Niupeng Harbor to Qinglonggang in Haimen; and other ports offer connections with Wusong and Chongming District's two other islands.

You can still reach Chongming by taking a ferry boat from Wusong Kou in Baoshan District. Chongming Island itself has three Yangzi River ports on its south shore serviced by ferries from Baoshan.   **South Gate Port** (Nan Men Matou) in Chengqiao Town [城桥镇] is the closest to the key sights of Jin Ao Shan, the Study Palace (Xue Gong) and Dongping Forest Park.   **Xinhe Port** (Xinhe Matou) is about the same distance from Dongping Park as Nan Men, but not as close to Golden Turtle Hill and the Study Palace. **Baozhen Port** (Baozhen Matou) is the closest one to the **Dongtan Bird Sanctuary** (Dongtan Niaolei Ziran), but is twice as far away from Jin Ao Shan and the Dongping Forest Park as the island's other two main ports.

The City God Temple (Shanghai Chenghuang Miao) [上海城隍庙]

The Shanghai City God Temple (Shanghai Chenghuang Miao) [上海城隍庙] is a Taoist Temple (Daojiao gongguan) [道教宫观] that dates from the early Ming Dynasty [明代] (1368-1644).   It is unusual for having once been dedicated to as many as three city gods: **Huo Guang** [霍光] (d.68 B.C.), **Qin Yubo** [秦裕伯] (1295-1373), and **Chen Huacheng** [陈化成] (1776-1842).

The first hall is devoted to **Huo Guang** [霍光] (d.68 B.C.), who is considered the god who saved Shanghai from being flooded by the sea.   He was an official of the **Western Han Dynasty** (Xi Han) [西汉] (206 B.C. – 8 A.D.) who was later deified in the **Three Kingdoms** (San Guo) [三国] (220-280 A.D.) period as a god who could stop the sea from flooding low lying coastal areas.   In fact, the pailou entrance gate facing the street known as Fangbang Zhong Lu [方浜中路] is inscribed "Guarding the Seas."

This first hall also used to contain a statue of **Chen Huacheng** [陈化成](1776-1842), who died at Wusong Mouth (Wusong Kou) [吴淞口] while leading the doomed resistance to the British naval invasion of Shanghai in mid-June 1842.   However, in 1985 a separate Chen Ancestral Hall (Chen Gong Ci) [陈公祠] (aka Chen Huacheng Ci) [陈化成祠] was established on the forested grounds of the Square Pagoda Park (Fangta Gongyuan) in Songjiang Town. Also, in 1992 there was yet another Chen Huacheng Memorial Hall (Chen Huacheng Jinian Guan) [陈化成纪念馆] erected at Linjiang Park (Linjiang Gongyuan) [临江公园] in Baoshan District.

Behind the **Huo Guang Hall** [霍光殿] is a long corridor known as the **Hall for Gods of the Sexagenary Cycle** (Yuanchen Dian) [元辰殿].   Both sides of this corridor are lined with glass cases containing statutes of 30 gods on either side, for a total of 60.   Each of these gods represents different birth years in the Chinese 60-year cycle calendar and is supposed to watch over people born during their years.   If you know which god protects those born in your birth year, it is good luck to kneel down and pray before the appropriate statue.

Behind the Sexagenary Cycle Hall is a small courtyard surrounded by halls on three sides. On the left is the **God of Wealth Hall** (Caishen Dian) [财神殿] containing statues of the **War God** (Guandi) [关帝] in the center, the **God of Wealth** (Caishen) [财神] on his right, and the **God of Literature** (Wenchang) [文昌] on Guandi's left.   On the right side of the courtyard is the **Goddess of Mercy Hall** (Guanyin Dian) [观音殿] containing statues of three variations of the female goddess Guanyin, including the **Goddess of the Sea** (Mazu) [妈祖].

On the North side of this courtyard stands the **City God Hall** (Chenghuang Dian) [城隍殿], which contains a statue of the city god **Qin Yubo** [秦裕伯] (1295-1373).   He is shown with a dark red face and long black beard, wearing a high black hat and red robes. The room to the left contains a statue of his wife, and that to the right has two statues of his parents.   **Qin Yubo** [秦裕伯] (1295-1373) was a Jinshi scholar who out of loyalty to the fallen Yuan Dynasty [元朝] (1279-1368) refused three invitations from the first Ming Dynsasty Emperor Hongwu [洪武] (1368-1398) to serve him at his new capital in Nanjing.   When Qin died in 1373 the Hongwu Emperor ordered the first shrine erected to Qin as Shanghai's new city god.

A City God Temple dedicated to Qin Yubo [秦裕伯] (1295-1373) was constructed during the Yongle reign [永乐](1403-1424) of the third Ming Dynasty emperor Zhu Di [朱棣] (1360-1424), and later rebuilt in 1602 during the reign of the Ming Emperor Wanli [万历] (1573-1620).   After the Pan family sold the Yu Garden (Yu Yuan) [豫园] in 1760, it became the property of the neighboring **City God Temple** (Chenghuang Miao) [城隍庙], along with the **Inner Garden** (Nei Yuan) [内园], and was opened to the public.   The present City God Hall (Chenghuang Dian) [城隍殿] was added in 1836 during the Daoguang reign [道光] (1821-1850) of the Qing Dynasty.   The Huo Guang Hall [霍光殿] was rebuilt after the Taiping Rebellion (Taiping Tianguo) [太平天国](1850-1864).   The existing halls were renovated in 1926 and again in 1994.

After Shanghai's Liberation (Jiefang) by the Red Army in May 1949, all the halls of the Shanghai City God Temple were closed to the public, but their interiors were not touched and all the religious statues inside were left intact. However, in 1956 the temple halls were reopened again.

In 1965 the Yuyuan Bazaar (Yuyuan Shangcheng) [豫园商城], (aka Yuyuan Shangchang) [豫园商场] was first opened in the area surrounding the Shanghai City God Temple.   At this time, the City God Temple's Rear Hall (Hou Dian) [后殿] facing the small lane of Anren Jie [安仁街] was occupied by a store.

During the Cultural Revolution (Wenhua Da Geming) [文化大革命] (1966-1976) the interior of the temple was completely destroyed (pohuai) [破坏], including all of the statues of gods (shenxiang) [神像] that had been housed inside it, but the basic structure and its exterior survived.   In April 1966 an official government announcement was issued for all religious activities at the Shanghai City God Temple to cease from then on.   In August 1966 the temple buildings were occupied by the Red Guards (Hongweibing) [红卫兵], who cleaned out the interior of all its religious articles, took them outside, and set them on fire, leaving no trace of them.   The empty temple buildings were turned into a warehouse for the surrounding Yuyuan Bazaar (Yuyuan Shangchang) [豫园商场] and not reopened as a temple until January 1995.

On November 28, 1994 the Yuyuan Bazaar (Yuyuan Shangcheng) [豫园商城] returned the usage rights (shiyongquan) for part of the old temple compound to the Shanghai City God Restoration Committee (Shanghai Chenghuang Miao Xiufu Weiyuanhui), including the Main Hall (Da Dian) [大殿], the Yuanchen Hall [元辰殿], the Caishen Hall [财神殿], the Cihang Hall [慈航殿], the Chenghuang Hall [城隍殿], the Queen Mother of the West Hall (Niangniang Dian) [娘娘殿], and the inner courtyard (neiyuan).

On January 26, 1995 new statues of City God Qin Yubo [秦裕伯] (1295-1373) and his wife were installed in the temple, and on January 31, 1995 the Shanghai City God Temple finally reopened to the public for religious purposes for the first time since April 1966, nearly 30 years earlier.   Once again the temple consisted of a Main Hall (Da Dian) [大殿], Yuanchen Hall (Yuanchen Dian) [元辰殿], God of Wealth Hall (Caishen Dian) [财神殿], Compassionate Ship Hall (Cihang Dian) [慈航殿], City God Hall (Chenghuang Dian) [城隍殿], and Queen Mother of the West Hall (Niangniang Dian) [娘娘殿], covering an area of 1,216 square meters.   However, restoration work was not fully completed until April 29, 1996, after which Taoist priests returned to the site and began performing religious ceremonies there again.

It's worth noting that within the greater Shanghai municipality there are also at least three other City God Temples located in Qingpu Town, Zhujiajiao Ancient Town, and Jiading Town.

Shanghai City God Temple
Address: 249 Fangbang Zhong Lu [方浜中路 249]
Phone: (021) 6386-5700
Web Site: http://www.shchm.org
Nearest Metro Station: Old West Gate (Lao Xi Men) [老西门] Station on Line 8.

The City Wall (Chengqiang) [城墙]

In 1554 the residents of the Shanghai county town (Shanghai xiancheng) [上海县城] finally succeeded in petitioning the Ming Dynasty Emperor Jiajing [嘉靖] (1521-1567) to build a town wall (chengqiang) [城墙] and moat (huchenghe) [护城河] around an area that later became known as the Nanshi district [南市区].   The Shanghai county town had never had a defensive wall before this time, and the fortifications gave it added security against the repeated lootings it had suffered from Japanese pirates (woko) [倭寇].   However, this wall was smaller in size compared with those around other Chinese cities of the day.   It was roughly ten meters in height and five kilometers in circumference.   A city map from the Tongzhi [同治] reign (1861-1875) of the Qing Dynasty shows that the town wall then had seven land gates (chengmen) [城门], four water gates (shuiguan) [水关], and four watch towers (genglou) [更楼].   One land gate faced North (Bei Men), one to the Northwest (Xiao Bei Men) [小北门], one to the West, the Old West Gate (Lao Xi Men) [老西门], one to the East (Dong Men) [东门], one to the Southeast (Xiao Dong Men) [小东门], and two to the South (Nan Men and Xiao Nan Men).   The four watch towers all faced to the North, Northwest and Northeast, giving the impression that attacks from this direction were considered more likely than from anywhere else.

The purpose of the four water gates was to allow the canalized streams (bang) [浜] flowing through the old town to pass through the wall as they entered and exited the town.   One water gate faced East, two to the Southeast, and one to the West.   The **Zhaojiabang** [肇嘉浜] canal which flowed from the Xujiahui [徐家汇] neighborhood to the Huangpu River entered the old town through the West Water Gate (Xi Shui Men) and exited out the Southeast Water Gate (Dongnan Shui Men).   The street **Fuxing Dong Lu** [复兴东路] now takes the exact same route as that formerly followed by the Zhaojiabang canal through the old walled town.   A second main canal, the **Fangbang** [方浜], also ran from West to East, and exited out of the walled town through the East Water Gate (Dong Shui Men).   The route of this canal later became what is now **Fangbang Zhong Lu** [方浜中路] and **Fangbang Dong Lu** [方浜东路], one of the main East-West roads across the old town.

Between 1912 and 1914 Shanghai's city walls were all torn down, and the moat was filled in, although the circular pattern of the former wall and surrounding moat can still be seen in the location of Renmin Lu and Zhonghua Lu, which were built in their place.   None of the water gates or watch towers have survived.   Of the original seven land gates, only the **Small North Gate** (Xiao Bei Men) [小北门] still stands next to the **War God Temple** (Guan Di Miao) [关帝庙], aka Dajing Ge Pavilion [大境阁] on Dajing Lu [大境路], despite the fact that some neighborhoods are still known by the names of city gates that no longer exist, such as Loa Xi Men, Lao Dong Men, etc.

Inside the **War God Temple** (Guan Di Miao) [关帝庙] at 259 Dajing Lu [大境路], intersection with Renmin Lu, there used to be a **City Wall Museum** (Chengqiang Bowuguan) with old photographs and a scale model replica of Shanghai's city wall and the entire Nanshi District as it looked in Qing Dynasty times.   Outside the **War God Temple** (Guan Di Miao) [关帝庙], a row of shops along Renmin Lu were torn down in 2004 to reveal an unobstructed view of the last remaining original section of city wall, upon which the temple stands.

Confucius Temple (Wen Miao) [文庙]

Devoted to the worship of Confucius (Kong Fuzi) [孔夫子] (551-479 B.C.), the Shanghai Confucius Temple (Wen Miao) [文庙] is located on Confucius Temple Road (Wen Miao Lu) [文庙路] one block from Zhonghua Lu in the Old West Gate (Lao Xi Men) [老西门] area.

Although Shanghai County had first established a Confucius Temple (Shanghai Xianxue Wen Miao) [上海县学文庙] as early as 1294, during the Yuan Dynasty, it was not until during the 5th year of the Xianfeng reign [咸丰] (1850-1861) of the Qing Dynasty in 1855 that a temple was built here at this present location, which was then near the West Gate in the county town's surrounding protective wall.   Chinese sources say the temple was "moved" here (qianyi) [迁移], after the previous one was destroyed during the rebellion by the Small Swords Society (Xiaodaohui) [小刀会], which is somewhat misleading, since brand new structures were built at this new location.   After the 1911 Revolution, the temple was repaired in 1914, and continued to serve its original purpose.   However, from 1927 to March 1931 the site was rebuilt as a public park known as **Confucius Temple Park** (Wenmiao Gongyuan) [文庙公园].   After that, its administration was handed over to the Shanghai Municipal Education Bureau (Shi Jiaoyu Ju) [上海市教育局].   In December 1931 the temple was renamed the **Shanghai People's Education Hall** (Shanghai Minzhong Jiaoyu Guan) [上海市民众教育馆].   In June 1932 the Zunjing Pavilion (Zunjing Ge) [尊经阁] was converted into the first **Shanghai Municipal Library** (Shanghai Shi Shili Tushuguan) [上海市市立图书馆].   In May 1949 it was occupied by the Red Army and turned into the **Shanghai Municipal People's Cultural Hall** (Shanghai Shi Renmin Wenhua Guan) [上海市人民文化馆].   All of the previous historic structures were completely demolished and torn down (chaichu) [拆除] during the Cultural Revolution (1966-1976). The present buildings were all reconstructed completely from scratch, from the ground up, during a major reconstruction project that started in April 1997 and was completed in September 1999.   It was not until the year 2002 that the site was listed as a city-level protected cultural relic.

The one surviving historic structure is the **Kuixing Ge** [魁星阁], a heavily restored three-story wooden tower in the southeast corner of what was previously the Confucian Academy (Shuyuan) [书院], where aspiring scholars studied to pass the imperial examinations.

The temple is most popular on Sundays when a traditional weekly used book fair (jiushu jiaoyi shichang) [旧书交易市场] is held on its grounds.   This tradition dates back to 1931 when the first Municipal Library of Greater Shanghai was founded here.   The book fair lapsed during the Cultural Revolution (1966-1976), but was revived again in 1986.

The walled compound occupies an area of 17 mu and is divided up into three parallel rows of gates and halls.

The western axis is that devoted to the worship of Confucius (Kong Fuzi) [孔夫子] (551-479 B.C.), and begins with a three-portal, stone gate called the **Lingxing Gate** (Lingxing Men) [棂星门], which leads to a second wooden gate known as the **Da Cheng Gate** (Da Cheng Men) [大成门].   Unlike most Confucius Temple's, including the one in Jiading Town, there is no half-moon pool (Pan Chi) [泮池] crossed by three stone foot bridges in between these two gates, although according to a map of the site from the Tongzhi reign [同治] (1861-1875), there used to be.   Following this is a courtyard containing the **Da Cheng Bell** (Da Cheng Zhong) [大成钟], and a statue of Confucius (Kong Fuzi) [孔夫子] (551-479 B.C.), before you reach the main hall known as the Da Cheng Dian [大成殿].   The **Da Cheng Hall** (Da Cheng Dian) [大成殿] is where traditionally sacrifices to Confucius would be held twice a year in the spring and autumn.   Along the eastern and western sides of the axis are stele corridors containing inscribed stone tablets.   Behind the Da Cheng Hall (Da Cheng Dian) [大成殿] is an ancestral temple called the **Chongsheng Ci** [崇圣祠].

The middle and eastern axis contain halls that would have been part of the **Confucian Academy** (Shu Yuan) [书院] devoted to study and preparation for the imperial civil service exams.

The middle axis begins with the **Study Gate** (Xue Men) [学门], followed by the **Ceremony Gate** (Yi Men) [仪门], then the **Minglun Hall** (Minglun Tang) [明伦堂], followed by the **Zunjing Pavilion** (Zunjing Ge) [尊经阁].

The eastern axis begins with the three-story **Kuixing Pavilion** (Kuixing Ge) [魁星阁], then the **Sky Cloud Reflecting Pool** (Tianguang Yunying Chi) [天光云影池], on the left side of which is the **Listening to the Rain Hall**, straight ahead is the **Confucius Studies Bueau** (Ruxue Shi) [儒学署] facing the square pool of water, and finally the Used Book Market (jiushu jiaoyi shichang) [旧书交易市场].

The site is bordered by four roads, on the south by Confucius Temple Road (Wen Miao Lu) [文庙路]; on the east by Study Palace Lane (Xue Gong Jie) [学宫街]; on the north by Flower Dream Lane (Menghua Jie) [梦花街]; and on the west by Old Road Front Lane (Lao Dao Qian Jie) [老道前街].

It's worth noting that there is a separate Confucius Temple (Kong Miao) [孔庙] located in Jiading Town, which is a much better preserved, genuine historic relic than this one in downtown Shanghai.   There is also a former Confucian academy known as the Study Palace (Xue Gong) [学宫] on Chongming Island.   Other than those three sites, no other Confucius Temples have survived within the boundaries of the Shanghai Municipality.

Address: 215 Wen Miao Lu [文庙路 215 号], former Nanshi District, now Huangpu District [黄浦区].
Phone: (021) 6377-1815, Fax: (021) 6377-9101
Web Site: http://www.confuciantemple.com E-mail: wenmiaosh@163.com
Nearest Metro Station: Old West Gate (Lao Xi Men) [老西门] Station on Line 8.

D

Dajing Pavilion (Dajing Ge) [大境阁]

The Dajing Pavilion (Dajing Ge) [大境阁] is also known as the **War God Temple** (Guan Di Miao) [关帝庙].   It stands on top of the last remaining section of the Shanghai county town's red brick Ming Dynasty city wall.   Between 1912 and 1914 Shanghai's city walls were all torn down, but this one section was preserved because this temple stood on top of it.

By walking around the perimeter outside, and looking up at the roof tops one can see that the eaves are decorated with many intricate statues of characters from Chinese mythology, including the Fulushou [福, 禄, 寿] and the Eight Immortals (Baxian)[八仙].   A row of shops along Renmin Lu [人民路] were torn down in 2004 to reveal an unobstructed view.

Beside the entrance a new stone tablet describes it as the "Old City Wall of Shanghai and Dajing Taoist Temple" (Shanghai Gu Chengqiang he Dajing Daoguan) [上海古城墙和大境道观].   The date of May 4, 1984 records when the site was designated a municipal protected cultural relic, but is not the date the stone tablet was erected.

Passing through the entrance, to your left there is a small arched doorway in the base of the brick wall.   Straight ahead is a flight of steps going up a sloping diagonal ramp to the terrace on top of the wall.   The outdoor terrace is surrounded on three sides by parapet and in the center stands a wooden flag pole supported by two stone blocks.   Look closely at these two stone blocks and you will see that they are covered with Chinese inscriptions on all sides.   One inscription is dated "Minguo Liu Nian" [民国六年], meaning the sixth year of the Republic of China, which would have been 1917.

Entering the pavilion and walking down a dark, narrow passageway leads you into the main room, which a few years ago used to house a small City Wall Museum (Chengqiang Bowuguan) with old photographs and a scale model replica of Shanghai's city wall, but is now used as a War God Temple (Guan Di Miao) [关帝庙].   There aren't any Taoist priests nor any realy worship going on here, but the five statues of various deities from Chinese mythology are quite fascinating.   In the center sits a giant statue of Guan Yu [关羽], a general of the Three Kingdoms (San Guo) [三国] (220-280) period who was later deified as the God of War in the Ming Dynasty. He is depicted with a bright red face and long black beard. Flanking him on either side are two standing warrior disciples.   To the right of Guanyu is a statue of the God of Longevity (Shouxing) [寿星].   To the left of Guanyu is another statue of a man with black face who is possibly supposed to be his sworn brother Zhang Fei [张飞].

Standing beside the Dajing Pavilion (Dajing Ge) [大境阁] on Dajing Lu [大境路] is a stone gate covered on all sides with Chinese inscriptions.   The inscription on the main horizontal beam at the top has two characters that read Dajing [大境], but local residents have always referred to this as the Small North Gate (Xiao Bei Men) [小北门].   When I first visited this site local residents used to hang their wet laundry on it to dry out in the sunshine, but now it is kept safely locked up inside its own fenced in enclosure, which unfortunately makes it hard to see the inscriptions on the back side.

Address: 259 Dajing Lu [大境路 259], intersection with Renmin Lu [人民路].

Duolun Lu Culture Street [多伦路]

Duolun Lu [多伦路] is a half-kilometer long, L-shaped street which oddly enough connects with Sichuan North Road (Sichuan Bei Lu) [四川北路] at both ends.   It is about one city block south of **Lu Xun Park** (Lu Xun Gongyuan) [鲁迅公园], which was formerly Hongkou Park [虹口公园].   From 1911 to 1943, when it was part of the International Settlement, it was previously known as Darroch Road.   In 1998 the road was converted into a pedestrian only (buxing jie) [步行街] "culture and famous people street" (wenhua mingren jie) [文化名人街] celebrating the role the Hongkou neighborhood played as home to **Lu Xun** [鲁迅] (1881-1936) and other left-wing intellectuals during the 1920s and 1930s.

The North entrance to the street is now marked by a new brick and masonry gate over the red brick paved road.   Beside the North entrance gate to Duolun Lu is a row of bronze plaques commemorating the Chinese writers **Ding Ling** [丁玲] (1904-1986), **Mao Dun** [茅盾] (1896-1981), **Guo Moruo** [郭沫若] (1892-1978), and **Lu Xun** [鲁迅] (1881-1936), as well as the Japanese bookseller who sold them imported publications, Uchiyama Kanzo (1885-1959).   Further down the street one can visit the site where the **League of Leftist Writers** (Zhongguo Zuoyi Zuojia Lianmeng) [中国左翼作家联盟] was founded on March 2, 1930 inside a French mansion built in 1924 on a small side lane branching off of the main road at Duolun Lu, Lane #201, Building #2 (Duolun Lu 201 long, 2 hao) [多伦路 201 弄 2 号].

In addition to sights related to China's writers of the 1920s and 1930s, there are the former homes of at least three Guomindang leaders, **H.H. Kung** (Kong Xiangxi) [孔祥熙] (1880-1967), **Bai Chongxi** [白崇禧] (1893-1966), and **Tang Enbo** [汤恩伯] (1899-1954), the last Guomindang military commander of Shanghai before it fell to the Communists in May 1949.

The Kong Residence (Kong Guju) [孔故居] at #250 Duolun Lu [多伦路 250 号] was built in 1924 by **H.H. Kung** (Kong Xiangxi) [孔祥熙] (1880-1967), the sometime Finance Minister of the Guomindang regime and husband of **Song Ailing** [宋蔼龄] (1889-1973).   The two-story white stone structure bears an incredible resemblance to an Islamic mosque, with its rows of arabesque arcades and columns, both inside and out.

The **Bai Residence** (Bai Guju) [白故居] at #210 Duolun Lu [多伦路 210 号] was built by **Bai Chongxi** [白崇禧] (1893-1966), the Guangxi warlord who was one of the key military commanders of the Guomindang regime between 1927 and 1949.   His Shanghai house has four massive round white Greco-Roman columns which stand two stories high.

The Tang Residence (Tang Guju) [汤故居] of Guomindang General **Tang Enbo** [汤恩伯] (1899-1954) built in 1920 is located at Sichuan North Road, #2023 Lane, Anzhi Fang #35 [四川北路, 2023 弄, 志安坊 35 号].

The former **China Art University** student dormitory (Zhonghua Yishu Daxue sushe jiuzhi) [中华艺术大学宿舍旧址] built in 1920 still stands at # 145 Duolun Lu [多伦路 145 号].   Since 1989 it has served as a memorial hall dedicated to the League of Leftist Writers (Zuolian Jinianguan) [左联纪念馆].

Beside the **Old Film Café** (Lao Dianying Kafei Guan) [老电影咖啡馆] at #123 Duolun Lu [多伦路 123 号] stands the **Xi Shi Bell Tower** (Xi Shi Zhong Lou) [夕拾钟搂] at 119 Duolun Lu [多伦路 119 号].   The 18 meter high, six story, red brick tower's current name comes from the title of a book of collected essays by Lu Xun [鲁迅] (1881-1936) entitled "Dawn Blossoms Plucked at Dusk" (Zhaohua Xishi) [朝花夕拾], but it looks as if it may have once belonged to a church, although its exact history remains a mystery.

The **Hongde Protestant Church** (Hongde Tang Jidu Jiaotang) [鸿德堂基督教堂] at #59 Duolun Lu [多伦路 59 号] was first built in 1928, was originally called Fitch Memorial Church after George F. Fitch (1845-1923), stopped holding religious services in 1966 at the start of the Cultural Revolution, was repaired in 1990, then resumed holding weekly church services again in August 1992, and was designated a municipal protected building in March 1994. Its amazing bell tower (zhong lou) [钟楼] and fascinating architecture make it a perfect example of the Chinese renaissance neo-classical style of architecture common to the Guomindang era in which modern elements of style then common in the West were combined with Ming dynasty elements.   The result in this case is a red brick church with bright red round pillars and a roof featuring enormous upturned eaves.   The main hall (libai tang) [礼拜堂] can hold from 500 to 1,000 people.

Location: Duolun Road (Duolun Lu) [多伦路] Hongkou District (Hongkou Qu) [虹口区]
Nearest Metro Station: Hongkou Stadium Station on Metro Lines 3 and 8.

Du Yuesheng's Da Gong Guan [杜月笙大公馆]

The East Lake Hotel (Donghu Binguan) [东湖宾馆] occupies a total of seven buildings in several historic gated compounds on both sides of Donghu Lu [东湖路], near its intersection with Huaihai Middle Road (Huaihai Zhong Lu), in an area that was formerly part of the French Concession.   Donghu Lu was built in 1902 and originally named Route Doumer.   It runs for a short distance of only 500 meters from Huahai Middle Road (Huaihai Zhong Lu) to Changle Road (Changle Lu), crossing Xinle Road (Xinle Lu) on the way.

The five-story main building located at #70 Donghu Lu [东湖路 70 号] was built in 1934 as two connected villsa and is reputed to have once belonged to infamous crime boss Du Yuesheng [杜月笙] (1888-1951).   A commemorative plaque on the wall outside the front entrance claims that this was Du's residence.   However, the same claim is made another much more interesting old house located across the street.   Du abandoned the building in August 1937 when the Japanese attacked Shanghai and he fled first to Hong Kong and then to Chongqing.   During the Japanese occupation (1941-1945) the house belonged to the Finance Minister in the Wang Jingwei puppet regime.   During the post-war period from 1945 to 1949 it was used first as offices of the Guomindang Bureau of Investigation and Statistics run by secret police chief Dai Li, and later as the U.S. Conslate.   This building has belonged to the Donghu Hotel since 1986 and is officially known as Buildings 1 and 2.   The hotel restaurant still claims to serve Du's favorite dishes made from his chef's secret recipes.

Across the street, located at #7 Donghu Lu [东湖路 7 号], next door to a comparatively newer wing of the East Lake Hotel (Donghu Binguan) [东湖宾馆], is a hidden gateway guarded by a pair of enormous iron gates leading into a triangular walled garden containing a historic house known as the Da Gong Guan [大公馆] mansion, which the current management claims formerly belonged to infamous crime boss Du Yuesheng [杜月笙] (1888-1951), among a host of other celebrities.   Thus, it is also sometimes known as Du Gong Guan [杜公馆], a name which is still etched into the glass doors of the side entrance leading in from the covered carport.

Until May 2002, this historic mansion had never been opened to the public during its nearly 100 year history, and its existence had remained a well-kept secret hidden behind its surrounding garden's high walls.   Only then did the local government, which continues to own it, open it up to outsiders.   A three-story French Renaissance Baroque style mansion surrounded by a triangular garden originally built by Jewish merchant **Ray Joseph** in 1925, this former residence has during its lifetime sequentially hosted a Chinese gangster, the Guomindang secret police chief, a famous Chinese movie star, diplomatic representatives of the Soviet Union, members of the infamous Gang of Four political clique, and even an American president.

In 1934 the houses that now belong to the Donghu Hotel were purchased by Green Gang crime boss **Du Yuesheng** [杜月笙] (1888-1951).   According to one story about how he got the money to purchase both the house at #7 Donghu Road and the even larger one at #70 Donghu Road, Guomindang central government Minister of Finance Song Ziwen appointed Du Yuesheng to run a national aviation lottery (hangkong jiangquan) [航空奖券] in order to raise funds to finance the purchase of airplanes for China's new airforce.   Many people purchased these lottery tickets (caipiao) [彩票] out of patriotism, but ultimately Du was the one who "won the lottery," when the holder of the winning ticket mysteriously gave Du most or possibly even all of the money.

However, Du didn't have long to enjoy his mansions as he fled Shanghai for the safety of Hong Kong in November 1937, after the Japanese had attacked the Chinese administered parts of Shanghai in August 1937, and later fled Hong Kong for the safety of Chonqing in December 1937 after Hong Kong was also captured by the Japanese.

After the August 1945 Victory over Japan, in 1946 Du gave the house at #7 Donghu Road as a gift to Guomindang secret police chief **Dai Li** [戴笠] (1897-1946), whose real name was Dai Chunfeng [戴春风], in the hopes that Dai would repay the favor by helping Du become Mayor of Shanghai, a dream which was shattered when Dai died in a plane crash soon afterward.   Before his death, Dai apparently gave the house to movie star **Hu Die** [胡蝶] (1908-1989), aka "Butterfly Wu," but whose real name was Hu Ruihua [胡瑞华], in an attempt to woo her as his mistress, even though she was already happily married.   After 1949 the house was taken over by the new city government.   From May 1952 to December 1962 it was occupied by representatives of the Soviet Union's cultural affairs and commercial affairs bureaus.   Shanghai's first post-Liberation Mayor **Chen Yi** also reportedly hosted VIP visitors here.   Later, during the Cultural Revolution it was occupied by **Zhang Chunqiao** [张春桥] (1917-2005), Shanghai Revolutionary Committee Chairman (Shanghai Shi Geming Weiyuanhui Zhuren) [上海市革命委员会主任] February 24, 1967-October 6, 1976, member of the Gang of Four (Siren Bang) [四人帮].   In 1972 U.S. President **Richard M. Nixon** met Chinese Prime Minister **Zhou Enlai** [周恩来](1898-1976) here for the negotiations (tanpan) that resulted in the 1972 "Shanghai Communique," although the agreement was not signed here.   Since the 1990s, it has been one of the buildings under the management of the East Lake Hotel (Donghu Binguan) [东湖宾馆], which uses the date 1934 in their logo, commemorating both the year that Du Yuesheng purchased the historic mansion at # 7 Donghu Lu and the year the main building was constructed at #70 Donghu Lu.

In May 2002 this house was opened to the public for the first time as **The 7 Restaurant and Bar** (Qi Hao Canting yu Jiuba) [七号餐厅与酒巴], named after its street address, #7 East Lake Road (Donghu Lu Qi Hao) [东湖路七号].   It featured an English language menu, and a live jazz band that performed nightly, but in between their performances you had to listen to canned recordings of the Bee Gees performing all their 1970s disco hits.   At that time I was able to make several visits to it and explore the inside.   However, when I revisited in October 2018, I discovered that the restaurant and bar had been closed, and instead a company had occupied the house and was using it as its office space.   The main entrance doors were locked, and a watchman who answered the door told me it is no longer open to the public, which is a real shame.   Oddly enough, the Donghu Hotel still prominently features photos of this old house in all of their marketing materials, including brochures, pamphlets, booklets, etc., even though it is no longer open to the public.   You can walk around the outside and look at it but you can no longer go inside to see the amazingly well-preserved historic interior.

What follows is a description of the interior based on previous visits in 2002 and 2003. Picture windows in the bar and dining rooms face the garden.   The main side entrance featured a covered carport driveway with a hanging chandelier.   Beside the entrance is a commemorative plaque claiming that the house was built in 1925.   Above the front door was a wooden sign with three Chinese characters reading, "Da Gong Guan" [大公馆]. This was the name given to the house by Du Yuesheng [杜月笙] (1888-1951), and it is supposedly the original name board which he had placed there.   The restaurant's current management is referring to it by this name.   Unfortunately, since the restatuarnt closed this sign has been removed.

Stepping inside, the cloakroom had an antique wooden coat rack fastened to the wall where many famous hats may have hung.   The lobby was surrounded by walls covered in polished wood paneling, ceilings decorated with plaster ornamentation, and hanging chandeliers.   The various bars, sitting rooms and dining rooms seemed to be furnished with the original wooden tables and chairs, certainly they are genuine antiques at least.   The walls were decorated with a host of antique artworks, including one work of calligraphy said to have been written by Li Hongzhang [李鸿章] (1823-1901). Wood-burning fireplaces were found in every room, and even in the hallways.   Colorful stained-glass windows decorated the stairwells.

Overall, this house had been one of the best preserved of any in Shanghai, as it was not damaged during either the Japanese occupation (1941-1945) nor the Cultural Revolution (1966-1976), and until recently had not suffered the type of ill conceived restoration that has become all too common during Shanghai's last two decades of economic prosperity in which historic buildings have had their original interiors completely gutted.   Unfortunately, after reopening as a restaurant and bar in 2002, the exterior of the building was altered on the side facing the great lawn, an extra layer of steel and glass like you would find in a green house was added to the ground floor to create a sunroom for patrons to sit at tables. The circular driveway leading to the house used to pass through the garden and exit out the walled enclosure through either of two gates, one on Donghu Lu, the other on Huaihai Middle Road (Huaihai Zhong Lu), but the later gate has been dismantled, leaving only the four gate posts, as the city reclaimed a slice of land along the road to create a public park.

It is said that nearly every business negotiation held in this house has been a success.   In 1927 the American businessman Sterling Fessenden, then Chairman of the Shanghai Municipal Council, visited Du's house and agreed to support the crime boss' Green Gang in their suppression of the local Communists.   In 1972 the Shanghai Communiqué was successfully negotiated here between U.S. President Richard M. Nixon and Chinese Prime Minister Zhou Enlai [周恩来](1898-1976), although it was actually signed in the Grand Hall of the Jinjiang Hotel on Moaming Nan Lu.

Some people claim that either this house at #7 Donghu Lu or the larger building across the street at #70 Donghu Lu was Du Yuesheng's main former residence (guju) [故居].   However, it should be noted that Du owned many properties in Shanghai.   Several historians claim that Du's real residence (zhenzheng juzhu) [真正居住] where he and his four wives actually lived was a three-story stone gate house (shikumen) [石库门] built in 1926 at present day 182 Ninghai Xi Lu [宁海西路 182 号], what was then known as 180 Rue Wagner in the French Concession, but which has since been torn down.   This housee was reportedly a gift given to Du by his partner in crime Huang Jinrong [黄金荣](1868-1953).   In 1951 the house was occupied by the East China Beijing Opera Group (Huadong Jingju Tuan) [华东京剧团].   In 1973 it was occupied by a company.   In the mid 1990s, the house was dismantled to make room for construction of the Yanan Zhong Lu Elevated Expressway (gaojia) [高架].　Some parts of the house were purchased by a Canadian Chinese collector who stored them in a warehouse in Tongli, Jiangsu.

Another competitor for the claim of Du's residence is **The Mansion Hotel** (Shanghai Shouxi Gongguan) [上海首席公馆] building at 82 Xinle Lu [新乐路 87 号], which also calls itself Du's Gong Guan, but this was actually offices of his Sanxin Company [三鑫公司].

Address:　#70 East Lake Road (Donghu Lu) [东湖路 70 号], and #7 East Lake Road (Donghu Lu Qi Hao) [东湖路七号].

F

Fazang Jiang Buddhist Temple (Fazang Jiang Si) [法藏讲寺]

This Buddhist temple was first built in 1923, and then later closed during the 1966-1976 Cultural Revolution, when it was turned into a factory.   It did not reopen until the year 2000. It has been beautifully restored with new statues and ornaments covered in gold leaf.

This is now a very active temple always full of worshippers practicing elaborate ceremonies on weekends.   A large community of resident monks lives here.   The worshippers and monks are friendly and welcome the chance to explain their faith to visitors.

They belong to the Pure Land Sect (Jingtu Zong) which worships the Amitabha Buddha (Emituofo).   This sect has an almost Christian belief in an after-death rebirth in a Western Land or Pure Land similar to heaven.   The Jingtu Sect was founded by the monk Hui Yuan in 384 A.D. at East Grove Buddhist Temple (Donglin Si) on Mount Lushan in Jiangxi province.   The temple takes its name from the story told in the Amitabha Scripture (Emituo Jing) of how Amitabha Budda (Emituofo) began life as the Buddhist monk Dharmakara (Fazang), was later elevated to the status of a bodhisattva, and then one day achieved total enlightenment and was transformed into a Buddha.   During his stage as a bodhisattva Fazang made 48 vows which are still celebrated in songs sung by the worshippers at Fazang Jiang Si today.

Fazang Jiang Si is easy walking distance from Huaihai Middle Road (Huaihai Zhong Lu) [淮海中路] and the Huangpi Nan Lu metro station.   You can see its bright yellow-painted walls from a long distance away.

Address: The intersection of Ji'an Lu and Fuxing Lu.
Phone: (021) 6311-4971

159

The French Club (Faguo Zonghui) [法国总会]

Although this is now the modern high-rise Okura Garden Hotel (Huayuan Fandian) [花园饭店], the first two floors over the main lobby and the surrounding spacious gardens are the surviving remnants of the former French Club, aka Cercle Sportif Francais (Faguo Zonghui) [法国总会], built on this same site in 1926.

In 1903 this location was the site of the German Club (Deguo Julebu) [德国俱乐部].   In 1914 the territory of the French Concession was expanded for the third time to include this area.   After the Germans defeat in the First World War in 1918, the French seized control of the former German Club.   After protests from the Chinese government, the French purchased the large plot of land laying between Shanxi Nan Lu and Changle Lu.

There had previously been a French Club located on Route Vallon, present-day Nanchang Lu [南昌路], near the French Park that is now known as Fuxing Park, but in 1924 construction of a new French Club began on the site of the former German Club and was completed two years later in 1926.   The old French Club on Nanchang Lu became the French High School "College Municipal Francais," which still stands but is now known as the Science Hall (Kexue Huitang) [科学会堂].

The new French Club featured a restaurant, multiple banquet rooms of various sizes, indoor swimming pool, and bowling alley on the first floor, with the Grand Ballroom on the second floor.   A grand staircase led from the first to the second floor. The oval-shaped Grand Ballroom was famous for its sprung wooden floor that would bounce up and down beneath the dancers' feet, and the stained glass domed ceiling overhead that was shaped like the bottom of a boat.   The walls were decorated with bas relief sculptures of naked bathing girls. Chandeliers imported from Vienna, Austria hung from the ceilings.   There were two pavilions in the garden, where tennis matches and picnics were held.   The club was a popular venue for garden parties in the summer and tea parties in the winter.

During the Second World War, the French Club was occupied by the Japanese military, but after the war ended in August 1945 it became the U.S. Navy Club (Meiguo Haijun Julebu) [美国海军俱乐部].   The U.S. military added a second outdoor swimming pool covered with a sliding roof that was later used on a regular basis by Mao Zedong, who insisted that the roof be sealed shut for safety.

After the May 1949 Liberation of Shanghai by the Communists, all of the foreign recreational clubs were gradually forced to shut down, but the French Club was one of the last to remain open.   On December 31, 1953 Shanghai's remaining foreign community held their final New Year's Eve party here, after which it was immediately taken over by the Shanghai city government the next day, January 1, 1954.

Officially, the former French Club became known as the Shanghai Municipal Culture Club (Shanghai Shi Wenhua Julebu) [市文化俱乐部] in 1954, and came under the management of the nearby Jinjiang Hotel (Jinjiang Fandian) [锦江饭店] across the street in 1960. However, unofficially, from 1954 to 1976 it was apparently used as a private playground for **Mao Zedong** and his inner circle of Communist party leaders, who dug a network of bomb shelters underneath the garden in order to be safe from an expected American air raid. There were underground pedestrian tunnels connecting the former French Club with the

Jinjiang Hotel (Jinjiang Fandian) [锦江饭店], the former Grosvenor House built by Victor Sassoon in 1934, across the street, so that Mao could stay at the Grosvenor House and visit the French Club to go swimming in its pool and hang out there without having to walk across the street.   Mao Zedong met with British Field Marshal Bernard L. Montgomery here at the former French Club on May 27, 1960, in a meeting immortalized by a photo showing them shaking hands.

In 1980 the building was converted back into a recreational club for the foreign businessmen who were starting to return to Shanghai in small numbers.   Under the name the **Jinjiang Club** (Jinjiang Julebu) [锦江俱乐部], it continued to serve this purpose until 1985, when the site was purchased by the Japanese owners of the site's current occupant, the five-star high rise **Okura Garden Hotel** (Huayuan Fandian) [花园饭店], which was completed in 1989 and opened for business on March 20, 1990.

The new main building is a 33 story cement high rise structure standing behind the two-story former French Club building, which has largely been preserved but repurposed as the hotel's front entrance and lobby.   The French Club's former ballroom on the second floor is now the hotel's banquet hall, which still features some of the original decorations, including the oval-shaped stained glass ceiling overhead, and the nude bas relief sculptures of the bathing girls, which had been covered up with wooden boards to hide them from destruction during the Cultural Revolution.   The former bowling alley on the first floor has been turned into the Rose Coffee Shop, but you can still see the original pillars that hold up the floor of the ballroom above.   Both the original indoor swimming pool and the outdoor swimming pool added by the U.S. military, have been removed and replaced with a new swimming pool in another new annex building, built to resemble the previous ones with a sliding glass roof. The gazebo that now stands in the garden, with its dome and Greco-Roman columns, is actually a copy that was erected in 1959 to replace the previous two pavilions that were removed at some point after 1949.   Oddly, the former French Club was not included on the city's list of historic buildings until 1994, long after the whole site had already been rebuilt. The hotel occupies 3.7 hectares of land, of which the garden covers 2.8 hectares, taking up one whole city block of prime downtown real estate in between Huahai Zhong Lu, Maoming Nan Lu, Changle Lu, and Shanxi Nan Lu.

Address: 58 Maoming Nan Lu [茂名南路 58 号], near Huaihai Middle Road (Huaihai Zhong Lu), Huangpu District

The French Concession (Shanghai Fa Zujie) [上海法租界]

The French Concession started in the east with a very narrow mouth along the Huangpu River, wedged in between the International Settlement to the North and the Chinese walled city of Nanshi district to the South.   This bottleneck only had three streets, Avenue Edward VII (Yanan Dong Lu), Rue Du Consulat (Jingling Dong Lu) and Avenue des Deux Republiques (Minguo Lu/Renmin Lu).   **Rue Du Consulat** (Jingling Dong Lu) was named after the French Consulate, which stood at the intersection of this street and the Bund.   It still has its distinct buildings, which hang over the covered sidewalks running past them. **Avenue Edward VII** (Yanan Dong Lu) marked the northern boundary with the International Settlement.   It was shaped like a snake because it followed the course of the former **Yangjing Bang Creek**, which was filled in when the road was built.   **Avenue des Deux Republiques** (Minguo Lu/Renmin Lu) marked the concession's southern boundary and wound around the circular pattern of the Nanshi town wall.   A narrow stretch of French territory known as the **French Bund** or **Quai de France** did extend along the Huangpu River as far south as **Fangbang Dong Lu**, but this was less than one block wide due to the existence of the Chinese walled city directly behind it.   The **Gutzlaff Signal Tower**, which was used to communicate with the Xujiahui Observatory and pass on weather reports to the ships at sea, originally stood on the French Bund before it was moved to its present location that makes it appear as if it had been located within the International Settlement.

Once past the obstacle of the Nanshi district's walled town, the French Concession at its peak expanded much more widely to the south, west and north.   **Avenue Edward VII** (Yanan Zhong Lu) continued to be the border with the International Settlement, but the way the road veered far to the North at a diagonal angle gave the French room to expand in this direction as well.   Where Avenue Edward VII (Yanan Zhong Lu) became the **Great Western Road** (Yanan Xi Lu), the French Concession's western boundary followed **Avenue Haig** (Huashan Lu) to the Xujiahui [徐家汇] area.   The furthest western limits of French control extended almost as far as the French Roman Catholic community at **Xujiahui** [徐家汇], which technically lay just outside of its boundaries.   The southern limit was **Route de Zikawei** (Xujiahui Lu and Zhaojiabang Lu), which followed the course of **Siccawei Creek**, then large enough for sailing houseboats all the way out to Sheshan Hill in Songjiang District. Veering north from Siccawei Creek and following the winding **Rue de Captaine Rabier**, part of which lay on what is now a southern section of Xizang Nan Lu, the French Concession's southern border connected with the western side of the Chinese walled city at the intersection of **Rue Millot** (Fangbang Xi Lu) on the French side and **Fangbang Zhong Lu** on the Chinese side.

The French used a similar road building strategy as the British and Americans in order to expand their concession's boundaries.   The French started out with just 3,800 feet of waterfront along the Huangpu River.   However, in **1861** they won a small extension of 23 acres of riverfront along the Huangpu, south of their original area and east of the Chinese walled town.   On January 27, **1900** the French received a larger extension of 171 acres to the west of their original Concession.   Finally, on July 31, **1914** the French received their third and last extension of 2,167 acres of new territory to the west of their existing concession.   This extension of 1914 took their western boundary all the way to **Avenue Haig** (Huashan Lu) and the edge of **Xujiahui** [徐家汇].   At its height after 1914 the French Concession covered 3.9 square miles of present day downtown Shanghai.

The French concession was largely a residential area of leafy, tree-lined suburbs dotted with impressive mansions, whereas the International Settlement was more commercial and industrial.   As a result, most of the surviving historic architecture in this area consists of villas, mansions, apartment buildings, churches, and residential houses.   Its main street was **Avenue Joffre** (Huaihai Lu), followed by Hengshan Lu in second place of importance.

Key surviving historical sights of the former French Concession include the former French Club, French Park, French High School, French Municipal Council Director's home, and Aurora University.

French Municipal Council Director's Home

This three-story French Renaissance style mansion was built in 1905 on Fenyang Lu, the former Route Pichon of the French Concession, and in some ways resembles the White House in Washington, D.C.   It was originally the home of the French Municipal Council's Director of la Compagnie Francais des Tramways et d'Eclairage Electriques de Shanghai. At the end of the Sino-Japanese War in 1945 the French Concession was dissolved, and the house was handed over by the Guomindang government to the **United Nations World Health Organization**.   Immediately after the Communist occupation of Shanghai in May 1949, the mansion became the residence of Shanghai'a first Communist mayor, **Chen Yi** (1901-1972), who had led the Red Army's capture of the city.   When Chen moved out of the house in 1954 to take up his new post as Vice-Premier in Beijing, the house became the offices of the **Sino-Soviet Friendship Organization**.   Ever since the Sino-Soviet split of 1960, the mansion has been the offices of the **Shanghai Arts & Crafts Research Institute**, which despite recently being renamed the friendlier sounding Arts & Crafts Museum still seems mainly dedicated to creating oil portraits of China's Communist leadership. However the institute did have to move out for one brief three-year period when Lin Liguo, the son of **Lin Biao** [林彪] (1908-1971), lived here from 1969 to 1971.   In 1971 he was forced to move out after his father attempted a coup d'etat and died while fleeing the country. Afterwards the institute moved back in.

The covered driveway just inside the gate marks the main entrance to the house. The rear of the rectangular, white building is divided into two wings by a circular round tower and round veranda.   Two sweeping flights of external steps lead down from the veranda to the green lawn behind the house.   The exterior is richly ornamented with Corinthian columns, while Greco-Roman urns line the balustrades of the veranda.   At the base of the veranda is a water fountain with a spout in the shape of a brass lion's head.   A water pool in the garden takes the form of a mock river winding across the estate.

The interior of the house features polished, exposed, heavy, wooden ceiling beams and crystal chandeliers.   French doors open from the second floor onto the veranda.   Plaster ornaments decorate the ceilings.   The walls of the second floor dining room are covered in polished wood paneling.   The shelves and fireplace are hewn from pure marble.   Floor to ceiling windows allow natural sunlight to stream into the room from the garden outside. Sliding wooden doors separate the living room and dining room.   The smell of wood fills the air.

A spiral staircase ascends to the third floor through a tower-like rotunda.   One room is devoted to an exhibit of Peking Opera costumes, including facemasks, robes, and weapons.

Address: 79 Fenyang Lu and Taiyuan Lu.
Phone: (021) 6431-1431
Fax: (021) 6437-3454
Nearest Metro Station: Hengshan Lu [衡山路] Station on Line 1.

Gardens (Yuanlin) [园林]

Although the Yu Garden (Yu Yuan) [豫园] in the center of the old walled Shanghai county town area once known as Nanshi District is by far the city's most famous garden, Shanghai has a number of other equally beautiful traditional landscape gardens, most of which are located outside the city center in the suburban districts.   The most notable one within the city center is **Guilin Park** (Guilin Gongyuan) [桂林公园], the former **Huang Garden** (Huangjia Huayuan) [黄家花园] of Huang Jinrong [黄金荣](1868-1953), which will be described separately in its own section after this.   Five gardens in Shanghai are known as the **Shanghai Five Classical Gardens** (Shanghai Wu Da Gudai Yuanlin) [上海五大古典园林].   In addition to the Yuyuan, these include four more notable gardens located in the suburbs, such as the **Garden of Drunken Poet Bai's Pool** (Zuibaichi Yuan) [醉白池园] in Songjiang, the **Garden of Autumn Clouds** (Qiuxia Pu) [秋霞圃] in Jiading Town, the **Garden of Ancient Splendor** (Guyi Yuan) [古漪园] in Nanxiang Town, and the **Garden of Zigzag Water** (Qushui Yuan) [曲水园] in Qingpu Town.   These are also the same five Shanghai gardens covered in _Famous Gardens South of the Yangzi River_ (_Jiangnan Mingyuan_) [江南名园] (2002).   In addition, there is also the **Dragons Meeting Pool Garden** (Huilongtan Gongyuan) [汇龙潭公园] in Jiading Town. Of course there's also the **Grand View Garden** (Da Guan Yuan) [大观园] on the shores of Lake Dianshan Hu in rural Qingpu District, which was only built 30 years ago from 1980-1988, but is a fairly authentic depiction of the traditional Chinese cultural scenes found in the Ming Dynasty novel "_A Dream of Red Mansions_" (Hong Lou Meng) [红楼梦].

The **Garden of Drunken Poet Bai's Pool** (Zuibaichi Yuan) [醉白池园]

Located at the intersection of Renmin Nan Lu and Songhui Lu in Songjiang Town is a Qing Dynasty walled garden dedicated to the Tang Dynasty [唐代] (618-907) poet **Bai Juyi** [白居易](772-846).

As early as the Northern Song Dynasty (Bei Song) (960-1127), in 1091 the Jinshi [进士] degree holder **Zhu Zhichun** [朱之纯] reportedly built a villa on this site and named it Guyang Yuan [谷阳园].   During the Wanli [万历] (1573-1620) reign of the Ming Dynasty [明代] (1368-1644), the famous calligrapher and painter **Dong Qichang** [董其昌], who also served as the Minister of Rites, came to live here in 1620.

During the Shunzhi [顺治] (1644-1661) and Kangxi [康熙] (1661-1722) reigns of the Qing Dynasty, the garden was rebuilt by the Minister of Public of Works and famous painter **Gu Dashen** [顾大申], a scholar official who had passed the civil service exam for the Jinshi [进士] degree.   Gu first came here in 1652, the ninth year of the Shunzhi reign [顺治] (1644-1661) of the Qing Dynasty, and renamed the garden in honor of the Tang Dynasty poet and scholar official Bai Juyi [白居易](772-846).

In 1797, the seconed year of the Jiaqing reign [嘉庆] the garden's name was changed from Zuibaichi Yuan to Yuying Tang [育英堂], but after the Liberation of Shanghai in May 1949 the name was changed back again.   In 1959 the garden was repaired, extended, and opened to the public.   In 1983 the Deer Pavilion (Shanglu Ting), Magnolia Courtyard (Yulan Yuan), the Deep Willow Book Reading Hall (Shen Liu Dushu Tang), and the Carved Hall (Diaohua Ting) were all constructed.

It now covers an area of five hectares full of flora and fauna such as singing birds, fish jumping in the ponds, pine, cedar, gingko, and deciduous trees.   The oldest tree is a 250-year-old gingko that requires three people to link arms in order to embrace its trunk. One could spend hours here wandering the pathways, stone arched footbridges and corridors amongst the many pavilions, halls, courtyards, landscape rockeries, man-made hills, five lakes, lotus ponds, and various types of trees.

The **Straw Hut Over the Pool** (Chishang Caotang) [池上草堂] is literally built over a canal which flows into the rectangular Zuibaichi pool.   It was rebuilt in 1909, during the Xuantong reign [宣统] (1909-1911) of the last Qing Dynasty Emperor Puyi [溥仪].   It is sometimes described as "*ban shan, ban shui, ban shu, ban chuang,*" meaning, "*half hill, half water, half books and half windows.*"   Next door is the **Square Hall** (Si Fang Ting) which also faces the Zuibaichi pool.   It was reportedly built by Dong Qichang, the garden's original owner and a prime minister during the **Wanli** reign (1573-1620) of the Ming Dynasty.

On the other side of the Zuibaichi pool is one of the garden's more fascinating sights, the **Famous People Corridor** lined with 30 stone engraved portraits of Qing scholars with their elaborate costumes shown in great detail.

To the east of the Zuibaichi pool is the original entrance gatehouse to the garden, the outside of which is decorated with an incredible array of intricate wood carvings that illustrate people in traditional costumes and depict traditional stories from Chinese history.   In the western corridor of the garden is hall dedicated to the Wu king Shou Men who called this place **Deer Town** (Lu Cheng) because of the many deer which roamed here then. Near the Zuibaichi pool is a separate walled courtyard featuring the **Snow Sea Hall** (Xue Hai Tang) [雪海堂], which dates from 1909.   Two stone lion statues mark the entrance to this impressive hall.   **Sun Yat-Sen** (Sun Zhongshan) [孙中山] (1866-1925) gave a speech here on December 26, 1912.

In between the Zuibaichi pool and the main entrance gate is the **Flower Carving Hall** (Diaohua Ting), a courtyard complex that features an amazing array of intricate wood carvings along the roof beams and doors of all its buildings.   The carvings illustrate stories from the Three Kingdoms (San Guo) era.

Phone: (021) 6785-3551
Website: http://www.shzuibaichi.com/

The **Garden of Autumn Clouds (Qiuxia Pu)** [秋霞圃]

In Jiading Town there is a Ming Dynasty garden located just behind the **Jiading City God Temple** (Jiading Chenghuang Miao) [嘉定城隍庙] and is entered via the same gate at 314 Dong Da Jie.   This garden was originally constructed in 1502 by Gong Hong, a scholar-official who was then the Minister of Public Works.   This makes it the oldest garden in Shanghai, even older than the more famous Yu Garden (Yu Yuan) [豫园].   It was reopened in the year 1987, along with the adjoining Jiading **City God Temple** (Jiading Chenghuang Miao) [嘉定城隍庙], after having been closed for an indefinite period of time dating back to at least 1966 when the Cultural Revolution began.   The original area of the Gong Garden (Gong Yuan) has now been merged with two other formerly separate private family gardens, the Shen Yuan and the Jin Yuan and covers an area of 3.2 hectares.

The first sight of the garden's **Peach Blossoms Pond** (Taohua Tan) leaves one absolutely stunned at its beauty.   Man-made hills and rockeries (jiashan) on either side of the pond create the feeling of a small valley, while thick foliage creates the atmosphere of a natural forest.   Waterside pavilions such as the **Hall of the Immovable Boat** (Zhou Er Bu You Xuan Dian), the **Biwu Xuan**, and the **Biguang Ting** are tastefully decorated with traditional Chinese furniture and landscape paintings on hanging scrolls.   Stone footbridges crossing the streams seem to be genuine historic relics.   A watch tower, the **Wanxiang Ju**, rises beyond the southern hill.   There are several rock grottoes and hills which are penetrated by twisting, turning tunnels, some long enough that they are pitch dark halfway through to the other side.   The **Immortals Cave** (Xianren Dong) penetrates the hill beneath the Wanxiang Ju tower, while the **Guiyun Dong** cave tunnels beneath the **Jishan Ting** pavilion on the other side of the lake.   The whole Tao Hua Tan area covers 5,200 square meters. And this is just the first third of the garden.   The other two-thirds of the garden featuring two more lakes, the **Sanying Tang** hall and the **Bei Men** northern gate are hidden on the other side of a wall to the North of the **Peach Blossoms Pond** (Taohua Tan) which can only be passed through via two small gates at the East and West end of the wall that divides the area in half.

The Garden of Ancient Splendor (Guyi Yuan) [古漪园]

Located at 218 Zhen Nan Lu (aka Huyi Gonglu) in Nanxiang Town (Nanxiang Zhen) [南翔镇] of Jiading District [嘉定区], it was first constructed in the Ming Dynasty [明代] (1368-1644) during the reign of Emperor Jiajing [嘉靖] (1573-1620). However, legends about this location go back as far as the Liang Dynasty [梁朝] (502-552) of the sixth century, and the garden now features a number of genuine stone relics from the Tang [唐代] (618-907) and Song [宋代] (960-1279) dynasties which were later moved here from elsewhere in the town.

Originally named the Magnificent Garden (Yi Yuan) [漪园], the name was changed in the year 1746, during the 11th year of the reign of Qng Dynasty Emperor Qianlong [乾隆], to Ancient Magnificent Garden (Guyi Yuan) [古漪园], and in the 13th year of Qianlong the garden was extensively rebuilt. In 1788, the 53rd year of the Qianlong reign of the Qing Dynasty, the garden was acquired by the Nanxiang City God Temple (Nanxiang Chenghuang Miao) [南翔城隍庙] and became known as the Temple Garden (Miao Yuan) [庙园]. This fits a pattern of Shanghai's classical gardens being transferred from private ownership to being attached to the local City God Temples during the late Qing Dynasty, a pattern that also occurred with the Yu Yuan in Shanghai County Town (Shanghai Xiancheng), the Garden of Zigzag Water (Qushui Yuan) in Qingpu Town, and the Garden of Autumn Clouds (Qiuxiapu) in Jiading Town. However, between 1860 and 1862, Nanxiang Town changed hands many times in the military struggle between the Taiping rebels based in Nanjing and the Qing Dynasty armies and foreign volunteers defending Shanghai, during which the garden was destroyed. After the Taiping Rebellion was over, the garden was rebuilt over a long period from the Tongzhi reign (1861-1875) through the Guangxu reign (1875-1908) of the Qing Dynasty.

During the Republic of China period (1911-1949) the garden was destroyed two more times, but was always rebuilt afterward. In March 1932 the Japanese occupied Nanxiang Town for two months, during which the garden's buildings and rockeries collapsed, the trees were j all chopped down, and all the flowers and plants dried up. In May 1933 a garden repair committee was established to raise funds for its reconstruction. During this reconstruction the Missing Corner Pavlion (Quejiao Ting) [缺角亭] was built. However, when the Japanese invaded Shanghai again in August 1937 the whole garden was destroyed once more. After the Victory (Shengli) [胜利] over Japan in 1945, the garden was turned into a public park.

Since the Liberation (Jiefang) [解放] of Shanghai in May 1949 the garden has experienced numerous renovations and expansions in area, including from March to October 1957, and again from 1958 to October 1959. At the start of the Cultural Revolution in August 1966 many historic relics inside the garden were destroyed or smashed. In January 1967 the garden's name was changed to Nanxiang Park (Nanxiang Gongyuan). In 1973 the garden was repaired again. In 1977 the garden was repaired again and its former name of Guyi Yuan was reinstated. In 1979 it was rebuilt and expanded again. In 1981 the garden's area was expanded again and the Big South Gate (Da Nan Men) was built. In 1982 the Big North Gate (Bei Da Men) was built. In 1985-1987 there was another major expansion. Today it covers 85,000 square meters and is considered one of Shanghai's five big classical gardens (Shanghai Wu Da Gudian Yuanlin) [上海五大古典园林], even though it is located 21 kilometers from the city center.

Most of the genuine historic sites are in the northern half of the park, including many traditional style pavilions and halls. The small hilltop **Missing Corner Pavilion** (Quejiao Ting) [缺角亭] was first built in 1933 to commemorate the September 18, 1931 Japanese occupation of Manchuria. Although the pavilion does in fact have four corners, if you look closely you can see that three of the corners of the roof have a defiant clenched fist raised up in the air, but the northeast corner does not because it symbolically represents Japanese-occupied Manchuria (Dong Bei) [东北]. Inside there is a fascinating dragon motif on the ceiling. It is perched on top of the **Bamboo Hill** (Zhuzi Shan) [竹枝山] looking down upon the **Floating Bamboo Pavilion** (Fuyun Ge) [浮筠阁] and the **Stone Boat** (Buxi Zhou) [不系舟] in a pond below. The front side is approached by a long, straight flight of stone steps with a carved stone balustrade on both sides, while the back side is approached by another more winding pathway of stone steps.

Several pavilions were originally used by the scholar official who built the garden and lived there. The **Reclusive Hall** (Yiye Tang) [逸野堂] was the pavilion where the original owner of the garden used to receive his guests. It was destroyed during the Japanese invasion of 1937, and last rebuilt in 1982. The **South Pavilion** (Nan Ting) [南亭] was where the garden's owner actually slept and lived. Unfortunately that pavilion is inside its own walled compound with a gate that is usually kept locked shut. The **Plum Blossom Hall** (Meihua Ting) [梅花厅] was first built in 1789, but destroyed during the Japanese invasion of Shanghai in 1932, and then later rebuilt in 1962.

The **White Crane Pavilion** (Baihe Ting) [白鹤亭], which fittingly enough is decorated with a statue of a white crane standing on top of its roof, has a fascinating legend associated with it. According to the story, workers digging an excavation during the reign of Emperor Wu Di of the Liang Dynasty (502-577) discovered a large white rock which they erected as an ornament. After this, a flock of white cranes become coming to rest on this rock every year. The pavilion is decorated with ornamental white cranes on its roof, and faces a stone stele standing in the water of the nearby pool with an inscription telling the story. In Chinese culture, white cranes have traditionally been seen as a symbol of longevity and good luck.

Besides the Missing Corner Pavilion, the garden's main attraction is the four ancient Buddhist stone towers that have been moved here from other places.

Just beside the Plum Blossom Hall (Meihua Ting) [梅花厅] sits the **Lotus Pond** (Hehua Chi) [荷花池] in the middle of which stands an inscribed stone pillar dating from the Song Dynasty [宋代] (960-1279) known variously as the **Song Dynasty Stone Tower** (Song Dai Shi Ta) [宋代石塔], or according to a sign at the site, simply the Putong Ta [普同塔]. This six-sided stone tower has seven levels and dates from 1222 A.D., the 15th year of the Jiading [嘉定] (1208-1224) reign of the Song Dynasty, which of course gave Jiading District its name. The pool is thick with lotus plants (lianhua) which partly obstruct the view of the stone tower, which can only be viewed from a distance while standing on the surrounding lake shore. The lotus plants' tall, broad leaves blow back and forth in the wind, at one moment hiding the tower and at another moment suddenly revealing the stone carvings on it. This makes trying to look at it both a frustrating and somewhat mysterious experience. Around the tower there are stone carvings of people in dressed in historic costumes such as long flowing robes. This tower does seem shorter than other three in the park, and it's not clear if it used to be taller.   Possibly what remains was once only the top part of a taller column. The Song Dynasty Stone Tower was moved here from the nearby Yunxiang Buddhist Temple (Yunxiang Si) [云翔寺] on October 1, 1959, along with the two Tang Dynasty Buddhist Stone Towers now located in other parts of the garden.   According to a plaque nearby, the Song Dynasty Stone Tower was listed as a protected cultural relic by the Jiading County Government in 1961 and again in 1981.

Located in between the **Stone Boat** (Buxi Zhou) [不系舟] and the **Little Sound Attic** (Weiyin Ge) [微音阁] is a completely intact **Tang Dynasty Sutra Pillar** (Tang Dai Jingchuang) [唐代石经幢], similar to the one which still stands in Songjiang Town.   This is an octagonal stone pillar carved with pictures of Buddhas, Buddhist saints known as Arhats (Luohan), the Four Heavenly Kings (Si Da Tian Wang) [四大天王], and lotus flowers (lianhua).   The tower has seven separate sections and stands 30 feet high.   It was carved in 875 A.D., the second year of the Qianfu [乾符] reign of the Tang Dyansty (618-907), and was moved here from Yunxiang Buddhist Temple (Yunxiang Si) [云翔寺] on October 1, 1959.

A second **Tang Dynasty Sutra Pillar** (Tang Dai Jingchuang) [唐代石经幢] is also located in this same garden, and stands just outside the **South Pavilion** (Nan Ting) [南亭], but it is less intact, missing its top part.   This second Tang Dynasty pillar was carved in 867 A.D. during the 8th year of the Xiantong [咸通] reign of the Tang Dynasty.   It is also has an octagonal shape, and used to have seven parts, with a total heigh of 30 feet, before the top part was lost in 1968, supposedly from a thunder and lightning storm.   This one was also moved here from Yunxiang Buddhist Temple (Yunxiang Si) [云翔寺] on October 1, 1959.

The East end of the park is a newer development constructed in 1985-1987, which nonetheless has an extremely pleasant environment, despite it's largely lacking of genuine historic relics.   One genuine historic relic in this part of the park is an octagonal stone Buddhist tower with Buddha images known as the **Wanan Ta** [万安塔], which was moved here in 1988 from the site of the Wanan Buddhist Temple (Wanan Si) [万安寺], once located elsewhere in the southwest corner of Nanxiang Town.

Overall, the garden is full of man-made ponds, pools, lakes, creeks, streams, and rivers, many of which are crossed by picturesque foot bridges, such as the Bridge of Nine Turnings (Jiu Qu Qiao), as well as man-made hills, rockeries, and curiously shaped stones from Lake Tai (Tai Hu), the most notable being the five stones names The Five Old Peaks (Wu Lao Feng).

Walking through the **Bamboo Forest** (Zhuzi Senlin) of the East Garden, one can hear the young bamboo saplings creek in the wind, and be reminded of the old Chinese saying that bamboo bends but it doesn't break.   A motto meant to inspire courage when faced with adversity.   The **Longevity Stele** (Guishou Bei) is a new monument balanced on the back of a turtle sculpture which stands at the summit of Turtle Hill (Gui Shan) [龟山] on Turtle Head Island (Gui Tou Dao) [龟头岛] in Turtle Hill Lake (Gui Shan Hu) [龟山湖],

The Garden of Zigzag Water (Qushui Yuan) [曲水园]

Located on Public Park Road (Gongyuan Lu) [公园路] in Qingpu Town is a Qing Dynasty [清朝] (1644-1911) garden constructed in 1745, the 10th year of the reign of Emperor Qianlong [乾隆] (1735-1796).   From 1860, the 10th year of the Xianfeng reign of the Qing Dynasty, until 1862, the first year of the Tongzhi reign of the Qing Dynasty, the Taiping rebels occupied Qingpu Town. During the 1862 reconquest of the town by a combination of Qing Dynasty and Western troops, the garden was destroyed.   In 1884, the 10th year of the Guangxu reign of the Qing Dynasty, the garden was repaired and extended. In the 13th year of the Guangxu reign it was rebuilt again.   In the 15th year of the Guangxu reign the Moon Pavilion (Yue Xuan) was added.   In 1910, the second year of the Xuantong reign of the Qing Dynasty, the garden was repaired and extended.   A perimeter wall and the Animal Releasing Pool (Fangsheng Chi) were added then.   At the start of the Second Sino-Japanese War (Kang Ri Zhanzheng) [抗日战争] (1937-1945), the garden was blown up by bombs dropped from Japanese airplanes. When the Qingpu city wall (chengqiang) [城墙] was torn down in 1952, it became possible to expand the size of the garden all the way to the city moat (huchenghe) [护城河].   The garden was declared a county-level protected cultural relic in 1959 and again in 1979. During the Cultural Revolution (1966-1976), in 1969 anti-aircraft defenses were erected in several parts of the garden, causing damage to some of the traditional sights.   In 1984 the Shanghai city government allocated funds to repair and extend the garden, and the work was completed two years later in 1986.

Over the years the garden has had at least five different names.   The garden was originally named the **Ling Yuan** [灵园].   However, because it was attached to the **Qingpu City God Temple** (Qingpu Chenghuang Miao) [青浦城隍庙] established in 1573, the first year of the Wanli reign of the Ming Dynasty, which still stands next door but is now separated from it by a high wall, it was sometimes referred to simply as the **Temple Garden** (Miao Yuan) [庙园], in a situation quite similar to the Guyi Yuan in Nanxiang Town.   However, because each town resident supposedly contributed one coin towards the garden's construction and maintenance, it was also unofficially sometimes known as the **Yiwen Yuan** [一文园].   The official name was changed from Ling Yuan [灵园] to the present **Qushui Yuan** [曲水园] in 1798, the 3rd year of the Jiaqing reign [嘉庆] (1796-1820) of the Qing Dynasty [清朝] (1644-1911).   From 1927 until 1980 the garden was known as **Zhongshan Park** (Zhongshan Gongyuan) [中山公园] in honor of Sun Yat-sen (Sun Zhongshan) [孙中山] (1866-1925), the first president of the Republic of China (Minguo) [民国] (1912-1949).   After being repaired in 1980 the garden reverted to its previous name of Qushui Yuan [曲水园].

The northern and eastern boundary of the garden follows the curving line of the city moat (huchenghe) [护城河], and a traditional covered wooden roof corridor (changlang) [长廊] which runs along the water's edge makes for a pleasant walk.   The garden has two lakes, the Lotus Pond (Hehua Chi) [荷花池] and the Water Lily Pond (Shuilian Chi) [睡莲池], a tea house (chalou) [茶楼], and a three-story square tower on top of a small man-made hill (jiashan) [假山] known as the Small Peak that Flew from Afar (Xiao Feilai Feng) [小飞来峰], after its much larger namesake in Hangzhou.   The lakeside pavilions tend to be full of the town's older residents, chatting and playing cards.

There are now many pavilions in the garden, most of them of recent construction due to the many previous waves of destruction the place has suffered.   The west end of the garden contains the Red Sunset Half Pavilion (Xiyanghong Ban Lou) [夕阳红半楼] constructed using stones from Lake Tai (Taihu Shi), with a man-mad cave downstairs and two flights of stone steps leading up to it, as well as the Moon Pavilion (Yue Xuan) [月轩].   The east side of the garden has the Thinking Hall (Jue Tang) [觉堂] first built in 1745 during the 10th year of the Qianlong reign of the Qing Dynasty and rebuilt in 1889 during the 15th year of the Guangxu reign of the Qing Dynasty.   This is the building with the oldest history in the garden.   There is also the Buddhist Valley Pavilion (Fogu Ting) and the Triangle Pavilion (Sanjiao Ting). On top of the Big Rockery (Da Jiashan), also known as the Small Peak that Flew from Afar, stands the Nine Peaks Overview Pavilion (Jiu Feng Yilan Ge), Mirror Center Hut (Jingxing Lu), Bamboo Pavilion (Zhu Xie), Clear Sound Mountain House (Qinglai Shanfang), Peony Pavilion (Mudan Ting) [牡丹亭], the Ji Cloud Pavilion (Ji Yun Ting) named after the writer Lu Ji [陆机] (261-303).

The garden is located on the North side of Gongyuan Lu, just after it crosses a bridge over the round city moat (huchenghe) [护城河].

Address: 650 Public Park Road (650 Gongyuan Lu) [公园路 650 号]

The Great World Amusement Center (Dashijie Youle Zhongxin) [大世界游乐中心]

The Great World Amusement Center (Dashijie Youle Zhongxin) [大世界游乐中心], usually just known as Great World (Dashijie) [大世界] for short, is Shanghai's former pleasure palace and an architectural gem. This entertainment center is notable for its 55.3 meter high tower, which resembles a round wedding cake, with its four successive stages supported by white columns, but was not added to the building until 1924. The enormous structure stretches for an entire city block from Yanan Dong Lu [延安东路] to Ninghai Dong Lu, with the main façade facing Tibet South Road (Xizang Nan Lu) [西藏南路].

The building was originally constructed in 1917 in an area that was then part of the French Concession (Shanghai Fa Zujie) [上海法租界] by its first owner **Huang Chujiu** [黄楚九] (1872-1931), who had previously been involved in the Louwailou Entertainment Center [楼外楼游乐场] in 1913, and established the New World Amusement Center (Xinshijie Youlechang) [新世界游乐场] on Nanking Road (Nanjing Dong Lu) two years earlier in 1915. Huang ran a tobacco company, a pharmaceutical company, and operated several banks that were the first ones in Shanghai to stay open all day long. He headed the pharmaceutical trade association and was a member of the standing committee of the Shanghai Chamber of Commerce (Shanghai Shi Zong Shanghui) [上海市总商会]. In 1928 he still had the resources to rebuild the Great World. However, after the global Great Depression started in 1929, his business began to suffer, and there was a run on his bank as depositors all tried to withdraw their funds at once in a panic.

When Huang Chujiu [黄楚九] died in January 1931 he was bankrupt, which allowed the Great World to be easily takne over in May 1931 by the famous Shanghai gangster **Huang Jinrong** [黄金荣](1868-1953), one of the three leaders of the notorious Green Gang (Qing Bang) [青帮].

In the 1920s and 1930s it was a famous center for live entertainment, including Peking Opera performances by famous actors, acrobats, martial arts, folk music, puppet shows, and magicians, all performing on the stages of its many indoor theaters as well as the large outdoor stage in the courtyard. It even included movie theaters, ballroom dance halls, restaurants, snack shops, and a hotel. However, it was also considered the most famous den of iniquity in the whole city, where prostitution and gambling were practiced openly. Along with the hordes of regular city residents who enjoyed going there for entertainment, estimated to number 10,000 per day, it was also reputed to be inhabited by various prostitutes, dancing girls, gangsters, hoodlums, and rogues engaging in immoral behavior. On August 14, 1937 it was accidentally hit by a bomb dropped by a plane belonging to the Chinese air force during the Sino-Japanese battle for Shanghai, which caused a civilian massacre, although the building itself survived largely intact.

Its heyday came to end when it was taken over by the Shanghai Municipal Government's Cultural Bureau on July 2, 1954, a year after its previous owner Huang Jinrong [黄金荣](1868-1953) had passed away. On May 1, 1955 it was renamed as the People's Amusement Center (Renmin Youlechang) [人民游乐场], but the name was changed back again in January 1958. Shortly after the start of the Cultural Revolution, on November 6, 1966 the Great World was attacked by a mob who destroyed its sign board. As a result, the name was changed again to the East is Red Amusement Center (Dongfanghong

Youlechang) [东方红游乐场].   Then it was turned into a warehouse until 1974 when it became the Shanghai Youth Palace (Shanghai Shi Qingnian Gong) [上海市青年宫].

On January 25, 1981 the name was changed back to Great World again, and it resumed its previous role as a public center for traditional Chinese live entertainment.   When I first arrived in Shanghai in 1999 it was still hosting live Peking Opera and acrobatic performances that were popular with the local native residents.   Until its closure for renovation in 2003, old black and white photos of past performances lined its dusty corridors and daily performances of acrobatics were still being held on the outdoor stage in the central courtyard, while Peking Opera performances by costumed actors accompanied by an orchestra of musicians playing traditional Chinse musical instruments could still be seen on the indoor stage upstairs.   There was also an old ball room with surrounding circular balcony reached by two sweeping flights of stairs. It was one of the few places left in the city where you could still get a feeling of old Shanghai.

In May 2003 the Great World was closed for renovations that were supposed to take only two years.   The interior was completely gutted down to its bare bones and even the old wooden window frames were replaced.   However, as of March 2009 it was still closed and the entire exterior was covered with scaffolding.

After 14 years of restoration, the Great World finally reopened to the public on March 13, 2017.   When I revisited the site for the first time in nearly 15 years on December 24, 2017, after paying a 60 Rmb admission fee I found the actual structure of the building to be quite intact, but the interior of all the rooms had been completely changed.   Most of all, the atmosphere had become quite sterile.   There were no longer any live performances by the traditional musicians, opera singers, actors, and acrobats that used to be seen here.   There were no longer any indoor theaters, like the one where I used to watch live Peking Opera performances, their stages and seats having been removed.   The outdoor stage in the courtyard where I used to sit and watch the acrobats perform now featured a large electronic screen showing a recorded video of a singing performance.   The security check at the entrance was as tight as that at an airport, and an army of uniformed security guards were on vigilant watch seemingly everywhere, standing only a few feet apart from each other, watching each visitor's every move, as if they were expecting a terrorist attack.   Elevators had been installed, but access to the top floor and the roof was forbidden.   A few other local old people like me who had probably frequented the place during its livelier days could be seen wandering the halls lost in thought, trying to recapture the spirit of the place, with disappointed looks on their faces.   The only part of the interior that had not changed was the funhouse mirrors in the lobby that distort your image to make you look taller or fatter, etc.

Address: 1 Tibet South Road (Xizang Nan Lu) [西藏南路].
Phone: (021) 6326-3760, 6374-6703.
Nearest Subway Station: People's Square Station on Lines 1, 2 and 8, or Da Shi Jie Station on Line 8.

The **Green Gang** (Qing Bang) [青帮]

The most notorious of the Chinese crime organizations to emerge was the Green Gang (Qing Bang) [青帮] led by the triumvirate of Huang Jinrong [黄金荣](1868-1953), Zhang Xiaolin [张啸林] (1877-1940) and Du Yuesheng [杜月笙] (1888-1951). Although they started out their careers as dealers of illegal narcotics, particularly opium, the Green Gang played a crucial role during the political events of 1927 by helping the Guomindang suppress an abortive Communist uprising in the city, with the tacit approval of the local British and French authorities. Eventually they became respected as legitimate businessmen and titans of industry, particularly in the fields of banking and finance. In the beginning, Huang and Zhang were the two more senior partners, while Du was merely their young apprentice, but later the relationship changed as Du assumed the leading role.

Huang Jinrong [黄金荣](1868-1953) had joined the French Concession police force in 1892 at the age of 24. He later became a Detective, then Inspector and finally in 1919 Chief Superintendent. In 1920 Huang formed the Sanxin Company [三鑫公司] along with his partners in crime Zhang Xiaolin [张啸林] (1877-1940) and Du Yuesheng [杜月笙] (1888-1951). The company's main purpose was to monopolize the opium trade. Huang was involved in an infamous incident during which he was kidnapped and held hostage at Longhua Garrison by Lu Yongxiang [卢永祥] (1867-1933), the military governor (dujun) [督军] of Shanghai, over a dispute Huang and Lu's playboy son Lu Xiaojia [卢筱嘉] had over a mistress, Lu Lanchun [露兰春] (1898-1936), who was an actress at Huang's theater (Shanghai Gong Wutai) [上海共舞台]. Huang had to be rescued by his junior partner in crime Du Yuesheng [杜月笙] (1888-1951), who paid a large ransom to secure his release, after which Du assumed a much more dominant leadership role over the criminal Green Gang (Qing Bang) [青帮]. Chinese sources say this incident occurred in 1922, but English language sources tend to say it was in 1924, while many sources in both languages avoid mentioning an exact date. In 1925 Huang resigned from the French police force and retired to his private garden now known as Guilin Park (Guilin Gongyuan) [桂林公园], but in 1931 he acquired the Great World Amusement Center (Dashijie). Surprisingly, Huang chose to stay in Shanghai after the Communist's captured the city in May 1949, even while his former business partner Du Yuesheng fled to Hong Kong and his friends in the Guomindang leadership fled to Taiwan. On May 7, 1951 he submitted to the new authorities a completed written confession of his crimes (zibaishu) [自白书], which is still held in the Shanghai Municipal Archives (Shanghai Dang'an Guan) [上海档案馆]. He finally died in Shanghai on June 20, 1953 at the ripe old age of 85. Two sights in Shanghai related to Huang Jinrong [黄金荣](1868-1953) that can still be seen today include the **Great World** Amusement Center (Dashijie) [大世界], which he acquired in 1931, and the traditional Chinese garden he started building in 1925, previously known as the Huangjia Huayuan [黄家花园], but now called **Guilin Park** (Guilin Gongyuan) [桂林公园].

Du Yuesheng [杜月笙] (1888-1951) was originally an uneducated peasant from the backwoods village of Gaoqiao in Pudong.   His name was first mentioned in the local Shanghai media in late 1924 when a letter to the editor of the North China Herald accused him of being "an opium and arms smuggler."   Du's power over the underworld took a huge leap after he rescued his mentor Huang Jinrong [黄金荣](1868-1953), who had been held hostage by the local military governor Lu Yongxiang [卢永祥] (1867-1933).   Du reached an agreement with French Concession authorities in 1925 which gave Du what Brian Martin calls "an official monopoly" on opium trade in the concession and allowed him to sell it on "an open basis," and this was reaffirmed in a second agreement of February 1927.   A similar agreement had been reached between Du and Shanghai Municipal Council Chairman Stirling Fessenden for "non-operation of the opium laws" in the International Settlement.   Du also reached an agreement with the Guomindang central government in 1932 that maintained his opium monopoly in the Chinese districts of Shanghai.   In July 1935 Du was ironically made one of the three standing committee members of the Shanghai Municipal Opium Suppression Committee, which simply allowed him to protect his own opium business.

However, it was Du's ability to develop a career as a local politician that set him aside from his fellow Green Gang leaders.   When the French Concession Chinese Ratepayers Association was established in January 1927 Du was among its leaders.   In July 1929 he was appointed by the French Consul to the Provisional Commission, the French Concessions' equivalent to a Municipal Council.   When in November 1930 the French Consul agreed to allow the Chinese Ratepayers Association to elect the Chinese members of the Provisional Commission, this effectively gave Du control over the commission's Chinese membership, since he already controlled the association.

Du's political career in the French Concession suffered a setback when he was forced to resign from the Provisional Commission on February 15, 1932.   Shortly thereafter, in mid-February 1932, one of the most notorious events of Du's life occurred when the entire leadership of the French Concession succumbed to fatal or near fatal illnesses immediately after having dinner together at Du's house.   The victims included the French Consul General Koechlin; the commander of French military forces, Colonel A. Marcaire; and the French Chief of Police, Etienne Fiori.   Fiori later recovered, but among the other fatal victims of Du's dinner party was M. du Pac de Marsoulies, the first owner of the **Marshall House**, aka Taiyuan Villa (Taiyuan Bieshu) [太原别墅], which still stands today at #160 Taiyuan Road (Taiyuan Lu).

In the 1930s Du's political career expanded out of the French Concession and into the Chinese administered Shanghai municipality.   Du took over chairmanship of the Shanghai Civic Association in November 1934, and in July 1936 Du was elected to the five-man standing committee of the Shanghai Chamber Commerce (Shanghai Shi Zong Shanghui) [上海市总商会].

In addition to his career as a local politician, Du's transformation from opium dealer was remarkable for his entry into legitimate fields of respectable business, most notably banking. Du was either a founder or later joined the Board of Directors of at least six commercial banks in Shanghai.   He was involved in the 1928 establishment of the Pudong Commercial Bank, of which he later became Chairman;   established the Zhonghui Bank in March 1929 and served as its Chairman of the Board; joined the Board of Directors of the Commercial Bank of China in June 1932, and later became its Chairman of the Board; founded the Minfu Union Commercial Bank in 1933; helped establish the Bank of Asia in 1934; was one of the founders of the China Investment Bank in 1935; and acquired the Jiangsu-Zhejiang Commercial and Savings Bank In 1936.   His two greatest achievements in the banking industry came in 1935 when he was appointed by the Guomindang central government to the Board of Directors of both the Bank of China (Zhongguo Yinhang) and the Central Bank of China (Zhongyang Yinghang) [中央銀行].

The main historic sights related to Du's life that can still be seen today include several buildings belonging to the **Donghu Hotel**, including Du's former mansion at #7 Donghu Lu, which since May 2002 had been used as the **Da Gongguan** [大公馆] bar and restaurant, but as of 2018 had been closed to the public and converted into office space for a private company that does not allow visitors.   The **Mansion Hotel** (Shanghai Shouxi Gongguan) [上海首席公馆] at 82 Xinle Lu [新乐路] also makes the claim that it was Du's gongguan [公馆] or "club house," although the official records simply state that the building constructed in 1932 served as the offices of the Sanxin Company [三鑫公司] jointly owned by Du and his partners in crime Huang Jinrong [黄金荣](1868-1953) and Zhang Xiaolin [张啸林] (1877-1940).   Du's original primary residence was torn down several years ago, but the pieces were rescued by Canadian Chinese collector Huang Xiuzhi, who has yet to reassemble them at his architectural museum in Tongli, Jiangsu.

Grosvenor House

Grosvenor House was an 18-story apartment building constructed by Sir Victor Sassoon and completed in 1934.   It housed 77 apartments that were once occupied by the upper class of Shanghai's foreign and Chinese community.   By the end of 1949 only 10 of the 77 units were inhabited as virtually all the foreigners and the Chinese upper class had fled the city to escape from the new Communist regime.   The new regime allocated apartments in this building to new members of the urban middle class who it felt would be loyal to them, including left-wing intellectuals and writers, but most of these people were arrested in 1957 during the Anti-Rightist Campaign.   After this the Grosvenor House building was incorporated into the Jinjiang Hotel (Jinjiang Fandian) complex, which in 1951 had already occupied the neighboring 13-story former Cathay Mansions building that had also been constructed by Sir Victor Sassoon back in 1929.   During the 1950s and 1960s, Mao Zedong used to enjoy staying here, as it gave him convenient access to the swimming pools, tennis courts, and garden of the former French Club, now the Okura Garden Hotel, which is located directly across the street and could be reached via an underground pedestrian tunnel.   When U.S. President Richard M. Nixon visited Shanghai in 1972, he and his delegation stayed at the Jinjiang Hotel (Jinjiang Fandian) and the famous Shanghai Communique was signed in the hotel's Grand Hall, which had been added to the complex in 1959.   The hotel's buildings were renovated in 1998 and in the year 2000 it received a five-star rating.   The Grosvenor House building still stands on present-day Maoming South Road (Maoming Nan Lu).

The former **Cathay Mansions** apartment building completed in 1929 is now known as the North Building of the Jinjiang Hotel (Jinjiang Fandian). It features a Sikh doorman dressed in full regalia, and the **Shanghai Moon** restaurant.   Other restaurants include **J.J. Mariachis** (Mexican), **Tandoor** (Indian), and **Latina** (Brazilian barbecue).

The former **Grosvenor House** apartment building completed in 1934 is now the South Building of the Jinjiang Hotel (Jinjiang Fandian).

The hotel's complex includes a total of five buildings occupying a whole city block, including the **Jinjiang Grand Hall** where U.S. President Richard M. Nixon signed the famous Shanghai Communiqué in 1972.

This Jinjiang Hotel is not to be confused with the newer Jinjiang Tower Hotel nearby, built in 1988.

Address: 59 Maoming Nan Lu
Phone: (021) 6258-2582
Fax: (021) 6472-5588
Web Site: http://www.jinjianghotelshanghai.com
E-mail: jinjiang@public2.sta.net.cn

Guilin Park (Guilin Gongyuan) [桂林公园]

This beautiful traditional style Chinese landscape garden covers 3.55 hectares in Shanghai's southwestern suburbs, and was once known as the **Huang Garden** (Huangjia Huayuan) [黄家花园] because it was the private suburban retreat of famous Shanghai gangster, **Huang Jinrong** [黄金荣](1868-1953), one of the three founders of the notorious **Green Gang** (Qing Bang) [青帮] and owner of the **Great World Amusement Center** (Dashijie) [大世界], whose dream was to live the life of a Confucian scholar official.

Huang started construction of this garden in 1929, and it was finally completed in 1932. However, many of the structures were destroyed during the 1937 Japanese attack on Shanghai.   The former **War God Temple** (Guandi Miao) [关帝庙], the Jing Guan House, the original **Inside House** (Nei Zhai) [内宅] where Huang lived, and even many of the flowers and trees were lost during the 1937 battle for Shanghai.   After the Sino-Japanese War ended in August 1945, Huang tried to restore his private garden to its former glory, but it once again suffered serious damage during the May 1949 capture of Shanghai by the Communists.

Huang chose to stay in Shanghai after the Communist's captured the city in May 1949, and on May 7, 1951 he submitted to the new authorities a complete written confession of his crimes (zibaishu) [自白书], which is still held in the Shanghai Municipal Archives.   He finally died in Shanghai in June 1953.

Four years later the Huang Garden underwent a complete restoration in 1957 and was renamed Guilin Park (Guilin Gongyuan) [桂林公园].   In August 1958 the newly renovated park was opened to the public for the first time.   Further expansion of the park occurred in 1981 and 1985 when areas to the East of the original Huang Garden were acquired.   This new **East Garden** (Dong Yuan) was opened to the public in October 1988, complimenting the original area of the Huang Yuan on the West side of the park, which is now known as the **Central Garden** (Zhong Yuan)[中园].

The current structures in the park include the **Four Teachings Pavilion** (Sijiao Ting) [四教厅], also known as the Big Pavilion; **Relaxation Pavilion** (Yi Ting) [颐亭], also known as the Mid-Lake Pavilion (Huxin Ting) [湖心亭]; **Goddess of Mercy Pavilion** (Guanyin Ge) [观音阁], also known as the War God Temple (Guandi Miao) [关帝庙]; **Twin Cranes Pavilions** (Shuang He Ting) [双鹤亭]; **Deer Pavilion** (Lu Ting) [鹿亭]; **Stone Boat** (Shi Fang) [石舫]; **Wisdom Hall** (Banruo Fang) [般若舫]; the **Inside House** (Nei Zhai) [内宅], also known as the Yuanyang Lou [鸳鸯楼]; the Welcoming Pavilion (Yingbin Ting) [迎宾厅]; the Osmanthus Pavilion (Guihua Ting) [桂花厅]; the Relaxing Month Pavilion (Song Yue Ting) [松月亭]; The Laughing Pavilion (Haha Ting) [哈哈亭]; Lingyun Pavilion [凌云亭]; Feixiang Pavilionl [飞香厅]; and the Nine Turnings Long Corridor (Jiuqu Changlang) [九曲长廊].   Many of these structures are covered with intricate wood carving designs depicting stories from Chinese mythology.   If you look up at the top of the pavilions, many of their roofs are topped with sculptures of animals such as white cranes (baihe) and deer (lu), both symbols of longevity. Many man-made grotto caves, grotesque rockeries (jia shan) [假山] and large Lake Tai stones (Tai Hu Shi) dot the landscape.

Entering the garden from South Main Gate (Da Nan Men) [大门] you pass through the Huang Yuan's original Gate House (Men Lou) [门楼], with its large single arched portal and two large wooden gates.   From here you follow the **Twisting Corridor**, a road between two high Dragon Walls (Long Qiang) [龙墙], until it stops at a "half pavilion" (ban ting) [半亭] known as the **Fragrant Pavilion** (Tian Xiang Ting) [天香亭].   Here you have the choice of either turning right into the newer **East Garden** (Dong Yuan), or left into the **Central Garden** (Zhong Yuan)[中园], the original area of the Huang Yuan, located on the west side of the park.   The entrance to the Central Garden (Zhong Yuan) [中园] is marked by a second original Gate House (Men Lou).   Its tiled roof is decorated with statues of two elephants and two dragon fish.   Both the East Garden (Dong Yuan) and the Central Garden (Zhong Yuan) [中园] have tea houses, but the Zhong Yuan's tea house is by far the more impressive.

In the center of the former Huang Yuan stands the **Four Teachings Pavilion** (Sijiao Ting) [四教厅], als known simply as the Big Pavilion (Da Ting) [大厅], now used as a tea house. This pavilion supposedly got its name because Chiang Kai Shek (Jiang Jieshi) [蒋介石] (1887-1975) taught Huang Jinrong [黄金荣](1868-1953) four principles to live by, including literature; behavior; loyalty; and honesty (wenxing zhongxin) [文行忠信].   This is by far the most impressive building in the whole park.   Intricate wood carvings cover its doors, walls and roof beams.   If you look up you can see the three original enormous copper chandeliers still hanging from the ceiling.   Despite being a well-known criminal, Huang's close relationship with the economic, political and cultural leaders of his day is attested by the large collection of inscribed wooden signboards (bian) that once hung on display inside the tea house which were received as gifts from these celebrities.   Included in the collection were inscribed wooden signboards (bian) given to Huang by the President of the Republic of China Li Yuanhong, Finance Minister Kong Xiangxi, Finance Minister Song Ziwen, Chen Lifu, and Yu Youren.   An outdoor veranda runs all along all four sides of the pavilion providing rattan tables and chairs where one can sit comfortably enjoying a cup of tea while feasting your eyes on the flowers, trees and landscape rockeries of the garden around you.   The tea house serves many unusual types of tea, including Chrysanthemum Flower Tea (Juhua Cha) [菊花茶].

Facing south from the tea house you see the green lawn (caoping) [草坪] and **Eight Immortals Terrace** (Ba Xian Tai)[八仙台].   During the Cultural Revolution (1966-1976), the original marble statues were destroyed, and since then this terrace had been empty for years.   It was still empty when I first saw it in 1999, but recently new statues of the Eight Immortals were placed here.   West of the tea house are the **Twin Cranes Pavilions** (Shuang He Ting) [双鹤亭] balanced atop man-made rockeries (jia shan) [假山], each with a statue of a white crane (baihe) on the peak of their roofs.   East of the tea house are two enormous Lake Tai stones (Tai Hu Shi) [太湖石] known as the old man and old woman stones (Shi Gong Shi Po) [石公石婆], and the **Deer Pavilion** (Lu Ting) [鹿亭], with a statue of a deer standing on its roof.

Walking north from the Deer Pavilion (Lu Ting) [鹿亭] you come to the **Goddess of Mercy Pavilion** (Guanyin Ge) [观音阁], a large rectangular masonry hall atop a forested man-made hill looking down on a pond below.   This pavilion was previously known as the War God Temple (Guandi Miao) [关帝庙].   The rocky man-made hill (jia shan)[假山] upon which the temple building stands has a bombshelter built underneath it, with a pair of very heavy steel doors covering two hidden entrances at the north and south ends.   Crossing the pond (Yuanbao Chi) [元宝池] at the foot of the hill are two arched stone foot bridges (shuang qiao) [双桥] whose reflections in the water's surface are known as the **Twin Rainbows** (Shuang Hong Wobo) [双虹卧波].   On the northern shore of this pond is the **Stone Boat** (Shi Fang) [石舫], with its large pavilion, followed by the **Wisdom Hall** (Banruo Fang) [般若舫].

On the northern border of the park stands the two-story **Inside House** (Nei Zhai) [内宅], known also as the Yuanyang Lou [鸳鸯楼].   This is the building where Huang lived when he visited his garden and stayed over night.   When I first saw it in 1999 it was largely unrestored, right down to the original tile floors.   There were historic black and white photos of how the garden had looked hanging framed on the walls.   It was actually composed of two buildings linked together with a garage in the middle where Huang used to park his car. Climbing up steps to a terrace on the roof of the two-story building provided wonderful views of the whole garden.   However, it has recently been turned into a restaurant known as Guilin Gongguan [桂林公馆].   The original interior was destroyed during the redecoration, the historic photos disappeared, and the garage was changed into the entrance to the restaurant. Restaurant staff don't like visitors to go up to the rooftop terrace now unless they are paying customers using the private dining rooms that have been installed up there.   The Four Teachings Pavilion and the Inside House are linked by the Nine Turnings Long Corridor (Jiuqu Changlang) [九曲长廊], a long, winding, open air, covered walkway with carved woodwork that prominently features the Chinese character for "Double Happiness" (shuangxi) [双喜] that's written like this 囍.

Address: The North Main Gate (Da Bei Men) is at 128 Guilin Lu [桂林路], on the corner with Caobao Lu, but the original Main South Gate (Da Nan Men) is at the rear of the park at 128 Caohejing Jie Dao, Xuhui District. The whole garden is surrounded by an undulating, white Dragon Wall (Long Qiang) [龙墙] with windows featuring the Buddhist backwards swastika symbol (wan) [卍].
Phone: (021) 6436-0042
Nearest Metro Station: Caobao Lu Station on Line 1, or Guilin Lu Station on Line 9.

H

Hengshan Road (Hengshan Lu) [衡山路]

Hengshan Road [衡山路] was first built in 1892, and then rebuilt after it became part of the French Concession in 1922, when it was renamed **Avenue Petain**. The road stretches for 2.3 km. from its intersection with Dongping Lu in the East to the Xujiahui [徐家汇] neighborhood in the West, where the road's name changes to Cao Stream North Road (Caoxi Bei Lu) [漕溪北路]. Both sides of the road are lined with a total of 460 Phoenix Trees (Wutong Shu) planted by the French, creating a leafy canopy over it. Nowadays Hengshan Lu [衡山路] is a popular nightlife district. The street is lined on both sides with over 200 restaurants, sidewalk café's, and bars, but the names of these change frequently. However, as the second most important road of the French Concession, Hengshan Lu [衡山路] still features a number of historic sites.

The former **Song Family Compound** still stands at the intersection of Hengshan Lu [衡山路] and Dongping Lu, and includes the former homes of two of the three Song sisters, Meiling [美龄], Ailing [蔼龄], and Qingling [庆龄], along with their husbands Chiang Kai-shek (Jiang Jieshi) [蒋介石] (1887-1975), and H.H. Kung (Kong Xiangxi) [孔祥熙] (1880-1967), as well as their brother T.V. Soong (Song Ziwen) [宋子文] (1894-1971). T.V. Soong's former home built in 1921 is located at #11 Dongping Lu. The former home of Chiang Kai-shek (Jiang Jieshi) [蒋介石] (1887-1975) and Song Meiling [宋美龄] (1898-2003) built in 1930 is located at #9 Dongping Lu just inside the gate of the Shanghai Conservatory of Music. Next door at #7 is the former home of Kong Xiangxi [孔祥熙] (1880-1967) and Song Ailing [宋蔼龄] (1889-1973). For over 20 years T.V. Soong's former home at #11 Dongping Lu was occupied by the upscale Sasha's Restaurant that was quite popular with expats and tourists, but in November 2018 they announced that they were being forcibly evicted after a strange incident in which several patrons were injured when a drunk driver crashed his car through the compound's metal gates and into the side of the building.

The Gothic style **Community Church** (Guoji Libai Tang) [国际礼拜堂] at #53 Hengshan Lu [衡山路] was built by protestant Americans from 1924 to 1925 and is once again open to the public for worship services.

The former **Shanghai American School** located at #8-10 Hengshan Lu [衡山路] was built from 1922 to 1923 and used by the school from then until 1949. It was designed by American architect Henry K. Murphy, who also designed Ginling College in Nanjing. Murphy intended it to resemble Philadelphia's Independence Hall, and it still has its distinctive steeple intact.

The Art-Deco **Washington Apartments** built in 1928 stand at #303-307 Hengshan Lu [衡山路], and at the road's intersection with Wuxing Lu stands the **Wuxing Garden**, formerly a private garden residence but now open to the public as a restaurant.

Farther up the street, the Art-Deco style **Hengshan Hotel** (Hengshan Binguan) [衡山宾馆], formerly the Picardie Apartments stands at #534 Hengshan Lu, opposite from the similarly Art-Deco **Kevin Apartments and Café'** at #525 designed by Palmer and Turner architects and built as Cavendish Court. Both buildings were constructed from 1933 to 1934, and together they form a sort of Art-Deco gateway at the intersection of Hengshan Lu and Wanping Lu.

At the intersection of Hengshan Lu [衡山路] and Guangyuan Lu stands **Hengshan Park** (Hengshan Gongyuan) [衡山公园], established in 1925 as Petain Park, and a monument erected by the state of Illinois in 1991 dedicated to the Chinese workers who helped build the railroads in the U.S.A.

At #811 Hengshan Lu [衡山路] stands **La Villa Rouge**, known in English as the Little Red House (Xiao Hong Lou). This was the only structure left standing along this section of Hengshan Lu between Wanping Lu and Tianping Lu when Xujiahui Park was constructed in the spring of 2001 on the former site of a smelly old factory, whose tall smoke stack has been preserved in a corner of the park. The two-story red brick structure with overhanging Mansard roof was built in 1921 and once served as recording studios for the French Pathe record label, a subsidiary of EMI. China's present-day national anthem, "March of the Volunteers" (Yiyongjun Jinxingqu) [义勇军进行曲], was supposedly written and first recorded here by composer Nie Er [聂耳] (1912-1935), whose statue stands nearby on Huaihai Middle Road (Huaihai Zhong Lu) [淮海中路]. Today it is a French restaurant.

Huaihai Road (Huaihai Lu) [淮海路]

Huaihai Road (Huaihai Lu) [淮海路], formerly the **Avenue Joffre** of the French Concession, travels a distance of 4 km. and is one of the two longest East-West roads cutting across the city, along with the roughly parallel Nanjing Road. Huaihai Road was first built in 1900, and celebrated its 100th anniversary in the year 2000. During the brief interlude from 1945 to 1949 when all of Shanghai was under Guomindang control, and the concessions had been abolished, Avenue Joffre's name was changed to **Lin Sen Lu** [林森路], after the former Guomindang president **Lin Sen** [林森] (1868-1943). The name was changed again after the May 1949 Liberation of Shanghai to the present-day Huaihai Lu [淮海路], named after a critical battle fought of the Chinese civil war which was won by the Communists. The November 7, 1948-January 12, 1949 **Battle of Huaihai** (Huaihai Zhanyi) [淮海战役] was a crucial turning point after which the Communist victory seemed inevitable.

The stretch of Huaihai Lu from Xizang Nan Lu to Changshu Lu is mostly office towers, department stores and shops. The section West of Changshu Lu does have some old French mansions, but most of these are closed to the public. Huahihai Road's reputation as being the most fashionable shopping street in the city has in recent years been somewhat replaced by the rise of Nanjing West Road (Nanjing Xi Lu) [南京西路]. The sight of Huaihai Road's arched gateways decorated with flashing lights used to make a night time visitor feel like a peasant in Las Vegas, but those have been removed.

A good sightseeing itinerary for Huaihai Road (Huaihai Lu) [淮海路] would include the following sights on or near the road, in order from west to east: Song Qingling's former home (Song Qingling Guju) [宋庆龄故居] at 1843 Huaihai Zhong Lu [淮海中路]; a statue of the Chinese national anthem's composer Nie Er [聂耳] (1912-1935) at the intersection of Huaihai Zhong Lu [淮海中路] and Fuxing Lu; crime boss Du Yuesheng's former club house (Da Gongguan) at # 7 Donghu Lu; the Russian Orthodox Church (Dongzhen Jiaotang) [东正教堂] at the intersection of Xinle Lu [新乐路] and Xiangyang Bei Lu; the former headquarters of the Sanxin Company [三鑫公司] owned by the three Green Gang leaders which is now the Mansion Hotel (Shanghai Shouxi Gongguan) [上海首席公馆] at 82 Xinle Lu [新乐路]; Sun Yat-sen's former home (Sun Zhongshan Guju) [孙中山故居] at the intersection of Xiangshan Lu and Sinan Lu; Xintiandi in between Huangpi Nan Lu, Madang Lu, and Taicang Lu; the Chinese Communist Party's First Congress Hall at the intersection of Xingye Lu and Huangpi Nan Lu; and the stone gate houses (shikumen) [石库门] on Danshui Lu.

The Huangpu River (Huangpu Jiang) [黄浦江]

The **Huangpu River** (Huangpu Jiang) [黄浦江] flows 114 km. from its head waters in Dianshan Lake in Qingpu District and Taihu Lake in Jiangsu province to its confluence with the Yangzi River at Wusong Kou. The distance from Wusong Kou to the north end of the Bund (Waitan) is about 29 km. On average the Huangpu is 400 meters wide and 9 meters deep. Traditionally this river has separated the older western half of Shanghai (Puxi) from the newer eastern half (Pudong).

As long ago as 1936, the Mayor of Shanghai, **Wu Tiecheng** [吴铁城] (1888-1953), had proposed building a bridge across the Huangpu from Puxi to Pudong. Nonetheless, the first bridge crossing the river wasn't completed until 55 years later with the opening of the Nanpu Bridge (Nanpu Da Qiao) [南浦大桥] in 1991. As recently as 1999 the easiest way to cross the Huangpu River from the West side (Puxi) to the East side (Pudong) was still to use the age-old method of floating across on the cross-river ferry (duchuan) for 0.5 Rmb. There were only two bridges and one tunnel to choose from, and both of those had steep toll gate charges of 15 Rmb each just to get to the other side. There was no subway connection then at all.

Today Pudong and Puxi are becoming increasingly integrated into a single whole through an ever growing network of cross-river transportation links, including a growing number of bridges and tunnels for motor vehicles, as well as an ever increasing number of subway lines. As of July 2009, there were six motor vehicle tunnels beneath the Huangpu River, with six more tunnels under construction and expected to be completed by 2010. By the year 2010 there will be a total of 17 bridges and tunnels open for motor vehicle traffic to cross the Huangpu River between Puxi and Pudong.

Huangpu River Bridges

The **Nanpu Bridge** (Nanpu Da Qiao) [南浦大桥] is a steel cable suspension highway bridge, and was the very first one to ever cross the Huangpu River when it was completed on December 1, 1991. The full length of the structure is 8,346 meters, including the main span of 423 meters. The bridge is 30 meters wide. H-shaped towers at each end hold up the 180 steel suspension cables and rise to a height of 154 meters. When it was completed it was considered the longest suspension bridge in China. It connects Zhongshan Nan Lu in Puxi with Longyang Lu in Pudong.

The **Yangpu Bridge** (Yangpu Da Qiao) [杨浦大桥] is a steel cable suspension highway bridge that was completed in October 1993, and was the second one to cross the Huangpu after the earlier Nanpu Da Qiao. The Yangpu Da Qiao [杨浦大桥] connects Yangpu District with Pudong. With a total length of 7,654 meters, including a main span of 602 meters, it was then the longest steel cable bridge in the world. It is held up by 256 steel cables.

The **Lupu Bridge** (Lupu Da Qiao) [卢浦大桥] was opened for traffic on June 28, 2003. It connects the Chongqing Nan Lu elevated expressway (gao jia) in Puxi with Yaohua Lu in Pudong. The bridge took three years to complete and cost $301 million U.S. dollars to build. Unlike the other bridges built across the Huangpu, the Lupu Bridge (Lupu Da Qiao) [卢浦大桥] is the only one built with a steel arch. The Nanpu, Yangpu, and Xupu bridges are all supported by steel suspension cables. In fact, the Lupu Bridge (Lupu Da Qiao) [卢

浦大桥] is the world's highest steel arch bridge, at a height of 550 meters.   Although the total length of the bridge is 3,900 meters, the main span is only 750 meters long.   The surface of the bridge hangs at an elevation of 46 meters above the water down below.

The Xupu Bridge (Xupu Da Qiao) [徐浦大桥] is a steel cable suspension highway bridge that forms part of the southern section of the Outer Ring Road (Wai Huan Lu).   It connects the southern end of Longwu Lu and the town of Huajing in Puxi with Jiyang Lu in Pudong.

Huangpu River Tunnels

The Bund Sightseeing Tunnel (Guanguan Suidao)

The "Bund Sightseeing Tunnel" was opened to the public in October 2000.   Traveling under the Huangpu River to connect Pudong (East River) with Puxi (West River), it has a length of 646.7 meters.   Although it seems no different from the Metro Line Two subway tunnel which also connects the two sides of the river, this one costs about ten times more to use.   You can get on board on the Bund at the foot of Nanjing Lu or on Lujiazui Lu at the foot of the Pearl Oriental T.V. Tower in Pudong.

Huangpu River Boat Rides

The **Shanghai Pujiang Company** operates a fleet of 17 sightseeing ships and provides an assortment of river boat cruises from their ticket office and dock facilities on the Bund (Waitan).   The shorter and cheaper cruises only travel up and down between the Nanpu and Yangpu Bridges, but longer and more expensive cruises south to the Lupu Bridge (Lupu Da Qiao) [卢浦大桥] and even as far north as the Huangpu's confluence with the Yangzi River at Wusong Kou are also available.
Address: 127 Zhongshan Dong Er Lu.
Phone: 6323-7755, 6318-8888
Web Site: http://www.SHPJYL.com

Cross-River Ferry (Huangpu Duchuan) [黄浦渡船]

The most enjoyable way to cross the Huanpgu River from west to east is still the good old fashioned ferry boat (duchuan) which thankfully is still running despite the increased competition it faces.   For the price of a few coins you can take a boat ride across the river, with the return trip costing the same.   This is without question the best bargain in Shanghai.   From the outside deck of the ship you get the best view of the historic buildings along the Bund (Waitan), which really can't be appreciated as well from up close.   This offers perfect perspective for photographers wanting to get a shot of the whole Bund.   The main ferry dock can be found at a spot historically known as **Shiliupu**, near the intersection of Zhongshan Dong Er Lu and Jinling Lu.

The International Cemetery (Wanguo Gongmu) [万国公墓]

Established as a private garden in 1909, then becoming an International Cemetery (Wanguo Gongmu) [万国公墓] in 1914 that was taken over by the Shanghai city government in 1934, until the 1949 revolution this was the special burial ground for foreign residents of Shanghai. In the 1930s upper class Chinese, such as the Song family, also gained admission to the site. The parents of Song Qingling [宋庆龄] (1893-1981), her father Song Jiashu (Charlie Soong) (1866-1918), and his wife (d. 1933) were buried here. The famous Chinese writer Lu Xun [鲁迅] (1881-1936) was originally buried here in 1936, before his remains were moved in 1956 to their current home in Hongkou District's Lu Xun Park.

Foreigners were still being buried here as late as May 1950. However, the foreigners' graves and Song family tombs were destroyed at the start of the Cultural Revolution in 1966. Finally, in 1981 the cemetery was reconstructed as a monument to Song Qingling [宋庆龄] (1893-1981).

The so-called Foreigners' Tomb Area (Waijiren Muyuan) [外籍人墓园] now occupies just one small corner of the grounds. The names of those buried here represent many nationalities, including British, American, French, Spanish, Korean, and Vietnamese. However, very few of the gravestones contain the dates of birth and death, with some only featuring the initials of the person's name. Furthermore, almost all the 28 rows of graves feature uniform headstones with no variation in size, style, lettering or material. Clearly, these are not the original grave stones, but replicas dating from the 1981 reconstruction. In 2002 there was still a pile of original broken tombstones in one corner of the park. They contained English language names and dates, with the earliest dated 1870 and the latest 1950. Many of the names were Jewish. Unfortunately, in 2004 this pile of broken relics disappeared, and that corner of the park was turned into a car wash and parking lot.

The most famous names found on the existing gravestones are the four dedicated to members of the Sassoon and Kadoorie families. Sir Victor Sassoon, who built the Peace Hotel in 1929 and whose house is nearby, is not buried here, but three other members of his family are, including Joseph Sassoon (d. 1946), Aaron Sassoon (d. 1946) and Charles Sassoon (d. 1941). The Kadoorie headstone is by far the largest and most impressive in the foreigners' area. It is dedicated to both Sir Elly Kadoorie (d. February 8, 1944) and his wife Lady Laura Kadoorie (d. 1918). It contains the interesting inscription, "The true grave of the dead is in the heart of the living." The Kadoorie's were famous for constructing the famous Marble Hall, which is now the Shanghai Children's Palace (Shanghai Xiaonian Gong) on Yanan Xi Lu. All four gravestones include English and Hebrew inscriptions.

Address: 21 Songyuan Lu, Changning District.
Phone: (021) 6275-4034, 6275-4145

The **International Settlement** (Shanghai Gonggong Zujie) [上海公共租界]

From 1854 to 1862 the three foreign settlements cooperated under one municipal government headed by the Shanghai Municipal Council (Shanghai Gongbu Ju) [上海工部局] established in 1854, but after the French dropped out of this arrangement in 1862, the British & American settlements merged into the unified International Settlement (Shanghai Gonggong Zujie) [上海公共租界] in 1863.

In the beginning, the International occupied most of the Bund (Waitan) waterfront along the Huangpu River, as well as parts of what are now Hongkou and Yangpu districts North of the Suzhou River.   The main street of the International Settlement was Nanking Road, now Nanjing East Road (Nanjing Dong Lu) [南京东路], which at its intersection with Tibet Road (Xizang Lu) changed its name to Bubbling Well Road (Nanjing Xi Lu).   The northern limits were clearly marked by Suzhou Creek west of Xizang Zhong Lu and the appropriately named Boundary Road (Tianmu Lu) in the Zhabei district.   Shanghai's North Train Station sat just across the Settlement's northern boundary, in the same place where the modern station stands today.   The Settlement's eastern limit was the Huangpu River, and the southern limit the boundary with the French Concession along what was originally a canal known as the Yangjingbang but later became Yanan Dong Lu and Yanan Xi Lu.   In 1853 the western boundary of the British Concession had been considered to follow the North-South line of Defence Creek, where present day Xizang Zhong Lu (Tibet Middle Road) runs, but since this boundary had not actually been clearly marked in the original agreements with Chinese authorities, over time the International Settlement was able to continue expanding in a westward direction.

One method of covert expansion was an aggressive road building program, which consistently extended far outside the settlement's established boundaries.   Once a new road was built, the Settlement authorities would insist that all residents and businesses located along it must pay taxes to the Shanghai Municipal Council.   In turn, as taxpayers they were then entitled to Settlement police, fire and militia protection.   The Settlement authorities would then appeal to the Chinese government that these taxpayers and roads outside the concession boundaries should be brought inside by extending the boundary to include them.   Use of this method over time resulted in extending the Settlement's official western boundary as far as the Buddhist temple Jingan Si on Bubbling Well Road (Nanjing Xi Lu), near the latter's convergence with Yanan Xi Lu.

A series of four diplomatic agreements gradually enlarged the official boundaries of the International Settlement.   Starting with an area of only 138 acres in 1846, the British concession had already grown to 470 acres in 1848.   The merger of the British and American concessions in 1863 gave the newly established International Settlement a total area of 1,779 acres.   In May 1899 the Shanghai Municipal Council concluded successful negotiations with the Chinese authorities that extended the Settlement boundaries to its farthest limits, including almost all the roads previously built outside the boundaries.   This 1899 extension added 1,896 acres North of the Suzhou River and 1,908 acres to the West of the existing Settlement.   At its maximum size after the 1899 extension, the International Settlement covered 8.3 square miles of what is now downtown Shanghai, including 31,000 feet of prime waterfront along the Huangpu River.   Its western boundary was now just past Jingan Si, and roughly followed the north-south line of today's Yan Ping Lu, just west of Jiao Zhou Lu, from the intersection of Huashan Lu and Changshu Lu in the south to Suzhou Creek in the north.

J

The **Jade Buddha Temple** (Yu Fo Chan Si) [玉佛禅寺]

The origins of the **Jade Buddha Temple** (Yu Fo Chan Si) [玉佛禅寺] date back to 1882, but it has changed locations, been rebuilt, and expanded several times since then. Although the temple's name is usually shortened to simply Yufo Si [玉佛寺] in colloquial speech, the word "Chan" indicates that this temple belongs to the Zen Meditations sect of Chinese Buddhism known in Chinese as Chan Zong [禅宗]. It's considered one of the big three Buddhist temples (San Da Si) [三大寺] located in the Shanghai city center, along with Longhua Si and Jingan Si.

In 1882, the 8th year of the Guangxu reign of the Qing Dynasty, Hui Gen [慧根法师], a monk from the Sacred Buddhist island of Putuoshan [普陀山] in Zhejiang province, traveled to Burma. On his return he brought back seven jade Buddha statues with him, sending five of them to Putuoshan and leaving two of them in Shanghai. Of the latter two, one was a seated Buddha (Yu Fo) [玉佛] while another was a reclining Buddha (Yu Wo Fo) [玉卧佛], both carved entirely from single blocks of jade. A temple was built in 1882 to house these statues in Shanghai's Jiangwan Town, a different location than it presently occupies, but later it was moved to the present location. In 1900 a train station on the railway line from Jiangwan Town to Wusongkou was built right beside the Jade Buddha Temple's original location, and this proved fateful later, as it made it a very strategic site. During the 1911 Revolution (Xinhai Geming) that overthrew the Qing Dynasty, the original buildings of the Jade Buddha Temple located in Jiangwan Town were completely destroyed by the fighting between different factions of soldiers, while the Jade Buddha statues themselves just barely survived.

In 1918 the temple moved to its current location and construction started on new buildings. Like all other temples in Shanghai, the Jade Buddha Temple was closed to the public during the ten-year Cultural Revolution, but unlike the others the Yufo Si somehow managed to prevent its Buddha statues and religious articles from being destroyed, and the Buddhist monks may even have been allowed to remain inside, while at all other temples they were "sent home." As a result, after the Cultural Revolution ended in 1976 it was able to quickly reinstate normal religious practices only three years later in 1979, being the very first temple of any kind to reopen in Shanghai.

Entering the temple compound from the main gate on Anyuan Lu, the first courtyard is sandwiched between the **Heavenly King's Hall** (Tian Wang Dian) [天王殿] to the south and the **Hall of the Great Hero** (Da Xiong Bao Dian) [大雄宝殿] on the north side. The Tian Wang Dian [天王殿] contains incredibly impressive statues of the Four Heavenly Kings (Tian Wang) [四天王], while the Da Xiong Bao Dian [大雄宝殿] houses three gilded statues of various incarnations of Buddha (Fo) [佛], including the Medecine Buddha (Yaoshifo) [药师佛] , Sakyamuni (Shijiamouni) [释迦牟尼], and Amitabha (Emituo Fo) [阿弥陀佛].

Walking counter clockwise around the temple compound takes you past the **Meditation Hall** (Chan Tang) [禅堂] courtyard on the east side to the entrance into the courtyard of the two-story **Jade Buddha Building** (Yu Fo Lou) [玉佛楼] housing the seated Jade Buddha (Yu Fo) [玉佛]. You have to buy a separate 10 Rmb ticket to enter this inner sanctum. Photos are not allowed of the jewel encrusted 1.92 meter high seated Jade Buddha (Yu Fo) [玉佛] statue housed on the second floor.

Exiting this inner courtyard continue in a counter clockwise direction along the west side of the original temple compound back towards the first courtyard at the south end. Walking this way will take you past the separate courtyard of the **Reclining Jade Buddha** (Yu Wo Fo) [玉卧佛] on the west side. Photographs are allowed of this statue housed in a ground floor hall of the two-story building. In fact, the Reclining Buddha (Yu Wo Fo) [玉卧佛] on display is a copy of the jade original, which is kept from public view. The original Reclining Jade Buddha [玉卧佛] was only 96 cm. long, but the new copy is 4 meters long and was a gift from Singapore in 1989.

The **Shanghai Buddhist Association** is located here, as is a Buddhism School (Fo Xue), which enrolls about 30 monks each year. There is also a famous vegetarian restaurant.

In March 2003 Yu Fo Si [玉佛寺] began a major expansion and renovation that was finally completed in November 2004 at a cost of $15.7 million USD. The area of the temple grounds grew by an additional 4,000 sq. meters to a total of 12,700 sq. meters. Thanks to this expansion, the temple's Abbot Jue Xing hoped to double enrollment in the Buddhism School to 60 students per year. He also planned on sending monks to attend English classes at local universities in order to better handle the foreign tourists among the 4,000 visitors the temple received each day.

The main hall of the **Jade Buddha Temple** (Yufo Si) [玉佛寺] was moved 30 meters on tracks in September 2017 in order to create a larger courtyard that could hold more visitors, much like the **Shanghai Concert Hall** was previously moved over 66 meters back in 2004, but unlike the **White Cloud Taoist Temple** (Baiyun Guan) [白云观], which was torn down to make room for the 2010 Expo, after which a fake copy of the same name was built elsewhere, despite inaccurate claims that it too was "moved."

Address: 170 Anyuan Lu [安远路 170 号], at the corner with Jiangning Lu, Putuo District (Putuo Qu) [普陀区].
Nearest Metro Station: Nanjing West Road (Nanjing Xi Lu) [南京西路] Station on Line 2.
Phone: (021) 6266-3668

Jewish Monuments

When the Communists occupied Shanghai in May 1949, the city had four main synagogues. The Sephardic **Ohel Rachel Synagogue** at 500 Shaanxi Bei Lu [陕西北路 500] (formerly Seymour Road) was founded by Sir Jacob Sassoon in 1920. Although it still stands it is no longer a functioning house of worship. Although it was being used as office space by the Shanghai Education Commission, it has officially been closed to public visitors since April 2002. The **Ohel Moshe Synagogue** at 62 Changyang Lu [长阳路 62] (formerly Ward Road) was founded by Russian Jews in 1907, and later moved to its present site in 1927. The **Beth Aharon Synagogue** on Huqiu Lu [虎丘路] (formerly Museum Road) was established by Silas A. Hardoon in 1927, and housed the Mir Yeshiva during the 1937-1945 Japanese occupation, but was demolished in 1985. The **New Synagogue** was built on Xiangyang Nan Lu [襄阳南路] (formerly Route Tenant de la Tour) by Russian Ashkenazim in 1941. After 1953 it was the only functioning synagogue still in operation. Services continued until 1956, making it not only the last built before the 1949 revolution, but also the last to be closed down by the new Communist regime. After its closure over 4,000 Jewish books were shipped from Shanghai to Israel. In 1993 the New Synagogue was also demolished.

Jewish Refugee Museum (Youtai Nanmin Jinian Guan) [犹太难民纪念馆]

Shanghai was the only city in the world that welcomed Jewish refugees (Youtai nanmin) [犹太难民] from Germany with open arms during the 1930s, accepting an estimated 20,000 to 30,000 Jewish refugees from Europe before 1941. By Pan Guang's estimate, at the end of 1941 the city contained a total of 25,000 Jewish refugees, most of them living in the Yangpu and Hongkou districts of the city. On February 18, 1943 the Japanese proclaimed what was officially known as the "Designated Area for Stateless Refugees," but was unofficially called the Hongkou Jewish ghetto. By 1956 the Jewish refugees had all left Shanghai.

The former **Ohel Moishe Synagogue** in Yangpu district now hosts a small museum devoted to the Jewish refugees who came here. The synagogue (Youtai Jiaotang) [犹太教堂] is a three-story red brick building built by Russian Ashkenazi Jews on **Ward Road** (Changyang Lu) [长阳路] of the International Settlement in 1927. The congregation was led by Rabbi Meir Ashkenazi from the synagogue's founding in 1927 until it was closed down in 1949. It is no longer a functioning synagogue although it is open to the public as a musem with exhibits of black and white photographs.

There is also a small memorial to the Jewish refugees in nearby **Huoshan Park** (Huoshan Gongyuan) [霍山公园] located at 118 Huoshan Lu [霍山路 118], formerly known as **Wayside Road**. The monument contains information about the "Designated Area for Stateless Refugees," otherwise known as the Jewish ghetto, which existed in this area during the 1937-1945 Japanese occupation. The trilingual inscription is written in English, Chinese and Hebrew. The monument states that the Designated Area for Stateless Refugees was bounded by Gongping Lu in the west, Tongbei Lu in the east, Huiming Lu in the south, and Zhoujiazui Lu on the north.

Address: 62 Changyang Lu [长阳路 62], near Zhoushan Lu, Yangpu District [杨浦区].
Phone: (021) 6541-5008, 6512-0229

Jiading City God Temple (Jiading Chenghuang Miao) [嘉定城隍庙]

The Jiading City God Temple (Jiading Chenghuang Miao) [嘉定城隍庙] was originally built during the Southern Song Dynasty (1127-1279), shortly after Jiading Town became the new county seat in 1218, and was then located on South Big Lane (Nan Da Jie).   Later it was moved to its present location in 1370, two years after the founding of the Ming Dynasty. The main hall (Da Dian) which stands today was last rebuilt in 1882 during the Qing Dynasty. The temple was re-opened in 1987 after having been closed for at least 20 years since at least the start of the Cultural Revolution in 1966.   It is in excellent condition, with a fair balance between restored features and original historic relics.

Walking east down the cobblestone East Big Lane (Dong Da Jie) from Bole Lu, a canal runs beside you on the south side of the lane, and you begin to see street vendors selling religious trinkets such as incense sticks, red candles, and paper lotus flowers. Approaching the South Gate (Nan Men) of the temple's walled compound, the first sight is of two ancient Stone Pavilions (Jing Ting) standing outside either side of the gate.   Looking up you can see that the roof eaves of each pavilion are decorated with rows of countless figurines depicting Confucian scholars dressed in their robes.

Passing through the South Gate, you approach the temple along a long pathway lined with trees.   The courtyard in front of the main hall has a golden incense burner where the local inhabitants can be seen burning incense sticks and red candles.

Looking up at the roof of the Big Hall (Da Dian) you can see that it is decorated with larger statues of Confucian scholars reading books.   Inside in the center of the hall is a large golden statue of the Jiading city god, **Liu Jiashu**, who is depicted as a Confucian scholar. Along both sides of the hall are 60 smaller statues of lesser individuals.   Some are depicted in quite curious ways, including one man who for some reason has two feet sticking out of his eyes, and another with a rabbit on his head.   Prayer cushions on the floor in front of the statues are signs of active worship.

This temple sits just in front of the Ming Dynasty **Qiuxiapu** garden and is entered via the same gate on East Big Lane (Dong Da Jie).   The garden can be reached by walking north from Pagoda City Road (Ta Cheng Lu) on Bole Lu, and then turning east onto the cobblestone East Big Lane (Dong Da Jie).   Alternatively, you could walk several blocks directly east from the Lotus Scripture Pagoda (Fahua Ta) (aka Jinsha Ta), or south from City Middle Road (Chengzhong Lu).

Address: 314 East Big Lane (Dong Da Jie), Jiading Town, Jiading District
Phone: (021) 5991-2440, 5953-1949
Nearest Metro Station: Line 11.

Jiading Confucius Temple (Jiading Kong Miao) [嘉定孔庙]

The Jiading Confucius Temple (Jiading Kong Miao) [嘉定孔庙] was originally constructed in 1219 during the Southern Song (Nan Song) Dynasty (1127-1279), but did not reach its full scale until 1603, the 31st year of the Wanli reign of the Ming Dynasty, after which it continued to be an active center of Confucian worship up till the end of the Qing Dynasty in 1911. Although it was damaged during both the Small Swords Society (Xiaodao Hui) and Taiping rebellions of the 19th century, it had been repaired afterward. When Elizabeth Crump Enders visited in 1925 she described it as already being abandoned, "the empty corridors and rooms were quite deserted in their melancholy solitude." Nonetheless her description closely matches the way it still looks today, right down to the ancient gnarled trees in the courtyard, the stone gates, and rows of stone lions. During the later years of the Republic of China (Minguo) (1911-1949), apparently after Enders' 1925 visit, the temple buildings were reportedly occupied by a rice factory. Then, it was bombed by the Japanese air force during the Second Sino-Japanese War (1937-1945). From 1959 to 1963 the temple was subjected to a massive reconstruction project by the local government, which included repairing the three memorial archways (paifang), the Lingxing Gate, the Da Cheng Men, the Da Cheng Dian, the Minglun Tang, and the Danghu Shuyuan. During this time the Jiading Museum occupied the site in 1961. Unfortunately, only a few years after this restoration project was completed, during the Cultural Revolution (1966-1976) some parts of the temple compound were completely torn down, while other parts were damaged, and it was covered with political posters. From 1981 through 1985 the whole site went through extensive repairs and reconstruction. In 1990 stautes of Confucius' 72 disciples were placed inside the main hall. In the year 2000 the bridges over the Pan Chi were repaired. Today, this is by far the best preserved Confucius temple within the Shanghai municipality. By comparison, the Confucius Temple (Wen Miao) [文庙] in downtown Shanghai is an entirely new reconstruction dating from 1999, while the Study Palace on Chongming Island is much smaller in scale.

A cobblestone road leading off of South Big Lane (Nan Da Jie) passes through the immense ancient stone memorial archway (paifang) [牌坊] covered with a tiled roof of upturned eaves known as the West Gate. Beyond it stand two more similar ancient stone memorial archways (paifang) [牌坊. The South Memorial Archway (Yanggao Fang) [仰高坊] leads directly to the Dragon's Meeting Pool (Huilong Tan) [汇龙潭] and is guarded by two large statues of lions, while the East Memorial Archway (Xingxian Fang) [兴贤坊] leads to a single arch stone foot bridge known variously as either the Guests Permitted Bridge (Binxing Qiao) [宾兴桥] or the Dragon Gate Bridge (Longmen Qiao) [龙门桥] over the Hengli He [横沥河] canal and the gate house entrance to Dragon's Meeting Pool Park (Huilong Tan Gongyuan) [汇龙潭公园]. Each gate has a two-character inscription in its horizontal stone lintel. The West Memorial Archway (Yucai Fang) [育才坊] facing South Big Lane (Nan Da Jie) is inscribed with the two characters "Yu Cai" [育才], meaning roughly education and talent, while the South Memorial Archway (Yanggao Fang) [仰高坊] facing the Dragons Meeting Pool (Huilong Tan) [汇龙潭] bears the two characters, "Yang Gao " [仰高], meaning high admiration, and the East Memorial Archway (Xingxian Fang) [兴贤坊] facing the Guests Permitted Bridge (Binxing Qiao) [宾兴桥] over the Hengli He [横沥河] has the two characters for "Xing Xian" [兴贤], meaning to encourage virtuous persons. These inscriptions are appropriate since education and respect for those above you in the social hierarchy were important facets of Confucianism. Rows of small figurines of robed Confucian scholars grace the upturned eaves of the stone gates tiled roofs. The cobblestone road is lined with a stone balustrade decorated with 72 statues of small stone lions (shi shiezi) [石狮子].

The six pillar, three portal, stone **Star Gate** (Lingxing Men) [棂星门] features stone columns with cloud pattern carvings at the top. However, a close look reveals that the top parts of these columns all appear to be separate pieces that have been glued on to the lower part. My guess is that the lower parts of the stone columns are new, while the upper parts with the cloud pattern carvings are real relics. In addition, there are no horizontal inscriptions where there should be. Immediately inside the gate you can see what may be the original stone pillars laying on the ground.

Passing through this entrance to the Confucius Temple, one enters a large courtyard, in the center of which is a half-moon shaped pool of water known as the **Pan Chi** [泮池] crossed by three parallel stone footbridges (Hongji Shiqiao) [泓及石桥]. Although the stone balustrades of the bridges seem be of recent reconstruction, their arches underneath appear to be original. The central bridge is kept roped off because it has an ornate stone carving on its floor.

Crossing the pool, you come to the rectangular wooden gate hall known as the **Da Cheng Men** [大成门]. Sheltered under the eaves of this hall is a collection of stone stele tablets inscribed with lengthy inscriptions. Seven of the stele stand atop stone turtles in Ming-style, while a dozen more smaller tablets are cemented into the walls of the hall. If one looks around the walled perimeter of this first courtyard you can find the broken remains of many more stone carved relics that have been piled up there.

Exiting out of the **Da Cheng Men** [大成门] gate hall, you enter a second much larger rectangular courtyard lined with side halls along both the West and East sides, with the main hall of the temple, the Da Cheng Dian [大成殿], straight ahead at the North end. These east and west side halls used to serve as ancestral temples (ci) for respected deceased local residents and government officials, but now hold museum exhibits. Standing in the courtyard are rows of ancient gnarled grey cedar trees. Many more inscribed stone tablets are cemented into the walls in various places.

Standing at the north end of the courtyard, the main hall, known as the **Da Cheng Dian** [大成殿], is notable for its immense tiled roof which rises up to an impressively high central ridge, with a very steep slope and upturned eaves. Parts of the stone balustrade around the hall's front terrace seem to have once been repaired with concrete, but at least half of it is composed of the original stone pieces. Inside the main hall is dominated by a wooden statue of Confucius (Kong Fuzi) [孔夫子] (551-479 B.C.) seated inside a wooden shrine. In front of the statue is a collection of ancient musical instruments, including a set of bronze bells.

The Da Cheng Dian stands in what we could call the Western courtyards. Running parallel to these, but separated from them by a high wall, is another set of Eastern courtyards that contained the Confucian academy (shuyuan) described in the next section.

Address: 183 South Big Lane (Nan Da Jie 183 hao) [南大街 183 号], Jiading Town, Jiading District
Nearest Metro Station: Line 11

Jiading Confucian Academy (Jiading Shuyuan) [嘉定书院]

Separated by a long internal wall from the Confucius Temple next door, stretching along the full length of the eastern end of the walled compound, beside the Hengli He, is a series of four courtyards and four buildings that collectively formed the Jiading Confucian Academy used to prepare candidates to take the imperial civil service examinations, which were based on a knowledge of the Confucian classics.

In the southeast corner of the Jiading Confucius Temple compound, in between the East Memorial Archway (Xingxian Fang) [兴贤坊] and the Guests Permitted Bridge (Binxing Qiao) [宾兴桥] or the Dragon Gate Bridge (Longmen Qiao) [龙门桥] over the Hengli He [横沥河], there is a separate gate house that once led into the Confucian Academy.   However, this gate is now kept closed.   There is no inscription or signboard over this gate, so we can't be sure of its name, but at other Confucian academies this would have been called the Rites Gate (Yi Men) [仪门] or the Study Gate (Xue Men).

Separated from the gate house by a small courtyard is a small walled compound containing two buildings.   According to maps of the site, this first hall should have been for the Confucianism Bureau (Ruxue Shu) [儒学署], but a Chinese language sign beside the entrance to this second courtyard calls it the **Dang Lake Academy** (Danghu Shuyuan) [当湖书院] established in 1765 during the Qianlong reign (1736-1795) of the Qing Dynasty.   It is also attributed to the modern-day Shanghai Association for Confucianism Studies, and the Autumn Glow Academy Library established in September 2009.   Inside this hall there are three rooms of exhibits devoted to Confucian academies all around China, including the White Deer Cave Academy (Bailu Dong Shuyuan) at the foot of Mount Lushan in Jiangxi Province. Oddly, there is a third courtyard and building behind this one that is kept closed.

Following a separate corridor between these three halls of the Confucian Academy and the Pan Chi [泮池] takes you to the Etiquette Gate (Li Men) [礼门] which leads into one large courtyard containing the Minglun Tang [明伦堂], behind which are replicas of the tiny examination rooms (kaochang) [考场].   Behind the Minglun Tang [明伦堂] is a building for the temple administration offices.   Between the back of this office building and the compound's outer wall one can find some broken stone relics, as is often the case with temples in China that have been restored.   Oddly, there is no inscribed signboard on the Minglun Tang [明伦堂] bearing its name, nor is there one on the Etiquette Gate (Li Men) [礼门], so this information has to be inferred from other sources.   Inside the Minglun Tang [明伦堂] has been turned into a museum devoted to the Chinese imperial civil service examination system.

For centuries the imperial civil service exams provided the only way to become a government official, which was also almost the only path of upward mobility in society, up until the time they were finally abolished in 1905, just before the end of the Qing Dynasty in 1911. There were three levels of examinations and corresponding degrees: county level (Xiucai)[秀才], provincial level (Juren) [举人], and national level (Jinshi) [进士].   The candidate (Shengyuan) [生员] who scored the highest on the national level examinations in any given year was given the special title of Zhuangyuan [状元].

Because the test questions were based on the Confucian classics, the shuyuan [书院] schools which helped students prepare for the exams were usually located beside the town's Confucius Temple.   According to the administrative hierarchy, these schools were sometimes called the Xian Xue, Fu Xue, Sheng Xue, Guo Xue, etc.

Although there had previously been more volumes, since the neo-Confucian reforms of Zhu Xi [朱熹](1130-1200) during the Song Dynasty, the Confucian Classics had come to be known as the Four Books and Five Classics (Sishu Wujing) [四书五经], with the main emphasis being on the Four Books (Sishu) [四书] , including the Great Learning (Daxue) [大学], the Doctrine of the Mean (Zhongyong) [中庸], the Analects (Lunyu) [论语], and Mencius (Mengze) [孟子].

The main test question involved writing was known as an eight-legged essay (baguwen) [八股文].   Successfully passing these tests usually guaranteed a job in the government bureaucracy, but the rote memorization required for successful preparation usually also killed any creativity or critical thinking skills.

Since January 2006 these eastern courtyards have been converted into the **China Imperial Examination Museum** (Zhongguo Keju Bowuguan) [中国科举博物馆].   The exhibits are fairly interesting, and depict what the examination process was like for the participants, who were confined to tiny cubicles while taking the tests.   There are also samples of the special mandarin robes that each degree holder was entitled to wear.

Address: 183 Nan Da Jie, Jiading Zhen, Jiading District.
Phone: (021) 5953-0379, (021) 5953-3789, (021) 5991-9581.
Nearest Metro Station: Line 11

Jiading Dragons Meeting Pool Park (Huilong Tan Gongyuan) [汇龙潭公园]

The Jiading Dragons Meeting Pool Park (Huilong Tan Gongyuan) [汇龙潭公园] was created in 1588 during the 16th year of the Wanli reign (1573-1620) of the Ming Dynasty, when five canals were joined together in this spot, surrounding the man-made island hill known as **Yingkui Shan** [应奎山]. The Hengli He [横沥河] flows all the way from the **Lotus Sutra Pagoda** (Fahua Ta) [法华塔], past the Jiading **Confucius Temple** (Jiading Kong Miao) [嘉定孔庙] to the **Dragons Meeting Pond** (Huilong Tan) [汇龙潭].

From 1928 to 1945 the park was known as Kuishan Gongyuan [奎山公园], and included the nearby Confucius Temple (Kong Miao). From 1976 to 1978 the park was rebuilt and expanded with a large investment from the Jiading county government. On January 6, 1979 the rebuilt park opened to the public as Huilong Tan Gongyuan [汇龙潭公园]. In 1980 the Jiading No. 1 Rice Mill Factory was demolished in order to make way for a second expansion of the park's area to the east of the canal. In December 1982 the eastern expansion was supposedly completed, but the new extension of the park did not open to the public until March 1984.

Nowadays the park extends one whole city block in length, stretching from Pagoda City Road (Ta Cheng Lu) in the North to Shaxia Lu [沙霞路] in the South. It can be entered from either a gate on Pagoda City Road (Ta Cheng Lu), which is usually kept closed, or by taking the cobblestone road from South Big Lane (Nan Da Jie) which passes by the Confucius Temple (Kong Miao) and crosses the single-arch stone footbridge known as the Binxing Qiao or the **Dragon Gate Bridge** (Longmen Qiao) [龙门桥] over a canal known as the Hengli He to the park's West Gate House, which is also known as the **Literary God Pavilion** (Wenchang Ge). Beside the park's ticket booth is the only good bilingual map I've seen of Jiading Town and all its historic sights. Immediately inside the gate is a Chinese language map of the park and a bilingual introduction.

In the southeast corner stands a one-story square structure designed as a Peking Opera stage for theater performances, with one of its four sides open facing the lawn. It is known variously as the **Beating & Singing Terrace** (Da Chang Tai) [打唱台], or the **100 Birds Sunrise Terrace** (Bainiao Chaoyang Tai) [百鸟朝阳台], **All Birds Looking at the Phoenix Terrace** (Bainiao Chaofeng Tai) [百鸟朝凤台]. It was supposedly first built in 1888 during the 15th year of the Guangxu reign of the Qing Dynasty and then later moved here from another location in 1976. Stepping inside and looking upward one can see that it has a gilded wooden dome (zaojing) [藻井] spiraling upward in the ceiling. Beside this there is a memorial obelisk known as the Hou Huang Jinian Bei first erected in 1961 and restored in 1981.

In the center of the park is a stone carved Buddhist tower sometimes known simply as the **Stone Tower** (Shi Ta) [石塔], other times called the **Ten Thousand Buddha Tower** (Wan Fo Bao Ta) [万佛宝塔]. It stands four meters tall and has stone carvings of Buddhas on three sides, but the fourth side is curiously blank. In 1980 it was moved here to this park from its previous location outside the town's South Gate (Nan Men wai) on Stone Tower Lane (Shi Ta Long) [石塔弄]. A plaque that simply refers to it as the Stone Pagoda (Shi Ta) [石塔] notes that it was declared a Jiading county level protected relic in 1961 and again in 1981.

In the southwest corner of the park is a two-story square pavilion known as the **Kuixing Ge** [魁星阁], which stands on a round peninsula that juts out into the dragon pool. Its first floor has four round wooden gates, each with an inscription above it. The gate inscriptions refer to four sacred animals which represent the four divisions of the 28 constellations (sixiang) [四象], including the blue dragon (canglong [苍龙], white tiger (baihu) [白虎], vermillion bird (zhuque) [朱雀], and black tortoise (xuanwu) [玄武]. Normally, every Confucian academy (shuyuan) [书院] had a Kuixing Ge [魁星阁] pavilion which would be ascended by the scholar who received the highest score in that year's imperial examinations. A photo taken of this same spot by Elizabeth Crump Enders and published in her book "*Temple Bells and Silver Sails*," (1925) shows the Jiading Kuixing Ge [魁星阁] looking remarkably identical to the way it does today. Miraculously, visitors are able to climb up the wooden stairs inside the pavilion to the outdoor veranda from which you can pretend to be announcing yourself to the world as the top scholar.

The three-story octagonal pavilion known as the **Champion Bell Tower** (Zhuangyuan Zhong Lou) [状元钟楼] stands on the summit of a 40 meter high hill called **Yingkui Shan** [应奎山], which is on a rocky island in the middle of the Huilong Tan dragon pool. In imperial China, the candidate who scored the highest on the palace examinations was called the Zhuangyuan [状元]. Thus, the name of this pavilion is related to the imperial examination system and refers to the Confucian tradition of having the student who received the best test score ascend to a high tower where he could be honored. At other Confucius Temples, such as the Wen Miao [文庙] in downtown Shanghai, this role was performed by the Kuixing Ge [魁星阁], but here the role seems to have been taken by the Zhuangyuan Zhong Lou.

The Huilong Tan dragon pool was originally a part of the nearby Jiading Confucian Academy (Jiading Shuyuan) [嘉定书院] and Confucius Temple (Jiading Kong Miao) [嘉定孔庙] next door, although now the majority of the park is separated from them by the Hengli He [横沥河] canal. Although the Huilong Tan, Kuixing Ge, and Yingkui Shan can be seen from the Confucius Temple's front gate, in order to enter the park one must pass through the East Memorial Archway (Xingxian Fang) [兴贤坊], cross the Binxing Qiao stone foot bridge over the Hengli He [横沥河] canal, and pass through another gate house known a the Literary God Pavilion (Wenchang Ge) where you must buy a separate ticket. After that it takes crossing two more stone foot bridges before you can finally reach the island in the center of the lake.

The North Gate of the park facing Pagoda City Road (Ta Cheng Lu) is marked by the **Changguan Lou** [畅观楼], a two-story wooden house dating from the Tongzhi reign of the Qing Dynasty which was moved here in 1980 as part of the park's 1980-1983 second expansion. Just inside this northeast entrance gate you can find a wall map of the park and a wall poster of key sights in the park, both labeled in Chinese. Also located in the center of this newer eastern extension area is the small carved stone relic known as the **Ten Thousand Buddha Pagoda** (Wanfo Baota) [万佛宝塔], similar to the one found in the Garden of Ancient Splendor (Guyi Yuan) in Nanxiang Town, but the origins of which are somewhat mysterious.

Address: North Gate at 299 Pagoda City Road (Ta Cheng Lu 299 hao) [塔城路 299 号] or West Gate at 183 South Big Lane (Nan Da Jie 183 hao), Jiading Zhen, Jiading District. Nearest Metro Station: Line 11.

Jiading Town (Jiading Chengqu) [嘉定城区]

As the capital city of Jiading County (Jiading Xian) [嘉定县], it was officially known as Jiading Xiancheng [嘉定县城], but colloquially could also be called Jiading Zhen [嘉定镇].   After Jiading County was elevated to the status of a district, it became known officially as Jiading Urban District (Jiading Chengqu) [嘉定城区], or colloquially as Jiading City (Jiading Chengshi) [嘉定城市].   It may seem odd that one city could belong to another city, as Qingpu City belongs to Shanghai City, but in modern China this administrative structure has become quite common as the previous term prefecture (fu) has fallen out of use since 1949. For example, in nearby Jiangsu province, Kunshan city belongs to Suzhou city, Danyang city belongs to Changzhou city, Jiangyin city belongs to Wuxi city, and Gaoyou city belongs to Yangzhou city.   Nonetheless, since these suburban district capital cities still look and feel more like small towns than cities I think I will continue to use the term town as more appropriate.

Jiading Town used to be called Lianqi Town [练祁镇] in the Tang Dynasty (618-907), after the Lianqi River (Lianqi He) [练祁河].   Sandwiched in between the Wusong River [吴淞江] to the south and the Liu River (Liu He) [浏河] to the north, other notable rivers or canals that cross the Jiading area include the Hengli He [横沥河], Yangshu Bang [杨树浜], and the Xiang Jing [项泾].   The Hengli He [横沥河] flows from northwest to southeast all the way from the north City Moat (Hucheng He), through an intersection with the west-east canal known as the Lianqi River (Lianqi He) [练祁河], past the **Lotus Sutra Pagoda** (Fahua Ta) [法华塔], underneath Pagoda City Road (Ta Cheng Lu), past the Jiading **Confucius Temple** (Jiading Kong Miao) [嘉定孔庙] to the **Dragons Meeting Pond** (Huilong Tan) [汇龙潭], then flows out of the pond, underneath Shaxia Lu [沙霞路], all the way to the south City Moat (Hucheng He).

Lianqi Town [练祁镇] (aka Jiading Town) became the county seat of the newly established Jiading County (Jiading Xian) of Suzhou Prefecture (Suzhou Fu) in 1219, during the 12th year of the Jiading reign of the Southern Song (Nan Song) Dynasty.   Shortly after its designation as a county seat, a **City God Temple** (Chenghuang Miao) and a **Confucius Temple** (Kong Miao) were built, both of which still stand today. Like the similar ancient towns of Qingpu and Songjiang, Jiading Town was once a circular walled city.   Jiading Town's brick city wall [城墙] was first built in 1358, during the Shundi reign of the last Yuan Dynasty emperor Toghon Temur, aka Yuan Zhizheng, by the rebel leader **Zhang Shicheng** [张士诚] (1321-1367) who had made nearby Suzhou his capital city two years earlier in 1356.   Later Jiading's city wall was enlarged to a circumference of about four miles in 1553 during the 32nd year of the Jiajing reign of the Ming Dynasty.   At its peak the Jiading city wall had four land gates and four water gates.

After the fall of the Ming Dynasty capital of Beijing in May 1644, Jiading became an important stronghold of Ming loyalist resistance against the Manchus newly established Qing Dynasty.   Even after the Southern Ming (Nan Ming) capital of Nanjing was captured by the Manchus on June 8, 1645, the walled city of Jiading refused to surrender.   Finally, on August 24, 1645 almost the entire population of the town, an estimated 20,000 people, was massacred by the enraged Manchu conquerors in an incident described by Jerry Dennerline in his book *The Chia-Ting Loyalists,* published by Yale University Press in 1981.

During the Taiping Rebellion (1850-1864), when the Taipings made Nanjing their capital city and nearby Suzhou was also a major stronghold of theirs, Jiading Town was the first town within the modern day Shanghai municipality captured by the Taipings during their first offensive against Shanghai in June 1860, and the last one they abandoned at the end of their third Shanghai offensive in October 1862.   Lianqi Town's name was not officially changed to Jiading Town until 1928, and it was not until 1958 that the entire Jiading County was finally separated from Jiangsu Province and made a part of the Shanghai municipality.

Jiading Town was once surrounded by a circular city wall (chengqiang) [城墙].   The city wall and its gates are long gone, but street names remain to commemorate where they were, and the circular city moat (huchenghe)[护城河] is still completely intact.   When Elizabeth Crump Enders visited in 1925, Jiading Town was still surrounded by a city wall (chengqiang) [城墙], which could be entered on board a boat passing through a water gate (shui men). The city walls were reportedly still completely intact at the time of Shanghai's liberation in May 1949, but were torn down thereafter.   Although they were torn down long ago, the former round shape of the city walls can be still be seen from the former city moat (huchenghe) which continues to surround the center of the modern-day town.   In order to get in or out of town, you still must cross a bridge over the former city moat (huchenghe), which is now used as a canal for barge traffic.   The wide city moat now has a green park and paved pedestrian pathway which run along its inner side.   A network of smaller canals crossed by stone foot bridges still criss-cross the area of the old walled town within the surrounding circular moat.

Jiading Town was listed in the Shanghai development plan as one of the municipality's four officially designated historic towns.   However, it was also designated as the site for one of the 11 New Towns, and the termination point of a new Metro line extension.   Much the same as with Songjiang and Qingpu Towns, a Jiading New City (Jiading Xincheng) has been constructed outside the old town lying within the city moat in order to preserve as much historical heritage as possible from the ravages of economic development.   Thus there is now an old city and a new city side by side, with the subway station and new highrise apartment buildings being located in the new city.   This is a model for combining economic development with historic preservation that was first pioneered in Suzhou, but sadly has not been implemented everywhere in China.   Line 11 was under construction from Jiading Town to Jiangsu Lu in the city center in May 2009, but was not expected to be completed until 2012.

As the former county seat for Jiading County, and current capital of Jiading District, it has many well preserved gardens and temples dating back to the Southern Song (Nan Song) Dynasty (1127-1279) , including the Jiading **Confucius Temple** (Jiading Kong Miao) [嘉定孔庙] and its attached **Dragons Meeting Pond Park** (Huilong Tan Gongyuan) [汇龙潭公园], as well as the Jiading **City God Temple** (Jiading Chenghuang Miao) [嘉定城隍庙] and its attached **Garden of Autumn Clouds** (Qiuxiapu) [秋霞圃].   One of the main areas of concentrated sights to see is the one square city block in between South Big Lane (Nan Da Jie) [南大街] to the West, Bole Lu [博乐路] to the East, Shaxia Lu to the South and Pagoda City Road (Ta Cheng Lu) [塔城路] to the North.   Within this area you will find the **Lotus Sutra Pagoda** (Fahua Ta) [法华塔] beside the Hengli He [横沥河] canal, **Wellington Koo Memorial Hall**, stone foot briges over Lianqi River (Lianqi He) [练祁河] and Hengli He [横沥河] canals, Jiading Confucian Temple (Jiading Kong Miao), and Jiading Museum (Jiading Bowuguan).   After having occupied the Jiading Confucius Temple since July 1961, the

Jiading District History Museum (Jiading Bowuguan) [嘉定博物馆] moved into a brand new modern facility that opened in June 2013 at 215 Bole Lu [博乐路 215 号], but the Jiading Confucius Temple continues to house the **China Imperial Examination Museum** (Zhongguo Keju Bowuguan) [中国科举博物馆].   The historic center of Jiading Town (Jiading Laocheng Qu) [嘉定老城区] is crisscrossed by a network of canals which are crossed by stone arched foot bridges, particularly in the part known as the **Zhou Bridge Scenic Area** (Zhouqiao Fengmao Qu) [州桥风貌区].   In this area you can also find a historic **Roman Catholic Church** [天主堂] located right beside the Lianqi He [练祁河] canal on cobblestone Zhongxiatang lane [中下塘街].

The **Jiading Roman Catholic Curch** [嘉定天主堂] at 99 Zhongxiatang Lane [中下塘街 99 号], near its intersection with City Middle Road (Chengzhong Lu), was constructed in Gothic style in 1932, and replaced an earlier church built by French Jesuits on the same site back in 1864.   Nowadays it is colloquially known as the Gongbao Bridge Catholic Church (Gongbao Qiao Tianzhu Tang) [宫宝桥天主堂], but originally it was called Sacred Heart Hall (Shengxin Tang) [圣心堂].   The current name comes from a bridge that crosses the Lianqi River (Lianqi He) [练祁河] on the church's north side.   At the start of the Cultural Revolution in 1966 it was damaged, closed down, occupied by the county government, and turned into a dining hall.   Restoration work began in February 1984 after it was returned to the local religious authorities.   The grand reopening ceremony was held on Christmas Eve December 24, 1984.   It was renovated and extended again in 1991 and 2005 and now occupies an area of 1,500 square meters.   You have to enter the compound from the West Gate (Xi Men), which is somewhat hidden around a corner from what would otherwise appear to be the front gate but is kept closed.

Not far from Jiading Town is the equally fascinating historic town of Nanxiang, which has its own separate entry in this book under the letter N.

Jiangnan Arsenal

The Jiangnan Arsenal, known in Chinese officially as the Jiangnan Machine Manufacturing Central Office (Jiangnan Jiqi Zhizao Zongju) [江南机器制造总局], was established in 1865 by Jiangsu Provincial Governor **Li Hongzhang** [李鸿章] (1823-1901), a leader of the **Self-Strengthening Movement** (Ziqiang Yundong) [自强运动], when he purchased the American Qiji Iron Factory in Shanghai's Hongkou District.   He merged it with the Foreign Gun Factory and equipped the factory with machines that **Rong Hong** had purchased in the U.S.   However, two years later the factory was moved in 1867 to a new location then known as Gaochang Miao in Shanghai's former Luwan District, beside the Huangpu River.   The armory set up there included a machine-making plant, copper foundry, shipyard, gun plant, cannon plant, powder plant, steel-making plant, administrative division, foreign language school and a translation bureau.   The translation bureau was headed by **John Fryer** (Fu Lanya) [傅兰雅] (1839-1928) from 1868 to 1876.   It focused on translating scientific works from English into Chinese.

The Jiangnan Arsenal became China's largest modern military industrial enterprise of the Qing Dynasty.   The arsenal was the first factory in China for the production of modern guns, rifles, canons, and ammunition.   Later it also added a shipyard, and shipbuilding eventually became its primary focus.   In the 19th century, Jiangnan focused on producing muskets, artillery shells, large-caliber guns, Remington breech-loading rifles, and gunboats.   In 1888, Jiangnan successfully cast the first Armstrong breech-loading steel cannon made in China. By 1898, Jiangnan had made 19 cannons of this type.

This arsenal played an important role in the local nationalist uprisings of 1911, 1913 and 1916.   Each time it was a key target of the revolutionaries.   It was successfully captured by Chen Qimei and Jiang Jieshi in November 1911 during the Xinhai Revolution that overthrew the Qing Dynasty, but the same two military officers failed to recapture it again in July 1913 during the so-called Second Revolution against Yuan Shikai.

A 2,733 kilowatt steam engine manufactured here in 1914 was the biggest marine engine in China at that time. Later, this engine was installed on one of China's earliest cargo ships, the Guanfu.

The arsenal's shipyard was renamed Jiangnan Shipbuilding Works (Jiangnan Zaochuansuo) [江南造船所] in 1911, while the other portions of the arsenal were renamed the Shanghai Munitions Factory (Shanghai Binggongchang) [上海兵工厂] in 1917.   The Chinese cruiser Pinghai was made by the Jiangnan Shipbuilding Works during the 1930s.   With a displacement of 2,400 tons and 110 meters long, cruiser Pinghai was delivered to the Chinese navy in 1937.   It served as the flagship of the Chinese fleet. Unfortunately, the fleet was destroyed in September of the same year by the invading Japanese navy while defending the Jiangyin forts on the Yangzi River, downstream from Nanjing in Jiangsu province.

It was renamed Jiangnan Shipyard (Jiangnan Zaochuanchang) [江南造船厂] after 1949. The cargo and passenger ship Minzhong was launched here on September 3, 1953. The 1,540 ton ship was the first to be built after the founding of the PRC.   It was suitable for river sailing and was able to accommodate 968 people and 700 tons of cargo.

The first domestically-made submarine, the Type 03, was built here for the Chinese navy. It was an upgrade of the former Soviet Union's Type 613 submarine. On January 10, 1956, Mao Zedong paid a visit to this submarine and that's how the submarine got its pennant number 56-110. By 1964, Jiangnan had made 13 submarines of this type

In 1996 it was transformed into the state-owned Jiangnan Shipyard (Group) Company Limited (Jiangnan Zaochuan Jituan Youxian Zeren Gongsi) [江南造船集团有限责任公司], a subsidiary of the China State Shipbuilding Corporation (CSSC).

In August 2003 it was reported that the Jiangnan Shipyard would move to Changxing Island (Changxing Dao) [长兴岛]near the mouth of the Yangzi River in order to make way for the 2010 World Expo. This motivated me to explore the site before it was too late.

On a November 9, 2007 exploration I found that most of the original shipyard site was still functioning and continuing to produce new ships, including one huge ship known as the Iran Pasardan.   The compound of the shipyard and former arsenal still covered a huge area bounded on the west by Luban Lu and the Lupu Bridge (Lupu Da Qiao) [卢浦大桥] over the Huangpu River, on the north by Longhua East Road (Longhua Dong Lu) and Gaoxiong Lu, on the south by the Huangpu River and on the east by the tail end of Tibet South Road (Xizang Nan Lu), which became Jiangban Lu at its intersection with Bansongyuan Lu. Jiangban Lu ran all the way to the water's edge at an abandoned old ferry dock, providing views of the large ocean-going ships under construction in the river at the shipyard next door. The main gate to the shipyard was at the intersection of Longhua East Road (Longhua Dong Lu) and Gaoxiong Lu, where a large bilingual sign used to say, "*Welcome to Jiangnan Shipyard.*"   A bilingual commemorative plaque on the exterior wall of the gate said: "*Jiangnan Arsenal.   Built 1865.   Administration Office.   Command Building.   Plane Plant. Shipyard.*" However, the welcome ended there as visitors were not allowed to go inside. Standing outside the gate one could see that some historic buildings were still standing then. It was pretty frustrating to not be allowed inside to photograph them right when they were on the eve of destruction.   Visible just inside the gate was a large wall map of the compound, but numerous other public signs warned in English and Russian that taking photographs was not allowed.   A second gate stood at 150 Longhua East Road (Longhua Dong Lu).   Both gates were post-1949 structures.   The original fortress-style gate to the arsenal shown in some historic photos seemed to have already been lost.   The oldest building in this riverside industrial area actually seemed to be at 592 Bansongyuan Lu, inside a separate compound that was not a part of the shipyard.

By 2007 a museum dedicated to the Jiangan Arsenal had been established, but this was not located on the site of the old shipyard itself, although it was fairly nearby.   Rather it was located inside a new highrise office building at the intersection of Luban Lu and Zhongshan Nan Yi Lu.   Furthermore the museum was only open by appointment on weekdays and closed on weekends.   You must call them first before going.   Their collection includes a steel cannon made by Jiangnan Arsenal during the Qing Dynasty. It was unearthed on May 8, 2001 when workers were rebuilding docks.

In 2008 the whole former site of the Jiangna Arsenal & Shipyard was completely cleared to make way for the 2010 World Expo.   All the historic buildings were torn down and the shipyard was moved to Changxing Island (Changxing Dao) [长兴岛] in the Yangzi River, with three dry docks the only remaining relics at the earlier site, which is now considered part of the new West Bund art district, which includes the former Longhua Airport (Shanghai Longhua Jichang) [上海龙华机场].

Shanghai Jiangnan Shipbuilding Museum
Address: Jiangnan Shipyard Company Building, 600 Luban Road, Luwan District, F2 & F3
Phone: (021) 6315-1818 x 2439 (call for appointment first)
Hours: Monday to Friday: 9am – 11:30am, 1:00pm-4:30pm
E-mail: jninfo@shipyard.com.cn

Jiangwan Town (Jiangwan Zhen) [江湾镇]

Soon after the Guomindang set up a new national government in Nanjing in April 1927, the Chinese-controlled parts of Shanghai were raised from the level of a county attached to Songjiang to that of a city for the first time in history. The first Shanghai municipal government was established on July 14, 1927 and included a mayor and a municipal council. The **Municipality of Greater Shanghai** covered an area of 320 square miles, completely surrounding the foreign concessions in the city center, which remained outside its control. One of the new municipality's first projects was to begin construction of a new civic center in Jiangwan Town (Jiangwan Zhen) [江湾镇] of Yangpu District (Yangpu Qu) [杨浦区]. Eventually it included a museum, library, stadium, and city hall, all of which were designed by the Chinese architect **Dong Dayou** (1899-1873), a University of Minnesota graduate who had worked with Americn architect Henry K. Murphy. He combined traditional Chinese and modern Western architecture in a Ming Dynasty revival style that was also used for the central government buildings of the Guomindang regime in Nanjing.

The former **Shanghai Municipal Administration Building** (Shanghai Tebie Shizhengfu Dalou) [上海特别市政府大楼] was constructed between 1931 and 1933 as Shanghai's new city hall, but now sits inside the campus of the Shanghai Sports College (Shanghai Tiyu Xueyuan) [上海体育学院], where it serves as the school's Administration Building (Xingzheng Lou) [行政楼]. The long, rectangular building has a traditional Chinese style sloping, glazed tiled roof with upturned eaves, supported by dougong [斗拱] brackets, colorfully painted roof beams, and red columns. A map of Shanghai is embedded in the floor of the main lobby. Address: 650 Qingyuanhuan Lu [清源环路650 号], Jiangwan Town (Jiangwan Zhen) [江湾镇], Yangpu District [杨浦区].

The former **Shanghai Municipal Museum** (Shanghai Shili Bowuguan) [上海市立博物馆] was built between 1934 and 1935, but now sits inside the compound of the Shanghai Second Army Medical University (Shanghai Di'er Jun Yike Daxue) [上海第二军医科大学], and the Changhai Hospital (Changhai Yiyuan) [长海医院]. In 2009 it was heavily restored and surrounded by the hospital's massive reconstruction project. The building's key feature is a traditional pavilion on top. Address: 174 Changhai Lu [长海路 174 号], Jiangwan Town (Jiangwan Zhen) [江湾镇], Yangpu District [杨浦区].

The former **Shanghai Municipal Library** (Shanghai Shili Tushuguan) [上海市立图书馆] located in Jiangwan Town [江湾镇] was designed by famous Chinese architect Dong Dayou [董大酉](1899-1973). Construction started in 1934 and was completed in 1935. The most interesting architectural feature is a stone pavilion on top that resembles the Ming Dynasty Bell Tower (Zhong Lou) in Beijing, or possibly a Ming Lou Tower at a Ming emperor's tomb. Later it became part of the Tongji Middle School (Tongji Zhong Xue), which moved out in the year 2000. Despite plans that had been announced for its restoration, when I visited the site in May 2009, it was still in a derelict state. After 17 years of restoration efforts it was announced in March 2017 that the building had officially been reopened to the public as the new Jiangwan Public Library. However, when I visited the site on New Year's Day 2018, the gates were still locked and an attendant security guard told me that it would actually not be open to the public until May 2018. Still, at least the high surrounding wall that used to completely hide it from view had been taken down so that the building's exterior was fully open to view from the new perimeter fence. Restoration had considerably changed the building's appearance.   The pavilion on top seemed to have been completely replaced, while the stone walls had been completely airbrushed, all the political slogans once painted on the walls had been removed, and it appeared that four brand new wings had been built as extensions of the original structure. (See the Appendix for more details on this building.)

Address: 181 Heishan Lu [黑山路 181 号], Jiangwan Town (Jiangwan Zhen) [江湾镇], Yangpu District [杨浦区].

The Former Shanghai Municipal Stadium (Shanghai Shili Tiyuchang) [上海市立体育场] was completed in 1935 and is still serving its original purpose.   Two other buildings at the site built in similar style include the Jiangwan Gymnasium and Jiangwan Swimming Pool. All the buildings in the recreation area were designed in the Ming Dynasty revival style popular with the Guomindang and feature the stone arched gateway entrances typical of this style. Address: 346 Guohe Lu [国和路 346 号], Jiangwan Town (Jiangwan Zhen) [江湾镇], Yangpu District [杨浦区].

The former museum, library and city hall are all located one block from the intersection of Changhai Lu and Hengren Lu, and only two blocks walking distance from each other.

Jingan Buddhist Temple (Jingan Si) [静安寺]

Unfortunately, there's really not anything worth seeing at this site nowadays, due to an ill-advised reconstruction project described in more detail below, but since the temple has played an important role in the city's history, and still provides the name for one of the city's main urban districts, Jingan District, it seems worthy of at least recounting its history here.

Jingan Si was supposedly first founded in 247 A.D. by Sun Quan [孙权], the King of the Eastern Wu Kingdom (Dong Wu) [东吴] Wu during the Three Dynasties (San Guo) [三国] (220-280).   However, like similar claims made for Longhua Temple, this seems impossible as maps of Shanghai's geological history contained in Zhou Zhenhe [周振鹤], *Shanghai Historic Maps Collection* (*Shanghai Lishi Ditu Ji*) [*上海历史地图集*], Shanghai: Shanghai People's Publishing House (Shanghai Renmin Chubanshe) [上海人民出版社] (1999) show that most of this area was underwater until the Tang Dynasty (618-907).   Records do seem to prove the establishment of a temple named Jingan Si in a different location in 1008 during the Zhenzong reign (997-1022) of the Northern Song Dynasty (960-1126), but it was not "moved" to the present location until 1216, during the Ningzong reign (1195-1224) of the Southern Song Dynasty (1127-1279), giving the temple an authentic history of approximately 800 years.

The previous buildings were all destroyed during the Taiping Rebellion (1851-1861), after which it was rebuilt, but the temple suffered another disaster when a mysterious fire broke out in 1972, at a time when the temple was closed due to the Cultural Revolution. Nonetheless, until the hideous 2001-2004 total reconstruction of the site, there were still several existing structures dating from the 1880 reconstruction during the Guangxu reign (1875-1908) of the Qing Dynasty (1644-1911).

Before 1949 Shanghai's foreign residents used to call Jingan Si by the name Bubbling Well Temple because this stretch of Nanjing West Road (Nanjing Xi Lu) [南京西路] was then known as Bubbling Well Road, named after a famous well that once stood across the street but has long since been filled up and lost to memory.   One of the more peculiar events in the temple's history was the brief revival of the heterodox **Secret Sect** (Mi Zong) [密宗] of Vajrayana Tantric Buddhism by the Abbot Chi Song in 1953.

Jingan Si used to have some precious historic relics, such as the inscribed Imperial Stele (Yu Bei) of Emperor Gaozong of the Southern Song Dynasty, and a big iron bell made in the 2nd year of the Hongwu reign of the Ming Dynasty.   As late as 1999 there was still at least one genuine brick and wood temple hall, outside of which was a wall of stone carvings depicting the eight famous scenes from the temple's history, such as the man disgorging a live fish from his mouth, but that wall has now disappeared.

Because of its urban location, this temple used to be a good example of how not only little old ladies were participating in China's revival of its traditional religions.   You could see fashionably dressed teenagers and businessmen in suits praying here.   During the **Mid-Autumn Festival** (Zhongqiu Jie) many local residents visited this temple to buy its special moon cakes as gifts for friends and family members.

Unfortunately, a massive reconstruction project that started in 2001 and was mostly completed by 2004 forever altered the temple's original appearance.   Two rather gaudy enormous concrete pavilions were placed just inside either side of the front gate in 2002. These new buildings resemble Himeji Castle in Osaka, Japan.   The much smaller quaint authentic brick and wooden halls behind them were completely destroyed.   In January 2003 a series of monstrous concrete high-rise towers began going up directly behind the two new traditional style pavilions.   Finally a giant, garish, golden tower with a ram's head on top of it was erected outside the front gate; a type of tower not seen at any other Buddhist temple, and more suitable to some kind of pagan religion.

All previous historic brick and wood structures have been replaced with new concrete ones, even the earth beneath them turned over to dig a subway station underneath, and really not even one genuine historic relic is left remaining.   Essentially, Jing An Temple as it was once known has ceased to exist, even as a shadow of its former self.   Professor Zheng Shiling of Tongji University [同济大学] has publicly criticized the reconstruction project as "a move that doesn't respect history," and complains that the temple, "has lost its original flavor." The whole site is now dominated by new construction erected during 2001-2004.   A subway station lays directly beneath it, rows of commercial shops are embedded in the exterior walls of its compound, all the structures are built of cement rather than traditional brick and wood, while the all the statues inside are brand new and kept under glass.

Address: 1686 Nanjing West Road (Nanjing Xi Lu) [南京西路 1686 号].
Phone: (021) 6256-6365, 6256-6366.

Jinze Ancient Town (Jinze Gu Zhen) [金泽古镇]

Jinze [金泽] is another well-preserved ancient water town, similar to Zhujiajiao [朱家角镇], both of which are located in Qingpu District, but its unique beauty is that it is the only town of this type in the Shanghai area that has yet to be re-discovered and promoted by tour operators.   This means it is so far unspoiled, untrampled by hordes of tourists led by megaphone wielding guides, and unvisited by tour busses.   In a way Jinze today resembles Zhujiajiao the way it was 20 years ago before it began to be destroyed by its own success in attracting tourism and development.   Jinze Town is located at the far western boundary of Qingpu District (Qingpu Qu) and Zhejiang Province (Zhejiang Sheng), at the very end of the Huqingping Highway, in the southwest corner of Shanghai Municipality (Shanghai Shi), 22 kilometers from Qingpu Town, 50 kilometers from Hongqiao Airport and 62 kilometers from People's Square in downtown Shanghai.   It is the last town on the A9 Expressway running between Jinze Town and the A20 Outer Ring Road.   For some reason, Jinze was not listed in the Shanghai development plan as one of the officially designated historic towns in the municipal region, even though it rivals the four that were listed in its collection of authentic historic sights.   However, maps in the development plan show it lying within a large greenbelt which will be maintained around the shores of Dianshan Lake (Dianshan Hu) [淀山湖], so it is likely that the town's special charm will be preserved.

Jinze Ancient Town (Jinze Guzhen) [金泽古镇] is criss-crossed by a network of half a dozen canals, which are crossed by ancient stone arched footbridges (shigong qiao) [石拱桥] of various sizes, ranging from small to enormous.   There were originally 42 stone foot bridges built in Jinze [金泽] during four dynasties, the Song, Yuan, Ming and Qing [宋元明清].   Of these, 21 have survived, although only seven of them are grouped together in the town center, the rest being scattered about the surrounding countryside.   The bridges' dates of construction range from 1267 at the earliest to 1698 at the latest, with the majority of them having been built in the 13th and 14th Centuries.

Eight bridges can be seen by following the two ancient flagstone paved pedestrian lanes known as **Above the Dyke Lane** (Shangtang Jie) [上塘街] on the east side, and **Below the Dyke Lane** (Xiatang Jie) [下塘街] on the west side, of the main north-south canal known simply as the **Jinze River** (Jinze Tang) [金泽塘].   The historic old town forms a corridor along the north-south Jinze River (Jinze Tang) [金泽塘], and is bisected by the modern town's east-west main street of **Jinxi Lu** [金溪路], as well as the east-west **North Victory Creek** (Beisheng Bang) [北胜浜], which both divide the old town into two northern and southern halves on either side of them.

Starting from the town's modern-day east-west main street of **Jinxi Lu** [金溪路] and walking north on **Below the Dyke Lane** (Xiatang Jie) [下塘街] along the west side of the north-south Jinze River (Jinze Tang) [金泽塘] to the east-west **North Victory Creek** (Beisheng Bang) [北胜浜] takes you to the three-arched stone **Heavenly Kings Bridge** (Tianwang Qiao) [天王桥], also known as the **Heavenly Emperor's Pavilion Bridge** (Tianhuang Ge Qiao) [天皇阁桥].   It was built in the Ming Dynasty (1368-1644), and then later rebuilt in 1698 during the Kangxi reign (1661-1722) of the Qing Dynasty.   It is apparently named after a building that no longer exists, the Heavenly King Pavilion (Tianwang Ge) [天王阁] or Heavenly Emperor's Pavilion (Tianhuang Ge) [天皇阁].

Continuing northward from **North Victory Creek** (Beisheng Bang) [北胜浜] along the western path, the **Below the Dyke Lane** (Xiatang Jie) [下塘街] then leads you to the western approach to the single stone arched **Rest Assured Bridge** (Wanan Qiao) [万安桥] with its graceful sloping hump, which crosses the Jinze River (Jinze Tang) [金泽塘]. The Wanan Qiao was built during the Jingding era (1260-1264) of the Lizong reign (1224-1264) of the Southern Song (Nan Song) Dynasty (1127-1279). It measures 29 meters in length, and 2.6 meters wide.

Following the **Below the Dyke Lane** (Xiatang Jie) [下塘街] further northward along the west side of the Jinze River (Jinze Tang) [金泽塘] will lead you to the single arched stone **Old Lin Bridge** (Lin Lao Qiao)[林老桥], which crosses another east-west side canal. It was built during the Zhiyuan reign (1264-1294) of Khubilai Khan, founder of the Yuan Dynasty (1279-1368). It is named in honor of a Mr. Lin who contributed money to its construction. Because there is a small **War God Temple** (Guandi Miao) [关帝庙] located at the north end of the bridge it is also sometimes known as the **War God Bridge** (Guandi Qiao) [关帝桥]. Past this point there is still a small neighborhood of old houses, but no more stone bridges. Once you reach **Peian Lu** you've arrived at the northernmost boundary of the historic area and should turn around to head back.

Alternatively, starting from the east-west main street of Jinxi Lu [金溪路], you could walk north on **Above the Dyke Lane** (Shangtang Jie) [上塘街] on the east side of the Jinze River (Jinze Tang) [金泽塘] until you reach the east-west **North Victory Creek** (Beisheng Bang) [北胜浜]. Here you would have to cross the **Pagoda Confluence Bridge** (Tahui Qiao) [塔汇桥], a stone foot bridge over North Victory Creek (Beisheng Bang) [北胜浜]. This bridge is not a genuine historic relic, but rather a more recent construction, although it replaces a historic bridge that was once here. Looking west from this bridge you can see the intersection of the Jinze River (Jinze Tang) [金泽塘] and North Victory Creek (Beisheng Bang) [北胜浜],. You can catch a glimpse of the **Heavenly Emperor's Pavilion Bridge** (Tianhuang Ge Qiao) [天皇阁桥] to the west, but you can't get a very good view of it from this east side of the Jinze River (Jinze Tang) [金泽塘]. Looking straight ahead on the northwest side of **North Victory Creek** (Beisheng Bang) [北胜浜] stands the **Champion Tea House** (Zhuangyuan Gulou) [状元古楼], named after a top scorer in the imperial civil service examinations. Continuing north on the east side of the Jinze River (Jinze Tang) [金泽塘], Above the Dyke Lane (Shangtang Jie) [上塘街] is lined on both sides with small, old, two-story wooden residential houses. Eventually you pass the eastern approach to the **Rest Assured Bridge** (Wanan Qiao) [万安桥] over the Jinze River (Jinze Tang) [金泽塘]. Finally, at the north end of Above the Dyke Lane (Shangtang Jie) [上塘街], you reach The **Two Kings Temple** (Er Wang Miao) [二王庙] on the east-west **Jinying North Road** (Jinying Bei Lu) [金鹰北路]. Straight ahead to the north you can see the tall steeple of the modern day **Jinze Catholic Church** (Jinze Tianzhu Jiaotang) [金泽天主教堂] standing on the east side of the Jinze River (Jinze Tang) [金泽塘], but the pathway does not seem to continue in that direction. To the east Jinying North Road (Jinying Bei Lu) [金鹰北路] leads to the gated compounds of two old factories. From outside the locked metal gates of the factory compound due east at #311 Above the Dyke Lane (Shangtang Jie 311 hao) [上塘街 31 号], you can catch a glimpse of what appears to be the brick façade of a much older, historic Catholic Church hidden inside, but the guard at the gatehouse refuses to let any visitiors enter the site.   To the west, the modern **Jinying Bridge** (Jinying Qiao) [金鹰桥] crosses over the Jinze River (Jinze Tang) [金泽塘] to the site of the **Old Lin Bridge** (Lin Lao Qiao)[林老桥] crossing a small tributary east-west side canal.

Starting from the town's modern-day east-west main street of **Jinxi Lu** [金溪路] and walking south on **Below the Dyke Lane** (Xiatang Jie) [下塘街] along the west side of the Jinze River (Jinze Tang) [金泽塘], the first bridge you see crossing the river is the **Puqing Qiao** [普庆桥], a single arched wooden bridge (mugong qiao) [木拱桥] made entirely of logs that somehow bend in a graceful curve that rises and falls over a high central hump. Without any vertical supporting pillars, the bridge seems to float in mid-air over the water like a ribbon.   Along both sides of the bridge are curious animal face masks.   This bridge only dates from 1999, but is so impressive that it has been featured in the PBS television program NOVA produced by WGBH Boston. It was designed to imitate the bridge in the famous Song Dynasty painting "*Qingming Shanghe Tu*" [清明上河图] by Zhang Zeduan [张择端] (1085-1145). Beside the eastern approach to the bridge is a Chinese language stone tablet dated October 1999 that was erected by the town government.   The bridge measures 16.8 meters long and 4 meters wide.

Crossing the Puqing Qiao [普庆桥] to the east side of the Jinze River (Jinze Tang) [金泽塘], and walking southward along **Above the Dyke Lane** (Shangtang Jie) [上塘街] on its eastern shore, takes you to a succession of four historic stone arched foot bridges.   First comes the **Universal Help Bridge** (Puji Qiao) [普济桥], a single arch stone bridge built in 1267 during the Yanchun era of the Duzong reign (1264-1274) of the Southern Song (Nan Song) Dynasty (1127-1279), repaired in 1723, and last repaired in 1982.   It is also known as the **Purple Stone Bridge** (Zishi Qiao) [紫石桥] because of the purple color of its stone blocks. The bridge measures 27 meters long, and 2.75 meters wide.   Beside one approach to the bridge is a Chinese language stone tablet dated December 1987 that was erected by the city government.

Continuing southward on **Above the Dyke Lane** (Shangtang Jie) [上塘街] along the eastern shore of the Jinze River, next you come to the single arch stone **Animal Releasing Bridge** (Fangsheng Qiao) [放生桥], which crosses an east-west side canal flowing into the north-south Jinze River.   The Animal Releasing Bridge (Fangsheng Qiao) was built during the Chongzhen reign (1628-1644) of the Ming Dynasty.   It is sometimes also known as the **Military General Bridge** (Zong Guan Qiao) [总管桥] because the **Military General Temple** (Zong Guan Miao) [总管庙] is located at its northern foot.   The bridge measures 26.7 meters in length, and 2.75 meters wide.

Crossing the Animal Releasing Bridge (Fang Sheng Qiao) and continuing southward on **Above the Dyke Lane** (Shangtang Jie) [上塘街], following the shady path lined with tall Cedar trees, one comes to the single arch stone **Ruyi Bridge** (Ruyi Qiao) [如意桥], which crosses another east-west side canal flowing into the north-south Jinze River.   The Ruyi Bridge [如意桥] was built between 1335 and 1340, during the Shundi reign (1333-1368) of the last Yuan Dynasty ruler Toghon Temur, and is sometimes also known as the **Ancestor Bridge** (Zushi Qiao) [祖师桥] because there was once an **Ancestor Temple** (Zushi Miao) [祖师庙] located here.   From the top of the Ruyi Bridge one can look eastward and see a glimpse of the yellow and orange walls of the **Yang Zhen Temple** (Yang Zhen Miao) [杨震庙] in the distance.　The bridge measures 20.8 meters in length and 3.4 meters wide. The last foot bridge at the south end of the Jinze River is the somewhat unimpressive **Auspicious Welcome Bridge** (Yingxiang Qiao) [迎祥桥], which has been propped up with ungraceful concrete supports.　It was first built in the the Zhiyuan [至元] reign (1335-1340) of the Yuan Dynasty.　It measures 34.25 meters in length, and 2.14 meters wide.

To the south of the Yingxiang Qiao is the **Auspicious Welcome Pavilion** (Yingxiang Ting) [迎祥亭] and a modern day stone tablet erected by the town government in January 1994 with a lengthy introduction to the town written in Chinese on the back side of it. Immediately behind this stone tablet is the modern day **Jinze River Bridge** (Jinze Tang Qiao) [金泽塘桥] over the north-south **Jinze River** (Jinze Tang) [金泽塘], across which crosses the east-west highway known as **Jin South Road** (Jin Nan Lu) [金南路].　There are no more historic sights to see south of this point, so rather than wandering aimlessly around the countryside it is advisable to turn around here and head back northward.

Nearby, beside the eastern pathway along the Jinze River known as **Above the Dyke Lane** (Shangtang Jie) [上塘街], there are two more modern informational signs that I discovered on my October 2018 visit, but which were not there on my previous visits.　One is a very useful color "Jinze Ancient Town Scenic Guide Map," and the other is a very lengthy bilingual "Introduction of Jinze Ancient Town."　These were the only examples of these two particular signs that I saw although other bilingual directional and infiormational signs had appeared throughout the town's historic corridor as of my most recent visit in October 2018, whereas there had been no English signage whatsoever at the time of my earlier first visits. This marks the south end of the historic corridor, city official may have expected visitors to begin their walking tours here, but actually most people will start at the midpoint east-west main street of Jinxi Road [金溪路] or else at Yihao Chansi on Jin Middle Road (Jin Zhong Lu) [金中路].

The various types of religious faiths found in China are well represented in Jinze Town, which has a fairly large Buddhist temple, both Catholic and Protestant Christian churches, and a large number of smaller traditional shrines scattered all about the town.

The new **Catholic Church** (Jinze Tianzhu Jiaotang) [天主教堂] is located at the extreme northern end of **Above the Dyke Lane** (Shangtang Jie) [上塘街] on the east side of the Jinze River (Jinze Tang) [金泽塘].　Although it has an imposing tower, the building is brand new.

The older Protestant (Jidu Jiao) [基督教] **Jesus Church** (Yesu Tang) [耶稣堂] can be found at #107 **Below the Dyke Lane** (Xiatang Jie 107 hao) [下塘街 107] on the west side, of the Jinze River (Jinze Tang) [金泽塘] at the southern foot of the **Heavenly Emperor's Pavilion Bridge** (Tianhuang Ge Qiao) [天皇阁桥].

At the northern end of **Old Lin Bridge** (Lin Lao Qiao)[林老桥] stands a small but active one-room shrine known as the **War God Temple** (Guandi Miao)[关帝庙], devoted to **Guan Yu**, who was deified as Guandi, the God of War.

The **Two Kings Temple** (Er Wang Miao) [二王庙] is a small one-room shrine that stands at the northern end of **Above the Dyke Lane** (Shangtang Jie) [上塘街] on the east side of the Jinze River, past the **Rest Assured Bridge** (Wanan Qiao) [万安桥], its bright yellow walls within sight of the **Old Lin Bridge** (Lin Lao Qiao)[林老桥] on the west side of the river.   The three characters on the front of the building are written in reverse order to the norm nowadays, from right to left, using traditional characters rather than simplified ones.   A metal plaque on the left side of the alcove provides a Chinese language history of the building, but it is also oddly written in traditional characters rather than the simplified characters usually used on the mainland.   According to this sign the temple was rebuilt in September 2012.

Yihao Buddhist Temple (Yihao Chansi) [颐浩禅寺]

This is a functioning Buddhist temple with several resident monks.   As the name implies they belong to the Zen meditation sect (Chan Zong).   The temple was rebuilt in April 1994, but has a history going back to the Southern Song (Nan Song) Dynasty (1127-1279). There are a total of six buildings, with two larger halls each flanked by two smaller ones on either side, and a courtyard in between them.   Inside the front entrance hall is a wooden **Maitreya Buddha** (Milefo) image inside an intricately carved wood and glass case.   At the west end of the hall is a small statue of the War God (Guan Di), and at the east end a gift shop offering a remarkable assortment of local souvenirs.   This is the only place in town where you can purchase books on the local history of Jinze.   East of the **Maitreya Buddha Hall** (Milefo Dian) is the small **Buddhist Reading Room** (Fo Shu Yuan Lan Shi), which despite its name seems to be full of families drinking tea and playing cards.   Nonetheless, it's worth trying to squeeze inside the crowded space to catch a glimpse of the wonderful watercolor paintings of Jinze's historic sights hanging on the walls.   One painting replicates a fascinating historic map of the town as it once looked.

Stepping into the courtyard, there are several historic relics, including inscribed tablets embedded in the walls, and an ancient stone wall decorated with a cloud pattern.   The **Everlasting Cloud Stone** (Buduan Yunshi) [不断云石] is a low wall encircling a square pool. The wall is completely covered with a cloud pattern.   Although parts of it have been repaired with cement, some of it obviously dates back to the original built in the Yuan Dynasty between 1290 and 1300 A.D.

Opposite the cloud wall is an enormous 700-year old Gingko tree (gu yinxing) [古银杏] planted during the Southern Song (Nan Song) Dynasty.   The tree stands 25 meters high, and 4.5 meters in circumference.   It used to be part of a pair of trees, but the other one was chopped down.

On the far side of the courtyard are the three main halls of worship.   The **Precious Hall of the Great Hero** (Da Xiong Bao Dian) in the center is the largest hall of the temple.   Inside is a nice collection of silk temple banners hanging from the ceiling, and an iron bell hung from a wooden frame with a suspended log for ringing it.   Behind the beautifully engraved and gilded wooden altar sits one large Buddha statue flanked on either side by two Arhats. Other paraphanalia of worship are present, such as the wooden fish (muyu) used to keep the rhythm for chanting.   On my October 2018 visit, a walk around to the area behind this main hall revealed a back courtyard containing a dozen stone pedestals that seemed to be real relics that once held up the wooden pillars of another long-gone temple hall.

East of the Da Xiong Bao Dian is the small but impressive **Goddess of Mercy Hall** (Guanyin Dian). Inside is a beautiful golden statue of Guanyin seated on a lotus flower with her hands pressed together in prayer wearing a golden silk robe. Beside her is a second image wearing a white silk robe.

West of the Da Xiong Bao Dian is the **Kshitigarbha Hall** (Dizang Dian) containing a golden statue of Dizang and rows of small funeral boards along the walls.

Directly beside the existing compound, a second temple building had just been razed to the ground when the author visited in March 2003, and only colorful yellow, red and blue broken fragments could be seen.

From the Puqing Qiao on the Jinze River to the west, a path leads through a gatehouse at #1 Yingxiang Jie [迎祥街 1] and directly to the **Yihao Buddhist Temple** (Yihao Chansi) [颐浩禅寺]. Alternatively you could approach from the temple from the east via Jin Zhong Lu [金中路] and Yingxiang Jie [迎祥街]. At the intersection of Yingxiang Jie [迎祥街] and Jin Zhong Lu [金中路] a foot bridge crosses a canal, the same canal as crossed by the Fangsheng Qiao, you walk through a stone gateway, across the bridge and up the road to #12 Yingxiang Jie [迎祥街 12]. Due to its central location and the fact that you can park a car here this also makes for a good starting point for your journey.

The small single-hall **Military General Temple** (Zong Guan Miao) [总管庙] is located in the southern section of the historic corridor at #8 **Above the Dyke Lane** (Shangtang Jie ba hao) [上塘街 8 号], No.4 Lane (Si Long) [四弄], on the east side of the Jinze River, at the north end of the Animal Releasing Bridge (Fangsheng Qiao) [放生桥]. The inside is surprisingly impressive, with three statues of Confucian scholar officials dressed in ornate, colorful silk robes, wearing head dresses. Two of the three statues are life-sized, and the one in the center is quite frightening, with a black face and long black beard, this one being Mr. Zongguan Laoye [总管老爷], also known as Mr. Jin Yuanqi [金元七], who was a native of Kaifeng [开封] in Henan Province, which was the capital of the Northern Song Dynasty. This temple supposedly dates from the Ming Dynasty. In the 1950s its previous statues were destroyed. In the 1960s it was turned into a warehouse. In the 1990s the temple was restored by the Qingpu County government. Nowadays the temple sits inside its own walled compound beside a canal. You must pay a small fee to enter at the entrance gate.

The **Yang Zhen Temple** (Yang Zhen Miao) [杨震庙] is located at #61 Peiyu Lu [培育路 61 号] in the midst of open fields southeast of the town center, a fairly long walk up the same side canal crossed by the Ruyi Qiao. Follow the concrete path along the side canal from the two-lane highway through open fields being encroached on by new factories to the large temple complex on the water's edge.

Inside the surrounding yellow walls is an enormous courtyard containing an incense burner in the center with one main hall and a single side hall at the far end. A half-circle canal surrounds the backside of the main canal. The signboard on the outside of the main hall's entrance bears the four characters for, "*Long Live Yang Ye.*"

The inside of the main hall, known as the Yang Zhen Hall (Yang Zhen Dian) [杨震殿] is dominated by a single life-size statue of Mr. Yang Zhen [杨震], again depicted in frightening fashion as black-faced with a long black beard, dressed in flowing silk robes. The hall also contains many other curious objects meant to represent Yang Zhen's personal possessions. These include his bed, his wooden boat, and the bridal sedan chair with silk curtains used to carry his wife. The side hall has three bedrooms for his three wives, including their statues and ornate beds.

The temple is dedicated to a gentleman named Mr. Yang Zhen [杨震] aka Yang Laoye [杨老爷]. Yang supposedly lived during the Eastern Han Dynasty (Dong Han) [东汉](25-220 AD.) and came from Shanxi Province [陕西省]. There is a Peking Opera (Jingju) [京剧] about Yang called "Caocao and Yangxiu," (Caocao yu Yangxiu) [曹操与杨修] which is still occasionally performed at the Yifu Theater in downtown Shanghai.

Yang Zhen Temple (Yang Zhen Miao) [杨震庙] was built in the year 2000, and you can still see the stone tablet listing the names of all those who contributed money to its construction. Some people only gave 200 Rmb, while one person contributed 5,000 Rmb.

Views of the temple are now somewhat obstructed from the nearest main road of **Peiyu Lu** Peiyu Lu [培育路] because it is now hidden behind the new Jinze Middle School (Jinze Zhongxue) [金泽中学], which I believe was constructed after I first visited the temple itself. The current temple supposedly stands in the same spot as a previous Taoist temple known as the Dong Yue Miao [东岳庙].

In addition to bridges and temples, the town has one museum, the **Showroom of Bridge Culture**, located just across the street from Yi Hao Chan Si. Unfortunately, the building seems to always be closed. A sneak peak through the museum's windows reveals a wonderful collection of old black and white photos of the town's bridges, as well as several scale models of what the town looked like centuries ago. One can only hope the museum is opened to the public soon.

The town has two fairly unobtrusive foreign owned factories outside the old town, one Japanese and the other Taiwanese, which together employ most of the residents. At quitting time hordes of young teenage girls can be seen heading home wearing their ubiquitous photo I.D. name cards and their metal lunch spoons dangling from their necks. Nonetheless, the residents rarely if ever see Westerners, and the author was alternately chased and ran from by mobs of residents in a mixed mass hysteria response of curiosity and fear when he visited there alone in March 2003. One seemingly friendly family who provided shelter actually invited a running stream of all their friends to come over to the house and see the foreigner. However, Jinze might be a good place for long-term downtown Shanghai residents to find a weekend villa (bieshu). In the case of the local home visited by the author in 2003, it turned out that the residents only paid 100 Rmb per month in rent for a two-story, four-room house with its own private courtyard right beside the canal.

Jinze Logistics

The fact that Jinze has yet to be discovered also means that there is no easy way of getting to or from there.   There is a **Jinze Bus Station** (Jinze Qiche Zhan) [金泽汽车站] on the **Huqingping Highway** (Huqingping Gonglu) [沪青平公路] at its T-intersection with the town's main street of **Jinxi Lu** [金溪路], but these public buses tend to be very croweded with standing room only, and only seem to travel back and forth between Jinze Town and Qingpu Town, the capital of Qingpu District, following a very slow milk run route of stopping at every village along the way.   As of 2018, the Shanghai subway system had been extended all the way to Zhujiajiao Ancient Town, and even the Oriental Green Boat amusement park, but it's doubtful whether it will ever reach Jinze Town.   Without long-distance bus service or a train station, the easiest and fastest way to get there from the city center is to hire a taxi.   The challenging part of a day trip to Jinze is getting back to the Shanghai city center at the end of the day, especially since there still don't seem to be any modern hotels in the town, which is also still lacking the modern conveniences of a Starbucks, KFC, or McDonalds.   It's highly unlikely that you would be able to find a taxi to take you back to the city when you've finished your sightseeing.   Your best choice will be taking a public bus from the Jinze bus station back to Qingpu Town, where you'll need to transfer to another bus, the subway line, or a taxi, for the remainder of the journey back to the city center.   Keep in mind that Qingpu District taxis are legally not allowed to leave Qingpu District, so even if you could catch one, you would still have to transfer later to a city taxi in order to cross the Qingpu border into Minhang District.

L

Libraries (Tushuguan) [图书馆]

Formerly housed in the old Shanghai Race Club building at #325 Nanjing West Road (Nanjing Xi Lu) [南京西路 325 号] from 1952 to 1996, the present-day Shanghai Library (Shanghai Tushuguan) [上海图书馆] opened the doors of its spacious new facility on Huaihai Middle Road (Huaihai Zhong Lu) in 1996.   The Shanghai Library is the largest public facility in China, and one of the ten largest in the world, with a collection of 48.5 million items.   It has much more in common with the Library of Congress in Washington, D.C. than your typical municipal library, both in the shear size of the facility and in the way it functions, as well as the quantity of its collections.   The library's motto, "*Knowledge is Power*," is inscribed into all the walls, and although this would seem an Orwellian irony to the uninitiated, the library in fact fulfills its mission quite well to those who know how to utilize its vast resources.   A quick glance at the shelves is misleading, as most of the collections are kept in storage.   Specific items have to be requested for retrieval in writing and cannot be taken out of the building.

During the Republic of China (Minguo) era of 1911-1949, the Chinese city government had made two attempts at establishing a Shanghai municipal public library (Shanghai Shi Shili Tushuguan) [上海市市立图书馆].   The first attempt was when the former Shanghai Confucius Temple (Wen Miao) was converted into a public library in June 1932.   The second attempt was when a new public library building was constructed in Jiangwan Town in 1935.   Unfortunately, the latter collection was destroyed during the Sino-Japaense War, and the building heavily damaged, although it survived to be restored later. . See the section on Jiangwan Town for more details.   In addition, the Shanghai Municipal Council of the International Settlement operated its own public library.

However, most of the libraries in Shanghai before 1949 were private collections that belonged to membership associations such as the R.A.S., private clubs such as the Shanghai Race Club, churches such as the St. Ignatius Cathedral, Christian missionary universities such as St. John's, and government institutions such as the China Maritime Customs Service.

When the Shanghai Library first opened in 1952 it somehow managed to already have a collection of 700,000 volumes.   The question is, where did these books come from?   The official library history states that in 1950 a "*campaign to collect books*" was started by the local government, which resulted in many "*donations*" of previously privately held books being made to the library, which was established two years later.

Many volumes from Shanghai's pre-1949 private libraries wound up in the Shanghai Library's collection.   Based on library stamps that can still be found inside their covers, this included titles from St. John's University Low Library, the Shanghai Race Club Library, the Shanghai Municipal Council Public Library, the U.S. Information Service Shanghai Branch Library, and the publishing house of Kelly & Walsh.   They seem to have acquired all the collections previously belonging to the Christionary missionary universities in Shanghai before they were all shut down in 1952.

In at least four cases, the Shanghai Library acquired entire intact pre-Liberation library collections, such as those once belonging to the **Royal Asiatic Society Library**) (Yazhou Wenhui Tushuguan) [亚洲文会图书馆], the **Zikawei Bibliotheca Major** (Xujiahui Cangshu Lou) [徐家汇藏书楼], the **Maritime Customs House Library** (Haiguan Tushuan) [海关图书馆书], and the **International Settlement's Shanghai Municipal Council Public Library** (Shanghai Zujie Gongbuju Gonggong Tushuguan) [上海租界工部局公共图书馆],. This is known because in the 1950s the Shanghai Library published a series of printed catalogs that recorded these acquisitions in great detail. See the section on Shanghai's pre-1949 libraries in my Bibliography for specific citations.

The RAS Library building at #20 Museum Road (Huqiu Lu) [虎丘路] was taken over by the Shanghai Library in 1952, and in February 1955 its collection then estimated at including 94,000 volumes was merged into that of the Shanghai Library. The Shanghai Library published a catalog of this collection in 1955, but most of these books were considered too controversial to allow public access to them. The fate of the RAS Library collection had been so unknown in the West that in 1990 Harold M. Otness published a scholarly article on the history of the collection which ended by saying, "what became of its collection is not known to this writer." In November 2002 Shanghai Library staff revealed to me their plans for the old RAS collection to be housed and made publicly available for the first time since 1966 in the newly reopened Zikawei Library. True to their word, nine months later, starting in Juiy 2003 they were housed in the newly reopened **Zikawei Bibliotheca Major** at Cao Stream North Road (Caoxi Bei Lu) [漕溪北路 80 号] in Xujiahui, which once belonged to the Roman Catholic Cathedral of St. Ignatius next door. The RAS Library building itself served as storage space for the Shanghai Library until 1996, when the new Shanghai Library building made this unnecessary, and at that time the RAS Library building was rented out as office space to private companies. Since 2010 it has been converted into the **Rockbund Art Museum** (Shanghai Waitan Meishuguan) [上海外滩美术馆]. For more information see the entry for the R.A.S. Building in the section on The Bund Waitan Yuan Area under the letteter B in this book.

The **Zikawei Bibliotheca Major** (Xujiahui Cangshu Lou) [徐家汇藏书楼] at 80 Cao Stream North Road (Caoxi Bei Lu) [漕溪北路 80 号], which had been established by French Jesuit priests in 1847, was taken over by the Shanghai Library in November 1955. At that time the collection included a total of 210,000 volumes, of which 120,000 were written in Chinese, and another 90,000 in various Western languages, mainly English and French. Although the Zikawei Library building was reopened in 1956 as a branch reading room of the Shanghai Library, and a catalog of its holdings was published in 1957, only small parts of its original collection were made available to the public. When subway Line 1 was constructed directly beneath the building in 1990, it was almost torn down, and was just barely saved from demolition by a public campaign led by famous Chinese writers and intellectuals such as Ba Jin [巴金] (1904-2005). Still, when the street in front of the building was widened the public sidewalk was routed directly through the arched arcades of the library's north building. In 1996, on the 100th anniversary of its construction in 1896, the Zikawei Library building was closed down, and left seemingly abandoned until a restoration project started seven years later in 2002. It was reopened to the public again in July 2003, with the former RAS Library and Zikawei Library collections included in its stacks and finally available to the public. It now reportedly has a collection of 320,000 foreign language publications printed between the years 1477 and 1950 in 20 different langauges, including Latin, French, English,

German, Russian, and Japanese. For more information see the entry for the Xujiahui Library (Xujiahui Cangshu Lou) [徐家汇藏书楼] under the letteter X in this book.

In 1936 the **Maritime Customs House Library** (Haiguan Tushuan) [海关图书馆书] reportedly housed 16,000 volumes of publications, and in 1957 the Shanghai Library published a catalog of its holdings, but most of its collections eventually ended up in the China Second National Archives in Nanjing. The original Customs House Library building constructed in Shanghai in 1931 was fully restored and opened to the public in August 2015, albeit stocked with new copies of the original publications it once housed. It is located at 1708 Xinzha Lu [新闸路 1708 号] in Jingan District [静安区] (former Zhabei District).

The Shanghai Library also has a complete set of original issues of the **North China Daily Herald**, which must be requested in writing and are only available Monday through Friday.

The Shanghai Library has a massive collection of nearly 9,000 historic maps published before 1949, of which 1,000 are English or French language documents. Again, these are not available on weekends, and must be requested in writing from Monday through Friday. A sample of 66 of these historic maps was published by the library in June 2001 in a volume entitled, "*The Album of Shanghai During the Past 150 Years (Lao Shanghai Ditu) [老上海地图]*," edited by the library's resident map expert, Professor Huang Gourong.

During the Cultural Revolution (1966-1976) the Shanghai Library and its collections were largely closed to the public. However, its collections continued to grow as more than four million volumes of books confiscated from private individuals by the Red Guards ended up being put in storage here.

Because no English maps of the facility are available, and the English signage is somewhat ambiguous, a description of the library's floor plan may be useful for those who would like to conduct research here. Furthermore, English titles are kept in a bewildering maze of different locations, collections and reading rooms. The Ground Floor has an **Internet Cafe**, cafeteria, and office for Reader's Card registration. Keep in mind that before you can even begin to use the facility you must apply for a Reader's Card, which requires showing your passport and paying an annual fee, and then wait several weeks before it is ready to be picked up.

The First Floor, and those above, is divided into East and West wings. The West Wing has a **Book Shop** which sells mainly Chinese language books, but also offers some useful bilingual maps of Shanghai and China, as well as some bilingual local history books. Beside the book store is a **Gift Shop** which is always stocked with the most recent editions of the local English language newspapers, the Shanghai Star and Shanghai Daily. At the far end are the computer terminals where you can access the library's catalogue if you can read the Chinese interface. These terminals are closed down at 5:00 p.m. every day, but normally the on-line catalogue can be accessed from any computer connected to the Internet 24 hours per day.

Around the corner is the **General Reading Room** and the desk for submitting your written requests for books kept in storage in the closed stacks.   You must present your reader's card to request books or enter any of the reading rooms.   The GRR does not have any shelved books kept in it, but merely serves as a place to read titles requested from storage. This General Reading Room tends to be noisy and overcrowded, but you can take books received from storage to other quieter parts of the library and read them there.

No bags or luggage can be taken inside any of the reading rooms, so you should know that the so-called Cloak Room just East of the main entrance is a locker room for storing your personal effects.   You must have a one Rmb coin to rent a locker.

The First Floor's East Wing is devoted to what signs somewhat misleadingly call **Shanghai Literature**, and **1911-1949 Literature**.   In fact, it is the Reference Desk here where you can request old Shanghai maps and pre-1949 English language Shanghai newspapers. Copies of historic maps can be professionally made for you at a cost of 20 to 100 Rmb. However, the map service is only available on weekdays, Monday through Friday from 9:00 to 5:00 p.m.   Around the corner is the Shanghai local history reading room, which makes a pleasant quiet retreat from the mob scene typical in other parts of the library.   Here you can find some volumes of Shanghai maps, old street name indexes, and gazetteers compiling the history of Shanghai's various towns (zhen zhi) districts (qu zhi) and counties (xian zhi). These gazetteers contain useful maps of the past and present, chronologies of events, and photographs, although they are of course written in Chinese.

The Second Floor's West Wing has a **Reference Books Reading Room** which contains many recently published English language titles on Chinese history and travel.   Next to it is the **Chinese Social Sciences Periodicals Reading Room**.   This reading room has many Chinese language magazines on Chinese religions and philosophy, including Buddhism, Taoism and Christianity.   You can find *Taoism Today* as well as the *Nanjing Theological Review*.   In between these two reading rooms is a photocopy center where you can have any books or periodicals you want copied for you.   You are not allowed to make copies yourself, which sometimes results in waiting in a long line to be served.   The copy center closes at 5:00 P.M.

The Second Floor's East Wing contains **Chinese Ancient Books, Ancient Documents, and Rare Books**.   In this section you can find 90,000 local histories (difang zhi) [地方志] for various towns, counties and prefectures all across China, as well as 2,000 ancient book manuscripts and 3,000 old imperial examination essays (zhujuan) from the Ming and Qing dynasties.

The main attraction on the Third Floor is the **Manuscript Library of Chinese Cultural Celebrities**.   This section includes 3,000 original book manuscripts by famous authors, including some by **Mao Dun**, as well as 108,000 personal letters and 100,000 personal archives of important people such as the Qing Dynasty official **Li Hongzhang**.

Most foreigners will probably be attracted to the Fourth Floor, as it is here that the majority of English publications not kept in storage are available.   However, even on this one floor the English titles are subdivided into an array of separate collections.   The five separate English collections on this one floor include Foreign Newspapers and Periodicals; the **Foreign Publications Reading Room**, the United Nations Depository; the San Francisco Friendship Library; and the Art Books Reading Room.

The Foreign Newspaper collection here is probably the only place in China where you can read the Washington Post and New York Times, as well as the more commonly available International Herald Tribune. The Foreign Periodicals shelves are well stocked with scholarly journals such as the Journal of Asian Studies, the Journal of the Royal Asiatic Society, the Middle East Journal; and the International Journal of Middle East Studies, as well as foreign news magazines such as Time and Newsweek.

Address: 1555 Huaihai Middle Road (Huaihai Zhong Lu).
Phone: (021) 6445-5555.
Website: http://www.library.sh.cn/english/

Longhua Airport (Shanghai Longhua Jichang) [上海龙华机场]

The site of the Longhua Airport (Shanghai Longhua Jichang) [上海龙华机场] (1917-2013) is considered the birthplace of Chinese aviation. The land along the Huangpu River was first acquired by the Beiyang Army in 1915 for use as a military base that included barracks and a drill ground. An airfield was constructed alongside the training ground and barracks in 1917. In 1922 the Beiyang Army ordered the first ten foreign airplanes, which were based here. However, in June 1929 the airport was taken over by the Civil Aviation Bureau of the newly established Guomindang central government in Nanjing and in 1930 more land was acquired to extend the runways. During the Republic of China (Minguo) era, it was one of only four international airports in mainland China and was considered the largest international airport in all of East Asia.

Longhua Airport was the base of operations for both **Eurasia Aviation Corporation** (Ouya Hangkong Gongsi) [欧亚航空公司] (1931-1943), a Sino-German joint venture founded in 1930 in agreement between the Chinese Ministry of Transportation and the German Lufthansa Company which began operations in 1931, and the **China National Aviation Corporation** (Zhongguo Hangkong Gongsi) [中国航空公司] (1929-1949), commonly known as CNAC, which had been founded in 1929 in a partnership with American investors operating as China Airways Federal Inc. and the Ministry of Communications of the Chinese national government in Nanjing, and was partly acquired by Pan American Airways in 1933. Both airlines operated ari mail, freight, and passenger, services. In addition to regular aircraft, there were some seaplanes flying "the Yangtze River route" that would land in and take off from the Huangpu River. In 1936 both airlines asked the government to extened the Longhua south-north runway to a length of 1,200 meters.

In November 1937 Longhua Airport was occupied by the Japanese military, who expanded it to two runways, one running south-north and the other east-west, with enough parking space for a fleet of 100 heavy bombers and 10 support aircraft. When the Japanese surrendered in August 1945, the airport was taken over by the Guomindang air force (Zhonghua Minguo Kongjun) [中华民国空军], who also allowed the U.S. Air Force to use it, but the U.S.A.F. soon moved their operations to Shanghai's **Jiangwan Airport** (Jiangwan Jichang) [江湾机场].

In 1946 Longhua Airport returned to civil aviation use when a new cement south-north runway measuring 1,829 meters in length was built and it became the headquarters of both the **China National Aviation Corporation** (Zhongguo Hangkong Gongsi) [中国航空公司] and the **Central Air Transport Co.** (Zhongyang Hangkong Yunshu Gongsi) [中央航空运输公司] (1943-1949), a Chinese state owned enterprise that had been formed in 1943 out of the ashes of the bankrupt **Eurasia Aviation Corporation** (Ouya Hangkong Gongsi) [欧亚航空公司] (1931-1943).   A third major airline to regularly use the Longhua Airport during this post-war time period was **Civil Air Transport** Inc. (Minhang Kongyun Gongsi) [民航空运公司] (1946-1975), which had been established in 1946 by Claire Chennault, formerly the commanding officer of the Flying Tigers (also known as the 14th Air Force), and was later acquired by U.S. intelligence services who used it for their covert purposes until 1975.

Flights in and out of Longhua used to make dramatic take offs and landings directly over the Huangpu River and get a bird's eye view of the buildings on the Bund (Waitan) down below, or sometimes they would approach directly over the Longhua Pagoda (Longhua Ta) of Longhua Buddhist Temple, which was considered by pilots to be a potential hazard.   In at least one case, a passenger plane crashed into the river during take off, with no survivors, and the wreckage had to be fished out of the water.

The worst civil aviation disaster occurred on December 25, 1946, known as "Black Christmas" (Heise Shengdan) [黑色圣诞], when three civil aviation passenger airplanes crashed in Shanghai all in one day due to low visibility caused by thick fog, two while trying to land at Longhua Airport, a third while trying to land at Jiangwan Airport, and a fourth just barely landed safely by diverting to Jiangwan Airport, which had more modern radar equipment installed that allowed the control tower to talk the pilot down.   Originally all four had been scheduled to land at Longhua Airport, which did not even have any runway lights for pilots to see where to land, let alone the modern radar equipment at Jiangwan Airport.

As in the Fall of 1937 when it served as the escape route from the advancing Japanese invasion, in May 1949 it was from this airport that the Chinese middle and upper classes tried to flee from the mainland to the safety of Hong Kong in the face of the Red Army's rapid advance.

It was taken overy by the Red Army in May 1949, but returned to at least partial civilian use by the end of 1950.   By some accounts it served joint civilian and military purposes.   In 1952, Longhua Airport began serving as the site for the Shanghai Military Commission's Civil Aviation Administration station.   In 1952 and 1955 the south-north and east-west concrete runways were both repaired.   From 1950 to 1964 Longhua Airport was the only civil aviation airport in Shanghai.   There were about a dozen domestic civil aviation air routes to other cities in China at this time.

However, in November 1963 the central government approved the extension of the Hongqiao Airport into an international airport, and in August 1966 all scheduled civil aviation flights were transferred from Longhua Airport to Hongqiao Airport.   After this, Longhua Airport was mainly used for civil aviation pilot training.

In 1983 the facility included an Air Terminal (hangkong zhan) [航空站], Shanghai Airplane Manufacturing Factory (Shanghai Feiji Zhizhaochang) [上海飞机制造厂], Shanghai airplane research institute/graduate school (Shanghai Feiji Yanjiusuo) [上海飞机研究所], Civil

Aviation Factory 102 (Minhang 102 Chang) [民航一○二厂], Civil Aviation Vocational School (Minhang Zhongzhuan Jixiao) [民航中专和技校], and the Shanghai Parachute Club (Shanghai Shi Tiaosan Julebu) [上海市跳伞俱乐部].

Longhua Airport sort of gradually disappeared one piece at a time, without there ever being any grand closing ceremony or formal announcement of its demise, making it difficult to pinpoint an exact ending date to its century-long history.   In the early 2000s there was much discussion about possibly reviving the Longhua Airport for some new purpose, such as helicopters, charter flights, or small private airplanes.   When I visited the site in 2008 the old Terminal Building and the main north-south runway were still fully intact and there was even a small collection of historic airplanes on display, although the east-west runway had already disappeared.   There was also a small old train station across the street from the old Terminal Building.

However, in 2008 the middle of the north-south runway was damaged during the construction of the **Longyao Road Tunnel** (Longyao Lu Suidao) [龙耀路隧道], which opened for traffic in April 2010.   By some accounts, the last take offs and landings at the airport occurred in June 2011.   In 2013 the former route of the south-north runway was completely built over with a new road, **Yunjin Road** (Yunjin Lu) [云锦路], and a new public park known as **Runway Park** (Paodao Gongyuan) [跑道公园].

As of late September 2018 all that remained of the airport was the former **Terminal Building** (Houji Lou) [候机楼] (or hangkong zhan) [航空站], which still stands at #1 Longhua West Road (Longhua Xi Lu yi hao) [龙华西路 1 号] facing Fenggu Road (Fenggu Lu) [丰谷路], and had been occupied for many years by the **Shoaxing Restaurant** (Shaoxing Fandian) [绍兴饭店] which was scheduled to move out for the building to be renovated and possibly converted into a district public library.   Oddly, the building had no commemorative plaque denoting its historical significance, and it has proven impossible to date exactly when it was built except that it appears to be from the late 1940s.   None of the many written sources I consulted mention it, and it appears in very few archival photographs.   However, the restaurant's interior was decorated with a large painting of a large passenger airplane taking off and framed historical photos of the airport lined the corridors.   The front façade had been completely redecorated to make it resemble a hotel, with the most revealing artifact being the curving, sloping driveways that approached the front entrance from both sides. However, the back side had not been changed.   By walking around the back of the building one could see that the original air traffic control tower on top of the building was still intact, with a forest of radar and radio transmitter antennae still installed all around it.   Some of the surviving aircraft hangars (jike) [机库] have been turned into art galleries as part of the **West Bund** development.   The collection of three or four historic airplanes that was still here in 2008 seems to have disappeared, but may have been moved inside the campus of the **Shanghai Civil Aviation College** (Shanghai Minhang Zhiye Jishu Xueyuan) [上海民航职业技术学院] located across the street from the old Terminal Building.   A nearby residential community is still known as **Airport New Village** (Jichang Xincun) [机场新村].

Address: #1 Longhua West Road (Longhua Xi Lu yi hao) [龙华西路 1 号] facing Fenggu Road (Fenggu Lu) [丰谷路], Longhua Town, Xuhui District, Shanghai.

Longhua Buddhist Temple (Longhua Si) [龙华寺]:   A Brief Description

Longhua Si [龙华寺] is a functioning Buddhist temple with a large resident monk population belonging to the Zen meditation sect (Chan Zong) [禅宗] of Mahayana Buddhism.   It is by far the largest one in Shanghai.   Located southwest of Xujiahui [徐家汇], in Longhua town, the main temple complex sits on the North side of Longhua Lu, while the seven-story Longhua Pagoda (Longhua Ta) [龙华塔] stands by itself across the street on the South side.

Popular local legends say the temple and pagoda were both supposedly first built in 242 A.D. by **Sun Quan** [孙权], the King of Eastern Wu (Dong Wu) [东吴], during the Three Kingdoms (San Guo) [三国] (220-280), and then later destroyed during the Qianfu [乾符] reign (874-879) of the Tang Dynasty [唐代] (618-907).   Other sources claim that the temple was first built in 977 A.D. by King **Qian Hong** [钱弘] of the Wu Yue Kingdom [吴越], during the second year of the Taiping Xingguo [太平兴国] reign of Emperor Taizong [太宗] (976 – 997) of the Northern Song Dynasty (Bei Song) [北宋] (960-1127).   However, its documented history really begins with the Northern Song Dynasty (Bei Song) [北宋] (960-1127) reign of Emperor **Yingzong** [英宗] (1063-1067), when the temple is recorded as having been renamed **Kongxiang Si** [空相寺] in 1066.   Later, Ming Dynasty Emperor **Yongle** [永乐] (1403-1424) completely rebuilt the temple and changed its name back to the original **Longhua Si** [龙华寺].

The temple was completely destroyed, and later rebuilt, numerous times in its long history.   These cycles of destruction and reconstruction usually followed the rise and fall of imperial dynasties and political regimes.   Except for the pagoda, most of the LonghuaTemple buildings were destroyed during the **Taiping Rebellion** (Taiping Tianguo) [太平天国] (1850-1864), during which the rebels launched three attacks on Shanghai from 1860 to 1862.   After the **1911 Revolution** (Xinhai Geming) [辛亥革命] overthrew the Qing Dynasty and established a Republic, in 1912 all the monks were forced to move out by armed soldiers who moved in and used the temple as a barracks.   The temple reopened ten years later in 1922 when the soldiers moved out and all the monks came back.   In 1928 gardens to the west of the temple that had previously belonged to it were converted into a public park known as **Longhua Park** (Longhua Gongyuan) [龙华公园], which nowadays is known as **Longhua Martyrs' Cemetery** (Longhua Lieshi Lingyuan) [龙华烈士陵园].   The temple was badly damaged on September 11, 1937 when nine Japanese airplanes dropped 30 bombs on the Longhua area during the Japanese attack on Shanghai.   It underwent extensive repairs in 1953-57, when the main halls were repaired, a new **Scripture Hall** (Cangjing Lou) [藏经楼] was completely rebuilt, and duplicate copies of all the Buddhist statues were supposedly made.

However, at the start of the **Cultural Revolution** (Wenhua Da Geming) [文化大革命] (1966-1976) the Red Guards (Hongweibing) [红卫兵] destroyed all of the temple's Buddha statues, library of books, Buddhist scriptures, treasures, ancient relics, and art work.   Even the Ming Dynasty bronze bell in the **Bell Tower** (Zhong Lou) [钟楼] was cut into pieces and melted down as scrap metal.   In 1967 the temple's buildings were all rented out as warehouse storage space to a company.

In 1978 the former compound of Longhua Temple was put under the administration of the Shanghai municipal government's Garden Bureau (Shanghai Shi Yuanlin Guanli Ju) [上海市园林管理局]. It was not until January 1982 that Shanghai's mayor Wang Doahan [汪道涵] (1915-2005) decided to return the Longhua Temple compound to the control of the Shanghai Buddhist Association (Shanghai Shi Fojiao Xiehui) [上海市佛教协会], and the actual handover did not occur until September 1, 1982. At some point in 1982 the Buddhist monk Ming Yang (Ming Yang Fashi) [明旸法师] was appointed as the temple's new Abbot (Fangzhang) [方丈]. Thus, it was only after these events of 1982 that repairs to the temple began and it reopened to the public as a house of worship for the first time since the Cultural Revolution had started 16 years earlier in 1966. The grand re-opening ceremony did not occur until January 1983. In 1983 the temple was listed by the State Council as a national protected cultural relic.

Nowadays, passing through the **Shan Men** [山门] gateway built in 1998, visitors enter into the orange-walled compound to the first of six successive courtyards which separate the six main halls on the south-north central axis. Most of the existing temple buildings were rebuilt from 1878 to 1895, during the Guangxu [光绪] reign (1875-1908) of the late Qing Dynasty [清朝] (1644-1911), following the destruction of the temple during the three Taiping rebel attacks on Shanghai from 1860 to1862. The six main halls on the central axis are in order from South to North as follows: the **Maitreya Hall** (Mile Dian) [弥勒殿] dedicated to the Maitreya Buddha (Mile Fo) [弥勒佛]; the **Hall of the Four Heavenly Kings** (Tianwang Dian) [天王殿] devoted to four-meter high statues of the Four Heavenly Kings (Sida Tianwang) [四大天王], with two on each side of the hall, and a statue of the guardian warrior Weituo [韦陀] facing the back door; the **Precious Hall of the Great Hero** (Da Xiong Bao Dian) [大雄宝殿], featuring three statues facing the front door of Sakyamuni Buddha (Shijiamouni) [释迦牟尼] standing in the center flanked on the left by the bodhisattva Samantabhadra (Puxian) [普贤] seated on an elephant and on the right by the bodhisattva Manjusri (Wenshu) [文殊] seated on a blue lion; with statues of 20 saints (Zhutian) [诸天] (or Tianshen) [天神] and 16 Arhats (Luohan) [罗汉] along the sides of the hall, and a statue of the Goddenss of Mercy (Guanyin) [观音] standing on an island in the sea facing the back door; the **Three Saints Hall** (Sansheng Dian) [三圣殿], containing statues of Amitabha Buddha (Emituo Fo) [阿弥陀佛] in the center, flanked on the left by the bodhisattva (pusa) [菩萨] Dashizhi [大势至] and on the right by the bodhisattva (pusa) [菩萨] Guanshiyin [观世音]; the **Abbot's Quarters** (Fangzhang Shi) [方丈室] inside its own private walled courtyard sometimes known as the Hualin Zhangshi [华林丈室] that is usually not open to the public; and finally the **Scripture Hall** (Cangjing Lou) [藏经楼].

The second courtyard is flanked on the left side by a two-story wooden **Drum Tower** (Gu Lou) [鼓楼] and on the right by the matching two-story wooden **Bell Tower** (Zhong Lou) [钟楼], each with three layers of upturned roof eaves. On the first floor of the Bell Tower (Zhong Lou) [钟楼] is a glass case holding a golden effigy of the Boddhisatva Kshitigarbha (Dizang) [地藏], who is the patron deity of the sacred Buddhist mountain of Jiuhua Shan in Anhui Povince. The bell in the tower is rung 108 times on New Year's Eve. Ringing the bell is considered so lucky that the right to strike is auctioned off to the highest bidders, some of whom fly in from overseas. On the first floor of the Drum Tower (Gu Lou) is a glass case containing a golden effigy of **Guan Yu** [关羽], the God of War.

Behind the Drum Tower is a round gateway in the wall leading to a secluded side garden that contains an original stone boundary marker used to mark the boundaries of the temple's grounds, but this small walled garden is usually kept locked shut. Outside the gate stand two stone carved animals known as Spirit Beasts (Ling Shou) [灵兽].

On the East side of the Abbot's Quarters is the small **Tomb Pagoda Garden** (Mu Ta Yuan) [墓塔园] containing a broken stone tomb pagoda erected in 1667 during the Qing Dynasty in honor of **Tao Ming** [韬明], who was the Master of Longhua Temple from 1647 to 1666. Sometimes this small pagoda is called the Tao Ming Fashi Lingta [韬明法师灵塔]. Unfortunately, on my last visit in 2018, this courtyard had become the smoking area, and a new rear gate had been opened up in the back corner wall to allow visitors to enter from the parking lot that used to belong to the former hotel next door. At the rear of the Tomb Pagoda courtyard is the monk's **Dining Hall** (Zhai Tang) [斋堂], not to be confused with the separate **Vegetarian Restaurant** (Sucai Guan) [素菜馆] intended for public visitors located on the right side of the Hall of the Great Hero (Da Xiong Bao Dian) [大雄宝殿] beneath the sign of the long wooden fish (muyu) [木鱼] hanging from the rafters. Althgough it may go by the same name, this is not the same as the much smaller and differently shaped wooden fish (muyu) [木鱼] used by Buddhist monks as a percussion instrument during temple ceremonies. Beside the suspended wooden fish is a suspended metal gong shaped like a cloud.

On the west side of the Abbot's Quarters, in the northwest corner of the temple's walled compound, is another area closed to the public where the monk's dormitories are.

On the east side of the walled temple compound, behind the Dining Hall and Vegetarian Restaurant, is a parallel walled compound containing the buildings of the former **Longhua Hotel** (Longhua Binguan) that went bankrupt and now seems to have been taken over by the temple. New gates have been opened up in the temple compound's eastern wall in at least three places to allow access to the former hotel compound. A large new Buddhist assembly hall that had been added here as of 2018 may have originally been a ballroom or lobby belonging to the hotel. It has a very high ceiling, a stage at one end, and seating for a large number of people, resembling in some ways a church more than a traditional Buddhist temple hall. The garden containing the southwest corner stone of Kongxiang Si [空相寺] is in the southeast corner of this parallel compound.

Two long barracks-like halls run along almost the full length of the western side of the temple compound and are divided up into many small Buddhist chapels. The major ones include the **Arhat Hall** (Luohan Tang) [罗汉堂], and the **Goddess of Mercy Hall** (Guanyin Tang) [观音堂]. The Arhat Hall (Luoan Dian) [罗汉殿] was added sometime during 2002. It features small golden statues of 500 arhats or Buddhist saints. The Goddess of Mercy Hall (Guanyin Tang) [观音堂] is on the left side of the fourth courtyard and features an impressive golden statue of Guanyin [观音], who is depicted as facing in all four directions, and has 1,000 arms. Many of her hundreds of hands hold objects of special significance.

A second long barracks-like hall hidden behind the first one is known as the **Jade Buddha Hall** (Yu Fo Dian) [玉佛殿], which contains an unusual **Reclining Jade Buddha** (Yu Wo Fo) [玉卧佛] like the one at the Jade Buddha Temple (Yu Fo Si) [玉佛禅寺].

Diagrams that map out all the buildings within the Longhua Temple compound can be found in the appendix of Pan Mingquan [潘明权] (1996) and on p.59 of Pan Mingquan [潘明权] (2003), both of which are locally published Chinese language sources.

Address: 2853 Longhua Road [龙华路 2853 号], Longhua Town, Xuhui District [徐汇区].

Longhua Pagoda (Longhua Ta) [龙华塔]

The 40.64 meter high, octagonal, wooden Longhua Pagoda (Longhua Ta) [龙华塔], has orange walls with red cross-timbers, upturned eaves and wood railing balconies at each level, and a metal spiral spire on top.   Depending on who you believe, it may have been built in 247 A.D. during the Three Kingdoms (San Guo) [三国] (220-280), in 1066 during the Northern Song Dynasty (Bei Song) [北宋] (960-1127) or in the late Qing Dynasty [清朝] (1644-1911).   After extensive research, I have concluded that the current pagoda may possibly be the same as the Xin Baota [新宝塔] constructed in 1066 by the Northern Song Emperor Yingzong [英宗] (1063-1067), but could not be the same as that supposedly first built in 247 A.D. by King Sun Quan [孙权] (222-252) of the Eastern Wu Kingdom (Dong Wu) [东吴].   In 1984 the pagoda underwent a massive restoration during which the entire tower was covered with scaffolding, and a giant boom crane dropped a brand new copper spiral ornament onto the tower's roof.

In the 1930s visitors could still ascend to the top of this tower, but after 1949 it was closed to the public for over 55 years until it was finally reopened on October 1, 2006.   Plans for reopening the pagoda were delayed for nine years when it was discovered in 1998 that the tower was leaning 1.04 meters to the East.   Ascending the pagoda is a challenge due to the interior staircase' 75 degree angle, and narrow 40 centimeter width.   At the time of its reopening visitors were being charged a rather exorbitant ticket price of 100 Rmb.   The pagoda garden at the base is encircled by an orange brick wall with a gate.   Unfortunately, during a visit in early 2007 it was found that the walled pagoda garden was closed once again.   As of 2018 it is still closed, although faithful visitors can be seen walking around its walled area in circles while chanting prayers.   It seems that it will only be opened to the public on special occasions.

Beside the pagoda garden is the remains of an earlier Shan Men entrance gate to the temple's walled compound in the form of two stone pillars.

Address: 2853 Longhua Lu [龙华路 2853 号], Longhua Town, Xuhui District [徐汇区].
Phone: (021) 6456-6085

How Old is Longhua Temple?　The Temple's Long History

Longhua Buddhist Temple (Longhua Si) [龙华寺] undoubtedly has a long history, but the question is how long?　The answer is debatable.　In all likelihood it is about 900 years old, rather than the 1800 years sometimes claimed for it.　Very little evidence exists to support the often heard claims that the temple and pagoda were supposedly first built in 242 A.D. and 247 A.D. by Sun Quan [孙权] (r.222-252), the King of the Eastern Wu Kingdom (Dong Wu) [东吴], during the **Three Kingdoms** (San Guo) [三国] (220-280).　Furthermore, maps of Shanghai's geological history contained in Zhou Zhenhe [周振鹤], *Shanghai Historic Maps Collection* (*Shanghai Lishi Ditu Ji*) [*上海历史地图集*], Shanghai:　Shanghai People's Publishing House (Shanghai Renmin Chubanshe) [上海人民出版社] (1999) show that most of this area was underwater until the Tang Dynasty (618-907).　Some sources also make vague claims that the temple was built by the Tang Dynasty Empress Wu Zetian [武则天] sometime during her reign (690-705 A.D.), but later destroyed at some unspecified date during the rebellion of Huang Zhao (879-884 A.D.) against the Tang Xizong Emperor (873-888).　The first specific year to appear in most accounts is a supposed rebuilding of a new temple on the same site as the earlier Three Kingdoms (San Guo) [三国] (220-280) and Tang Dynasty temples by the Wu Yue [吴越] regional kingdom in 977 A.D.　If these earlier versions of LonghuaTemple did in fact exist, they were ephemeral and have left no lasting traces.

Substantial documented evidence of the temple's origins begins to appear during the Northern Song Dynasty (Bei Song) [北宋] (960-1127).　In the year 1066 the Northern Song Emperor **Yingzong** (1063-1067) built a new **Big Buddha Hall** (Da Fo Dian) [大佛殿] and the **New Precious Pagoda** (Xin Bao Ta) [新宝塔] on this same site.　Although at that time it was named **Kongxiang Si** [空相寺], it is from this date that LonghuaTemple's history can accurately be traced through a continuous progression of events up to the present day.　In fact, it is even possible that the 11th Century Xin Bao Ta [新宝塔] is the same pagoda which still stands today, albeit after having been repeatedly repaired and restored countless times.

During the Lizong [理宗] reign (1224-1264) of emperor Zhao Guicheng [赵贵诚] at the end of the Southern Song Dynasty (1127-1279), four boundary stones were erected in 1262, one in each of the four corners of the temple's property.　Two of these supposedly still exist today, and one of them could until recently actually be seen in the **Tomb Pagoda Garden** (Mu Ta Yuan) [墓塔园], lying on the ground beside the Tao Ming Tomb Pagoda (Tao Ming Mu Ta) [韬明墓塔].

In the **Yuan Dynasty** (1279-1368) the temple was given several land grants which added considerably to its territory.　However, at the end of the Yuan Dynasty the temple buildings were completely destroyed during a battle, except for the pagoda (bao ta) [宝塔], which is recorded as somehow miraculously surviving the conflagration, as it supposedly would in many similar situations throughout the temple's history.

The third Ming Emperor **Yongle** [永乐](1403-1424) completely rebuilt the temple from the ground up between **1410-1416**, and also changed its name from the Northern Song Dynasty name of **Kongxiang Si** [空相寺] to the present day name of **Longhua Si** [龙华寺].　Later, the **Shan Men** [山门] front gate was built between 1506 and 1521.

The structures built by Yongle [永乐](1403-1424) had a relatively short life span of only 140 years as the whole temple was destroyed during an invasion by Japanese pirates (Woko) [倭寇] in **1553**.   Nonetheless, after the destruction of the Woko [倭寇] pirates, the Ming Dynasty began a reconstruction project which lasted for about ten years, from 1563 to 1574. However, during the late Ming Dynasty the temple suffered from neglect and only one new hall, the **Scripture Storage Pavilion** (Cangjing Ge) [藏经阁], was built in **1611**.   A Cangjing Ge [藏经阁] is used by a temple to store the Tripitaka (Sanzang) [三藏] scriptures.

In the early Qing Dynasty Longhua Temple received considerable attention in the form of repairs to the existing buildings and construction of new ones.   A major construction project started in 1647 resulted in the completion of the Abbot or Temple Master's Room (Fangzhang Shi) [方丈室] and the **Weituo Hall** (Weituo Dian) [韦陀殿], as well as the repair of the Scripture Storage Pavilion (Cangjing Ge) [藏经阁].

It will be recalled that during the Yuan Dynasty the temple experienced a massive expansion in the size of its territory, if not its actual structures.   In 1672 the Qing authorities measured the size of the immediate area around the temple halls as occupying 93 mu of land, plus an additional 74 mu of open land in the surrounding area which was used to plant vegetables. It was this later open space which gradually evolved into first **Longhua Park** (Longhua Gongyuan) [龙华公园], and then the present day **Longhua Martyr's Cemetery** (Longhua Lieshi Lingyuan) [龙华烈士陵园].

During a 155 year period in the middle of the Qing Dynasty, from 1672 to 1827, no new construction, reconstruction or repairs were recorded.   This begs the question as to why the temple was dormant during such a long period of time.   Was it lack of imperial sympathy for Buddhism in general, or simply the absence of wars and destruction requiring later rehabilitation during this relatively peaceful time?

After a century and a half of dormancy, the **Taiping Rebellion** finally provided the opportunity or the need for new construction and repairs.   Between 1860 and 1862 the Taiping rebels attacked Shanghai three times, during which records say vaguely that most of the LonghuaTemple buildings were destroyed.   On August 18, 1860 the Taiping rebels captured Xujiahui, and it was probably then when the nearby Longhua Temple was destroyed.   Although no list is provided of exactly which buildings were destroyed, we can infer from later lists of the structures rebuilt afterwards that this included the **Great Sadness Hall** (Da Bei Dian) [大悲殿], the **Precious Hall of the Great Hero** (Da Xiong Bao Dian) [大雄宝殿], the **Heavenly Kings Hall** (Tian Wang Dian) [天王殿], the **Three Saints Hall** (San Sheng Dian) [三圣殿], the **Maitreya Buddha Hall** (Mile Dian) [弥勒殿], the **Drum Tower** (Gu Lou) [鼓楼], the **Bell Tower** (Zhong Lou) [钟楼], and the **Big Buddha Hall** (Da Fo Dian)[大佛殿].   Basically every previously existing key structure is mentioned as having been rebuilt after this period of destruction, with the exception of the die hard **Precious Pagoda** (Bao Ta) [宝塔] and the **Master's Room** (Fangzhang Shi) [方丈室], raising the possibility that the two structures which stand today are both authentic originals.

Restoring the damage done by the three years of Taiping destruction required a massive reconstruction project which lasted for nearly 30 years from 1871 to 1899.   In addition to rebuilding the previous structures, several new halls which had not existed before were added during this time, including the **Guest Hall** (Ke Tang) [客堂] and the **Dining Hall** (Zhai Tang) [斋堂] in 1887; the **Goddess of Mercy Hall** (Guanyin Dian) [观音殿], **Ancestors Hall** (Zushi Dian) [祖师殿], and the **Kshitigarbha Hall** (Dizang Dian) [地藏殿] in 1890; and finally the **500 Arhats Hall** (Wubai Luohan Tang) [五百罗汉堂] in 1896.

The Republican Era (Min Guo) [民国], 1911-1949

At the beginning of the Republic (1912), all the monks were forced to move out by armed soldiers who moved in and used the temple as a barracks. The soldiers looted the golden statues from the temple, and wooden parts of the temple such as window frames were used by the soldiers to make cooking fires. However, in 1920 the temple and the pagoda were both repaired, and after being closed for a whole decade the temple finally officially reopened in 1922 when all the monks came back. Holmes Welch's otherwise authoritative 1967 study of Buddhism in China mistakenly states that LonghuaTemple was occupied by the Chinese military for the entire Republican period. Nobel laureate author Rabindranath Tagore visited Longhua Temple in April 1924. Photos from D.C. Burn's brief 1926 study of the temple show that the Qing Dynasty **500 Arhat Hall** (Wubai Luohan Tang) [五百罗汉堂] was still intact then, although it no longer exists now.

Longhua Temple enjoyed 15 years of peace and tranquility until September 11, 1937 when the temple was badly damaged during the Japanese attack on Shanghai. Nine Japanese airplanes dropped 30 bombs on the Longhua area. Most likely they were targeting the nearby **Longhua Airport** and the Guomindang's **Longhua Garrison** military camp next door, but they accidentally caused severe damage to the temple. Before the attack there had been 80 monks living in the temple, but afterward there were only 7 monks remaining.

During the first five years of the **Sino-Japanese War**, 1937-1942, the internal affairs of the temple were confused and disorganized, with rival masters claiming the post of Abbot, and unqualified persons claiming to be Buddhist monks for the sake of seeking safe haven in the temple. On September 9, 1942 a reorganization committee was established to restore order within the temple's community of resident monks. In 1944 this committee restored the Precious Hall of the Great Hero (Da Xiong Bao Dian) [大雄宝殿], and the next year, 1945, the Pagoda (Bao Ta) [宝塔]. Once the Sino-Japanese War had ended, in 1946 life in the temple returned to a resemblance of its pre-war normalcy. However, the tranquility which existed within the temple for the next three years was suddenly disrupted when the Communist's captured Shanghai in May 1949 and proclaimed the People's Republic in October 1949. With all the disasters the temple had survived over the previous 900 years, the worst was yet to come.

People's Republic, 1949-2018.

In June 1949, one month after their capture of Shanghai, the new Communist government took over the temple, and on October 1, 1949, the day celebrating the establishment of the People's Republic of China, the Red flag of the P.R.C. was flown from the top of the pagoda. The temple grounds were drastically reduced in size by at least two-thirds when their garden area was seized by the state and converted into **Longhua Park** (Longhua Gongyuan) [龙华公园] in 1954. The temple's halls were temporarily appropriated by the government in January 1956 for a series of meetings held between local government officials and Chinese businessmen to explain and then celebrate the new policy of abolishing private enterprise in favor of a new system of joint private-state companies.   The celebration involved a party for 2,000 people.

In the summer of 1966 Longhua Temple suffered a devastating series of events over a one month period which destroyed nearly all vestiges of its centuries old heritage.   On August 24, 1966 a mob of more than 1,000 Red Guards (Hongweibing) rushed into the temple and in one day destroyed all of the temple's Buddha statues, library of books, treasures, and art work.   The next day, August 25, the Red Guards returned with the intention of destroying the Longhua Pagoda (Longhua Baota) [龙华宝塔], which we've seen had probably been built in the Northern Song Dynasty (960-1126).   First they tied ropes around the base of the pagoda and tried to pull it down, but when this failed they poured oil all around it's base, intending to set it on fire and burn it down.   At this stage the account recorded in the Longhua Town local records (*Longhua Zhen Zhi*) *[龙华镇志]* states rather mysteriously that "the strong opposition of the residents and other people" forced the Red Guards to give up. Thanks to the intervention of these nameless people, the pagoda repeated its performance of having miraculously survived many upheavals throughout the temple's history.

Nonetheless, the destruction of the relics within the temple halls continued for another month. On September 3rd an estimated 103 antique relics found in the temple were looted.   This was followed on September 14th by the intentional destruction of the *Da Cangjing* [大藏经], a sacred Buddhist scripture which weighed 1,763 kilograms before it was shredded into waste paper.   Finally, on September 30th the Ming Dynasty bronze bell in the Bell Tower (Zhong Lou) [钟楼], which weighed 2,574 kilograms, was cut into pieces and melted down as scrap metal, as was the last remaining Buddha statue, which had been a gift of Ming Dynasty Emperor Wanli, and weighed 334 kilograms.

Having now been destroyed as a functioning temple, all that remained were the empty buildings.   In 1967 the temple buildings were all rented out as warehouse storage space to the China Rice and Oil Import Export Co.   The one exception was the Master's Room (Fangzhang Shi) [方丈室], in which some monks may have continued to live a hidden existence.

In 1978 the former compound of Longhua Temple was put under the administration of the Shanghai municipal government's Garden Bureau (Shanghai Shi Yuanlin Guanli Ju) [上海市园林管理局].   It was not until January 1982 that Shanghai's mayor Wang Doahan [汪道涵] (1915-2005) decided to return the Longhua Temple compound to the control of the Shanghai Buddhist Association (Shanghai Shi Fojiao Xiehui) [上海市佛教协会], and the actual handover did not occur until September 1, 1982.   At some point in 1982 the Buddhist monk Ming Yang (Ming Yang Fashi) [明旸法师] was appointed as the temple's new Abbot (Fangzhang) [方丈].   Thus, it was only after these events of 1982 that repairs to the temple began and it reopened to the public as a house of worship for the first time since the Cultural Revolution had started 16 years earlier in 1966.   The grand re-opening ceremony did not occur until January 1983.   In 1983 the temple was listed by the State Council as a national protected cultural relic.

The government tried to make further amends in 1983 by giving the temple a new set of scriptures known as the _Long Cang_ [龙藏], which had been preserved in the Shanghai Library.   In 1984 the Longhua Pagoda (Bao Ta) [宝塔] was repaired, and these repairs continued with the restoration of the Three Saints Hall (San Sheng Dian) [三圣殿] in May 1986.

In 2001 a giant new shopping center called **Longhua Tourist City** was built behind the pagoda.   Surprisingly, this did not damage the environment, but added the convenience of additional restaurants in the area at which one could rest after a long day's exploration of the temple complex.   One other positive result of the new development was that the section of Longhua Lu which passes in between the walled temple compound and the pagoda was closed to vehicular traffic, unless you count motorcycles, and turned into a pedestrian mall. However, by 2018 all the modern buildings in the entire surrounding area had been completely demolished in a major reconstruction of Longhua Town.

Longhua Temple's Current Structures

The 40.64 meter high octagonal wooden pagoda, **Longhua Ta** [龙华塔], has orange walls with red cross timbers, upturned eaves and wood railing balconies at each level, and a metal spiral spire on top.   Depending on who you believe, it may have been built during the Three Kingdoms (San Guo) [三国] (220-280), the Northern Song Dynasty (Bei Song) [北宋] (960-1127) or the late Qing Dynasty [清朝] (1644-1911).   After extensive research into the local histories (difang zhi) [地方志], the author has concluded that the current pagoda may possibly be the same as the **Xin Bao Ta** [新宝塔] first constructed in 1066 by the Song Emperor **Yingzong**, but could not be the same as that supposedly first built in 247 A.D.   In 1984 the pagoda underwent a massive restoration during which the entire tower was covered with scaffolding, and a giant boom crane dropped a brand new copper spiral ornament onto the tower's roof.

As late as 1934 visitors could still ascend to the top of this tower, but after 1949 it was closed to the public and could not be entered or ascended for over 55 years until it was finally reopened on October 1, 2006.   Plans for reopening the pagoda were delayed for nine years when it was discovered in 1998 that the tower was leaning 1.04 meters to the east. Ascending the pagoda is a challenge due to the interior staircase' 75 degree angle and narrow 40 centimeter width.   At the time of its reopening visitors were being charged a rather exorbitant ticket price of 100 Rmb.   The pagoda garden at the base is encircled by an orange brick wall with a gate.   Unfortunately, during a visit in early 2007 it was found that the walled pagoda garden was closed again.   It seems that it will only be opened to the public on special occasions.

The grand front entrance gateway (Shan Men) [山门] to the temple complex is one of the most impressive sights it has to offer, with its six stone pillars, five portals, upturned roof eaves on top, and inscribed signboard overhead, but it's a relatively new structure that was built in 1998.   A photo in Pan Mingquan [潘明权] (1996) shows that the current gate did not yet exist then.   The five-gate pai lou has a granite stone frame with five wooden double gates, above which are three inscribed wooden signboards, all of which is covered by an enormous three-tiered wooden roof with multiple layers of upturned eaves, itself supported by layers of intricate wooden brackets.   The top of the roof is covered with tiles and decorated with dragon-fish ornaments.   Each wooden gate is one-foot thick, which would have made the temple impregnable to attack during times of unrest, but according to a photo in Pan Mingquan [潘明权] (1996), this gate had not yet then been built.   However, it was there when I first visited the temple in the spring of 1999.

Passing through this outer gateway, you enter the first of six successive courtyards which separate the six main halls on the central axis.   All told there are about a dozen halls, towers, and pavilions, each containing golden effigies of a wide variety of various Buddhist deities.   This goes well beyond the typical scale of the average Buddhist temple which normally has only three main halls and sometimes just one.

In this first courtyard are two stone lions and two octagonal stone lanterns, all four enclosed by stone railings.   New replacements for earlier versions of all four of these were installed in 2007.   Two large trees in the courtyard were transplanted here in January 2004.   On the right side of the courtyard is a new expanded gift shop (shu dian) added in January 2004.   It offers not only Buddhist trinkets, but a fine selection of Chinese language books containing histories of Longhua Temple and Buddhist scriptures.   Until 2004, there was not a single published history of Longhua Temple available for sale here, but late in December 2003 no less than three new well-researched titles on this topic were published, several of which can be found here.   Opposite the gift shop is an identical rectangular hall newly added in 2007.

Just past the book shop, on the right side of the first courtyard, is a round moon gate leading into a separate walled garden.   The entrance gate is protected by two stone statues of mythical animals known as Spirit Beasts (Ling Shou) [灵兽].   These two were part of the four Spirit Beast (Ling Shou) [灵兽] statues that used to stand in the Tomb Pagoda Garden (Mu Ta Yuan) at the northeastern rear corner of the temple compound.   One of the two statues has obviously been broken in half and then glued back together again.   On either side of the gate are a number of gold metal signs with black letters advertising this garden as belonging to various organizations including the **Hualin Museum** (Hualin Bowuyuan), the **Hualin Art Institute** (Hualin Meishuyuan), and **Shanghai Poem Association**.   Oddly the English names on the sings use the incorrect phonetic Pinyin translation of "Hualing." However, this garden's real importance is that it contains one of the original four stone boundary markers for Longhua Temple's predecessor, Kongxiang Si [空相寺].   The stone tablet dating from the year 1262 of the late Southern Song Dynasty (1127-1279) is housed inside a small open-air wooden pavilion beside a pond of water.   According to the still legible two column 14 character inscription, this stone was used to mark the southwest corner of Kongxiang Si [空相寺].   The first five characters in the right column read "Kongxiang Si Xinan….[空相寺西南]"   The top right corner of the tablet has been broken off. This garden was apparently not opened to the public until early 2007.   On my last visit to the temple in December 2017 the garden's gate was padlocked shut.

The first main hall is the one-story **Maitreya Buddha Hall** (Mile Dian) [弥勒殿].   This hall dates from an 1884 reconstruction, when it was rebuilt to replace an earlier structure destroyed during the Taiping rebels attacks on Shanghai in 1860-1862.   The hall was last restored in 1981.   It is dedicated to the Maitreya Buddha of the future, known in China as **Mile Fo** [弥勒佛], and depicted here as the fat laughing Buddha of the Song Dynasty (960-1279).   This Mile Fo [弥勒佛] image is a golden effigy, seated on a square stone base and protected by a glass case.   He is depicted as having a third eye in the center of his forehead.   Until 2007 the Buddha could be seen from the first courtyard through a partially open gate on the south side of the hall, but the hall itself could not be entered without passing through the adjoining orange wall into the second courtyard and entering from the north side.   In October 2007 the southern entrance to the **Maitreya Hall** (Mile Dian) [弥勒殿] was opened to the public for the first time.   Although Mile Fo usually does occupy the first hall of many temples, he often has to share his space with the Four Heavenly Kings (Sida Tianwang) [四大天王].   In this case he has the whole hall to himself, the kings occupying a separate building of their own.   Until January 2004 he had to share his home with the temple gift shop and book store (shu dian) [书店], but this has now been moved out to a separate new hall in the first courtyard.

The second courtyard is flanked on the left side by a three-story wooden **Drum Tower** (Gu Lou) [鼓楼] and on the right by the matching three-story wooden **Bell Tower** (Zhong Lou) [钟楼].   On the first floor of the Bell Tower (Zhong Lou) [钟楼] is a glass case holding a golden effigy of **Kshitigarbha** (Dizang) [地藏].   Dizang [地藏] is the bodhisattva who has the special power to rescue departed souls from Hell, and thus plays an important role in Buddhist funeral ceremonies.   He is the patron deity of the sacred Buddhist mountain of Jiuhua Shan [九华山] in Anhui Province.   Upstairs on the second floor is the bronze bell which can be rung for a fee of 50 Rmb.   On New Year's Eve this bell is rung 108 times at midnight.   It is considered good luck to be there to hear it ring, and even better luck to be the one who rings it.   The Bell Tower (Zhong Lou) [钟楼] was rebuilt by Qing Dynasty Emperor Guangxu in 1895, following the Taiping destruction of the temple in 1860-1862. The bell itself was made in 1894, during the 18th year of the Guangxu reign of the Qing Dynasty.   Beside the Bell Tower (Zhong Lou) [钟楼] is a Ming Dynasty-style stone stele with a partially legible inscription which has been damaged.

On the first floor of the Drum Tower (Gu Lou) [鼓楼] is a glass case containing a golden effigy of **Guan Yu** [关羽], the God of War.   In the Ming and Qing dynasties Guan Yu had temples dedicated exclusively to him in every city in China.   Shanghai's former War God Temple (Guandi Miao) [关帝庙] can still be visited in Shanghai's former Nanshi District. The second floor of the Drum Tower (Gu Lou) [鼓楼] cannot be ascended, and it no longer seems to contain a drum. Beside the Drum Tower (Gu Lou) [鼓楼] is a Ming Dynasty-style stone stele with a lengthy inscription in very good condition.   The present Drum Tower (Gu Lou) [鼓楼] dates from an 1895 reconstruction, following the Taiping destruction of the temple in 1860-1862.

Across the second courtyard from the Maitreya Hall (Mile Dian) [弥勒殿] is the **Heavenly Kings Hall** (Tian Wang Dian) [天王殿].   This hall dates from an 1881 reconstruction, when it was rebuilt to replace an earlier structure destroyed during the Taiping rebels' attacks on Shanghai in 1860-1862.   The hall was last restored in 1981.   The hall contains enormous gilded wooden statues of all four kings, two on each side of the hall.   All four wear crowns on their heads and are dressed in heavy armor.   One holds a four string guitar and has a light green face, another holds a sword in his right hand and has a black face, a third holds an umbrella in his right hand and a small stupa in his left hand, and has white face, while a fourth holds a snake and has a black face.   This depiction is somewhat different than in the past.   In the center of the Heavenly Kings Hall (Tian Wang Dian) [天王殿] are two glass cases containing golden effigies of two rather obscure Buddhist deities.   An unusual variant incarnation of the Maitreya Buddha (Mile Fo) [弥勒佛] known as **Tianguan Mile** [天官弥勒] is depicted as seated, holding a long-stemmed lotus flower with a small temple perched on the blossom, and has a third eye in the center of his forehead.   **Weituo Pusa** [韦陀菩萨] is represented by a golden statue in which he poses wearing armor and holding a drawn sword. Weituo is the protector of all Buddhist temples. Behind the Heavenly Kings Hall (Tian Wang Dian) [天王殿] stands a pair of tall wooden flagpoles, each supported by two stone carved stones, which could date from when the temple was used as military base during the Republic of China.

On the other side of the Heavenly Kings Hall (Tianwang Dian) [天王殿] is the third courtyard, on the far side of which is the **Precious Hall of the Great Hero** (Da Xiong Bao Dian) [大雄宝殿]. This hall's origins date to an 1878-1879 reconstruction, when it was rebuilt to replace an earlier structure destroyed during the Taiping rebels attacks on Shanghai in 1860-1862. The hall was closed for a massive reconstruction and renovation in November 2002, but had been reopened by January 2004. The interior is now nothing less than spectacular. Three large Buddhas (San Fo) [三佛] are placed in the center. Sakyamuni Buddha (Shijiamouni) [释迦牟尼] stands in the center, flanked on the left by the bodhisattva Samantabhadra (Puxian) [普贤] seated on an elephant, and on the right by the bodhisattva Manjusri (Wenshu) [文殊] seated on a blue lion. Overhead the hall's ceiling is pierced by a massive wooden dome that spirals upward, looking much like the wooden domes (zaojing) [藻井] often found over traditional Peking Opera stages (Jingju Wutai) [京剧舞台]. Behind the San Fo [三佛] facing out the rear exit is a large Guanyin state in front of a floor to ceiling landscaped rockery covered with smaller figurines depicting the Buddhist heaven and hell. Along the side walls stand 36 quite expressive human statues of the Buddhist saints, 18 on each side of the hall. This is an unusual number, which seems to include 16 Arhats (Luohan) [罗汉] and 20 Devas (Zhutian) [诸天], and an assortment that includes such non-Buddhist figures from Chinese tradition as Confucius (Kong Fuzi) [孔夫子], the War God (Guandi) [关帝], the God of Literature (Wenchang) [文昌], the Kitchen God (Zaoshen) [灶神] (aka Zaowang) [灶王]; Hindu gods such as Brahma (Fantian) [梵天], Indra (Yintuoluo) [因陀罗], and Yama (Yanluo) [阎罗]; as well as Buddhist deities such as the Four Heavenly Kings (Sida Tianwang) [四大天王] and the bodhisattva Weituo [韦陀] as well. The hall also houses one of Longhua's three bronze bells, this one dating from 1586. With all the times I've visited the temple since 1999, it was only my December 2017 visit that I noticed what appears to be an original corner stone dating from the Republic of China (Minguo) [民国] on the southeast corner of the **Precious Hall of the Great Hero** (Da Xiong Bao Dian) [大雄宝殿].

Looking to your right here you can see both the cloud shaped metal gong and the long wooden fish suspended from the side corridor. Both are used as time keeping devices and are struck to announce meal times and other events during the monk's daily schedule. On the wall below the fish is a convenient Chinese language map of the temple's layout.

On the other side of the Precious Hall of the Great Hero (Da Xiong Bao Dian) [大雄宝殿] is a fourth courtyard. On the far side of this fourth courtyard is the **Precious Hall of the Three Saints** (San Sheng Bao Dian [三圣宝殿]. This hall is dominated by enormous floor to ceiling golden statues of three Buddhas (San Fo) [三佛] who appear side by side in an unusual standing position with golden flames rising up behind them. In the center is Amitabha Buddha (Emituo Fo) [阿弥陀佛], to your left is the bodhisattva Dashizhi [大势至], and on your right is the bodhisattva Guanshiyin [观世音]. While Guanyin [观世音] has compassionate mercy for those in need, it is Dashizhi [大势至] who possesses the power to actually carry out her acts of kindness.   The Three Saints Hall (San Sheng Dian) [三圣殿] houses by far the oldest of Longhua's three bronze bells, this one supposedly dating from 1132, which would also make it the oldest historic relic the temple possesses today.   The hall itself dates from an 1884 reconstruction, when it was rebuilt to replace an earlier structure destroyed during the Taiping rebels attacks on Shanghai in 1860-1862.   The hall was last restored in 1986.

Immediately behind the Three Saints Hall (Sansheng Dian) [三圣殿] is a walled garden with trees which unfortunately is closed to the public.   Inside this walled garden is a fifth main hall, the **Abbot's Quarters** (Fangzhang Shi) [方丈室], which is for the private use of the resident monks and their master, the Fangzhang [方丈].   It was the only hall which the monks maintained control of during the Cultural Revolution.   Normally it is kept off limits to the public and cannot be visited.   However, the author was able to steal a glimpse and found that the hall was furnished with rows of large armchairs, and lacked any large statues.   Possibly it is a modern day form of the Meditation Hall (Chan Tang) [禅堂], which the temple otherwise lacks, which is odd for one belonging to the Zen sect (Chanzong) [禅宗].   At the far left end of the hall was a small office decorated with framed color photos of the temple's Buddhist leaders posing with Communist Party leaders such as Jiang Zemin [江泽民].

Behind the Abbot's Quarters is the sixth and final courtyard, and the sixth hall on the central axis, the newly built two-story **Scripture Hall** (Cangjing Lou) [藏经楼].   This modern building holds most of the temple's few genuine relics, including a library of 7,000 Qing Dynasty volumes; a Ming Dynasty gold seal given to the temple in 1598 by the emperor Wanli (1573-1620); a Ming Dynasty gold-plated bronze Buddha statue; Tang Dynasty scriptures; and a copy of the Heart Sutra (Xin Jing) [心经] dating from the year 1098, the fifth year of the Zhezong [哲宗] reign (1085-1100) of emperor Zhao Xu [赵煦] of the Northern Song Dynasty (960-1126).   Exactly how these relics survived the destruction of the Taiping Rebellion, the lengthy military occupation of the Republican era, and the Cultural Revolution is unclear.   Possibly they were donated to the temple sometime later.   Unfortunately the public is not welcomed to visit this sixth hall, and the relics are kept hidden from view, although photographs of them have appeared in pamphlets sold at the temple's book store.

Hidden in a once seldom visited northeast corner of the temple grounds on the east side of the Fangzhang Shi's walled garden is a smaller garden which is open to the public, the **Tomb Pagoda Garden** (Mu Ta Yuan) [墓塔园], so named for the **Tao Ming Tomb Pagoda** (Tao Ming Mu Ta) [韬明墓塔], a broken stone tomb pagoda dating from the year 1667 in the reign of Emperor Kangxi which stands in the center.   This Tomb Pagoda (Mu Ta) [墓塔] was erected in commemoration of Tao Ming [韬明], who was the Master of Longhua Si from 1647 to 1666.   The Tomb Paoda (Mu Ta) [墓塔] is a hexagonal stone pillar on a lotus flower with a round stone ball balanced on top decorated with dragon images wrapped around it.   Two faint inscriptions can be seen on either side of the pillar.   One of the four boundary stones of Longhua's predecssor Kongxiang Temple (Kongxiang Si) [空相寺] used to lay here but has been moved to the separate walled garden in the southeast corner of the former Longhua Hotel's compound, which for a while belonged to the now apparently defunct Hualin Art Gallery.   Similarly, the Tomb Pagoda Garden (Mu Ta Yuan) [墓塔园] once had four stone statues of a mythical animal known as a Spirit Beast (Ling Shou) [灵兽], but two of these are now protecting the entrance to the Hualin garden, and the other two have disappeared.

In one corner of the Tomb Pagoda Garden (Mu Ta Yuan) [墓塔园] courtyard is a corridor connecting with the former Longhua Hotel (Longhua Binguan) next door. At the rear of the courtyard is the monk's **Dining Hall** (Zhai Tang) [斋堂], not to be confused with the separate **Vegetarian Restaurant** (Sucai Guan) [素菜馆] intended for public visitors located on the right side of the Hall of the Great Hero (Da Xiong Bao Dian) [大雄宝殿] beneath the sign of the large wooden fish (muyu) [木鱼] hanging from the rafters.

Two long barracks-like halls run along almost the full length of the western side of the temple compound and are divided up into many small Buddhist chapels. The major ones include the **Arhat Hall** (Luohan Tang) [罗汉堂], and the **Goddess of Mercy Hall** (Guanyin Tang) [观音堂]. The Arhat Hall (Luohan Tang) [罗汉堂] is a new addition to the temple, added sometime during 2002. It features small golden statues of 500 arhats or Buddhist saints. This chapel has become quite popular with worshippers, but one woman who had just finished praying mistakenly told the author there were 800 arhats, testimony to the newness of this innovation. The **Guanyin Tang** [观音堂] is on the left side of the fourth courtyard and features an impressive golden statue of Guanyin, who is depicted as facing in all four directions, and has 1,000 arms. Many of her hundreds of hands hold objects of special significance.

In between the Luohan Dian and Guanyin Dian is yet another hall, seemingly nameless, which although devoid of architectural splendor does have three splendid gilded Buddha statues. These three include **Sakyamuni** Buddha (Shijiamouni) [释迦牟尼] in the center, **Manjusri** (Wenshu) [文殊] on your left, and **Guanyin** [观音] on your right. The interior walls of this hall are literally covered with memorial slips of paper and photographs meant to commemorate lost loved ones. It is also in this hall that one is most likely to see the resident monks performing ceremonies which include chanting and the use of musical instruments such as cymbals and drums.

A second long barracks-like hall hidden behind the first one is known as the **Jade Buddha Hall** (Yu Fo Dian) [玉佛殿], and contains other side chapels which are usually kept closed and only opened on special occasions. One of these is a chapel which contains an unusual **Reclining Jade Buddha** (Yu Wo Fo) [玉卧佛] like the one at the Jade Buddha Temple (Yu Fo Si) [玉佛寺]. Above this chapel is a seconf floor with another image inside a glass case, and windows looking down on the gardens of Longhua Park (Longhua Gongyuan) [龙华公园] next door.

The monks' residence is in a separate set of buildings in a back corner of the complex and is off limits to visitors. Through the windows of the second floor can be seen their private library stacked with books.

Approximately 90 resident monks lived here in 2003, with another 30 student monks in apprenticeship. At that time the temple's abbot was Master Ming Yang (Ming Yang Fashi) [明旸法师]. At least one resident foreign monk was noticed living here in January 2004, made obvious by his large crooked nose, white skin, and wide girth, as well as his lateness for morning prayers.

The monks of Longhua supposedly belong to the Chan Zong sect (Zen) of Chinese Buddhism.   However, the vast array of gilded effigies here, representing the whole Buddhist pantheon of deities, makes one wonder about the accuracy of this claim or the status of Chan Buddhism in China today.   Chan was originally an iconoclastic sect which prohibited use of images of any kind.

According to the October 24, 2007 Shanghai Daily newspaper, the temple has a Library and Museum, but these are normally closed to the public.   There are three relics known as the "Longhua Three Treasures."   These include a tripitaka (sanzang) [三藏] scripture dating back to the reign of Emperor Qianlong of the Qing Dynasty; a gold Buddha statue from the Ming Dynasty; and a gold seal given by Emperor Shenzong of the Ming Dynasty.   This is all confirmed in my section on the **Scripture Hall** (Cangjing Lou) [藏经楼] above.

Address: 2853 Longhua Lu [龙华路 2853 号], Longhua Town, Xuhui District [徐汇区].
Phone: (021) 6456-6085

Longhua Guomindang Military Garrison HQ (Songhu Jingbei Silingbu) [淞沪警备司令部]

In a corner of the Longhua Martyr's Cemetery (Longhua Lieshi Lingyuan) [龙华烈士陵园] is the site of the Guomindang's old **Longhua Military Garrison** (Songhu Junshi Gongshu) [淞沪军事公署] first established in 1912.　After the Guomindang General **Bai Chongxi** [白崇禧] (1893-1966) occupied it on March 21, 1927, the Longhua Garrison became the Shanghai headquarters used by the Guomindang military until the Japanese invasion of Shanghai in August 1937.　Longhua Town was the closest the Guomindang army could get to the southern city limits of downtown Shanghai then occupied by the British and French concessions.　It was also conveniently located close to the Longhua Airport (Shanghai Longhua Jichang) [上海龙华机场] and the Jiangnan Arsenal.

The original monumental entrance gate (Songhu Jingbei Silingbu Menlou) [淞沪警备司令部门楼] was built in 1920 and restored in 1991.　The entrance to the compound has sometimes been referred to as the "Gate of Darkness," because many who went in never came out alive.　After the **Chiang Kai-shek** (Jiang Jieshi) [蒋介石] (1887-1975) right wing coup of April 12, 1927, known as the April 12, 1927 Shanghai Massacre (Siyier Canan) [四一二惨案], the Longhua Garrison was turned into a kind of concentration camp for opponents to the Guomindang regime.

This is where the famous five left-wing Chinese writers and nineteen others were arrested on January 17, 1931 and executed by the Guomindang on the night of February 7, 1931.

Address:　2577 Longhua Lu [龙华路 2577 号], Longhua Town [龙华镇], Xuhui District [徐汇区] Nearest Metro Station:　Longcao Lu Station on Line 3.

Longhua Revolutionary Martyrs Cemetery (Longhua Lieshi Lingyuan) [龙华烈士陵园].

Located on Longhua Lu next door to the Longhua Si Buddhist Temple, this area had belonged to the temple since the 13th Century Yuan Dynasty when it was suddenly turned into a public park by the Communist government in 1954.　The temple walls still have gates, now kept closed, leading into the park.　**Longhua Park** (Longhua Gongyuan) [龙华公园] began another transformation in 1990 when construction started on the memorials, monuments and museum of the new Revolutionary Martyrs Cemetery (Longhua Lieshi Lingyuan) [龙华烈士陵园].　The newly completed memorial park was opened to the public on July 1, 1991.

The new memorial park now includes a large multi-floor museum devoted to the Chinese Revolution.　In addition to Communist Party members, the museum honors some Qing Dynasty and Guomindang individuals who are now considered to have been national heroes for their efforts to resist foreign invasions.

Outside the museum are rows of graves of Communist martyrs who died during the revolution from 1927 to 1949.   Many of the gravestones have photos mounted on them. From these photos you can see how the demographic composition of the revolution evolved over time from a diverse one including middle class urban intellectuals in the 1920s and 1930s to a more monolithic one of Mao suit wearing peasants by the late 1940s.   The whole site is a giant park containing green grass and many flowering trees, making it a nice place for a picnic in the spring or summer.

Address: 2887 Longhua Lu, Longhua Town
Phone: (021) 6468-3059, (021) 6468-5995   Fax: (021) 6438-2775
Web Site: http://www.slmmm.net, E-mail: slhmc@online.sh.cn.
Nearest Metro Station: Longcao Lu Station on Line 3.

Lu Xun's Former House (Lu Xun Guju) [鲁迅故居]

One block east of Lu Xun Park is the house where the famous Chinese writer Lu Xun [鲁迅] (1881-1936), aka Zhou Shuren [周树人] lived during the last three years of his life from April 11, 1933 to his death on October 19, 1936.   The simple three-story row-house structure still stands on a narrow lane which branches off of Shanyin Lu, the former Scott Road.   A sign at the entrance to the lane reads, "Continental Terrace," in English.

Lu Xun nicknamed his house the Qie Jie Ting, which translated literally means Half Concession Pavilion and was meant as a humorous reference to the fact that Scott Road as an Outside Area Road (Yuejie Zhulu) was neither inside nor outside the International Settlement.   Although Scott Road was officially located outside the International Settlement boundary, it was built, owned, and policed by the Shanghai Municipal Council as part of its network of Outside Roads (Yuejie Zhulu), and was connected to the Settlement by similar Outside Roads such as Sichuan Bei Lu.   This gave Lu Xun a certain amount of protection from the political persecution of the Guomindang, who after April 1927 had banned all of his publications.

Lu Xun's house is the second from the last on the dead-end lane.   The three-story red brick house has a small balcony on the third floor and a very small courtyard enclosed by a wall in front of the first floor entrance.   Although it is fairly tall, the house is quite narrow, just one-room wide on each floor.   The interior of the house is furnished with what is supposedly the original furniture, including desks, tables, and beds.   Oddly enough, his own study/bedroom where he worked and lived was on the second floor, while his wife and son had their bedrooms on the top floor above his.   From the third floor steps lead up to the roof, where Lu Xun was once able to sit outside, but which is now closed to visitors.   The calendar in his bedroom is supposedly the last one he used himself, and has been left open to the date he died.   A Japanese kimono-clad figurine in the living room reflects his long friendship with Japanese people and culture, dating from his years of residence there.

This house was the original site of the Lu Xun Museum founded in January 1951, but in October 1956 the museum moved to its then new facility in Hongkou Park (Lu Xun Park), where a vastly remodeled and expanded version of it still stands.

Tickets for Lu Xun Guju can be bought next door at house # 8.   The charge includes a guided tour of the house by a guide who speaks only Chinese.   The ticket office also houses a bookstore offering some English translations of Lu Xun's works, as well as his official biography which can be purchased.

Shanyin Lu runs parallel to the eastern boundary of Lu Xun Park, from Sichuan Bei Lu in the South to Ouyang Lu and Dalian Xi Lu in the North.
Address: House #9, Lane # 132, Shanyin Lu, Hongkou District
Phone: (021) 5666-2608
Nearest Metro Station: Hongkou Stadium Station on Lines 3 and 8.

Lu Xun Museum (Lu Xun Jinian Guan) [鲁迅纪念馆]

This museum is devoted to China's most famous modern writer, Lu Xun [鲁迅] (1881-1936), aka Zhou Shuren [周树人], who spent the last ten years of his life living in Shanghai.

When the museum was originally founded on January 7, 1951 it was located at Lu Xun's former residence (Lu Xun Guju) [鲁迅故居] on Shanyin Lu.   In 1956 the museum was moved to its present site inside the former Hongkou Park, which was renamed Lu Xun Park in 1988.   The museum underwent a massive renovation and expansion in August 1998, and was reopened in its current form on September 25, 1999.   The present building is a two-story structure modeled after the architectural style of Jiangnan water towns such as Lu Xun's home town of Shaoxing in Zhejiang Province.

On the first floor of the museum is a wide screen T.V. showing black and white film footage of Shanghai in the 1920s and 1930s.   Beside the T.V. is a bronze statue of a seated Lu Xun smoking a cigar.   The statue is a bit chunky and crude, not as graceful as the one at Lu Xun's Tomb located nearby.

The second floor exhibits include one whole room whose walls are impressively decorated from floor to ceiling with rows of nearly all the book covers of Lu Xun's published works, as well as translations, anthologies, and biographies about him.   A first edition of Edgar Snow's edited volume, _Living China_, which contained seven essays by Lu Xun, is given a special display case of its own.

Several other halls are devoted to photographs of Lu Xun's hometown of Shaoxing, as well as his other former residences in Japan, Beijing and Shanghai.   An impressive collection of first editions of his works and samples of manuscript pages are also displayed.

Personal possessions of Lu Xun on display in the museum include his reading glasses, umbrella, fedora felt hat, mandarin gown, and even his v-neck sweater and socks.   Lu Xun's typical style of dress, in a Western hat, Western shoes, and a traditional Chinese gown, seemed to itself convey his inner combination of Western and Chinese ideas.

A movie theater on the second floor shows black and white film footage of Lu Xun's funeral procession in 1936, and his burial ceremony at the International Cemetery (Wanguo Gongmu) [万国公墓] on Hongqiao Lu.   Just outside the theater is Lu Xun's white plaster face mask made while he lay on his deathbed.   Most fascinating of all is the original tombstone erected at Lu Xun's grave in the International Cemetery (Wanguo Gongmu) [万国公墓] in 1937.   It was decorated with a photo of Lu Xun and an inscription from his son. Unfortunately armed guards are quite vigilant at preventing visitors from taking photographs of the exhibits.

There is a small book store on the second floor.

Address: 2288 Sichuan Bei Lu, Hongkou District.
Phone: (021) 6540-4573, 6540-2288.
Nearest Metro Station: Hongkou Stadium Station on Lines 3 and 8.

Lu Xun's Tomb (Lu Xun Mu) [鲁迅墓]

The famous Chinese writer Lu Xun [鲁迅] (1881-1936) was originally buried in the Shanghai Municipal Council's International Cemetery (Wanguo Gongmu) [万国公墓] out on Hongqiao Lu after his death in October 1936. However, in October 1956 his remains were moved to what was then still known as Hongkou Park, and later the park was renamed after him in 1988.

His tomb is marked by a black bronze statue of him seated in a wicker arm chair, holding a book in his left hand, wearing Western dress shoes but a Mandarin's gown. The statue is amazingly life-like right down to his moustache and gives you the feeling of being in the man's presence. It sits atop a granite pedestal which bears no inscription except for the dates of his birth and death. The statue was erected in 1961 on the 80th anniversary of his birth, at the same time as a small granite block was placed at the foot of it, a few yards away, stating simply in gold letters that this is "Lu Xun's Tomb." The nearby Lu Xun Museum (Lu Xun Jinian Guan) [鲁迅纪念馆] has Lu Xun's original tombstone which was moved there from the International Cemetery (Wanguo Gongmu) [万国公墓].

Address: Lu Xun Park (Lu Xun Gongyuan), 146 Jiangwan Dong Lu.
Phone: (021) 5666-7122
Nearest Metro Station: Hongkou Stadium Station on Lines 3 and 8.

M

The **Maglev Line**

In 2002 a magnetic levitation train line was constructed in Pudong, covering a 30 km. distance from the Longyang Lu Station on the Metro Two Line to the Pudong International Airport.   By August 2002 the rail line's basic infrastructure had already been completed, and the first three Maglev rail cars arrived from Germany.   The inaugural run of the train was held on New Year's Day 2003.   During the February 2003 Spring Festival tourists were charged a whopping 150 Rmb per ride one-way, but prices were later lowered.   The Maglev train usually runs at an average speed of 430 km. per hour, and is capable of a maximum speed of 500 km per hour.   Although the technology had been invented years earlier, this was the first commercial use of a magnetic levitation train anywhere in the world.   It was designed by German engineers of the Krupp corp.

Unfortunately, the much-heralded Maglev ended up being a bit of a white elephant, as its use required transferring to or from the subway line at one end, and a long walk to or from the airport terminal at the other end.   In August 2006 one of the trains caught fire in an unexplained accident.   Plans to build a second Maglev line between Shanghai and Hangzhou were also cancelled.   The Maglev is set to become even more of a white elephant once the Metro Two Line is extended east to the Pudong International Airport and west to Hongqiao Airport.

Nearest Metro Station: Longyang Lu Station on Line 2.

The **Marble Hall**

Sir Elly Kadoorie's famous residence, the so-called Marble Hall, was built in 1924 and continued to serve as the Kadoorie family home until 1949.

The wealthy Sephardic Jewish merchant Sir Eleazer (Elly) Silas Kadoorie spent 14 years constructing this mansion, which was finally completed in 1931.   At the time it was nicknamed, "the Marble Hall," and referred to as such in the local media.   Kadoorie had been born in Baghdad in 1867, and originally came to China in 1881 as an employee of David Sassoon & Co., before founding his own family firm of Sir Elly Kadoorie & Sons.

Marble Hall's structure is a long, rectangular, two-story box the size of a football field.   It sits on an estate composed mainly of an enormous green lawn.   Despite its impressive size, the exterior architecture is rather plain and lacking ornamentation.   Four Greco-Roman Corinthian columns face the lawn from the center of the building, while large French windows dominate the rest of the exterior.   A second floor veranda runs the full length of the building.   The overall appearance is rather like an American high school from the 1950s.

The current entrance to the house is from a long lane on the east side, which leads to a covered driveway.   Stepping inside, one is immediately struck by how much more impressive the interior is compared to the exterior.   The inside of the house is dominated by the first floor ballroom, which features a two-story high, vaulted ceiling and a concert stage. The walls and columns are nearly all pure white marble, hence the house's nickname, although some of the current columns seem to be plastic replicas.

Twin flights of marble steps lead up to the second floor through a circular rotunda, which protrudes from the back of the house. The most peculiar feature of the second floor is the French doors that open up onto the ballroom down below. Mirrors on the walls add a bit of a touch of Versailles. However, once outside the ballroom the impression once again returns that this is a cavernous but rather plain structure. It is difficult to imagine that one married couple lived here alone in such an enormous space.

Sir Elly Kadoorie (d. 1944) and his wife Lady Laura Kadoorie (d.1918) were both buried in the **International Cemetery** (Wanguo Gongmu) [万国公墓] on Songyuan Lu, near its intersection with Hongqiao Lu, which is now part of the Song Qingling Tomb Garden (Song Qingling Lingyuan). Although their original tombs were later vandalized during the Cultural Revolution, an impressive replica of their tombstone now commemorates them there.

Nowadays the Kadoorie mansion is used as the **Shanghai Municipal Children's Palace** (Xiaonian Gong). You can spend a pleasant afternoon watching children performing classical music with their violins on the ballroom stage, and practicing ballet dance steps in some of the other side rooms while dressed in colorful costumes of China's ethnic minorities. No one seems to mind the presence of interloping visitors watching them, and no tickets are required. It is located on Yanan Xi Lu, near its intersection with Huashan Lu, across the street from the Equatorial Hotel.
Address: 64 Yanan Xi Lu [延安西路 64 号].
Phone: (021) 6248-1850.

The Marshall House, aka Taiyuan Villa (Taiyuan Bieshu) [太原别墅].

This 1920s era mansion was originally the home of a pair of French aristocrats, the Count du Pac de Marsoulies and his wife the Countess Virginie Blanche, who moved to Shanghai in 1918. The Count du Pac de Marsoulies suffered a sudden and mysterious death in February 1932, just after having had dinner with Green Gang (Qing Bang) crime boss Du Yuesheng at his home. Almost the entire leadership of the French Concession were also victims of poisoning at this same dinner. After the demise of her husband, the Countess inherited the house and the Count's fortune, becoming known about town as "the merry widow." She continued to live in the house until 1940 when she picked a wise time to sell it. From 1941 to 1945 it was occupied by the Japanese.

After the war was over, it became the home of U.S. General **George C. Marshall** for over a year when he served as mediator for the December 1945-January 1947 negotiations between the Guomindang and the Communist Party. Marshall's goals were to achieve a cease-fire in the Chinese civil war that had resumed as soon as the Japanese were defeated, a coalition national government to include both the Guomindang and the Communist parties, and the merger of their respective military forces into one national army. The ultimate failure of these talks and U.S. President Harry Truman's recall of Marshall on January 6, 1947 led to the resumption of a full-scale Chinese civil war resulting finally in the Communists 1949 victory.

In the decades after the revolution, the mansion was used as a state guesthouse for visiting dignitaries from friendly socialist countries, such as Ho Chi Minh, Kim Il Sung, Nehru, and Sukarno.   Later the house became home to Mao Zedong's wife, **Jiang Qing**, from whence she directed the actions of her infamous Gang of Four during the 1966-1976 Cultural Revolution.   Jiang reportedly had the master bedroom completely furnished in her favorite color, green, including the carpets, curtains and furniture.

The house is now open to the public as a hotel known as Taiyuan Villa (Taiyuan Bieshu) [太原别墅], which actually now belongs to the larger Shanghai Intercontinental Ruijin Hotel (Shanghai Rujin Zhouji Jiudian) [上海瑞金洲际酒店] located nearby.   When entering the main gate of the hotel compound on Tai Yuan Lu, visitors are first greeted by a new wing housing the **Marshall Café Bar**.   The historic estate is actually inside a separate walled enclosure next door, reached by passing through a second gate to the rear of the modern complex. The original grounds feature a circular driveway that winds through a thick forest of trees and green lawns.

The three-story red brick house has a covered carport and several wings.   A Mansard roof over the main wing is pierced by dormer windows and topped with at least five chimneys emerging from the many fireplaces inside.   In the back of the house a round tower with conical pointed roof encloses the spiral staircase within.   The main house is connected to a carriage house and servants quarters behind it.   On the side of the main house is a brick elevator shaft added by Jiang Qing during her residence here.

On the other side of the house, an outdoor first floor veranda accented with two Ming Dynasty style stone lions faces an expansive green lawn.   In the garden are two bamboo gazebos, which cover bomb shelters and escape routes installed by Jiang Qing.   Walking on the floor of the gazebos you can feel the hollow spots underneath where the hidden entrances lie.

Passing through the wrought iron and glass double front doors, one climbs a flight of marble steps that lead into the lobby.   The entrance room features a massive granite fireplace, grand piano, exposed polished wood ceiling beams, and polished wood paneling on the walls.   The entrance hall fireplace has the Count de Marsoulies' family crest inside it with an oval design topped by a crown, below which stands a cow at the foot of a deciduous tree. To the left of the first floor entrance hall is an enormous dining room running the full length of the house with fireplaces at both ends and floor to ceiling windows facing the lawn outside.

A spiral staircase with wooden steps and brass railing winds up through the circular tower to the second and third floors.   Imagine yourself trodding the same worn wooden steps as General Marshal and Jiang Qing.   A separate flight of hidden servants' stairs makes the same journey from the kitchen.   Oddly enough, each of the bedrooms has glass doors with only curtains protecting the guests' privacy.

The Roosevelt Steakhouse (Lousifu Niupaiguan) [罗斯福牛排馆] founded by Franklin D. Roosevelt III, and one of the most expensive restaurants in the city, used to be located here from 2007 until May 2018, but it has since relocated to Shanghai Intercontinental Ruijin Hotel (Shanghai Rujin Zhouji Jiudian) [上海瑞金洲际酒店].

Address: 160 Taiyuan Lu [太原路 160 号], between Yongjia Lu [永嘉路] and Jianguo Xi Lu, Xuhui District [徐汇区].

The **Mid-Lake Pavilion Teahouse** (Huxin Ting Chalou) [湖心亭茶楼]

A traditional Qing Dynasty two-story wooden pavilion, it was first built in 1784, during the 49th year of the Qianlong reign, and is undoubtedly the oldest teahouse in Shanghai.   However, it has been restored and rebuilt several times.   The current structure probably dates from 1855, the 5th year of the Xianfeng reign, which is when it first became a public tea house. The tea house had several earlier names, including Yeshi Xuan and Wanzai Xuan, before adopting is present day name of Mid-Lake Pavilion (Huxin Ting) [湖心亭].   It sits in the middle of a man-made lake reached by crossing the famous **Bridge of Nine Turnings** (Jiuqu Qiao) [九曲桥], and is located just outside the walls of the **Yu Yuan Garden** (Yu Yuan) [豫园], near the Shanghai **City God Temple** (Shanghai Chenghuang Miao) [城隍庙].   This teahouse served as the model for the 19th century willow pattern porcelain.

Address: Bridge of Nine Turnings (Jiuqu Qiao) [九曲桥], Yu Yuan Bazaar
Phone: (021) 6373-6950
Nearest Metro Station: Old West Gate (Lao Xi Men) [老西门] Station on Line 8.

Moganshan Lu Artists Colony

This area of art gallerys housed inside old warehouses and abandoned factories located on a peninsula jutting out into Suzhou Creek is collectively known as **Moganshan Lu**, although some of the buildings are located down long one lane roads that branch off of Moganshan Lu and head deep into the old industrial area.   From a historical standpoint, the most impressive view of the site can be had by walking the long one-lane road that leads from #120 Moganshan Lu to the **Island 6 Arts Center** (http://www.island6.org.).   This road starts at a gate beside which is a wall plaque providing some brief historical information about how the **Fuxin Flour Mill** occupied this site in the 1930s.

Following the road you enter a wide open space in which stands the incredible sight of the baroque-style, two-story structure of the former **Moganshan Hotel**, complete with flagpole on top.   It is boarded up, closed and dark now, but the Min Guo-era architecture is one of the most impressive in Shanghai.   Some workers are living inside.   On a November 2007 afternoon they opened up a side door and allowed me to tour the inside.   The interior had yet to be renovated.   One large room that must have been the lobby occupies the ground floor, with the whole front wall consisting of a series of folding wooden panels with the original glass panes still intact.   In the center of the building is a two-story courtyard surrounded by verandas with interesting woodwork.   The second floor is divided up into fairly small spaces that clearly could have once been hotel rooms.   The workers themselves knew nothing about the building's history.

Continuing up the road through a wide open area that feels like it's in the countryside rather than the city, you finally reach the tall five story brick warehouse housing the **Island 6 Arts Center** at the very end of the road.   This is officially known as Building #6 within the 120 Moganshan Lu compound. Standing here at night with a full moon in the sky the site is remarkably peaceful, dark and quiet for being in the center of China's biggest city.   Across the river on the north side you can see the North Railway Station and the high tower of the Holiday Inn Hotel.   Surprisingly, the Oriental Pearl T.V. Tower (Dongfang Mingzhu Guangbo Dianshi Ta) [东方明珠广播电视塔] in Pudong is visible in the distance, seemingly straight ahead, although a walk along the Suzhou River (Suzhou He) follows all its winds and curves back and forth.

The Island 6 gallery is indeed a bit isolated in the middle of overgrown fields and still abandoned buildings, at the end of a dead end road on the very tip of a peninsula surrounded on three sides by a curving bend in the Suzhou River.   By far most of the art galleries are located at the much busier, hipper and popular **50 Moganshan Lu** compound, which includes over a dozen galleries, such as the Big Warehouse Gallery, Bizart Space, Eastlink Gallery, Elephant Art Loft, Gallery 55, m97 Gallery, New B Gallery, Nutshell Art, ShanghART Gallery, Shine Art Space, Twocities, Xie Rong Art Studio, and YB2 Gallery. This is also where you will find several hip coffee shops, and no they are not Starbucks.

Address: 50 & 120 Moganshan Lu

Moller Mansion (Moller Dasha)

Built in 1936 as the private residence of the mysterious Swedish shipping tycoon Eric Moller, this three-story red brick structure is easily noticed for its Gothic style featuring several steeples topped by pointy peaked roofs resembling witches hats.   Moller's main profession was running the Moller Line, a steamship service which transported passengers and goods up and down the Yangzi River.   In 1925 he owned a fleet of three steamships, but by 1929 the number had increased to five, each one named after a family member, such as the Daisy Moller, the Erica Moller, the Isabel Moller, the Minnie Moller, and the Nancy Moller.   However, he was also an active participant in the local horseracing scene of the 1930s, spending a lot of time and money at the racetrack where People's Park (Renming Gongyuan) [人民公园] now stands.

After 1949 the house became the headquarters of the Communist Party Youth League.   In May 2002 it was finally opened to the public for the first time as a luxury hotel and renamed the Hengshan Moller Villa.   Rooms in the mansion are decorated in British, French, Italian and Spanish style.   A one night stay can run as high as 4,000 Rmb ($485 USD).   A new wing known as building #2 offers 45 much more affordable rooms, but without the same ambience.

A visit to the coffee bar presents a much more affordable opportunity to explore the mansion's inside.   Upon entering the first floor lobby you are greeted by the sight of marble columns, crystal chandeliers, polished mahogany wood paneling, and intricate wood carving decorations.   Wooden staircases wind up to the second floor.   The coffee bar offers a view of the garden and green lawn behind the house.   In the middle of the green lawn stands a bronze statue of Moller's favorite horse.   Several stone relics in the garden appear to be pieces of a gateway from a Chinese temple.

Located on Shanxi Nan Lu, beside the Yanan Lu expressway.
Address: 30 Shanxi Nan Lu [陕西南路 30 号]

Morris Garden (Malisi Huayuan) [马立斯花园]

This enormous, green compound containing four historic villas was originally known as the Morris Garden (Malisi Huayuan) [马立斯花园], named after its original owner, the British businessman Mr. **Henry E. Morris, Sr.** (Lao Malisi) [老马立斯], who first arrived in Shanghai in 1867 as an employee of the Hong Kong and Shanghai Bank (Huifeng Yinhang) [汇丰银行], earned a fortune by investing in real estate, and later purchased a controlling stake of 47% of the newspaper *The North China Daily News* (Zilin Xibao) [字林西报] in 1901, allowing him to become its Chairman of the Board.   He was a fan of horse racing and served as a member of the board for the Shanghai Race Club (Paoma Zonghui).   This collection of colonial era mansions set in well-manicured gardens with green laws and a forest of trees, covers 60,000 square meters, taking up nearly one whole city block in the middle of downtown Shanghai.   Morris Sr. chose this location for his family's estate in the French Concession on the former Avenue Pere Robert, now Ruijin Second Road (Rujin Er Lu). The compound is so large that it has a West Gate (Xi Men) facing Maoming South Road (Maoming Nan Lu), and two North Gates (Bei Men) facing Fuxing Middle Road (Fuxing Zhong Lu), as well as the main entrance to the East facing Ruijin Second Road (Ruijin Er Lu).

In 1917 Mr. **Henry E. Morris, Sr.** (Lao Malisi) [老马立斯] constructed **Villa No. 1** (Yihao Lou) [一号楼], which became his residence and is still known as the Main Building (Zhu Lou) [主楼].

Mr. **Henry E. Morris, Jr** . (Xiao Malisi) [小马立斯], who had ben born in Shanghai in 1883, but spent 10 years being educated overseas from 1896-1906, inherited his father's business and wealth when **Henry E. Morris, Sr.** (Lao Malisi) [老马立斯] died in 1920 leaving his son with a small fortune.   During 1920 and 1921 Henry E. Morris, Jr . (Xiao Malisi) [小马立斯] served as a member of the Shanghai Municipal Council of the International Settleement. From 1921 to 1924 he also torn down the previous three-story wooden building at #17 on the Bund (Waitan) and rebuilt a completely new nine-story headquarters building for the North China Daily News.

Meanwhile, Henry E. Morris, Jr. (Xiao Malisi) [小马立斯] continued to expand on his father's palatial estate.   **Villa No. 2** (Er Hao Lou) [二号楼], also known as the Auxiliary Building (Fu Lou) [辅楼], and **Villa No.3** (San Hao Lou) [三号楼], also known as the Beatiful Thoughts Building (Qisi Lou) [绮思楼], were both constructed in 1920.

The site of **Villa No.4** was sold by the Morris family to the Japanese Mitsui Company (Sanjing Yanhang) [三井洋行] in 1924, after which it became known as the Sanjing Garden (Sanjing Huayuan) [三井花园].

In 1928 Henry E. Morris, Jr. (Xiao Malisi) [小马立斯] opened the Canidrome (Yiyuan Paogouchang) [逸园跑狗场], a combined dog racing track, stadium, and ballroom, located on the other side of the compound's West Gate (Xi Men) facing Maoming South Road (Maoming Nan Lu), but that's a whole 'nother story deserving its own section, which it has in this book under the letter C.

During the December 1941- August 1945 Japanese occupation of the Shanghai city center, the compound was occupied by the Japanese army. This set off a chain reaction in which each successive regime felt it was legitimate to occupy the compound as one of the victor's spoils of war.

After the Victory over Japan in August 1945, at least part of the compound was occupied by the Guomindang Encouragement Society (Lizhi She) [励志社], which was actually a shorter code name for the Huangpu Classmates Association (Huangpu Tongxue Hui) [黄埔同学会], whose members were all graduates of the Whampoa Military Academy in Guangzhou, which had once been headed by Chiang Kai-shek (Jiang Jieshi), and thus this was really an organization of Guomindang military officers who owed their loyalty to Jiang. .

Despite being the owners of a newspaper that reported on all the latest events happening all around China, the Morris family apparently failed to see the end approaching for their way of life, as **Villa No.3** has a set of stained glass windows dated as having been made and installed in 1949. This is one of the few surviving examples of a stained glass window made at the Catholic orphanage of Tou-Se-We (Tushanwan) [土山湾] in Xujiahui.

The North China Daily News continued to publish until its last edition on March 31, 1951, when it was shut down by the Shanghai city government, who also took over its building on the Bund.

One of the sons of Mr. Henry E. Morris, Jr. (Xiao Malisi) [小马立斯], Gordon Morris, supposedly continued to live on the family's estate for several years after the Communist takeover in May 1949 until his death in 1952. According to legend, during the final years of his life he was forced to move out of the villas and live in the Gate House, which you can still see on the grounds today. Some sources incorrectly state that it was his father, who had already passed away before the Liberation, rather than Gordon, who stayed on here until the bitter end. Other sources say H.E.M. Jr. stayed until 1951.

Later the estate was seized by the new regime and became a private retreat for high ranking Chinese Communist Party officials. Shanghai's first post-Liberation mayor, Chen Yi, supposedly had his residence and office here, but that same claim has also been made for a number of other former colonial mansions in the city, including Du Yuesheng's former villa now on the grounds of the Donghu Hotel, and the former French Municipal Council Director's home. It has also been said that Mao Zedong, Liu Shaoqi, Zhou Enlai, Zhu De, and Dong Biwu all stayed here at various times. It was also used as a **State Guest House** (Guo Binguan) [国宾馆] that welcomed visiting leaders of friendly socialist and non-aligned countries during the Cold War, including Ho Chi Minh of Vietnam, Kim Il Sung of North Korea, Suharto of Indonesia, and Nehru of India. Because it was being used by Chinese party and government officials, as well as visiting foreign heads of state, the historic compound avoided being damaged by Red Guards during the Cultural Revolution, which helps explain its miraculously pristine conditon today.

In 1979 the Shanghai municipal government opened up the estate to the public for the first time as the very up market **Ruijin Hotel** (Ruijin Binguan) [瑞金宾馆].

Villa No.1 was placed on the list of protected historic buildings by the Shanghai municipal government in 1989, and Villa No. 3 joined the same list in 1999.   Apparently Villas No. 2 and No.4 have not been considered worthy enough of this honor.

From the late 1990s until they were finally forced to move out in November 2006, Villa No. 4 was home to The Face Bar, which was a very popular night spot with the local expatriate population and foreign tourists.

In 2008 the Rujin Hotel constructed a new modern guest room building (Xin Dalou) [新大楼] on the estate grounds, along with a new Conference Center building (Huiyi Zhongxin) [会议中心] in preparation for the 2010 World Expo.

In 2012 a new joint venture partnership was formed between the domestic Donghu Hotel Group and the overseas Intercontinental Hotel Group to jointly manage the hotel, and from 2012 to 2013 the whole compound underwent extensive renovations.   It reopened in 2013 as the renamed Shanghai Intercontinental Ruijin Hotel (Shanghai Zhouji Rujin Jiudian) [上海瑞金洲际酒店].   In May 2018 the Roosevelt Steakhouse (Lousifu Niupaiguan) [罗斯福牛排馆] relocated here from its original location at the Taiyuan Villa (Taiyuan Bieshu) [太原别墅].

The **Taiyuan Villa** (Taiyuan Bieshu) [太原别墅], which is located nearby but outside the original Morris family garden compound and has its own completely separate history, and thus its own entry in this book under the letter M for **Marshall House**, is now considered a branch building of the Ruijin Hotel and is thus officially known as the Ruijin Hotel Taiyuan Villa (Rujin Binguan Taiyuan Bieshu) [瑞金宾馆太原别墅.

For such a notable family in Shanghai's modern history, it is odd how little detailed information there is available about the Morris family.   The sources that do exist all seem to contradict each other on key details.   There is no consistent agreement on whether the Morris family name should be spelled with one s or two, most English sources fail to distinguish Morris Sr. from Morris Jr., sources contradict each other on the dates when the four villas were constructed, sources disagree on which of the family members stayed behind in Shanghai after the Liberation, precise dates for their births and deaths are also often unavailable, and sources published in China refer to a so-called "Benjamin" Morris that overseas sources do not.   I've done my best to sift through the contradictions and fill in the gaps.   Generally speaking I find Chinese language sources are a more accurate source of information on China, whereas most English language sources on China tend to be full of the same salacious anecdotal stories, lacking in corroboration from primary sources or support from hard facts, which they merely copy from each other.   The prominent family is not mentioned in George F. Nellist, ed., _Men of of Shanghai and North China_ (1933).

On a side note, located in the garden of the Ruijin Hotel are two stone animal statues that some have speculated may have originally come from a Song Dynasty Chinese temple usually referred to as the Fresh Well Temple (Danjing Miao) [淡井庙].   There was a lengthy article on this published in the _Liberation Daily_ (Jiefang Ribao) [解放日报] on May 11, 2018, entitled "Does the Ruijin Hotel have Shanghai's oldest City God Temple?" [瑞金宾馆里居然有上海最老的城隍庙?].

Address: 118 Ruijin Er Lu [瑞金二路 118 号], Huangpu District [黄浦区], formerly Luwan.

Mosques (Qingzhen Si) [清真寺]

Islam entered China in a peaceful process through two main trade routes.   The most well known of these was the overland "Silk Road" through Xinjiang and the Gansu corridor to Xian (Changan), the capital in the Tang Dynasty.   However it also spread via a maritime trade route from the ancient sea port of Quanzhou in Fujian Province, and from there to Hangzhou in Zhejiang, then up the Grand Canal (Da Yunhe) through Northern Jiangsu province to Huaian, where it turned west towards the Northern Song Dynasty capital at Kaifeng in Henan province.   Later when the Yuan Dynasty moved the national capital from Kaifeng to Beijing, the Grand Canal's route was changed to run in more of a straight line north from Huaian through Shandong & Hebei provinces to Beijing, Islam spread through these areas as well.   Today there are many surviving ancient mosques (Qingzhen Si) [清真寺] and Muslim communities all along both the old and new routes of the Hangzhou-Beijing Grand Canal (Jinghang Da Yunhe), as well as the more famous overland Silk Road.

As a historically important sea port for both coastal and inland maritime trade, Shanghai has three historic mosques, as well as a dozen newer modern ones.   In the old walled city area there is the small **Fuyou Road Mosque** (Fuyou Lu Qingzhen Si) [福佑路清真寺], and not far from it stands the much larger **Little Peach Garden Mosque** (Xiaotaouan Qingzhen Si) [小桃园清真寺].   The largest and oldest mosque in Shanghai is the **Songjiang Ancient Mosque** (Songjiang Qingzhen Gu Si) [松江清真寺] located on Zhongshan Road in Songjiang Town, but this is described later in its own entry under the letter S.

The **Fuyou Road Mosque** (Fuyou Lu Qingzhen Si) [福佑路清真寺]

This mosque was built in 1870, the 9th year of the Tongzhi reign of the Qing Dynasty, and was rebuilt and extended at least four times after that, in 1899, 1905, 1936, and 1979.   In 1909 the Shanghai Muslim Association (Shanghai Yisilan Dongshi Hui) [上海伊斯兰董事会] was established here, and 1911 an anti-Qing Dynasty Muslim association was organized here as well.   During the Cultural Revolution it was turned into a warehouse.   In Novemer 1979 it was restored and reopened again.

From the street of Fuyou Lu, at #378 you can see a small arched gate leading into an alley. Above the gate are inscribed three-characters for Qingzhen Si [清真寺], meaning a mosque, and below that a line of Arabic script.   Beside the gate is a nondescript three-story white masonry building with a domed tower standing on top of a raised terrace on the roof.   This domed tower is the mosque's **Watching the Moon Pavilion** (Wangyue Ting) [望月亭], but the rest of the building apparently no longer belong to the mosque, although when it was first built in 1936 it reportedly did.   In 1993 a commercial trading company occupied the lower floors of this three-story building facing the street.

Entering the gate and taking a short walk down a narrow alley in between the buildings facing the street leads you to the big surprise that a genuine Qing Dynasty mosque is hidden behind them in the back.

Beside the entrance to the compound containing the actual mosque halls, outside stands a small shop that offers an amazing array of Islamic items for sale.   Included in their inventory are Arabic and Chinese versions of the Quran (Gulan Jing) [古兰经], many bilingual Arabic-Chinese books on Islam (including ones that use illustrations to show Muslims the correct way to pray), buteqa hats, and woven carpets with patterns illustrating the Kaaba (Ke'erbai) [克尔白] in Mecca (Maijia) [麦加].

Stepping with your right foot into the mosque compound itself, you find a row of three one-story wooden Qing Dynasty halls connected together.   Round red wood pillars support the wooden roofs of the three halls.   The first hall is known simply as the Main Hall (Zheng Dian) [正殿], that in the middle is the Second Hall (Er Dian) [二殿], and the third hall is known as the Third Hall (San Dian) [三殿], or the Big Hall (Da Dian) [大殿], or more officially the **Prayer Hall** (Libai Da Dian) [礼拜大殿].   A chalk board on the wall of the Third Hall (San Dian) bears the times for the five daily prayers, as well as the time of sunrise and sunset. This is updated every day.

The far wall of the **Prayer Hall** (Libai Da Dian) [礼拜大殿], aka Third Hall (San Dian) [三殿], has an inscribed stone tablet (shibei) embedded in it.   Unfortunately, the inscription has been completely worn off, but the top is still decorated by two stone carvings of white cranes (xianhe).   This tablet supposedly originally recorded the history of the construction of the mosque 135 years ago in 1870.

In the Second Hall (Er Dian) [二殿] is an office and small library of Qurans and other Islamic books, with framed woven carpets hanging on the walls depicting the Kaaba in Mecca. Here you'll find friendly Chinese Muslims in white buteqa caps willing to explain the site to you.   They confirm orally that the mosque was built more than 130 years ago during the Qing Dynasty.   A glass case in the corridor outside contains a brief Chinese language history of the site with the dates 1870, 1935, and 1979.

The mosque is surrounded on all sides by modern buildings and new construction projects that dwarf it.   It's amazing that this genuine Qing Dynasty structure has so far survived.   It is quite active with worshippers, especially on Fridays, most of whom seem to be Xinjiang Uighurs and Hui Chinese (Hui Min).

Address: 378 Fuyou Lu [福佑路], near Henan Nan Lu, formerly Nanshi District, now Huangpu Qu.
Phone: (021) 6328-2135.

————————————————

The **Little Peach Garden Mosque** (Xiaotaoyuan Qingzhen Si) [小桃园清真寺]

The land for this mosque was purchased in 1917 and the construction of the buildings was completed in 1925.   Little Peach Garden Lane (Xiaotaoyuan Jie) [小桃园] branches off of Fuxing East Road (Fuxing Dong Lu) [复兴东路] to the south and travels in a straight line to the mosque.   This entire lane is lined with Muslim establishments, including Islamic restaurants serving Halal food and Muslim schools.   The gate house is a three-story yellow masonry structure with arched gateway.   Above the gate is a line of flowing Arabic script, a quote from the Quran (Gulan Jing) [古兰经], plus the three Chinese characters for Qingzhen Si [清真寺], and the date 1343.   To the west of this gate house is the main mosque building, which features four corner towers topped by domes.   In the center of its roof stands the square, open-air **Watching the Moon Pavilion** (Wangyue Ting) [望月亭] with a golden roof topped by a high pole bearing the Muslim crescent moon symbol.   Inside is the 500 square meter **Prayer Hall** (Libai Da Dian) [礼拜大殿], which can house 500 worshippers at one time.   Today this is a functioning mosque, which also serves as the headquarters of the **Shanghai Islamic Association**.

Address: 52 Xiaotaoyuan Jie [小桃园], south of Fuxing Dong Lu [复兴东路].
Phone: (021) 6377-5442

Museums (Bowuguan) [博物馆]

The Shanghai Museum (Shanghai Bowuguan) [上海博物馆]

The **Shanghai Museum** (Shanghai Bowuguan) [上海博物馆] located in the middle of People's Square (Renmin Guangchang) [人民广场] is the most well known in the city, but probably has the least interesting exhibits.   In fact, you won't learn anything about Shanghai's history at the Shanghai Museum, as it focuses on traditional Chinese art works collected from all around China's other provinces.

Construction of the present Shanghai Museum began in 1993 on the site of the former race course in the middle of People's Square.   The first three galleries opened in December 1995, but the entire project was not completed until a grand opening was held for the other eight galleries on October 12, 1996.   The building covers 39,200 square meters and takes the unusual shape of a round top over a square base, symbolizing the traditional Chinese belief that the Earth is square and the sky is round.   The museum has 11 galleries for displaying its permanent collection, plus three exhibition halls for special temporary visiting exhibits.   Underneath the building a model of a traditional Chinese garden has been built in the basement for the entertainment of VIP visitors.   There is also a library of 200,000 rare volumes, which is open only to museum staff and professional scholars, but a well-stocked book shop on the ground floor is open to the public.   What is most peculiar about the Shanghai Museum is that it exhibits no items related directly to the history of Shanghai itself, but rather focuses on artwork from the various dynasties of China's ancient imperial past.

Address: 201 People's Avenue (Renmin Da Dao 201 hao) [人民大道 201 号].
Phone: (021) 6372-3500.
Fax: (021) 6372-8522
Nearest Metro Station: People's Square Station on Lines 1, 2, & 8.

Shanghai Municipal History Museum (Shanghai Shi Lishi Bowuguan) [上海市历史博物馆]

The Shanghai Municipal History Museum (Shanghai Shi Lishi Bowuguan) [上海市历史博物馆] has been relocated numerous times over the past 30 years.   From 1991 to 1998 it was located at 1286 Hongqiao Road, but three years after that site had closed in 1998, it was installed inside the basement of the Oriental Pearl T.V. Tower (Dongfang Mingzhu Guangbo Dianshi Ta) [东方明珠广播电视塔] in Pudong in May 2001.   Most recently, in March 2018 it moved into the former Shanghai Race Club building at 325 Nanjing West Road (Nanjing Xi Lu) [南京西路] in Puxi, after two years of preparations that had begun in 2015, three years after the Shanghai Art Museum had moved out of that building in 2012.

The Pudong facility had many exhibits about the city's history, but few if any authentic relics or artifacts.   The focus was on using wax figures to act out scenes from the city's history.

There were 10,000 square meters of exhibits, but very few genuine historic relics on display. Two floors of exhibits consisted of wax figure mannequins posing in simulated models of historic situations, such as various types of shops, and models of historic houses and buildings in the city.   English captions were provided for all the displays, but the names of Chinese people and places had been transliterated in the antiquated Wade-Giles phonetic system rather than the Pinyin system in use today.

260

One fascinating exhibit was devoted to **Hardoon Garden**, the former garden residence of Silas A. Hardoon, which no longer exists. The large amount of space dedicated to the Hardoon Garden included a scale model of the entire grounds, plus a wall map, and about 36 black and white photos. This garden was destroyed in 1954 and made the location of the new Sino-Soviet Friendship Palace which still stands there today. Similarly, a fairly large exhibit was devoted to the Holy Trinity Cathedral (Sheng Sanyi Tang) [圣三一堂], the oldest Christian church in Shanghai, even though this church was until recently off limits to visitors as it was still serving as Communist Party office space.

The most impressive historic relic in the museum was one of the two bronze lions which once guarded the entrance to the Hong Kong and Shanghai Bank building on the Bund. The lion on display was the roaring one, while the lion at rest was still hidden from view somewhere. The roaring lion's nose shows the signs of all the thousands of hands which have touched it for good luck over the years, making it shine golden like brass, while the rest of the lion's body is a much darker color.

At the very end of the tour was a book store near the exit which has a fairly good selection of publications on Shanghai history, although most of them were written in the Chinese language rather than English.

Those wishing to learn more about the historic development of Shanghai as a city would probably have learned more by visiting the Urban Planning Exhibition Center on People's Avenue (Renmin Da Dao) [人民大道], across the street from People's Square.

By most accounts, the museum's new facility on Nanjing West Road (Nanjing Xi Lu) [南京西路] is considered a big improvement. First of all, there is much more space available for exhibits, which allows the museum to display much more of its collection than before, including both bronze lions that had stood in front of the HSBC building on the Bund, boundary markers from the international settlements, a wedding sedan chair, and a rickshaw. All together there are more than 1,100 cultural relics on display over 9,800-square-meters of space.

The museum's permanent exhibits in the main building, known as the East Wing, are organized into three sections presented in chronological order on four floors: special exhibitions on the ground floor; ancient Shanghai on the 2nd floor; and modern Shanghai on both the 3rd and 4th floors. At least 80% of the descriptions are now bilingual. In addition, visitors are now allowed to go up to the roof, an area that was once forbidden. There are also temporary exibhits in a second building next door, known as the West Wing.

Address: 325 Nanjing West Road (Nanjing Xi Lu) [南京西路 325 号]
Phone: (021) 6323-2504.
Nearest Metro Station:

The **Shanghai Urban Planning Exhibition Hall** (Chengshi Guihua Zhanlan Guan) [城市规划展览馆] across the street from People's Square on People's Aveneue (Renmin Dadao) [人民大道] has informative exhibits showing how the city has already changed and how it will look in the future, including a large scale model.

The **Bund** (Waitan) has two small but interesting museums, one located at the North end of the Bund in the basement of the tripod-shaped Victory Monument in **Huangpu Park** (Huangpu Gongyuan), and another inside the **Gutzlaff Signal Tower** at the South end of the Bund.   In addition, there is the Bund Branch of the Shanghai Archives (Shanghai Shi Dangan Guan), which has some useful exhibits.

Surprisingly, the most interesting collection of genuine historic artifacts related to the city's history can be found inside the exhibition hall at the site of the **First Congress Hall of the Chinese Communist Party** on Xingye Lu, beside the new Xintiandi complex.

The Shanghai Railway Museum (Shanghai Tielu Bowuguan) [上海铁路博物馆]

Unlike the steel and concrete box built in 1987 that has served as Shanghai's main train station since then, the original **Shanghai North Train Station** (Shanghai Bei Huoche Zhan) [上海北火车站] built in 1909 featured beautiful architecture of arabesque arcades, arches and columns.   Unfortunately, as the center of heavy fighting during the 1932 Japanese invasion of Shanghai, the building was so severely damaged by bombs, artillery and bullets that it collapsed shortly after, only to be replaced by a new train station that was itself blown up by the Japanese again during their second invasion in 1937.

The **Shanghai Railway Museum** (Shanghai Tielu Bowuguan) [上海铁路博物馆] located at 200 Tianmu Dong Lu [天目东路 200 号] was constructed on the original site of Shanghai's **Old North Train Station** (Lao Bei Zhan) [老北站] and opened to the public in August 2004. The museum building's architecture bears a striking resemblance to the earlier structure built in 1909.   Inside there are copious photographic exhibits relating to the history of railroad construction in China.   Parked outside are several examples of authentic historic steam locomotives and passenger cars once used in China.

Address: 200 Tianmu Dong Lu [天目东路 200 号], former Zhabei District, now Jingan District.
Phone: (021) 5122-1575

District Museums

Some of the outlying suburban districts, such as Songjiang, Qingpu, and Jiading, also have their own district museums.   The Songjiang District Museum is located right beside the main entrance to the Square Pagoda Park (Fangta Gongyuan) on Zhongshan Lu.   Qingpu District recently completed construction of a modern new district museum located in Qingpu New Town.

There are also many memorial halls (jinian guan) [纪念馆] devoted to famous celebrities, such as Lu Xun and Song Qingling.

N

Nanjing East Road (Nanjing Dong Lu) [南京东路]

This two-mile stretch of road between the Bund (Waitan) and Tibet Middle Road (Xizang Zhong Lu) was the main street of the International Settlement, when it was known as Nanking Road.   It was the first modern shopping street in China, with a string of four Western-style department stores erected here in the early 20th century.   On October 1, 1999 Nanjing East Road (Nanjing Dong Lu) [南京东路] was turned into a pedestrian only mall (buxing jie) between the cross streets of Tibet Middle Road (Xizang Zhong Lu) and Henan Middle Road (Henan Zhong Lu).

The **Sincere Department Store** (Xianshi Gongsi) erected in 1917 was the first modern department store to be founded in Shanghai.   Its five-story building featured four floors of shopping space and was topped by a four-story, round clock tower decorated with Greco-Roman columns that looked like a Western wedding cake.   The bright white building still stands on the North side of Nanjing East Road (Nanjing Dong Lu) [南京东路] at #640-700, at its intersection with Zhejiang Middle Road (Zhejiang Zhong Lu).   It's now known as the **Shanghai Fashion Co.** (Shanghai Shizhuang Gongsi) [上海时装公司]. Although other buildings later tried to imitate its style, particularly the feature of having a baroque or Greco-Roman tower on top, the former Sincere Co. is still the most impressive building on the whole street.

The six-story **Wing On Department Store** (Yongan Gongsi) was erected in 1918, directly across the street from their main competitor, the Sincere Co.   The Wing On building was topped with a slightly smaller three-story round tower meant to rival that of Sincere's.   It was the first store in Shanghai to have signboards outside illuminated by neon lights, a sight so common today as to make the street seem like Las Vegas.   The yellow building still stands on the South side of Nanjing East Road (Nanjing Dong Lu) [南京东路] at #635, at its intersection with Zhejiang Middle Road (Zhejiang Zhong Lu).   It is now known as the **Hualian Commercial Building** (Hualian Shangsha) [华联商厦].   However the original facade of the northeast corner was altered during a 1987 renovaton in which gold colored glass panels were installed over the four middle floors.   In 2003 it was announced that $1.2 million U.S. dollars would be spent to restore the exterior completely to its original appearance.

The **Sun Sun Department Store** (Xinxin Gongsi) at #720 opened for business in 1926. The building still stands on the North side of Nanjing East Road (Nanjing Dong Lu) [南京东路] at its intersection with Guizhou Road (Guizhou Lu).   Although the building has a two-story square tower on top, this resembles more the pilot house of a ship and pales in comparison to the towers of Sincere and Wing On.   The store is now a state owned enterprise until recently called the **No. 1 Provisions Store** (Shanghai Shi Diyi Shipin Shangdian) [上海市第一食品商店].   The store's name has been somewhat modernized as the **Shanghai First Food Store**.

Da Sun Department Store (Daxin Gongsi) at #830 was the last of the four pre-war modern department stores to be built in Shanghai.   Although it came later than the other three, it was by far the biggest at ten stories high, and it had probably the best location, standing right at the northeast corner of Nanking Road and Tibet Road.   Construction started in 1934, but the doors didn't actually open until 1936.   Da Sun was the first store in Shanghai to offer central heating and had the first escalator in the city.   However, it's the only one of the big four pre-revolution department stores to not have a Western wedding cake-style tower on top.   The building is now a state owned enterprise called the **No. 1 Department Store** (Shanghai Shi Diyi Baihuo Shangdian) [上海市第一百货商店].

Nearest Metro Station: People's Square Station on Lines 1, 2, & 8 or Nanjing East Road (Nanjing Dong Lu) [南京东路] Station on Line 2.

Nanjing West Road (Nanjing Xi Lu) [南京西路]

Before the 1949 Communist revolution, Nanjing West Road (Nanjing Xi Lu) [南京西路] was known as **Bubbling Well Road**.   It stretches from Tibet Middle Road (Xizang Zhong Lu) in the East to the Jingan Buddhist Temple (Jingan Si) [静安寺] in the West.   A number of historic hotels, theaters and other structures line its sidewalks, but in recent years it has become the site of new modern skyscrapers housing hotels, restaurants, shopping centers and upscale luxury boutique shops.   Walking from East to West, historic sights along this road include in order the **Pacific Hotel** (Jinmen Dajiudian) [金门大酒店] located at #108 built in 1926 as the luxurious China United Apartments; the former **Foreigner's YMCA** (now the Shanghai Sports Mansion) completed in 1933 and located at #150 is notable for its Arabesque arcades of pillars and arches; the **Park Hotel** (Guoji Dajiudian) [国际饭店] built in 1934 and located at #170; the **Grand Movie Theater** (Da Guanming Dianyingyuan) [大光明电影院] designed by Laszlo Hudec and built in 1932; the former **Shanghai Race Club** (Paoma Zonghui) [跑马总会] built in 1934, which was later used as the **Shanghai Library** (Shanghai Tushuguan) [上海图书馆] from 1953 until 1996, and then became the **Shanghai Art Museum** (Shanghai Meishuguan) [上海美术馆] until October 2012, is located at # 325; the Brethren Buildings, two matching French palace-style, three-story homes designed by Palmer & Turner architects that once belonged to the Guo brothers, Guo Le and Guo Shun, who owned the Wing On Department Store, stand side by side at #1418; while across the street is the former site of the Hardoon Garden (Hatong Huayuan) [哈同花园], built between 1904 and 1909 by the Baghdadi Jewish merchant Silas Aaron Hardoon (1851-1931), which once covered 30 acres of land where the **Sino-Soviet Friendship Hall** built in Stalinist-Byzantine architectural style in 1954 stands today at the intersection of Tongren Lu (formerly known as Hardoon Road) and Nanjing West Road (Nanjing Xi Lu) [南京西路].   At the time of his death in 1931 Hardoon was described by newspaper headlines as the "Orient's Richest Individual."   The last sight of interest on Nanjing West Road (Nanjing Xi Lu) [南京西路] is the **Jingan Buddhist Temple** (Jingan Si) [静安寺]. The entire length of Nanjing Road from the Bund (Waitan) to Jingan Buddhist Temple (Jingan Si) [静安寺] stretches 5.5 km.

Nearest Metro Station: People's Square Station on Lines 1, 2, & 8 or Nanjing West Road (Nanjing Xi Lu) [南京西路] Station on Line 2.

Nanxiang Steamed Dumplings (Nanxiang Xiaolong Bao) [南翔小笼包]

Located on the corner of Guyi Yuan Lu [古漪园] and Zhen Nan Lu in Nanxiang Ancient Town (Nanxiang Gu Zhen) [南翔古镇], on a section of road also known as the Huyi Highway (Huyi Gonglu), inside the main South Gate of the Guyi Yuan [古漪园] is a famous local restaurant which takes up half a dozen large traditional style halls and pavilions.   It specializes in serving the Nanxiang steamed dumplings which won an award at the fourth world Chinese cuisine competition held in Kuala Lumpur, Malaysia in 2002.   Prices for the dumplings rang from 2 to 40 Rmb.   The restaurant is quite packed with visitors on weekends, compared to the garden itself which is relatively sedate and peaceful.   Most of the cars and busses you see in the garden's parking lot in fact belong to people going to eat in the restaurant.   There are also many other competing steamed dumpling restaurants located up and down both sides of Guyi Yuan Lu [古漪园].

Nanxiang Ancient Town (Nanxiang Gu Zhen) [南翔古镇], Jiading District.

The Old Shanghai County Town (Shanghai Xiancheng) [上海县城]

Bounded by the two roads Renmin Lu [人民路] and Zhonghua Lu [中华路] that follow the circular route marking where the town wall once stood, Shanghai's old county town area has come under increasing pressure from urban development in recent years, with high-rise apartment buildings and office towers sprouting everywhere.   In the year 2000 the Nanshi District (Nanshi Qu) [南市区] was elminated and merged into Huangpu District (Huangpu Qu) [黄浦区].   In the the same year all the old houses along Fangbang Middle Road (**Fangbang Zhong Lu)** [方浜中路] were torn down and replaced with Ming-Qing style new replicas, after which the road was renamed as "*Shanghai Old Street*" (Shanghai Laojie) [上海老街].   In order to make space for the 2010 World Expo, the original century-old buildings of the **White Cloud Taoist Temple** (Baiyun Guan) [白云观] in the Old West Gate (Lao Xi Men) [老西门] neighborhood were demolished and replaced with sterile replicas in a new location far from the previous site, next door to the War God Temple and Small North Gate (Xiao Bei Men) [小北门], on land that had until then been occupied by a block of old Stone Gate Houses (Shikumen), which were torn down to make room for it.

Nonetheless, a half dozen noteworthy sights have survived, including the **War God Temple** (Guandi Miao) [关帝庙], also known as the **Dajing Pavilion** (Dajing Ge) [大境阁], the **Small North Gate** (Xiao Bei Men) [小北门] standing beside it inside a fenced enclosure, the **Fuyou Road Mosque** (Fuyou Lu Qingzhen Si) [清真寺], the **Chenxiang Ge** [沉香阁] **Buddhist Temple**, **Jingyi Church** (Jingyi Tang) [敬一堂], the Shanghai **City God Temple** (Shanghai Chenghuang Miao) [城隍庙], the **Mid-Lake Pavilion Teahouse** (Huxin Ting Chalou) [湖心亭茶楼], the **Bridge of Nine Turnings** (Jiuqu Qiao) [九曲桥], the **Yu Garden** (Yu Yuan) [豫园], and the **Small World** Building (Xiaoshijie) [小世界], once a rival to the more famous Great World Amusement Center (Dashijie), which has a pedestrian gateway leading into the north end of the Yu Yuan Bazaar.

The Shanghai **Confucius Temple** (Wen Miao) [文庙] was completely destroyed during the Cultural Revolution, with the existing one being a completely new replica rebuilt in 1999 on the vacant lot where the previous one had stood.   However, there is another Confucius Temple (Jiading Kong Miao) [嘉定孔庙] in suburban Jiading Town which is a more authentic relic, as well as a Confucian Academy (Xue Gong) on Chongming Island.

Nearest Metro Station: Old West Gate (Lao Xi Men) [老西门]
Station on Line 8.

Pagodas (Baota) [宝塔]

Pagodas (baota) [宝塔] are tower structures associated with Buddhist temples. They evolved over time from the smaller domed stupas of India into their present tower form found in China. The average pagoda has seven storeys and an octagonal shape, but there are some as tall as 13 storeys and occasionally they can be hexagonal or square shaped. All the pagodas in Shanghai are seven-storey, octagonal structures. .Pagodas were usually constructed with a brick or stone block core that was then covered with a plaster and wooden exterior of balconies and upturned roof eaves at each level. Over time the wooden exterior would often be destroyed, burned off, or disintegrate, leaving only the brick and stone core left standing. Often the wooden halls of the temple beside it would completely disappear, leaving only this brick and stone monument as a reminder that it was there. Pagodas that have been restored by having their wooden exterior rebuilt look deceptively new, although their inner core may be hundreds of years old, while those left in a ruined state appear to be much more authentic historic relics. Restored pagodas are more pleasing to Chinese eyes, but Westerners tend to appreciate unrestored ruins more.

According to Pan Mingquan [潘明权] (b.1947) of Shanghai Finance and Economics University in his encyclopedic work, _Shanghai Buddhist & Taoist Temples_ (_Shanghai Fosi Daoguan) [上海佛寺道观],_ " (2003), there were then 16 historic pagodas in the greater Shanghai municipality. However, most of them are located out in the suburban districts of Songjiang, Qingpu, and Jiading. His list in order of importance includes the following: 1) Longhua Ta in Longhua Town of Xuhui District; 2) Li Ta in Shihudang Town of Songjiang District; 3) Qinglong Ta in Qinglong Village of Baihe Town in Qingpu District; 4) Mao Ta in Qingpu District; 5) Nanxiang Shuang Ta in Nanxiang Town of Jiading District; 6) Xiudaozhi Ta on Sheshan in Songjiang District; 7) Xingshengjiao Si Ta, aka the Fang Ta [方塔], in Songjiang Town of Songjiang District; 8) Huzhu Ta on Tianma Shan in Songjiang District; 9) Fahua Ta in Jiading Town of Jiading District; 10) Xilin Ta in Songjiang Town of Songjiang District; 11) the 50 meter high Huayan Ta in Jinshan District, which was rebuilt in 1999; 12) Wanshou Ta in Qingpu Town of Qingpu District; 13) Zhenhai Ta in Chengqiao Town of Chongming County; 14) Baoen Ta in Pudong New District; 15) the 32 meter high Xingjue Si Ta in Jinshan District, which was rebuilt in 1996; 16) the 53 meter high Zhenru Ta in Putuo District, which completed on December 24, 1999.

Since the 1980s there have continued to be new pagodas built in Shanghai. In some cases these are considered to be reconstructions of historic pagodas that once stood in the same spot but had been completely destroyed and disappeared, as in the cases of the Zhenru Ta in Putuo and the Anfang Ta in Sijing Town, or in other cases they are simply considered attractive decorations for a park, such as the pagoda in the Grand View Garden on the shore of Dianshan Lake in Qingpu District.

There are also seven genuinely ancient stone Budhist towers (shi ta) dating from the Tang and Song dynasties spread out throughout the Shangahi municipality. Four of these now stand inside the Guyi Yuan in Nanxiang Town of Jiading District, 1 is inside a public park beside the Jiading Confucius Temple in Jiading Town, another is inside the walled compound of Longhua Buddhist Temple, and one is in Songjiang Town.

In my own personal opinion, which is slightly different to that of Pan Mingquan, the 14 most significant pagodas in Shanghai are as follows:

1) Longhua Pagoda (Longhua Ta) [龙华塔]

Located inside its own small walled compound across the street from the much larger walled compound of Longhua Buddhist Temple (Longhua Si) [龙华寺] in Longhua Town, this pagoda stands 40.64 meter high and was most likely constructed in 1066 during the Northern Song Dynasty.   It was almost destroyed in 1966 during the Cultural Revolution, and was completely restored in 1984.   This is the only historic pagoda in the downtown city center area.   Look under the L section for more information on Longhua Temple and Longhua Pagoda.

2) The **Green Dragon Pagoda** (Qinglong Ta) [青龙塔]

Located in Green Dragon Village (Qinglong Cun) [青龙村] of White Crane Town (Baihe Zhen) [白鹤] out in the rural countryside of Qingpu District.   Today this is the oldest existing pagoda still standing within the Shanghai municipality.   A Buddhist temple called Baode Si [报德寺] was first built at this site as early as 743 A.D., the second year of the Tianbao [天宝] reign of the Tang Dynasty.   However, the adjoining octagonal, seven-story brick and stone pagoda was first built nearly 80 years later between 821 and 824 A.D. during the Changqing reign of the Tang Dynasty.   The pagoda's original official name was Longfu Si Ta [隆福寺塔], but it was also commonly known as (Qinglong Ta) [青龙塔].

By some accounts Qinglong Town marks one of the first two most important locations of human settlement within the boundaries of the modern day Shanghai municipality, the other being the site of Hudu village at the confluence of Suzhou Creek and the Huangpu River. During the Tang Dynasty, Qinglong village was a thriving commercial port on a river, but nowadays the water has dried up to barely a trickle flowing in a small creek beside the tower.

In the Northern Song Dynasty the Buddhist temple was renamed Longfu Si [隆福寺], and the adjoining pagoda was rebuilt between 1041 and 1048, after having been previously damaged by fire during wartime.   The tower was repaired again in 1644, the last year of the Ming Dynasty.   In 1715 the Kangxi emperor visited Qinglong Temple during his southern journey (nanxun) and renamed it Jiyun Chan Si.   At the time of the Guangxu Qingpu Xianzhi publication, the temple's structures included a Hall of the Great Hero (Da Xiong Bao Dian), a Dizang Hall (Dizang Dian), a Weituo Hall (Weituo Dian), Meditation Hall (Chan Tang), Dining Hall (Zhai Tang), Abbot's Quarters (Fangzhang Shi), and many other buildings. However, in 1798, the third year of the Jiaqing reign of the Qing Dynasty, the temple caught on fire and the main halls burned down.   In the early years of the Daoguang reign some attempts were made at reconstruction, but in 1860, during the 10th year of the Xianfeng reign, the temple was burned down again, this time by soldiers, most likely as part of the Taiping Rebellion.   In 1956 the top of the pagoda was blown off in a typhoon.   In 1959 and 1960 it was classified as a county-level and city-level histori relic.

The pagoda has not been restored since the end of the Ming Dynasty in 1644.   Much like the Wanshou Ta was until 2009, and how the Huzhu Ta still is, the current remnants of the Qinglong Ta are merely the hollow inner brick core, all of the wooden parts such as the eaves, balconies, and roof having long ago disappeared, likely as a result of the fires of 1798 and 1860 that destroyed the rest of the temple.

The pagoda stands inside its own small walled compound, the gate of which never seems to be open.   The separate walled compound of the recently rebuilt Green Dragon Buddhist Temple (Qinglong Si) [青龙寺] now stands nearby.

Location: Green Dragon Village (Qinglong Cun) [青龙村], White Crane Town (Baihe Zhen) [白鹤], Qingpu District.

3) The **Nanxiang Twin Pagodas** (Nanxiang Shuang Ta) [南翔双塔]

Nanxiang Town, Jiading District.   Each one of theset two identical brick pagodas is only 11 meters high.   They probably date from the Northern Song (Bei Song) Dynasty (960-1126). Chinese historian Pan Mingquan [潘明权] (b.1947) guesses that they were built in 980 A.D. In 1766, during the 31st year of the Qianlong reign, the adjoining buildings of the associated Buddhist temple were completely burned down in a big fire, and only the two brick pagodas were left standing. It is known that they once stood inside the gates of the original **Baihe Nanxiang Si** Buddhist Temple before it burned to the ground in 1766.   They were fully restored from 1985 to 1986.

Address: Xianghua Qiao, intersection of Renmin Jie and Shuangyong Jie, Nanxiang Ancient Town (Nanxiang Guzhen) [南翔古镇], Jiading District.

4) The **Square Pagoda** (Fang Ta) [方塔]

Also known as the Xingshengjiao Buddhist Temple Pagoda [兴圣教寺塔], this tower is a nine-story brick Pagoda Park (Fangta Yuan) [方塔园].   It was originally built between 1068 and 1094 during the Northern Song Dynasty.   It was extensively restored to its present condition between 1975 and 1977.   Also on the park grounds is a Ming Dynasty Screen Wall (zhaobi) [照壁] dating from 1370 that once belonged to the Songjiang City God Temple (Songjiang Chenghuang Miao), which was blown up by the Japanese in WWII and no longer exists, a Tianfei Temple (Tianfei Gong) [天妃宫] supposedly dating from 1853, which was moved here in 1980, a Sacred Way (shendao) of carved stone statues that once belonged to a tomb dating from the Ming Dynasty, and Shanghai's oldest stone foot bridge, the Wangxian Qiao [望仙桥], dating from 1193 in the Southern Song Dynasty.   In 1985 a Chen Ancestral Hall (Chen Gong Ci) [陈公祠] (aka Chen Huacheng Ci Tang) [陈化成祠堂] was established within the park in memory of Chen Huacheng, the defender of Shanghai during the British invasion.

Address: 235 Zhongshan Dong Lu, Songjiang Town, Songjiang District.

5) The **Pearl Guarding Pagoda** (Huzhu Ta) [护珠塔]

also known as the Baoguang Ta [宝光塔] Tianma Shan [天马山], Songjiang District.   This octagonal brick structure was built in 1079 during the Northern Song Dynasty.   In 1788, the 53rd year of the Qianlong reign of the Qing Dynasty, the pagoda caught on fire and all the wooden parts of the structure were completely burned off, including the eaves, balconies, roof, floors, and stairs, leaving only a hollow brick core left standing.   It was restored to its present condition in 1982.   It leans sharply at an angle of 6 degrees, which is one degree more than the leaning tower of Pisa in Italy.

6) The **Fahua Pagoda (Fahua Ta)** [法华塔]

The seven-story, square-shaped Fahua Pagoda (Fahua Ta) [法华塔] also known as the Golden Sands Pagoda (Jinsha Ta) [金沙塔], stands 41 meter high, is made of brick and wood, and was first built between 1205 and 1207 in the Southern Song Dynasty (Nan Song). It was last restored in 1996, during which an underground chamber containing Buddhist relics was discovered. Its square shape gives it a resemblance to the Square Pagoda (Fang Ta) [方塔] in Songjiang Town. It has been completely restored to give it a deceptively new appearance that includes wooden eaves on each floor, and a tall pinnacle on top. It is located in the historic Zhou Bridge (Zhou Qiao) neighborhood of Jiading Town, the administrative capital of Jiading District.

Oddly enough, beside the pagoda is a memorial hall (jinian guan) [纪念馆] devoted to the Guomindang diplomat **Wellington Koo** (Gu Weijun) [顾维钧] (1888-1985) (1888-1985), a native of Jiading who graduated from St. John's University in Shanghai in 1904, and earned a Ph.D. at Columbia University n New York in 1912. After his 1912 graduation, he returned to China and began a long career as a diplomat, representing first the Beijing warlord regime from 1912 to 1927, and later the Guomindang government established in Nanjing in 1927. He served as China's plenipotentiary to the 1919 Paris Peace Conference, where he refused to sign the Versailles Treaty because of its cession of Shandong province to Japan. He participated in drafting the League of Nations charter in 1919, and was China's delegate to the League of Nations in 1920. Later he acted as Foreign Minister in the Beijing government from 1922 to 1924.

Koo joined the Guomindang regime in Nanjing as its Foreign Minister in 1931, and in 1932 hosted the League of Nations' Lytton Commission which investigated Japans' occupation of Manchuria. He served as China's delegate to the League of Nations throughout the 1930s. After WWII, he attended the 1945 San Francisco Conference, which established the United Nations, and spoke before the very first U.N. General Assembly in January 1946. He capped off his distinguished career with a stint as a judge on the International Court of Justice from 1961 to 1967.

Despite his being a Guomindang diplomat, the Wellington Koo memorial hall received a favorable mention in the July, 5, 2013 edition of the government-run newspaper China Daily, which pointed out his refusal to sign the Versailles Peace Treaty in 1919.

Address: 349 Big South Lane (Nan Da Jie) [南大街], North Branch (Beiduan) [北端], Zhou Bridge (Zhou Qiao), Jiading Town, Jiading District.

7) The **West Grove Pagoda** (Xilin Baota) [西林宝塔]

Also known as the Yuanying Ta [圆应塔], this pagoda was first built between 1265 and 1274 during the Southern Song Dynasty (Nan Song) (1127-1279), but was rebuilt in 1982. It is an octagonal, seven storey structure, and stands 40 meters high. It is located within the walled compound of West Grove Zen Buddhist Temple (Xilin Chan Si) [西林禅寺], Songjiang Town, Songjiang District.

Address: 666 Zhongshan Zhong Lu, Songjiang Town.

8) The **Longevity Pagoda (**Wanshou Ta) [万寿塔]

Qingpu Town, Qingpu District. It was built in 1743 A.D., the 8th year of the Qianlong reign of the Qing Dynasty, in honor of the emperor. This seven-story, square-shaped, wood and brick structure is located right beside the outer side of the still existing Qingpu city moat (huchenghe), right across the water from the former site of the South Gate (Nan Men) of the Qingpu city wall (chengqiang). As a result, it is sometimes also called the South Gate Pagoda (Nan Men Ta) [南门塔]. In 1883, the ninth year of the Guangxu reign of the Qing Dynasty, it caught fire and all the wooden parts were burned up, including the floors, the steps, the eaves, the balconies, and the roof, leaving only a hollow brick core still standing. In 1959 it was classified as a county-level cultural relic, but remained unrestored. It used to take quite a long walk from the main highway of Qingsong Gonglu to reach the site, passing through a village of farmers' houses and their fields, then required walking through the comcould pound of an abandoned factory. Once inside the pagoda's ground floor you look all the way up at the sky above, as it was completely hollow. However, after having been an unrestored historic relic for 126 years, in July 2009 it was covered with scaffolding as part of a restoration process that included mounting a new roof and metal spiral on top, as well as rebuilding the wooden eaves and balconies on each level, all of which completely changed its outward appearance. By 2017 the factory had been completely demolished, as had most of the surrounding farmers' houses, leaving a clear sight of the tower from a distance. It stands inside a walled compound with a wooden gate that is often kept locked, so it's no longer always possible to get inside. You can also get good views of it from several highway bridges crossing the city moat. Address: 406 Qingsong Gonglu, Qingpu Town, Qingpu District.

9) **Mao Pagoda** (Mao Ta) [泖塔]

This is a Tang Dynasty (618-907) pagoda built during the Qianfu era (874-880) of the Xizong reign (873-888). The original five-story, sqare-shaped, wood and brick structure was placed on an island in the middle of **Mao Hu** lake, which is in reality formed by two branches of the **Mao He** [泖河] river. It was last restored in November 1995. This pagoda stands at the southeastern tip of Sun Island (Taiyang Dao). You can reach Sun Island by driving South from Zhujiajiao Town on the Zhufeng Highway, which runs between Zhujiajiao and the town of Fengjing in Jinshan District. Maps contained in the Shanghai development plan show the Sun Island area lying within a large greenbelt which will be maintained around the shores of Mao Hu, so this should mean that the natural environment here will be preserved. However, the designation of this area as a greenbelt hasn't prevented the construction of the large **Sun Island Resort** development at the northwestern tip of Sun Island, on the opposite end from the Mao Ta.

Address: Shenxiang Town (Shenxiang Zhen) [沈巷镇], Zhangjiawei Village (Zhangjiawei Cun), Qingpu District (Qingpu Qu).

10) **Xiudaozhi Pagoda** (Xiudaozhi Ta) [秀道者塔]

The **Xiudaozhi Pagoda** (Xiudaozhi Ta) [秀道者塔] is a seven-story, octagonal structure that stands 30 meters high.   According to a sign nearby, it was originally built in 978 A.D. during the Northern Song Dynasty (Bei Song) [北宋]. However, according to the Songjiang District Annals (Songjiang Quzhi) [松江区志] it was constructed in the Northern Song Dynasty (Bei Song) [北宋] during the Taiping Xingguo [太平兴国] reign (976 – 984) of Zhao Guangyi [赵光义], whose temple name was Emperor Taizong [宋太宗] (976-997), by a Taoist monk named Xiu [秀], in whose memory it was named.   However, it is also known as the Yueying Ta [月影塔].   According to the Songjiang Prefecture Annals (Songjiang Fuzhi) [松江府志] during the Ming Zhengde [正德] reign (1491-1521) there was a Buddhist temple here called Puzhao Si [普照寺], later known as Xuhua Si.   When the famous Ming Dynasty traveler **Xu Xiake** [徐霞客] (1587-1641) visited Sheshan for the third time in 1636 he recorded that the temple was already in ruinous condition, as recorded in his travel diaries (Xu Xiake Youji) [徐霞客游记].   In 1864 French Catholics purchased all the land on Sheshan and tore down the then existing Xuhua Si Buddhist Temple and Xiudaozhi Pagoda here in order to build a Christian church (jiaotang).   After political and cultural reforms began in 1979, there was apparently a struggle between local Christians and Buddhists over which religion would get possession of the Sheshan site.   As part of a compromise solution, reconstruction of the present pagoda began in 1997 and was completed in December 1998.   As a result of these renovations, the pagoda now has a deceptively new appearance, but if you look at photos of it from earlier in the 1980s and 1990s, you can see that prior to its restoration it was a genuine historic relic with nothing left but the weathered brick and stone core.   Each of the eight corners of the octagonal pagoda are now hung with small bells that chime naturally when the wind blows.   The sound of their delicate chimes ringing in a random pattern with the wind is quite relaxing.   The pagoda is surrounded by a menagerie of Ming Dynasty-style stone animal sculptures, including horses, rams, cats, and lions, all of which once formed part of the Sacred Way (shendao) leading to a tomb.   Nearby stands a two story Bell Tower (Zhong Lou) with a golden Maitreya Buddha (Milefo) seated inside the first floor, but a full scale Buddhist temple has not been rebuilt.

Location: The West Peak (Xi Sheshan) [西佘山] of **Sheshan National Forest Park** (Sheshan Guojia Senlin Gongyuan).

11) Li Pagoda (Li Ta) [李塔]

The Li Ta [李塔] is a seven-story, square-shaped pagoda built in Tang Dynasty style, made of brick and wood, and standing almost 41 meters tall.

The origins of the pagoda have not been well documented. Despite legends of an earlier origin, it probably dates from the Song Dynasty at the earliest, although it is built in Tang Dynasty style. Even the source of its name is debatable. It has three variant names, including the Li Ming Ta [李明塔], the Li Ta [李塔] or even the Li Ta [礼塔]. According to one popular legend, it is named after the Cao King Li Ming (Cao Wang Li Ming) [曹王李明], who was either the 13th or 14th son of Li Shimin [李世民] who reigned as the Tang Dynasty Emperor Taizong [唐太宗] (626-649). Li Ming [李明] once served as the governor of nearby Suzhou Prefecture and according to legend built a navigation light house for ships sailing the maze of inland waterways in this area. The location is sometimes referred to as Li Pagoda Confluence (Li Ta Hui) [李塔汇] because two rivers converge here, the Henglaojing [横潦泾] and the Mao He [泖河]. In keeping with this tradition, on the east side of the pagoda there is an ancestral temple devoted to Li Ming [李明] known as the Ming King Temple (Ming Wang Miao) [明王庙]. However, the earliest historical references to this ancestral temple only date from the Ming & Qing dynasties.

The earliest documented reference to the pagoda that I could find was when it was supposedly "repaired" in 1852 and then again later a record that it was still standing in 1913, after which there is no mention of it again until 1985. In 1985 the Li Ta [李塔] pagoda was classified as a Songjiang county-level cultural relic. A 1995 investigation by a team of experts trying to document its history was inconclusive. The pagoda was restored in 1997. In 2002 the Li Ta [李塔] pagoda was classified as a Shanghai city-level cultural relic.

The Li Ta pagoda is now associated with **Yanshou Buddhist Temple** (Yanshou Si) [延寿寺], which has a slightly better documented history. During the Southern Song Dynasty a Buddhist monk first came to this site in 1213 in order to establish a temple, but at first only a small hut known as Yuan An [圆庵] was built. Between 1265 and 1274 Yuan An [圆庵] changed its name to Yanshou Yuan [延寿院]. However, in 1308 this small temple was destroyed, although no mention is made of the pagoda. In 1573, during the Wanli reign of the Ming Dynasty, the small temple of Yanshou Yuan [延寿院] was rebuilt again. It is recorded as ungoing large scale repairs in 1659, the 16th year of the Shunzhi reign of the Ming Dynasty. In 1740, the 5th year of the Qianlong reign of the Qing Dynasty, two new temple halls were constructed, a Precious Hall of the Great Hero (Da Xiong Bao Dian) [大雄宝殿] and a Flexible Hall (Yuantong Dian) [圆通殿]. In 1821, the first year of the Daoguang reign of the Qing Dynasty, the Meditation Hall (Chan Tang) [禅堂] was repaired. During the Xianfeng reign of the Qing Dynasty, the temple was destroyed, but in 1852 repairs started on the Entrance Gate (Shan Men) [山门], Precious Hall of the Great Hero (Da Xiong Bao Dian) [大雄宝殿], Abbot's Quarters (Fangzhang Shi) [方丈室] and the pagoda (baota) [宝塔]. In 1913 major repairs were made to the Flexible Hall (Yuantong Dian) [圆通殿], Maitreya Hall (Mile Dian) [弥勒殿], Suspended-in-Mid-Air Hall (Xuankong Dian) [悬空殿] and Entrance Gate (Shan Men) [山门]. The Li Ta pagoda was reportedly still standing fully erect at that time. However, during the Second Sino-Japanese War of 1937-1945, the temple halls were all destroyed, although no mention is made of the pagoda itself.

The temple was officially re-established (huifu) [恢复] in 1999, but not opened to the public until 2001.   The temple halls currently include a Precious Hall of the Great Hero (Da Xiong Bao Dian) [大雄宝殿], Heavenly Kings Hall (Tian Wang Dian) [天王殿], Three Saints Hall (San Sheng Dian) [三圣殿], Hall of Great Sadness (Da Bei Dian) [大悲殿], Goddess of Mercy Hall (Guanyin Dian) [观音殿], Dizang Hall (Dizang Dian) [地藏殿], Bell Tower (Zhong Lou) [钟楼], Drum Tower (Gu Lou) [鼓楼], etc.

What's strange about thet temple's historic records is that the pagoda is seldom mentioned. When recording times of destruction and reconstruction the pagoda is not specifically mentioned.   Its specific date of original construction is not recorded.   It is only specifically mentioned as being repaired in 1852 and still standing in 1913, after which there is no mention until 1985 when it was listed as a county level relic.   As a result, the official assumption has been that the pagoda was already there when the temple was built in the Southern Song Dynasty, and survived each wave of destruction.

Location: 130 Li Pagoda Lane (Li Ta Jie 130 hao) [李塔街 130 号], Pagoda Confluence Community (Ta Hui Shequ) [塔汇社区], Shihudang Zhen [石湖荡镇], Songjiang District, about 10 kilometers southwest of Songjiang Town, on the Shanghai – Hangzhou railway line (Hu-Hang Tielu) [沪杭铁路] and near the Mao He [泖河], Ba He [坝河], Yaojinghe [姚泾河] and Henglaojing [横潦泾] rivers. The closest other significant town is Xiao Kunshan Zhen [小昆山镇].   Prior to 2001 its location was considered to lay within Li Pagoda Confluence Town (Li Ta Hui Zhen) [李塔汇镇], but in January of that year Li Pagoda Confluence Town (Li Ta Hui Zhen) [李塔汇镇] was lowered in status, renamed Pagoda Confluence Community (Ta Hui Shequ) [塔汇社区] and merged with Shihudang Zhen [石湖荡镇].

12) Anfang Pagoda (Anfang Ta) [安方塔]

The Anfang Ta [安方塔] was rebuilt in 2001 at the same location where a previous pagoda had stood 600 years earlier in Sijing Town of Songjiang District.   It is associated with the Buddhist temple Futian Jingsi [福田净寺], which is located across the street in a separate walled compound.   The pagoda stands inside its own small walled compound beside a river. Beautiful views of the pagoda can be seen from a nearby highway bridge crossing the river.

Standing at the western end of Kaijiang Zhong Lu is undoubtedly the town's most impressive sight, its seven-story octagonal wooden pagoda.   The entrance to the pagoda's walled garden is located at #411 Kaijiang Lu.   An impressive stone gate, similar to that found at the Longhua Bao Ta [宝塔], marks the spot.

Tickets include a brief Chinese language description printed on the back of it.   The name "An Fang Ta" can be translated as quiet or peacefule square pagoda.   The square part of the name seems odd because, unlike the Fang Ta in Songjiang town, this one has eight sides rather than four.   The pagoda used to belong to the former Dongtian Chan Si Buddhist Temple, which no longer exists, but was recently replaced with the newly built Futian Jing Si nearby.   The An Fang Ta stands 35.18 meters high.   It cost more than 6 million Rmb to build/rebuild it.   The ticket does not say when it was built or rebuilt, but a shi bei inside the ground floor is dated 2001.

Amazingly the seven story structure is solid wood, including its roof eaves and balconys. The wooden dou gong brackets supporting the roof eaves are quite intricate in their design. The wood is a curious dark brownish red color. Four of the pagoda's eight sides have wooden gates on the ground floor, one of which is left open allowing entrance inside. From the ground floor the pagoda can be ascended all the way to the top via parallel flights of wooden stairs, one flight for going up the other for going down. There are windows and balconys on each floor providing wonderful views of the sourrounding area. Curiously steps from the ground floor also lead down into a dark basement. Inside the ground floor stands a new shibei tablet dated in Chinese as December 18, 2001.

It's hard to get a good angle for taking photographs of the tall structure from either the front gate or the road outside it. Fortunately the pagoda garden has a long arm extending to the west. Walking westward to a small pavilion containing a well (jing ting), and then turning around, from this spot you can get excellent photograph's of the pagoda's full structure, with unobstructed blue sky in the background. Walking over to a long covered corridor on the south side of the garden, you discover that a long canal or river flows beside it here.

The Buddhist temple located in a separate walled compound across the street was first established as Dongtian Chansi [东田禅寺] in 1008, during the Zhenzong reign of the Song Dynast, and rebuilt in 1776, during the 41st year of the Qianlong reign of the Qing Dynasty. After 1949, local authorities compiling the Sijing Town Annals (Sijing Zhenzhi) [泗泾镇志] researched the temple'history back to the Song Dynasty, but by 1958 there was almost nothing left of the temple buildings except for some ruins (yiji) [遗迹]. In the year 2000 it was decided to rebuilt the temple under the new name of Futian Jingsi [福田净寺]. By August 2006 many new temple buildings had been completed, including a Tian Wang Dian, Zhong Lou, Gu Lou, Dining Hall (Zhai Tang), Gongde Tang. The Wisdom Hall (Faru Tang) was completed in January 2008, and in April 2008 a grand opening ceremony was held. Since then a Yuantong Boadian, Qianfo Tang, Guanyin Dian and a vegetarian restaurant (Suzhai Tang) have been added.

Location: #411 Kaijiang Zhong Lu, Sijing Town [泗泾镇], Songjiang District

13) Guard the Sea Tower (Zhenhai Ta) [镇海塔]

Inside Golden Turtle Hill Park (Jin Ao Shan Gongyuan) [金鳌山公园] on Chongming Island stands the **Guard the Sea Tower** (Zhenhai Ta) [镇海塔], which was first built in 1893, the 19th year of the Guangxu reign of the Qing Dynasty, and restored in 1986. It is a nine-story, windowless, octagonal pagoda with plaster walls painted red. Its appearance is quite similar to the Homeward Looking Tower on Ming Shan in Fengdu. The top floor contains a Lighthouse (Deng Ta) for giving directions to passing ships at night. Nearby stands the Tang Yicen Memorial Hall (Tang Yicen Jinian Guan) devoted to a county magistrate who died defending the island against an attack by Japanese pirates (woko) in 1554. Tang's tomb was first built here during the 33rd year of the Jiajing reign (1522-1567) of the Ming Dynasty, and later rebuilt during the Yongzheng reign (1723-1735) of the Qing Dynasty.

Address: Golden Turtle Hill Park (Jin Ao Shan Gongyuan) [金鳌山公园], Chengqiao Town, Chongming Island

14) **Zhenru Pagoda (Zhenru Fota) [真如佛塔]**

Although the Zhenru Buddhist Temple (Zhenru Si) [真如寺] associated with this pagoda has a history dating back to the Tangy Dynasty, the current pagoda only dates from 20 years ago. In September 1998 construction began on bulding a completely new Zhenru Pagoda (Zhenru Fota) [真如佛塔], which was completed on December 24, 1999 when a ceremony was held to celebrate.   The square-shaped, wooden pagoda is 51 meters tall with nine floors, and designed in a combination of Song and Yuan dynasty style.   Although it is mostly made of wood, it does have a cement framework.

Location: 399 Lanxi Lu [兰溪路 399 号], Putuo District [普陀区]

The **Park Hotel** (Guoji Dajiudian) [国际饭店]

The Park Hotel was designed by Hungarian architect **Laszlo Hudec** (1893-1958), who designed many buildings in Shanghai during his 26 years of residence in the city from 1919 to 1945.   Advertised as "the tallest building outside North America" when it first opened for business in December 1934, this 24-story Art Deco hotel was still the tallest building in all of China until the economic development of the 1980s.   The China Press carried a full page advertisement for the Park Hotel on December 1, 1937, declaring it to be, "Shanghai's tallest building."   It was also once promoted as having "the fastest elevator in Shanghai."   On May 19, 1937 two of the Song sisters, Ailing and Meiling, inaugurated long-distance telephone service between China and the U.S. when they placed a call to President Franklin D. Roosevelt from the 15th floor of the Park Hotel.   The hotel is also the official geographic center of the Shanghai municipality.

A Viewing Gallery on the 22nd floor originally offered panoramic views of the city, including the horseracing track that lay just across the street where People's Park (Renmin Gongyuan) [人民公园] now stands.   However, until March 2003 neon billboards had long covered up all four sides of the building's top four floors, including the former Gallery.   When the signs were finally removed the building's dramatically telescoping summit was revealed for the first time in years.   Decent views of the old Shanghai Race Club (Paoma Zonghui) [跑马总会] and People's Park (Renmin Gongyuan) [人民公园] can be had from the 14th floor Sky Terrace, now occupied by a family style Chinese restaurant which often hosts wedding parties.   At the time of the hotel's opening in 1934 the "Sky Terrace ballroom" was advertised as offering "dancing on the roof of Shanghai…"   The Banquet Hall on the 15th floor is the highest space open to the public.   It has spectacular views of People's Park and People's Square down below.   The 18th floor is the highest one reached by the elevator, but highest floors are occupied by luxury suites and can not be reached without a key card, so apparently there are some guestrooms are suites up there.

The hotel's interior last underwent major renovations in 1997, which resulted in a gleaming new lobby with an atrium open to the second floor mezzanine.   The Park Hotel is managed by the Jinjiang Group.

Address: 170 Nanjing Xi Lu [南京西路　170 号]
Nearest Metro Station: People's Square Station on Lines 1, 2, & 8.

People's Park (Renmin Gongyuan) [人民公园]

Just across People's Avenue (Renmin Da Dao) from the much larger People's Square, this park occupies 120,000 sq. meters and sits between the new Municipal Government building on Renmin Da Dao and Nanjing Xi Lu. This was once a part of the famous horseracing course built by the British in 1862, and it sits directly below the site of the former grandstand, which once sat atop a building that until 2012 was occupied by the Shanghai Art Museum (Shanghai Meishu Guan) [上海美术馆]. In 1952 it was opened as a public park, after all vestiges of the racetrack had been erased. In more recent years it was known for its weekly Sunday English Corner. Foreign visitors to the park should be warned that they may be highjacked as volunteer English teachers by the crowds that gather there to practice their language skills. There is also a matchmaking area where parents of unwed children post advertisements for them to find a suitable spouse. The park was closed in the year 2000 as part of the construction of a Metro Two subway station lying beneath it, but was reopened in spring 2001 with a much improved environment, including a small lake.

Phone: (021) 6327-1071
Fax: (021) 6372-5545
Nearest Metro Station: People's Square Station on Lines 1, 2, & 8.

People's Square (Renmin Guangchang) [人民广场]

People's Square occupies a 140,000 square meter area, which until 1951 formed part of the site of the city's horse racing track laid out by the British in 1861 and built in 1862 on 466 mu of former Chinese farm land. The other half of the race track was located where People's Park now stands. After 1951 People's Square was constructed as a rather barren, paved, open space intended for holding political rallies and marches. The People's Square area received a major face lift between 1993 and 1999, before taking on its current appearance. Nowadays the square bears much more resemblance to a park, with lush green grass, trees, plants, and water fountains.

Located in the center of People's Square (Renmin Guangchang) [人民广场], construction of the 39,200 sq. meter **Shanghai Museum** started in 1993 and wasn't completed until its grand opening in 1996. The building has an unusual shape of a round top over a square base, symbolizing the traditional Chinese belief that the Earth is square and the sky is round. The round top also has four handles.

Across the street on the other side of People's Avenue (Renmin Da Dao), three important new city buildings were erected between 1994 and 1999 as part of the overall redevelopment of the People's Square area. These included the 1,800-seat **Shanghai Grand Theater** (Shanghai Da Juyuan) [上海大剧院] built from 1994 to 1998, the Shanghai Municipal Government headquarters, and the **Shanghai Urban Planning Exhibition Center** [城市规划展览馆] completed in 1999. Directly underneath People's Square are several underground shopping centers with retail shops and restaurants, as well as pedestrian tunnels leading to the subway station. The square is bordered by Tibet Middle Road (Xizang Zhong Lu) to the East, Huangpi North Road (Huangpi Bei Lu) to the West, People's Avenue (Renmin Da Dao) to the North, and Yanan West Road (Yanan Xi Lu) to the South. Nearest Metro Station: People's Square Station on Lines 1, 2, & 8.

Pudong New Area (Pudong Xinqu) [浦东新区]

In 1990 the formerly deserted wasteland on the east side of the Huangpu River was selected by the local government as the home of a new economic development zone named the Pudong New Area (Pudong Xin Qu).   Within this zone were established many smaller development districts devoted to specialized economic pursuits, such as the Lujiazui Financial District, the Waigaoqiao and Jinqiao Export Processing Zones, and the Zhangjiang Hi-Tech Park (Zhangjiang Gaoke).   In one of the first steps, the **Shanghai Stock Exchange** (Shanghai Zhenquan Shichang) was moved from the old Pujiang Hotel (Pujiang Fandian) [浦江饭店] in Puxi to a new facility at 528 Pudong Nan Lu in Lujiazui. Construction of the 468-meter-high **Oriental Pearl T.V. Tower** (Dongfang Mingzhu Guangbo Dianshi Ta) [东方明珠广播电视塔] located at #1 Century Avenue (Shiji Dadao) started in 1991 and was completed in 1994.   In March 1999 the 420.5-meter-high, 88-floor **Jinmao Tower** (Jinmao Dasha) opened for business at #88 Century Avenue (Shiji Dadao) in Lujiazui.   Convention facilities were developed in the form of the **Shanghai International Convention Center**, which hosted both the 1999 Fortune 500 Forum and 2001 APEC Conference events. Tourism facilities came in the form of new hotels such as the **Shangri-La** and the **Grand Hyatt**, the latter occupying the upper 36 floors of the Jinmao Tower, thus making it the world's highest hotel at that time.   After 11 years of efforts, the **Shanghai World Financial Center** (SWFC) [上海环球金融中心] building was completed in 2008, having been under construction since 1997.   Standing at a height of 492 meters, with 101 floors, the SWFC dwarfed its next door neighbor the Jinmao Tower.   However, not wanting it to be exclusively a business area, the local government has also promoted Pudong as a good place to live, building the enormous **Century Park** (Shiji Gongyuan) covering 100 hectares of land on Jinxiu Lu in 1999, the Lujiazui Greenland, and Binjiang Park along the Huangpu River waterfront.   **Century Boulevard** (Shiji Dadao) stretches all the way from the east end of the Yanan Dong Lu tunnel to Century Park.

The success of all this development has hinged on making the East side of the Huangpu River (Pudong) easily accessible from the West side (Puxi).   Before 1990 there had never been any other way of getting across the Huangpu River except by boat.   By December 2002 there were four bridges and nine tunnels crossing the Huangpu River.   As of March 2009, seven new tunnels were under construction beneath the Huangpu River, all of which were completed by 2010.   By the year 2010 there were a total of 17 bridges and tunnels open for motor vehicle traffic to cross the Huangpu River between Puxi and Pudong. Nearest Metro Station: Lujiazui Station on Line 2.

The Shanghai Tower (Shanghai Zhongxin Dasha) [上海中心大厦]

The second tallest building in the world, and the tallest one in China, 127 floors, 632 meters/2,073 feet high.   It is so tall that it can be clearly seen with the naked eye over 30 kilometers away in Qibao Town of Minhang District.   Observation Deck on the 118th floor at 546 meters/1,791 feet.   "Shanghai Eye" on the 125th and 126th floors.   The foundation is 86 meters/282 feet deep underground.   The exterior of the building spirals upward like a snake. It twists about one degree per floor to offset the wind effect on higher altitude. The tower sports two glass facades, an inner one and an outer one.

Address: 501 Yincheng Zhong Lu, Lujiazui, Pudong New District

The Jin Mao Tower (Jinmao Dasha) [金茂大厦]

When it opened in March 1999, the Jinmao was the tallest building in China, and the third tallest building in the world.   After September 11, 2001 it was elevated in status to the world's second tallest, but has seen its ranking fall since then with the recent completion of its taller next door neighbors, the Shanghai World Financial Center and the Shanghai Tower.

Standing 420.5 meters high, it has a total of 88 floors.   The lower 50 floors are used as office space, while the upper 36 floors contain the Grand Hyatt Hotel, once considered the highest hotel in the world.   The view inside of the building looking up from the Grand Hyatt's 56th floor coffee lounge to the top is of an enormous hollow tubular atrium, rising up 33 stories, around which circle the hotel's hallways.   According to some, this atrium was inspired by the style of a Chinese pagoda.   The Grand Hyatt's swimming pool on the 57th floor was the highest swimming pool in the world when it was built.   The 88th floor houses a special Observation Deck, which can be reached by taking a special express elevator in just 45 seconds.

Since 2001 security has become extremely tight.   Special electronic pass cards must be requested at the first floor in order to board the elevator for the office tower.   However, access to the hotel floors does not have the same restrictions.   An express elevator travels from the ground floor to the hotel reception desk floor without stopping, bypassing the office floors.
Address: 88 Century Avenue (88 Shiji Dadao), Lujiazui, Pudong.
Phone: (021) 5047-5101, 5047-5002 Fax: (021) 5047-2608, 5047-5004
Nearest Metro Station: Lujiazui Station or Dongchang Road Station, both on Line 2.

The Oriental Pearl T.V. Tower
(Dongfang Mingzhu Guangbo Dianshi Ta) [东方明珠广播电视塔]

Construction started in 1991 and was completed in 1994.   It is 468 meters high, making it the tallest T.V. tower in Asia, and the third tallest in the world.   Eleven balls of different sizes are connected by an axis.   The main observation deck is 263 meters high.   However, tickets can be purchased for the first ball, second ball, or the top, at different prices, which rise the higher up you go.   It is located near the Lujiazui Metro Two Station and the Pudong exit from the Huangpu Sightseeing Tunnel.   In addition to the original restaurants, coffee shops and observation decks, from 2001 to March 2018 the tower hosted the Shanghai History Museum, which has now moved out to its new location at 325 Nanjing West Road (Nanjing Xi Lu) [南京西路] in Puxi.

Address: 1 Century Avenue (1 Shiji Dadao), Lujazui, Pudong.
Phone: (021) 5879-1888
Nearest Metro Station: Lujiazui Station on Line 2.

The Shanghai World Financial Center (Shanghai Huanqiu Jinrong Zhongxin) [上海环球金融中心]

After 11 years of stop and go efforts, the Shanghai World Financial Center (SWFC) building was finally completed in 2008, having been under construction since 1997. Standing at a height of 492 meters, with 101 floors, the SWFC became the second tallest building in the world upon its completion, overshadowing its next door neighbor the Jinmao Tower. In 2008 it contained the world's highest observation deck at a height of 474 meters on the 100th floor, as well as the world's highest five-star luxury hotel, the Park Hyatt, which occupies the 79th to 93rd floors. The building was designed by the Mori Building Co. of Japan according to their concept of a "Vertical Garden City." Most of its records for being the highest this or that have since been broken by the nearby Shanghai Tower.

Address: 100 Century Avenue (100 Shiji Dadao), Lujiazui, Pudong New Area
Nearest Metro Station: Lujiazui Station or Dongchang Road Station, both on Line 2.

Qingpu Town (Qingpu Chengqu) [青浦城区]

Qingpu Town was established in 1573 when the administrative center of Qingpu County (Qingqpu Xian) [青浦县] was moved here from its previous location in Qinglong Town.   As the capital city of Qingpu County (Qingqpu Xian) [青浦县], it was officially known as Qingpu Xiancheng [青浦县城], but colloquially could also be called Qingpu Zhen.   After Qingpu County was elevated to the status of a district, it became known officially as Qingpu Urban District (Qingpu Chengqu) [青浦城区], or colloquially as Qingpu City (Qingpu Chengshi) [青浦城市].   It may seem odd that one city could belong to another city, as Qingpu City belongs to Shanghai City, but in modern China this administrative structure has become quite common as the previous term prefecture (fu) has fallen out of use since 1949.   For example, in nearby Jiangsu province, Kunshan city belongs to Suzhou city, Danyang city belongs to Changzhou city, Jiangyin city belongs to Wuxi city, and Gaoyou city belongs to Yangzhou city.   Nonetheless, since these suburban district capital cities still look and feel more like small towns than cities I think I will continue to use the term town as more appropriate.

Qingpu Town was once surrounded by a circular city wall (chengqiang).   The city wall and its gates are long gone, but street names remain to commemorate where they were, and the circular city moat (huchenghe)[护城河] is still completely intact.   Just within the circular moat a ring road known as Huancheng Lu (literally "around the city road") follows roughly the same route as the city wall once did.   During the Taiping Rebellion (1850-1864), Qingpu Town changed hands countless times between 1860 and 1862.   In June 1862 Frederick Townsend Ward had the entire town burned to the ground in order to prevent the Taipings from using it as a base.   Qingpu Town was liberated by the Red Army on May 14, 1949.

In order to get in or out of town, you still must cross a bridge over the former city moat (huchenghe)[护城河], which is now connected to a network of canals used by fleets of barges transporting various goods.   A stroll along the tree-lined ring **East Ring Road** (Huancheng Dong Lu**)** which runs beside the southern half of the moat makes for a pleasant walk and provides views of the Qing Dynasty **Longevity Pagoda** (Wanshou Ta) [万寿塔] on the other side.

On the north side of Park Road (Gongyuan Lu), just after crossing the city moat, stands the **Garden of Zigzag Water** (Qushui Yuan) [曲水园], and the former **Qingpu City God Temple** (Qingpu Chenghuang Miao) [青浦城隍庙] to which it was once attached.   On the West side of the Qingpu City God Temple (Qingpu Chenghuang Miao) [青浦城隍庙], the old residential neighborhood has completely disappeared and been replaced by a Yu Yuan Bazaar type pedestrian mall, featuring many resaurants, including a Pizza Hut, as well as brand name clothing stores you would find in any shopping mall in downtown Shanghai.   The pedestrian mall runs all along the West side of the City God Temple and Garden of Zigzag Water (Qushui Yuan), clear to the North side of the round city moat.   A new **Qingpu District Museum** (Qingpu Bowuguan) [青浦博物馆] opened in 2004 in a brand new facility in a very modern science-fiction kind of building outside the old walled city in the east end of the new town at 1000 Huaqing South Road (Huaqing Nan Lu).   The museum features a scale model of the old Qingpu City Wall.

The half of the town located south of Park Road (Gongyuan Lu) [公园路] seems to have preserved more historic houses than the much more modern northern half.   The most picturesque street is probably **Juxing Jie**, a narrow lane that runs from Park Road (Gongyuan Lu) [公园路] in the center of town all the way to the Ring Road (Huan Cheng Lu) and the southern half of the city moat.   Some of the streets and lanes are still named after the city gates that once stood there, such as **South Gate Lane** (Nan Men Jie) and **Big West Gate Street** (Da Xi Men Lu).   Across the city moat from the site of the former South Gate (Nan Men), one can see the **Longevity Pagoda** (Wanshou Ta) [万寿塔].

Qingpu Town is located just off of the Huqingping Highway, on the way to **Zhujiajiao Ancient Town** [朱家角古镇], **Dianshan Lake** (Dianshan Hu) [淀山湖], the **Grand View Garden** (Da Guan Yuan) [大观园],   and the even further **Jinze Ancient Town** [金泽古镇]. It's also on the way to Qinglong Village, the site of the Tang Dynasty **Green Dragon Pagoda** (Qinglong Ta) [青龙塔] and **Green Dragon Buddhist Temple** (Qinglong Si), in Baihe Town [白鹤镇].   There is a long-distance bus station in Qingpu Town where you can catch buses headed back to downtown Shanghai at the intersection of Park Road (Gongyuan Lu) and the Waiqingsong Highway.   Be aware that much like Shanghai's other suburban districts, Qingpu District has its own fleet of taxis with distinct markings that are not allowed to leave the district or drive into the city center.   After three years of construction that started in 2014, at the end of Decemer 2017 Qingpu Town was finally connected to the Shanghai subway system by Line 17, which runs for 35 kilometers (22 miles) from Hongqiao Railway Station [虹桥火车站] in Minhang District, through Xujing Town [徐泾镇], Qingpu Town, and Zhujiajiao Ancient Town [朱家角古镇], all the way out to Oriental Green Boat (Dongfang Luzhou) [东方绿舟], a large amusement park covering 56 square kilometers (21 square miles) that opened in the year 2000 on the Huqingping Highway and on the shores of Dianshan Lake [淀山湖].   You could choose to stay overnight in Qingpu Town at the Qingpu Hotel (Qingpu Binguan), located at the intersection of Park Road (Gongyuan Lu) and Chengzhong Bei Lu at the heart of the old walled city.

Address: Huqingping Highway, Qingpu Town, Qingpu District (Qingpu Qu).

The **Garden of Zigzag Water** (Qushui Yuan) [曲水园]

The **Garden of Zigzag Water** (Qushui Yuan) [曲水园] is a Qing Dynasty garden constructed in 1745, the 10th year of the reign of Emperor Qianlong.   The garden was originally named the **Ling Yuan** [灵园], and was attached to the Qingpu City God Temple (Qingpu Chenghuang Miao) [青浦城隍庙], which still stands next door but is now separated from it by a high wall.   The name was changed from Ling Yuan [灵园] to the present Qushui Yuan [曲水园] in 1798, the 3rd year of the Jiaqing reign of the Qing Dynasty.   During the Taiping Rebellion the original garden was completely destroyed in 1860, the 3rd year of the Xianfeng reign of the Qing Dynasty.   After the Taiping rebels had been defeated, the Garden of Zigzag Water (Qushui Yuan) [曲水园] was rebuilt using private contributions to the Qingpu City God Temple (Qingpu Chenghuang Miao) [青浦城隍庙].   In 1927, the 16th year of the Republican era (Minguo) [民国] (1911-1949), the Garden of Zigzag Water (Qushui Yuan) [曲水园] was renamed as Zhongshan Park (Zhongshan Gongyuan) [中山公园] in honor of the Republic's first president, Sun Yat-sen (Sun Zhongshan) [孙中山] (1866-1925).   However, most of this Minguo [民国] park was in turn destroyed during the Sino-Japanese War (1937-1945).   After the 1949 Revolution the park was rebuilt again in the 1950s.

It is located on the North side of Park Road (Gongyuan Lu) [公园路], just after it crosses a bridge over the city moat.   The northern and eastern boundary of the garden follows the curving line of the city moat (huchenghe) [护城河], and a traditional covered wooden roof corridor which runs along the water's edge makes for a pleasant walk.   The garden has two lakes, a tea house, and a three-story square tower on top of a small hill.   The lakeside pavilions tend to be full of the town's older residents, chatting and playing cards.   Although not an unpleasant place to visit, it pales in comparison to other gardens in Shanghai, such as the Garden of Autumn Clouds (Qiuxiapu) [秋霞圃] in Jiading Town and the Drunken Poet Bai's Garden (Zuibaichi Yuan) [醉白池园] in Songjiang Town.

When I revisited it five years later in June 2008, the Garden of Zigzag Water (Qushui Yuan) [曲水园] had clearly gone through a significant renovation, which it actually needed, and now it looks much better than before.   Tickets were still only 5 Rmb.   A new inscribed stone tablet (shi bei) outside it is dated May 2001, but the reconstruction undoubtedly happened after that.

You can find more information about the Garden of Zigzag Water (Qushui Yuan) [曲水园] under the letter G in the section of this book on Gardens.

Address: 650 Park Road (650 Gongyuan Lu) [公园路650号], Qingpu Town, Qingpu District (Qingpu Qu).
Phone: (021) 5973-2996, (021) 5972-8861

Qingpu City God Temple (Qingpu Chenghuang Miao) [青浦城隍庙]

Qingpu Town's former City God Temple (Qingpu Chenghuang Miao) [青浦城隍庙] stands right beside the Garden of Zigzag Water (Qu Shui Yuan), only separated from it by a wall. Although next door, its entrance gate is actually a few yards back from the main street of Park Road (Gongyuan Lu) and can be reached by several narrow lanes, including Miao Qian Lu , "the road in front of the temple," and Juxing Jie.

The Qingpu City God Temple was founded in 1573, rebuilt in 1745, but mostly destroyed during the Taiping Rebellion, rebuilt again in 1895, later became the Qingpu County Museum [青浦县博物馆], until finally on December 28, 2005 a restoration project was completed and it was reopened once again as the Qingpu City God Temple.   After moving out of the Qingpu City God Temple, a new **Qingpu District Museum** (Qingpu Bowuguan) [青浦博物馆] opened in 2004 at 1000 Huaqing South Road (Huaqing Nan Lu).   The museum features a scale model of the old Qingpu City Wall.

When I first visited it in 2003, it was no longer a functioning temple, and there were no signs of active religious worship here.   Instead, the former temple had been converted into the Qingpu Museum (Qingpu Bowuguan).   Unfortunately, although the museum's offices were staffed with employees working here, there were no exhibits then open to the public and not much had been done to organize the few relics they had on hand.

The arched entrance gate passed through the first floor of the first two-story hall leading you into a courtyard lined with side halls on both sides and the main halls straight ahead.   The main two-story halls seemed to be concrete reconstructions dating from sometime after 1949.   Since the main halls were currently closed, and seemed to be empty anyway, the main asset they then possessed was to offer a birds' eye view of the neighboring Garden of Zig Zag Waer (Qu Shui Yuan) from their second floor balconies.   It's up here on the second floor that you would also find the offices of the museum staff, who did seem fairly willing to answer questions about local history.

If you looked closely around the courtyard, you could find a three-piece iron canon laying on the ground.   Several stone tablets also leaned up against the inner walls of the entrance gate house.   Peering through the windows of the closed side halls, piles of moldering old books and mothballed exhibits including a scale model of the old walled city were partly visible.   It was clear then that if the few items available were organized and displayed better this place might be worth a visit.

When I returned in June 2008, the Qingpu City God Temple (Qingpu Chenghuang Miao) [青浦城隍庙] had been completely rebuilt.   When I had first seen it 5 years earlier it had been an abandoned ruin, used as office space by district officials, and once had been the town museum.   A bridge crosses a small moat running along the South side of the temple and the garden next door.   Now it clearly looks like a temple once again, with three main halls on a central axis all inside a walled compound.   Unfortunately it was closed when I arrived because it was past 4:30 p.m.   A new plaque outside is also dated May 2001, but the reconstruction actually happened after that.

Address: 650 Gongyuan Lu, Qingpu Town, Qingpu District (Qingpu Qu).
Phone: (021) 5972-8441, (021) 5973-2341

The Qingpu South Gate Old Town (Nan Men)

When I first visited in 2003, the narrow lane of Juxing Jie was lined with old two-story wooden houses and was home to a flourishing street market of vendors selling all manner of items.   The lane was not wide enough for motor vehicles, which limited its use to pedestrians and the occasional motorcycle.   It was a real street market intended for the local residents, and not one simply designed for tourists.   It ran from Gongyuan Lu in the center of town all the way to the East Ring Road (Huancheng Dong Lu) and the southern half of the city moat (huchenghe).   About halfway down the length of the lane, after it had crossed Chengzhong Dong Lu, you could hear the sounds of worshippers singing at a makeshift Buddhist temple set up in a house to the right of the lane.   There was no sign outside, and the interior decorations were quite simple, but the faith of the worshippers was impressive.   Sitting in long rows of wooden benches, they sang in chorus praises to "E-mi-tuo-fo," while focusing on looking at very simple Buddhist ornaments in the front of the room.   It seemed to be run entirely by the worshippers themselves without the aid of any professional monks.

Back on the main lane, the name changed imperceptibly somewhere along the way to South Gate Late (Nan Men Jie**)** by the time you reached the city moat (huchenghe), thus revealing that this was once where the city's South Gate (Nan Men) once stood.   Emerging from the lane onto the East Ring Road (Huancheng Dong Lu) and the city moat (huchenghe), you found that this was where the fleets of canal barges tied up for the night, giving you an opportunity to see up close what life is like for the people who lived on these boats.   These boat dwellers were some of the thousands of *Shui Shang Ren Jia* who lived on board an estimated 1,224 unlicensed house boats moored on the inland waterways of the Shanghai municipality.   Best of all, from this spot you could catch some incredible views and camera angles of the impressive **Longevity Pagoda** (Wanshou Ta), which today still stands across the moat on the other side, albeit now in a greatly restored state due to its 2009 reconstruction.

When I revisited this area in 2008 after an absence of five years I found the most disturbing changes were happening along the three connected old outdoor market streets of Juxing Jie, Matou Jie, and Nan Men Jie, which despite their three names form one continuous lane running from the old town center to the South city moat.   Juxing Jie was still an outdoor shopping street, but featured more mass-produced items than the local arts and crafts it had before.   After crossing the next East-West main street, I noticed for the first time that the lane name changed to Matou Jie.   Matou means boat dock in Chinese.   Clearly this road once led to the town's main boat dock at the South city moat, which is connected to the region's maze of canals.   About halfway to the South city moat, the lane's name changes yet again to Nan Men Jie, meaning South Gate Street, further evidence that the South City Gate once stood where this lane connects with the East Ring Road (Huancheng Dong Lu) running along the South city moat.   The sad part was that most of the old houses along Matou Jie and Nan Men Jie were in the process of being torn down.   Some of these houses were worthy of being called mansions, two stories high, built of stone blocks, with corner stone inscriptions, and in one case a high tower with a captain's landing.   Since this was the main lane leading to the South City Gate and the Boat Dock, it seems possible that this was once the main street, and a place where the local wealthy merchants lived.   Many simpler wooden frame houses were in a state of half-collapse, their wooden log frames exposed to public view like a skeleton.   In fact, Nan Men Jie disappeared into an open overgrown grassy field for about the last third of its route to the East Ring Road (Huancheng Dong Lu).

Strangely, when I revisited the area again in 2017 not much had changed. There were still large open, overgrown areas, empty lots, where buildings had once stood when I first visited 15 years ago in 2003, but at least a half dozen of the largest, most impressive, historic houses were also still standing. The neighborhood Buddhist temple and barber shop were still functioning, but most of the hair salons had shut down or disappeared.

Longevity Pagoda (Wanshou Ta) [万寿塔]
This is described under the letter P in the section on Pagodas.

Qingpu District Government
100 Gongyuan Lu
(021) 5973-2890

Qingpu Town Government
4530 Huqingping Highway
(021) 5971-0420

Other Sights in Qingpu District

If you've already made it as far as Qingpu Town, other sights you could visit in the rest of Qingpu District outside the town would include the Longevity Pagoda (Wanshou Ta) [万寿塔], Qinglong Pagoda (Qinglong Ta) [青龙塔] and Qinglong Buddhist Temple (Qinglong Si) in Baihe Town (Baihe Zhen)[白鹤镇], Mao Ta Pagoda, Zhujiajiao Ancient Town (Zhujiajiao Guzhen) [朱家角古镇], Jinze Ancient Town (Jinze Guzhen) [金泽古镇], and Grand View Garden (Da Guan Yuan) [大观园] on the shore of Dianshan Lake (Dianshan Hu) [淀山湖]. These sights are described in detail in other alphabetically organized sections of this book.

The **Shanghai Concert Hall** (Shanghai Yinyue Ting) [上海音乐厅]

Formerly known as the **Nanking Theater** when it was built in 1930, the architecture features a row of Greco-Roman columns along the front entrance.   Before 1949 this was where Hollywood movies such as Tarzan had their China premier.   After 1949 the name was changed to the more politically correct Peking Theater, and then later adopted it present name in 1959. In recent years the theater has been the concert hall for the **Shanghai Symphony Orchestra**.   Its original location was at the corner of Yanan Dong Lu and Longmen Lu.   However, in July 2002 plans were announced to move the entire 5,650-ton building as part of the construction of the new Yan Zhong green belt around People's Square. The move had been completed by June 18, 2003, with the new location 66.4 meters southeast of the original site, in the middle of the new park between Jinling Zhong Lu and Ninghai Xi Lu.   The new open space of this surrounding park now provides unobstructed views of several other historic buildings nearby, including the Great World (Dashijie) and the YMCA Hotel (Qingnian Hui Binguan) [青年会宾馆] built in 1931 on Tibet South Road (Xizang Nan Lu).

The now heavily restored hall has a deceptively new appearance, and the original structure has in fact been enlarged to four times its previous size, including a two-meter extension of the auditorium's rear wall.   A set of 24 huge springs have been installed under the ground floor to insulate the hall from vibrations caused by the underground subway line that runs beneath it.   Despite the changes, efforts have been made to maintain the building's interior design.   During the restoration it was discovered that the original color scheme had been blue and gold, so the interior has been newly decorated in these same colors.   The thin sheets of real gold used as a layer over the ceiling cost 300,000 Rmb alone.   The hall will be celebrating its 75th anniversary in 2005.

Address: 523 Yanan Dong Lu [延安东路 523 号]
Phone: (021) 6386-9153
Nearest Metro Station: Peoples Square Station on Lines 1, 2, & 8.

Shanghai Municipal Council Headquarters

(Gonggong Zujie Gongbu Ju) [公共租界工部局]

The former headquarters building of the International Settlement's Municipal Council built in 1922 still stands on an entire city block bounded by Hankou Lu to the North, Jiangxi Zhong Lu to the East, and Fuzhou Lu to the South.   This council had been established in 1854 as the self-governing body for the British settlement, and after 1863 it continued to govern the newly merged International Settlement.   The Shanghai Municipal Council delegated to itself the powers of taxation, and with this revenue financed a police force, jails, hospitals, public works department responsible for building and maintaining roads and bridges, education department in charge of municipal schools, and a fire brigade.   This headquarters building formally opened in November 1922, after eight years of construction.   In addition to containing 400 offices for all the city bureaucracy, it quartered the local foreign militia known as the Shanghai Volunteer Corps.

After the International Settlement was abolished by a treaty with Britain in 1943, when the Guomindang returned to Shanghai from Chongqing in 1945 and began administering Shanghai's downtown core for the first time they made this building their new municipal government headquarters, replacing the earlier one in Jiangwan Town (Jiangwan Zhen) [江湾镇].   On the night before the city fell to the Communists on May 24th 1949, observers saw trucks being loaded with cases of documents and driven away to the airport, which was still open.   Later, some of these documents, including the old S.M.C. police files, ended up in the U.S. National Archives and Library of Congress.

The Communists also made this proud trophy their first municipal government headquarters, and it was from here that the city's fist Communist mayor General Chen Yi directed Shanghai's six year transition from capitalism to communism.   In 1955 the Shanghai People's Municipal Government moved their offices to the even more impressive trophy of the Hong Kong and Shanghai Bank (Xianggang Shanghai Huifeng Yinhang) [香港上海汇丰银行] building on the Bund (Waitan).

Nowadays, the former Shanghai Municipal Council building is still home to the Municipal Administration Engineering Office (Shizheng Gongcheng Ju) [市政工程局], and until recently still housed the Civil Affairs Bureau.

Inside the northeastern main entrance facing Hankou Lu, the first and second floor lobbies contain a photo exhibition of historic black and white pictures with English captions.   In addition to portraits of Chen Yi, one finds surprising testaments to the building's pre-1949 history.   One portrait proudly displayed on the second floor shows the entire membership of the Shanghai Municipal Council posing for a photo in 1936.   Although several of the members depicted are Chinese, obviously the majority are British and American.   The picture hangs on a wall near where it was taken, but the inscriptions on the marble wall monument have obviously been changed since then.

Address: 215 Hankou Lu and Jiangxi Zhong Lu.
Nearest Metro Station: Nanjing East Road (Nanjing Dong Lu) [南京东路]
Station on Line 2.

R

The **Race Club Building** (Paoma Zonghui) [跑马总会]

This historic old building was originally built in 1934 as the Shanghai Race Club (Paoma Zonghui) [跑马总会], on the same site as the previous horse racing club first constructed by the British in 1863.   Grandstands once provided a bird's eye view of the horse races held on the oval track where People's Park (Renmin Gongyuan) [人民公园] is now.   From grandstands up on the roof, fans once watched the horse races held on the large race track in the area down below, which is now People's Park (Renmin Gongyuan) [人民公园] and People's Square (Renmin Guangchang) [人民广场]

Later the building served as the Shanghai Library (Shanghai Tushuguan) [上海图书馆] from 1953 to 1996, when it moved to its current facility on Huaihai Road, then housed the Shanghai Art Museum (Shanghai Meishuguan) [上海美术馆] until it moved out in October 2012.   Most recently, after two years of renovation that had started in 2015, in March 2018 the Shanghai Municipal History Museum moved in.

The fascinating Race Club building is immediately noticeable for its trademark clock tower. If one looks closely at the outside and inside one can still find many emblems with the insignia SRC, standing for Shanghai Race Club.

Outside the north entrance, two original corner stones are still intact on both sides of the doorway.   According to an inscription on the left side, the foundation stone was laid on May 20, 1933 by Mrs. Katharine Burkill.   The inscription on the right lists all the race club officers by name, including the chairman, treasurer, and "clerk of the course," as well as the architects and engineers responsible for building the structure.

Inside, the main staircase is decorated with iron railings in the shapes of horses' heads, with their main's blowing in the wind.   Old black and white photographs of the horse racing course and grand stands hang on the walls of the stair well.   In the front stair well on the third floor there is even a bronze "Roll of Honour," which seems to be a European war monument devoted to those Shanghailanders who died in World War I.   28 individuals are listed by their full name and military rank.

In 2004 a new restaurant was added to the roof top of this building, on the same spot where this author was apprehended by uniformed police for taking photographs in 2002. **Kathleen's Five Restaurant** was owned by That's Shanghai magazine co-founder Kathleen Lau.   Its roof top location offered excellent views of the city, especially People's Park (Renmin Gongyuan) [人民公园], Nanjing West Road (Nanjing Xi Lu) [南京西路], and People's Square (Renmin Guangchang)[人民广场].   You could choose to sit outside on open-air deck or inside a glass covered atrium space.   However, it's now been replaced with a new fifth floor restaurant known as Roof 325.

Address: 325 Nanjing West Road (Nanjing Xi Lu) [南京西路].
Nearest Metro Station: People's Square Station on Lines 1, 2, & 8.

S

Sheshan Hill [佘山]

Sheshan National Forest Park (Sheshan Guojia Senlin Gongyuan) [佘山国家森林公园] is located in Songjiang District, 26 kilometers southwest of Hongqiao Airport and 38 kilometers from People's Square in downtown Shanghai. It has two main peaks, separated by a highay in a valley in between, known as the West Peak (Xi Sheshan) [西佘山] and the East Peak (Dong Sheshan) [东佘山], although there are a total of eight or nine hills in the immediate area. The national park was first approved by the Forestry Ministry in June 1993, but it did not officially open until the end of 1998.

The West Peak (Xi Sheshan) [西佘山] is by far the more interesting of the two, as it is here that most of the historic sights are located, including the Sheshan Observatory, Sheshan Cathedral, the Pilgrim's Trail, the Middle Church, and the octagonal, seven story, 20 meter high, Buddhist Pagoda Xiudaozhe Ta on the southeast slope built of brick and wood in the Northern Song Dynasty Taiping Xingguo reign [北宋太平兴国], among others. With an elevation of 97 meters above sea level, the West Peak (Xi Sheshan) [西佘山] has often been considered to be the highest hill in Shanghai, but actually the highest one is Tianma Shan, located about 7 kilometers away, which measures just slightly higher at 99.5 meters in height.

Some people subdivide the park into four main sections; East Sheshan Park (Dong Sheshan Yuan) [东佘山园], West Sheshan Park (Xi Sheshan Yuan) [西佘山园], Heavenly Horse Hill Park (Tianma Shan Yuan) [天马山园], and Little Kunshan Park (Xiao Kunshan Yuan) [小昆山园]. Officially, the boundaries of Sheshan National Forest Park contain 12 hills within a nine kilometer radius, including Heavenly Horse Hill (Tianma Shan) [天马山], Phoenix Hill (Fenghuang Shan) [凤凰山], Hengyun Shan [横云山], Little Kunshan Hill (Xiao Kunshan) [小昆山], Xiaoji Shan [小机山], Zhongjia Shan [钟贾山], Chen Shan [辰山], Xue Shan [薛山]、 Shegong Shan [厍公山]、 and Beigan Shan [北竿山]. However, in reality most people consider Heavenly Horse Hill (Tianma Shan) [天马山] to be a separate destination, and in fact it does usually have far fewer visitors due to its more isolated location. As such, you can find a detailed description of it in its separate entry under the letter T. For practical purposes, most people consider Sheshan to only be the two West and East peaks already mentioned.

The beauty of Sheshan's natural surroundings is impressive, with its network of canals, their glistening water, everywhere bisecting the flat, open fields, criss-crossed by bridges. The trail around the base of the southern slope passes through a bamboo forest and past repeated examples of old red brick vaulted chambers with openings protruding from the hillside. These chambers usually appear in sets of three and appear to have once been tombs, although they are all open now.

The part of the park incorporating Sheshan West Peak (Xi Sheshan) [西佘山] has three main entrance gates. The main entrance from Waiqingsong Gonglu [外青松公路] is actually the **North Gate** (Bei Da Men), and requires the longest walk to reach the historic sights on the summit and the south slope, although it also allows you to see the Buddhist Pagoda that most people otherwise miss. In December 2018 this gate was closed for repairs. As of 2018, there is also now a new **East Gate** (Dong Da Men) that enters the park from Waiqingsong Gonglu [外青松公路] before the road enters the pass between the two peaks.   The trail from here is fairly steep and leads up to the site of the Buddhist Pagoda. Alternatively, you could enter the park through either the **South Gate** (Nan Da Men) or the **Pilgrims' Gate** (Jiaoyou Men) [教友门] at the southern foot of the hill on the Mountain Ring Road (Huanshan Lu) [环山路].   This is the shortest route on foot and allows you to follow the Pilgrim's Trail past all the Roman Catholic sights along the south slope directly up to the summit.   If you have your own car, you could also drive all the way to the summit on a narrow, winding mountain dirt road paved with stone slabs that begins at the **West Gate** (Xi Da Men), or hike in that way.   The road follows the most gradual ascent and descent.   If you're driving up the road, you should be aware that there are two turnoffs onto branch roads, one going to the new Astronomical Observatory (Tianwen Tai), which is closed to the public, and a second going to a spot just below the Catholic Cathedral.   Be sure to park your car in the parking lot at the entrance to the Asronomical Observatory Museum (Tianwen Tai Bowuguan).

If you want to stay overnight there, your best choice in terms of price and location is the three-star Shanghai Sheshan **Forest Hotel** (Shanghai Sheshan Senlin Binguan) [上海佘山森林宾馆] located on the Waiqingsong Gonglu [外青松公路] highway right in the narrow gap between Sheshan's East and West Peaks [http://www.shforesthotel.com/].   The much more modern, but somewhat misleadingly named Sofitel Sheshan Hotel opened in 2009. However, despite the name it is actually located nowhere near the mountain, so don't be deceived.

Since 2008 it's been possible to get relatively close to Sheshan by taking Line 9 of the subway system, but the nearest station is still not within walking distance of the mountain, so you'll still need to transfer to a local taxi.   Ironically, Dongjing Station [洞泾站] is the closest one to the mountain, not the incorrectly named Sheshan Station [佘山站], so don't be fooled again.

Address: Sheshan National Forest Park (Sheshan Guojia Senlin Gongyuan) [佘山国家森林公园], 9258 Waiqingsong Gonglu [外青松公路 9258 号],   Songjiang District
Phone: (021) 5765-1609, (021) 5765-1651, (021) 5765-1521
Nearest Metro Station: Dongjing Station on Line 9 (Ditie Jiu hao Dongjing Zhan) [地铁 9 号洞泾站].
Tickets: It used to cost 30 Rmb to enter the Sheshan West Peak area (Xi Sheshan), but it was free in 2009, and it has always been free if you enter by the Pilgrims' Gate at the southern foot of the mountain on the Mountain Ring Road (Huanshan Lu) [环山路].

Sheshan Observatory (Sheshan Tianwentai) [佘山天文台]

Beside the Sheshan Cathedral on the west peak of Sheshan (Xi Sheshan) [西佘山] stands a collection of late Qing Dynasty buildings that once belonged to the Sheshan Astronomical Observatory (Sheshan Tianwentai) [佘山天文台], established in 1900 by the same French Jesuits who also operated the Meteorological Observatory set up in Xujiahui in 1872. Its first director was French missionary Stanislaus Chevalier, known in Chinese as Cai Shangzhi.

A separate Geomagnetic Observatory originally established at Xujiahui [徐家汇] in 1874 was moved from Lujiabang to Sheshan mountain out in Songjiang District in 1932. It published a total of 105 volumes of geomagnetic reports, including 76 volumes published from 1932 to 1999.

The former Geomagnetic Observatory is the first hall visitor's see, and now houses exhibits devoted to the history of time keeping and calendars in China. It includes photographs and models of various time devices dating back to the Han Dynasty, such as water clocks (aka clepsydra), prismatic astrolabes, pendulum clocks, quartz clocks, global-positioning-system (GPS) clocks, and atomic clocks. From 1951 to 1981 the Sheshan Astronomical Observatory was responsible for providing the standard clock-time for all China, despite the standard being officially called "Beijing time." In 1981 this responsibility was shited to another observatory in Shaanxi province.

Walking along an outdoor terrace from the first exhibition hall to the observatory's main building some ancient astronomical instruments such as armillary spheres, celestial globes and sun dials can be seen on display.

Inside the main building of the old Sheshan Observatory there is now an Astronomical Museum established in 2004. Exhibits on the first and second floors cover the history of astronomy in China, including pictures of Xu Guangqi and Matteo Ricci, as well as Ming Dynasty astronomical instruments in Beijing and at the Zijin Shan Observatory in Nanjing. There is a copy of the 137 volume calendar created by Xu Guangqi for the Chongzhen emperor in 1634. Other exhibits of old black and white photos document the construction of the Sheshan Observatory in 1900.

On the third floor of the Observatory, halfway up the steps to the roof, you can see the gigantic double astrograph refracting telescope imported from France by Stanislaus Chevalier at a cost of 100,000 French Francs in1900. The telescope has an aperture of 40 cm, a focal length of 7 m, and weighs over three tons. At the time of its installation in 1900 it was the largest telescope in all of East Asia. It has a large armchair for the observer to sit in which can be raised up and down on a vertical track using push button controls. The telescope is under a giant retractable metal dome with a slit that can open to view the night sky above. It is equipped with a camera that can take pictures of the night stars, and photographed Haley's Comet in both 1910 and 1986. It also took the first photos in China of a solar eclipse on January 14, 1907

From the third floor you can continue climbing up flights of wooden steps to the outdoor promenade on top consisting of a narrow walkway encircling the observatory dome. It has a bird's eye view of the Sheshan Cathedral next door.

The historic buildings of the former observatory are now operated as a museum known as the Sheshan Astronomical Observatory Museum (Sheshan Tianwen Tai Bowuguan) [佘山天文台博物馆], for which you must buy a separate admissions ticket at the parking lot down below. As of December 2018 the price of a ticket was 12 Rmb. Note that the ticket seller goes to lunch at 11:30 a.m., and after that ticket sales halt for an hour until she finishes eating.   Try to time your arrival accordingly, otherwise you'll be locked out for up to an hour while you sit around waiting to get in.

In the 1980s a new Sheshan Astronomical Observatory was built, equipped with a 25m radio telescope, a 1.56m optical telescope; and a 60cm satellite laser-ranging system.   This newer observatory is still in use today, but is not open to the public.   You can see views of it down below from the end of the side road leading to the cathedral.

Sheshan Roman Catholic Cathedral (Sheshan Tianzhu Jiaotang) [佘山天主教堂]

French Roman Catholic Jesuit (Yesuhui) [耶酥会] missionaries first started coming to Sheshan in 1863, when they built five small houses and one Small Church (Xiao Tang) [小堂] on the southern slope (nanpo) and began using part of the mountain as a holiday resort. They also built a small hexagonal pavilion on the summit of the mountain containing a statue of the Virgin Mary (Sheng Mu) [圣母].   At that time they referred to the place as Zo-Se, rather than the current name of Sheshan.   A comparatively Big Church (Da Tang) [大堂] was constructed here by the missionaries from 1870 to 1873, to give thanks to the Virgin Mary for supposedly protecting the Catholics in Shanghai from the effects of the June 1870 Tianjin Massacre (Tianjin Jiao'an) [天津教案].   In 1894 the missionaries added a Middle Church (Zhong Tang) [中堂] at a spot halfway up the mountain (ban shan shang) [半山上]. In front of this Middle Church (Zhong Tang) [中堂] they built a Virgin Mary Pavilion (Shengmu Ting) [圣母亭], Sacred Heart Pavilion (Shengxin Ting) [圣心亭], and a St. Joseph Pavilion (Ruose Ting) [若瑟亭].   A mountain trail (dengshan lushang) [登山路上] with 14 "road of suffering" pavilions (kulu ting) [苦路亭] representing the 14 Stations of the Cross modeled on the Via Dolorosa was also built from here to the summit of the mountain.

Ever since then every year on May 24th there has been a pilgrimage (chaosheng) [朝圣] by followers up the mountain trail to the summit, which has become a sort of holy land (sheng di) [圣地] for Roman Catholics.   The annual pilgrimages had actually started even earlier in 1874 with encouragement from Pope Pius IX.   Visitors used to come here all the way from the French Roman Catholic community of Xujiahui [徐家汇] by boat along the network of rivers and canals that connected Songjiang with Xuhui District.

As the number of Roman Catholic converts in Shanghai grew to an estimated 10,000 peoplein the early 20th Century, the previous churches on Sheshan became too small, and it was decided to build a larger New Church (Xin Tang) [新堂] right on the highest summit (shanding) [山顶] at the very top of the mountain's west peak.   On April 24, 1925 a groundbreaking ceremony was held for the New Church.   The entire project ended up taking ten years before it was completed in November 1935.   The stone, timber, bricks, marble, ceramic tiles, and concrete used in the construction were all transported to the foot of Sheshan by boat, and then carried to the summit on the shoulders of the Chinese workers. The resulting Sheshan Cathedral, then formally known as the **Basilica Minor of St. Mary** (Sheshan Shengmu Tianzhutang) [佘山圣母天主堂], had a cross-shape that measured 56 meters long from east to west, 25-35 meters wide from south to north.   The interior ceiling was 17 meters high, while the exterior roof spine reached 22 meters high, but the square-shaped Bell Tower (Zhong Lou) [钟楼] topped by a dome stood 38 meters tall in the southwest corner. 16 pillars supported the vaulted ceiling on the inside.   The whole cathedral had stained glass windows (caise boli chuang) all around.   The interior could seat 3,000-4,000 people.   The main entrance was at the southwest corner, while at the back was a semicircular (banyuanxing) extension.   On top of the Bell Tower (Zhong Lou) [钟楼] dome stood a 4.8 meter tall copper statue of the Virgin Mary (Shengmu) [圣母] holding the baby Jesus (Xiao Yesu) [小耶酥] that weighed 1,800 kilograms.   The exterior walls were red brick, while the inside was granite, and the altar was made of marble.   The building covered 1,400 sq. meters.   The architectural style incorporated elements of Greek, Roman, Middle Eastern, Gothic, and Spanish architecture.

During the Cultural Revolution (1966-1976) the Cathedral was closed and suffered severe damage at the hands of Red Guards.   All of its stained glass windows were destroyed.   The statue of the Virgin Mary on top of the Bell Tower was removed and destroyed.   The annual pilgrimages were halted for more than 15 years from 1966 until they were resumed in May 1983.

In 1981 the Cathedral was returned to the Roman Catholic diocese of Shanghai, but repairing the damage and restoring it to its original condition have been a continuing process ever since.   The initial repairs lasted for two years from 1982 to 1984.   In the year 2000 a new copper statue of the Virgin Mary holding the baby Jesus was installed on top of the Bell Tower to replace the one that had been removed and destroyed.   Only a few of the stained glass windows have been replaced so far.

Despite its official reopening, the cathedral has always kept peculiar, limited hours of operation.   Although I have visited the mountain countless times between 1999 and 2018, there has only been one single time when I found the compound's metal gates open, and was able to actually go inside the cathedral building.   Every other time I have visited the metal gates of the cathedral's fenced in compound have been padlocked shut.   On my December 2018 visit I found the gates once again locked shut.   While I was hanging around, the warden briefly opened them to let in some construction workers and I tried to sneak in with them but he caught me and told me to stay out.   Apparently it is undergoing yet another round of renovation work.   Chinese language signs that refer to the cathedral simply as the **Summit Big Hall** (Shanding Dadian) [山顶大殿] state that it closed for renovations on September 1st 2018 and is expected to reopen sometime in 2019.

The pilgrims trail to the cathedral starts at a stone gate with six pillars and five portals known as the Church Members' Gate or **Pilgrims' Gate** (Jiaoyou Men) [教友门]] located at #3 Mountain Ring Road (Huanshan Lu 3 hao) [环山路 3], at the southern foot of the hill, near the modern **South Gate** (Nan Da Men), and right beside the separate compound of the so-called **Earthquake Platform** (Dizhen Tai) [地震台].   The gate has a horizontal four-chacter inscription that reads from left to right "*You Zhi Jiao Jing*" [友之教迳], which could be translated as "church member's path."   The fact that the inscription reads left to right indicates that it does not date from before 1949, when Chinese characters were instead written from right to left.   Besides the one stone block bearing this inscription, most of the gate's stone framework does appear as if it could date from before 1949, but there is a white statue of an angel now standing atop the center of the gate which seems to be a new addition that I don't recall seeing prior to my December 2018 visit.   The remains of the canal on which pilgrims used to approach the site by boat can still be seen across the street from the gate, but no longer seems to be in use by any sort of water transport.

The trail ascends upward on flights of stone steps through forests, past a back gate entrance into the so-called **Earthquake Platform** (Dizhen Tai) [地震台], and a "Religious Objects Store" that is usually closed, until you reach the halfway point up the mountain where the red brick **Middle Church** (Zhong Tang) [中堂] built in 1894 which still stands on the right, and the three Roman Catholic pavilion shrines (San Sheng Ting) [三圣亭] on the left.

The chapel at the halfway point is nowadays known variously as the **Middle Church** (Zhong Tang) [中堂], Mid-Mountain Church (Zhongshan Jiaotang) [中山教堂], or simply the the Small Church (Xiao Tang) [小堂], in contrast to the Big Church (Da Tang) [大堂] on the summit.   Despite its smaller size, the Middle Church is quite an impressive structure by itself, and is a genuine relic of the late Qing Dynasty dating from 1894.   It can hold 500 people and is well stocked with two book cases full of Chinese language Bibles (Shengjing) [圣经].   In stark contrast to the cathedral on the summit, which seems to almost always be closed, the Middle Church has always been open to visitors every time I have been there.

The three shrines on the left are known as the **Three Saints Pavilions** (San Sheng Ting) [三圣亭], and are dedicated to Jesus (Yesu) [耶酥], the Virgin Mary (Shengmu) [圣母], and St. Joseph (Ruose) [若瑟].

After this the trail zigzags up the hill along the 14 **Stations of the Cross** with kiosk type structures each containing a small shrine until finally it reaches the Cathedral (Da Tang) [大堂] on the summit.

The Three Saints Pavilions and the 14 Stations of the Cross were originally added to the Pilgrims' Road in 1894, at the same time as the Middle Church was built, but the ones that exist now seem to be new replacements of the originals.

Alternatively, instead of hiking up the pilgrims trail from the south, you could drive all the way to the summit on a winding mountain road that begins at the **West Gate** (Xi Da Men), or hike in from the **North Gate** (Bei Da Men).   The latter route allows visitors to see the seven-story Buddhist Pagoda known as the **Xiudaozhi Ta.**

The **Sheshan Roman Catholic Seminary** (Tianzhujiao Sheshan Xiuyuan) [天主教佘山修院] is now located in a separate compound of new buildings at the southwestern foot of the hill on Mountain Ring Road (Huanshan Lu) [环山路], although it previously occupied the older buildings behind the Middle Church (Zhong Tang) [中堂] halfway up the hillside from 1982 to 1986.   It was reopened in 1981 and by 1987 was training 127 new priests.   The main hall was constructed between May 1985 and September 1986.

The Song Family Compound

Two of the of the famous three Song sisters and their brother once lived with their spouses in a row of three houses within the same walled compound at the corner of Dongping Lu [东平路] and Hengshan Lu [衡山路], in the former French Concession. The compound has now become the campus of the Shanghai Conservatory of Music, but all three houses are still there with at least their exteriors intact, if not their original interiors.

The former Shanghai residence of Jiang Jieshi (Chiang Kai Shek) [蒋介石] (1887-1975) and his wife **Song Meiling** [宋美龄] (1898-2003) is the middle house in between the other two, facing Dongping Lu [东平路], on the North side of the school's gate. Jiang would have periodically stayed here during visits to Shanghai after his December 1927 marriage to Meiling, although their primary residence was in the Guomindang capital city of Nanjing.

The home of **H.H. Kung** (Kong Xiangxi) [孔祥熙] (1880-1967) and his wife **Song Ailing** [宋蔼龄] (1889-1973), whom he married in 1914, was the house on the South side of the compound's main gate facing Dongping Lu. Kung was a rich banker from Shanxi Province who claimed to be a direct descendant of Confucius. He replaced his brother-in-law T.V. Soong as Guomindang Finance Minister and Governor of the Central Bank (Zhongyang Yinhang) [中央银行] of China in November 1933, and held the posts until he was suddenly dismissed in June 1944.

The home of Jiang's brother-in-law, **T.V. Soong** (Song Ziwen) [宋子文] (1894-1971), sits on the North side of Jiang's house on the corner of Hengshan Lu [衡山路] and Dongping Lu [东平路]. T.V. Soong served off and on as Guomindang Finance Minister from 1924 to November 1933 and later became Chairman of the Board of the Bank of China in March 1935. During the Sino-Japanese War, T.V. Soong became Chiang Kai Shek's personal representative to the U.S. in June 1940, and then Foreign Minister in January 1942. In May 1945 T.V. Soong was again made Finance Minister, as well as Foreign Minister and Premier. However, in 1947 he was demoted to Governor of Guangdong Province, from where he fled to exile in the U.S. via Hong Kong in January 1949. T.V. Soong's house has not been included in the music school, and instead has been turned into the fashionable and pricey Sasha's Restaurant.

Address: 7, 9, and 11 Dongping Lu [东平路], formerly Route Francis Garnier.
Nearest Metro Station: Hengshan Lu [衡山路] Station on Line 1.

Song Jiaoren's Tomb (Song Jiaoren Muyuan) [宋教仁墓园]

Song Jiaoren [宋教仁] (1882-1913) was assassinated on March 20, 1913 at Shanghai's **Old North Train Station** (Shanghai Bei Huoche Zhan) [上海北火车站] (aka Lao Bei Zhan) [老北站].   At that time he was the leader of the Guomindang [国民党] political party, which had just won a majority of legislative seats in the January 1913 elections for the Parliament based in Beijing.   When he died he was boarding a train headed for Beijing, where many expected him to be chosen as Prime Minister.   Subsequent investigations by the police and judiciary of the International Settlement revealed that the assassins were tied to the administration of President **Yuan Shikai** [袁世凯] (1859-1916).   His death lead directly to the failed July 1913 **Second Revolution** (Erci Geming) [二次革命], in which revolutionaries such as **Chen Qimei** [陈其美] (1878-1916) who had supported the 1911 Revolution tried unsuccessfully to seize power from Yuan Shikai.

Song is important to modern Chinese history for a number of reasons.   He played a leading role in the **1911 Revolution** (Xinhai Geming) [辛亥革命], spending time together with **Huang Xing** [黄兴] (1874-1916) organizing revolutionary actions in Wuhan and Nanjing during the actual fighting with Qing Dynasty troops, unlike Sun Yat-sen (Sun Zhongshan) [孙中山] (1866-1925) who in many ways missed the revolution entirely because he was overseas then.   He was the Attorney General during the brief Nanjing regime of provisional president Sun Yat-sen in 1912.   Later he reorganized Sun's secret revolutionary organization the Alliance for Democracy (Tongmenghui) [同盟会] into a real political party known as the Guomingdang [国民党], and led them to victory in the 1913 parliamentary elections.

When first established in June 1914, the park was known as Song Jiaoren Tomb Garden (Song Jiaoren Muyuan) [宋教仁墓园], but when the park was repaired in September 1923, the name was changed to Song Park (Song Gongyuan) [宋公园], and in 1946 the name was changed again to Jiaoren Park (Jiaoren Gongyuan) [教仁公园].   In 1959 the park was extensively rebuilt and its name was changed for a fourth and final time to Zhabei Park (Zhabei Gongyuan) [闸北公园].   The tomb was destroyed during the Cultural Revolution (1966-1976), but was rebuilt again in 1981.   The site was repaired once again over a period of four months in 2011.

Today Song Jiaoren's tomb (Song Jiaoren Lingmu) [宋教仁陵墓] still stands inside Shanghai's **Zhabei Park** (Zhabei Gongyuan) [闸北公园].   The impressive sacred way leading to his tomb begins with an inscribed tablet dated August 25, 1981, recording the date when it became a municipal protected cultural relic.   Next comes a tall stone obelisk with a very impressive stone carved statue of Song Jiaoren [宋教仁] (1882-1913) seated on top of it.   In this statue Song looks quite young.   He has a moustache and is wearing a Western style suit, unlike many intellectuals of his day who still wore Mandarin gowns, including even such reformers as Lu Xun [鲁迅] (1881-1936) and Cai Yuanpei [蔡元培] (1868-1940).   He strikes a pose with his chin rested on one hand, as if he is pondering the solutions to China's troubles, looking not unlike Rodin's thinker.   Although the base of the obelisk looks new, the torso of the stone column and the statue atop it appear to be genuine historic relics from the Minguo era.   The front of the column bears his name in calligraphy and the back of the column bears a lengthy inscription.

A few yards distant from the obelisk is a short flight of steps leading up to a stone terrace on which stands the stone dome covering his actual tomb.　Atop the tomb's dome is perched a soaring Eagle with its wings spread.　Another tablet stands in front of the tomb.　The terrace on which the dome stands is obviously brand new, as is possibly the dome itself. Beside the steps leading up to it stands a new memorial tablet dated 2002.

Oddly, Zhabei Park is now in Jingan District due to the elimination of Zhabei District.

Adddress:　Zhabei Park (Zhabei Gongyuan) [闸北公园], 1555 Gonghe Xin Lu [共和新路 1555 号], former Zhabei Distrct, now Jingan District.
Phone:　(021) 5662-6010.

Song Qingling's Former House (Song Qingling Guju) [宋庆龄故居]

Song Qingling [宋庆龄] (1893-1981) became the wife of modern China's founding father Sun Yat-sen (Sun Zhongshan) [孙中山] (1866-1925) in 1915 when she was only 22 years old. After Sun's premature death in 1925, she used his name to lead the democratic opposition against the Guomindang right wing of Chiang Kai-shek (Jiang Jieshi) from 1927 to 1948. She welcomed the Communist's victory in 1949, and was appointed one of six Vice-Presidents of the new People's Republic of China. Two weeks before she died in Beijing at the age of 90 on May 29, 1981 she was made honorary President of the People's Republic of China. Her former Shanghai home was almost immediately declared a memorial to her, but it was not opened to the public until May 14, 1988. Since then the site has gone through several major renovations, and is kept in pristine condition.

This two-story Western-style wood and brick house was built on the former Avenue Joffe of the French Concession in 1920. After the Sino-Japanese War ended in 1945, Song Qingling returned to Shanghai and the Guomindang government gave her this house in 1948. After the 1949 revolution, Song Qingling chose to remain in China while the rest of her family fled the country. She accepted a post as one of the People's Republic's six vice-presidents, and as a reward for her valuable service as a well known figure head, the Communist government allowed her to keep this house in Shanghai for the rest of her life, as well as another house in Beijing at 46 Houhai Beiyan which was given to her when she moved there in April 1963. Photographs exist of her meeting with Mao Zedong at this house in Shanghai on May 11, 1961.

The Shanghai house is surrounded by a huge garden estate, with camphor trees and a large green lawn behind it. The rear of the house has a long veranda for enjoying the garden in the comfort of a wicker chair in the shade. The front of the house has a covered carport in front of the entrance, where her black Russian Zil limousine is still kept parked. The interior of the house is supposedly furnished the same as when she lived here. The ground floor rooms include a kitchen, dining room, and living room, while upstairs on the second floor are her bedroom, office, and the bedroom of her faithful servant Li Yaner. The rooms are decorated with gifts she received from foreign heads of state, including Sukarno, Kim Il Sung, Sihanouk and Stalin.

A separate Exhibition Hall was constructed in 1997 and opened on May 29th of that year. The museum inside is devoted entirely to her, and contains some intriguing looking documents on display under glass. Many of the documents are English language correspondence she exchanged with world leaders during the period before 1949, a time when she was campaigning for some sort of third way political compromise between the two extremes of the Guomindang on the right and the Communists on the left. Unfortunately, the way the documents are displayed, only portions of them can be read. It would be fascinating to know the full story of this powerful woman's thoughts.

Address: 1843 Huaihai Middle Road (Huaihai Zhong Lu) [淮海中路].
Phone: (021) 6437-6268, 6474-7183
Nearest Metro Station: Xujiahui Station on Line 1.

Song Qingling's Tomb Garden (Song Qingling Ling Yuan) [宋庆龄陵园]

The tomb of Song Qingling [宋庆龄] (1893-1981), the wife of China's first President Sun Yat-sen (Sun Zhongshan) [孙中山] (1866-1925), is located inside a very large park formally known as the Song Qingling Tomb Garden (Song Qingling Ling Yuan) [宋庆龄陵园], but often referred to simply as the Song Garden (Song Yuan) [宋园]. The garden was formerly the site of Shanghai's International Cemetery (Wanguo Gongmu) [万国公墓]. After the death of Song Qingling in Beijing on May 29, 1981, this whole site was rebuilt to serve as her family's tomb garden, and the site was opened to the public in January 1984.

The **Song Qingling Mausoleum** (Song Qingling Mu) [宋庆龄墓] is presided over by a larger than life white marble statue of Song Qingling [宋庆龄] (1893-1981) seated on a chair. Behind her statue are four white marble gravestones marking the final resting place for herself, her parents, and her servant. Her parents' original graves here were purposefully destroyed by Red Guards in 1966 during the Cultural Revolution (1966-1976). The current mausoleum dates from a reconstruction of the site in 1981.

Nearby, the air-conditioned **Song Qingling Memorial Hall** (Song Qingling Jinian Guan) [宋庆龄纪念馆] houses six rooms of impressive exhibits devoted to telling her whole life story. Many of her personal belongings are on display, including samples of her clothes, such as a seductive qipao with mesh neckline exposing her cleavage and back, her eyeglasses, writing brushes, a bottle of her favorite cherry brandy, and her Underwood portable typewriter. There are copies of books written by her and about her. Most impressive is the selection of old black and white photographs. There are quite a few photos of Song Qingling [宋庆龄] (1893-1981) posing with **Chiang Kai-shek** (Jiang Jieshi) [蒋介石] (1887-1975), as well as her husband **Sun Yat-sen** (Sun Zhongshan) [孙中山] (1866-1925). One remarkable photo shows all three of them together in June 1924; Qingling in the center flanked by Sun and Jiang on either side, with the crossed Guomindang flags overhead. Another rare photo dated March 1927 shows the entire membership of the ill-fated left Guomindang regime in Wuhan. There are also photos of Qingling and Jiang attending the 1929 funeral held for Sun at his newly completed tomb in Nanjing.

A so-called **Celebrities Tomb Area** (Mingren Muyuan) [名人墓园] seems dedicated to Chinese who supported the Communist Party in various ways.

The Song Qingling Mausoluem is located on the same site as the former **Foreigners' Cemetery** (Wanguo Gongmu) [万国公墓], which was owned and operated by the International Settlement's Shanghai Municipal Council before 1949. This was completely destroyed during the Cultural Revolution (1966-1976), but the rebuilt replica of it is now known as the Foreigners' Tomb Area (Waijiren Muyuan) [外籍人墓园].

Address: 21 Songyuan Lu [宋园路 21 号], or 1290 Hongqiao Lu [虹桥路 1290 号], Changning District.
Phone: (021) 6275-4034, 6275-4145
Nearest Metro Station: Hongqiao Lu Station on Line 3.

Songjiang Ancient Mosque (Songjiang Qingzhen Gu Si) [松江清真古寺]

The **Songjiang Ancient Mosque** (Songjiang Qingzhen Gu Si) [松江清真古寺] was built during the Yuan Dynasty [元朝] (1279-1368). Although the exact date of construction is debated, most sources agree that it was constructed by a Mongol general (Daluhuachi) [达鲁花赤] during the Zhizheng [至正] reign (1341-1368) of Toghan Temur (Tuohuan Tiemuer) [妥欢铁木儿], the last emperor of the Yuan Dynasty, making it over 600 years old, and the oldest of the nearly 20 mosques in Shanghai. However, other sources claim it was founded 46 years earlier in 1295 by local Mongol military commander Nasulading [納速拉丁], whose tomb the mosque still claims to have. It was rebuilt in the 24th year of the Hongwu reign [洪武] (1368-1398) of the first Ming Dynasty emperor, and thereafter is recorded as having been repaired & expanded many times, including in 1407, the 5th year of the Yongle reign [永乐](1403-1424); 1535, the 14th year of Jiajing reign [嘉靖](1521-1567); the 10th year of the Wanli reign [万历] (1573-1620); the 15th year of the Shunzhi reign [顺治] (1644-1661)of the Qing Dynasty; 1677 & 1683, the 16th & 22nd year of the Kangxi reign [康熙] (1661-1722); 1812, the 17th year of the Jiaqing reign [嘉庆] (1796-1820); and the 2nd year of the Daoguang reign [道光] (1821-1850).

In more recent years it's had its ups and downs. In 1961 it was made a county-level protected relic, but it was closed during the Cultural Revolution (Wenhua Da Geming) [文化大革命] (1966-1976). A four-year restoration project that started in 1981 and finished in 1985 allowed the mosque to reopen for religious services again in 1987, after a pause of 20 years. Meanwhile, in 1982 it had been raised to a municipal-level protected relic. A more recent restoration project was completed in 2003-2004.

The compound has many genuine historic relics from the Yuan, Ming and Qing Dynasties. The total area of the walled compound covers 4,446 square meters, of which only 2,126 square meters are occupied by buildings, while the rest of the area is composed of a half dozen spacious walled courtyard gardens. The most impressive structures include the **Bangke Men Lou** [邦克门楼] gate tower, the **Yao Dian** [窑殿] pavilion tower, the **Prayer Hall** (Libai Da Dian) [礼拜大殿], the **Ancient Muslim Cemetery** (Gu Muyuan) [古墓园] and the tomb of the mosque's supposed founder, Nasulading [納速拉丁], known as the Ancient Virtuous Tomb (Xianxian Gu Mu) [贤贤古墓].

Hidden behind the **Outer Screen Wall** (Waizhao Bi) [外照壁] is the entrance known as the **North Main Gate** (Bei Da Men). After this comes the **Inner Screen Wall** (Neizhao Bi) [内照壁]. Next, on your right, is the **Ancient Virtuous Tomb** (Xianxian Gu Mu) [贤贤古墓] of the mosque's founder, the Yuan Dynasty general Nasulading [納速拉丁]. His tomb consists of a horizontal stone tube or stone tomb ridge, characteristic of Muslim tombs in China, behind which stands an inscribed stone tablet (mubei).

308

A second gate leads you North into the **Ancient Stone Tablet Garden** (Gu Bei Yuan) [古碑园] courtyard, which has four arched portal gates, one facing in each compass direction, and is surrounded by a winding, undulating, serpentine, white Dragon Wall (Long Qiang) [龙墙]. Inside the courtyard are four inscribed stone tablets (beiji) [碑记], collectively known as the "Lidai Beiji" [历代碑记] dating back as far as the 17th Century.   Although their inscriptions are no longer legible, modern day signs beside them provide their dates as 1677, 1812, and 1821.   One stele is the "Chongxiu Zhenjiao Si Beiji" [重修真教寺碑记] recording the repair of the mosque in 1677, the 16th year of the Kangxi reign of the Qing Dynasty.   A second stele from 1812 records the mosque's repair in the 17th year of the Jiaqing reign [嘉庆] (1796-1820).   A third is the "Qingzhen Si Juanshu Beiji" [清真寺捐输碑记] from 1821, the first year of the Daoguang reign [道光] (1821-1850).   Of the four gates the most impressive is the **Bangke Men Lou** [邦克门楼] Gate Tower.   This is a brick gate with a pavilion built atop it that has layers of upturned roof eaves.   It bears an Arabic language inscription over its arched portal.

The Bangke Men Lou [邦克门楼] gate leads West into another courtyard where the mosque's **Prayer Hall** (Libai Da Dian) [礼拜大殿] is flanked by two side halls, the **North Lecture Hall** (Bei Jiang Tang) [北讲堂] and **South Lecture Hall** (Nan Jiang Tang) [南讲堂], both of the latter now being used as exhibition halls.

The **Prayer Hall** (Libai Da Dian) [礼拜大殿] houses ornate gilded Arabic wooden signs, with colorful carpets on the floor.   There is a clock on the inside wall, and a set of five more clocks with Arabic labels on the outside porch.   If you wait around at this spot, you will see the local faithful coming to prayers five times a day, wearing their white buteqa skull caps, and hear the muezzin singing the call to prayer from a microphone at the speaker's podium. This is not only a museum, but an active place of religious worship. Inside Muslim worshippers can be seen actively kneeling and praying on carpeted floors, facing a wall engraved with rows of flowing Arabic script, led by a turbaned Imam (Jiaozhang) [教长]. Some of the worshippers are dark skinned Turkic Uighurs from Xinjiang, but most are ethnic Han Chinese Hui Muslims (Huimin) [回民].   The Prayer Hall supposedly dates from 1407, the 5th year of the Yongle reign [永乐](1403-1424) of the Ming Dynasty.

The **South Lecture Hall** (Nan Jiang Tang) [南讲堂] has some English signs on the mosque's history, as well as displays on Songjiang Town's history, including a map of the old city wall.   A photo of the mosque's entrance gate bears the dates 1295 and 1341, denoting both of the two foundation stories.   Pictures of the mosque's restoration in the early 1980s have the dates 1980 and 1985, denoting when the restoration started and finished, and show black & white shots of before the restoration started in 1980 and color shots of after it finished in 1985.   It says the mosque dates from the 14th Century of the Yuan Dynasty, without giving a specific date of founding, supporting the conclusion that no specific date has yet been agreed upon.   The exhibition hall's wooden cross timber framework structure of round logs makes it look like an authentic historic relic. There is also an original three-character gilded signboard hanging on the rear wall inside.

The exhibition in the **North Lecture Hall** (Bei Jiang Tang) [北讲堂] contains Chinese language displays on the other mosques in the Shanghai area.

In the **Ancient Bai Tree Garden** (Gu Bai Yuan) [古柏园], on the north side of the Prayer Hall (Libai Da Dian) [礼拜大殿], is home to a 400-year-old tree called the Guguibai [古桧柏], and another historic pavilion tower known as the **Yao Dian** [窑殿].   It is quite similar in style to the Bang Ke Men Lou, and equally impressive.   This tower has a triangular shaped roof that faces four directions and has multiple layers of roof eaves.   Unfortunately it seems that it can not be entered.   You can also find three ancient stone wells (Gu Jing) hidden in the bushes of the Gu Bai Yuan [古柏园].

Behind the Prayer Hall is the **Ancient Muslim Cemetery** (Gu Mu Yuan) [古墓园].   The cemetery is L-shaped and zig zags around a corner of the walled compound's southwestern permimeter.   Brick walled rectangular tombs rise above the ground with inscribed stone tablets bearing both Chinese and Arabic inscriptions.   There are a total of about 50 graves with inscribed stone markers dating back centuries.   The graves are built in a curious way with brick walls supporting a mound of earth piled above ground.   Each grave is marked by a stone tablet which features an inscription written in flowing Arabic script at the top and a text inscribed in Chinese characters below.   The people buried here are reportedly mainly ethnic Han Chinese Hui Muslims (Huimin) [回民].

The exterior wall that once surrounded the larger outer garden area that logically should be called the East Garden (Dong Yuan) but instead is known simply as the **Yuanlin**, located on the East side of the **Ancient Stone Tablet Garden** (Gu Bei Yuan) [古碑园], has unfortunately now been torn down and replaced by a two-story building containing shops and restaurants that have windows allowing people to look directly into and down upon the mosque compound, thereby destroying the privacy and serenity the site previously had. There is still one other important Muslim tomb in the Yuanlin outer garden.   A new side **East Gate** (Dong Men) exits out of the mosque compound from the Yuanlin outer garden and onto a new side street that has replaced the once narrow twisting high walled lane that was there before.   However, only local Muslim residents are supposed to use this gateway, and not tourists.

This is not just a museum, but continues to be a functioning houe of religious worship for the local Muslim community, with prayer services led by an Imam (Jiaozhang) [教长], so non-Muslim visitors should be respectful and expect streams of worshippers going in and out during prayer times, especially on Fridays for Jummah (Zhuma) [主麻], the main Muslim day of prayer each week.   Obvious rules apply, such as taking off your shoes before entering the Prayer Hall and not smoking or littering anywhere within the walled compound.

Tourists need to buy a ticket and enter the compound from the North Gate (Bei Men) entrance facing Zhongshang Middle Road (Zhongshan Zhong Lu) [中山中路], while practicing Muslims attending prayer services enter without buying a ticket from a separate modern East Gate (Xin Dong Men).   Previously, prior to the 2003-2004 restoration, all visitors used to enter from a South back door facing Gangbang Alley (Gangbang Xiang) [缸鬃巷], and then pass through the bathing building (paishui fang) [排水房] or bathing room (yushi) [浴室] where worshippers wash up (muyu) [沐浴] or simply wash their hands (xi shou) [洗手] before prayers, but this entrance is now kept closed.   Unlike other Chinese temples that follow a South-North axis in which the main entrance gate is always the South Gate (Nan Men), Chinese mosques follow and East-West axis so that worshippers in the main Prayer Hall will be facing Mecca when they pray.

The mosque's earlier names were Zhenjiao Si [真教寺] or Yunjian Baihe Si [云间白鹤寺]. Yunjian [云间] was an ancient name for Songjiang town. Baihe [白鹤] is a white crane. Zhongshan Road [中山路] has always been the main street (malu) [马路] of Songjiang Town.

Address: The previous entrance was at 21 Gangbang Alley (Gangbang Xiang) [缸甏巷], but the current entrance is at 365 Zhongshan Middle Road (Zhongshan Zhong Lu) [中山中路 365 号].

Nearest Metro Station: Songjiang New City Station (Songjiang Xin Cheng Ditie Zhan) on Metro Line 9.

Songjiang Town (Songjiang Chengqu) [松江城区]

As already discussed earlier in the introductory historical narrative, from the Song Dynasty through the Qing Dynasty, Songjiang Town was once a walled city surrounded by a moat that served as the political center of the entire modern-day Shanghai municipality. The town's name has changed over the years from Yunjian [云间], to the county town (xiancheng) [县城] of Huating County (Huating Xian) [华亭县] in 751 A.D. during the Tang Dynasty Tianbao reign, to the capital city (fucheng) [府城] of Songjiang Prefecture (Songjiang Fu) [松江府] in 1278 near the end of the Southern Song Dynasty, to the county town (xiancheng) [县城] of Songjiang County (Songjiang Xian) [松江县] in 1914, the third year of the Republic of China, to the present day capital city of Songjiang District (Songjiang Qu) [松江区] in 1998. After Songjiang County was elevated to the status of a district, it became known officially as Songjiang Urban District (Songjiang Chengqu) [松江城区], or colloquially as Songjiang City (Songjiang Chengshi) [松江城市].

Beside the old town, a whole **Songjiang New City** (Songjiang Xincheng) [松江新城] has been constructed. The idea had already been in the planning stages for several years, but development really began with the opening of the Line 9 light rail extension in December 2007.

It's important to keep in mind that **Songjiang District** (Songjiang Qu) [松江区] covers a huge area of approximately 605 square kilometers that includes nearly a dozen other smaller towns (zhen) [镇], such as Jiuting [九亭镇], Sijing [泗泾镇], Dongjing [洞泾镇], Sheshan [佘山镇], Xiao Kunshan [小昆山镇], Shihudang [石湖荡镇], Maogang [泖港镇], Xinbang [新浜镇], Xinqiao [新桥镇], etc. There are also at least half a dozen sub-districts (jiedao), such as Guangfulin [广富林街道]. Guangfulin [广富林街道] was the site of a major archeological discovery and has been in the process of being developed into a tourism resort destination for many years. Tianma Shan used to be classified as a town (zhen) [镇] in its own right, but ever since it was merged with Sheshan Town [佘山镇] in January 2001 it has officially been considered merely a township (xiang) [乡] called Tianma Xiang [天马乡]. This is odd since Sheshan Town really has no urban center but Tianma Township does. Also, Shihudang Town [石湖荡镇] has absorbed the previous Li Pagoda Town (Li Ta Zhen).

In addition, Songjiang District is also home to **Songjiang University City** (Songjiang Daxue Cheng) [松江大学城], located in between the old Songjiang Town and Sheshan Town. The roots of Songjiang University City go back to a 2004 decision, but its real development began with the opening of the Line 9 light rail extension in December 2007. It is now home to over a dozen university campuses, including Shanghai International Studies University (Shanghai Waiguoyu Daxue) [上海外国语大学], East China University of Politics & Law (Huadong Zhenfa Daxue) [华东政法大学], Donghua University (Donghua Daxue) [东华大学], etc.

Less than a decade ago, before the Line 9 light rail was completed in 2008, Songjiang District was still primarily a rural, agricultural area, covered with wide expanses of farmers' fields and open green spaces dotted with occasional small villages and towns. However, since then, the former farm land in the area between Sijing Town [泗泾镇], Dongjing Town [洞泾镇], and Jiasong Gonglu [嘉松公路] on the border of Sheshan Town [佘山镇] has now become a seemingly endless sea of new highrise apartment buildings, and Jiuting Town [九亭镇] has become the site of the worst traffic jams in the whole city.

While it's useful to point out the modern new developments, and people should be aware of Songjiang District's recent multipolar urbanization, for our purposes here, we're far more interested in looking at the historic sights within the urban area of the former Songjiang old town.   **Zhongshan Road** (Zhongshan Lu) [中山路] is the main street of the old Songjiang Town, running the whole length of the town from East to West.   Most of the town's many historic sights are located along this road, making an itinerary quite easy to follow.   It is divided up into three sections, labeled as east, middle, and west.   It's important to keep in mind that "Zhongshan" is an extremely common place name in China, since it was the name of the first President of the Republic of China, making it equivalent to the name Washington in the U.S.   The Inner Ring Road (Nei Huan Gaojia) encircling Shanghai's downtown city center is also known as Zhongshan Road (Zhongshan Lu) [中山路], so be sure you get the right one by specifying Songjiang.   Shanghai also has at least two People's Roads (Renmin Lu), one surrounding the former old town of former Nanshi District in downtown Shanghai, and one in Songjiang, as well as one People's Avenue (Renmin Dadao) downtown beside People's Square.

Songjiang Zhongshan East Road (Zhongshan Dong Lu) [中山东路]

Starting at the east end of Zhongshan Road is the **Square Pagoda Park** (Fangta Yuan) [方塔园] located at 235 Zhongshan Dong Lu.   The Square Pagoda (Fang Ta) [方塔], also known as the Xingshengjiao Buddhist Temple Pagoda [兴圣教寺塔], dates from the Northern Song Dynasty and stands on the shore of a beautiful blue lake.   Also on the park grounds is a **Tianfei Temple** (Tianfei Gong) [天妃宫] supposedly dating from 1853; Shanghai's oldest stone foot bridge, the **Wangxian Qiao** [望仙桥], dating from 1193 in the Southern Song Dynasty; and a sacred way (shendao) of stone statues from a tomb dating from the Ming Dynasty.   In 1985 a **Chen Ancestral Hall** (Chen Gong Ci) [陈公祠] (aka Chen Huacheng Ci) [陈化成祠] was established on the forested grounds of the Square Pagoda Park (Fangta Yuan) [方塔园].

You can find more information about the **Square Pagoda** (Fang Ta) [方塔] in this book under the Letter P in the section on Pagodas.

Next to the park's main entrance gate is the **Songjiang District Museum** (Songjiang Bowuguan) [松江博物馆] at 233 Zhongshan Dong Lu.

313

Heading west, a short distance up Zhongshan East Road is the **Songjiang Tang Dynasty Buddhist Stone Tower** (Songjiang Tang Dai Tuoluoni Jingchuang) [松江唐代陀罗尼经幢]. According to the Ming Chongzhen Songjiang Fuzhi, the tower was first built in 859 A.D., the 13th year of the Dazhong reign of the Tang Dynasty. This is supposedly the oldest historical relic in Shanghai. Tuoluoni [陀罗尼] is the Chinese translation of the Sanskrit word Dharani, meaning a religious chant, while Jing [经] means a sacred scripture, but a Jingchuang [经幢] is a Buddhist stone pillar. It is often referred to simply as the Songjiang Tang Jingchuang [松江唐经幢] for short. The tower has an octagonal shape and stands 9.3 meters high, with 21 different layers of stone carvings from the pedestal to the top, including dragons, Buddhas, lotus flower petals, lions, various flowers and plants, Bodhisattvas, clouds, the Four Heavenly Kings (Sida Tianwang), coiled dragons (panlong), blooming lotus flowers, relief sculptures of people that seem to include a monarch, stone carved balustrades (goulan) like you might see encircling a regular wooden pagoda. It has seven round stone discs that protrude from the pillar's main stem, in between the stone pedestal at the bottom and the stone top knot on top. One of the seven stone discs is carved to look like a balcony with a balustrade. When the tower went under its first major restoration from September 1962 to November 1964 it was completely dismantled and a number of copper and gold coins were discovered hidden inside it dating from the Tang and Song dynasties. When I visited the site again in 2018 I found that the tower was under scaffolding and undergoing a major restoration again. The tower is hidden behind some school buildings in the back of the walled compound of the **Zhongshan East Road Elementary School** (Zhongshan Dong Lu Xiaoxue) [中山东路小学] a short walk down the narrow Lane #43 from the main street of Zhongshan Dong Lu. There are two other very similar Buddhist Stone Towers located inside the Guyi Yuan in Nanxiang Town of Jiading District.

Songjiang Zhongshan Middle Road (Zhongshan Zhong Lu) [中山中路]

Zhongshan Middle Road (Zhongshan Zhong Lu) [中山中路] between People's Road (Renmin Lu) and West Grove North Road (Xilin Bei Lu) was reconstructed as a pedestrian mall known as **Huating Old Street** (Huating Laojie) [华亭老街] in 2003 and two new stone pailou memorial archways were built at either end of this section of the street. However, by 2018 both of the memorial gates had been removed and the street reopened to vehicular traffic.

The **Taoist East Peak Temple** (Dongyue Miao) [东岳庙] was rebuilt in 2003 on the same site where it was originally built 400 years ago at #9 on Lane #196 of Zhongshan Middle Road (Zhongshan Zhong Lu) [中山中路], a block from its intersection with People's Road (Renmin Lu).

Located at 365 Zhongshan Middle Road (Zhongshan Zhong Lu) [中山中路 365 号], near its intersection with People's South Road (Renmin Nan Lu), is the walled compound of the **Songjiang Ancient Mosque** (Songjiang Qingzhen Gu Si) [松江清真古寺] dating from the Yuan Dynasty (1279-1368).

You can find more information about this mosque in this book under the letter M in the section on Mosques, and in its own entry under the letter S for Songjiang.

At 666 Zhongshan Middle Road (Zhongshan Zhong Lu) [中山中路 666 号], near its intersection with West Grove North Road (Xilin Bei Lu), is the walled compound of the **West Grove Zen Buddhist Temple** (Xilin Chan Si) [西林禅寺] and its Yuanying Pagoda (Yuanying Ta) [圆应塔].   This temple was supposedly first founded in 872 during the Tang Dynasty and was then later rebuilt in 1265 during the Southern Song Dynasty. The pagoda was first built between 1265 and 1274 during the Southern Song Dynasty (Nan Song) (1127-1279.   Throughout its long history this temple was repeatedly destroyed and rebuilt again.   In 1959 the temple was turned into a warehouse and factory, and all its Buddha statutes were destroyed.   In 1963 the entire pagoda was completely torn down (chaichu) [拆除], after an incident in which some children who had been climbing on it accidentally fell to their deaths, but almost 20 years later the pagoda was rebuilt again in 1982.   The current structure has an octagonal shape, seven stories, and stands 46.5 meters high.   On November 15, 1986 the temple was officially reopened for the first time since it was closed in 1959, 27 years earlier.   Ever since 1986 this temple compound has been undergoing continuos, seemingly never-ending, extensive renovations during which the vast majority of the previous structures were torn down and replaced with new ones, and the pagoda itself was so heavily restored that its appearance changed dramatically.   As such, it's difficult to provide a detailed description of the existing structures within the compound.   Shanghai historian Pan Mingquan has recently published a new Chinese language book devoted exclusively to the history of this one temple, but I'm not sure why he chose to focus on it.

Songjiang Zhongshan West Road (Zhongshan Xi Lu)

When I first visited this area 15 years ago in 2003, Zhongshan West Road (Zhongshan Xi Lu) in between West Grove North Road (Xilin Bei Lu) and Yushu Road (Yushu Lu) used to be home to a more authentic historic neighborhood of lowrise old wooden buildings of only two or three stories high.   Open air shops along the street sold old-fashioned, hand-made, traditional snacks that you would never find downtown and other handicrafts.   However, since 2009 the old neighborhoods that used to stand here have gradually been demolished in approximately three stages.   The houses along the far western end of Zhongshan Road before crossing the bridge over the Shenjingtang River [沈泾塘] had been completely demolished by 2009, and in 2018 all the historic wooden buildings on the other side of the bridge over the Shenjingtang River [沈泾塘] had been shuttered and appeared about to be demolished.   Ironically, at the same time as the historic buildings are torn down, large street signs have been put up in the surrounding area advertising it as the **Songjiang Historic Warehouse District** (Songjiang Cangcheng Lishi Wenhua Fengmao Qu) [松江仓城历史文化风貌区], which means a fake Disneyland copy is probably on the way.

The remaining treasures of the road's western end are two ancient stone arched foot bridges crossing a canal known simply as the City River (Shi He) [市河].   The larger, but slightly newer, of the two bridges is the five-arched, Ming Dynasty, **Big Warehouse Bridge** (Da Cang Qiao) [大仓桥] standing on the east side of Yushu Lu.   This bridge was built during the Tianqi [天启] reign (1621-1627) of the Ming Dynasty. Its original name was the Yongfeng Qiao [永丰桥], but because it was located near the West Warehouse it was also known as the West Warehouse Bridge (Xicang Qiao) [西仓桥].   Because at the south end of the bridge there is a large building known as the Water Transport Warehouse (Caoyun Cang) [漕运仓], the bridge is also known as the Big Warehouse Bridge (Da Cang Qiao) [大仓桥]. The bridge span measures 50 meters in length, while it is 3 meters wide.

To the west of Yushu Lu is the smaller, but older, three-arched stone foot bridge known as the **Yunjian First Bridge** (Yunjian Diyi Qiao) [云间第一桥], Yunjian [云间] being the original name of Songjiang Town.   In the Song Dynasty there was an earlier bridge at the same location known as the Anjiu Qiao [安就桥], but this was destroyed during the Chenghua [成化] reign (1465-1489) of the Ming Dynasty, and replaced with the present bridge, which was renamed Yunjian First Bridge (Yunjian Diyi Qiao) [云间第一桥].   Today you can still find a five character inscription bearing this name on the east side of the bridge over the top of the central arch.   This inscription dates from the Tongzhi reign of the Qing Dynasty.   There is also another inscription on the stone railing of the same side of the bridge recording its repair by the Songjiang government in 1986.   According to an undated Chinese language sign beside it, the bridge measures 30 meters long, 8 meters high, 5 meters wide, and was listed as a district level protected cultural relic in 1985.   There is also a rock nearby bearing a Chinese language inscription telling a similar story that is dated April 2015.   When I first saw this bridge in around 2003 it was in the middle of a historic neighborhood, the second time in 2009 it stood in a desolate no man's land after the demolition of the surrounding old neighborhood, and the third time I visited in 2018 I found that this section of the canal was lined on the north side with the walled compound of a huge new condominium development that blocked access to the bridge on that side, requiring a long circular detour of a walk to the bridge along Huagong Lu [化工路]on the south side of the canal through one remaining old neighborhood.

Nearest Metro Station: Songjiang Xincheng Station on Metro Line 9.

St. John's University (Shanghai Sheng Yuehan Daxue) [上海圣约翰大学]

Located in between the former Jessfield Park, now known as Zhongshan Park (Zhongshan Gongyuan) [中山公园], and a winding bend in the Suzhou River (Suzhou He) [苏州河] that envelopes the campus on three sides making it seem like a peninsula, with its entrance gate facing the former Jessfield Road, now known as Wanhangdu Lu [万航渡路], in Changning District [长宁区] this 130-year old college originally founded by Protestant Christian misisonaries is still educating students today as Shanghai's oldest continuously functioning university. It was founded as **St. John's College** (Sheng Yuehan Shuyuan) [圣约翰书院] in April 1879 by Rev. **Samuel Isaac Schereschewsky** (Shi Yuese) [施约瑟], who was then the Bishop of Shanghai for the American Episcopal Church, and was later upgraded to university status in 1905, upon being incorporated in Washington, D.C., and became known as St. John's University (Sheng Yuehan Daxue) [圣约翰大学].

During the Republic of China (Minguo) (1911-1949) most of the Chinese economic and political elite were graduates of this university. Famous graduates included finance minister T.V. Soong (Song Ziwen) [宋子文] (1894-1971), diplomat Wellington Koo (Gu Weijun) [顾维钧] (1888-1985), architect I.M. Pei (Bei Yuming), novelist Eileen Chang (Zhang Ailing) [张爱玲] (1920-1995), and K.C. Wu, Mayor (Wu Guozhen) [吴国桢] (1903-1984) of Shanghai for three years from April 1946 to April 1949. On February 1, 1913 the first President of China, Sun Yat-sen (Sun Zhongshan) [孙中山] (1866-1925) gave a speech here.

By far the longest serving president was **Francis L. Hawks Pott** (Bu Fangji) [卜舫济] (1864-1947), the famous author of a classic 1928 history of Shanghai, who served as the university's president for 53 years, from 1888 to 1941. Hawks Pot was extremely successful at fundraising efforts targeting donors in the United States, and this enabled him to finance a continuing expansion of the university's growing complex of buildings. It was said that whenever he went to the U.S. he would come back to Shanghai with a new building for St. John's in his pocket. However, he was a strict disciplinarian who alienated much of the Chinese student body through his failure to understand the rising Chinese nationalism of the 1920s student movement.

Major protests by Chinese students occurred on the St. John's campus on at least three separate occasions; first during the 1919 May 4th Movement, then again during the 1925 May 30th Movement, and finally in response to the 1927 April massacre of Communists in Shanghai. During the 1919 May 4th Movement, disruption of normal campus life was so great at St. John's that the school administration decided to end the 1918-19 academic year early without holding any final exams, and simply closed the university down until the start of the 1919 Fall Semester. During the 1925 May 30th Movement, St. John's President H.L. Hawks Pott argued so violently with the demonstrating Chinese students that approximately 553 of them, amounting to at least half those enrolled, withdrew from the school and later founded a new rival institution known as Guanghua University (Guanghua Daxue) [光华大学], which was the origin of present day Donghua University (Donghua Daxue) [东华大学] located on Yanan Xi Lu. Once again, St. John's was forced for a second time to shut down before the normal end of the 1924-1925 academic year. Finally, protests by Chinese students in response to the 1927 April massacre caused St. John's to close down for a third time from April 1927 to September 1928. According to one story, during one of these protests a group of Chinese students tried to raise the Chinese national flag on the university flag pole, but were prevented from doing so by the Western faculty members.

When Hawks Pott retired in February 1941 his place was taken by William Z.L. Sung (Shen Siliang) [沈嗣良] (1896-1967), who served as president from 1941 to 1946.   Sung made the controversial decision to keep the university open during the Sino-Janese War (1937-1945) when the staff and students of ten other protestant Christian colleges in Japanese occupied China retreated to Sichuan Province along with the Guomindang national government in internal exile.   After the war, Sung was tried for collaboration with the enemy by the Jiangsu High Court and imprisoned for two years starting in 1946 until he was finally acquitted of all charges and released in 1948.   He left China in 1949 and moved to the U.S.

St. John's independent existence continued for another three years after the May 1949 Liberation of Shanghai, but in June 1952 St. John's University was shut down, 73 years after its founding, making the 1952 graduating class the very last one.   It's campus and buildings were occupied by the East China Politics & Law School (Huadong Zhengfa Xueyuan) [华东政法学院], now known as **East China Politics & Law University** (Huadong Zhengfa Daxue) [华东政法大学].   At the start of the Cultural Revolution in 1966 the university was closed and appears to have only reopened in 1979.   In 1992 the St. John's University Alumni Association held its annual reunion meeting at the original campus, with many Chinese alumni returning to China from overseas for the first time since 1949.   As a result, there was a big push to restore the campus to its previous condition as much as possible before the visitors arrived.   In 2017 The East China School of Politics and Law celebrated its 65th anniversary at this location.   As part of the celebration new bilingual plaques were placed on almost all the historic halls with information including their original names and dates of construction.   The current occupants' dedication to historical accuracy is refreshing.

At first glance, it seems as if virtually all of the original campus buildings still remain, including the red brick dormitories, classroom buildings, gymnasium, clock tower, and administration building.   Several of the surviving buildings still have plaques and foundation stones embedded in their walls with the original English language inscriptions and university coat of arms. However, when you look more closely you'll find that the Chapel built in 1884, the Schereschewsky Hall built in 1895, and the 50th Anniversary Memorial Gate erected in 1929, were all destroyed after 1952.   The latter two were later rebuilt in 1992 as convincing copies, but the chapel was not.

Entering the modern main gate on the former Jessfield Road now known as Wanhangdu Lu [万航渡路], a long, straight, tree-lined lane leads one through the center of the park-like campus grounds, with its fresh-cut lawns.   Walking north on the campus' tree-lined main avenue, the first major building on the east side to your right is the **Social Hall** (Jiaoyi Shi) [交谊室].   Construction started in 1919 and was completed ten years later in 1929, with the grand opening held on December 14, 1929.   It was dedicated to the memory of Huang Su'e [黄素娥], who had been the Chinese wife of university president Hawks Pott until she died in 1918.   The building's architecture is a classic example of 1930s Chinese renaissance style, similar to those found in Nanjing and Shanghai's Jiangwan Town (Jiangwan Zhen) [江湾镇]. The massive roof has upturned eaves and is covered in glazed red ceramic tiles.   Thick, red, pillars support the roof.   The red brick walls are pierced by oval, Ming Dynasty-style, stone archway doors.   It is now known simply as Building # 3 [San Hao Lou] [三号楼].

To your left, on the west side of the main campus avenue, standing beside the green lawn (da caoping) [大草坪], is the two-story wooden **Administration Building**, built in 1898, or according to some accounts 1911. A combination of Victorian and Qing architectural styles, it features a roof with upturned eaves and intricate lattice-work wood carvings running the length of the house. This is sometimes referred to as the President's Office Building (Yuanzhang Bangong Lou) [院长办公楼] or Campus Office Building (Xiao Ban Da Lou) [校办大楼]. It's also known simply as Building #4 (Si Hao Lou)[四号楼].

Just to the west of the Administration Building is the former **Low Library** (Luoshi Tushuguan) [罗氏图书馆], now known as the **Red Building** (Hong Lou) [红楼], the Old Library (Lao Tushuguan) [老图书馆] or more officially as Building # 5 (Wu Hao Lou) [五号楼]. Construction started on December 20, 1913 and was completed in the early summer of 1916. Although the building was originally intended to commemorate the 25th anniversary of F.L. Hawks Pott as university president, and as such was initially referred to as "The Anniversary Building," it was ultimately named in honor of **Seth Low** (1850-1916), mayor of New York City and president of Columbia University. On the east side door is a three character Chinese inscription reading from right to left in traditional characters "Tushuguan" [图书馆] meaning library. The university's Low Library building held a collection of 23,000 volumes of books in 1925. By June 1935 this collection had grown to 105,741 volumes, of which 24,052 were in Western languages. Some of these are now held in the collection at the Xujiahui Library (Xujiahui Cangshu Lou). Although a new highrise library building was constructed in 1984, today the Low Library building is still used as the Foreign Languages Library. Amazingly the interior seems untouched with the original wooden steps and carved wood balustrades leading up to the second floor reading room, with its high roof supported by exposed wooden beams. However, there is a spot outside where the original corner stone has obviously been covered up with white plaster or cement.

In between the Adminstration Buidling and the Old Library is Building 63 (Liu San Lou).

Although the three-arched stone **Memorial Gate** (Jinian Fang) [纪念坊] originally set up in December 1929 in commemoration of the school's 50th anniversary was torn down (chaichu) [拆除] in May 1955, it was replaced by a fairly convincing replica erected at the same spot in October 1992. On the back side of the gate are two horizontal Chinese inscriptions in the center. The upper one reads from right to left, "Sheng Yuehan Daxue," being the Chinese name of St. John's University. The lower one reads from right to left, "Guang yu Zhenli" [光与真理], being the Chinese translation of St. John's University old motto, "Light and Truth."

The original **Chapel** (Libai Tang) [礼拜堂] aka (Jiao Tang) [教堂] built in 1884 was also destroyed at some point, and has not been rebuilt. According to some Chinese language sources it was torn down during the Cultural Revolution, but according to others it was demolished later in the 1980s, in order to make room for the current modern highrise library building. As a university founded by Protestant Christian missionaries, St. John's originally required mandatory attendance by all students at religious services held in the chapel every Sunday, but in 1931 this became voluntary.

The **Taofen Building** (Taofen Lou) [韬奋楼] is named in honor of **Zou Taofen** [邹韬奋] (1895-1944), who graduated from St. John's in 1921, and stands just behind the stone Memorial Gate (Jinian Fang) [纪念坊]. Its four-story, brick clock tower chimes its bells on the hour.   Below the clock tower is an arched gateway that tunnels through the tower into a large inner courtyard.   In the middle of the courtyard stands a bronze statue of Zou Taofen [邹韬奋] (1895-1944) wearing a Western-style business suit with a necktie and eyeglasses. On the base of the statue is inscribed the dates of his life.

At first glance, the **Taofen Building** (Taofen Lou) [韬奋楼] appears to be the same as the original **Scherechewsky Hall** (Huaishi Tang) [怀施堂], which was built on this same site between January 1894 and February 1895, and was named in honor of the school's founder Rev. Samuel Isaac Schereschewsky (Shi Yuese) [施约瑟], although in common practice it was often shortened to simply **S.Y. Hall**.   In March 1951 the original **Scherechewsky Hall** (Huaishi Tang) [怀施堂] was renamed the **Taofen Building** (Taofen Lou) [韬奋楼]. Nowadays this is also known simply as **Building #41** (Sishiyi Hao Lou) [四十一号楼].

However, by comparing photos from the past and present side by side, it is clear that at least the clock tower (Zhong Lou) [钟楼] is not the same as before.   For example, the original clock face was a round circle inside an eigh-sided octagon, but now it is square. The tower used to be topped with a double eaved roof that featured sharply upturned corners, but now it's a very plain looking single eaved roof.   It's possible that only the clock tower (Zhong Lou) [钟楼] was destroyed, and then was rebuilt, while the rest of the original two-story courtyard (siheyuan) building survived, but that's pure speculation.

Facing the green lawn, the **Yen Hall** (Si Yan Tang) [思颜堂], dedicated to a former faculty member named Reverend Y.K. Yen (Yan Yongjing) [颜永京] (1838-1898), and now known simply as Building #40 (Sishi Hao Lou) [四十号楼].   Constructed in 1903-04, it is a three-story, red brick building with arcades of arched verandas.   It still has a visible foundation stone with a readable English language inscription.   The inscription reads, *"St. John's College, Erected 1903."*   Below the inscription is the seal of the school's coat of arms, which seems to have once been covered up with wet cement, but is now partially visible.   When I revisited in December 2017, the foundation stone could no longer be found, but a new bilingual plaque had been mounted on the wall claiming that the building opened on October 1, 1904, and once included a 600-seat auditorium (Da Hui Tang) [大会堂], but was converted to a student dormitory (xuesheng sushe) [学生宿舍] in March 1953.   There is also another Chinese language plaque dated 1995 which commemorates a visit to the campus by China's first President Sun Yat-sen (Sun Zhongshan) [孙中山] (1866-1925) when he gave a speech here on February 1, 1913.   The interior of the building is amazing for its original wooden hand rails and wooden steps in the stairwell.   Nowadays it is known simply as Student Dormitory # 4 (Xuesheng Sushe Si Hao Lou) [学生宿舍四号楼].

To the west of Yen Hall (Si Yan Tang) [思颜堂] is the two-story **Small White House** (Xiao Bai Lou) [小白楼], with its row of seven colonial columns and second floor veranda, known more formally as Building #17 (Shi Qi Hao Lou) [十七号楼], it houses the College of Postgraduate Education.   Despite its impressive appearance, it's one of the few historic buildings lacking a memorial plaque, and also has no original inscriptions, so it's unclear what its original name and purpose was.

The former **Mann Hall** (Si Meng Tang) [思孟堂], built in 1908, is notable for the original inscriptions that can still be found on it.   Another example of the school's original crest can be found embedded in an English language plaque on the Si Meng Tang [思孟堂] building on the far side of the tennis courts.   This plaque has an inscription that states, *"St. John's University, Mann Hall, Erected 1908,"* followed by the quotation, *"The Earth shall be full of knowledge of the Lord as the waters cover the sea."*   In the center of the plaque is the school's seal, a round circle divided into three pie slices by a y-shaped bar.   On the three bars of the Y are the words, "St. John's University Shanghai."   At the bottom of the outer circle is the school's motto, "Light and Truth."   Around the top of the outer circle is an inscription in Chinese characters.

Mann Hall (Si Meng Tang) [思孟堂] is also notable for the story behind how it got its original name.   A new modern plaque recently beside the original one explains that this dormitory was originally named in honor of Arthur S. Mann, a teacher who began work at St. John's in 1904, but who during a July 1907 visit to Mt. Lushan in Jiangxi province drowned while trying to rescue another swimmer in the Jade Pool (Yu Chi), near Guanyin Bridge (Guanyin Qiao) on the southern slopes of the mountain.   The building first opened in September 1909, and originally featured a bronze tablet sent as a gift by Yale University, which was Mann's alma mater.   According to a new bilingual plaque beside the entrance, the name was changed to Peace Hall in March 1951, then Student Dormitory #2 (Xuesheng Sushe Er Hao Lou) [学生宿舍二号楼] in March 1953, and eventually regained its original name of Mann Hall in June 1998.   It is also known simply as Student Dormitory #5 (Xuesheng Sushe Wu Hao Lou) [学生宿舍五号楼].

Standing beside the tall Water Tower (Shui Ta) [水塔], the former **Cooper Memorial Gymnasium** (Gufeide Jinian Tiyushi) [顾斐德纪念体育室] built in 1918-19 still has an original corner stone (yushi) [隅石] with an English inscription that reads, *"Cooper Memorial Gymnasium, Erected MCMXVIII By the alumni, students and friends."*   The other side of the corner stone bears an original Chinese inscription written in six vertical columns of characters.   This inscription translates Cooper's name as "Gufeide" [顾斐德] and states simply that he was a science professor at St. John's.   Actually, F.C. Cooper was the Head of the Science Dept. in 1894.   The inscription is dated *"Minguo Qi Nian, Liu Yue,"* or in other words the six month of the 7th year of the Minguo era, which would have been June 1918. Over the main entrance there is also an original three character Chinese inscription dated 1918 that reads from right to left "Tiyushi" [体育室], a rather unusual naming for what would nowadays usually be called a "Tiyuguan" [体育馆].   A new bilingual plaque beside the entrance says the building opened on November 15, 1919, and originally featured a basketball court, volleyball court, and an indoor swimming pool with a glass roof. Amazingly enough, it is still in use as the school's gymnasium today. The sound of students playing basketball inside drifts out the windows.

Seaman Hall (Xi Men Tang) [西门堂] was completed in 1924 and located far in the back of the campus at the north end of the peninsula near the bridge over the Suzhou River. It still has an original corner stone dated 1923, marking when construction started, although it was actually completed in 1924. Seaman Hall was named after John Seaman, and the original Chinese name was merely a phonetic rendering of it, which should not be translated literally as West Gate, as the campus has never had a west gate since it's surrounded by water on three sides. During the Cultural Revolution, the name was changed to East Wind Building (Dongfeng Lou) [东风楼], which is still the name used today.

Other historic buildings still standing on the St. John's campus include the **Science Hall** (Gezhi Lou) [格致楼] completed in 1899, and now used as a student dormitory.

The St. John's campus is surrounded on three sides by a winding bend in the Suzhou River (Suzhou He) [苏州河] that makes it feel like a peninsula and creates a very peaceful environment cut off from the rest of the city. In the back of the campus a foot bridge known simply as the **Campus Bridge** (Xiaoyuan Qiao) [校园桥] crosses the Suzhou River to several other campus buildings on the other side, including the **New Science Hall**, built on the North side of the creek in 1919 at 1347 Guangfu Xi Lu. It is now used by the Ministry of Justice Institute of Forensic Sciences. During the period from December 1937 to December 1941 the Suzhou River (Suzhou He) [苏州河] formed the boundary between the Japanese occupied Shanghai on the other side, and the International Settlement on the campus side. Because of this the school was in great danger of being accidentally bombed. As a precaution, a giant American flag was stretched across the tennis courts to ward off air attacks.

Address: Located in between the former Jessfield Park, now known as Zhongshan Park (Zhongshan Gongyuan) [中山公园], and the Suzhou River (Suzhou He) [苏州河] at 1575 Wanhangdu Lu [万航渡路 1575 号] in Changning District [长宁区].
Phone: (021) 6251-2497
Nearest Metro Station: Zhongshan Park Station on Metro Lines 2, 3 & 4.

Stone Gate Houses (Shikumen) [石库门]:

The frequent social upheavals and political instability in the rest of China during the late 19th century and early 20th century caused Shanghai to experience a huge growth in population, as well as a corresponding boom in construction to build housing for all the new immigrants. Prior to 1860, the foreign concessions had not permitted Chinese residents to live within their boundaries, but during the uprising of the **Small Swords Society** (Xiaodao Hui) [小刀会] from September 1853 to February 1855, and the **Taiping Rebellion** (1850-1864) during which Shanghai was attacked three times between 1860 and 1862, an estimated 110,000 Chinese refugees were allowed in who later elected to stay.   During the warlord era of 1911 to 1927, compared to the rest of the country Shanghai offered relative security of investment for the Chinese middle and upper classes, as well as a safe haven for political leaders of various factions and parties.

Although they were at first reluctant to accept Chinese as permanent residents of the concessions, foreign residents soon realized there was money to be made in selling and renting housing to these new residents.   Once the temporary refugees became permanent residents, more substantial housing for them had to be constructed.   It was this real estate market that later created the wealth of such landlord tycoons as Silas A. Hardoon and the Sassoon family.   With the birth of Shanghai's real estate market came the creation of whole new neighborhoods of **Shikumen** [石库门] stone gate houses, which are unique to this city. These are rows of two-story brick and cement houses, which are connected together and face inward towards a common courtyard or lane (lilong [里弄] or longtang [弄堂]) that is entered from the main street via a stone gate inscribed with the name of the house.

As late as 1949 three-quarters of the residential housing in Shanghai still consisted of lane houses of various types such as lilong fangzi [里弄], longtang fangzi [弄堂] and Shikumen [石库门] Since then four-fifths of the Shikumen [石库门] houses have been demolished, but an estimated 1 million residents still live in such traditional old houses.

The **Xintiandi** [新天地] restaurant and retail complex developed in 2001 was proclaimed by its developers as a good example of the preserveration of historic Shikumen houses [石库门], but in fact the development has been so sanitized that it bears no resemblance to a real living Shikumen [石库门] neighborhood.

However, only a short walk from Xintiandi, in 2009 you could then still find a real Shikumen [石库门] neighborhood still standing on the short section of Danshui Lu between Zizhong Lu to the north and Fuxing Lu to the south.   Here wet laundry was hung out to dry naturally in the sun on long bamboo poles, chamber pots were emptied of human waste every morning, and groups of local residents idled away their spare time playing cards on the sidewalk. Each house had a gate decorated with a floral pattern on both sides of its masonry frame and black double wooden gates.   In addition, each narrow side lane had a larger gate with the three-character name of the lane inscribed above, and often the year of construction. The Danshui Lu neighborhood's Shikumen lane houses were constructed in 1925, and were 85 years old in 2010.

In 2009 the former Luwan District (Luwan Qu) [卢湾区] still had at least 30 intact Shikumen [石库门] lanes, and an estimated 2,000 Shikumen [石库门] houses, the most of any district in the city.   In May 2009 the district government announced plans to renovate at least 800 of them by the end of the year.

Two well known Shikumen [石库门] neighborhoods in the former Luwan District (Luwan Qu) [卢湾区] are the **Cite Bourgogne** (Bu Gao Li) [步高里] community on Shaanxi Nan Lu and the **Tianzi Fang** [田子坊] community on Taikang Lu.

Cite Bourgogne (Bu Gao Li) [步高里] was built in 1930 in what was then the French Concession (hence its French name), and is located at the intersection of Shaanxi Nan Lu and Jianguo Xi Lu.   The large compound has five gates, four of them facing Shaanxi Nan Lu and one facing Jianguo Xi Lu.   The two most impressive gates are designed like traditional Chinese pai lou, and bear both the three-character inscription for the neighborhood's Chinese name, Bu Gao Li [步高里], and its French name, Cite Bourgogne, with the date of construction A.D. 1930.   You can enter the compound at either Shaanxi Nan Lu lane #287 or Jianguo Xi Lu lane # 172, the other three less impressive gates being kept closed.   Inside the compound there are four lanes running east to west, and one central lane running north to south.   Although the compound has been restored, average local people still live here, and continue to hang their laundry out to dry in the sunshine, which gives it a less sterile atmosphere than Xintiandi.   Although it was originally meant to house only 78 families, it is now home to 450 households.

Tianzi Fang [田子坊] is located on Lane (long) # 210 of Taikang Lu in Luwan District.   The houses here are at least 80 years old.   Since 1998 it has gradually been turned into an artists' colony, with occupants including the famous photographer Er Dongqiang (aka Deke Erh).   Unfortunately, it has also become a bit of a tourist trap, with busloads of foreign visitors unloading here daily.   As a result, the restaurants and coffee shops here charge exorbitant prices, and the atmosphere feels a bit fake and phony in contrast to Bu Gao Li [步高里].

The Subway System (Ditie) [地铁]:

Shanghai's subway system started in 1995 with the construction of Line 1 running from Shanghai North Railway Station through People's Square to Xinzhuang Town in Minhang. By the start of 2003 there were three Metro lines in Shanghai. These included the two underground lines, 1 and 2, and the above ground light rail line 3. By 2008 there were eight Metro lines operational, with a total of 12 lines expected to be completed by 2010. More lines are in the pipeline, with the total number of planned routes having reached 18.

As of March 2008 the system had 227 km. of tracks, with 161 stations. However, 100 new stations were then under construction. The new lines are now branching far out of the city center, connecting the downtown area with the satellite towns in the outlying rural districts of Minhang, Songjiang, Qingpu, Jiading, and even Chongming Island. In addition, the previously completed lines are being extended further. Line One's northern end has been extended from its former terminus at Shanghai Railway Station all the way to Baoshan District. Similarly, Line Three's northern terminus has been extended from Jiangwan Town (Jiangwan Zhen) [江湾镇] to the Yangzi River port of Baoyang in Baoshan District.

Fares are quite reasonable, ranging from 3 to 8 Rmb depending on the distance. One of the conveniences for foreign visitors is that on-board public announcements are made in English as well as Chinese, telling you the name of each stop. The names of each stop are also posted in the stations in the phonetic Pinyin writing script, as well as Chinese characters. The system for buying and using tickets is automated and quite similar to that used in Washington, D.C.

Line One runs for a distance of 38.1 km. from North to South and has 28 stations. It was originally completed in April 1995 with a distance of only 16.1 km. and just 13 stations. In 1996 the southern end of the line was extended from Jinjiang Park to Xinzhuang Town in Minhang District, for an additional 5.3 km. and three stations. At the end of December 2004 it was extended at its northern end by an additional 12.4 km. and 9 stations. At the end of December 2007 its northern end was extended again by another 4.3 km. and 3 additional stations. It now runs from Fu Jin Lu in Baoshan District to the North through Shanghai Circus World Station, Shanghai Railway Station, People's Square, and Xujiahui Station all the way to Xinzhuang town in Minhang district to the South.

Line Two runs for a distance of 26.0 km. from East to West and has 17 stations. It was originally completed in October 1999 with only 12 stations, but was extended at its eastern end in December 2000, and extended again at its western end in December 2006. It now runs from Zhang Jiang Hi-Tech Park (Zhangjiang Gao Ke) in the East through People's Square and Zhongshan Park Station to Song Hong Lu in the West. Line Two will eventually link the city's two airports, Hongqiao Airport in the west and Pudong International Airport in the east, making the Maglev Line completely superfluous.

Line Three runs for a distance of 40.3 km. from North to South and has 29 stations. It was originally completed in December 2000 with 19 stations, but extended with a further ten stations added in December 2006. It now runs from Jiang Yang Bei Lu in Baoshan district to the North through Jiangwan Town (Jiangwan Zhen) [江湾镇], Hongkou Stadium Station, Shanghai North Railway Station, Zhongshan Park Station, and Caoxi Bei Lu [漕溪北路] Station, all the way to Shanghai South Railway Station (Shanghai Nan Huoche Zhan) in Minhang District.

Line Four runs for 34.2 km. and makes a complete ring around the urban city center, following the route of Line Three for a distance of 11.9 km., but also passing through Yangpu District and Pudong. It passes beneath the Huangpu River twice. It has 26 stations, of which 9 are shared with Line Three. It was completed at the end of December 2007.

Line Five runs for a distance of 17.2 km. from Xinzhuang Town in Minhang District to the Minhang Development Zone. It has 11 stations. It was completed in November 2003.

Line Six runs for a distance of 31.5 km. from south to north along the Pudong side of the Huangpu River. Most of the line runs underground, but 12.1 km. run above ground. It has 27 stations, with a southern terminus at Ling Yan Nan Lu, and a northern terminus in the Wai Gao Qiao Free Trade Zone. There is a transfer hub at Century Avenue (Shi Ji Da Dao) Station, where Line Six connects with Lines Two and Four. It was completed at the end of December 2007.

Line Seven runs for a distance of 35 km. from Qihua Lu in Baoshan district, through Jingan Si station, to the 2010 World Expo site on the Huangpu River in Luwan district and Pudong on the east side of the river. It is nick named as "the Expo Line," and will connect with Lines 1, 2, 4, 6, and 8. As of May 1, 2009 the tracks and tunnels had been completed but none of the stations had been built yet.

Line Eight runs for a distance of 22.6 km. from south to north along the Puxi side of the Huangpu River, connecting the Dongjiadu area in the south with Yangpu District in the north. It has 20 stations, all of which are underground. There is a transfer hub at People's Square (Renmin Guangchang) Station, where Line Eight connects with Lines One and Two. It was completed at the end of December 2007.

Line Nine opened to the public in January 2008 and runs for a distance of 29.1 km. from Gui Lin Lu Station in Xuhui District, passes through Qi Bao Town in Minhang District, and ends up at Songjiang New City in Songjiang District. More than half of the line, 16 km., runs above ground South of Jiuting station. Originally there were 12 stations, but a 13th station was opened at the intersection of Yi Shan Lu and Zhongshan Xi Lu in 2009, providing a transfer hub with Lines 3 and 4. The future northeastern extension of the line is expected to connect it with Xujiahui Station on Line 1 by the end of 2009.

Sun Yat-Sen's Residence (Sun Zhongshan Guju) [孙中山故居]

This house was formerly owned by Sun Yat-sen (Sun Zhongshan) [孙中山] (1866-1925), the founder of the Guomindang party and first president of the Chinese Republic from January to April 1912.   Sun lived here in this house with his second wife, Song Qingling [宋庆龄] (1893-1981), off and on between 1918 and 1925.   The Shanghai house served as a safe refuge for Sun during his repeated periods of political exile from his power base in Guangzhou (Canton), where he served as the president of three successive regimes in opposition to the officially recognized government in Beijing.

It was during one such period of poltical exile spent at this house from the Spring of 1918 to the Fall of 1920 that he wrote his work, *Plan for National Reconstruction (Jianguo Fang Lue),* which emphasized ideas for China's economic development and ignored politics.   His most important political documents, the *Three Principles of the People (San Min Zhu Yi)* and the *Five-Power Constitution (Wu Quan Xian Fa)* had been written earlier in his life, the first in 1905 and the second in 1912.

Sun was more politically active during his second period of exile in Shanghai from 1922 to 1923.   It was during this time that his increasingly frequent contacts with diplomatic representatives of the Soviet Union culminated in a series of meetings with Adolfe Joffe at Sun's Shanghai house which concluded with the signing of the January 26, 1923 **Sun-Joffe Agreement**.   The result was the first United Front between the Guomindang and Chinese Communist political parties in which Communists joined the Guomindang and participated in its organizations. At the end of February 1923 Sun was able to return to Guangzhou yet again, to head a third national opposition regime.

On his final journey to Beijing in December 1924, Sun stopped off in Shanghai just long enough to irritate the entire foreign community by publicly calling for the abolition of the foreign concessions.   After Sun's premature death in Beijing in March 1925, his wife Song Qingling returned to their Shanghai house, where she continued to live periodically until the Sino-Japanese War broke out in 1937.

Sun's Shanghai house is now treated as a national shrine much like George Washington's house at Mt. Vernon.   It has been decorated with period furnishings, black and white photographs of its former occupants, and some original household items.   The library contains photographs of the books which were once kept there.   You can see the wide variety of titles read by Dr. Sun, including books on the U.S. Constitution and the multinational Habsburg Empire.   The garden in back was where many famous visitors once had their photographs taken with Sun and Song Qingling, including the likes of Lu Xun and George Bernard Shaw.   The house next door contains a separate exhibition of photographs included in the price of admission.

Sun's former home is located at the intersection of Sinan Lu and Xiangshan Lu.   The original address was 29 Moliere Road of the French Concession.   Xiangshan Lu ends at a wall separating it from Fuxing Park, the former French Park.
Address: 7 Xiangshan Lu [香山路 7 号].
Phone: (021) 6437-2954, (021) 6385-0217
Nearest Metro Station: Huangpi Nan Lu Station on Metro Line 1.

Suzhou Creek (Suzhou He) [苏州河]

Suzhou Creek (Suzhou He) [苏州河], also known as the Wusong River (Wusong Jiang) [吴淞江], starts in the Wujiang area of Jiangsu province and flows through Wuxian and Kunshan before entering Shanghai, where it passes through the districts of Qingpu, Jiading, Putuo, Jingan, Zhabei, Hongkou and Huangpu before flowing into the Huangpu River. It has a total length of 125 km, of which 54 km. flows through Shanghai.

Suzhou Creek has experienced a dramatic revival over the last ten years, thanks largely to a massive environmental clean up that cost millions of dollars. In 1998 its waters were black and emitted a hideous stench. Long lines of barges clogged the artery. Nobody wanted to live here then. Between 1998 and 2007 more than 10 billion RMB was spent eliminating the stench and black color. Now the water is blue and smells clean. Fewer boats ply its waters now than before, but the occasional barges can still be seen and heard chugging along, especially at night. Some new high rise apartment buildings have been built along its banks. In short, the area along the creek has become a desirable place to live. In 2007 another 3 billion RMB was budgeted for the final phase of the clean up expected to be completed in 2009.

At the confluence of Suzhou Creek and the Huangpu River stands the historic **Garden Bridge** (Waibaidu Qiao) [外白渡桥], which leads from the Bund (Waitan) [外滩] to Daming Road (Daming Lu) [大名路] of Yangpu District. The steel bridge was built in 1907, and celebrated its 100th anniversary in 2007, making it the oldest bridge across Suzhou Creek. It measures 104 meters long and 18 meters wide. Its name has been translated as "free ferry," a reference to the tolls paid to cross an earlier wooden bridge built on the same site in 1856. After November 1937, the center of the **Garden Bridge** (Waibaidu Qiao) [外白渡桥] was the borderline between Shanghai's Japanese occupied districts and the "Isolated Island" of the International Settlement. On February 14, 2008 plans were announced to dismantle the historic **Garden Bridge** (Waibaidu Qiao) [外白渡桥] over Suzhou Creek (Suzhou He) in order to restore it piece by piece. The restoration took one year, after which the bridge was returned to its previous location in March 2009.

Immediately west of the **Garden Bridge** (Waibaidu Qiao) [外白渡桥] was the more modern **Wusong Road Water Gate Bridge** (Wusong Lu Zha Qiao) [吴淞路闸桥]. A system of steel water gates was built beneath the Wusong Road Bridge, preventing boats from passing in or out of the Huangpu River via Suzhou Creek. A sort of boat harbor had been developed here in the section of Suzhou Creek (Suzhou He) in between the Zhapu Road Bridge and Wusong Road Bridge, since this was the farthest East that barges could travel down the creek before having to turn around and go back. However, in 2009 the Wusong Road Water Gate Bridge was demolished, and replaced in 2010 by the so-called Bund Tunnel which now carries road traffic underneath Suzhou Creek (Suzhou He) instead of over it.

Continuing westward up the Suzhou Creek (Suzhou He), a short distance upstream from the Wusong Road Bridge (Wusong Lu Zha Qiao) [吴淞路闸桥] stand a pair of historic bridges, the **Zhapu Road Bridge** (Zhapu Lu Qiao) built in 1927, and the **Sichuan Road Bridge** (Sichuan Lu Qiao) constructed in 1922. At the north end of the Sichuan Road Bridge stands the historic Baroque-style **Post Office Building** built in 1924.

The **Zhejiang Lu Bridge** is an interesting artifact, a now rarely seen steel frame structure with a high peak in the center of its span. Crossing it into Huangpu District takes you down a lane lined with historic low-rise buildings that had yet to be demolished.

At the north end of the **Xizang Lu Bridge** stands the Number Four Company Warehouse (Sihang Cangku) [四行仓库] located at No. 1 Guangfu Lu, where a Guomindang unit of fewer than 500 men led by General Xie Jinyuan [谢晋元] (1905-1941) defied an entire division of the invading Japanese army for a week in October 1937. Xie Jinyuan [谢晋元] died in 1941 and was reburied in Shanghai's Song Qingling Cemetery (Song Qingling Lingyuan) in 1983.

The Swire Mansion (Swire Dasha)

This mansion was originally built by the owner of **Butterfield and Swire**, a powerful British shipping and trading firm sometimes known by its Chinese name "Taikoo" or "Tai Ku" (Tai Gu) [太古]. Although the company initially bore the names of its two founding partners, it was in fact owned and run by the Swire family for most of its history, and eventually changed its name to Swire & Sons, Ltd., a company which still exists today.

Opening their Shanghai head office soon after the Taiping Rebellion ended in 1864, by 1891 they had opened offices in the Yangzi River ports of Zhenjiang (1890), Wuhu (1884), Jiujiang (1885), Hankou (1885), and Yichang (1891). They operated two fleets of steamships, starting with their purchase of the **China Navigation Co**. in 1872, which sailed a fleet of ships up and down the Yangzi River as far as Yichang. By 1929 the China Navigation Co. had a fleet of 87 ships sailing China's inland and coastal waters, making it by far the largest in China. Their second shipping line was officially called the **Ocean Steamship Co.** but was informally known as "the Blue Funnel Line," and handled ocean-going cargo and passengers between Shanghai and Europe.

Over time the company expanded into many other lines of business, and acquired great political power. At one time they had representatives on the Board of Directors of the Hong Kong & Shanghai Bank, as well as the Union Insurance Co. of Canton. Their power in local Shanghai politics was second only to their main rival in the shipping business, Jardine and Matheson. From 1923 until the International Settlement was dissolved in 1943 they usually had a seat reserved for one of their representatives on the Shanghai Municipal Council, as did Jardine Matheson. Their first representative on the Council, Edward F. Mackay, was actually selected to serve as Council Chairman during his first term as a member.

George Swire, the then owner of the firm who lived in London, had the plans for this Shanghai estate drawn up in 1925, and it was finally completed in 1934. The two-story house features a row of massive round white Greco-Roman columns facing the rear lawn, a covered driveway in front, and a semi-circular wooden staircase inside the front hall. Oddly enough, Mr. Swire never lived in the house and only visited it once upon its grand opening before returning to London. Even the architect who designed it, C. Williams-Ellis, never laid eyes on it, conducting the work from London. Nonetheless, a brass plaque dedicated to the architect is still mounted in the wall of the entry way, just to your left as you walk inside.

The Swire Mansion is now Building #1 of the **Radisson Plaza Xingguo Hotel**, which has taken possession of the entire one square block estate which lies in between Huashan Lu to the west, and Xingguo Lu to the east.   The vast majority of the hotel's guest rooms are in a new high-rise tower on the north side of the estate, but rooms are also available in the seven colonial era villas which occupy the expansive grounds.   The walled estate can be entered from either the west or east gates.   The Swire Mansion would seem to be the main raison d'etre and crown jewel of the new hotel, but in fact the building has yet to be restored and has an abandoned appearance both outside and inside.   Although rooms here are available to be rented to guests, the mansion is not even mentioned in the hotel's marketing materials and seems to be a well-kept secret.

Address: 72 Xingguo Lu
Phone: (021) 6212-9998
Fax: (021) 6212-9996
Web Site: http://www.radissonasiapacific.com

T

Taoist Temples (Dao Guan) [道观]

According to Pan Mingquan [潘明权] (b.1947) of Shanghai Finance and Economics University in his encyclopedic work, *Shanghai Buddhist & Taoist Temples* (*Shanghai Fosi Daoguan) [上海佛寺道观],* " (2003), there were then 11 Taoist temples (Daojiao Gonguan) in the greater Shanghai municipality.   Two of these were City God Temples (chenghuang miao), one in the former Nanshi District, and one in Zhujiajiao Ancient Town (Zhujiajiao Guzhen) [朱家角古镇] of Qingpu District, and one was the White Cloud Taoist Temple (Baiyun Guan) [白云观] later destroyed to make way for the 2010 World Expo (see below). However, Zhou Fuchang [周富长], ed. *Shanghai Zongjiao Zhilu [上海宗教之旅]* (2004) lists 13 Taoist temples within Shanghai, ranked and categorized by district.   Many of these lay outside the downtown city center in the surrounding suburbs and rural districts.   Zongjiao Zhilu ranks the White Cloud Temple (Baiyun Guan) [白云观] first and the Shanghai City God Temple (Shanghai Chenghuang Miao) second in importance.   After that it lists 5 Taoist temples in the Pudong New Area, 2 in Nanhui District (which has since been merged into Pudong New Area), 1 in Fengxian District, a War God Temple (Guandi Miao) in Minhang District, the City God Temple (Chenghuang Miao) in Zhujiajiao Town of Qingpu District, and the Dongyue Miao in Songjiang Town of Songjiang District.   From this list we can see that 8 of the 13 Taoist temples in Shanghai are located in the area east of the Huangpu River, and only 5 are on the West side.

The largest and most significant ones are as follows:

White Cloud Taoist Temple (Baiyun Guan) [白云观]

This functioning Taoist temple is also the headquarters of the **Shanghai Taoist Association**. It has a more famous sister temple by the same name in Beijing.   The Shanghai Baiyun Guan [白云观] was founded by the Taoist monk Xu Zhizheng, a native of Jiading, and built on this spot just outside the Old West Gate (Lao Xi Men) [老西门] of the City Wall in 1882.   Six years after its construction, in 1888 the Qing Dynasty gave the temple a library of 8,000 volumes, including the sacred Taoist scriptures *Zhengtong Dao Cang*, and *Wanli Xu Dao Cang*.

Until June 2004 the temple was located at #8 of Lane #100 on Xilin Hou Lu [西林后路 100 弄 8 号], a long narrow alleyway which began near the Old West Gate (Lao Xi Men) [老西门] police station just off of Tibet South Road (Xizang Nan Lu).   A large multi-story pavilion gate stood over the alleyway's entrance.   At the end of the long alleyway plain looking walls on the outside disguised the beautiful Qing Dynasty wooden courtyard structures within. Buildings included the Linggong Dian, Lingxiao Dian, Laojun Dian, and Thunder God Hall. Looking upward at the rooftops one could see ornaments of historical figures brandishing weapons and wearing traditional clothes, as well as nature scenes of sacred animals.

The Shanghai Baiyun Guan [白云观] was a living community center that would attract residents from all over the old city to watch the Taoist monks performing elaborate ceremonies and rituals that included the use of musical instruments, something you would never see in a Buddhist temple.   It was a colorful, lively place full of magic.

In June 2004 official Chinese news media reports stated that the temple was being "moved" to a new location. However, when the author visited the old location, he found that the temple's pavilion gate had already been torn down, and preparations were under way to demolish the remaining buildings. A visit to the new site revealed that an entirely new Taoist temple had already been constructed there to replace the old one. Clearly, none of the original structures were moved. The old temple was simply replaced with a new one, located on Dajing Road beside the **War God Temple** (Guandi Miao) [关帝庙], aka the Dajing Pavilion (Dajing Ge) [大境阁], on a spot that had previously been occupied by a row of Stone Gate Houses (Shikumen) that were torn down to make way for it.. Unfortunately, the new Taoist temple seems sterile and abandoned, devoid of the lively activities of the previous one, and no longer serving as a genuine community center for local residents.

Address: 239 Dajing Lu [大境路]
Phone: (021) 6385-5366.
Nearest Metro Station: Old West Gate (Lao Xi Men) [老西门] on Metro Line 8, or Huangpi Nan Lu Station on Metro Line 1.

Shanghai's **City God Temple** (Chenghuang Miao) [城隍庙] in the Yu Yuan Bazaar (Yuyuan Shangcheng) [豫园商城] is also staffed by Taoist monks.

East Peak Temporary Palace (Dongyue Xinggong) [东岳行宫] (

Previously known as the East Peak Temporary Palace (Dongyue Xinggong) [东岳行宫], this Taoist temple claims to be the largest and oldest one in Shanghai, but is actually a brand new compound of structures constructed in 2007, when it was given the new name of (Shanghai Qinci Yangdian Daoguan)[上海钦赐仰殿道观], which most sources roughly translate as "Shanghai Royal Yangdian Taoist Temple."

Claims that the temple dates back to the reign of King Sun Quan [孙权] of the Eastern Wu Kingdom (Dong Wu) [东吴] (222-252) in the Three Kingdoms (San Guo) period cannot be believed because geological history proves the area was under water then.

More realistically, there may have previously been a Taoist temple at this location as early as the Qianlong reign (1736-1795) of the Qing Dynasty.

it is the only Taoist temple in the Pudong New Area. An impressive collection of 600 statues can be found in its one dozen halls.

Address: 476 Yuanshen Lu, Pudong New Area
Closest Subway Station: Yuanshen Stadium on Line 6

Songjiang East Peak Temple (Songjiang Dongyue Miao) [松江东岳庙]

The Taoist **East Peak Temple** (Dongyue Miao) [东岳庙] on Zhongshan Zhong Lu of Songjiang Town was rebuilt in 2003 on the same site as it originally stood 400 years ago.

In February 2008 the author discovered that a new Dongyue Miao Taoist Temple [东岳庙] had suddenly appeared on Zhongshan Zhong Lu, just east of the road's intersection with Renmin Bei Lu.

The temple is actually located on a back alley hidden behind the row of modern buildings facing the main street.   The exact address is #9 Zhongshan Zhong Lu, Long #196.   One massive new temple hall stands in between two-story barracks-style dormitories on either side.   According to the gate keeper, the temple was built in 2003, although this was the first I had ever seen or heard of it.   He claimed that this was actually a reconstruction of the original temple that had stood on the same spot, and as evidence pointed to the remains of a pair of two gnarled, blackened 400-year old gingko trees standing outside the front gate. According to him there are now 60 Taoist monks living here.

In Taoist nomenclature, Dongyue means "the East Peak," and is an alternate name for the sacred Mount Tai Shan in Shandong province.   Dongyue Temples serve the purpose of worshipping the God of Mt. Tai Shan, and are modeled on the Dai Miao Temple in Tai An city at the foot of Tai Shan.

Back in the Qing Dynasty every major city in China had their own Dongyue Miao [东岳庙], but during the Cultural Revolution these were prime targets for destruction by the Red Guards, who particularly despised Taoism above all other religions.   Until recently the only genuine surviving Dongyue Miao outside of Tai An was the one located in Beijing. However, in the past few years a nationwide revival has started, with Dongyue Temples being rebuilt in Hangzhou and Songjiang.

Address: #9 Zhongshan Zhong Lu, Long #196, Songjiang Town

Theaters

The **Paramount Ballroom** (Bailemen Da Fandian Wuting) [百乐门大饭店舞厅] located at 218 Yuyuan Lu [愚园路 218 号], just around the corner from Jingan Buddhist Temple (Jingan Si), was built between 1931 and 1932 and opened for business in 1933. It once had the most fashionable ballroom dances in town, complete with a live jazz band and dancing girls, and was frequented by such celebrities as Mayor Wu Tiecheng [吴铁城] (1888-1953), Chinese General Zhang Xueliang, and American General Claire Chennault. But in 1954 it was taken over by the government and turned into the **Red Capital Theater** (Hong Du Xiyuan) [红都戏院], and shortly thereafter converted into a movie theater (dianyingyuan) [电影院]. In 1990 the movie theater was closed after an accident in which part of the building's façade collapsed, and in 2001 Taiwanese businessman Mr. Zhao Shichong acquired the premises, restored its former name, and completely redecorated the interior. It reopened as a place where diners could watch showgirls perform while they eat. Since then it has gone through too many waves of restoration and changes in ownership to mention. The building itself is notable for its wedding cake spire on top, covered with neon lights that make it look waterfalls cascading down over its three tiers.

Address: 218 Yuyuan Lu [愚园路 218 号]
Phone (021) 6249-8866
Website: www.sh-paramount.com

The **Lyceum Theater** (Lanxin Da Xiyuan) [兰心大戏院] at 57 Maoming Nan Lu was built in1930 and last renovated in 2003. It now offers traditional Kunqu Opera performances, such as "The Peony Pavilion," performed by the Shanghai Kunqu Opera House.

Address: 57 Maoming Nan Lu [茂名南路 57 号]
Phone: (021) 6374-8445, 6437-7756, 6256-4738

The **Majestic Theater** (Meiqi Da Xiyuan) [美琪大戏院] at 66 Jiangning Lu is a granite Art-Deco structure built in 1941 on the site of the former Majestic Hotel where Chiang Kai-shek (Jiang Jieshi) [蒋介石] (1887-1975) held his December 1, 1927 wedding party when he married his third wife Song Meiling [宋美龄] (1898-2003). It now offers Peking Opera performances by the Jiangsu Peking Opera Troupe with traditional stories about Southern Song dynasty military heroes such as Yue Fei and Yang Zongbao.

Address: 66 Jiangning Lu [江宁路 66 号]
Phone: (021) 6217-4409

The **Yifu Theater** (Yifu Wutai) [逸夫舞台] at 701 Fuzhou Lu is home of the Shanghai Yueju Opera troupe and offers traditional Peking Opera performances nightly. Popular shows have include "Cao Cao and Yang Xiu," "The Glorious Zhen Guan Years of the Tang Dynasty," and "The Monkey King."

Address: 701 Fuzhou Lu [福州路 701 号].
Phone: (021) 6351-4668.

The Guotai Movie Theater (Guotai Dianying Yuan) [国泰电影院] at 870 Huaihai Zhong Lu [淮海中路] was formerly known as the **Cathay Theater**. Built in 1931, this is the longest running and most famous movie theater in Shanghai, and it still shows movies every week. In June 2003 the 72-year-old theater completed a six-month renovation that changed the interior considerably by dividing the previous single hall into three separate theaters. However the exterior remains substantially the same.
Address: 870 Huaihai Zhong Lu [淮海中路 870 号], Phone: (021) 5403-2980

The **Shanghai Concert Hall** (Shanghai Yinyue Ting) [上海音乐厅] at 523 Yanan Dong Lu [延安东路 523 号], intersection with Xizang Nan Lu, offers performances by the Shanghai Symphony Orchestra. [See its separate listing under the letter S for more details.]

The **Shanghai Grand Theater** (Shanghai Da Juyuan) [上海大剧院] located across the street from People's Square (Renmin Guangchang) [人民广场] is an 1,800 seat theater is where the biggest entertainment events take place, including Peking Opera shows such as Dream of Red Mansions (Hong Lou Meng) which are too popular for the smaller Yi Fu Theater. Construction started in 1994 and was completed in 1998.

Address: 300 Peoples Avenue (Renmin Da Dao 300 hao) [人民大道 300 号] on the corner with Huangpi Nan Lu. Phone: (021) 6372-8701, 6372-8702, 6372-3833.

The **Grand Movie Theater** (Da Guanming Dianyingyuan) [大光明电影院] at the intersection of Nanjing West Road (Nanjing Xi Lu) [南京西路] and Huanghe Lu was designed by architect Laszlo Hudec and built in 1932. In 1941 it was one of the first buildings in Shanghai to install air conditioning. The building has two floors containin six movie theaters, including a big hall that can seat 800 people and five smaller halls. Before 1949 this was the place to see Hollywood films.

Flying Horse Hill (Tianma Shan) [天马山]

Although Sheshan is the most famous mountain in Shanghai, the highest one is actually Tianma Shan [天马山], which stands 99.8 meters tall and is located 7 kilometers away from Sheshan. You can reach Tianma Shan [天马山] from the foot of Sheshan by taking the Shetiankun Highway (Shetiankun Gonglu) [佘天昆公路], a narrow two-lane paved road through green fields, lined on both sides with rows of trees white-washed at their base to serve as street lights.   After passing several other small foothills, you arrive at a sign welcoming you to "Sheshan National Forest Tianma Shan Park."   You can get a good view of the Huzhu Ta [护珠塔] pagoda on top of the hill if you stop at just right the spot on the Shetiankun Highway (Shetiankun Gonglu) [佘天昆公路] a few minutes drive away to the East of the mountain.

The name Tianma Shan [天马山] means "Flying Horse Hill," so called because its shape looked like a flying horse to those who first named it.   It is the highest and largest of all the nine peaks which together make up Sheshan National Forest Park.   It covers an area of 96 hectares.

Tianma Shan West Gate (Tianma Shan Xi Da Men) [天马山西大门]

The West Gate (Xi Da Men) of the park is just opposite the small village of Tianma, at the intersection Shetiankun Highway (Shetiankun Gonglu) [佘天昆公路] and Heavenly Residence Road (Tianzhai Lu) [天宅路].   There's a parking lot here where you can park your car if you have one, or ask your taxi driver to wait for you, which would be a good idea since there's no other transportation options for getting to or from here except motor vehicle. Along with Jinze Town and Qinglong Village in Qingpu District, this is still one of the few places in Shanghai that has yet to experience economic development and has not yet been connected to the public transportation system.   The old Tianma village was in the process of being torn down at the time of my December 2018 visit.   A somewhat shabby but newer more modern town had been built across the bridge on the other side of a river.

As of December 2018 a ticket admission of 10 Rmb was required.   After buying your ticket, a pretty steep flight of steps from the West Gate ascends to a ridge line where trails lead to the left and right.   There's a convenient sign here with a map and list of sights to see on the mountain.   On this map the pagoda is referred to in Chinese as the Pearl Guarding Precious Light Pagoda (Huzhu Bao Guang Ta) [护珠宝光塔], but in English it's called the Leaning Tower of Pisa of China.   To see the main sight of the Huzhu Ta [护珠塔] Pagoda you want to turn right and follow the trail up the ridge line, past another trail that turns off to the left, until you see the entrance gateway to the pagoda's walled compound.

On the left side of the entrance gate is a Chinese language plaque dated January 2016 which notes that these are the ruins of a former Buddhist temple once known as the **Circular Wisdom Religion Temple** (Yuanzhi Jiao Si) [圆智教寺], but also more commonly known as the **Middle Peak Buddhist Temple** (Zhong Feng Si) [中峰寺], in contrast with two other Buddhist temples that were also once on the mountain known as the Lower Peak Buddhist Temple (Xia Feng Si) [下峰寺] and Upper Peak Temple (Shang Feng Si) [上峰寺].   The three-character Chinese inscription over the gate says simply Pearl Guarding Pagoda (Huzhu Ta) [护珠塔].

The Pearl Guarding Pagoda (Huzhu Ta) [护珠塔]

Sitting half-way up the hill is the impressive ruin of the Pearl Guarding Pagoda (Huzhu Ta) [护珠塔], also known as the Precious Light Pagoda (Baoguang Ta) [宝光塔]. Oddly enough, the tower is not on the summit of the hill, but on a false summit at the foot of a long ridge that continues to ascend up the peak.

It was first built in 1079, the second year of the Yuanfeng [元丰] era (1078-1085) of Zhao Xu [赵顼] aka Song Shenzong [宋神宗] (1067-1085) of the Northern Song Dynasty (Bei Song), but was restored to its present condition in 1982.

The octagonal, seven story, tower stands 18.82 meters high.　It is "the most sloping tower in the world," leaning sharply at an angle of 6 degrees, 51', 52", which is one degree more than the leaning tower of Pisa in Italy, even before the latter's recent restoration.

Huzhu Ta [护珠塔] Pagoda is an all red brick, octagonal construction with no wooden beams at all.　It has seven stories, with a flat top, and has an enormous hole of fragmented brick blown out of one corner of the base, causing it to in effect be a tripod standing on three legs. Before the hole was made, it's clear that it once had four doorways on the ground floor, but now only two doorways are intact. Windows in the tower alternate floors.　You cannot ascend Huzhu Ta [护珠塔], as it has no stairs or ladder, but you can enter the base and look up all the way through the inside of the tower through the octagonal hole in the center that opens up at the top revealing the clear blue sky above.

The hole at the base looks as if it had been made by an explosion, possibly during the Taiping Rebellion, and seems as if it may have caused the sharp tilt it now has.　In fact, the village of Tianma Shan [天马山] was the scene of a fierce battle in June 1862 when Frederick Townsend Ward recaptured it from the Taiping rebels.

There are no inscriptions on the tower itself, having either been removed or worn off. However, there are a few modern inscribed tablets.　In front of the pagoda, at its base, stands a stone tablet erected by the Shanghai city government dated March 26, 1983 announcing the pagoda's status as a protected cultural relic.　On the far side of the pagoda, standing at its base, is another stone tablet that appears to be dated 1982 which details the history of the pagoda's construction in the year 1079.

The Huzhu Ta [护珠塔] Pagoda stands inside a walled enclosure with three buildings, all locked up and closed.　One building can be seen through the windows to contain a Guanyin and Buddha statue, while the one opposite it is set up to sell red candles and incense, but was also closed.　It seems to be a non-functioning Buddhist temple without resident monks or worshippers.　The third building is a tea house which was also closed.

An ancient stone well near the pagoda is known as the Fourth Spring Under Heaven (Tianxia Disi Quan) [天下第四泉].　.

Behind the well stands an ancient Gingko tree (Yinxiang Gushu) [银杏古树] that is supposedly 700 years old.　　.

A quite steep cobblestone trail ascends the ridge.   Just before reaching the summit one passes some real old broken stone pillars lying beside the trail to the left side, along with a still upright stone grave marker.

The Bronze Goddess of Mercy (Tong Guanyin) [铜观音]

At the summit of Tianma Shan [天马山] one finds a white walled enclosure, within which sits a golden statue of a seated Goddess of Mercy (Guanyin) [观音] with its right arm raised and its left arm lowered.   Signage here refers to it simply as the Bronze Goddess of Mercy (Tong Guanyin) [铜观音]. This statue is 3 meters high, weighs 1800 kg, and is made completely of bronze.   Curiously, it sits outdoors and there are no actual temple buildings inside the enclosure at all.   Although the whole facility seems brand new, on closer examination one finds the Guanyin is sitting on top of the remains of a genuinely old stone foundation surrounded by several stone pillar pedestals proving the previous existence of an earlier historic structure here.   This was previously the site of the **Upper Peak Buddhist Temple** (Shangfeng Si) [上峰寺] which no longer exists.

The North Peak Pavilion (Bei Feng Ting) [北峰亭]

This is a new two-story pavilion, which can be ascended to the top via an internal flight of stairs.   For some reason, a furry statue of a giant white horse sits inside the first floor, complete with saddle, stirrups, and soft white fur!   A circular doorway in the far wall frames a beautiful scenery of trees and a small octagonal two-story Qing Dynasty style pavilion on a lower peak across a small ridge that dips down and then back up again.   The view from the summit also features green farmland surrounding the mountain, two more completely separate forested hills in the near distance, and the long straight tree-lined road upon which I traveled here.   This northern area of the mountain is also known as the Sword Dance Terrace (Wujian Tai) [舞剑台].

Leaving the pavilion, the trail descending downward has the odd sign saying, "Too Secluded To Go Alone," "A Place With Wonderful Sounds of Pipa in the Special Moon Night."   This trail apparently descends down a long ridge which extends out into farmland that forms a small gap separating Tianma Shan [天马山] from yet another small forested hill in the near distance which can be probably be reached on foot this way.

Walking along the forested trail towards the East Gate, I found that Tianma Shan [天马山] has some of the same mysterious vaulted red brick chambers emerging from underground as does Sheshan.   A herd of three wild, unattended white billy goats surprised me and I them as them went scurrying away off down the hillside.

Just before descending down to East Gate I ascended a third peak of Tian Ma Shan [天马山] to find a very ugly modern seven story concrete block tower which although tall is a terrible eyesore with no architectural merit at all.   Worst of all it was locked shut giving it no purpose at all.   They should blow it up for it spoils the scenery.

Near the East Gate is the Tomb of Three High Officials (San Gao Shi Mu) [三高士墓], Yang Weizhen [杨维桢] (1296—1370), Qian Weishan [钱惟善] (d.1369), and Lu Juren [陆居仁].

Other sights on the mountain include the Sword Watching Pavilion (Kanjian Ting) [看剑亭], Can Xia Guan [餐霞馆]、Eight Immortals Slope (Ba Xian Po) [八仙坡], Liu Yun Wall (Liu Yun Bi) [留云壁]、Liu Yun Pavilion （Liu Yun Ge) [留云阁], Er Lu Thatched Cottage (Er Lu Cao Tang) [二陆草堂], Banzhu Nunnery (Banzhu An) [半珠庵]、Xiang Yan Jing Residence（Xiang Yan Jing She) [香岩精舍], Twin Pines Terrace (Shuang Song Tai) [双松台]、Zhuoyue Spring (Zhuoyue Quan) [濯月泉], Shangqqing Spring (Shangqing Quan) [上清泉]、Chaozhen Taoist Temple (Chaozhen Daoyuan) [朝真道院], Jade Emperor Hall (Yu Huang Dian) [玉皇殿]、Dongyue Temporary Palace（Dongyue Xinggong) [东岳行宫], and the Taixu Building (Taixu Lou) [太虚楼].

Tianma Shan East Gate (Tianma Shan Dong Da Men) [天马山东大门]

Although the East Gate is much further away from the main attraction of the Huzhu Ta [护珠塔] Pagoda than the West Gate, it offers a much clearer view of Tianma Shan's [天马山] composition in the form of three peaks.   Furthermore, much more visitor information seems to be available here, including free Chinese language maps of the mountain, and a detailed English language sign describing the mountains history.

Location: Tianma Township (Tianma Xiang) [天马乡], Sheshan Town, Songjiang District. Tianma Shan used to be classified as a town (zhen) [镇] in its own right, but ever since it was merged with Sheshan Town [佘山镇] in January 2001 it has officially been considered merely a township (xiang) [乡] called Tianma Xiang [天马乡].

U

Urban Planning Exhibition Center (Chengshi Guihua Zhanlan Guan) [城市规划展览馆]

Completed in 1999 as the last part of the People's Square renovations started in 1993, this four-story building is a curious piece of architecture, with a giant white hat on top that serves no purpose but decoration.   Despite the awkward name, this is a museum devoted to the past, present and future urban architecture of Shanghai.   Exhibits trace the history of Shanghai from the Song Dynasty (960-1279) to the present, and show urban planners visions of what the city may look like tomorrow.

On the Mezzanine level you find the "Historic City" exhibit.   Highlights include a Ming Dynasty map of the old Shanghai county town's city wall, the 1933 plans for development of the Jiangwan Town (Jiangwan Zhen) [江湾镇] civic center, and a multimedia display of the Bund (Waitan) which rotates through three time periods of its development, from roughly 1865 to 1937.   The 1937 shot is remarkable for its identical likeness with the scene you see today.   A computer photo database includes images of suburban towns in the Shanghai suburbs, such as Jiading and Nanxiang, and a large scale mode depicts the layout of the Square Pagoda Park (Fang Ta Yuan) [方塔园] in Songjiang Town.

Most of the third floor is taken up by an enormous scale model of the city, the size of an ice skating rink, with a pedestrian catwalk surrounding its perimeter.   The model is a mixture of the present and future, with some features that don't exist yet, such as the giant Ferris wheel planned for the Yangpu District's Huangpu River coastline.   Workers with hammers can be seen standing in "the river," making the endless changes to the model of the city skyline, which even the city planners can't keep up with.   On this floor you can also see artists' conceptions and street plans of the 11 New Towns proposed for the Shanghai countryside.

The fourth floor's main feature is an atrium hole in the floor allowing an overhead view of the scale model of Shanghai down on the floor below.   From this angle one can see more clearly that the former Nanshi District is nothing more than a sea of skyscrapers with the tiny island of the Yu Garden (Yu Yuan) [豫园] in the center.   Exhibits on this floor include a scale model of the man-made Yangshan Deep Sea Port (Yangshan Shenshui Gang) [洋山深水港] constructed in Hangzhou Bay, the Pudong Airport, the Suzhou River clean up project, and the Metro system expansion plan.   Nice views of People's Square can be had from the South facing windows.

The exhibition hall is located across the street from People's Square (Renmin Guangchang) [人民广场], just in front of People's Park (Renmin Gongyuan) [人民公园]

Address: 100 People's Avenue (Renmin Da Dao 100) [人民大道 100 号]
Phone: (021) 6318-4477
Fax: (021) 6372-2077
Web Site: http://www.supec.org
Nearest Metro Station: People's Square Station on Lines 1, 2, & 8.

W

West Bund (Xi Tan) [西滩]

Shanghai West Bund (Xi Tan) [西滩] is a relatively new geographical term that refers to a corridor running along the west bank of the Huangpu River in the southwest part of Xuhui District and former Luwan District.   This West Bund corridor has a shoreline of 11.4 km in length, and covers an area of 9.4 sq. km.

Until about 10 years ago, this had been an industrial area where historically speaking some of Shanghai's first industries were founded in the early 20th Century.   It had been the site of the Jiangnan Arsenal, Jiangan Shipyard, Longhua Airport (1917-2008), Shanghai Aircraft Factory (1950-2009), Shanghai Nanpu Railway Station (1907-2009), Beipiao Coal Wharf (1929-2009), and Shanghai Cement Factory (1920-2009).   With the exeption of only a few remaining relics such as the Terminal Building of the Longhua Airport and the dry docks of the Jiangnan Shipyard, the structures belonging to these former industrial sites were all torn down in 2008-2009 as part of the preparations for the 2010 World Expo, including the former airport runway, which is now in the process of being built over.

After the Expo was over, it was decided by the government to maintain this area as a waterfront green belt and also redevelop it into an arts district.   The Xuhui District 9th Party Congress held at the end of 2011 called for the creation of a "West Bund Culture Corridor." Since then, Shanghai West Bund has been officially used as the new name for the Xuhui waterfront area. Today more than 20 cultural and art institutions are located here, such as the Long Museum, Yuz Museum, Start Museum, Tank Shanghai, etc.   In 2017, the West Bund was listed in the Master Plan for Shanghai.

World Expo 2010

Shanghai won the right to host the 2010 World Expo in December 2002.   The 2010 World Expo took place in Shanghai over a six month period from May 1st to October 31st, 2010.

The theme for the expo was "Better City – Better Life."   The mascot was a blue cartoonish chracter known as "Hai Bao," whose image could be seen all over the city in the form of statues standing in parks, posters in subway stations, and banners hanging from light poles along the streets.

The expo site covered an area of 5.28 sq. km. along both sides of the Huangpu River between the Nanpu Bridge (Nanpu Da Qiao) [南浦大桥] and Lupu Bridge (Lupu Da Qiao) [卢浦大桥].

The west side of this section of the Huangpu River in Luwan district was previously the site of the Jiangnan Shipyard, which has been relocated to the small island of Changxing Dao in the Yangzi River estuary.   The shipyard's predecessor, the Jiangnan Armory was established on this same site back in 1867, and gradually evolved into the shipyard.   This west bank section of the Expo site has now become part of the new **West Bund** art district.

New subway lines, and extensions of existing lines, were constructed to provide public transportation to and from the expo site.   When the projects were completed, subway lines 4, 7, 8 and 13 connected to the expo site.   By May 1, 2009 all the tracks and tunnels of the newly constructed Line 7, nick named "the Expo Line," had been completed, but the subway stations for that line had not been built yet.

As of May 2009, 190 countries and 48 international organizations had committed to participate in the expo.   40 countries planned on building their own pavilions for the expo, and 18 of these were already under construction at this time.   Participating countries include at least 34 from North and South America, 45 from Europe, 50 from Africa, 45 from Asia, 16 from Oceania.   Foreign national pavilions were grouped into clusters based on the continents where those countries are located.   It was estimated that 70 million visitors would attend the expo, and that 5 per cent of these would be foreign tourists from overseas. The U.S. finally confirmed its plan to build a pavilion on July 10, 2009 after a long delay, making it the 240th confirmed participant.

Although expo rules usually require all pavilions to be temporary structures that are torn down after the event is over, the **China Pavilion** was preserved and later became the new home of the former Shanghai Art Museum, previously housed in the old Shanghai Race Club building on Nanjing West Road, which has since had its name changed to the China Art Museum.

Nearest Metro Station: Luban Lu Station on Line 4, Xizang Nan Lu Station on Lines 4 & 8, and Nanpu Bridge (Nanpu Da Qiao) [南浦大桥] Station on Line 8.

Xintiandi [新天地]

The Xintiandi [新天地] retail and restaurant development is the most well known part of the larger Taipingqiao Redevelopment Project launched by property developer Shui On Group in 2001 on 52 hectares of land in what was an old Shikumen residential neighborhood in the downtown city center of Shanghai.   The other twp parts of the project were the Taipingqiao Park, covering an area of 44,000 square meters, including a man-made lake of 12,000 square meters, and Corporate Avenue, a complex of modern office towers, hotels and other commercial properties.

The Xintiandi [新天地] part of the project covers an area of 30,000 square meters, with a floor space of 60,000 square meters.   It is divided into North and South Blocks, divided by the cross street Xingye Lu.   The North Block of Xintiandi lies between Taicang Lu to the north and Xingye Lu to the south, with Huangpi Nan Lu running along its eastern boundary and Madang Lu to the west.   The development is characterized by low-rise buildings featuring the restored red brick exterior facades of old stone gate houses (shikumen) [石库门], which have had their interiors entirely gutted and modernized to house upscale restaurants, bars and retail shops.   The North Block was completed first, and the South Block did not open for business until mid-2002.

There are a total of 44 restaurants offering French, American, German, British, Brazilian, Italian, Japanese, Taiwanese and Hong Kong cuisines.   Highlights include the American-style KABB restaurant founded by Kathleen Lau, the German beer house Paulaner Brauhaus, the Brown Sugar Jazz Club, and a branch of the Seattle-based Starbucks coffee shop chain.   There are also 25 fashionable clothing shops.   Cultural facilities include a Shikumen Museum and the Central Academy of Fine Arts Gallery. Tourists may find the Visitor Information Center on Xingye Lu a useful resource, as it is well stocked with pamphlets, brochures and books about the sights to see in Shanghai.

Xintiandi [新天地] has aroused two opposing points of view.   On one hand, the property developer claims that the historic houses' original bricks were used and that Xintiandi is a good example of the restoration and preservationof historic architecture, or *"adaptive re-use of old buildings"* in their words.   Shui On's slogan for the project is *"Yesterday meets tomorrow in Shanghai today."* Professors from the prestigious Tongji University [同济大学] Urban Planning faculty served as advisers to the project, which was designed by Boston-based architectural firm Wood and Zapata Inc.   Xintiandi has won several architectural awards, including the 2001 Innovation China Architecture Award, and the 2003 Award for Excellence from the Urban Land Institute in the U.S.

On the other hand, the complex of restored buildings looks brand new and certainly bears no resemblance to a real living residential neighborhood of Shanghai stone gate houses (shikumen) [石库门].   Furthermore, a total of 3,800 families were evicted from the old residential neighborhood.   As a witness who saw their evictions, I have to say these people did not look happy, despite the often heard argument that they would be better off moving to more modern housing.   Gone now are the chamber pots, communal cooking and washing areas, courtyard games of Chinese chess (weiqi) [围棋], the click clack sound of the mahjong [麻将] rolling dice and tiles rattling together, the music of Shanghai Opera (Huju) [沪剧] such as Dream of Red Mansions (Hong Lou Meng) [红楼梦] drifting out of open windows, neighbors shouting at each other in the local Shanghai dialect (Shanghai Hua) [上

海话]. Despite its peculiar smells, it is sad to see this special way of life disappear. Depending on how you look at it, the tangible archictecture may have been saved, but the intangible cultural heritage has been lost.

The First Congress Hall of the Chinese Communist Party where the Communist Party was founded in July 1921 at 76 Xingye Lu is now on the southern edge of Xintiandi's North Block. It's seems doubtful that Mao Zedong would have approved of such a capitalist shopping center enveloping such a revolutionary shrine.

Visitor Information Center
House 3, Lane 123, Xingye Lu, South Block,
Phone: (021) 6311-2288

Stone Gate House Museum (Shikumen Bowuguan)
House 25, Lane 181, Taicang Lu, North Block
Phone: (021) 3307-0337

Nearest Metro Station: Huangpi Nan Lu Station on Line 1.

Xujiahui French Roman Catholic Community [徐家汇]

In March 1847 French Roman Catholics established an entire community of their own on the far northwestern fringe of the French Concession at what is now known as Xujiahui [徐家汇], but which they called Zikawei or Siccawei, after their Romanization of the local Shanghai dialect name for the place.   The area was named after famous Ming Dynasty scientist **Xu Guangqi** [徐光启] (1562-1633), who is still buried there in a tomb located inside a public park on Nandan Lu [南丹路].   At its peak this settlement included an astronomical observatory, a Jesuit seminary, several convents, orphanages for boys and girls, a publishing house, library, museum, educational institutions ranging from grade school to university level, and the Cathedral of Saint Ignatius.   The Zikawei Canal used to flow in between the two main rows of buildings where the Cao Stream North Road (Caoxi Bei Lu) [漕溪北路] now runs.   Buildings that once belonged to the French Catholic community can still be found along both sides of Cao Stream North Road (Caoxi Bei Lu) [漕溪北路] stretching from Hongqiao Lu in the North to Nandan Lu in the South.   The name of this main south-north road implies that there was once a stream called the Cao Xi [漕溪] that flowed in between these rows of buildings on either side.   In fact, the name of the main east-west road known as Caobao Lu comes from the fact that it runs from the former Caoxi He in the east to Qibao Town in the west.   Nonetheless, foreigners usually referred to the stream as Siccawei Creek or Zikawei Creek.

It used to be possible to sail a boat from the Xujiahui French Roman Catholic Community to the foot of Sheshan Hill in Songjiang District, atop which stands another French Roman Catholic Cathedral, by following the route of the Puhuitang River (Puhuitang He) [蒲汇塘河] from its confluence with the Zhaojiabang [肇嘉浜] canal at its eastern end through Minhang and Songjiang districts to Sheshan at its western end.   However, in the 1950s the Xujiahui section of the river was filled in, paved over, and turned into today's Puhuitang Road (Puhuitang Lu) [蒲汇塘路], where I used to live for years, and where one can still find the site of the former Tousewei Orphanage.   Since the Zhaojiabang canal was also filled in and turned into a road, the eastern mouth of the Puhuitang River was rerouted to flow into the Huangpu River at Longhua Harbor (Longhua Gang) [龙华港].   Today it still continues to flow through Caohejing Town [漕河泾镇], Hongqiao Town [虹桥镇], and Qibao Town [七宝镇] in Minhang District, as well as Sijing Town [泗泾镇] in Songjiang District, although after that it doesn't seem to quite reach the foot of Sheshan anymore.   In the Minhang section of the river one can still see local fisherman lowering and raising large nets attached to bamboo pole frames in order to catch fish.

In the 1990s the Xujiahui area was developed into a major retail shopping hub, with a number of department stores and shopping malls being built there around the central intersection where the five roads Zhaoajiabang Lu, Hongqiao Lu, Caoxibei Lu, Hengshan Lu, and Huashan Lu all meet; including the Pacific Department Store, Oriental Department Store, the Metro City shopping mall, and the Grand Gateway shopping mall.   When I first visited the area in early 1999, Metro City, the Oriental, and the Pacific had already been built, but construction on the Grand Gateway had been temporarily halted due to the Asia Financial Crisis of 1997, with the concrete dome standing half-finished and the two towers not even started yet.   The construction of the large underground Xujiahui Subway Station for a while threatened the destruction of some of the historic buildings, which in the end were preserved due to a public outcry.

Xujiahui Cathedral (Xujiahui Tianzhu Jiaotang) [徐家汇天主教堂]

This red brick and stone building was constructed from 1906 to 1910.   It was originally known to foreigners as **St. Ignatius Cahthedral.**   The main hall is 83 meters long, with a 26 meter high vaulted ceiling supported by 64 stone columns.   The hall can hold as many as 3,000 people.

During the Cutural Revolution (1966-1976) the cathedral was closed, its stained glass windows were destroyed, and its two towers were torn down.   After the cathedral reopened in 1979 the existing two towers were rebuilt in 1982 at a height of 56 meters, ten feet shorter than the original ones.   In 2004 a massive ongoing restoration project began to install new stained glass windows.

Xujiahui Cathedral was under scaffolding yet again in 2015 for more of the seemingly endless renovations to its exterior.   In December 2017 the whole public square in front of the cathedral was closed off and undergoing some sort of massive reconstruction project. [See more under the section Cathedrals and Churches.]

Address: 158 Puxi Lu [蒲西路 158 号].

The **Xujiahui Convent of the Holy Mother** (Xujiahui Niuxiu Daoyuan) [徐家汇女修道院]

This five-story white building just across the street from the Xujiahui Library was constructed between 1929 and 1931.   In addition to serving as a convent for Catholic nuns, it was also home to an orphanage for Chinese girls.   In 2004 the building was occupied by a restaurant known as Ye Olde Station.   Inside an upper floor of the building there is a still a chapel where weddings are sometimes performed.

Behind the convent is the site of a former Roman Catholic mission day school which until recently was still serving as a public school.   The entrance gate to the compound of red brick buildings faced Tianyaoqiao Road.

Address: #201 Caoxi Bei Lu [漕溪北路 201 号],

Xujiahui Library (Xujiahui Cangshu Lou) [徐家汇藏书楼]

Across the street from the former Convent of the Holy Mother, on the West side of Cao Stream North Road (Caoxi Bei Lu) [漕溪北路], stands a pair of buildings which were once the French Catholic community's library.   The library is known to foreigners as the **Zikawei Bibliotheca Major**, but called the Xujiahui Cangshu Lou [徐家汇藏书楼] by Chinese.   It is sometimes also called the St. Ignatius Catholic Library.   A smaller structure built on this site in 1847 was the first library ever established in Shanghai.   The present structure is a conglomeration of a two-story North wing and a three-story South wing connected like a letter L, plus a three-story western extension later added to the rear of the South wing.   The three-story South wing decorated with verandas on each floor was originally built in 1867 as the residence for the priests of the nearby cathedral, while the two-story North wing was added between 1896 and 1897.   According to a still visible cornerstone written in French, the western extension was added in 1931.

In 1935 the Zikawei Library had a collection of 200,000 volumes, of which 80,000 were in Western languages, making it the biggest library in all of Shanghai. When the Zikawei Library was taken over by the Shanghai government in December 1955 the collection included a total of 210,000 volumes, of which 120,000 were written in Chinese, and another 90,000 in various Western languages, mainly English and French.

The Zikawei Library served as a branch of the Shanghai Municipal Library from 1956 until 1996 when it was closed down. It was abandoned and derelict for six years until a full restoration began in 2002. The Xujiahui Library was finally reopened in August 2003. In January 2004 it was officially listed as a Xuhui District cultural relic.

The reopened Zikawei Library's collection consists of 560,000 Chinese and foreign language books, documents and maps published before 1949. In addition to the original Zikawei Library collection, this total also includes some of the city's other pre-1949 library collections, such as the 94,000 volumes that had been in the library collection of the **North China Branch of the Royal Asiatic Society (RAS)** (Yazhou Wenhui Bei Zhongguo Zhihui) [亚洲文会北中国支会].

Some of the highlights of the collection include complete sets of the Shanghai Municipal Council Gazette and Municipal Reports, all of the China Yearbooks edited by H.G.W. Woodhead from 1913 to 1939, Shanghai business directories for 1935 and 1941, and educational directories for 1917 and 1920. A casual look through the volumes displayed on the shelves reveals library stamps on the inside covers from St. John's University Low Library, the Shanghai Race Club Library, the Shanghai Municipal Council Public Library, the Royal Asiatic Society North China Branch Library, and even the U.S. Information Service Shanghai Branch Library.

A new electronic database of the Xujiahui collection has been created and is availble on line through the website of the Shanghai Library (Shanghai Tushuguan) [上海图书馆], but its interface is entirely in Chinese. In addition, the original English language RAS Library card catalogue stands in the hallway and can still be used to order volumes from storage.

Address: 80 Caoxi Bei Lu [漕溪北路 80 号], near Puxi Lu [蒲西路].
Phone: (021) 6487-4095 x 209
Nearest Metro Station: Xujiahui Station on Line 1.

Xujiahui Observatory (Xujiahui Guanxiangtai) [徐家汇观象台]

The Xujiahui Observatory (Xujiahui Guanxiangtai) [徐家汇观象台] , known in French as the "Observatoire Meteorlogique," was founded by French Jesuits at a meeting held in August 1872, although construction did not actually begin until February 1873. It continued to be operated by French Jesuits until 1947. By collecting information from coastal lighthouses, in July 1879 the Zikawei Observatory was able to correctly predict a typhoon in its first successful weather forecast (tianqi yubao) [天气预报]. In 1880 a three-story tower was added to the top of the building. On January 1, 1882 the Zikawei Observatory began publishing regular weather forecasts in the local newspapers.

Beginning in May 1884, the **Gutzlaff Signal Tower** (xinhaotai) [信号台] was established on the French Bund (Falanxi Waitan) [法兰西外滩] and connected to the Zikawei Observatory by a telegraph line, which was used to send regular weather reports to the waterfront and then relay them to the ships at sea. These weather reports were also sent to the Customs House (Jiang Hai Guan) on the Bund. It also published regular weather bulletins and annual weather almanacs.

In 1900 a new facility on **Sheshan Hill** (aka Zo-Se) [佘山] in Songjiang District took over the functions of the astronomical observatory (tianwentai) [天文台], but the site in Xujiahui continued to function as a weather observatory (qixiangtai) [气象台]. In 1900 a new building was constructed at 166 Puxi Lu, 100 meters away from the old one.

During the Sino-Japanese War (1937-1945) both the Sheshan and Xujiahui Observatory stopped functioning. The Sheshan Observatory stopped functioning at the end of 1937, while the Xujiahui Observatory stopped issuing weather forecasts and publications in 1941. On December 1, 1945 the Guomindang Chinese Central Meteorological Bureau took over the Gutzlaff Signal Tower on the Bund. In February 1947 the Guomindang Chinese government closed the Xujiahui Observatory and turned its work over to the Chinese Meteorological Bureau. In January 1951 the **Shanghai Meteorological Bureau** (Shanghai Shi Qixiangju) [上海市气象局] moved into the former Xujiahui Observatory. [

Although the building no longer functions as an observatory, until recently it was still used by the Shanghai Meteorological Bureau as their television broadcast station.

The building has now been completly restored, including placement of a replica of its original metal tower on top. It was officially opened to the public as the new Shanghai Meteorological Museum in July 2016, but public access is still extremely limited to only tour groups with a reservation on certain days of the week.

Address: the compound has two gates, one at 166 Puxi Lu [蒲西路 166 号], and another at 1 Nandan Lu [南丹路 1 号]. Nearest Metro Station: Xujiahui Station on Line 1.

St. Ignatius College, established in 1850, is now Xuhui High School (Xuhui Gaoji Zhongxue) [徐汇高级中学] located at #68 Hongqiao Lu.

The **Tomb of Xu Guangqi [徐光启]**

Xu Guangqi [徐光启] (1562-1633) was a famous Ming Dynasty scientist and astronomer who converted to Christianity after a meeting in Nanjing with the Jesuit Matteo Ricci (1552-1610). His tomb, known as the "Tombeau de Paul Zi" in French, is located inside a park at #17 Nandan Lu [南丹路 17 号]. It was rebuilt from June to December 2003 to include a new memorial hall (jinian guan)[纪念馆], a stone memorial archway (pailou) [牌楼], a sacred way (shendao) [神道] of eight stone statues leading to his five-peaked tomb mound, and a large white crucifix standing in front of the tomb mound. The present present-day layout supposedly duplicates the one it had in 1903 when French Jesuits redesigned it. The park itself was renamed from Nandan Gongyuan [南丹公园] to Guangqi Gongyuan [光启公园] in honor of Xu once the reconstruction of the site was completed. Prior to the 2003 reconstruction there had been no real historic relics remaining in the park besides the large earthen tomb mound, making it pretty clear that the original site had most likely been completely destroyed during the Cultural Revolution (1966-1976).   A statue of Xu Guangqi erected in 1994 stands outside the park at the intersection of Caoxi Bei Lu [漕溪北路] and Nandan Lu [南丹路].   The Xujiahui area is named after Xu, as this name basically means the Xu family home.

Address: #17 Nandan Lu [南丹路 17 号]

Tou-Se-We Orphanage Musuem (Tushanwan Bowuguan) [土山湾博物馆]

Established by French Roman Catholic missionaries in 1864, this orphanage was well known for training Chinese orphan boys in a variety of professional skills in various workshops that focused on painting, wood-working, book publishing, and making stained glass windows.   The stained glass windows originally installed in the Xujiahui Cathedral, and the Morris Mansion, were made here.   The publishing house here was responsible for printing many of the books published in Shanghai during the late Qing Dyansty and Republic of China (Minguo) time periods.   It was taken over by the state in 1953, when 200 orphans were still living there, and closed in 1960.   Shortly after first arriving in Shanghai in the late 1990s, I used to live in a highrise apartment building on Puhuitang Road, from the windows of which I could look down on the orphanage's former buildings, which were then being used as a public school.   In May 2010 the orphanage's last surviving historic building was reopened to the public as a museum.   It's most treasured item on display is the wood-carved memorial gate (pailou) that was made by orphans here in 1912-1913 and then sent to San Francisco to be displayed at the 1915 Panama Pacific Exposition.   It was also displayed at two other World Expos held in Chicago in 1933 and New York City in 1939. After spending decades overseas in the possession of various owners, it was finally returned to Shanghai in July 2009 after which it underwent seven months restoration work, and is now displayed in a special hall that was newly constructed just for it.

Since its establishment, this orphanage has been known to most foreigners by the name of "Tou-Se-We," with the full name in French being "Orphelinat de T'ou-Se-We," although in today's phonetic Pinyin system used in mainland China the correct spelling of the Chinese name should be Tushanwan [土山湾], which translated roughly means "earth hill bay." The "bay" part comes from the fact that this location was once near the confluence of the Puhuitang River (Puhuitang He) [蒲汇塘河] and the Zhaojiabang Canal [肇嘉浜], before their channels flowing through the Xujiahui area were filled in and paved over to become today's streets of the same name. The earthen hill referred to could possibly have been a reference to the large tomb mound of Xu Guangqi found about a block away on Nandan Road.

Address: 55 Puhuitang Road (Puhuitang Lu 55 hao) [蒲汇塘路 55]
Phone: (86) (021) 5424- 9688

Xujiahui Jesuit Seminary

This four-story, white bulding was originally constructed over a year between November 1928 and November 1929 to serve as the Zi-Ka-Wei Major Seminary, "Grand Seminaire" in French, for the Roman Catholic community of Xujiahui. After 1949, this building was occupied by the Shanghai city government and has up until the present day been used as a court house. Over a two year period from 2014 to 2016 the building did undergo significant restoration both inside and out to highlight its original appearance, but the government officials still have not moved out. In 2016 there was a so-called "soft opening" of just the ground floor, and only to organized tour groups on certain days of the week, but it now seems to be closed to the public once again. A notable attraction on the ground floor is supposedly a large auditorium. It would be nice to see what's inside, but considering the building's current occupants that seems a bit like putting your head in the lion's mouth, so I prefer to look at it safely from across the street.

The official address is #40 Nandan Lu [南丹路 40 号], but The main entrance gate to this high-security government compound actually faces Caoxi Bei Lu [漕溪北路], but public access for visitors to the former seminary, when it's available, is provided via a side gate facing Nandan Lu. It's also from Nandan Lu that one can get the best view of the historic building from outside the compound.

There was originally also a Minor Seminary, "Petit Seminaire" in French, in the same area, but that building no longer exists. It would have stood on the north side of Nandan Road, in between Coaxi North Road and Xu Guangqi Park.

Shanghai Film Studios

This was originally the site of the Roman Catholic St. Joseph's Convent of Carmel, a high-walled compound of several buildings constructed in 1874 and home to a group of resident nuns belonging to the Sisters of Carmel almost until 1950. A map of the Zi-Ka-Wei area from before 1949 shows this spot labeled as "Carmel," with half a dozen buildings.

In November 1949 the convent's compound was taken over by the Shanghai Film Studios, which preserved the original historic structures until January 2009 when they were suddenly completely demolished to make room for a new real estate development of highrise apartment towers. Shanghai Film Studios had itself been taken over by the much larger Shanghai Film Group in 2001, and the larger company was apparently less sentimental about this compound.

When I lived nearby on Puhuitang Road I often used to walk by the film studio compound's front gate, and along its northern wall where a very narrow pedestrian pathway ran in a zig zag route between two high walls, the buildings visible from that side covered with thick ivy, trying to sneak glimpses of what lay inside, and wonder about the movies that had been filmed there. It was a mysterious and intriguing place then.

In June 2013 a brand new Shanghai Film Museum was opened in small corner of the former site, surrounded by highrise apartment towers on all sides. It seems to feature mainly high-tech, interactive multi-media exhibits, rather than any genuine historic artifacts.
Address: 595 Caoxi Bei Lu [漕溪北路 595 号]

Y

Yangzi River Waterfront:

The Huangpu River flows into the Yangzi River at Wusong Kou [吴淞口] in Baoshan District (Boashan Qu) [宝山区].   This is where the British navy defeated Chinese defenders led by Chen Huacheng [陈化成](1776-1842) on June 16, 1842.   It was also the starting point of the Japanese naval invasions of 1932 and 1937, and scene of the Guomindang's last ditch effort to defend Shanghai against the Red Army in May 1949.   Until recently it had been largely a military controlled area, but increasingly scenic spots have begun to open up to the public. It is also the place to catch a ferry boat ride to Chongming Island.   Reaching Wusong Kou [吴淞口] has become easier with the extension of light rail Metro Line 3.

Wusong Battery Wetland Forest Park (Wusong Paotaiwan Shidi Senlin Gongyuan) [吴淞炮台湾 湿地森林公园]

In 2009 a section of the Wusong Kou [吴淞口] Yangzi River waterfront that had formerly been an industrial and military area was opened to the public as a beautiful new park.   The forested hill known as Paotai Shan [炮台山] where the Wusong Fort (Wusong Paotai) [吴淞炮台] and its gun emplacements once stood is still a military controlled area off limits to the public, but the new park surrounds its base.   Walking along the waterfront boardwalks and trails you can see all the ships on the Yangzi, as well as the ship traffic entering and exiting the narrow mouth of the Huangpu River.   An old lighthouse stands out in the middle of the water, marking the beginning of the Huangpu ship channel that is marked by a chain of smaller beacons, while a tall modern traffic control tower stands right at the confluence, directing the ship traffic in and out of the Huangpu River.   There is even one old wooden shipwreck beached on the shore of the park.   The park covers 110 hectares and stretches for a length of 2 km. along the Yangzi River coastline.   As of May 2009 it was only about half completed, but when finished it will stretch all the way from the mouth of the Huangpu River (Wusong Kou) [吴淞口] in the east to the Baoyang Road Ferry Dock (Baoyang Lu Matou) in the west.
Address: 206 Tanghou Lu, Baoshan District (Boashan Qu) [宝山区]

Wusong Port (Wusong Matou) [吴淞码头] resumed Yangzi River ferry service on July 24, 2009 after a ten year hiatus.   Passenger ships were scheduled to travel as far west as Jiujiang in Jiangxi province, the jumping off point for trips to Mt. Lushan, with stops at Yangzhou and Nanjing along the way.   Ferries also departed Wusong for Shanghai's two small islands of Hengsha and Changxing located in the Yangzi River estuary.   With the increasing number of other transportation options, passenger ferry services may have been discontinued by the time you read this, so be sure to check before relying on this type of transport.

Baoyang Road Ferry Dock (Baoyang Lu Matou) [宝杨路码头]
The main attraction for many visitors to Wusongkou may be in order to reach the ferry dock where boats depart for **Chongming Island** (Chongming Dao).   Ships leave for Chongming Island daily from 5:30 a.m. to 7:00 p.m.   There are two light rail stations nearby at Baoyang Lu and Youyi Lu on Metro Line 3.

Waterfront Promenade

West of the Baoyang Road Ferry Dock (Baoyang Lu Matou) [宝杨路码头] is a waterfront promenade that passes the River Viewing Pavilion (Wangjiang Lou) of Linjiang Park (Linjiang Gongyuan) [临江公园] and stretches all the way to Pangu Lu.   From 2007 to 2009 the Yangzi waterfront was widened here through a large landfill and construction of several new breakwaters east of the original one.   Parts of this promenade pass through what was once a military base, and some Chinese naval ships could still be seen tied up a dock here in May 2009.

Linjiang Park (Linjiang Gongyuan) [临江公园]

Inside Linjiang Park (Linjiang Gongyuan) [临江公园] is the 3-story Shanghai Songhu Anti-Japanese War Memorial Hall (Shanghai Songhu Kangzhan Jinian Guan) [淞沪抗战纪念馆] dedicated to the August-November 1937 Sino-Japanese battle for Shanghai.   Atop the hall is a four-sided tower with glass windows that can be ascended by elevator to the 10th floor for views of the Yangzi River and surrounding area.   The tower and hall were both opened to the public on January 28, 2000.   You can see the tower from far away in the distance as you approach along the waterfront promenade from the Baoyang Ferry Dock [宝杨路码头].

The park also has a memorial hall (jinian guan)[纪念馆] dedicated to Chen Huacheng [陈化成] (1776-1842) the Chinese scholar-official who died leading the defense of Wusong against the British invasion during the battle of June 16, 1842.   Two floors of exhibits about Chen are housed inside the former Da Cheng Hall of the Baoshan Confucius Temple (Baoshan Kong Miao Da Cheng Dian) [孔庙大成殿].   There are some real relics, including three bronze cannon apparently dating from the 1839-1842 Opium War.   Behind the hall stands a statue of Chen Huacheng [陈化成] (1776-1842).   Since he was blown to smithereens by British canon fire, and the remains of his body were never found, he has no actual tomb.   In addition to the memorial here, in 1985 a separate Chen Ancestral Hall (Chen Gong Ci) [陈公祠] (aka Chen Huacheng Ci) [陈化成祠] was established on the forested grounds of the Square Pagoda Park (Fangta Gongyuan) in Songjiang Town.

The park was first established in 1956 as Youyi Park [友谊公园], but had its name changed to Linjiang Park (Linjiang Gongyuan) [临江公园] in October 1965.   The Chen Huacheng Memorial Hall [陈化成纪念馆] was established in 1992.   The **River Viewing Pavilion** (Wangjiang Lou) was built in May 1993.   The **Shanghai Songhu Anti-Japanese War Memorial Hall** (Shanghai Songhu Kangzhan Jinian Guan) [淞沪抗战纪念馆] and its tower were added in the year 2000.   The park was been expanded three times, in 1991, 2004, and 2007, until it reached its current size of 107,703 sq. meters.

Address: 1 Youyi Lu [友谊路], Baoshan District
Nearest Metro Station: Baoyang Lu [宝杨路] or Youyi Lu Stations on Metro Line 3.

Yuan Ming Buddhist Lecture Hall (Yuanming Jiangtang) [圆明讲堂]

The Yuan Ming Buddhist Lecture Hall (Yuanming Jiangtang) was established in the autumn of 1934 by Master Yuan Ying [圆瑛法师] (1878-1953), who belonged to the Zen (Chan Zong) sect of Chinese Buddhism.   In 1940/1942 the Master Yuan Ming Society (Yuanming Fashi Hui) [圆瑛法师会] was set up to expound texts of Buddhism, and in 1942/1945 the Yuanming Lengyan Zhuanzong Xueyuan [楞严专宗学院], based on the Lengyan Jing scripture, and in 1942/1945/1948 a **Buddhism Institute** (Shanghai Yuanming Fo Xueyuan) [上海圆明佛学院] was established here.   In 1953 Master Yuan Ying [圆瑛法师] (1878-1953) became the first president of the **Chinese Buddhism Association** (Zhongguo Fojiao Xiehui) [中国佛教协会]. However, shortly thereafter on September 19, 1953 Master Yuan Yin [圆瑛法师] (1878-1953) died, and his disciple Master Ming Yang took charge of the Buddhist Rites Hall.   The institution was at least partly occupied by a wool clothes factory in 1958.

During the Cultural Revolution it was completely closed and suffered even more damage, until repairs finally started to be made in 1982.   In 1983 the Yuan Ming Buddhist Lecture Hall was recognized by the State Council as one of the key temples in China and reopened for religious purposes.   The Master Yuanming Memorial Hall [圆瑛法师纪念堂] and the Jade Buddha Hall [玉佛殿] both opened in 1983.   The **Buddhism Institute** (Fo Xue) [佛学] originally established in 1945 was resumed at the end of 1997.   At the end of 1999 the five-storey Hong Fa Building [弘法大楼] was set up covering a floor area of 2,399.6 sq. meters.

The yellow walls of the Yuan Ming compound are today sandwiched into a narrow space between the Yanan Xi Lu elevated expressway (gaojia) on the south and the high-rise Rendevous Hotel on the north.   The complex is composed of three main buildings containing many different halls.   Entering the Lecture Hall on the corner of Yanan Xi Lu and Zhenning Lu, you find inside a bookshop well stocked with many titles on Chinese Buddhism, as well as an exhibition of old black and white photos of Master Yuan Ying's activities during the Republic of China (Minguo) era.

Exiting this first building from its east side, you enter a courtyard that separates the other two buildings.   On your right is the original two-story Minguo hall built in 1934, and on your left is the newer five-story Hongfa Building constructed in 1999.   In the courtyard is a statue of the Maitreya Buddha (Milefo), and two interesting iron bells.   One of the bells is a very slender Tang Dynasty-style bell covered with inscriptions, quite similar in appearance to that found at Han Shan Buddhist Temple (Han Shan Si) in Suzhou, Jiangus.   The other bell has a more bulbous shape, with fewer inscriptions, but appears to be older.   These bells are relics that must have been moved here from somewhere else, but no one seems to know their origin.

The first floor of the original Minguo building is known as the Da Shi Da Bei Dian according to an inscribed sign board on its south side.   Inside a gilded class case in the center of the ground floor is a beautiful thousand-armed Guanyin statue that faces in all four directions. This version of Guanyin is known as Guanshiyin.   Along the side walls are many spirit tablets for the deceased, hence the great sadness (da bei) portion of the hall's name.   A statue of Weituo Pusa, the martial guardian of Buddhist temples, stands inside a class case outside the south side of the hall.

Although the wooden flights of steps leading up are normally kept closed, the second floor of this building contains the fascinating Ancestors' Hall (Zushi Tang), also known as the Yuan Ying Memorial Hall (Yuan Ying Jinian Guan).   Inside are shrines to all the temple's former deceased masters, including Yuan Ying and Ming Yuan.   A giant life-like statue of Yuan Ying stands at his shrine on the south side, and a photo of Ming Yuan graces a shrine dedicated to him at the north end.   This is a quite peaceful place for quiet meditation, despite the expressway being only a few feet away from the window.

From the Ancestor's Hall (Zushi Tang) two elevated pedestrian causeways connect with the five-story Hongfa Building across the central courtyard.   The ground floor of this building is occupied by the Jade Buddha Hall (Yufo Dian) containing a beautiful statue of a bejeweled white jade Buddha, sitting cross-legged, dressed in flowing golden robes, with a top knot of blue hair.   This statue is a near perfect replica of that at the Jade Buddha Temple (Yufo Si) in Shanghai.   The second floor of this building contains an extensive Library (Cangshu Lou) of Buddhist books and scriptures, which are amazingly open to the public for perusal.   The author counted 12 book cases of seven shelves each. In the center of the library stands another statue of a thousand-armed Guanyin.   The rest of the building is devoted to the monks' residential quarters.

This Buddhist site functions as both a place of Buddhist learning and religious worship for laymen.   It is quite popular with local lay Buddhists.   However, in contrast to many other Buddhist temples in Shanghai, the people here are quite friendly and willing to answer questions.   Because of the book shop in the Lecture Hall and the Library in the Hongfa Building, this is also an excellent place to learn more about Chinese Buddhism.   Even better, admission is free.

Address: 456 and 434 Yanan Xi Lu , intersection with Zhenning Lu.
Phone: (021) 6248-3968   Web Site: http://www.yuanming.org

Yu Garden (Yu Yuan) [豫园]

With beautiful pavilions, miniature lakes, bridges and rock formations, this walled garden is considered one of the most impressive examples of a Suzhou-style landscape garden.

The Yu Garden (Yu Yuan) [豫园] was first built during the Ming Dynasty by **Pan Yunduan** [潘允端] (1526–1601), a wealthy former Governor of Sichuan province, who dedicated it to his father, **Pan En** [潘恩].   Pan Yunduan was also responsible for building the first Chenxiang Ge Pavilion [沉香阁], and the Ever-Spring Hall (Shi Chun Tang) [世春堂], which later became Jingyi Church (Jingyi Tang) [敬一堂], possibly the first Catholic Church in Shanghai, and today one of the oldest buildings in the city.   Construction of the original Yu Garden (Yu Yuan) [豫园] started in 1559 and when it was finally completed in 1577 it covered 40 mu of land.

After the Pan family sold the Yu Garden (Yu Yuan) [豫园] in 1760 it was merged together with the neighboring **Inner Garden** (Nei Yuan) [内园] to create a total area of 70 mu.   The enlarged garden became the property of the **City God Temple** (Chenghuang Miao) [城隍庙] and was opened to the public.   The garden's **Mid-Lake Pavilion** Teahouse) (Huxin Ting Chalou) [湖心亭茶楼] became a popoular meeting place.

After the capture of Shanghai on July 19, 1842 during the First Opium War, the British military commander **General Sir Hugh Gough** and British plenipotentiary **Colonel Sir Henry Pottinger** used the Yu Garden (Yu Yuan) [豫园] as their military headquarters for about a week.

Later, on September 7, 1853, an offshoot of the Taiping rebels known as the **Small Sword Society** (Xiaodao Hui) [小刀会] captured the old walled town and held it for a year-and-a-half before being driven out on February 17, 1855.   During their occupation they established their headquarters in one of the Yu Yuan's halls, the **Hall of Heralding Spring** (Dianchun Tang) [点春堂], which now contains a small museum of artifacts dedicated to them.

Large-scale repairs started in 1956.   In 1959 it was classified as a city-level protected relic. In 1961 the garden was opened to the public for the first time.   In 1982 it was made a national-level protected cultural relic.

Today the Yu Garden (Yu Yuan) [豫园] covers an area of over two hectares, or 50,000 square meters, including the **Inner Garden** (Nei Yuan) [内园], which was not originally a part of the Pan family's garden.   While the Mid-Lake Pavilion (Huxin Ting) [湖心亭] and City God Temple (Chenghuang Miao) [城隍庙] were once connected to the Yu Yuan, they are now separated from it by a wall, and a special admission ticket must be purchased at one of two gates to enter the garden.

There are over 40 historic structures in the garden, and more than 30 trees which are over 100 years old.   Key sights in the garden include the dragon walls with their enormous fierce looking dragon heads, complete with bulging eyeballs, and the **Exquisite Jade Rock** (Yu Linglong) [玉玲珑] which stands erect in front of the **Hall Facing the Jade Rock** (Yuhua Tang) [玉华堂], which was the former owner's study.

The Yu Garden (Yu Yuan) [豫园] has six main scenic areas, centered around the **Three Ears of Corn Hall** (Sansui Tang) [三穗堂], the **Ten Thousand Flowers Chamber** (Wanhua Lou) [万花楼], **Hall of Heralding Spring** (Dianchun Tang) [点春堂], the **Scenery Gathering Tower** (Huijing Lou) [会景楼], the **Hall Facing the Jade Rock** (Yuhua Tang) [玉华堂], and finally the **Inner Garden** (Nei Yuan) [内园].

Address: 132 Anren Jie [安仁街]
Phone: (021) 6328-2465, 6326-0830
Nearest Metro Station: Old West Gate (Lao Xi Men) [老西门] Station on Line 8.

Z

Zhenru Buddhist Temple (Zhenru Si) [真如寺]

This temple was first built in the Tang Dynasty, but formerly at a town known as Da Chang Zhen, under the original name of Zhenru Yuan.   It was also known as Wanshou Si.   In the Song Dynasty the temple was rebuilt again at the original Da Chang Zhen site and under the same name.   However, in 1320, during the Yuan Dynasty, the temple moved to its present location at the confluence of two rivers and changed its name to Zhenru Si [真如寺].

During the Ming and Qing dynasties the temple continued to expand into a large complex of buildings that included a Main Hall (Zheng Dian), Guanyin Dian, Shi Wang Dian, Yoashi Dian, Dongyue Xinggong, Zhongxian Wang Dian, Chenghuang Xinggong, Dizang Dian, Weituo Dian, E Wang Dian, Luban Dian, Caishen Dian, Beifang Dian, Dabei Ge, Wenchang Ge, etc., many of which would be unusual to find at a typical Buddhist temple in China today. Although it was repaired many times, due to its location near the city center it managed to escape the destruction that other temples in the outlying districts suffered during the Taiping Rebellion.   By 1894 a commercial area known as Zhenru Town (Zhenru Zhen) had sprung up around the temple.

However, by May 1949 only the Main Hall (Zheng Dian) still survived.   In October 1950 government funds were provided to repair the Main Hall.   In May 1959 it was made a city-level protected relic.   In 1963 the Main Hall was rebuilt in order to restore its original Yuan Dynasty style architecture.   However, during the Cultural Revolution (1966-1976) the Main Hall was destroyed by a fire and all the remaining relics within and without it were smashed.   Reconstruction of the Main Hall began in 1979.   In November 1996 it was designated as a national level protected cultural relic.

In September 1998 construction began on bulding a completely new Zhenru Pagoda (Zhenru Fota) [真如佛塔], which was completed on December 24, 1999 when a ceremony was held to celebrate.   The square-shaped, wooden pagoda is 51 meters tall with nine floors, and designed in a combination of Song and Yuan dynasty style.   Although it is mostly made of wood, it does have a cement framework.

Location: 399 Lanxi Lu [兰溪路 399 号], Putuo District [普陀区]

Zhujiajiao Ancient Town (Zhujiajiao Gu Zhen) [朱家角古镇]

At least until 2018, when it became the terminus of the #17 subway line and was transformed by massive modern economic development and hordes of additional visitors, Zhujiajiao [朱家角] was a peaceful, traditional water town criss-crossed by six canals in an isolated, rural part of Qingpu District, far from Shanghai's downtown city center.　The center of town stood at the confluence of the **Caogang He** [漕港河] and **Zhumao He** [朱泖河] streams. The giant fresh-water lake, **Da Dian Hu** [大淀湖], is located on the northern edge of the town.　Along the sides of the canals and narrow cobble stone lanes are rows of ancient stone houses and shops.　The sights include a **Qing Dynasty Post Office** (Daqing Youju) [大清邮局] built in 1903 on West Lake Lane (Xihu Jie) [西湖街 35 号], the **Kezhi Garden** (Kezhi Yuan)[课植园] constructed in 1912 on Western Well Lane (Xijing Jie), the **Pearl Creek Garden** (Zhuxi Yuan) [珠溪园] originally built in 1584, small restaurants selling local delicacies, and shops with local handicrafts.　The **North Big Lane** (Bei Da Jie) [北大街] and **Front Line Lane** (Yixian Jie) [一线街] offer typical examples of local traditional architecture. Zhujiajiao also has historic religious institutions including a **City God Temple** (Chenghuang Miao) [城隍庙] from 1763 on Caohe Lane (Caohe Jie) [漕河街 69 号], **Yuanjin Buddhist Temple** (Yuanjin Chanyuan) [圆津禅院] originally built in 1341 and rebuilt in 2002, and a **Roman Catholic Church** (Tianzhu Jiaotang) [天主教堂] dating from 1898 on Caohe Lane (Caohe Jie) [漕河街 317 弄 27 号].

The half-dozen canals are spanned by a total of 36 stone-arched foot bridges dating from the 16th century, all of which are still used by local residents today to get from one part of town to the other.　The most impressive of these ancient stone bridges is the **Animal Releasing Bridge** (Fangsheng Qiao) [放生桥] built during the Ming Dynasty in 1571.　The Fangsheng Qiao has five arches and a very sharp-angled central peak.　At over 70 meters in length, nearly six meters in width, and more than 7 meters in height, it is the largest stone-arched bridge in Shanghai.　Built during the Ming Dynasty in the year 1571 the Animal Releasing Bridge (Fangsheng Qiao) [放生桥] crosses the stream known as the **Caogang He** [漕港河] located in the east end of town.　Its name commemorates the Buddhist practice of setting captive animals free, and was given by the Buddhist monk Xing Chao of Ci Men Temple who donated the money for the bridge's construction.

The local Zhujiajiao **City God Temple** (Chenghuang Miao) [城隍庙] is a Qing Dynasty structure dating from 1763.　A signboard hanging in the main hall was given to the temple by Emperor Qianlong [乾隆] (1735-1799) during one his famous journeys to the South down the Grand Canal (Jinghang Da Yunhe) from the capital in Beijing.　69 Caohe Lane (69 Caohe Jie) [漕河街 69 号].

Yuanjin Buddhist Temple (Yuanjin Chanyuan) [圆津禅院], originally constructed in 1341 during the Zhizhen reign (1341-1370) of the Yuan Dynasty, was recently rebuilt on the banks of the Caogang He [漕港河] in 2002.　It has one enormous central pavilion that stands four-stories high, with each level decorated by upturned roof eaves, and is surrounded by a yellow wall.　As the name implies it belongs to the Zen sect (Chan zong) [禅宗] of meditative Buddhism.　As recently as the year 2000 there was no trace of the original temple structures at all.　The current buildings have all been constructed since then, and were completed in 2002.

The Zhujiajiao **Roman Catholic Church** (Zhujiajiao Tianzhu Tang) [朱家角天主堂] dates from the 19th century, and was originally known as the Church of the Ascension. A smaller wooden church was first built on the same site in 1860. Later the present much larger structure was built here in 1898. The church's tall, square, Western-style, five-story, brick bell tower was not added until 1909. The main hall of the church is a one-story structure with a sloping tile roof made more imposing by a large, brick, Chinese-style facade resembling a pailou, which is covered with inscriptions. The church faces the stream known as the **Caogang He** [漕港河], and can be approached by boat. The buildings were last restored between 1992 and 1993. It is located at Caohe Lane, Alley # 317, Building #27 (Caohe Jie, 317 Long, 27 Hao) [漕河街 317 弄 27 号].

The **Kezhi Garden** (Kezhi Yuan) [课植园], located at 119-147 Well Lane (Xi Jing Jie) [西井街] in the northern part of Zhujiajiao town beside one of its canals, is a landscaped garden that was originally built in 1912. It is sometimes also called the **Ma Family Garden** (Majia Huayuan) [马家花园], after its original owner Ma Wenqing [马文卿]. One of its main features is the **Book Collecting House** (Cangshu Lou) [藏书楼]. The five-story tower **Full Moon Pavilion** (Wangyue Lou) [望月楼] was once the highest building in the whole town. Other structures include the Zou Ma Building and the Wu Chen Building. You must walk through the narrow lanes of Zhujajiao's old town to the gigantic **Animal Releasing Bridge** (Fangsheng Qiao) [放生桥], cross this ancient stone foot bridge over the stream known as the **Caogang He** [漕港河], and then turn left and head West up a narrow lane until you reach a small canal which flows in between **Eastern Well Lane** (Dong Jing Jie) [东井街] and **Western Well Lane** (Xi Jing Jie) [西井街]. Cross this canal over another small stone footbridge, then turn right and head due North up the cobblestone footpath known as Western Well Lane (Xi Jing Jie) [西井街] until you reach the entrance to the Kezhi Yuan [课植园]. From the garden it is but a short walk to an enormous fresh-water lake, **Da Dian Hu** [大淀湖].

Zhujiajiao Transportation

Zhujiajiao town is located in Qingpu District on the Huqingping Highway (Huqingping Gong Lu) [沪青平公路], about 6 km. from Qingpu Town, and 45 km. from People's Square (Renmin Guangchang). It takes about one hour to get there from downtown Shanghai by bus or taxi. You can catch a sightseeing bus from the Shanghai Stadium bus station. Since the end of December 2017 it has been the terminus of subway line #17 from Hongqiao Railway Station.

Zhujiajiao Town (Zhujiajiao Zhen) [朱家角镇] [2003 version]

This was a delightful old water town criss-crossed by six canals, upon which float traditional wooden boats.   A glance at a map shows that the center of town is actually on an island formed by the confluence of the **Caogang He** [漕港河] and **Zhumao He** [朱泖河] streams and a canal which runs between them.   The giant fresh-water lake, **Da Dian Hu** [大淀湖], is located on the northern edge of the town and is connected to the Caogang He via several of the town's canals.   Zhujiajiao is similar in style to the over-hyped water town of **Zhouzhuang,** but much more authentic, cheaper, less crowded and unspoiled.   Along the sides of the canals and narrow cobble stone lanes are rows of ancient stone houses and shops.   There is a Qing Dynasty Post Office (Daqing Youju) [大清邮局], traditional Chinese medicine shop, the **Kezhi Garden** (Kezhi Yuan) [课植园], the **Pearl Creek Garden** (Zhuxi Yuan) [珠溪园], small restaurants selling local delicacies, and shops offering local handicrafts.   **North Big Lane** (Bei Da Jie) [北大街] and **Front Line Lane** (Yixian Jie) [一线街] offer typical examples of local traditional architecture.   One can spend an entire day walking the narrow stone paved corridors which twist and turn in between the two-story stone houses, walking across the high-peaked stone arch foot bridges, sitting beside the canals at sidewalk restaurants, and riding in the wooden boats which take passengers around the town.

The half-dozen canals are spanned by a total of 36 stone-arched foot bridges dating from the 16th century of the Ming Dynasty which are still used by local residents today to get from one part of town to the other.   The most impressive of these ancient stone bridges is the **Animal Releasing Bridge** (Fangsheng Qiao) [放生桥], a very large Ming Dynasty stone structure with five arches and a very sharp-angled central peak.   At nearly 71 meters in length, almost six meters in width, and more than 7 meters in height, it is the largest stone-arched bridge in Shanghai.   Built in the year 1571, the fifth year of the Longqing reign of the Ming Dynasty, the Animal Releasing Bridge (Fangsheng Qiao) [放生桥] crosses the **Caogang He** [漕港河] stream in the East end of town, and connects North Big Lane (Bei Da Jie) [北大街] on one side with Eastern Well Lane (Dongjing Jie) [东井街] on the other side. Its name commemorates the Buddhist practice of setting captive animals free, and was given by the Buddhist monk Xing Chao of Ci Men Temple who donated the money for the bridge's construction.   It is the largest stone arched bridge within the Shanghai municipality.

The single-arched moon-shaped **Tai An Bridge** (Tai An Qiao) [泰安桥] located in the middle section of North Big Lane (Bei Da Jie) [北大街] was built in the year 1584, the 12th year of the Wanli reign of the Ming Dynasty, and was until recently the second oldest bridge in Zhujiajiao after the Animal Releasing Bridge (Fangsheng Qiao).   It stood in front of the Yuanjin Chansi Buddhist Temple.   It was notable for having the steepest angle of any bridge in Zhujiajiao.   The stone balustrades on both sides were decorated with the classic cloud pattern.   However, on the night of August 19, 2003 this 419 year old bridge suddenly collapsed without warning.   Although local authorities claimed that the bridge had been restored' by October 1st, photographs taken after the accident show that in fact the entire span had totally collapsed into the water and needed to be completely rebuilt from scratch.

The covered wooden **Huimin Bridge** (Huimin Qiao) dates from the Jiaqing reign of the Qing Dynasty. Its eastern end connects with the North Big Lane (Bei Da Jie) [北大街], and the western end with Temple Front Lane (Miao Qian Jie)/Caohe Lane (Caohe Jie) [漕河街]. It is the only wooden bridge in this town full of stone bridges.

Xi Shan Bridge (Xi Shan Qiao), also called Lucky Star Bridge (Fuxing Qiao) [福星桥], was built in the year of 1774, the 2nd year of the Yongzheng reign of the Qing Dynasty. It is located on the western branch of East Lake Lane (Donghu Jie Xi Duan) [东湖街西段] in the west end of the town on the Hukai Gang canal.

Zhujiajiao has historic religious institutions representing a wide range of faiths and beliefs. Among these are a City God Temple, a Buddhist Temple, and a Roman Catholic Church.

The local **City God Temple** (Chenghuang Miao) [城隍庙] is an 18th century Qing Dynasty structure dating from 1763. It was originally located south of the town on the Xueyin Bang canal, but was moved to its present site on the Xiangning Bang canal in the year 1763, the 28th year of the Qianlong reign of the Qing Dynasty. A signboard hanging in the main hall was given to the temple by Emperor Qianlong during one his famous journeys to the South down the Grand Canal (Jinghang Da Yunhe) from the capital in Beijing. This temple was recently restored and is quite an active social center for the community. The ancient practice of sacrificing the whole heads of pigs on an altar before the city god can still be seen here. Another unusual feature is that statues in the main hall depict the city god side by side with his wife. The main hall is inside a large courtyard surrounded by side halls and corridors full of an amazingly wide array of gods and goddesses. One of the more curios statues is that of a man with a hood covering his head, so that you cannot see his face. It is said that if his face is ever uncovered terrible events may happen. Many of Zhujiajiao's older retired people like to spend their time in the courtyard here relaxing, chatting, and playing checkers. Look for the ancient story teller wandering about the halls to have the whole temple explained to you.
Phone (021) 5924-2597

Yuanjin Buddhist Temple (Yuanjin Chanyuan) [圆津禅院], originally constructed during the Zhizhen reign (1341-1370) of the Yuan Dynasty, was rebuilt on the banks of the Caogang He [漕港河] in 2002. It has one enormous central pavilion that stands four-stories high, with each level decorated by upturned roof eaves, and is surrounded by a yellow wall. As the name implies it belongs to the Zen sect (Chan zong) of meditative Buddhism. When I first visited in the year 2000 there was no trace of the original temple structures at all. The current buildings have all been constructed since then, and were completed in 2002.

The Zhujiajiao **Roman Catholic Church** (Zhujiajiao Tianzhu Jiaotang) [天主教堂] dates from the 19th century, and was originally known as the Church of the Ascension. A smaller wooden church was first built on the same site in 1860. Later the present much larger structure was rebuilt in 1898. The church's tall, square, Western-style, five-story, brick bell tower was not added until 1909. Entrance into the walled compound is through an arched gateway which tunnels through the tower's ground floor, the two other gates on either side of the tower being kept shut. The main hall of the church is a simple one-story structure with a sloping tile roof made more imposing by a large, brick, Chinese-style facade resembling a pai lou, which is covered with inscriptions. The church faces the **Caogang He** [漕港河]

canal and can be approached by boat.   The buildings were last restored between 1992 and 1993.

Although the Zhujiajiao church now has a quite active congregation, it has had a particularly tumultuous history over the past 50 years.   In 1949 Qingpu County had an estimated 10,000 Catholics.   The Zhujiajiao church was part of a parish which included several other Catholic churches in nearby towns, as well as a Catholic school.   However, from 1953 to 1958 a series of leftist campaigns against supposed counter-revolutionaries within the Catholic church severely reduced the number of active worshippers, until by 1964 the Zhujiajiao Catholic Church had only 100 regular members.

Then, when the Cultural Revolution started in 1966, all the Catholic Churches in Qingpu County were closed down, and remained shut for the next 14 years.   Finally, in December 1980 the Zhujiajiao Catholic Church was the first church in Qingpu County to be repaired and reopened.   An estimated 1,000 people attended the church's formal reopening on Christmas Day 1980.   Many of these people were multi-generation believers (shidai jiaotu) who were descendants of the pre-1949 generation of local Catholics, but in the years since the church reopened thousands of new believers have been baptized.

Outside of Zhujiajiao town lie wide-open fields of bright yellow flowers tended by farmers.   These flowers are used to make cooking oil.   A long walk down the dirt roads bisecting these fields is a great way to temporarily escape from the confines of life in the city.

Zhujiajiao is listed in the Shanghai development plan as one of the municipal region's four officially designated historic towns.   Nonetheless, in 2001 urban development arrived here when the center of town was razed for the construction of a large public square and parking lot.   Since 2012 about two-thirds of the town have been lost to modern developments such as gargantuan garish shopping malls, subway stations, flashy new five-star hotels, and expansive parking lots.   However most of the key historic sights of the old town still remain.

On July 1, 2003 a new five-year development plan was announced just for Zhujiajiao. According to this plan, the town would be divided up into three sectors, a so-called Ancient Town of less than 1 square km., an Old Town of 2.4 square km., and a New Town of 3.6 square km.   Motor boats will be banned from the Caogang He [漕港河], but homeowners will be able to meet historic preservation requirements under quite flexible standards allowing for the modernization of the interior of buildings as long as the exterior preserves the original style.   A new sewage system and electricity grid will be installed.

Kezhi Garden (Kezhi Yuan) [课植园]

Located in the northern part of Zhujiajiao town beside one of its half dozen canals, this landscaped garden was originally built in 1912.   It is sometimes also called the **Ma Family Garden** (Majia Huayuan) [马家花园], after its original owner Ma Wenqing [马文卿].   One of its main features is the **Book Collecting House** (Cangshu Lou) [藏书楼].   The five-story tower **Full Moon Pavilion** (Wangyue Lou) [望月楼] was once the highest building in the whole town.   Other structures include the Zou Ma Building and the Wu Chen Building. The garden cannot be approached directly by motor vehicle, but rather requires some walking to get there.   You must walk through the narrow lanes of Zhujiajiao's old town to the gigantic **Fangsheng Qiao**, cross this ancient stone foot bridge over the **Caogang He** [漕港

河] stream, and then turn left and head West up a narrow lane until you reach a small canal which flows in between Eastern Well Lane (Dong Jing Jie) [东井街] and Western Well Lane (Xi Jing Jie) [西井街].   Cross this canal over another small stone footbridge, then turn right and head due North up the cobblestone footpath known as Western Well Lane (Xi Jing Jie) [西井街] until you reach the entrance to the Kezhi Yuan [课植园].   From the garden it is but a short walk to an enormous fresh-water lake, **Da Dian Hu** [大淀湖].   Kezhi Yuan [课植园] can also be reached by a slightly shorter walk from the end of the Huan Hu Lu road.
Address: 147 Western Well Lane (Xi Jing Jie 147 hao) [西井街 147 号], Zhujiajiao Town, Qingpu District.

Zhujiajiao town is one hour away from Shanghai by bus or taxi, just past **Qingpu Town**, and before **Dianshan Lake** (Dianshan Hu) [淀山湖], which is about 15 minutes further driving away.

Address: Huqingping Highway (Huqingping Gonglu) [沪青平公路], Qingpu District (Qingpu Qu). Web Sites: http://www.zhujiajiao.com, http://zhujj.shqp.gov.cn

Appendix I: Bibliography

Early Shanghai:

[A prime source for this time period is the official government histories of each district and county, the so-called difangzhi [地方志].   I began consulting the printed hard copies of these at the Shanghai Library in the 1990s, but now they can easily be found online here: http://www.shtong.gov.cn/node2/node4/node2249/index.html.]

Elvin, Mark, "Market Towns and Waterways: The County of Shanghai from 1480 to 1910," in G. William Skinner, ed., *The City in Late Imperial China*, Stanford University Press, 1977.

Jingan District Official History (*Jingan Qu Zhi*) [*静安区志*], Shanghai, 1996. (Chinese)

Johnson, Linda Cooke, *Shanghai: From Market Town to Treaty Port*, 1995.

Johnson, Linda Cooke, ed., *Cities of Jiangnan in Late Imperial China*, Albany: SUNY, 1993.

Luwan District Official History (*Luwan Qu Zhi*) [*卢湾区志*], Shanghai: February, 1998. (Chinese).   Now available online: http://www.shtong.gov.cn/node2/node4/node2249/luwan/index.html

Lu Haiping [陆海平] ed., *Rivers of China: The Shanghai Region (Zhongguo Jiang He: Shanghai Pian)* [*中国江河: 上海篇*], Shanghai: Shanghai People's Fine Arts Publishing House (Shanghai Renmin Meishu Chubanshe) [上海人民美术出版社], 2000. (Includes a chapter on Qinglong Town.) (Chinese)

Montalto de Jesus, C.A., *Historic Shanghai*, Shanghai: Shanghai Mercury, 1909.

Nanshi District Official History (*Nanshi Qu Zhi*) [*南市区志*], Shanghai, 1997. (Chinese) Now available online: http://www.shtong.gov.cn/node2/node4/node2249/nanshi/node70266/index.html

Pan, Hongxuan [潘洪萱], *Ancient Bridges in Jiangnan (Jiangnan Guqiao)* [*江南古桥*], Hangzhou: Zhejiang Photography Publishing House (Zhejiang Sheying Chubanshe) [浙江摄影出版社], 1999. (Chinese)

Shanghai County Official History (Shanghai Xian Zhi) [*上海县志*], Shanghai. (Chinese)

Shanghai Old Town, Shanghai.

The Markets Below the Roof Eaves, Shanghai.

Longhua Town:

Burn, D.C.,   *A Guide to Lunghwa Temple: with Brief Notes on Chinese Buddhism*, Shanghai: Kelly and Walsh, Ltd., 1926.

The History of Longhua Town (*Longhua Zhen Zhi*) *[龙华镇志]*, Shanghai: December 1996. (Chinese)

Zhang Qinghua and Zhu Baikui, *Longhua [龙华]*, Guangling Shushe, Yangzhou: December 2003. (Chinese)

Pan Mingquan [潘明权] (b.1947), *Shanghai Buddhist & Taoist Temples (Shanghai Fo Si Dao Guan) [上海佛寺道观]*, 2003.   (Chinese)

Shanghai Tan [上海滩] magazine, Shanghai: October 2002, pp.38-42 on the history of Longhua Temple. (Chinese)

Suburban Shanghai Districts:

[A prime source for these areas is the official government histories of each district and county, the so-called difangzhi [地方志] or xianzhi [县志].   I began consulting the printed hard copies of these at the Shanghai Library in the 1990s, but now they can easily be found online here: http://www.shtong.gov.cn/node2/node4/node2249/index.html.]

Dennerline, Jerry, *The Chia-Ting Loyalists*, New Haven: Yale University Press, 1981. (Southern Ming resistance to the Manchus in Jiading.)

Famous Towns South of the Yangzi River (*Jiangnan Mingzhen*) *[江南名镇]*, Chapter 7 on Zhujiajiao , pp.84-98, Shanghai: Shanghai Book Store Publishing House (Shanghai Shudian Chubanshe), July 2003. ISBN#7-80678-062-9. (Chinese)

Kahler, William R., *Rambles Round Shanghai*, Shanghai: The Union, 1905.   211 pp.

Jiading County Official History (*Jiading Xian Zhi*) *[嘉定县志]*, Shanghai, 1992. (Chinese) Now available online: http://www.shtong.gov.cn/node2/node4/node2250/node4424/node34336/index.html

Meskill, John Thomas, *Gentlemanly Interests and Wealth on the Yangtze   Delta*, Ann Arbor, 1994. (The only English language source which focuses on the history of Songjiang County.)

Qingpu County Official History (*Qingpu Xian Zhi*) *[青浦县志]*, Shanghai, 1990.   (Chinese) Now available online: http://www.shtong.gov.cn/node2/node4/node2250/node4427/node34338/index.html

Ruan Yisan [阮仪三], *Canal Towns in Jiangnan Area (Jiangnan Shuixiang Guzhen) [江南水乡古镇]: Zhujiajiao*, Hangzhou: Zhejiang Photography Publishing House (Zhejiang Sheying Chubanshe) [浙江摄影出版社], September 2004. (Chinese)

Shanghai Tan [上海滩] magazine, Shanghai: August 2002, pp.24-28 on the history of Jiading Town. (Chinese)

Songjiang County Official History (*Songjiang Xian Zhi*) [松江县志], Shanghai: August 1991. (Chinese).   Now available online:
http://www.shtong.gov.cn/node2/node4/node2250/songjiang/index.html

Songjiang Town Official History (*Songjiang Zhen Zhi*) [松江镇志], Shanghai: May 1990. (Chinese)

Wilkinson, E.S., *Shanghai Country Walks*, 1932.

Shanghai Gardens

Ding, Liangcai, ed., *Yuyuan Garden*, Shanghai: 1999.

Famous Gardens South of the Yangzi River (*Jiangnan Mingyuan*) [江南名园], pp.79-112 on Shanghai gardens, Shanghai: Shanghai Book Store Publishing House (Shanghai Shudian Chubanshe), December 2002. ISBN#7-80622-971-X. (Chinese)

Shanghai in The First Opium War (1839-1842)

Cunynghame, Captain Arthur, *The Opium War: Being Recollections of Service in China*, Wilmington, DE: Scholarly Resources, 1972 reprint of 1845 edition.

Ouchterlony, John, *The Chinese War: An Account of All the Operations of the British Forces from the Commencement to the Treaty of Nanking*, London: Saunders and Otley, 1844.

Fay, Peter Ward, *The Opium War, 1840-1842*, Chapel Hill: University of North Carolina Press, 1975.

Holt, Edgar, *The Opium Wars in China*, London: 1964.

Waley, Arthur, *The Opium War Through Chinese Eyes*, London: Allen & Unwin, 1958.

Economic Shanghai (1842-1949):

Anderson, Irvine H., *The Standard Vacuum Oil Company and U.S. East Asian Policy, 1933-1941*, Princeton, 1975.

Bergere, Marie Claire, *The Golden Age of the Chinese Bourgeoisie, 1911-1937*, New York: Cambridge University Press, 1989.

Chan, Wellington K.K., "Selling Goods and Promoting a New Commercial Culture: The Four Premier Department Stores on Nanjing Road, 1917-1937," pp.19-36 in Sherman Cochran, ed., 1999.

Coble, Jr., Parks M., *The Shanghai Capitalists and the Nationalist Government, 1927-1937*, Cambridge, Mass.: Harvard University Press, 1980.

Cochran, Sherman, ed., _Inventing Nanjing Road: Commercial Culture in Shanghai, 1900-1945_, Ithaca, NY: Cornell University, 1999.

Cochran, Sherman, _"Commercial Culture in Shanghai, 1900-1945:   Improved or Invented? Cut Short or Sustained?"_ pp.3-18 in Sherman Cochran, ed., 1999.

Drage, Charles, _Taikoo_, London: Constable, 1970.   (A history of Butterfield and Swire.)

Fewsmith, Joseph, _Merchant Organizations and Politics in Shanghai, 1890-1930_, 1985.

Hou, Chi Ming, _Foreign Investment and Economic Development in China, 1840-1937_, Cambridge: Harvard University Press, 1965.

King, Frank H.H.,   _A Concise Economic History of Modern China, 1840-1961_, New York, N.Y. Praeger London Pall Mall, 1968.

King, Frank H.H.,   ed., _Eastern Banking: Essays in the History of the Hongkong and Shanghai Banking Corporation, Papers first presented at a conference sponsored by the Hongkong and Shanghai Banking Corporation, and held at the Centre for Asian Studies, University of Hong Kong, Dec. 1981_, London: Athlone Press, 1983.

King, Frank H.H.,   The History of the Hong Kong and Shanghai Banking Corporation, Vol. 1, The Hongkong Bank in Late Imperial China, 1864-1902: On an Even Keel, Cambridge: Cambridge University Press, 1987.

King, Frank H.H.,   The History of the Hong Kong and Shanghai Banking Corporation, Vol.2 , The Hongkong Bank in the Period of Imperialism and War, 1895-1918:   Wayfoong, the Focus of Wealth,   Cambridge: Cambridge University Press, 1988.

King, Frank H.H.,   The History of the Hong Kong and Shanghai Banking Corporation, Vol.3, The Hong Kong Bank Between the Wars and the Bank Interned, 1919-1945:   Return from Grandeur, Cambridge: Cambridge University Press, 1987.

King, Frank H.H.,   The History of the Hong Kong and Shanghai Banking Corporation, Vol.4, The Hongkong Bank in the Period of Development and Nationalism, 1941-1984:   From Regional Bank to Multinational Group, Cambridge: Cambridge University Press, 1991.

Levy, M.J., _The Rise of the Modern Chinese Business Class_, N.Y., 1949.

Liu, Kwang-Ching, _Anglo-American Steamship Rivalry in China, 1862-1874_, Cambridge: Harvard University Press, 1962.   (A great deal of information on the histories of the rival China traders Butterfield and Swire, Jardine Matheson, and Russell Co.)

Shai, Aron, _The Fate of British and French Firms in China, 1949-1954:   Imperialism Imprisoned_, London: Macmillan, 1996.

Sopher, Arthur, and Sopher, Theodore _The Profitable Path of Shanghai Realty_, Shanghai: Shanghai Times, 1939.

Tamagna, Frank M., *Banking and Finance in China*, N. Y.: Institute of Pacific Relations, 1942.

Taire, Lucian, *Shanghai Episode: The End of Western Commerce in Shanghai*, Hong Kong: Rainbow Press, 1957.

Shanghai Directory, Shanghai: North China Daily News and Herald, July 1941. (Contains a "List of Hongs," and a "Who's Who," as well as fascinating period advertisements.)

COMACRIB, Shanghai: 1935.

Shen Ji, *Lao Shanghai Nanjing Lu (Old Shanghai Nanjing Road)*, Shanghai: Shanghai Renmin Meishu Chubanshe, 2003.

The Taiping Rebellion in Shanghai

Abend, Hallett, *The God From the West: A Biography of Frederick Townsend Ward*, Garden City, N.Y.:   Doubleday, 1947.

Allen, Bernard M., *Gordon In China*, London: Macmillan, 1933.

Carr, Caleb, *The Devil Soldier: The Story of Frederick Townsend Ward*, New York: Random House, 1992.

Curwen, Charles A., *Taiping Rebel: the Deposition of Li Hsiu-Cheng (Li Xiucheng),* Cambridge: Cambridge University Press, 1977.

Gregory, J.S., *Western Reports on the Taiping: A Selection of Documents*, 1982.

Hail, William James, *Tseng Kuo Fan (Zeng Guofan)*, New Haven: Yale University Press, 1927.

Li, Hsiu Cheng (1823-1864), and Way, W. T. , tr., *The Autobiography of the Chung-Wang, Li Hsiu Cheng Kung Chuang (the Zhong Wang, Li Xiucheng)*, Shanghai: Presbyterian Mission Press, 1865.

Michael, Franz, *The Taiping Rebellion: History and Documents*, Seattle: University of Washington Press, 1972. 3 vols.

Spector, Stanley, *Li Hung Chang (Li Hongzhang) and the Huai Army*, Seattle: University of Washington Press, 1964.

The Foreign Settlements in Shanghai

Chinese Maritime Customs Service, _Documents Illustrative of the Origin, Development, and Activities of the Chinese Customs Service_, Vol. VII, _"Despatches, Letters, Memoranda, Index (1843-1937),"_ Shanghai: Inspectorate General of Customs, 1937.   Seven volumes.

Johnstone, William Crane, _The Shanghai Problem_, 1937.

Kotenev, A. M., _Shanghai: Its Mixed Court and Council_, Shanghai: North-China Daily News and Herald, 1925.

Kotenev, A. M., _Shanghai: Its Municipality and the Chinese, Being the History of the Shanghai Municipal Council and Its Relations with the Chinese, the Practice of the International Mixed Court, and the Inauguration and Constitution of the Shanghai Provisional Court_, Shanghai: North-China Daily News & Herald, 1927.

Kounin, I.I., _Eighty Five Years of the Shanghai Volunteer Corps_, Shanghai: Cosmopolitan Press, n.d., ca.1939.

Revolutionary Shanghai

Chen, Joseph T., _The May Fourth Movement in Shanghai: The Making of a Social Movement in Modern China_, Leiden: Brill, 1971.

Isaacs, Harold R., _The Tragedy of the Chinese Revolution_, Stanford: Stanford University Press, 1961, Second Edition.   (Chinese politics of the 1920s and 1930s as told by a man who lived in Shanghai during that time.)

Kuo, Thomas C., _Chen Tu Hsiu (Chen Duxiu) and the Chinese Communist Movement_, N.J., 1975.

Rudinger de Rodyenko, Stephen Piero Sergius, _The Second Revolution in China, 1913:   My Adventures of the Fighting around Shanghai, the Arsenal, Woosung Forts_, Shanghai: Shanghai Mercury, Ltd., 1914.

Cosmopolitan Shanghai (1842-1949):

Ben-Eliezer, Judith, *Shanghai Lost; Jerusalem Regained*, Israel: 1985.

Betta, Chiara, "Silas Aaron Hardoon and Cross-Cultural Adaptation in Shanghai,"

Betta, Chiara, *Silas Aaron Hardoon (1815-1931): Marginality and Adaptation in Shanghai*, University of London, Unpublished Ph. D. Dissertation, 1997.

Dicker, Herman, *Wanderers and Settlers in the Far East*, N.Y.: Twayne Publishers, 1962. (More about the earlier Sephardic immigrants than the later Jewish refugees.)

Ginsbourg, Anna, *Jewish Refugees in Shanghai*, Shanghai: China Weekly Review, 1941.

Heppner, Ernest G., *Shanghai Refuge: A Memoir of the World War II Jewish Ghetto,* Lincoln: University of Nebraska Press, 1993.

Jackson, Stanley, *The Sassoons: Portrait of a Dynasty*, London : Heinemann, 1989.

Pan, Guang, ed., *The Jews in Shanghai,* Shanghai: Shanghai Pictorial Publishing House, 2001. (The best one volume summary history of Shanghai's Jewish community.)

Reynders Ristaino, Marcia, *Port of Last Resort: Diaspora Communities of Shanghai*, Stanford: Stanford University Press, 2001. (The most detailed study of Shanghai's Russian community.)

Reinisch, George, *Shanghai Haven*, 1984.

Ross, James R., *Escape to Shanghai, a Jewish Community in Shanghai,* New York: Free Press, 1994.

Shanghai Architecture and Urban Planning:

Cai Yutian [蔡育天], ed. , preface by Han Zheng [韩正], *Tracing Back: The Excellent Architecture of Modern Times in Shanghai (Hui Mou: Shanghai Youxiu Jindai Baohu Jianzhu)* [回眸: 上海优秀近代保护建筑], Shanghai [上海]: Shanghai People's Publishing House (Shanghai Renmin Chubanshe) [上海人民出版社], May 2001. 386 pp. (Chinese).

Cody, Jeffrey W., *Building in China: Henry K. Murphy's Adaptive Architecture, 1914-1935*, Hong Kong: Chinese University Press, 2001.

Cody, Jeffrey W., *Exporting American Architecture 1870-2000*, Routledge, 2005. 304 pp.

Chen Congzhou [陈从周] and Zhang Ming [章明], ed., *A Draft History of Modern Shanghai Architecture (Shanghai Jindai Jianzhu Shigao)* [上海近代建筑史稿], Shanghai [上海]: Shanghai Joint Publishing (Shanghai Sanlian Shudian) [上海三联书店], 2002 reprint. [First published in 1988.] 229 pp. (Chinese).

Denison, Edward and Guang Yuren, *Building Shanghai: The Story of China's Gateway*, John Wiley & Sons, 2006.

Han Chaolu, "*The Seventy Two Tenants: Residence and Commerce in Shanghai's Shikumen Houses, 1872-1951,*" pp.133-184 in Sherman Cochran, ed., Inventing Nanjing Road: Commercial Culture in Shanghai, 1900-1945, Cornell University, 1999. 252 pp.

Huebner, Jon W., "*The Shanghai Bund's Missing Monuments,*" American Asian Review, Vol. VIII, No. 1, 1990, pp.88-97.

Johnston, Tess and Erh, Deke (Er Dongqiang), *A Last Look: Western Architecture in Old Shanghai*, Hong Kong: Old China Hand Press, 1993. 111pp.

Johnston, Tess and Erh, Deke (Er Dongqiang), *Frenchtown Shanghai: Western Architecture in Shanghai's Old French Concession*, Hong Kong: Old China Hand Press, 2000.

Lou, Rongmin, ed., *The Bund: History and Vicissitudes (Waitan: Lishi he Bianqian)*, Shanghai: Shanghai Pictorial Publishing House (Shanghai Huabao Chubanshe), 1998.

MacPherson, Kerrie L. , *"Designing China's Urban Future: The Greater Shanghai Plan, 1927–1937,"* Planning Perspectives, Volume 5, Issue 1, 1990, pages 39-62.

Novelli, Luigi, *Shanghai Architecture Guide: 100 Years, 100 Buildings (Shanghai Youzhe Zhongxi Bainian Jianzhu de Chengshi)*[上海: 有着中西百年建筑的城市], Shanghai: Bai Jia Publishing House (Baijia Chubanshe) [百家出版社] , 2001. 127 pp. ISBN# 9787806564790. (English)

Ye Shuping, *Old Photos of Shanghai aka Old Fashions of Shanghai (Shanghai Jiu Ying)* [上海旧影], Beijing: People's Fine Arts Publishing House (Renmin Meishu Chubanshe) [人民美术出版社], 1998. (Chinese).

Shanghai Municipal Tourist Administration, *A Tour of Shanghai's Historical Architecture*, Henan Fine Arts Publishing House, 1996.

Shanghai Municipality Xuhui District Housing Management Office (Shanghai Shi Xuhui Qu Fangwu Tudi Guanli Ju) [上海市徐汇区房屋土地管理局], *Old Houses Behind Phoenix Trees: Shanghai Xuhui District Historic Architecture Collection* (*Wutong Shu Hou De Lao Fangzi: Shanghai Xuhui Lishi Jianzhu Jjjin*) [*桐树后的老房子: 上海徐汇历史建筑集锦*], Shanghai [上海]: Shanghai Pictorial Publishing House (Shanghai Huabao Chubanshe) [上海画报出版社], 2001. 192 pp. (Chinese)

Shanghai Urban Planning Administrative Bureau, *The Comprehensive Plan of Shanghai, 1999-2020*, Shanghai, n.d., ca. 2002.

Shanghai Historic Maps:

Zhang Wei [张伟], *The Album of Shanghai During the Past 150 Years (Lao Shanghai Ditu)* [*老上海地图*], Shanghai Library (Shanghai Tushuguan) [上海图书馆], Shanghai Pictorial Publishing House (Shanghai Huabiao Chubanshe) [上海画报出版社], June 2001. 66 maps including some in English, French and Japanese.

Zhou Zhenhe [周振鹤], *Shanghai Historic Maps Collection* (*Shanghai Lishi Ditu Ji*) [*上海历史地图集*], Shanghai: Shanghai People's Publishing House (Shanghai Renmin Chubanshe) [上海人民出版社], 1999. 157 pp. ISBN# 9787208032859.

Shanghai Municipal Council, *Plan of Shanghai*, Shanghai: 1928. 1 vol. Fold-out Map.

Intellectual Shanghai:

Ding Ling

Alber, Charles J., *Enduring the Revolution: Ding Ling and the Politics of Literature in Guomindang China*, Westport, Conn.; London: Praeger, 2002.

Feuerwerker, Yi-tsi Mei, *Ding Ling's Fiction: Ideology and Narrative in Modern Chinese Literature*, Cambridge, Mass.: Harvard University Press, 1982.

Ding, Ling; Jenner, W.J.F., tr., *Miss Sophie's Diary and Other Stories*, Beijing: China International Book Trading Corp., 1985. 271 pp. A translation of nine short stories selected by the author: *Miss Sophie's Diary*; *Shanghai in the Spring of 1930*; *From Dusk to Dawn*; *The hamlet*; *A Certain Night*; Rushing; *The reunion*; *When I was in Xia Village*; *Night*.

Barlow, Tani E. with Bjorge, Gary J., ed. & tr., *I Myself Am a Woman: Selected Writings of Ding Ling*, Boston: Beacon Press, 1989.

Lu Xun

Lee, Leo Ou-fan, *Voices From the Iron House: A Study of Lu Xun*, Bloomington: Indiana University Press, 1987.

Lee, Leo Ou-fan, ed., *Lu Xun and His Legacy*, Berkeley: University of California Press, 1984.

Pollard, David E., *The True Story of Lu Xun*, Hong Kong: Chinese University Press, 2002.

Wang, Shiqing, *Lu Xun: A Biography*, Beijing: Foreign Languages Press, 1984.

Weiss, Ruth F., *Lu Xun: A Chinese Writer for All Times*, Beijing: New World Press, 1985.

Yang, Gladys, *Silent China: Selected Writings of Lu Xun*, London: Oxford University Press, 1973.

Yang, Gladys, *Selected Works of Lu Hsun*, Peking: Foreign Languages Press, 1956-1960. 4 vols.

Mao Dun

Mao Tun, *Midnight*, Peking: Foreign Languages Press, 1st ed. 1957, 2nd ed. 1979.

Mao Tun, *Spring Silkworms and Other Stories*, Peking: Foreign Languages Press, 1979.

Anthologies and Studies of Modern Chinese Literature

Denton, Kirk A., ed., *Modern Chinese Literary Thought: Writings on Literature, 1893-1945*, Stanford: Stanford University Press, 1996.   An anthology of important essays: Hu Shi, *"Some Modest Proposals for the Reform of Literature;"* Chen Duxiu, *"On Literary Revolution;"* Lu Xun, *"The Divergence of Art and Politics;"* Hu Feng, *"What Do the Broad Masses Demand of Literature?;"* Ding Ling, *"We Need the Zawen Essay;"* Mao Zedong, *"Talks at the Yan'an Forum on Literature and Art."*

Hsia, Tsi-an, *The Gate of Darkness; Studies on the Leftist Literary Movement in China,* Seattle : University of Washington Press, 1968.

Isaacs, Harold R., ed., *Straw Sandals: Chinese Short Stories, 1918-1933*, Cambridge: MIT Press, 1973.   Forward by Lu Xun.   Collection originally compiled in 1934.

Religious Shanghai:

Buddhist Treasure (Fo Bao), August 2003. (Chinese)

Dictionary of Buddhsim (Fojiao Da Cidian), December 2002. (Chinese)

Jin, Luxian, *Jinri Tianzhu Jiao Shanghai Jiaoqu (Catholic Church in Shanghai Today)*, Shanghai: Guang Qi She, 2000. (Chinese)

MacInnus, Donald E., *Religion in China Today: Policy and Practice*, Maryknoll: Orbis Books, 1989. (Sections on Qingpu County Catholics, Zhujiajiao and Sheshan Cathedral.)

Novelli, Luigi, *Shanghai: Religious Buildings*, Shanghai: Haiwen Audio-Video Publishers, 2002.

Pas, Julian F., Ed., *The Turning of the Tide: Religion in China Today*, RAS HK Branch and Oxford University Press: 1989.

Pan Mingquan [潘明权], *Shanghai Buddhist and Taoist Temples (Shanghai Fosi Daoguan) [上海佛寺道观],*" Shanghai: Shanghai Cishu Chubanshe, December 2003. (Chinese)

Pan Mingquan [潘明权], Shanghai Si Miao Ying Lian Dui Lian Ji *(Poems About Shanghai Buddhist and Taoist Temples)*, Shanghai: Shanghai Ci Shu Chubanshe, December 2003. (Chinese)

Stockwell, Foster, *Religion in China Today*, Beijing: New World Press, 1996.

Zhou Fuchang [周富长], ed., *Shanghai Zongjiao Zhilu [上海宗教之旅]*, Shanghai Encyclopedia Publishing House (Shanghai Cishu Chubanshe) [上海辞书出版社] (2004). (Chinese)

Xujahui:

American Jesuits in Shanghai, Nanking & Hai Chow, *Portraits of China* , Shanghai: Gonzaga College, 1936.

A Visit to Siccawei Observatory, Shanghai: North China Daily News, 1908. 12 pp.

Bell, G.J., *"Father Ernesto Gherzi, S.J., 1886-1973; An Appreciation, "* Journal of the Hong Kong Branch of the Royal Asiatic Society, Vol. 14, 1974, c. 1975, pp.85-91.
(Bell was Director of the Royal Observatory in Hong Kong.)

Borrell, Octavius William, *"A Short History of the Heude Museum,"* Journal of the Hong Kong Branch of the Royal Asiatic Society, Vol. 31, 1991, pp.183-191.

Kavanagh, D.J., *The Zi-ka-wei Orphanage*, San Francisco: James H. Barry, n.d. 24 pp.

Kearney, James F., *The Four Horsemen Ride Again*, Shanghai: Tou Se We, 1940.

Siccawei Catholic Mission, *The 0bservatory of Zi-ka-wei: Fifty Years of Scientific Work*, Shanghai: Hsu Chia Hui Mission, 1928.

The Story of Siccawei Observatory, Shanghai: North China Daily News, n.d.

Shanghai Tan [上海灘] magazine, October 2002, pp.18-21 on the history of Xujiahui. (Chinese)

Walsh, Reverend James Anthony, *Observations in the Orient*, NY: Catholic Foreign Mission Society of America, 1919.

Republican Shanghai (1911-1949):

Bergere, Marie-Claire, *Sun Yat-sen*, Stanford: Stanford University Press, 1998.

Chang, Jung with Halliday, Jon, *Madame Sun Yat-Sen (Soong Ching-ling)*, Harmondsworth, Middlesex, England: Penguin Books, 1986.

Eastman, Lloyd E., et al, *The Nationalist Era in China, 1927-1949*, New York: Cambridge University Press, 1991.

Epstein, Israel, *Woman in World History: Soong Ching Ling (Madame Sun Yat-sen)*, Beijing: New World Press, 1995, Second Edition.

Liew, K.S., *Struggle for Democracy: Sung Chiao-jen (Song Jiaoren) and the 1911 Chinese Revolution*, 1971.

Criminal Shanghai:

Martin, Brian G., The Shanghai Green Gang: Politics and Organized Crime, 1919-1937, Berkeley: University of California Press, 1996.

Hershatter, Gail, Dangerous Pleasures: Prostitution and Modernity in Twentieth-Century Shanghai, Berkeley: University of California Press, 1997.

Wakeman, Jr., Frederic, Policing Shanghai, 1927-1937, Berkeley: University of California Press, 1995.

Shanghai's pre-1949 Libraries:

Cordier, Henri, *The Life and Labours of Alexander Wylie*, n.p., n.d.   18 pp.

Otness, Harold M., *"A History of the Library of the North China Branch of the Royal Asiatic Society,"* Journal of the Hong Kong Branch of the Royal Asiatic Society, Vol. 28, 1988, c. 1990, pp.185-197.

Selected Archival Treasures of Shanghai," Orient Publishing Center, 1996.

Shanghai Library (Shanghai Tushuguan) [上海市图书馆], editor (bian) [编], *Former Royal Asiatic Society Library Catalog* (*Qian Yazhou Wenhui Tushuguan Tushu Mulu*) *[前亚洲文会图书馆图书目录]*, Shanghai: Shanghai Tushuguan, 1955. Two Volumes. (Catalog of the former RAS Library.)

Shanghai Library (Shanghai Tushuguan) [上海市图书馆], editor (bian) [编], (Xujiahui Library Warehouse Local Histories Draft Catalog) *Xujiahui Cangshu Lou Suocang Difangzhi Mulu Chugao [徐家汇藏书楼所藏地方志目录初稿]*, Shanghai: Shanghai Library (Shanghai Tushuguan) [上海市图书馆], 1957.   25 Volumes.   (A catalog of local histories in the Zikawei Library collection.)

Shanghai Library (Shanghai Tushuguan) [上海市图书馆], editor (bian) [编], *Xujiahui Library Western Languages Books Collection Draft Catalog* (*Xujiahui Cangshu Lou Xiwen Cangshu Mulu Chugao) [徐家汇藏书楼西文藏书目录初稿]*, Shanghai: Shanghai Library (Shanghai Tushuguan) [上海市图书馆], 1958.   29 volumes.   (A catalog of foreign language books held in the Zikawei Libary collection at that time.)

Shanghai Library (Shanghai Tushuguan) [上海市图书馆], editor (bian) [编], *Shanghai Library Warehouse Former Maritime Customs House Library Catalog* (*Shanghai Tushuguan Cang Qian Haiguan Tushuguan Shumu)[上海图书馆藏前海关图书馆书目]*, Shanghai: Shanghai Library (Shanghai Tushuguan) [上海市图书馆], 1959.   Two Volumes.   (A catalog of the former collection of the China Maritime Customs Service Library, which was previously located in Shanghai prior to 1950, but is apparently now part of the China Second National Archives in Nanjing.   This volume has been somewhat superseded by the new digital catalog for the China Maritime Customs Service collections held at the Second National Archives in Nanjing completed by the University of Bristol in the U.K.)

Shanghai Library, *Shanghai Library Catalog of Western Rare books*, Shanghai: Publishing House of Shanghai Academy of Social Sciences, 1992.

Shanghai Library (Shanghai Tushuguan) [上海图书馆], *40th Anniversary of the Founding of Shanghai Library, Collected Works, 1952-1992,(Shanghai Tushuguan Jianguan Sishi Zhounian Wenji, 1952-1992)* [上海图书馆建馆 40 周年文集], Shanghai: 1992.

Shanghai Tan [上海滩], magazine, October 2002, pp.18-21 on the history of Xujiahui and the Zikawei Library. (Chinese)

Stam, David H., ed., *International Dictionary of Library Histories*, Vol. II, Chicago: Fitzroy Dearborn Publishers.

Tan, Chu Yuan, *The Development of Chinese Libraries Under the Ch'ing Dynasty, 1644-1911*, Shanghai: Commercial Press, 1935.

Wong, V.L. , *The Low Library: A History*, Shanghai: St. John's University, 1924. (Reprinted from the *St. John's Echo*, February, 1924.)

Shanghai's Historic Universities

Aurora University Shanghai, Zi-ka-wei: Tou-se-we, 1935.   181 pp.

Bulletin of St. Ignatius University, San Francisco, 1914.   116 pp.

Chen, Kaiyi, *Seeds From the West: St. John's Medical School, 1880-1952*, 2001.   316 pp.

Chyne, W. Y. *Handbook of Cultural Institutions in China*, Shanghai: Chinese National Committee on Intellectual Cooperation, 1936.

The Educational Directory of China, Shanghai: Volumes for 1917 and 1920.

Forster, Lancelot, *The Universities Along the Yangtze*, Hong Kong: South China Morning Post, 1932.

Hayhoe, Ruth, *China's Universities, 1895-1995:   A Century of Cultural Conflict*, New York : Garland Publishing, 1996.

Hartnett, Richard A., *The Saga of Chinese Higher Education from the Tongzhi Restoration to Tiananmen Square: Revolution and Reform*, Lewiston, N.Y.:   E. Mellen Press, 1998.

Lamberton, Mary, *St. John's University, Shanghai, 1879-1951*, New York: United Board for Christian Colleges in China, 1955.

Lutz, Jessie Gregory, *China and the Christian Colleges, 1850-1950*, Ithaca: Cornell University Press, 1971.

Smalley, Martha; Johnston, Tess;   and Erh, Deke, *Hallowed Halls: Protestant Colleges in Old China*, Hong Kong: Old China Hand Press, 1998.

St. Francis Xavier's College Diamond Jubilee Album, 1934.

Yeh, Wen-Hsin, *The Alienated Academy: Culture and Politics in Republican China, 1919-1937*, Cambridge, Mass.: Council on East Asian Studies, Harvard University Press, 1990.

The Sino-Japanese Wars in Shanghai:

Dreyer, Edward L., *China at War: 1901-1949*, New York: Longman, 1995.

Five Months of War, Shanghai: North China Daily News & Herald, 1938.
(22 pp. of text, followed by 133 pp. of photos with detailed captions.)

Japan's War in China, Shanghai: China Weekly Review, n.d.
(A series of small volumes published between 1937 and 1939 summarizing daily news accounts of the Sino-Japanese war in booklet form with maps.)

Jordan, Donald A., *China's Trial by Fire: The Shanghai War of 1932*, University of Michigan Press, 2001.

Lee, Edward Bing-Shuey, *One Year of the Japan-China Undeclared War*, Shanghai, 1935.
(Chapter XVII, "The Attack on Shanghai," pp.229-260.)

Wasserstein, Bernard, *Secret War in Shanghai*, London: Profile Books, 1998.
(Shanghai during the Japanese occupation, 1937-1945.)

Woodhead, H. G. W. (1883-1959), Editor, *Shanghai in Torment, August-November, 1937 : A Complete Record of Sino-Japanese Hostilities Around Shanghai*, Shanghai: Woodhead, 1937. pp.119-378, ill. *Series* Oriental Affairs: A Monthly Review; vol. 8, Nos. 3-6.

Yeh, Wen-hsin, ed., *Wartime Shanghai*, London: Routledge, 1998.

Shanghai During the Cultural Revolution (1966-1976):

Terrill, Ross, *Flowers on an Iron Tree: Five Cities of China*, Boston: Little, Brown, 1975.

China International Travel Service, *China Travel: Shanghai, Hangzhou, Nanjing, Wuxi, Suzhou*, Beijing: China Travel and Tourism Press, 1975.

Shanghai Since 1979:

Hook, Brian, *Shanghai and the Yangtze Delta: A City Reborn*, Oxford University Press, 1998.

Isaacs, Harold R., *Re-Encounters in China: Notes of a Journey in a Time Capsule*, Armonk: M.E. Sharpe/East Gate Books, 1985. (The return to China of a 1930s expat.)

Yatsko, Pamela, *New Shanghai: The Rocky Rebirth of China's Legendary City*, New York: John Wiley & Sons, 2001. (Author was Shanghai resident correspondent for Far East Economic Review during the 1990s.)

General Histories of Shanghai:

Anonymous, *All About Shanghai and Environs: A Standard Guide Book*, Shanghai: The University Press, 1934. (Incredibly informative guidebook published anonymously by a local publisher in Shanghai.)

Baker, Barbara, ed., *Shanghai: Electric and Lurid City*, Hong Kong: Oxford University Press, 1998. (Anthology)

Couling, Samuel and Lanning, George, *History of Shanghai*, Shanghai: Published for the Shanghai Municipal Council by Kelly & Walsh, 1921.

Pott, F.L. Hawks, *A Short History of Shanghai*, Shanghai: Kelly & Walsh, 1929. (Author was president of St. John's College in Shanghai, now the East China University of Politics & Law.)

Sergeant, Harriet, *Shanghai*, London: John Murray, 1991.

Wei, Betty Peh-Ti, *Shanghai: A Crucible of Modern China*, Hong Kong: Oxford University Press, 1987.

General Reference Works:

Couling, Samuel, *Encyclopedia Sinica*, Shanghai: Kelly & Walsh, 1917.

Goodrich, L. Carrington, *Dictionary of Ming Biography, 1368-1644*, 1976. Two Vols.

Hummel, Arthur W., *Eminent Chinese of the Ching Period*, Washington, D.C.: Government Printing Office, 1944. Two Volumes. (Biographies of Chinese celebrities from the Qing Dynasty, 1644-1911.)

Hsu, Immanuel, *The Rise of Modern China*, New York: Oxford University Press, 1983.

Men of Shanghai and North China: A Standard Biographical Reference Work, Shanghai: The University Press, Second Edition, 1935.

Mote, Frederick W., *Imperial China: 900-1800*, Cambridge: Harvard University Press, 1999.

Moule, A.C., and Yetts, Percival W., *The Rulers of China, 221 B.C.-A.D. 1949: Chronological Tables*, N.Y.: Praeger, 1957. 131 pp.

Paludan, Ann, *Chronicle of the Chinese Emperors*, London: Thames & Hudson, 1998.

Twitchett, Denis, et al, ed., *Cambridge History of China*, 1978-1992. (15 Vols.)

Who's Who In China: Biographies of Chinese Leaders, Shanghai: China Weekly Review, 1936, 5th Edition. (The last of five editions issued between 1918 and 1936.)

Woodhead, H.G.W., *China Year Book*, 26 Volumes, Shanghai and Tianjin: 1913-1939.

Appendix II

Shanghai's Lost Foreigner Cemeteries
Text by Eric N. Danielson

Up until the 1949 revolution foreigners had been living in Shanghai for over a hundred years, ever since the 1842 Treaty of Nanjing opened up Shanghai as a treaty port. In fact, some foreign missionaries and businessmen continued to live here until they were kicked out en masse in 1952. During those 110 years that a significant number of foreigners lived in Shanghai, some of them obviously had to have died here. But, where are their graves now? Although I had initially assumed they were all destroyed during the Cultural Revolution, it now seems that from 1953 to 1959 almost all the foreigners tombs in the city center were moved to a site out in Xujing Town [徐泾镇] of Qingpu District [青浦区] that is now occupied by a Muslim Cemetery (Huimin Gongmu) [回民公墓] established in 1979, and a neighboring modern cemetery next door. It was only in 1966 that the Xujing foreigners' cemetery was destroyed, the tombstones being carried off by local villagers to use as construction materials in the surrounding villages where as late as October 2010 they could still be found dotting the landscape.

My calculations have concluded that there were as many as eleven foreigner's cemeteries in Shanghai. This conclusion comes from consulting various sources that each tell only part of the story. According to F.L. Hawks Pott, in his book *"A Short History of Shanghai,"* (1928), there were at least six foreign cemeteries in Shanghai at that time. The Shanghai Star newspaper published an article on the history of seven foreigners' cemeteries in 2001. The website of the University of Bristol's Chinese Maritime Customs Project says there were at least eight foreigners' cemeteries in Shanghai until 1949.

Almost every one of the eleven former sites of foreigner cemeteries in the Shanghai city center has now become a public park, including Jingan Park, Huaihai Park, Panyu Park, Pudong Park, etc. The site of the **Shandong Road Cemetery**, open from 1844 to 1871 and once containing 469 foreigners' graves including that of Mrs. H.M. Alcock, wife of the second British Consul in Shanghai, is now occupied by the Huangpu District Stadium. The **Pudong Sailors' Cemetery** open from 1859 to 1904, which once contained the graves of 1,783 foreign sailors, is now part of Pudong Park (Pudong Gongyuan) surrounding the Oriental Pearl T.V. Tower (Dongfang Mingzhu Guangbo Dianshi Ta) [东方明珠广播电视塔]. The **Mohawk Road Cemetery** established in 1862 as the first one exclusively for Shanghai's Jewish residents contained 304 graves before it was destroyed during the Cultural Revolution Revolution and is now the site of the J.W. Marriott Hotel. The **Eight Immortals Bridge Cemetery** (Ba Xian Qiao, aka "Pahsienjao") opened in 1863 and once contained the tomb of Henry Burgevine, who led the Ever Victorious Army against the Taiping Rebels after the death of the units original leader F.T. Ward. It is now Huaihai Park. **Bubbling Well Road Cemetery** open from 1880 to 1953 and once the home of 5,500 foreigners' graves is now Jingan Park. The **International Cemetery** (Wanguo Gongmu) [万国公墓] established at the intersection of Hongqiao Road and Songyuan Road in 1909 was destroyed by Red Guards at at the start of the Cultural Revolution in 1966, and has been the site of Song Qingling's Tomb Garden (Song Qingling Mu Yuan) since 1981. Although there is still a small Foreigners Tombs Tombs Area here, the headstones are all fake reproductions, many of them containing spelling errors, and most bearing very minimal information. The **Baikal Road Cemetery** established in 1917 on present day Weiming Lu was the largest Jewish one in the city containing 1,692 graves until they were moved out in 1958-59. The **Hongqiao Road Cemetery** established in 1926, and its neighboring **Columbia Road Cemetery** established in 1940 specifically for Jewish residents, were merged together in 1945, and are now the site of Panyu Park. The grounds of **Holy Trinity Cathedral** (Sheng Sanyi Tang) [圣三一堂] were the site of 110 foreigners' graves between 1937 and 1952. Finally, the **Point Road Cemetery** created for Jewish refugees in 1940 contained 834 graves before it was dismantled in 1958-59. Thus the stain of colonialism has been erased from the city.

Jewish historian Dvir Bar-gal had previously reported finding Hebrew language tombstones near a Muslim cemetery located somewhere in "western Shanghai" in a village called "Minzhu," using only the phonetic pinyin for the village's name and not the actual Chinese characters. Dvir discovered this site back in 2002, and had found 80 Jewish tombstones there since then. However, he's always been a bit reluctant to be more specific in his directions due to his fear of tomb raiders. Since Shanghai municipality is a big place, which in 2010 covered 18 districts and one county with 118 towns and nearly 6,000 villages in an area of 6,340 square km., these vague directions had made it a nearly impossible task for others to find the exact spot. Moreover, Dvir was only interested in collecting old Jewish headstones, whereas to me there was a larger fascinating question here of what happened to all of the foreigners' cemeteries that previously existed in the downtown city center before 1949. Therefore, during one long National Day holiday in October 2010 I set out to see if I could find this place on my own.

The First Day

The **Shanghai Muslim Cemetery** (Huimin Gongmu) [回民公墓] entrance gate stands at #508 Xiewei Lu near its intersection with Zhuguang Lu, close to the modern downtown of Minzhu Village (Minzhu Cun) [民主村] of Xujing Town (Xujing Zhen) [徐泾镇], Qingpu District (Qingpu Qu) [青浦区]. One block south runs the main highway of Huqingping Gong Lu. The official Chinese name is *Hui Min Gong Mu* [回民公墓], named after the Hui ethnic minority of Chinese Muslims. Several halls near the entrance gate are designed in traditional Arabic-Islamic architecture with onion domes on top. The phone number on their business card is (021) 3985-3286. Staff there told me that they had no website and no e-mail address.

In my first conversation with the clerk in the visitors' hall he said the cemetery had a history of 30 years (sanshi nian). Later, in a second conversation after I had explored the site he told me it was established in 1979, and that any tombstones with earlier dates than that had been moved there.

The site has a strange shape. After the main halls near the gate you enter a garden area (huayuan), after which the trail takes a diagonal jog sharply to the left and around this corner you enter the much larger tomb area. This area is divided up into sections labeled by signs, and there are Chinese language wall maps of the whole area posted in a few places.

The tombstones seem to be arranged roughly in chronological order. In the West First section (Xi Yi Qu) there were tombstones dating from 1980, and in the East First section (Dong Yi Qu) there were tombstones dating from 1979. The East First section (Dong Yi Qu) is the closest to the garden and thus the first section a visitor would come to. In this section there were also a few tombstones that dated from as early as 1966 and 1969, as well as some from the mid-1970s, but they looked newer than their dated age would imply, and I had already guessed that the few stones from before 1979 may have been moved there when this was later confirmed by the clerk at the visitors' center.

Dating the establishment of this Muslim Cemetery was important because according to Jewish historian Dvir Bar-gal this was previously the site of a Jewish Cemetery established in 1958, when the tombs of all Jews buried in Shanghai were moved here from four other sites, and before that an International Cemetery. The Jewish Cemetery was destroyed at some point during the Cultural Revolution (1966-1976), and the foreigners' tombstones were then scattered in surrounding villages where they were used by local residents as construction materials in building their small farm houses.

Dvir Bar-gal began researching, documenting and collecting these scattered tombstones in 2001. However, despite his 9 years of gallant efforts, on October 31, 2010 (Halloween Eve, appropriately enough) I was still able to locate 3 or 4 remaining foreigners' tombstones in the surrounding area before the sun went down on my first day of searching. Some of these still had legible English language and Russian inscriptions, and are not documented in the index of tombstones he has discovered on his website: http://shanghaijewishmemorial.com/.

As such, the history of this site is similar to that of the former Foreigners' Cemetery (Wanguo Gongmu) [万国公墓] on Songyuan Lu, now the Song Qingling Mu Yuan, which I previously wrote about in my books _Shanghai and the Yangzi Delta_ (2004), and _Discover Shanghai_ (2010).

Right next door to the Muslim Cemetery on Xiewei Lu stands another modern cemetery which had obviously been established within the previous 10 years. Within its huge expanse stands one large tombstone with a uniquely artistic design and a Russian language inscription. The dates on it are 1915-1939. It is the only non-Chinese language tombstone in the cemetery, and the only one dating from prior to the year 2000.

At 1568 Huqingping Gong Lu, near its intersection with Xiewei Lu, stood a large building full of "antique" furniture shops. Between the wall of this buildings compound and the wall of the modern Chinese cemetery ran a long narrow road unmarked by any signs. The road led all the way to the creek which runs behind the two cemeteries. Just before reaching the creek was an intersection at which the road to the left led to the remains of the old village of Minzhu Cun [民主村]. However, straight ahead on the left stood a large warehouse which an employee told me was a "furniture factory," but which seemed to be stockpiled with recycled wooden remains of old houses, and even a giant drum from a temple.

For our purposes the important point is that right beside the road in front of this warehouse lay lay a whole row of stone relics that obviously once belonged to the nearby foreigners cemetery. First I noticed about four long, rectangular stone carved troughs that may have once been water basins or contained flower beds. At the end of the row of relics were two stone blocks. One block bore a clearly legible English language inscription on the side facing upward: _"In memory of our beloved mother Laisa Berkovitch who died on January 21st 1936 age 63."_ It shocked me to find this laying right beside a paved road, and I was even more surprised when I discovered later that this tombstone was not yet included on Dvir Bar-gal's list on his website: http://shanghaijewishmemorial.com/.

Following the road branching off to the left (west) took me into the remaining ruins of the old village of Minzhu Cun [民主村]. This was where Dvir Bar-gal reported previously finding many many of the tombstones he discovered. Unfortunately, the village seemed to be in the process of being cleared away, and most of the houses had already been torn down, with only only a few left standing. In addition, the sun was going down and it got dark before I had finished searching. Nonetheless, I was still able to make several more discoveries of foreigners' tombstones in this area.

The houses in this area didn't have precise addresses, and the muddy dirt tracks between them had no names, so rough directions would have to do. At a spot where a fairly large house still stood surrounded by a wall with a gate, beside it was a goat herder who kept a flock of goats. In between the goat herder's shack and the large house ran a narrow dirt trail heading north towards the creek. In the courtyard of a small house behind the large one I found at least two foreigners' tombstones. At the far end of the courtyard beside the house was one extremely large tombstone, with decorative columns on both sides, but was laying face down so that it was impossible to read the inscription on the other side. It would have taken several men armed with iron crowbars to turn this over, or so I thought. At the near end of the house was another smaller one containing an English language inscription laying on its side, half buried in the ground. It was easy to miss because the inscription was facing sideways rather than upward. Half the inscription was buried under ground, but the half above ground was clearly legible. Unfortunately, by this time it was pitch black out as the sun had gone down, but I was able to photograph it using a flash. In fact, I took digital pictures of all the sights I had seen throughout the day.

Half the day was wasted simply wandering around on foot trying to locate the proper location of the site, but once I knew where it was, and considering what I had been able to find on the first day, I decided would like to go back and try my luck again. It was like a treasure hunt.

Dvir Bar-gal said he had moved all the significant foreigners' tombstones from this area to a "Buddhist Cemetery" near the Hongqiao Airport for safe keeping, but obviously he had missed a few.

The Second Day

Going back to the Minzhu Cun [民主村] site a second time in the daylight on Monday November 1, 2010, I found three foreigner's tombstones with English language inscriptions and one with a Hebrew inscription. These four added to the *Laisa Berkovitch* stone and the Russian language stone in the nearby modern day cemetery made a total of six foreigner's headstones with legible inscriptions that I had discovered in only two days of searching.

The first stone found on the second day was a square piece of marble with a round hole in the center from the top down.   It was then being used by a local family to cover a drinking water well. The English inscription here said, *"In memory of George Daniel ???hnhorst, born 1st October 1857, died 25th May 1912."* Unfortunately, the first three letters of the family name had been partly covered up with cement and were largely illegible, but I surmised that it may have said *Sharnhorst*. Later research confirmed that the June 1, 1912 issue of the North China Herald newspaper had announced the death in Shanghai on May 25, 1912 of a George Daniel Sharnhorst.

The three other tomb stones were found behind house #447. The house in front bore this address plate, while a second house behind it had no address number. The courtyard of this rear house was littered with tomb stones, many of which had been used to line the sides of a sewage/drainage channel. There were others which I was unable to excavate. Of the three tomb stones at this site that I did manage to excavate, one quite large marble tomb stone with decorative columns on either side was originally upside down until I used a shovel and bamboo poles to cantilever it into an upright position with the inscription facing up.

This English inscription read as follows: *"William Bennicke Loam, born in Devonshire England, ?th December 1848, died at Shanghai, 20th October 1889."*

At the intersection of two pathways half buried in a drainage ditch was another tomb stone with an English inscription which I fully excavated until I could read that it said, *"To the memory of the late Christian Hermann Simon Peter Minck, a native of Gluecksta Holstein. He departed this life in Shanghai December 14th 1884 at the age of 47."* This man had a long name, and at first it wasn't clear if the word Christian was meant to describe his religion or was his first name. Holstein is an area that straddles the German-Danish border, but we can assume this man was probably German. This is the oldest tombstone found at the Minzhu Cun site. Later research confirmed that the December 21, 1884 issue of the North China Herald newspaper reported the death of Mr. Christian Minck in Shanghai on December 14, 1884 at the age of 47. According to the newspaper report, Minck had "served with Colonel Gordon in the Ever Victorious Army and held the rank of Captain during the [Taiping] Rebellion." He was also a Freemason and a member of the Shanghai Fire Department.

To the left of this one, hidden in the bushes and half buried in a trash strewn sewage ditch, was a large Hebrew language tombstone with a star of David above the inscription facing away from the trail. Standing on the pathway you could not see that it was there. After discovering this one I reported it to Dvir Bargal, who upon examining photos I took of it commented that it may be one of the oldest Jewish headstones found in Shanghai, as well as one of the best preserved.

The people who lived in this village had an ambivalent attitude towards the foreigners' tombstones laying about their courtyards and gardens. On the one hand they couldn't read the foreign language inscriptions and the stones have no personal significance to them at all. On the other hand, as some of them started to realize that the stones were important to foreigners living today, they got the idea that they could make money off of these relics. One villager offered to help me dig up the headstones at a price of 100 Rmb each. I declined this offer and instead grabbed a shovel and some bamboo poles and excavated the tomb stones myself. Strangely, they didn't seem to mind me digging up their courtyard. Although he clearly felt that the tomb stones were his property, he was also willing to sell them to me for a price, and even followed me as I was leaving the site saying repeatedly in Chinese,"Do you want them or not (Yao bu yao)?" He offered to show me the location of some more headstones, claiming that there were many more yet to be found ("Zheli haiyou henduo zhege."). But once again, his help was only available in exchange for some financial reward. He made this quite clear by using the international body language of rubbing his fingers together as if clenching a coin. Dvir previously reported that on average he only paid 30 Rmb each to buy the tomb stones that he had previously collected, but the villagers obviously expected much more than that from me. I speculated that the few remaining foreigners'tomb stones might go for a much higher price for anyone willing to buy them.

Dvir told me that he planned to go out to Xujing to pick up this last remaining Hebrew headstone, although he was not interested in the tombstones of the non-Jewish foreigners. I'm glad that I was able to make a small contribution to his continuing efforts at documenting Shanghai's Jewish heritage. However, at that point I thought, after having had a nine year monopoly on exploration of the site, it was in the public interest for more people to know the location.

Now it can be told that the exact site was Minzhu Village (Minzhu Cun) [民主村] of Xujing Town (Xujing Zhen) [徐泾镇] in Qingpu District (Qingpu Qu) [青浦区].   Oddly enough, the place name means "Democracy Village."

The above part of this story was first published on my now defunct Yangziman blog in October 2011, a year after I had first visited the site.   Based on Google Analytics records of hits, it proved to be one of the most popular articles on my blog.   Several individuals even wrote to me with positive feedback on it and generously shared with me information that they had about the topic. Patti Gully of Vancouver, B.C., Nick Fielding of the U.K., and Paul S. Allen of the U.K. were my most notable correspondents.

March 2015 Third Visit:

Then, for the first time in four years, on Sunday February 15, 2015 I went out to the Minzhu Village (Minzhu Cun) [民主村] site in Xujing Town (Xujing Zhen) [徐泾镇] to revisit it and see what had changed.   What a surprise it was to find that the whole village had disappeared, the site had been completely bulldozed, and a new villa development was almost finished on the same site where the village had once stood.   The whole former village site was all surrounded by a high construction fence that made it difficult to even see inside, let alone get in, but by walking all the way around it I eventually found one gate where I managed to talk a Chinese guard into letting me inside to look around.

The one two-story house (#447) behind which I had found the three largest foreigner tombstones, including the Jewish one with the Hebrew inscription, was the last old house still standing, but the half dozen tombstones that had been behind it were all gone.   In fact, all the foreigner tombstones had disappeared from the whole area where the village had once stood, except for one that is embedded face down in an old cement pathway with the inscription on the bottom side that's not visible.   It would take a jack hammer to get that one out of there, which is probably why it's still there.

At any rate, it would now be a waste of time for any visitors to take all the trouble of going out there, as there is nothing left to see, so save yourself the time.   As I was leaving I could hear the security guard who had let me inside being severely criticized by his boss, so it's unlikely they'll be very welcoming next time.   Also, I nearly fractured a knee walking around the rubble.

In e-mail correspondence with Shanghai's resident Jewish heritage expert Dvir Bar-Gal, he assured me that most if not all the foreigner tombstones previously found in this village had been moved in an effort organized by him to "the parking lot of the Buddhist cemetery near the place."   Unfortunately, he has not responded to requests for a more detailed name and address of the place where the foreigner tombstones are now being kept, and the information he has provided is too vague to pinpoint the location.   He has not visited the site himself since April 2013, but says that the Israeli Consulate in Shanghai has been in correspondence with Qingpu district officials, asking them to preserve and protect the tombstones.   Let's hope those requests are being honored.

It's too bad that Shanghai has not followed the example of Beijing's restoration of the Jesuit Zhanlan Cemetery, which suffered similar waves of destruction in the 20th Century but has been gradually rebuilt since 1978.

Meanwhile, a while ago I notice that the original version of this blog post had been cited as a source of information in an article published on December 9, 2013 in the <u>Global Times</u> newspaper, "*Digging Up the Past*," written by Zhang Yu.   Here's the link to their website: http://www.globaltimes.cn/content/831024.shtml.

Shanghai's Lost Foreigner Cemeteries Bibliography:

Elliston, E. S., *Shantung Road Cemetery, Shanghai, 1846-1868: With Notes About Pootung Seamen's Cemetery [and] Soldiers' Cemetery,* Shanghai, December 1946. (51pp.)

Hawks Pott, F.L., *A Short History of Shanghai*, (1928). According to p.72, there were at least six foreign cemeteries in Shanghai at that time.

International Jewish Cemetery Project website describes the history of five Jewish cemeteries in Shanghai.

http://www.iajgsjewishcemeteryproject.org/china-inc-hong-kong-a-macao/shanghai.html

North China Herald, a former Shanghai newspaper, obituaries section.

Shanghai Guide website, http://www.shanghaiguide.org/Shanghai-Foreign-Cemeteries-2838.html.   This website documents the history of five foreigners' cemeteries in Shanghai.

<u>Shanghai Jewish Memorial</u> website run by Israeli historian Dvir Bar-Gal has an index listing all the Jewish tombstones he has found in Shanghai since 2002. http://shanghaijewishmemorial.com/ (Divr also reposted an entire earlier English only version of this article on his website in 2014 without asking me for permission, and without citing me as the author by using my real full name, but merely citing "Yangziman."

Shanghai Star newspaper, *"Foreign Ghosts, Lost and Found,"* April 5, 2001, documented the history of seven foreigners' cemeteries in Shanghai, as well as the destruction of the Shandong Lu Cemetery and its replacement with the Huangpu District Stadium. http://app1.chinadaily.com.cn/star/2001/0405/cu18-2.html

University of Bristol's Chinese Maritime Customs Project website states that there were at least eight foreigners' cemeteries in Shanghai. http://www.bristol.ac.uk/history/customs/ancestors/shanghai.html

University of Bristol's Chinese Maritime Customs Project website offers a pdf download of a file on Holy Trinity Cathedral (Sheng Sanyi Tang) [圣三一堂]. http://www.bristol.ac.uk/history/customs/ancestors/holytrinity.pdf

Visual Cultures in East Asia (VCEA) website contains a digital online library of photos of the tombstones of some of the more famous foreigners to be buried in Shanghai, including Mrs. H.M. Alcock and Mr. Henry Burgevine. http://www.vcea.net/Digital_Library/Images_en.php

Wei, Betty Peh-ti, *Old Shanghai*, (1993) p.51, "A Jewish cemetery constructed in 1862 on **Mohawk Road** was destroyed during the Cultural Revolution a century later." This is now the site of the J.W. Marriott Hotel according to the Urbanatomy website. http://www.thatsmags.com/shanghai/

Appendix III:

Guomindang Architecture in Jiangwan Town of Shanghai's Yangpu District
Eric N. Danielson
(10-23-17)

Preface

In the Republic of China (Minguo) [民国] era (1911-1949), during which the Nationalist Party (Guomindang) [国民党] controlled the central government based in Nanjing, the Greater Shanghai Plan (Da Shanghai Jihua) [大上海计划] for a new civic center in Jiangwan Town (Jiangwan Zhen) [江湾镇] of Shanghai's Yangpu District (Yangpu Qu) [杨浦区] featured government buildings designed by Chinese architect **Dong Dayou** [董大酉](1899-1973) in a unique style best described as "Chinese Renaissance," " Ming Dynasty revival style," or even "neo-classical Chinese style" of architecture.   Dong himself used the term "Chinese Renaissance style" to describe the buildings he designed.   I previously wrote about this topic in two of my books: *Shanghai and the Yangzi Delta, From Past to Present*, Vol. I of the New Yangzi River trilogy, Singapore (2004); and *Discover Shanghai: The City's History and Culture Redefined*, Singapore (2010), as well as in a more recent lengthy blog post published on a now extinct blog in January 2016.   This is an updated synthesis of all three of my previous publications on the topic.

Historical Introduction

The founding in April 1927 of a new Chinese central government by the Nationalist Party (Guomindang) [国民党] in their recently acquired capital city of Nanjing was soon followed on July 14, 1927 by the establishment of the Greater Shanghai Municipal Government (Shanghai Tebie Shizhengfu) [上海特别市政府].   The Chinese-controlled parts of Shanghai were raised from the level of a county attached to Songjiang to that of a city for the first time in history.   This municipal government was headed by a Chinese mayor appointed by the central government, who in turn appointed a Chinese municipal council.   Although the two foreign concessions in the center of Shanghai controlled by the British and the French were still outside of its boundaries, the **Municipality of Greater Shanghai** (Shanghai Tebie Shi) [上海特别市] covered an area of 320 square miles, including what were then the districts of Zhabei, Nanshi, and Pudong, all of which had formerly been considered parts of Jiangsu Province.   The new civic center was to be located in what is now **Jiangwan** Town [江湾镇] of Yangpu District [杨浦区], just north of Hongkou District, which was then controlled by the British-dominated International Settlement.   The "special" (tebie) [特别] way Shanghai's city government reported directly to the Guomindang's national government, rather than that of a provincial capital, was not unlike today's system of zizhishi [自治市] whereby the municipal governments of Shanghai, Chongqing, Tianjin, and Beijing all report directly to the Communist central government in Beijing.

In 1929 the City Planning Commission of Greater Shanghai was formed, consisting of 11 members appointed by the Mayor, with Dr. Shen Yi as its chairman and Dong Dayou [董大酉] serving as an advisor. On July 5, 1929 the city council chose the site for the new city. In October 1929 there was an open competition for the design of the new civic center of Greater Shanghai. One requirement was that the civic center be placed at the intersection of east-west and north-south axes, "taking the shape of a cross." The east-west axis was a boulevard running from the new train station to the Huangpu River. It was known as Three People's Principles Road (San Min Road) to the west of the civic center, and Five Rights Road (Wu Chuan Road) to the west. The north-south axis connected the new civic center with the International Settlement to the south. The civic center was to be formed by a group of nine buildings with the surrounding area decorated by fountains, reflecting pools, gardens, bridges, and monuments. Dong Dayu [董大酉] won the competition and was appointed Chief Architect. The site selected in Jiangwan was considered convenient because it lay in between the International Settlement to the south, the Yangzi river port and forts at Wusong in Baoshan district to the north, the Huangpu River to the east, and the Shanghai-Wusong railwa line to the west. On July 7, 1930 a Street Plan showing the layout of the street system was adopted. The plan was examined by several foreign experts, including American city planner Mr. Asa E. Philips.

Eventually the new civic center in Jiangwan included a museum, library, stadium, and city hall, all of which were designed by the Chinese architect **Dong Dayou** [董大酉](1899-1973), a University of Minnesota graduate who had worked with Henry K. Murphy on the Soul Valley Park (Linggu Gongyuan) [灵谷公园] in Nanjing. He combined traditional Chinese and modern Western architecture in a Ming Dynasty revival style that was also used for the central government buildings of the Guomindang regime in Nanjing. Dong himself used the term "Chinese Renaissance style" for the architecture of the new buildings, "a combination of the traditional Chinese style with modern comforts."

Plans for further development of this area were halted by the Japanese occupation of Chinese-administered Shanghai in November 1937, although the two contiguous foreign concessions in Shanghai's downtown city center continued to form a solitary island (gu dao) [孤岛] of territory not occupied by the Japanese until December 1941. The Japanese occupation of the Chinese-administered parts of Shanghai from 1937 to 1945 brought a premature halt to the construction project and caused considerable damage to the buildings that had been finished. After the war was over in 1945 the city government abandoned the pre-war municipal buildings in Jiangwan for ones located inside the former International Settlement.

All four of the main buildings constructed as part of the Guomindang's new civic center in Jiangwan [江湾] have miraculously survived to this day, but with only two of them still serving their original purpose, the others having been incorporated into surrounding universities, hospitals, middle schools, and office parks. All four of these key historic buildings are within a few blocks walking distance of each other, and the entire area can easily be reached by a short taxi ride from the Jiangwan Town Station (Jiangwan Zhen Ditei Zhan) [江湾地铁站] on the Metro 3 light rail line. A suggested walking tour itinerary would follow the order in which they are presented below.

The former **Shanghai Municipal Administration Building** (Shanghai Tebie Shizhengfu Dalou) [上海特别市政府大楼] was constructed between 1931 and 1933 as Shanghai's new city hall, but now sits inside the west side entrance to the campus of the Shanghai Sports College (Shanghai Tiyu Xueyuan) [上海体育学院], where it serves as the school's Administration Building (Xingzheng Lou) [行政楼].

Dong Dayou [董大酉] and his contemporaries sometimes referred to it as "the Mayor's Building." The foundation stone was laid on July 7, 1931 and it was completed in 1933. It measures 310 feet long and 100 feet wide in the middle. It has four floors with a total floor area of 90,000 square feet. The highest portion measures 100 feet from the ground. The exterior has been called "an adaptation of the traditional Peking palace style....," with an interior that reminds one of the "Peking palaces." It was designed according to the neo-classical Chinese style of architecture established in Nanjing as the form for Guomindang official structures

The long, rectangular building features a massive tiled roof with upturned eaves, supported by wooden tripod roof brackets (dougong), balanced atop granite block walls decorated with thick bright red round pillars. Glazed orange porcelain animals and tiles decorate the roof ridges. A stone balustrade surrounding the ground floor, and the monumental flight of stone steps leading up to the entrance seem to be new replacements of the originals. The building has in effect three wings. Two giant flagpoles out front seem to be the originals. A circular driveway passes underneath the front steps. All the entrances are in the style of round stone arched gateways with double doors. The back side of the building features an even more impressive pair of monumental stone staircases leading up to a large stone terrace, and it is here that newlyweds once customarily had their wedding photos taken.

When I first visited it in March 2003, the exterior was under renovation and covered with scaffolding. The original corner stone was still visible at the base of the front right corner of the central hall, but its inscription had been partly covered up with wet cement, leaving a few characters still visible.

The interior had been left largely untouched. Student guards dressed in red arm bands were curious but friendly guides. Stepping into the central lobby, I found that the floor was decorated with a map of the Shanghai municipality, including the street plan for the Guomindang's Jiangwan municipal center. Inside a separate entryway between the interior and exterior doors of the main entrance was a marble wall plaque which still contained the original dedication from when the building was first built. The lengthy inscription was in perfect condition and still legible, although the characters were quite small. It's amazing that it had not been defaced, as the corner stone was.

There are four floors of offices inside the building. The third and fourth floors both have a curious hump in the center where they pass over a room on the second floor above the lobby which seems to have a much higher raised ceiling and runs all the way from the front to the back side. This second floor room is kept closed, but due to its special position it seems possible that it may have once been the Shanghai mayor's office.

Behind the building on its North side was a new socialist realist statue balanced atop an original stone pedestal, on which once stood the original statue of Sun Yat-sen (Sun Zhongshan) erected in 1933, which had been removed by the Japanese in 1937. This statue was restored in December 2009.

In 2009, and again during the Spring Festival of 2015, I made return visits to this site to take more photographs of it.

The college's official address of 399 Changhai Lu [长海路399 号] actually means a much longer walk from the main entrance to the former city hall than entering from the side gate at the intersection of Hengren Lu [恒仁路] and Qing Yuan Huan Lu [清源环路].

Address: 650 Qing Yuan Huan Lu [清源环路650 号], Jiangwan Town [江湾镇], Yangpu District [杨浦区].

The former **Shanghai Municipal Museum** (Shanghai Shili Bowuguan) [上海市立博物馆] built between 1934 and 1935 now sits inside the compound of the Shanghai Second Army Medical University (Shanghai Di'er Jun Yike Daxue) [上海第二军医科大学], and the Changhai Hospital (Changhai Yiyuan) [长海医院].   Although a few soldiers man the gate house, the area is open to the public, and access is not a problem.   This building was heavily restored in 2009, and now has a deceptively brand new appearance.   A traditional wooden pavilion with glazed tile roof supported by wooden brackets and red pillars stands atop the central hall of the two-story white stone building.   Two wings branch out to the sides forming a horse shoe shape.   A stone arched gateway entrance into the center hall is flanked by two foundation stones with inscriptions, but due to the recent renovation it's impossible to tell if these have been altered or not.   Passing through the lobby, a second stone arched gateway leads into a large two-story interior courtyard with similar gateways branching off in all four directions. Skylights and colorful ceiling paintings of mythical birds hang overhead.   Two more exterior courtyards stand in the center of each of the building's two wings.   A two-story mezzanine lined with red columns also stands above the main lobby, and from the third floor a stone arched gateway leads out onto the roof.

Address: 174 Changhai Lu [长海路174号], Jiangwan Town [江湾镇], Yangpu District [杨浦区].

The former **Shanghai Municipal Library** (Shanghai Shili Tushuguan) [上海市立图书馆] was built between 1934 and 1935.   Later it was used by the Tongji Middle School (Tongji Zhong Xue) until they moved out in the year 2000.   After 17 years of abandonment and restoration efforts, it finally reopened to the public in March 2017 as the new Jiangwan Public Library.

The old library building and former school grounds take up almost the entire city block between Changhai Lu [长海路], Heishan Lu [黑山路], Zhengli Lu [政立路] and Hengren Lu [恒仁路].

My First Visit in 2003

When I first visited the site in 2003, views of the library building could be had through a surrounding fence from all four streets except Changhai Lu [长海路].   Although access to the inside of the school compound was not a problem, visitors were not allowed to actually enter the interior of the building.   I was able to enter the gate of the fenced-in grounds from Heishan Lu [黑山路] and walk all around the outside of the building, although I could not enter inside the closed buildings themselves.

Unlike the former museum building, the library building had not yet been restored then, and thus still showed a weathered appearance displaying its true age, making it seem all the more mysterious. The exterior granite walls were dark, mossy and heavily pitted, in contrast to the perfectly smooth bright white walls of the museum. The library had by far the most impressive looking exterior of the four historic Jiangwan municipal buildings. It resembled a Ming Dynasty fortress, completely made of stone, with no wooden parts except for the roof of the pavilion on top. The gate from Heishan Lu [黑山路] lead directly to the back of the building, and to see the front facade properly one had to walk all the way around to the other side through a series of playgrounds still swarming with amateur athletes engaged in various sports.

From the front side one could see that the building had a horse shoe shape, with two wings branching out from the center hall, plus another two wing extension which was connected to the back of the center hall, making a total of four wings. The center hall entrance was in the shape of a stone arched gateway, with a stone balcony hanging overhead from the second floor, and flanked by two octagonal windows on either side. There was a remarkable resemblance in some ways with the former RAS Library building on Huqiu Lu [虎丘路].

Above the two-story center hall was a two-story stone pavilion standing on a stone terrace surrounded by a stone balustrade with a long series of stone alligator heads protruding outward from the walls. It made me recall that I had seen this same alligator head motif at the Ming Xiao Ling tomb of the first Ming Dynasty emperor Zhu Yuanzhang in Nanjing. Atop the pavilion was a roof of glazed orange tiles with upturned overhanging wooden eaves supported by wooden tripod roof brackets.

Unfortunately, political censors had been at work here obliterating the historical record. Inscriptions on both of the two foundation stones had been intentionally chiseled off character by character. Also, four columns of bright yellow characters had been painted in large brush strokes all across the front facade. Higher up on the walls of the pavilion one could see where additional faded white characters were once painted. This defacement seemed inexplicable for a so-called "Municipal Preserved Building."

My Second Visit in 2009

When I revisited the site for a second time in May 2009 the school had completely moved out and the building sat empty and abandoned. Amateur athletes were no longer allowed to use the former school playgrounds, and nobody was allowed to enter the fenced-in compound at the Heishan Lu gate, which was kept locked shut and guarded. Thus, six years after my first visit public access had only become more restricted than before. One could only view the building from a long distance through the fence. Publicly announced plans called for its restoration, but as of May 2009 it was still in a derelict state and there were no signs that repair work had even started yet. The most interesting feature was still the stone pavilion on top that resembled the Ming Dynasty Bell Tower (Zhong Lou) in Beijing, or possibly a Ming Lou Tower at a Ming emperor's tomb.

My Third Visit in 2015

When I returned for a third time during the Spring Festival 2015, the whole site was closed to visitors and it was only possible to see it from the surrounding sidewalks by looking over a high fence.

Restoration: 2015-2017

An August 24, 2015 an unsigned post on the Shanghai city government's website, entitled "Discovered artwork aids library renovation," stated that plans called for the building to be renovated and opened to the public by "early 2017."   Not only the interior had to be restored. The stone facade that had enormous vertical columns of bright red and yellow slogans painted on it when it served as the Tongji Middle School had to have every piece removed and cleaned, while all the ceramic roof tiles also had to be replaced.

After 17 years of abandonment and restoration efforts, it finally reopened to the public in March 2017 as the new Jiangwan Public Library.

Address: 181 Heishan Lu [黑山路181号], Jiangwan Town [江湾镇], Yangpu District [杨浦区].

The Former Shanghai Municipal Stadium (Shanghai Shili Tiyuchang) [上海市立体育场] was completed in 1935.   Until the reopening of the Jiangwan Library in March 2017, it was the only one of the four historic Jiangwan municipal buildings still serving its original purpose as the only slightly renamed **Jiangwan Stadium** (Jiangwan Tiyuchang) [江湾体育场] .   The stadium itself is only one of four original buildings which make up an entire recreation area lying between Guohe Lu [国和路], Zhengli Lu [政立路], and Songhu Lu [淞沪路].   Two other buildings at the site built in similar style include the Jiangwan Gymnasium (Jiangwan Tiyuguan) [江湾体育馆] and Jiangwan Swimming Pool (Jiangwan Youyongguan) [江湾游泳馆].   All four buildings in the recreation area were designed in the Ming Dynasty revival style popular with the Guomindang and feature the stone arched gateway entrances typical of it. Address: 346 Guohe Lu [国和路346号], Jiangwan Town [江湾镇], Yangpu District [杨浦区].

The former museum, library and city hall are all located one block from the intersection of Changhai Lu [长海路] and Hengren Lu [恒仁路], and only two blocks walking distance from each other.   The stadium is a bit farther away on Guohe Lu [国和路].   The whole site can be reached from the Jiangwan Town Station (Jiangwan Zhen Ditei Zhan) [江湾地铁站] on Metro Line 3 by taking a short taxi ride down Zhengli Lu [政立路] to Guohe Lu [国和路].

Conclusion: The Post-War City Government

In 1945 the Chinese municipality's government offices were moved from their previous location in Jiangwan town to the former **Shanghai Municipal Council** headquarters of the Internatinal Settlement (which had been abolished in 1943) located on Jiangxi Lu where they remained until the Guomindang's evacuation to Taiwan in May 1949.   Some sources have claimed that the Shanghai city government moved into the HSBC building on the Bund (Waitan) in 1949, but this is incorrect, The Hong Kong and Shanghai Bank (HSBC) building on the Bund actually continued to be occupied by its original owners until April 1955, when they were evicted by the **Shanghai Municipal People's Government**, who became the new occupants until their current building at People's Square was completed in 1994.

The 1933 plans for development of the Jiangwan civic center can be seen on display at the Shanghai **Urban Planning Exhibition Center** (Chengshi Guihua Zhanlan Guan) [城市规划展览馆] at People's Square in the "Historic City" exhibit on the Mezzanine level.

Sources on Shanghai Architecture and Urban Planning:

I. English Books

Cody, Jeffrey W., *Building in China: Henry K. Murphy's Adaptive Architecture, 1914-1935*, Hong Kong: Chinese University Press, 2001.

Cody, Jeffrey W., Exporting American Architecture, 1870-2000, Routledge,   2005.   304 pp. "American Building & Planning in China, 1907-1937," pp.39-42, pp.109 – 121.

Cody, Jeffrey W., *Chinese Architecture and the Beaux-Arts*, University of Hawaii Press, 2011. 385 pp.

Croizier, Ralph, *"Review Article: Modern Chinese Architecture in Global Perspective,"* World History Connected, 2012.
http://worldhistoryconnected.press.illinois.edu/9.2/br_croizier.html

Danielson, Eric N., *Shanghai and the Yangzi Delta, From Past to Present*, Vol. I of the New Yangzi River trilogy, Singapore (2004)

Danielson, Eric N., *Discover Shanghai: The City's History and Culture Redefined*, Singapore (2010)

Denison, Edward and Guang Yuren, *Building Shanghai: The Story of China's Gateway*, John Wiley & Sons, 2006

Denison, Edward and Guang Yuren, *Modernism in China: Architectural Visions and Revolutions*, Wiley, 2008. 336 pp.

Nellist, George F., Dong Dayou biography, *Men of Shanghai and North China*, Shanghai: Oriental Press, 1933.

Novelli, Luigi, *Shanghai Architecture Guide: 100 Years, 100 Buildings (Shanghai Youzhe Zhongxi Bainian Jianzhu de Chengshi)[上海: 有着中西百年建筑的城市]*, Shanghai: Bai Jia Publishing House (Baijia Chubanshe) [百家出版社] , 2001. 127 pp. (Bilingual in English & Chinese)

Yeung Yue-man, *Shanghai: Transformation and Modernization Under China's Open Policy*, Hong Kong: Chinese University Press, 1996.   583 pp.

Shanghai Municipal Tourist Administration, *A Tour of Shanghai's Historical Architecture*, Henan Fine Arts Publishing House, 1996.

Shanghai Urban Planning Administrative Bureau, *The Comprehensive Plan of Shanghai, 1999-2020*, Shanghai, n.d., ca. 2002.

II. Chinese Books

Cai Yutian [蔡育天], ed., preface by Han Zheng [韩正], _Tracing Back: The Excellent Architecture of Modern Times in Shanghai (Hui Mou: Shanghai Youxiu Jindai Baohu Jianzhu)_ [回眸: 上海优秀近代保护建筑], Shanghai [上海]:   Shanghai People's Publishing House (Shanghai Renmin Chubanshe) [上海人民出版社], May 2001. 386 pp. (Chinese)

Chen Congzhou [陈从周] and Zhang Ming [章明], ed., _A Draft History of Modern Shanghai Architecture (Shanghai Jindai Jianzhu Shigao)_ [上海近代建筑史稿], Shanghai [上海]: Shanghai Joint Publishing (Shanghai Sanlian Shudian) [上海三联书店], 2002 reprint, first published in 1988. 229 pp. (Chinese)

Ye Shuping, _Old Photos of Shanghai aka Old Fashions of Shanghai (Shanghai Jiu Ying)_ [上海旧影], Beijing: People's Fine Arts Publishing House (Renmin Meishu Chubanshe) [人民美术出版社], 1998. (Chinese).

III. Periodicals

"Building a New Shanghai," Far Eastern Economic Review, Vol. 27, No.6., June 1931

Dong Dayou, _"Architecture Chronicle,"_ Tien Hsia Monthly, Vol. 3, November 1936.

Dong Dayou, _"Greater Shanghai – Greater Vision,"_ China Critic, Vol. 10, No. 5, August 1 1935, pp.103-106.

Dong Dayou, _"Greater Shanghai's New Million Dollar Stadium …,"_ China Reconstruction and Engineering Review, Vol. 4, No. 1, October 1934.

"Greater Shanghai," North China Herald, July 16 1927.

Lillico, Stuart, _"The Civic Center at Kiangwan,"_ The China Journal, Vol. 22, 1935.

MacPherson, Kerrie L., _"Designing China's urban future: The Greater Shanghai Plan, 1927–1937,"_ Planning Perspectives, Volume 5, Issue 1, 1990, pages 39-62.

IV. Historic Shanghai Map Collections

Zhou Zhenhe [周振鹤], _Shanghai Historic Maps Collection_ (_Shanghai Lishi Ditu Ji_) [上海历史地图集], Shanghai: Shanghai People's Publishing House (Shanghai Renmin Chubanshe) [上海人民出版社] , 1999.   157 pp.   ISBN# 9787208032859.   (Chinese)

Zhang Wei [张伟] , _The Album of Shanghai During the Past 150 Years (Lao Shanghai Ditu)_ [老上海地图], Shanghai Library (Shanghai Tushuguan) [上海图书馆], Shanghai Pictorial Publishing House (Shanghai Huabiao Chubanshe) [上海画报出版社], June 2001.   66 maps including some in English, French and Japanese.

Shanghai Municipal Council, _Plan of Shanghai_, Shanghai: 1928. 1 vol. Fold-out Map.

Appendix IV:

From: Eric N. Danielson
To: Simon Winchester
Date: September 22, 2010

Subject: ***Two Beautiful Days on the Bund***

Dear Simon,

Last year when I was writing and taking photographs for my latest book, Discover Shanghai (2010), the whole Bund area was one giant construction site, and it was very difficult to take decent pictures with all the cranes in the way and scaffolding covering up the facades of many historic buildings.

Although in my normal daily life here I seldom go out sightseeing, focused as I am on earning my daily bread, the Mid-Autumn Festival (Zhongqiujie) officially occurring today has given me a few days time off this week to reflect and re-explore the city once again.

Yesterday the weather here was absolutely picture perfect, with clear blue skies, and since I didn't have to work at my day job I took the opportunity to back down to the Bund and rediscover this area now that its renovation is finally complete.

What amazing surprises awaited me! Contrasting the way it looks now with when I first arrived here 12 years ago is mind boggling. Some changes are much for the better, while others seem to have been a mistake.

The jewel in the crown now is the renovated and reopened Shanghai Club at No. 2 Zhongshan Dong Yi Lu [中山东一路] on the Bund. Originally built in 1910 to replace an earlier structure of 1864, this beautiful building had just closed in 1998 when I first arrived here. Countless times I stood outside its locked iron gates and fantasized about what lay inside, but I was never able to get in until yesterday. Just last week, on Sept. 15th to be precise, the old Shanghai Club finally reopened as the new Waldorf Astoria Hotel. Thus I was able to get a look at it within a week of its reopening. Before going inside I was filled with excitement and trepidation that much like many other renovations here they may have completely gutted the interior and only left the exterior facade intact, but my fears were overcome with delight once I discovered that the interior renovation has kept the original design and appearance intact as much as possible. The lobby atrium is like a cathedral, lined with marble pillars on both sides, with a skylight and chandeliers overhead. They've even saved the two original metal cage elevators.

The lobby floor has a salon for women to the left and the famous Long Bar to the right. Of course I took the chance to enjoy a Long Island iced tea and a Reuben sandwich in the bar. The current wooden bar is indeed quite long, but I don't think it's the original one, as that one was at some point supposedly sawed in half into two pieces. Historic photos grace the walls of the bar. Surprisingly they weren't very busy at all and I almost had the place to myself. Prices were a bit steeper than I would normally pay, but well worth it for an experience that I waited a lifetime for. They have specials where all drinks are 88 Rmb and sandwiches 108, both being lucky numbers in Chinese.

Most of all, the staff were quite kind to this bearded, somewhat scruffy looking photographer, and gave me a guided tour around the main floor, but unfortunately they would not let me go upstairs to the second floor, which is occupied by a number of ballrooms with windows facing the Bund, as well as the club's former library, which they are now calling the "Writers' Room." Hotel suites now occupy the third and fourth floors, while a Chinese restaurant occupies the top fifth floor. Sine this was only the soft opening, I'm hoping to be able to go back later and explore the rest of the building. In the parts that I was allowed to see, I was also graciously permitted to take as many photographs as I wanted, unlike other places such as the former HSBC building where they always say, "No taking pictures!"

While that was certainly the climax of my day, I took the time to wander along the full length of the Bund from that starting point. Nearby, the Gutzlaff Signal Tower built in 1884 looks better than ever, marking a good starting point for a south-north walking tour of the whole Bund (Waitan). It had been covered up with construction cranes last time I tried to photograph it in 2009. I was also able to get good shots of the exterior of the Peace Hotel (1929), which last year (2009) had been completely covered up with scaffolding.

However, my main goal after having seen the Shanghai Club was to get down north to the Waitan Yuan redevelopment project area and see what was happening there. I found that it's now much easier to get views and side angle shots of the Garden Bridge (Waibaidu Qiao) built in 1907, as they have now cleared areas along Suzhou Creek (Suzhou He) on the south side and turned them into green space and an extended promenade around the Victory Monument. It used to be very hard to get side views of the bridge due to all the clutter in the way. In fact the entire Wusong Lu Water Gate Bridge (Wusong Lu Zha Qiao) [吴淞路闸桥] has been removed from where it once ran parallel to the Garden Bridge (Waibaidu Qiao) on its west side, thus blocking the view from that direction.

Along Suzhou Nan Lu, the old Rowing Club building has been restored, or by the looks of it possibly completely rebuilt. However, the old swimming pool building that still stood beside it last year is now gone. They left the pool itself but filled it in with soil and grass, creating a kind of weird modern art landscape, with the outlines of the pool still visible. Across the street, at the corner of Suzhou Nan Lu and Yuanmingyuan Lu, the old Union Church, which was built in 1886 but burned down in 2007, has now been completely rebuilt, along with the bell tower steeple that had been removed during the Cultural Revolution. The result, however, is a brand new building that appears sterile and fake, as opposed to a genuine historic relic that has been restored.

Nearby, Yuanmingyuan Lu has been turned into a brick paved pedestrian walking street. All the historic buildings along this street, many of which had been built and previously occupied by Christian missionary societies, have been saved and restored. The restoration of their exteriors has been completed, but they are all still empty inside and closed to visitors. Oddly, in the restoration of the exteriors they chose to inscribe the facade of each building with its English name, in a way which looks unnatural. A historic plaque would have been enough.

On the east side of Yuanmingyuan Lu the old British Consulate compound has also been renovated. The main building and the Consul's former residence both look pretty good from the outside, but these are the only two historic buildings remaining from what used to be a much larger group of old buildings that once stood inside the walled compound. When researching my Shanghai and the Yangzi Delta book in 2003, I noted that there were then eight buildings within the compound, at least three of which were original, and that historically the site used to include not only the consulate, but also consul's residence, supreme court, naval office, and so on. Now there are only two buildings left, but a much expanded garden. Although I was allowed to walk around the garden freely and photograph the exterior, once I approached the entrance and knocked on the door I was told quite coldly by one woman staff person who met me at the front door that, "This is private space," and not allowed to set foot inside. It seemed odd that a building constructed by a foreign government at the expense of British taxpayers, and then seized by the new Communist regime to serve as one of their local government office buildings, would today be described by a representative of its new owners as their "private space." When I inquired at the front desk of the Peninsula Hotel next door, which I thought also owned the former consulate, I was told that the Shanghai government still owned the consulate site, but that the Peninsula staff manage it, a rather confusing arrangement. They told me that they would get back to me later in response to my request to see the inside. In fact, I had been inside the building before it was restored back in 2002, and took photographs of the interior then, but at that time it was still used as city government office space and I had snuck in unbeknownst to anyone.

Originally I had planned to also re-explore the former Museum Road (Huqiu Lu), which runs parallel to Yuanmingyuan Lu, but I got too hot and tired and had to go home. Thus, I still haven't had a chance yet to investigate the interior of the former RAS Building, which finally reopened this summer as the new Rockbund Art Museum (RAM). That's another architectural treasure I never got to explore before its restoration, except for the lobby which the security guard once let me see.

Another restored site on my list to revisit is the Great World Amusement Center (Da Shi Jie) on the corner of Yanan Lu and Xizang Lu, with its wedding cake white tower on top. This used to be one of my favorite places to hang out when I first came to Shanghai in the 1990s, and at that time I felt it was one of the last places to still preserve an authentic atmosphere of old Shanghai. It was closed for seven years starting in 2003 and underwent a much delayed restoration project that did not finish until sometime this summer. I'm very eager to revisit it and see what they've done with the interior.

Yet another long closed and recently restored site in the Bund area on my list to revisit is the old Trinity Cathedral, used by the city government as office space from 1949 until last year (2009).

On Friday September 24, 2010, the last day of my four-day Mid-Autumn Festival (Zhongqiujie) vacation, I made a second journey into the city, taking subway Line 9 all the way from Sijing town in Songjiang District to its intersection with Line 8, which I then took two stops to the Shanghai Great World (Da Shi Jie) station, emerging from underground right at the Shanghai Concert Hall now located across the street due its move there in 2004.

It was yet another perfectly beautiful sunny day. I took some great shots of the Great World Amusement Center (Dashijie) from across the street and up close, but was shocked to discover that the interior was still visibly gutted as could be seen through the open windows, and the courtyard area was also still under reconstruction, as could be seen through the narrow alley separating the two parts of the building. The scaffolding had all been taken down, and the exterior renovation seemed complete, but the doors were still closed, with no sign posted outside informing as to when it might reopen. Seven years of reconstruction and it's still not done yet! The Shanghai Daily newspaper had twice earlier this year predicted that it would reopen in time for the 2010 World Expo, but it did not.

While I was there I also took a lot of exterior and interior shots of the old YMCA Hotel, built in 1931, which has had a thorough make over and is now called the Marvel Hotel in English, but in Chinese is still the Qingnian Hui Binguan [青年会宾馆].

Next stop was Huqiu Lu [虎丘路], where I finally got to see the restored outside and inside of the former Royal Asiatic Society (RAS) building, now the RAM Rockbund Art Gallery. The entrance is from the rear east side now, via a parking lot created by tearing down all the other old buildings that had stood between the RAS Building and the Christian Literature Society Building to the north. Passing through the modern eastern extension added on, I entered what had been the ground floor lobby of the original building, the one interior space I had managed to see before the renovation. There were the same steps leading upward that I had been denied access to before. The original Art-Deco staircase, complete with floor pattern and handrails, has been kept intact all the way from the ground floor up to the sixth floor. The original wooden interior doors also seem intact. Otherwise, the second and third floors have little of architectural or historical interest, but the 4th and 5th floors form one two-level atrium with a skylight overhead. The skylight may have been added later, but I imagine these two floors were the library. Up on the sixth floor there is a small cafe and an incredible roof deck on top of the eastern rear extension with a bird's eye view of the confluence of Suzhou Creek and the Huangpu River, including the Garden Bridge (Waibaidu Qiao), former Russian Consulate, Pujiang Hotel (Pujiang Fandian) [浦江饭店], and the new cruise ship port. Unfortunately, my camera had run out of digital memory by the time I got there, and I had been told before that no photos were allowed inside the building.

BTW, according to RAM staff they are also using the Union Church as exhibit space.

The most shocking discovery was the huge gap on Huqiu Lu's east side now separating the RAS Building from the Christian Literature Society Building, where a number of other historic buildings have obviously been torn down.

Fortunately the old New York club building is still standing, looking much the same except for missing its old neon marquee, but still closed, although a new turnstile door has been installed and a uniformed guard sits inside. Across the street next to the old tobacco building building that looks like an opera hall the old youth association building is almost the only one on the street that is still there and still looks the same as it did a year ago in 2009 when I last visited. The others are either gone or have been restored beyond recognition into shiny new new edifices.

On the way back we took Henan Zhong Lu on a bewildering journey through what used to be the "old city" of the former Nanshi District and Old West Gate (Laoximen) area. The one bright spot was the Small Peach Garden Mosque (Xiaotaoyuan Qingzhen Si), which was still there, but all else was now soaring skyscrapers where stone gate houses (shikumen) [石库门] and temples used to stand.

I don't know when you were last here, but if you haven't been back here in a while this update may prove interesting to you.

Here's wishing you the best. Take care.

Best Regards,
Eric N. Danielson
Shanghai, China

Appendix V:
Chongming Island Trip Report
Eric N. Danielson
(11-05-10)

On Thursday Nov. 4th, 2010 I took a trip all the way out to Chongming Island [崇明岛]. Although it's now possible to go there by bus or car via the new combination of bridges and tunnels connecting the Pudong area on the east side of the Huangpu River with first Changxing Island and then Chongming Island, I chose to go there the traditional way by boat from the port of Wusongkou in Boashan District.

The Shanghai subway system has so improved that it was possible for me to go from Sijing Town in Songjiang to Wusong Kou in only 1 hour and a half via Line 9 and then transferring to Line 3 at Yishan Lu Station. There was a slight delay when our train stopped prematurely at Changjiang Nan Lu Station on Line 3, and we had to wait for another one to come pick us up and take us the rest of the way to the end of Line 3. I chose to get off at the Baoyang Lu Station of Line 3, assuming that I could walk from there to the Baoyang Lu Ferry Boat Dock, and in fact there were street signs right across from the station pointing in that direction.

However, it turned out to be a very long walk and when I finally got to the spot where Baoyang Lu met the Yangzi River I discovered that a new International Passenger Ship Dock and Terminal were being constructed there. Walking west along the river I passed the abandoned old buildings of the Baoyang Dock Terminal, which were in the process of being torn down, and finally reached the brand new Baoyang Dock Terminal building, which is shaped like a ship with a smoke stack on top. The ticket window area was completely empty, and it was a pleasant surprise to find no chaotic lines of people waiting to buy tickets. The ticket windows were all clearly labeled with bilingual signs providing the choice of destinations, which were limited to only two. I purchased a ticket for South Gate (Nan Men) dock of Chengqiao Town at a price of only 18 Rmb and then had another 30 minutes to wait until the next boat left at 2:00 p.m.

I had arrived at the Baoyang Lu Station on Line 3 at 12:30 p.m., having left Sijing at 11:00 a.m. It was my one regret that an hour and a half of crucial time was lost in walking from the subway station to the boat dock. Fortunately, some time was saved when I discovered that the boat trip itself had been reduced down form an hour to only 30 minutes from Baoyang to Nan Men dock of Chengqiao Town. The boat was not only fast, but quite comfortable, although the dirty windows could not be opened, and we were not allowed to go outside on the deck during the voyage. As a result, it was not possible to take any photos during the boat trip, although I did take shots from the docks before leaving and after arriving.

From Nan Men dock in Chengqiao Town [城桥镇], August 1st Road (Ba Yi Lu) leads right into the town, and it was quite easy to travel the short distance to the Study Palace (Xue Gong) [学宫] on Ao Shan Lu [鳌山路]. Ao Shan Lu [鳌山路] is a very pleasant forested two-lane road lined with trees on both sides that form a green canopy overhead. It starts from the edge of Chengqiao Town and runs along the south coastline of the island. The area is quite flat, without even any hills, despite the road being named Turtle Hill (Ao Shan).

At the entrance to the walled Study Palace (Xue Gong) [学宫] compound are three stone gates standing side by side. The cloud design tops of all four vertical stone posts were a different color and had obviously been reattached, leading me to believe that they were previously broken off, and that these top parts are new whereas the rest of the gate may be real. On either side of the gate stand two gateways (pailou) with wooden brackets (dougong) supporting the roofs, their eaves arching sharply upward into the sky. There are also two 350 year old gingko trees. No ticket was required to enter the site, which used to be a Confucius Temple, but now serves as the Chongming Museum [崇明博物馆].

Entering the walled compound, the first courtyard contains a half moon pool crossed by a single stone foot bridge. Next comes the Cheng Men gate hall, the roof eaves of which protect three inscribed stone tablets (shi bei), all of which seem to be new replicas. Entering the second courtyard you see a sacred way (shen dao) of four stone statues, two on either side, with a stone statue of Confucius (Kong Fuzi) [孔夫子] (551-479 B.C.) straight ahead on the raised front terrace of the temple's main hall (Da Cheng Dian) [大成殿]. The stone statues all looked quite new, although they were well made. At first I assumed the four statues along the way were some of his most important disciples, but according to Chinese inscriptions at the bottom of all five statues, the first one on the right has the surname Kong, implying it is one of his sons, while at least one other seemed to be that of a woman.

While the exterior has the appearance of a Confucius Temple (Wen Miao) [文庙] or (Kong Miao)[孔庙], once inside the buildings you realize that this is no longer a functioning temple but a modern museum. The interior of the main hall (Da Cheng Dian) [大成殿] itself now contains exhibits related to the island's shipbuilding industry, including a lot of fascinating models of wooden sailing ships of various types, as well as some more modern ones. The exhibits are all labeled exclusively in Chinese, but there are brief English language introductions near the entrance to most of the exhibit halls. Other side halls along the second courtyard were dedicated to the local salt industry. Behind the main hall (Da Cheng Dian) [大成殿] were two small halls, side by side, containing wax mannequin exhibits depicting traditional folk life, such as weaving, churning butter, etc. Pretty boring stuff.

The most exciting discovery was that, as is usual with these rebuilt historic sites, the few real remaining broken stone relics were piled up in the back left corner of the walled compound, hidden from view in an area strewn with trash and littered with dog poop. There were some really beautiful and fascinating examples of stone carvings, which I photographed.

In the very back of the site there is a small hill or mound of earth.

A parallel pair of courtyards and halls beside the main one was deserted and pretty boring. The main hall contained a modern painting exhibition. There were two stele corridors along both sides of the second rear courtyard, but as usual these all seemed to be fake copies made from rubbings.

Directly across the street from the front entrance to the Study Palace (Xue Gong) [学宫] was the waterfront **Yingzhou Park** [瀛洲公园] with a pedestrian promenade along the Yangzi River.

While it had proven remarkably easy to find the Study Palace (Xue Gong) [学宫] site, it turned out to be a long distance down the same Ao Shan Road headed East to the site of the Calm Sea Tower (Zhen Hai Ta) at **Golden Turtle Hill Park** (Jin Ao Shan Gongyuan) [金鳌山公园]. The Golden Turtle Hill site is now hidden behind the newly constructed compound of the **Longevity & Peace Buddhist Temple** (Shou An Si) [寿安寺], which stands right beside the road. I had to walk along a muddy dirt road running beside the temple compound in order to reach the park hidden behind it. Once I arrived the sun was already going down and I found that it was being restored by construction workers, but still I could see that the surrounding grounds were designed in the way of a traditional Chinese landscape garden like the Yu Yuan [豫园] or those found in Suzhou. Within the landscaped garden there were streams crossed by stone and wood foot bridges, small forested hills, rockeries, caves, pavilions, and a number of Chinese inscriptions written on stone tablets (shi bei) and rocks.

Unfortunately, it soon got too dark to see and I had to make the long walk back to South Gate (Nan Men) dock of Chengqiao Town [城桥镇] in order to catch the last ferry boat back to the Shanghai mainland. Rather than returning me to my original starting point of the Boayang Lu Boat Dock at Wusongkou, this last late night boat landed me further West up the Yangzi River at a spot known as Shidongkou, which proved to be an absolutely horrible place, densely packed with heavy industry, tall smoke stacks belching clouds of air pollution everywhere, and no transportation. If it can at all be avoided, I strongly recommend against traveling through the Shidongkou port.

_____

Appendix VI: Bilingual Shanghai Historic Street Name Index
Eric N. Danielson
(02-08-19)

Non-Chinese language maps and written sources about Shanghai published before 1949 all used English and French street names which are no longer used today for those areas that were within the International Settlement and French Concession, and some English language histories of Shanghai have continued to do so to this day. In addition to their official English and French names, these streets also had Chinese names which were usually phonetic renderings of their foreign names. Some Shanghai streets were re-named as early as 1946 after the Guomindang took over control of the former foreign concessions for a brief three-and-a-half-year period. After May 1949 most, but not all, Shanghai's streets were given new Chinese names, including those which had just recently been renamed by the Guomindang. In the center of the International Settlement between Thibet Road (Xizang Zhong Lu) [西藏中路] and the Bund (Waitan) [外滩], few names were changed because the British had previously named the East-West streets after Chinese cities, and the North-South streets after Chinese provinces.

Most English language publications about Shanghai's history written by foreigners have continued to use the old pre-1949 street names, without providing their new post-1949 names, often because the authors themselves have never been to Shanghai and based their works solely on archival documents and books contained in the libraries of ivory towers overseas. This has made it difficult for foreign visitors to Shanghai to actually locate the historic sights that they've read about in English language books. This nomenclature confusion has only been compounded by the adoption in mainland China of the Pinyin phonetic system, and the simplified Chinese characters, both of which most authors in Taiwan and overseas still refuse to accept, instead preferring to use the antiquated Wade-Giles phonetic system and traditional Chinese characters.

In order to allow foreign visitors to be able to actually find Shanghai's historic sights located within the former concessions, I have compiled an index detailing the pre-1949 street names cross referenced with their current Chinese names in the phonetic Pinyin and simplified Chinese characters actually used in mainland China today. This chart is adapted and updated from an earlier one that appeared in my previous book, _Shanghai and the Yangzi Delta_, published in 2003. It would be impossible to include every single name every street in the city has ever had. For reasons of space it was only possible to include the most significant streets. I have a separate 147 page bilingual list of Shanghai's historic street names. Also, I have alphabetized the French street names as best as I can without actually being familiar with the language. Please pardon my French!

I. International Settlement (Shanghai Gonggong Zujie) [上海公共租界]

Pre-1945 English Name (From A to Z)	Post 1945 Chinese Name (Pinyin)	Today's Chinese Name (Characters)
Alcock Road	Anguo Lu	安国路
Baikal Road	Huimin Lu	惠民路
Boone Road	Tanggu Lu	塘沽路
Boundary Road	Tianmu Lu	天目路
Broadway	Daming Lu	大名路
Broadway East	Dong Daming Lu	东大名路
Bubbling Well Road	Nanjing Xi Lu	南京西路
The Bund	Zhongshan Dong Yi Lu	中山东一路
Canton Road	Guangdong Lu	广东路
Carter Road	Zhongzheng Bei Er Lu (1946-1949) Shimen Er Lu (after 1949)	中正北二路 石门二路
Elgin Road (Beside the Elgin Market)	Anqing Lu	安庆路
Foochow Road	Fuzhou Lu	福州路
Hankow Road	Hankou Lu	汉口路
Hardoon Road	Tongren Lu	铜仁路
Honan Road	Henan Zhong Lu	河南中路
Hong Kong Road	Xianggang Lu	香港路
Kiukiang Road	Jiujiang Lu	九江路
Mandalay Road	Jiangyin Lu	江阴路
Mohawk Road	Huangpi Bei Lu	黄陂北路
Moulme Road	Maoming Lu	茂名路

Museum Road	Huqiu Lu	虎丘路
Nanking Road	Nanjing Dong Lu	南京东路
Park Road (Beside the Park Hotel)	Huanghe Lu	黄河路
Peking Road	Beijing Dong Lu	北京东路
Peking Road	Beijing Xi Lu	北京西路
Point Road	Dinghai Lu	定海路
Range Road	Wujin Lu	武进路
Seymour Road	Shanxi Bei Lu	陕西北路
Soochow South Road	Nan Suzhou Lu	南苏州路
Soochow North Road	Bei Suzhou Lu	北苏州路
Szechuen Road	Sichuan Zhong Lu	四川中路
Thibet Road	Xizang Zhong Lu	西藏中路
Ward Road	Changyang Lu	长阳路
Wayside Road	Huoshan Lu	霍山路
Weihaiwei Road	Weihai Lu	威海路
Yangtszepoo Road	Yangshupu Lu	杨树浦路
Yates Road	Zhongzheng Bei Yi Lu (1946-1949) Shimen Yi Lu (after 1949)	中正北一路 石门一路
Yuen Ming Yuen Road	Yuan Ming Yuan Lu	圆明园路

2. Western Outside Roads Area (Huxi Yuejie Zhulu) [沪西越界筑路]

Pre-1949 English Name (From A to Z)	Today's Chinese Name (Pinyin)	Today's Chinese Name (Characters)
Amherst Avenue	Xinhua Lu	新华路
Brenan Road	Changning Lu	长宁路
Columbia Road	Panyu Lu	番禺路
Connaught Road	Kangding Lu	康定路
Edinburgh Road	Jiangsu Lu	江苏路
Gordon Road	Jiangning Lu	江宁路
Great Western Road	Zhongzheng Xi Lu (1946-1949) Yanan Xi Lu (after 1949)	中正西路 延安西路
Hungjao Road	Hongqiao Lu	虹桥路
Jernigan Road	Xianxia Lu	仙霞路
Jessfield Road	Wanhangdu Lu	万航渡路
Jordan Avenue	Lin Sen Lu (1946-1949) Huaihai Xi Lu (after 1949)	林森路 淮海西路
Keswick Road	Kaixuan Lu	凯旋路
Lincoln Road	Tianshan Lu	天山路
Monument Road	Suiyuan Lu	绥宁路
Robinson Road	Changshou Lu	长寿路
Rubicon Road	Hami Lu	哈密路
Warren Road	Gubei Lu	古北路
Yuyuen Road	Yuyuan Lu	愚园路

3. Northern Outside Roads Area (Hubei Yuejie Zhulu) [沪北越界筑路]

Pre-1949 English Name (From A to Z)	Today's Chinese Name (Pinyin)	Today's Chinese Name (Characters)
Darroch Road	Duolun Lu	多伦路
Dixwell Road	Liyang Lu	溧阳路
Scott Road	Shanyin Lu	山阴路
Szechuen North Road	Sichuan Bei Lu	四川北路

4. French Concession (Shanghai Fa Zujie) [上海法租界]

Pre-1949 French Name (From A to Z)	Today's Chinese Name (Pinyin)	Today's Chinese Name (Characters)
Avenue Dubail	Chongqing Nan Lu	重庆南路
Avenue Edward VII	Zhongzheng Dong Lu (1946-1949) Yanan Dong Lu (after 1949)	中正东路 延安东路
Avenue Foch East	Jinling Xi Lu	金陵西路
Avenue Foch West	Zhongzheng Zhong Lu (1946-1949) Yanan Zhong Lu (after 1949)	中正中路 延安中路
Avenue Haig	Huashan Lu	华山路
Avenue Joffre	Lin Sen Lu (1946-1949) Huaihai Zhong Lu (1949)	林森路 淮海中路
Avenue Petain	Hengshan Lu	衡山路
Avenue du Roi Albert	Shanxi Nan Lu	陕西南路
Boulevard des Deux Republiques	Minguo Lu (1946-1949) Renmin Lu (After 1949)	民国路, 人民路
Boulevard de Montigny	Xizang Nan Lu (north of Fangbang Xi Lu).	西藏南路
Moulmein Road	Maoming Bei Lu	茂名北路
Quai de France	Zhongshan Dong Er Lu	中山东二路
Route A. Charles Culty	Hunan Lu	湖南路
Route Alfred Magy	Wulumuqi Zhong Lu	乌鲁木齐中路
Route Amiral Courbet	Fumin Lu	富民路
Route Andre Cohen	Gaoan Lu	高安路
Route Bridou	Wuxing Lu	吴兴路 (南段)
Route Camille Lorioz	Taian Lu	泰安路
Route Cardinal Mercier	Maoming Nan Lu	茂名南路
Route Conty	Jianguo Dong Lu	建国东路
Route Dolfus	Nanchang Lu	南昌路
Route Doumer	Donghu Lu	东湖路
Route Dupleix	Anfu Lu	安福路
Route Emmanuel III	Shaoxing Lu	绍兴路
Route Francis Garnier	Dongping Lu	东平路
Route Ferguson	Wukang Lu	武康路
Route General Pershing	Wuxing Lu	吴兴路 (淮海中路至衡山路段)
Route Grouchy	Yanqing Lu	延庆路
Route Gustave Boissezon	Fuxing Xi Lu	复兴西路
Route Herve Sieyes	Yongjia Lu	永嘉路
Route Joseph Freupt	Jianguo Xi Lu	建国西路

Route J. Winling	Wanping Lu	宛平路
Route Kaufmann	Anting Lu	安亭路
Route Louis Dufour	Wulumuqi Nan Lu	乌鲁木齐南路
Route Mgr Maresca	Wuyuan Lu	五原路
Route Mgr. Prosper Paris	Tianping Lu	天平路
Route Marcel Magniny	Kangping Lu	康平路
Route Mayen	Huating Lu	华亭路
Route Paul Henri	Xinle Lu	新乐路
Route Pére Dugout	Yongnian Lu	永年路
Route Pere Huc	Yongfu Lu	永福路
Route Pere Robert	Zhongzheng Nan Er Lu (1946-1949) Ruijin Er Lu (after 1949)	中正南二路 瑞金二路
Route Picard Destelan	Guangyuan Lu	广元路
Route Pichon	Fenyang Lu	汾阳路
Route Pottier	Baoqing Lu	宝庆路
Route Ratard	Julu Lu	巨鹿路
Route Remi	Xingguo Lu	兴国路
Route Rene Delastre	Taiyuan Lu	太原路
Route Sayzoong	Changshu Lu	常熟路
Route des Soeurs	Zhongzheng Nan Yi Lu (1946-1949) Ruijin Yi Lu (after 1949)	中正南一路 瑞金一路
Route Stanislas Chevalier	Jianguo Zhong Lu	建国中路
Route Tenant de la Tour	Xiangyang Nan Lu	襄阳南路
Route Vallon	Nanchang Lu	南昌路
Route Zikawei	Xujiahui Lu & Zhaojiabang Lu	徐家汇路, 肇嘉浜路
Rue Amiral Bayle	Huangpi Nan Lu	黄陂南路
Rue Auguste Boppe	Taicang Lu	太仓路
Rue Baran Gross	Songshan Lu	嵩山路
Rue Bluntschli	Jinan Lu	济南路
Rue Bourgeat	Changle Lu	长乐路
Rue Brenier de Montmorand	Madang Lu	马当路
Rue Buissonnet	Shouning Lu	寿宁路
Rue Capitaine Rabier	Xizang Nan Lu (south of Fangbang Xi Lu).	西藏南路 (南段)
Rue Cassini	Taikang Lu	泰康路
Rue Chapsal	Danshui Lu	淡水路
Rue Consulat	Jingling Dong Lu	金陵东路
Rue Corneille	Gaolan Lu	皋兰路
Rue Eugine Bard	Zizhong Lu (east section)	自忠路 (东段)

Rue Hennequin	Dongtai Lu	东台路
Rue Hue	Zhejiang Nan Lu	浙江南路
Rue Lafayette	Fuxing Zhong Lu	复兴中路
Rue de la Laguerre	Yongan Lu	永安路
Rue Lieutenant Petiot	Chengdu Nan Lu	成都南路
Rue L. Lorton	Xiangyang Bei Lu	襄阳北路
Rue Marcel Tillot	Xingan Lu	兴安路
Rue du Marche	Shunchang Lu	顺昌路
Rue Massenet	Sinan Lu	思南路
Rue Mathieu	Shandong Nan Lu	山东南路
Rue Millot	Fangbang Xi Lu	方浜西路
Rue Moliere	Xiangshan Lu	香山路
Rue Montauban	Sichuan Nan Lu	四川南路
Rue Ningpo (Beside the Ningbo Guild)	Lin Sen Lu (1946-1949) Huaihai Dong Lu (after 1949)	林森路 淮海东路
Rue de la Observatoire	Hefei Lu	合肥路
Rue Palikao	Yunnan Nan Lu	云南南路
Rue Paul Beau	Chongqing Zhong Lu	重庆中路
Rue Pere Huc	Xinjiang Nan Lu	浙江南路
Rue Petit	Jiangxi Nan Lu	江西南路
Rue de la Porte du Nord	Henan Nan Lu	河南南路
Rue de la Porte de l'Ouest	Zizhong Lu	自忠路
Rue de Saigou	Guangxi Nan Lu	广西南路
Rue Soeur Allegre	Taoyuan Lu	桃源路
Rue de Taikoo	Gaoqiao Lu	高桥路
Rue Tourane	Fujian Nan Lu	福建南路
Rue Vouillemont	Puan Lu	普安路
Rue Wagner	Ninghai Xi Lu	宁海西路
Rue Wantz	Xingye Lu	兴业路

Appendix VII:
Bilingual Glossary of Key Vocabulary, People, and Place Names
Eric N. Danielson

City Wall

City Wall (chengchiang) [城墙]
City Moat (huchenghe) [护城河]
Shanghai county town (Shanghai xian cheng) [上海县城]
Nantao (Nandao) [南岛]
Nanshi District (Nanshi Qu) [南市区]
Japanese pirates (woko) [倭寇].
seven land gates (chengmen) [城门]
four water gates (shuiguan) [水关]
four watch towers (genglou) [更楼]
Renmin Lu [人民路]
Zhonghua Lu [中华路]
Old West Gate (Lao Xi Men) [老西门]
Small East Gate (Xiao Dong Men) [小东门]
Small North Gate (Xiao Bei Men) [小北门]

Shanghai's Evolving Names & Administrative Status

Shanghai Municipality (Shanghai Shi) [上海市]
The four directly governed municipalities (zhixiashi) [直辖市]
Green Dragon Town (Qinglong Zhen) [青龙镇]
The village of Hudu [沪渎]
Huating County (Huating Xian) [华亭县]
Songjiang Prefecture (Songjiang Fu) [松江府]
Shanghai County (Shanghai Xian) [上海县]
Shanghai county town (Shanghai xiancheng) [上海县城]
Region South of the Yangzi River (Jiangnan) [江南]

Famous Streets
Anren Jie [安仁街]
Zhaojiabang Lu [肇嘉浜路]
Fuxing East Road (Fuxing Dong Lu) [复兴东路]
Fangbang Middle Road (Fangbang Zhong Lu) [方浜中路]
Fangbang East Road (Fangbang Dong Lu) [方浜东路]
Nanking Road (Nanjing Lu) [南京路]
Shanghai-Nanjing Expressway (Hu-Ning Gaosu Gonglu) [沪宁高速公路].
Yuanmingyuan Lu [圆明园路]
Boulevard des Deux Republiques (until 1945) = Minguo Lu [民国路] (1946-1949), Renmin Lu [人民路] (After 1949)
Pedestrian only walking street (buxing jie) [步行街]
Culture and famous people street (wenhua mingren jie) [文化名人街]

Neighborhoods

Lujiazui [陆家嘴]
Xujiahui [徐家汇]
People's   Square (Renmin Guangchang) [人民广场]
Yu Yuan Bazaar (Yuyuan Shangcheng) [豫园商城]
Hongqiao [虹桥]
Wujiaochang [五角场]
West of the Huangpu River (Puxi) [浦西]
East of the Huangpu River (Pudong) [浦东]
Zhongshan Park (Zhongshan Gongyuan) [中山公园]
British Settlement (Shanghai Ying Zujie) [上海英租界]Y
Shanghai American Settlement (Shanghai Mei Zujie) [上海美租界]
International Settlement (Shanghai Gonggong Zujie) [上海公共租界]
French Concession (Shanghai Fa Zujie) [上海法租界]
Outside Roads Areas (Yuejie Zhulu) [越界筑路]
Western Outside Roads Area (Huxi Yuejie Zhulu) [沪西越界筑路]
Northern Outside Roads Area (Hubei Yuejie Zhulu) [沪北越界筑路]
Longhua Town (Longhua Zhen) [龙华镇]
Jiangwan Town (Jiangwan Zhen) [江湾镇]
Jiading Town (Jiading Zhen)[嘉定镇]
Qingpu Town (Qingpu Zhen) [青浦镇]
Qinglong Village (Qinglong Cun) [青龙村]
Jinze Ancient Town (Jinze Guzhen) [金泽古镇]
Zhujiajiao Ancient Town (Zhujiajiao Gu Zhen) [朱家角古镇]

Former Districts

Chuansha Qu [川沙区]
Luwan Qu [卢湾区]
Nantao (Nandao) [南岛]
Nanshi Qu [南市区]
Nanhui Qu [南汇区]
Zhabei Qu [闸北区]

Existing Districts

Pudong Xinqu [浦东新区]
Fengxian Qu [奉贤区]
Jinshan Qu [金山区]
Huangpu Qu [黄浦区]
Jingan Qu [静安区]
Xuhui Qu [徐汇区]
Changning Qu [长宁区]
Putuo Qu [普陀区]
Hongkou Qu [虹口区]
Yangpu Qu [杨浦区]
Boashan Qu [宝山区]
Minhang Qu [闵行区]
Jiading Qu [嘉定区]
Qingpu Qu [青浦区]
Songjiang Qu [松江区]
Chongming Qu [崇明区]

Temples

Church (Jiaotang) [教堂]
Chenxiang Ge Buddhist Temple [沉香阁]
City God Temple (Chenghuang Miao) [城隍庙]
Confucius Temple (Wen Miao) [文庙] or (Kong Miao) [孔庙]
Jingan Buddhist Temple (Jingan Si) [静安寺]
Jade Buddha Temple (Yufo Si) [玉佛寺]
Longhua Buddhist Temple (Longhua Si) [龙华寺]
Memorial Hall (Jinianguan) [纪念馆]
Mosque (Qingzhen Si) [清真寺]
War God Temple (Guandi Miao) [关帝庙], aka Dajing Ge Pavilion [大境阁]
Synogogue (Youtai Jiaotang) [犹太教堂]

Religions

Buddhism (Fo Jiao) [佛教]
Catholic Religion (Tianzhu Jiao) [天主教]
Chinese Muslims (Huimin) [回民]
Eastern Orthodox Church (Dongzhen Jiao) [东正教]
Islam (Yisilan Jiao) [伊斯兰教]
Judaism (Youtai Jiao) [犹太教]
Jesuits (Yesuhui) [耶稣会]
Muslims (Musilin) [穆斯林]
Protestant Religion (Jidu Jiao) [基督教]
Taoism (Dao Jiao) [道教]

Cast of Characters: Famous People
(Presented roughly in chronological order)

Huo Guang [霍光] (d.68 B.C.)

Sun Quan [孙权], King of Wu (222-252)

Bai Juyi [白居易] (772-846)

Qin Yubo [秦裕伯] (1295-1373)

Zhu Yuanzhang [朱元璋] (1328-1398), Hongwu [洪武] (1368-1398)

Zheng He [郑和] (1371-1433)

Zhu Di [朱棣] (1360-1424), Yongle [永乐](1403-1424)

Zhu Zhanji [朱瞻基] (1398-1435), Xuande [宣德] (1426-1435)

Zhu Houcong [朱厚熜] (1507-1567), Jiajing [嘉靖] (1521-1567)

Xu Guangqi [徐光启] (1562-1633)

Pan Yunduan [潘允端] (1526–1601) built the Yu Yuan, Chenxiang Ge, and Jingyi Tang.

Wanli [万历] (1573-1620)

Shunzhi [顺治] (1644-1661)

Kangxi [康熙] (1661-1722)

Yongzheng [雍正] (1722-1735)

Qianlong [乾隆] (1735-1796)

Jiaqing [嘉庆] (1796-1820)

Daoguang [道光] (1821-1850)

Xianfeng [咸丰] (1850-1861)

Tongzhi [同治] (1861-1875)

Guangxu [光绪] (1875-1908)

Chen Huacheng [陈化成] (1776-1842)

Li Xiucheng [李秀成] (1823-1864), the Taipings' Loyal King (Zhong Wang) [忠王]

Li Hongzhang [李鸿章] (1823-1901), Qing commander of the Huai Army (Huai Jun) [淮军].

Xuantong [宣统] (1909-1911) reign of the last Qing Dynasty Emperor Puyi [溥仪].

Sun Yat-sen (Sun Zhongshan) [孙中山] (1866-1925)

Yuan Shikai [袁世凯] (1859-1916)

Song Jiaoren [宋教仁] (1882-1913)

Chiang Kai-shek (Jiang Jieshi) [蒋介石] (1887-1975) aka Zhong Zheng [中正]

Charlie Soong (Song Jiashu) [宋嘉树](1864-1918)

Song Meiling [宋美龄] (1898-2003)

Song Qingling [宋庆龄] (1893-1981)

Song Ailing [宋蔼龄] (1889-1973)

T.V. Song (Song Ziwen) [宋子文] (1894-1971)

H.H. Kung (Kong Xiangxi) [孔祥熙] (1880-1967)

Bai Chongxi [白崇禧] (1893-1966)

Li Zongren [李宗仁] (1891-1969)

He Yingqin [何应钦] (1890-1987)

Wellington Koo (Gu Weijun) [顾维钧] (1888-1985)

Huang Chujiu [黄楚九] (1872-1931) [Original owner of Dashijie]

Du Yuesheng [杜月笙] (1888-1951)

Huang Jinrong [黄金荣](1868-1953)

Zhang Xiaolin [张啸林] (1877-1940)

The Green Gang (Qing Bang) [青帮]

Yu Qiaqing [虞洽卿](1867-1945), president of the Shanghai Chamber of Commerce.

Tongmenghui [同盟会] (founded 1905)

The Communists (Gongchandang) [共产党]

The Nationalists (Guomindang) [国民党] (founded 1912)

Huang Xing [黄兴] (1874-1916)

Chen Qimei [陈其美] (1878-1916), the uncle of Chen Guofu and Chen Lifu, aka CC Clique.

Song Jioaren [宋教仁] (1882-1913)

Lu Xun [鲁迅] (1881-1936), aka Zhou Shuren [周树人]

Mao Dun [茅盾] (1896-1981)

Ding Ling [丁玲] (1904-1986)

Ba Jin [巴金] (1904-2005)

Guo Moruo [郭沫若] (1892-1978)

Hu Shi [胡适](1891-1962)

Cai Yuanpei [蔡元培] (1868-1940)

Chen Duxiu [陈独秀] (1879-1942)

Li Dazhao [李大钊] (1889-1927)

Li Lisan [李立三] (1899-1967)

Mao Zedong [毛泽东] (1893-1976)

Cai Tingkai [蔡廷锴] (1892-1968)

Xie Jinyuan [谢晋元] (1905-1941)

Chiang Ching-kuo (Jiang Jingguo) [蒋经国] (1910-1988)

Tang Enbo [汤恩伯] (1899-1954)

William Z. L. Sung (Shen Siliang) [沈嗣良] (1896-1967)

Peng Dehuai [彭德怀](1898-1974)

Liu Shaoqi [刘少奇] (1898-1969)

The Red Guards (Hongweibing) [红卫兵]

Jiang Qing [江青] (1914-1991) Mao's fourth wife & leader of the Gang of Four.

Deng Xiaoping [邓小平] (1904-1997)

Modern Buildings

Jin Mao Tower (Jinmao Dasha) [金茂大厦]
Oriental Pearl T.V. Tower (Dongfang Mingzhu Guangbo Dianshi Ta) [东方明珠广播电视塔]
Shanghai Tower (Shanghai Zhongxin Dasha) [上海中心大厦]
Shanghai Grand Theater (Shanghai Da Juyuan) [上海大剧院]
Shanghai World Financial Center (Shanghai huanqiu jinrong zhongxin) [上海环球金融中心]
Yuyuan Bazaar (Yuyuan Shangcheng) [豫园商城]
Subway Station (Ditie Zhan) [地铁站]

Historic Buildings

Hong Kong & Shanghai Bank (Huifeng Yinhang) [汇丰银行]
Astronomical Observatory (Tianwentai) [天文台]
Meterological Observatory (Guanxiangtai) [观象台]
No.4 Company Warehouse (Sihang Cangku) [四行仓库]
Former Residence (Guju) [故居]
Memorial Hall (Jinian Guan) [纪念馆]
Wusong Forts (Wusong Paotai) [吴淞炮台]
St. John's University (Shanghai Sheng Yuehan Daxue) [上海圣约翰大学]
Great World Amusement Center (Dashijie) [大世界]
Huang Garden (Huangjia Huayuan) [黄家花园]
Shanghai Municipal Council (Shanghai Gongbu Ju) [上海工部局]
Gong Guan [公馆]
Zhenguang Dalou [真光大楼]

Traditional Architecture

Lane (lilong) [里弄] or (longtang) [弄堂]
Stone Gate House (Shikumen) [石库门]
Xintiandi [新天地]

Intangible Heritage

Shanghai Opera (Huju) [沪剧]
Shanghai Dialect (Shanghai Hua) [上海话]
Nanxiang Dumplings (Nanxiang Xiaolong Bao)
Xinghua Lou Moon Cakes (Xinghua Lou Yuebing)

Waterways

The Bund (Waitan) [外滩]
French Bund (Falanxi Waitan) [法兰西外滩]
Huangpu Jiang [黄浦江]
Suzhou He [苏州河]
Song River (Song Jiang) [松江]
Wusong River (Wusong Jiang) [吴淞江]
Wusong Mouth (Wusong Kou) [吴淞口]
Dianshan Lake (Dianshan Hu) [淀山湖]
Yangshan Deep Water Port (Yangshan Shenshui Gang) [洋山深水港]
Hangzhou-Beijing Grand Canal (Jinghang Da Yunhe) [京杭大运河]
Yellow River (Huang He) [黄河]
Yangzi River (Changjiang) [长江]
Yangjing Bang [洋泾浜]
Fangbang [方浜]
Puhuitang River [蒲汇塘河]

Bridges

East Sea Bridge to Yangshan (Donghai Daqiao) [东海大桥]
Garden Bridge (Waibaidu Qiao) [外白渡桥]
Wusong Lu Water Gate Bridge (Wusong Lu Zha Qiao) [吴淞路闸桥]
Lupu Bridge (Lupu Da Qiao) [卢浦大桥]
Yangpu Bridge (Yangpu Da Qiao) [杨浦大桥]
Nanpu Bridge (Nanpu Da Qiao) [南浦大桥]
Xupu Bridge (Xupu Da Qiao) [徐浦大桥]

Key Historical Events

Treaty of Nanking (Zhongying Nanjing Tiaoyue) [中英南京條約] 1842
The Taiping Rebellion (Taiping Tianguo) [太平天国](1850-1864)
The 1911 Revolution (Xinhai Geming) [辛亥革命]
The 1913 Second Revolution (Erci Geming) [二次革命]
The 1919 May 4th Movement (Wusi Yundong) [五四运动]
The 1925 May 30th Movement (Wusa Yundong) [五卅运动]
Northern Expedition (Bei Fa) [北伐] (1926-1928)
The April 12, 1927 Shanghai Massacre (Siyier Canan) [四一二惨案]
Sino-Japanese War (Kang Ri Zhanzheng) [抗日战争] (1937-1945)
Victory Over Japan (Shengli) [胜利] (August 1945)
Battle of Huaihai (Huaihai Zhanyi) [淮海战役] (November 1948-January 1949)
The Liberation of Shanghai (Jiefang) [解放] (May 27, 1949)
Land Reform Campaign (Tudi Gaige Yundong) [土地改革运动] (1950-1953)
Hundred Flowers Campaign (Baihua Yundong) [百花运动] 1956
Anti-Rightist Campaign (Fanyou Yundong) [反右运动] 1957
Great Leap Forward (Dayuejin) [大跃进] (1958-1960)
Cultural Revolution (Wenhua Da Geming) [文化大革命] (1966-1976)

Chinese Dynasties & Time Periods
(in chronological order)

Han Dynasty [汉代] (206 B.C.-220 A.D.)
Western Han [西汉] (206 B.C.-8 A.D)
Eastern Han [东汉] (25 A.D.-220 A.D.)
Three Kingdoms (San Guo) [三国] (220-280)
Eastern Wu Kingdom (Dong Wu) [东吴]
Jin Dynasty [晋朝] (265-420)
Western Jin [西晋] (265-316)
Eastern Jin [东晋] (317-420)
Southern Dynasties [南朝] (420-589)
Liang Dynasty [梁朝] (502-557)
Sui Dynasty [隋代] (581-617)
Tang Dynasty [唐代] (618-907)
Five Dynasties [五代] (907-960)
Ten Kingdoms [十国] (902-979)
Wu Yue Kingdom [吴越]
Northern Song Dynasty (Bei Song) [北宋] (960-1127)
Southern Song Dynasty (Nan Song) [南宋] (1127-1279)
Yuan Dynasty [元朝] (1279-1368)
Ming Dynasty [明代] (1368-1644)
Qing Dynasty [清朝] (1644-1911)
Taiping Rebellion (Taiping Tianguo) [太平天国](1850-1864)
Republic of China (Minguo) [民国] (1912-1949)
Isolated Island (Gu Dao) [孤岛] (1937-1941)
Peoples Republic of China (1949- Present)
Cultural Revolution (Wenhua Da Geming) [文化大革命] (1966-1976)
Economic Reform & Opening Up (Gaige Kaifang) [改革开放] (1979-Present)

Appendix VIII: List of Chairmen of the Shanghai Municipal Council (1854-1943)

Number	Name	Dates in Office	Nationality
1.	James Lawrence Man	July 11, 1854 – 1855	British
2.	Christopher Augustus Fearon	1855	British
3.	William Shepard Wetmore	March .1855	American
4.	William Thorbun	1855 - 1856	British
5.	James Lawrence Man	January 1856 – January 31, 1857	British
6.	George Watson Coutts	January 31, 1857 – January 1858	British
7.	John Thorne	January 1858 – January 1859	American
8.	Robert Reid	January 31, 1859 – February 15, 1860	British
9.	Rowland Hamilton	February 15, 1860 – February 2, 1861	British
10.	William Howard	February 2, 1861 – March 31, 1862	British
11.	Henry Turner	March 31, 1862 – April 4, 1863	British
12.	Henry William Dent	April 4, 1863 – April 25, 1865	British
13.	William Keswick	April 25, 1865 – April 18, 1866	British
14.	F.B. Johnson	April 18, 1866 – March 1868	British
15.	Edward Cunningham	M20rch 1868 – April 2, 1870	American
16.	George Basil Dixwell	April 2, 1870 – April 4, 1871	American
17.	John Dent	April 4, 1871 – January 1873	British
18.	Robert Inglis Fearon	January 1873 – April 16, 1874	American
19.	John Graeme Purdon	April 16, 1874 – 1876	American
20.	Alfred Adolphus Krauss	1876 – January 1877	British
21.	J. Hart	January 1877 January 16, 1879	American
22.	Robert "Bob" W. Little	January 16, 1879 – January 30, 1882	British
23.	H.R. Hearn	January 30, 1882 – 1882	British
24.	Walter Cyril Ward	1882 – 1883	British

25.	Alexander Myburgh	1883 – January 22, 1884	British
26.	James Johnstone Keswick	January 22, 1884 – January 22, 1886	British
27.	A.G. Wood	January 22, 1886 – 1889	British
28.	John Macgregor	1889 – May 1891	British
29.	John Graeme Purdon	May 1891 – January 1893	American
30.	John Macgregor	January 1893 – November 7, 1893)	British
31.	James Lidderdale Scott	November 1893 – January 26, 1897	British
32.	Edward Albert Probst	January 26, 1897 – April 21, 1897	British
33.	Albert Robson Burkill	May 12, 1897 – January 1898	British
34.	James S. Fearon	January 1898 – August 1899	American
35.	Joseph Welch,	August 3, 1898 – November 30, 1898	British
36.	Frederick Anderson	August 1899 – January 1900	British
37.	Edbert Ansgar Hewett	August 1900 – January 25, 1901	British
38.	John Prentice	January 26, 1901 – January 25, 1902	British
39.	William George Bayne	January 25, 1902 – 1904	British
40.	Frederick Anderson	1904 – January 25, 1906	British
41.	Cecil Holliday	January 25, 1906 – August 24, 1906	British
42.	Henry Keswick	August 24, 1906 – May 1907	British
43.	David Landale	May 1907 – January 17, 1911	British
44.	Harry De Gray	January 17, 1911 – January 24, 1913	American
45.	Edward Charles Pearce	January 24, 1913 – February 17, 1913	British
46.	Alfred Brooke-Smith	February 17, 1920 – March 17, 1922	British
47.	H.G. Simms	March 17, 1922 – October 12, 1923	British
48.	Stirling Fessenden	October 12, 1923 – March 5, 1929	American
49.	Harry Edward Arnhold	March 5, 1929 – 1930	British

50.	Ernest Brander Macnaghten	March 22, 1930 – 1932	British
51.	A.D. Bell	March 22, 1932 – March 27, 1934	British
52.	Harry Edward Arnhold	March 27, 1934 – April 1937	British
53.	Cornell Franklin	April 1937 – April 1940	American
54.	William Johnstone "Tony" Keswick	April 1940 – May 1, 1941	British
55.	John Hellyer Liddell	May 1, 1941 – January 5, 1942	British
56.	Katsuo Okazaki	January 5, 1942 – August 1, 1943	Japanese

Appendix IX. List of Shanghai Mayors (Shanghai Shi Shizhang) [上海市市长]

Republic of China (Minguo) [民国], 1911-1937

Number	Name	Lived	Dates in Office
1.	Chen Qimei [陈其美]	(1878-1916)	Military Governor of Shanghai (Hujun Dudu) [沪军都督], November 6, 1911 - July 31, 1912.
2.	Lu Yongxiang [卢永祥]*	(1867-1933)	SH Military Governor 1917-1924
	Huang Fu [黄郛]	(1880-1936)	SH Mayor, July 7, 1927 - August 14, 1927.
	Wu Zhenxiu [吴震修]	(1883-1966)	SH Mayor, August 15, 1927 - September 16, 1927.
	Zhang Dingfan [张定璠]	(1891-1945)	SH Mayor, September 17, 1927 - March 31, 1929.
	Zhang Qun [张群]	(1889-1990)	SH Mayor, April 1, 1929 - January 6, 1932.
	Wu Tiecheng [吴铁城]	(1888-1953)	SH Mayor, January 1932 - March 1937.
	O.K. Yui (Yu Hongjun) [俞鸿钧]	(1898-1960)	SH Mayor, April – November 1937.

*Lu Yongiang was a native of Shandong province and a member of the Anhui warlords military clique (Wanxi Junfa) [皖系军阀].   After the 1911 Revolution he became the Provincial Military Governor (dujun) [督军] of Zhejiang province [浙江省].   In 1917 he extended his authority over the present-day Shanghai area, then known as Song Hu [淞沪]. Lu was involved in an infamous incident in 1924 during which he imprisoned Huang Jinrong [黄金荣](1868-1953) over a dispute Huang and Lu's son had over a mistress, and Huang had to be rescued by his junior partner in crime Du Yuesheng [杜月笙] (1888-1951), after which Du assume a much more dominant leadership role over the criminal Green Gang (Qing Bang) [青帮]. After losing the Zhejiang-Jiangsu war, which returned control of Shanghai back to Jiangsu province, Lu retired to Tianjin where he passed away in 1933.

WWII Japanese Puppet Collaborator Mayors, 1937-1945

Number	Name	Lived	Dates in Office	Fate
1.	Su Xiwen [苏锡文]	(1889-1945)	SH Mayor, December 5, 1937 – October 15, 1938.	Died of illness in 1945.
2.	Fu Xiaoan [傅筱庵]	(1872-1940)	SH Mayor, October 16, 1938 – October 10, 1940	Assassinated on October 10, 1940, while still in office.
3.	Su Xiwen [苏锡文]	(1889-1945)	SH Mayor, October 11 – November 19, 1940.	Died of illness in 1945.
4.	Chen Gongbo [陈公博]	(1892-1946)	SH Mayor, November 20, 1940 – November 11, 1944.	After the war he was captured by the Guomindang, convicted of treason in a court room trial held in Suzhou in April 1946, sentenced to the death penalty, and executed on June 3, 1946.
5.	Wu Songgao [吴颂皋]	(1898-1953)	SH Mayor, November 12, 1944 – January 14, 1945.	Promoted to be the Minister of Justice in the puppet central government in Nanjing. After the war he was arrested by the Guomindang, escaped the death penalty, but was sentenced to life in prison, a sentence which the new Communist government continued to enforce after 1949, until Wu finally died in prison in 1953.

| 6. | Zhou Fohai [周佛海] | (1897-1948) | SH Mayor, January 15, 1945 – September 12, 1945. | He remained in office for a whole month after the war was over, per orders from Chiang Kai-shek (Jiang Jieshi) himself, but was still later arrested and put on trial by the Guomindang. On November 7, 1946 he was sentenced to the death penalty, but this was later reduced to life in prison. He died of a heart attack in a Nanjing prison on February 28, 1948. |

Post-WWII Guomindang Mayors, 1945-1949

Number	Name	Lived	Dates in Office
	Qian Dajun [錢大鈞]	(1893-1982)	SH Mayor, September 12, 1945 - April 19, 1946.
	K.C. Wu (Wu Guozhen) [吴国桢]*	(1903-1984)	SH Mayor April 20, 1946-April 30, 1949.

* Wu was a native of Hubei province.   He was a graduate of the Nankai Middle School in Tianjin, the Qinghua School in Beijing, and in 1926 he earned a Ph.D. from Princeton University in the U.S.   He served as Mayor of Hankou from 1932 to 1938, then Mayor of Chonqing from 1939 to 1942.   From 1943 to 1945 he was a deputy chief of the Foreign Affairs Ministry.   In 1945 he became head of the publicity department of the Guomindang party central committee.   During his three years as Shanghai mayor he lived in a house at 201 Anfu Lu.

Peoples Republic of China Mayors, 1949-2018

Number	Name	Lived	Dates in Office	Fate
1.	Chen Yi [陈毅]	(1901-1972)	PLA Marshal, SH Mayor May 28, 1949 - November 1958, also City Party Secretary 1950-1954,	Promoted to Foreign Minister 1958-1972.
2.	Ke Qingshi [柯庆施]	(1902-1965)	SH Mayor, November 1958 - April 9, 1965, also Shanghai City Party Secretary, 1954-1965.	
3.	Cao Diqiu [曹荻秋]	(1909-1976)	SH Mayor, November 1965 - February 24, 1967.	
4.	Zhang Chunqiao [张春桥]	(1917-2005)	Shanghai Revolutionary Committee Chairman (Shanghai Shi Geming Weiyuanhui Zhuren) [上海市革命委员会主任], February 24, 1967 - October 6, 1976. Member of the Gang of Four (Siren Bang) [四人帮], along with Mao's wife Jiang Qing [江青] (1914-1991), Yao Wenyuan [姚文元] (1931-2005), and Wang Hongwen [王洪文] (1935-1992).	He was arrested along with the rest of the Gang of Four immediately upon Mao's death on October 6, 1976 and expelled from the Communist Party in 1977. On January 25, 1981 he was convicted by the Supreme Court of counterrevolutionary activities and given a deferred death sentence. He finally died of natural causes in 2005.
5.	Su Zhenhua [苏振华]	(1912-1979)	Shanghai Revolutionary Committee Chairman October 1976 – January 1, 1979.	Note: Shanghai continued to be governed by a Revolutionary Committee and its Chairman until December 1979, when the positions of city government mayor and city party secretary were both revived.

6.	Peng Chong [彭冲]	(1915-2010)	Shanghai Revolutionary Committee Chairman January 1, 1979 – December 1979; then SH Mayor December 1979 - March 1981.	
7.	Wang Daohan [汪道涵]	(1915-2005)	SH Mayor, April 1981 – July 1985	
8.	Jiang Zemin [江泽民]	(1926-present)	SH Mayor, July 1985 - April 1988	Promoted to SH Party Secretary, and later President and Party Secretary of China in Beijing.
9.	Zhu Rongji [朱镕基]	(1928-present)	SH Mayor, April 1988 - April 1991,	Promoted to SH Party Secretary, and later Prime Minister of China in Beijing, 1998-2003.
10.	Huang Ju [黄菊]	(1938-2007)	SH Mayor, April 1991-February 1995,	Promoted to SH Party Secretary until 2002, Vice-Premier of China in Beijing, 2002-2006.
11.	Xu Kuangdi [徐匡迪]	(1937-present)	SH Mayor, February 1995 - December 7, 2001.	Dismissed from office in a coup d'etat by his successor Chen Liangyu.
12.	Chen Liangyu [陈良宇]	(1946-present)	SH Mayor, December 7, 2001 - February 21, 2003, promoted to SH Party Secretary until September 24, 2006.	Arrested and dismissed from office in September 2006. Convicted & imprisoned in 2008.
13.	Han Zheng [韩正]	(1954-present)	SH Mayor, February 21, 2003 - December 26, 2012. Promoted to SH Party Secretary 2012 - October 29, 2017.	Promoted to Politburo Standing Committee in Beijing in 2017 and central government Vice-Premier in 2018.

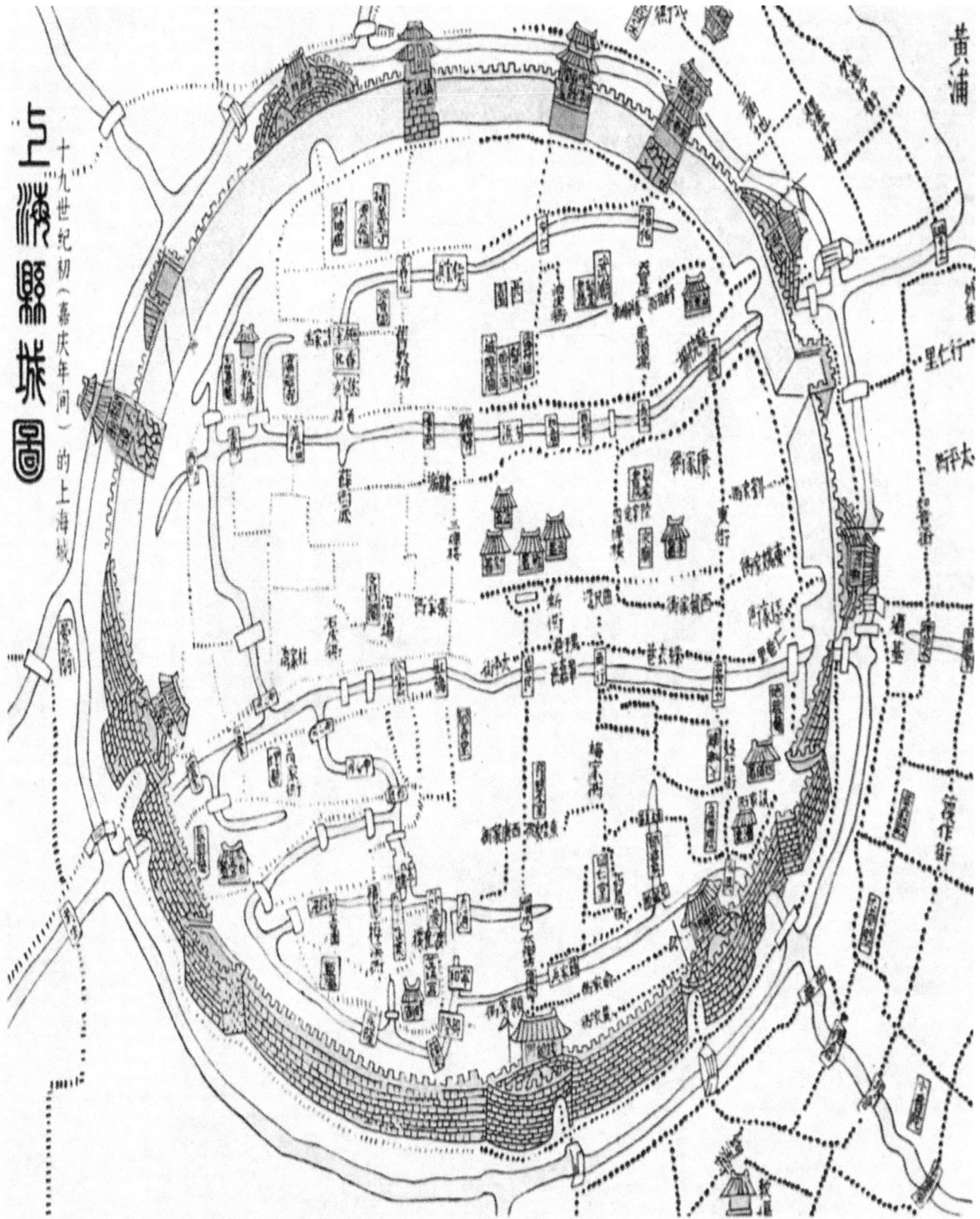

1820 Map of the Shanghai City Wall

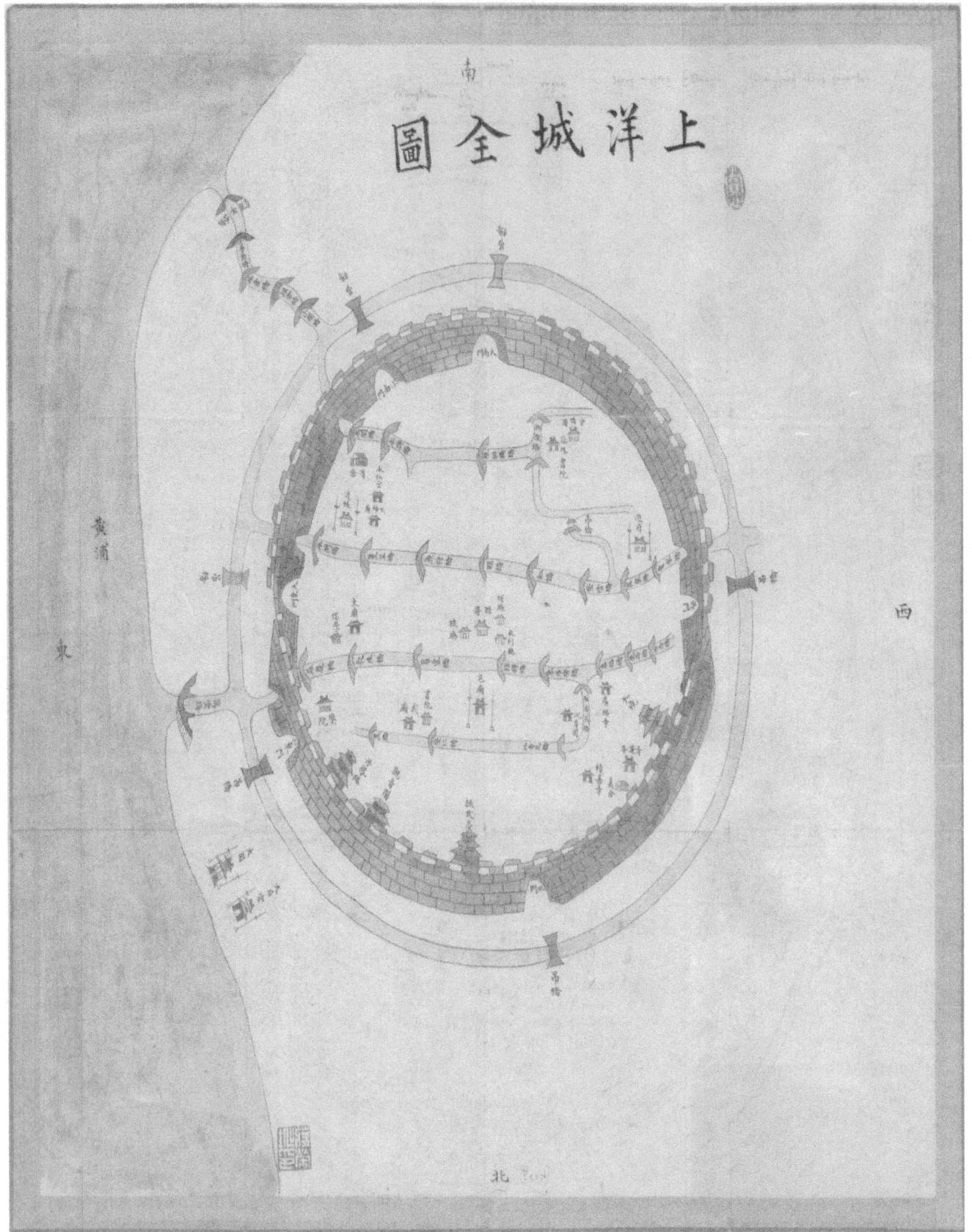

1870 Map of the Shanghai City Wall

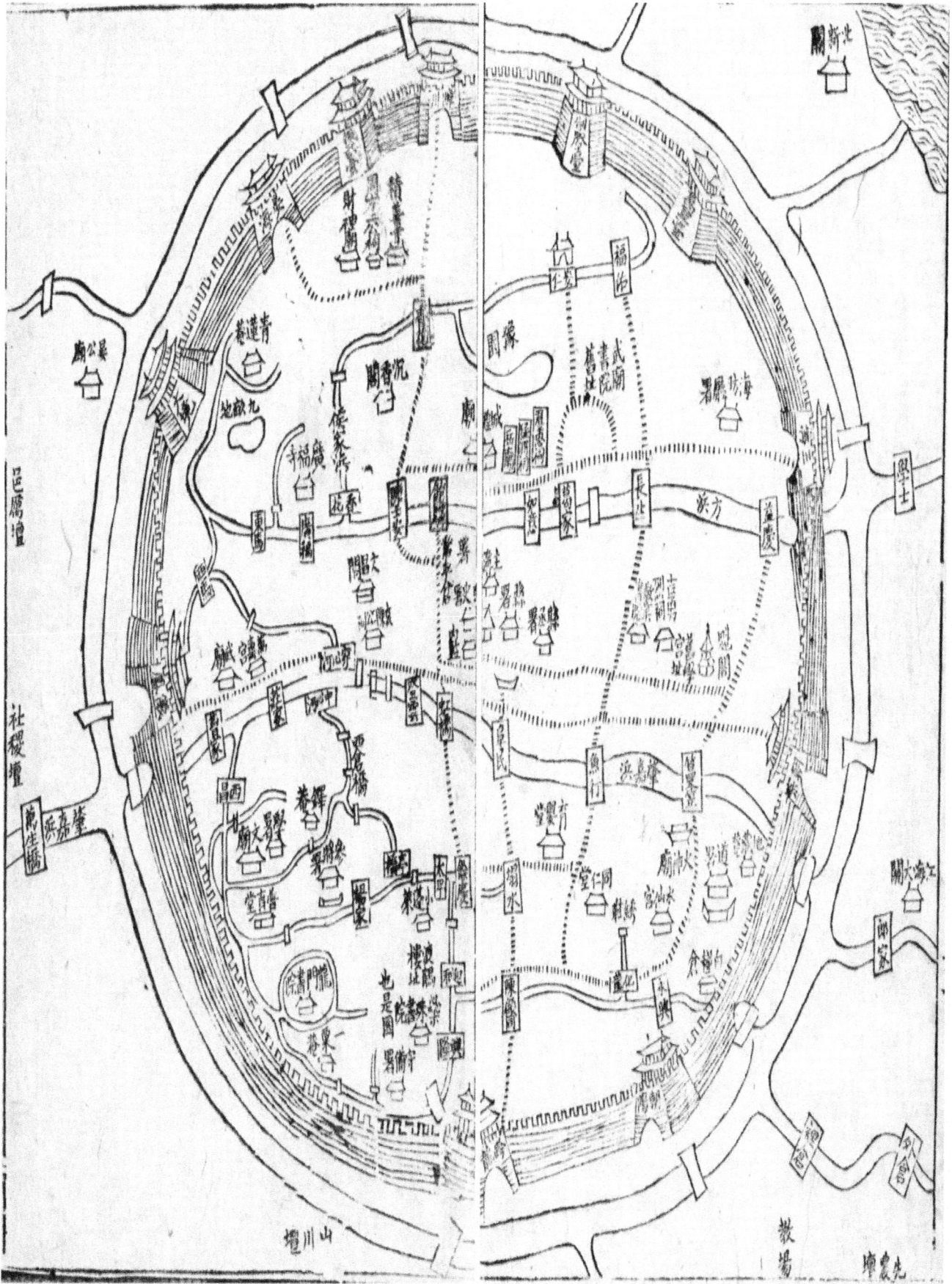

1882 Map of the Shanghai City Wall

SHANGHAI

Shanghai 1902 Map

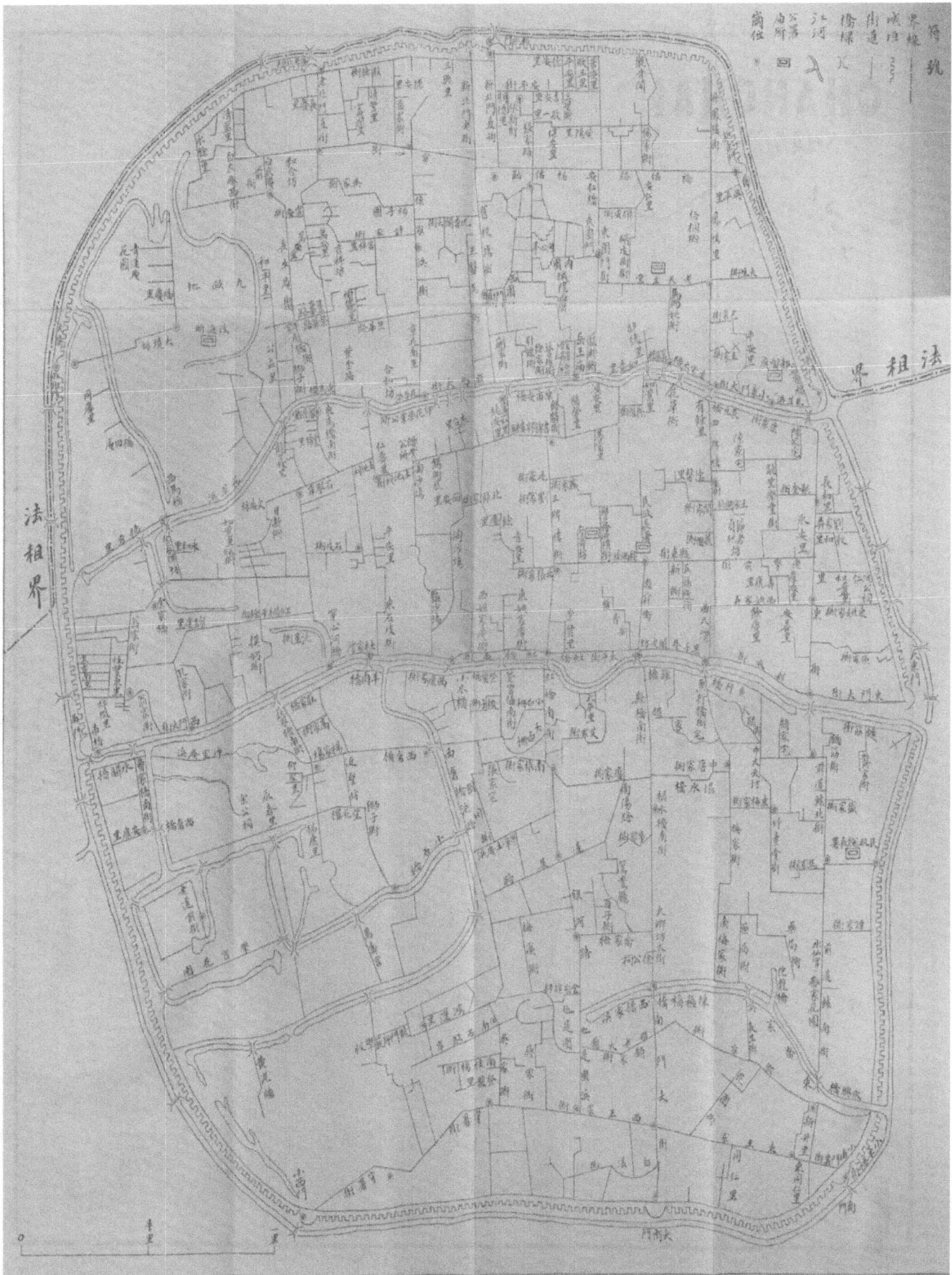

1912 Map of Shanghai walled city.

CHANGHAI
SHANG·HAI

SHANG-HAI — The Settlements — The Chinese City.

1912 French Map of Shanghai.

1929 Map of the former Shanghai walled city area.

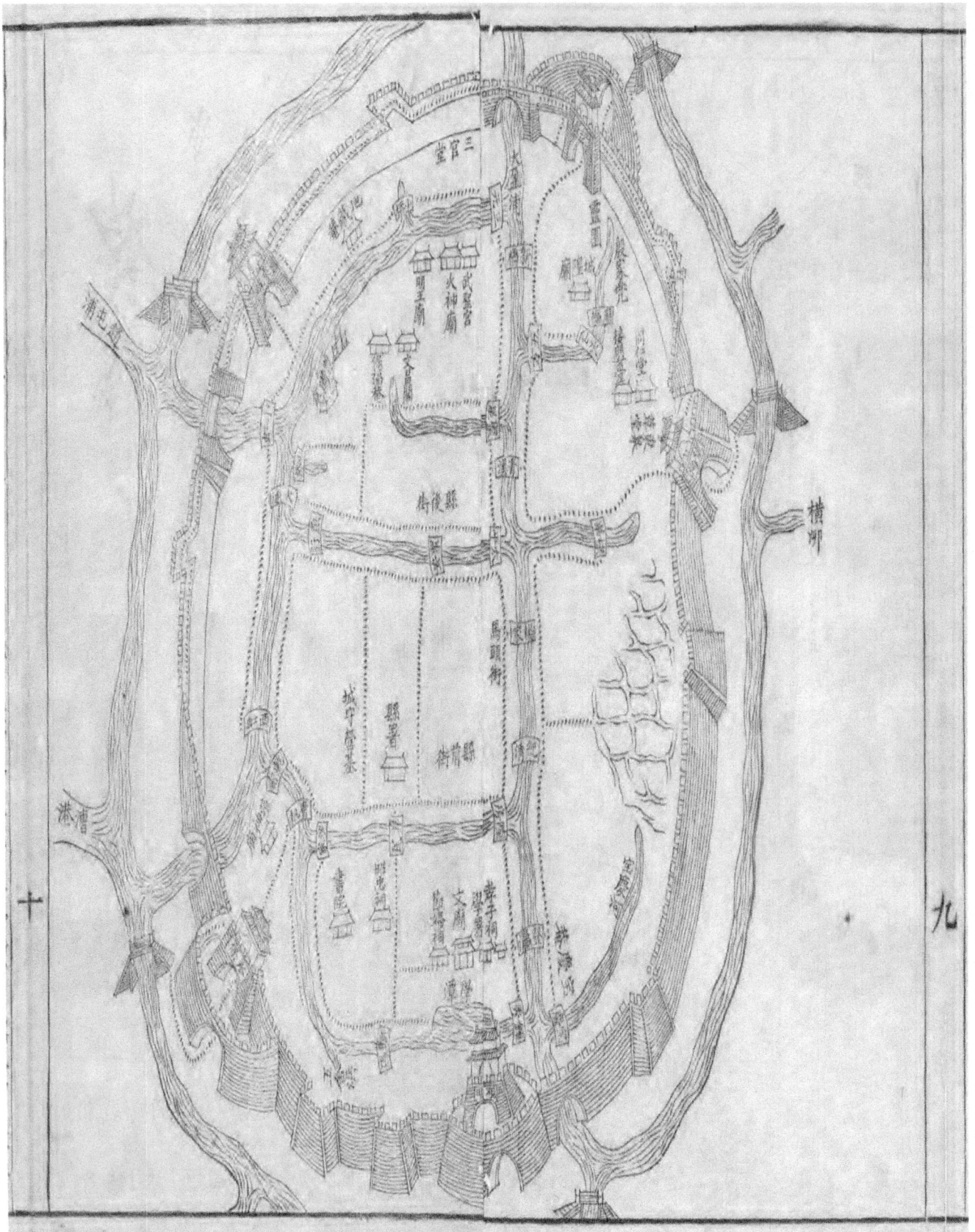

1879 Map of Qingpu Town city wall.

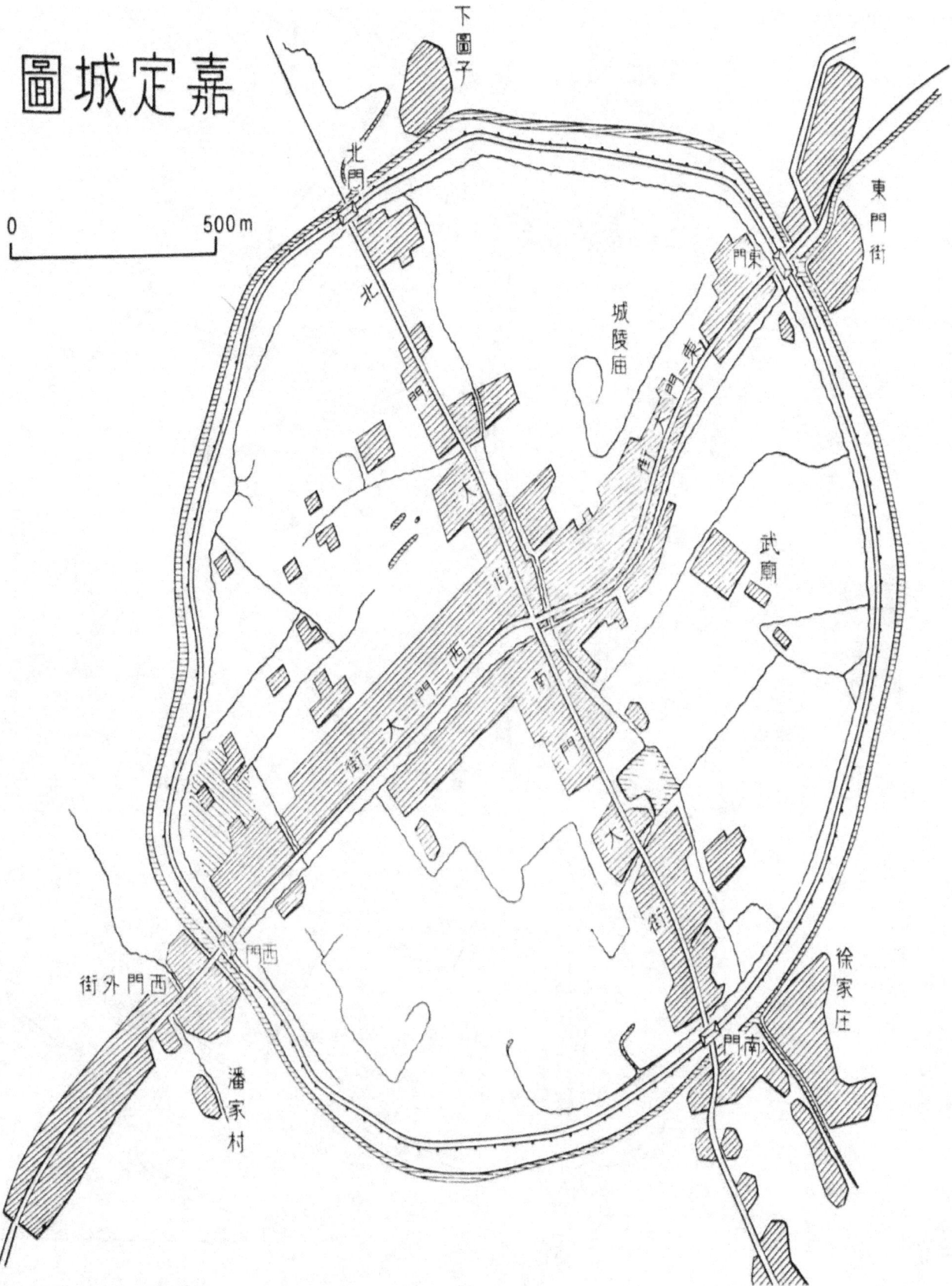

圖城定嘉

0　　　　　500 m

下圖子

北門

東門街

門東

城陵庙

武廟

街一門大西

門西

街外門西

潘家村

門南

徐家庄

1941 Map of Jiading Town showing the city wall and moat.

441

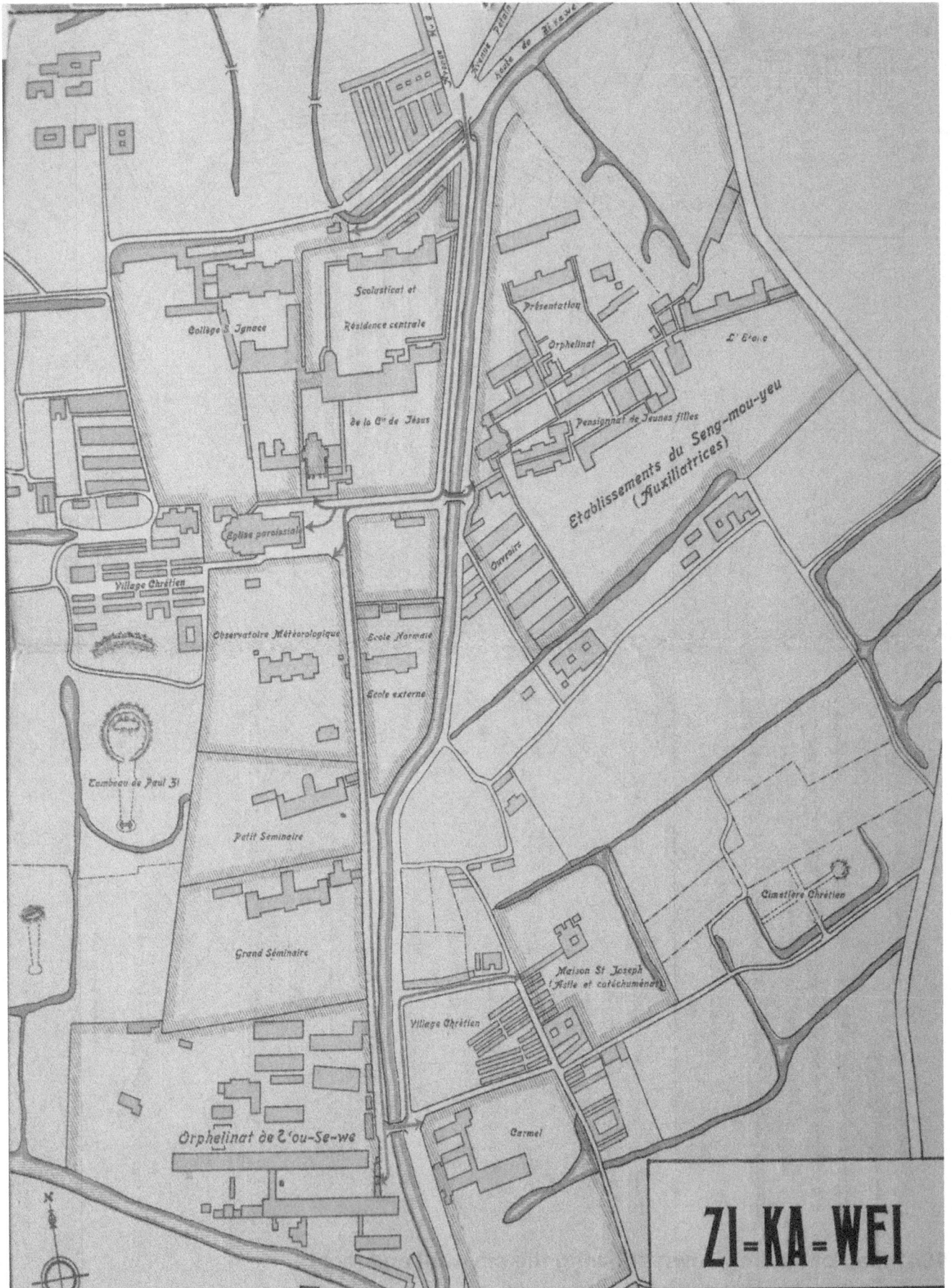

Pre-1949 Map of Xujiahui (Zikawei).

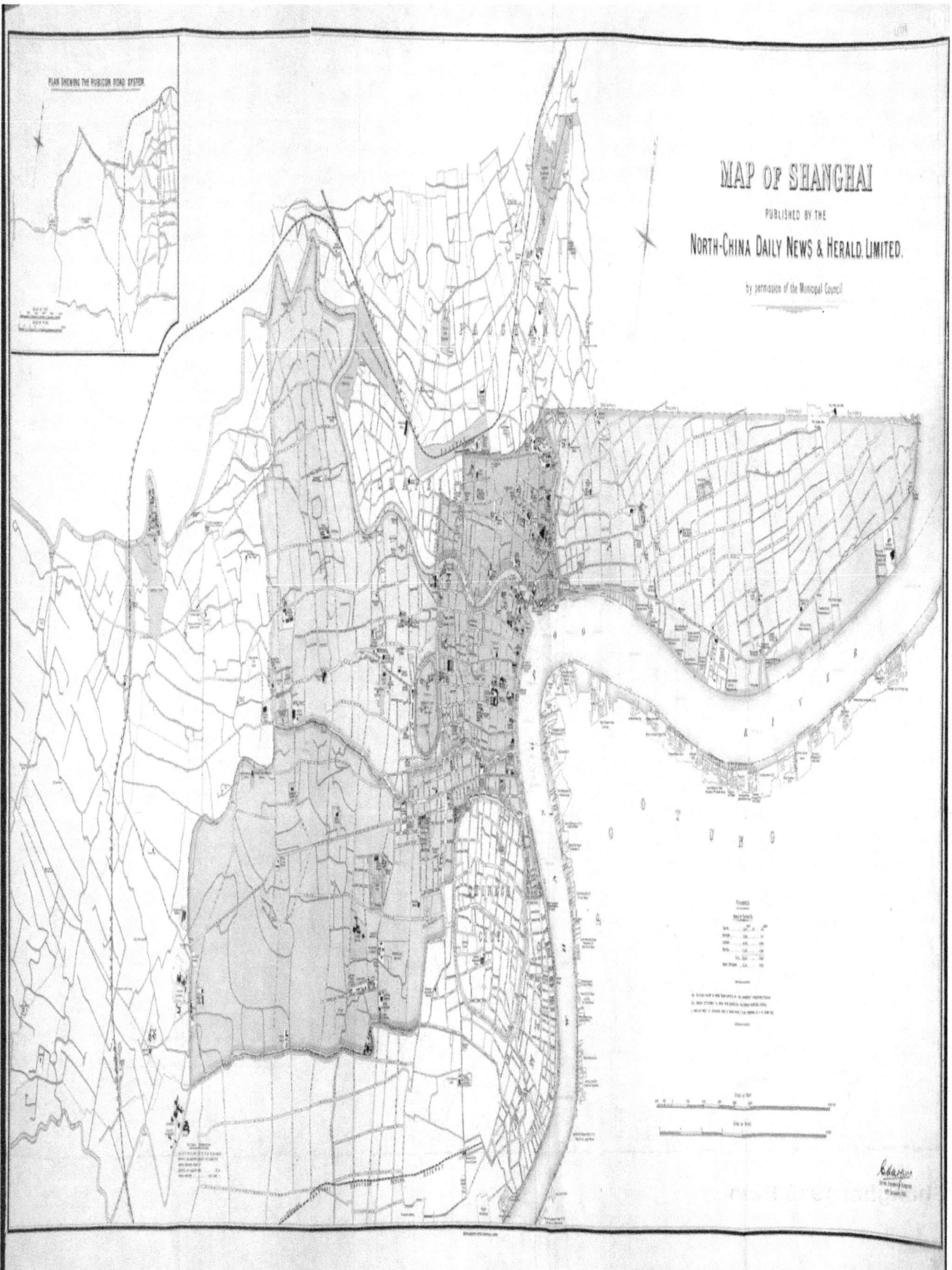

Shanghai 1918 Plan

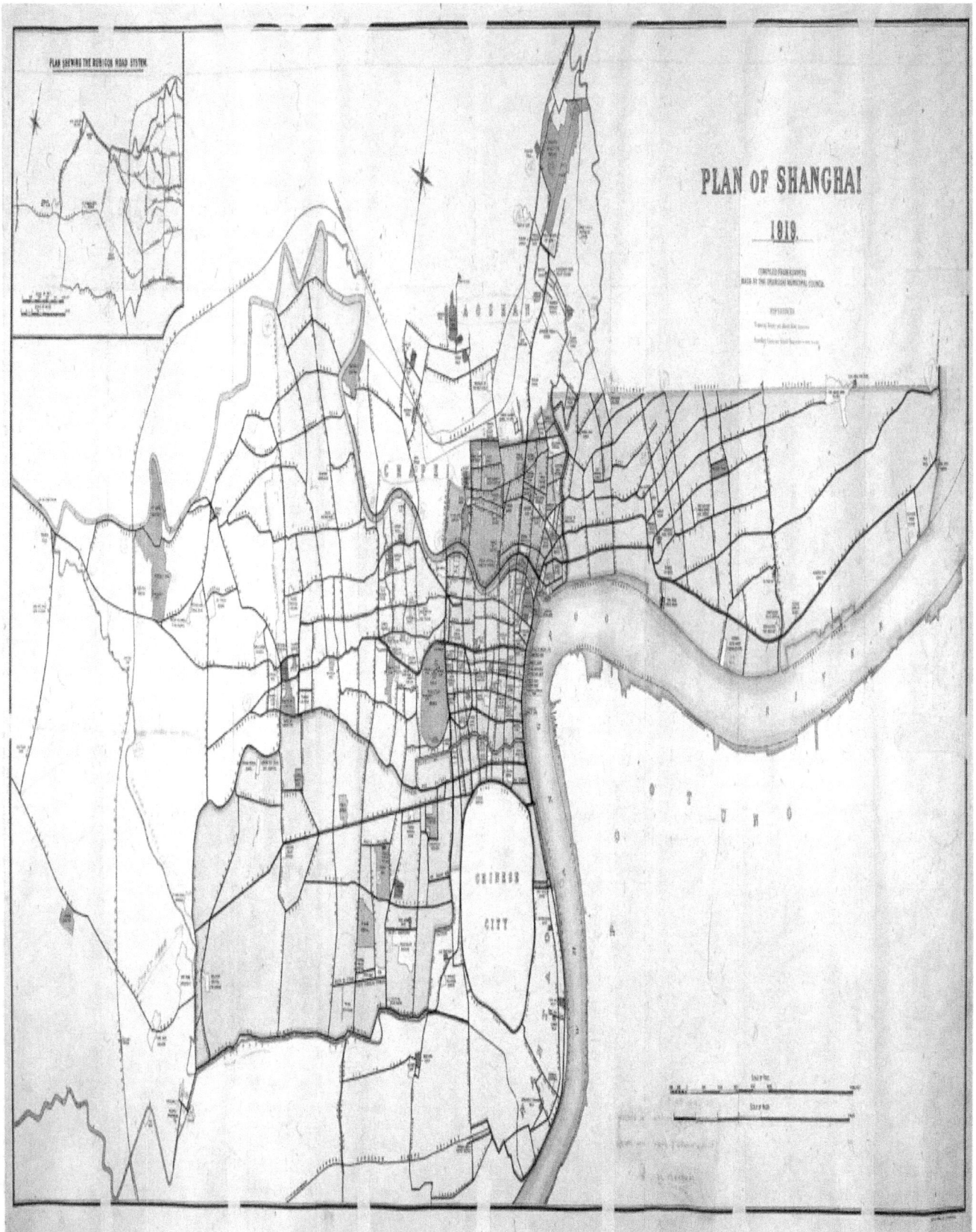

Shanghai 1919 Plan

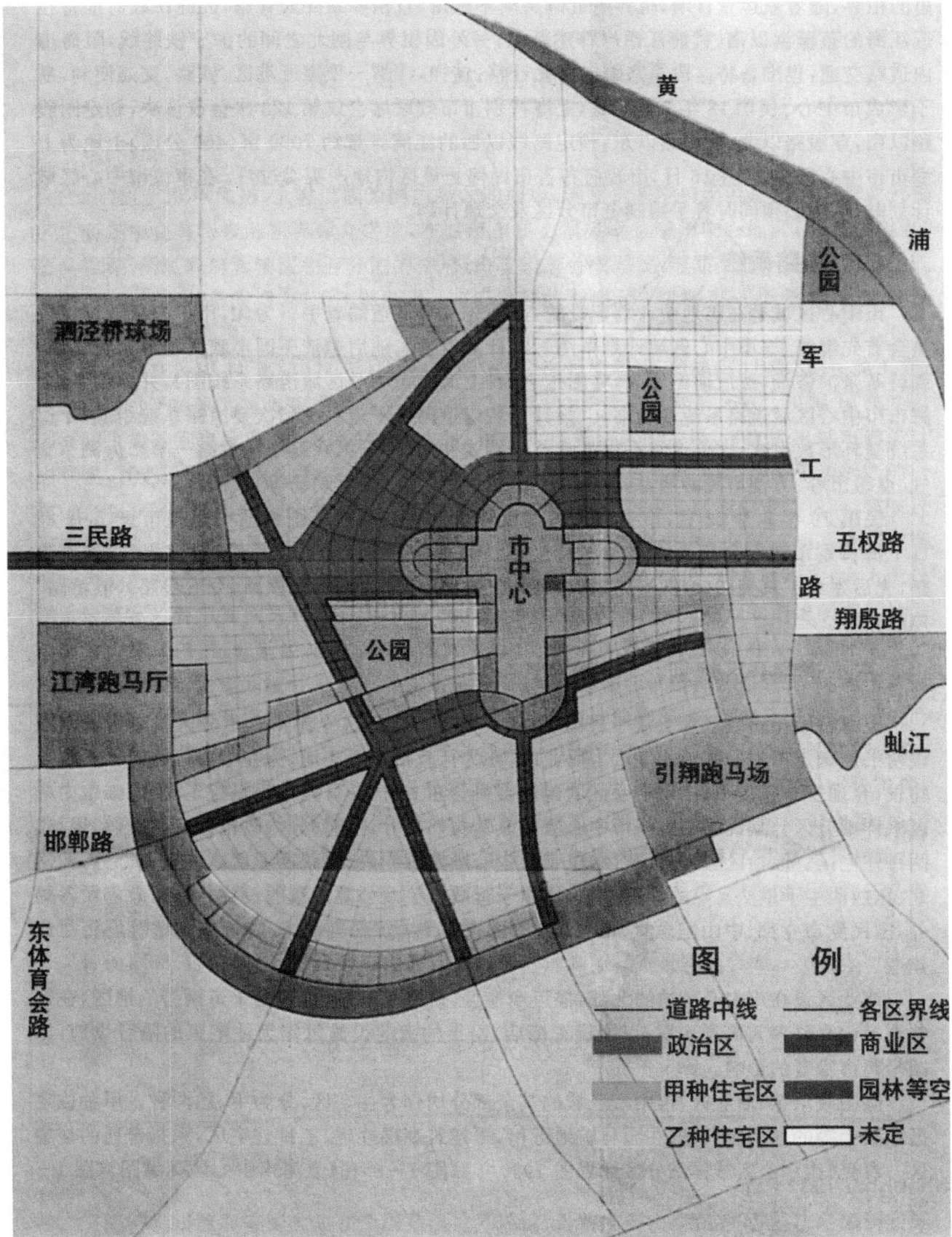

黄

浦

公园

军

工

路

五权路

翔殷路

虹江

酒泾桥球场

公园

三民路

市中心

公园

江湾跑马厅

引翔跑马场

邯郸路

东体育会路

图 例

——— 道路中线 ——— 各区界线
政治区 商业区
甲种住宅区 园林等空
乙种住宅区 未定

图1-8 市中心区域详细分区计划图(1930年)

Greater Shanghai Plan for new Jiangwan civic center, 1930

445

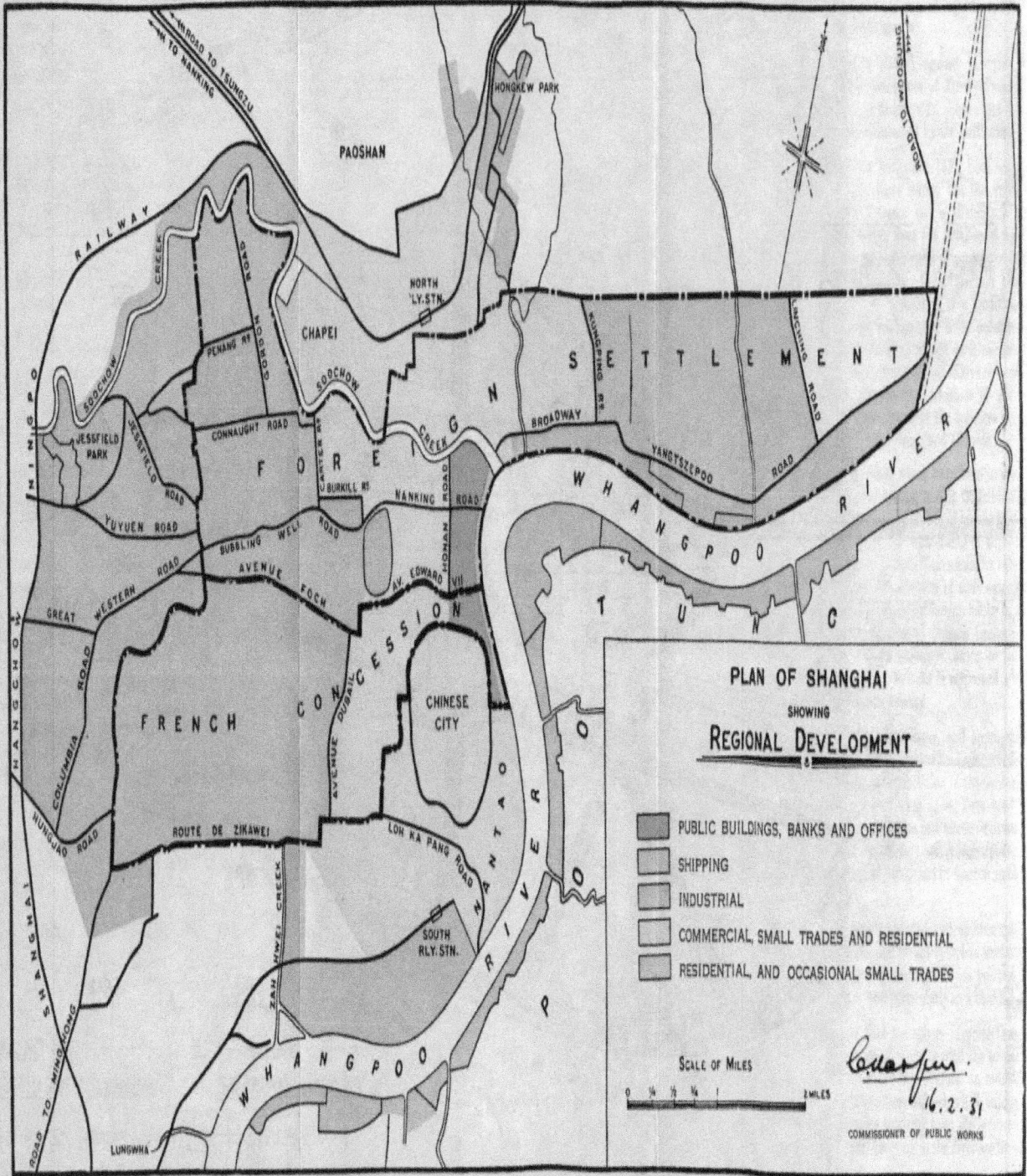

Shanghai 1931 Plan

PLAN OF SHANGHAI
SHOWING
REGIONAL DEVELOPMENT

PUBLIC BUILDINGS, BANKS AND OFFICES

SHIPPING

INDUSTRIAL

COMMERCIAL, SMALL TRADES AND RESIDENTIAL

RESIDENTIAL, AND OCCASIONAL SMALL TRADES

SCALE OF MILES

COMMISSIONER OF PUBLIC WORKS

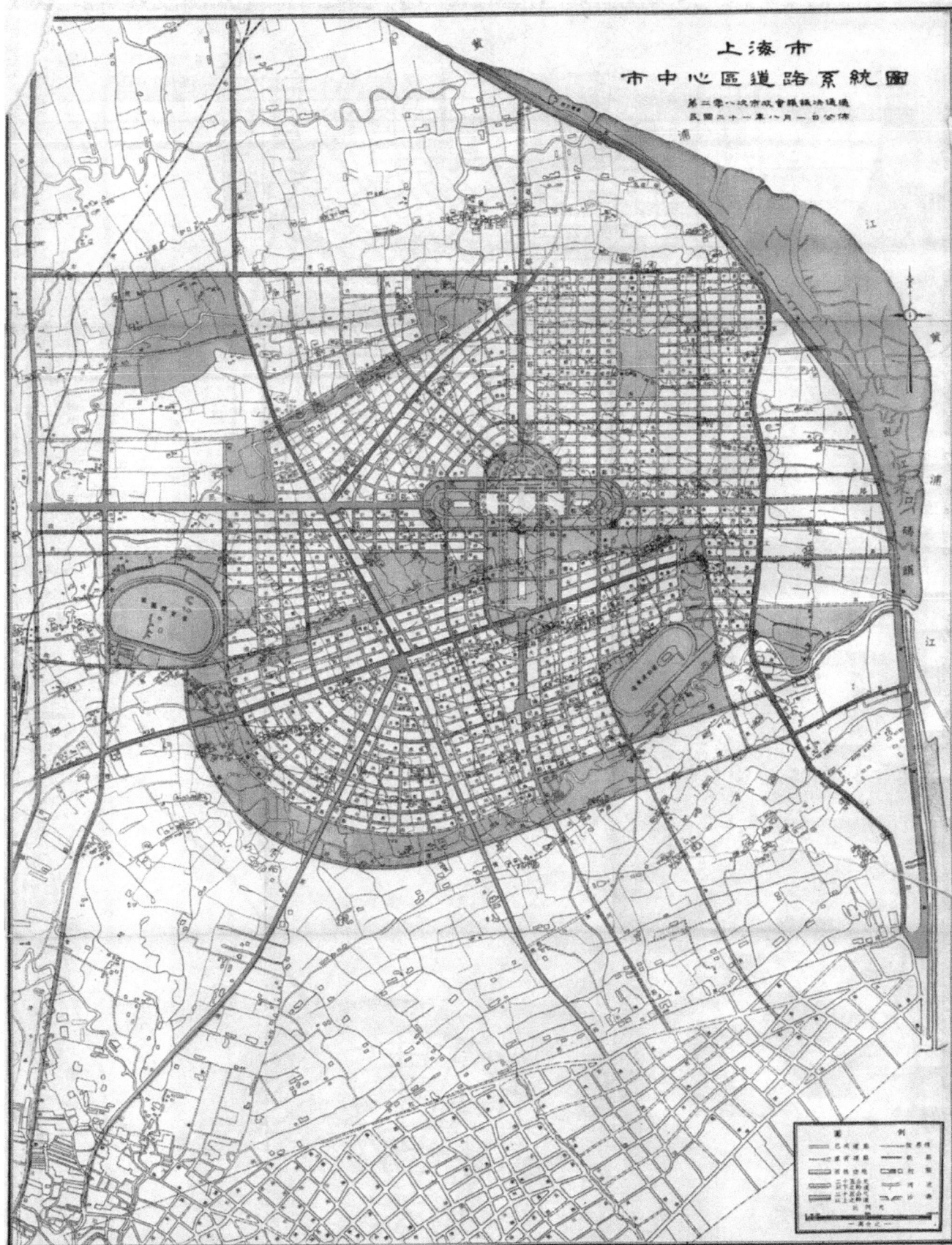

Greater Shanghai Plan for new civic center in Jiangwan Town, 1932.

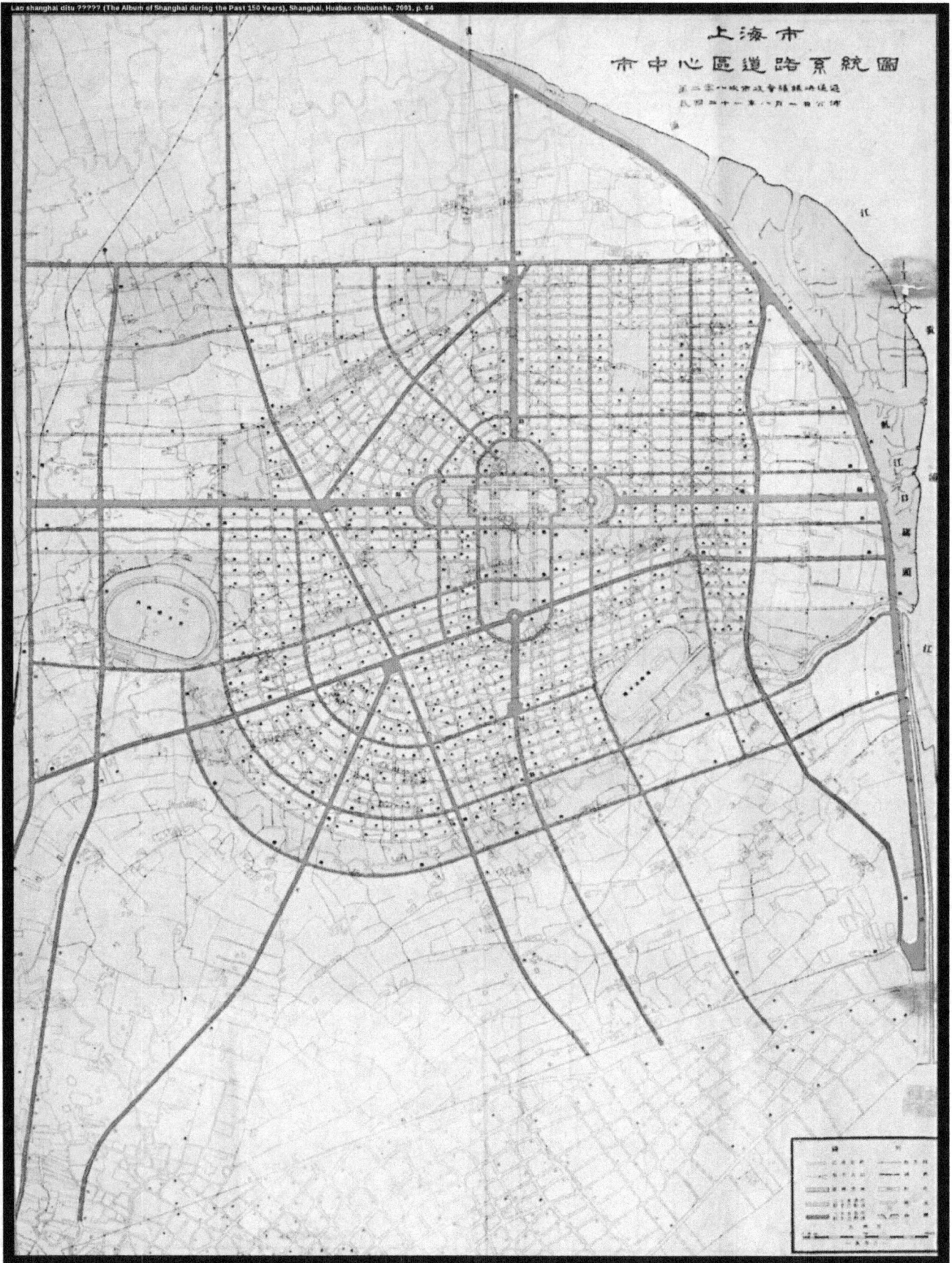

Greater Shanghai Plan for new civic center in Jiangwan Town, 1932.

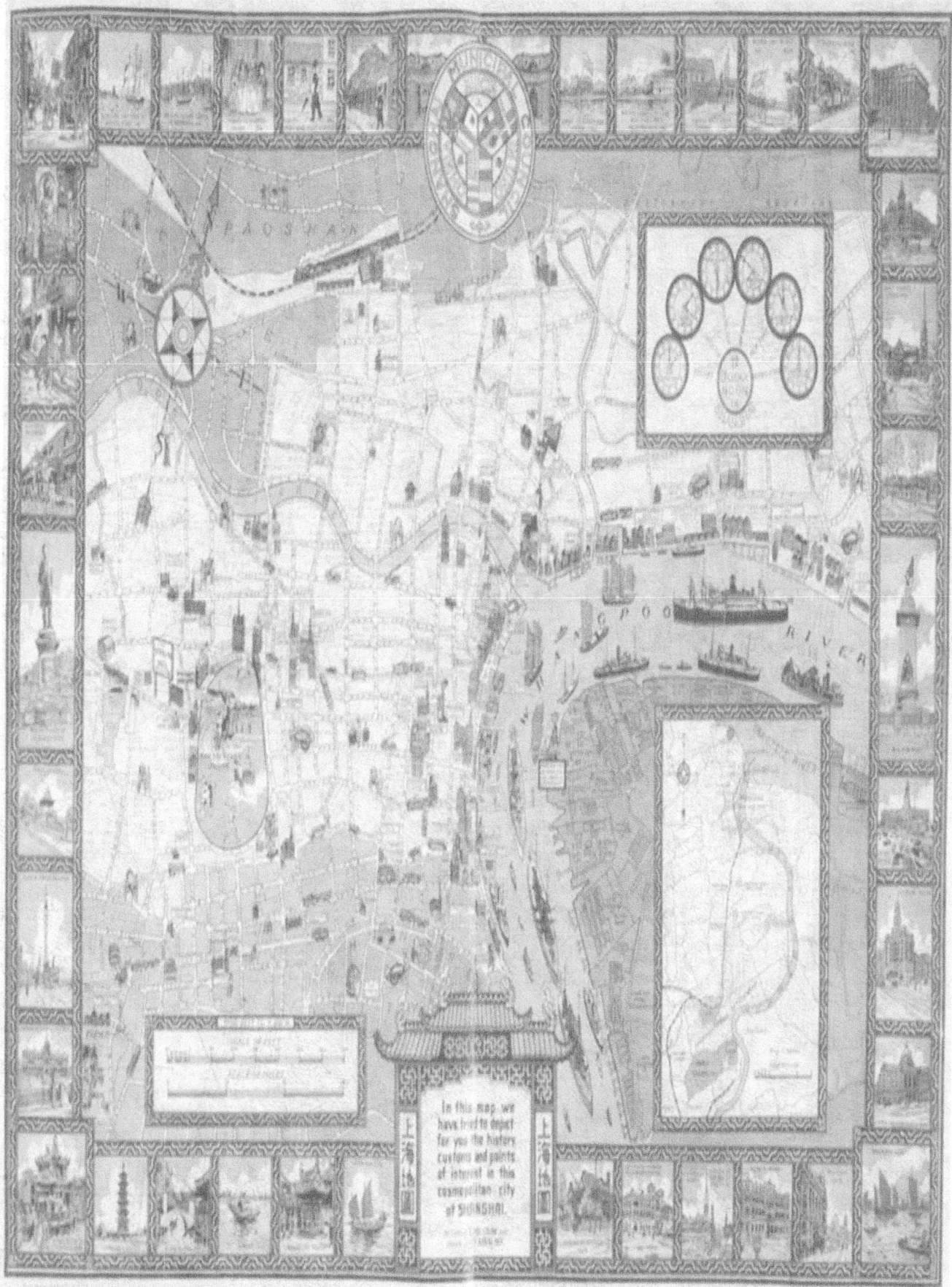

Shanghai 1932 Map

449

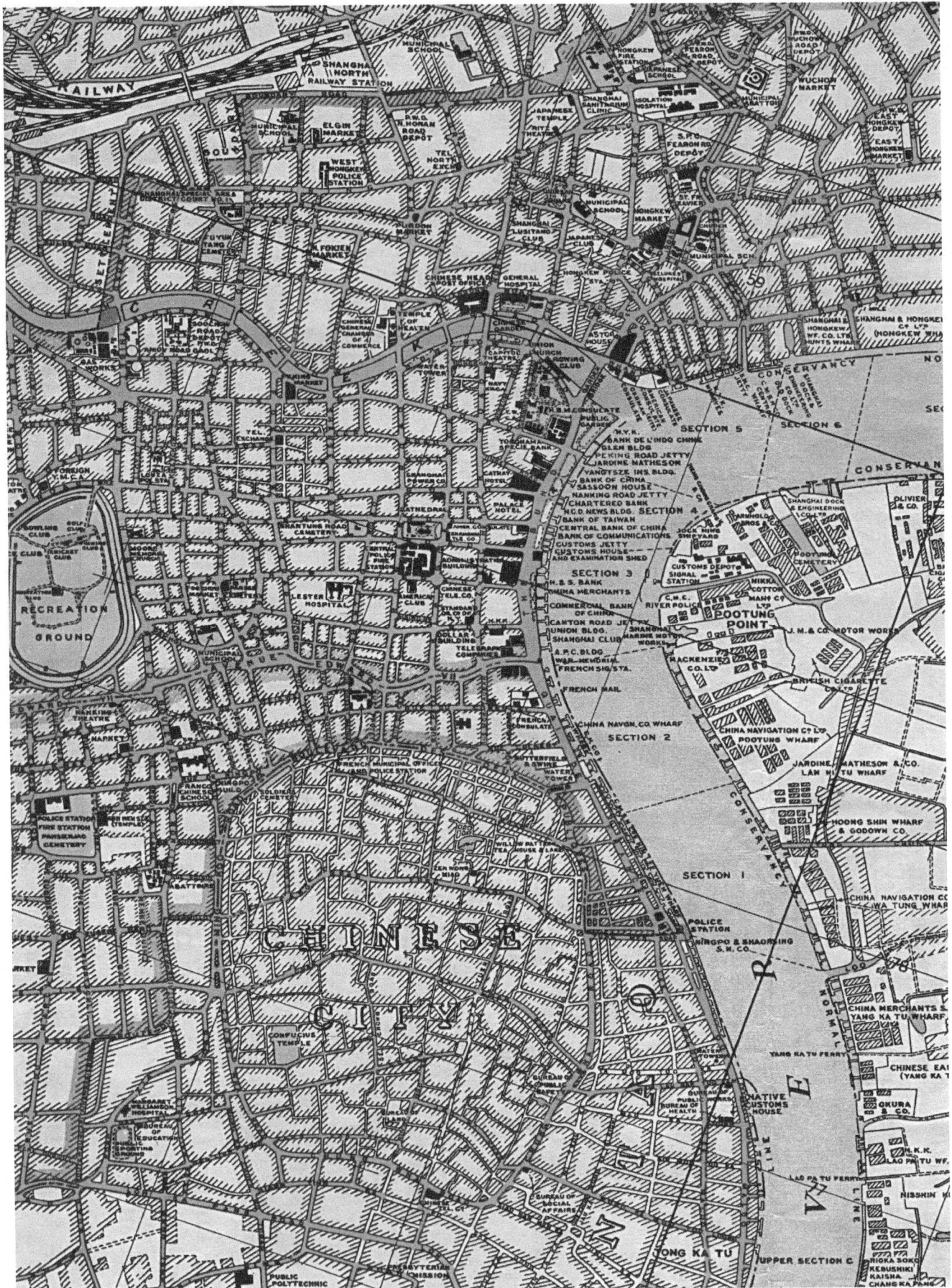

Shanghai 1933 Map

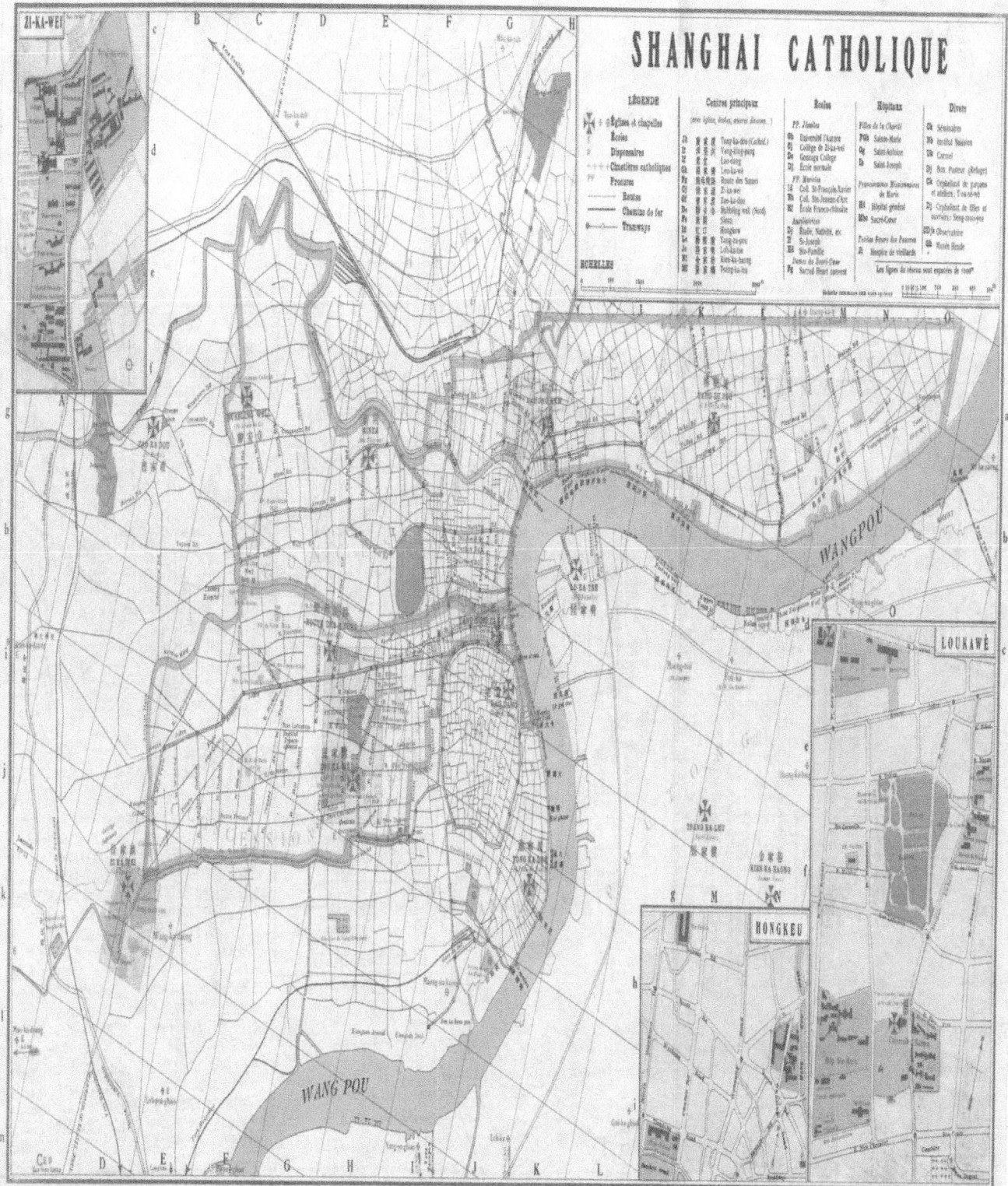

Map of Catholic Churches in Shanghai in 1933.

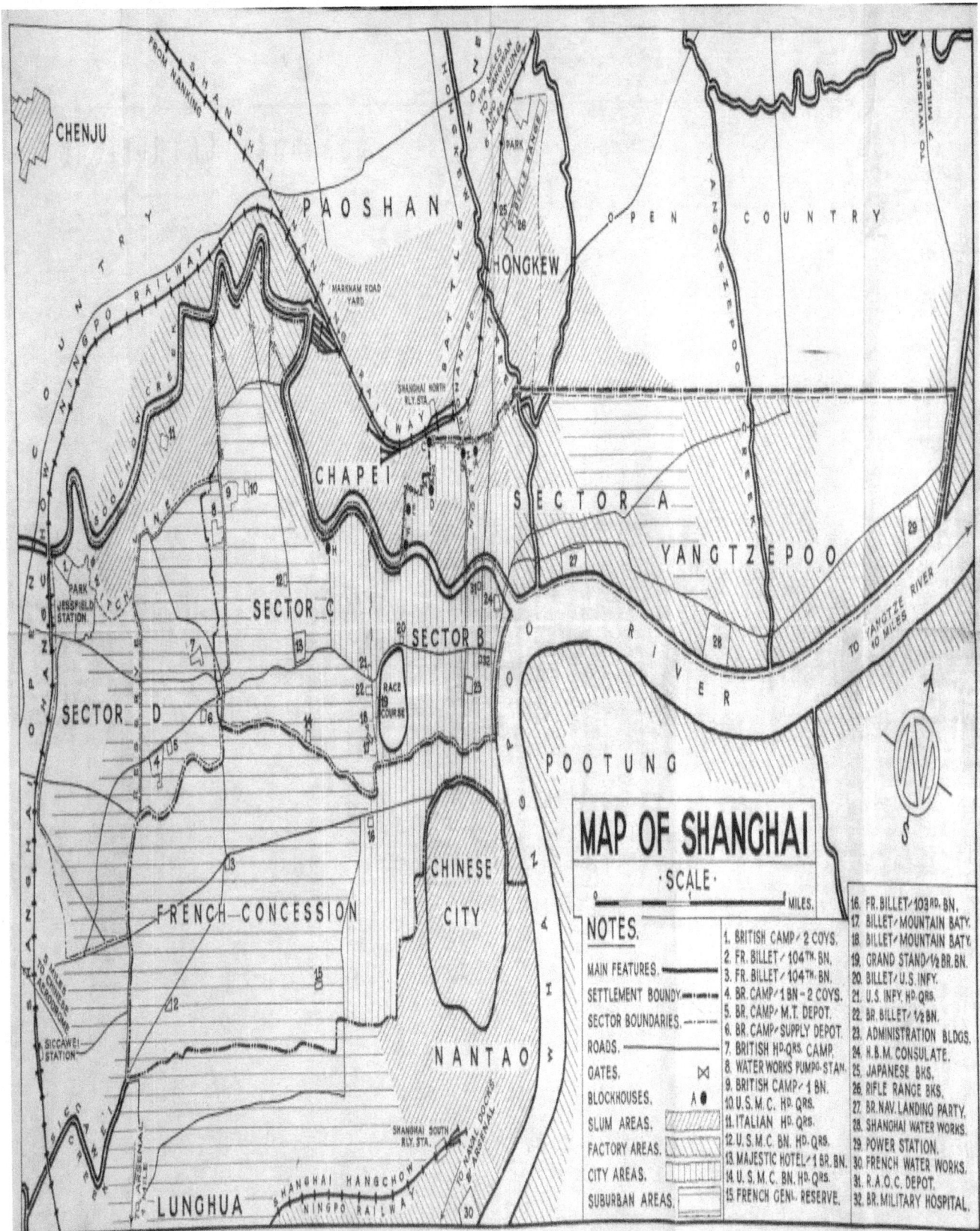

Shanghai 1935 Map

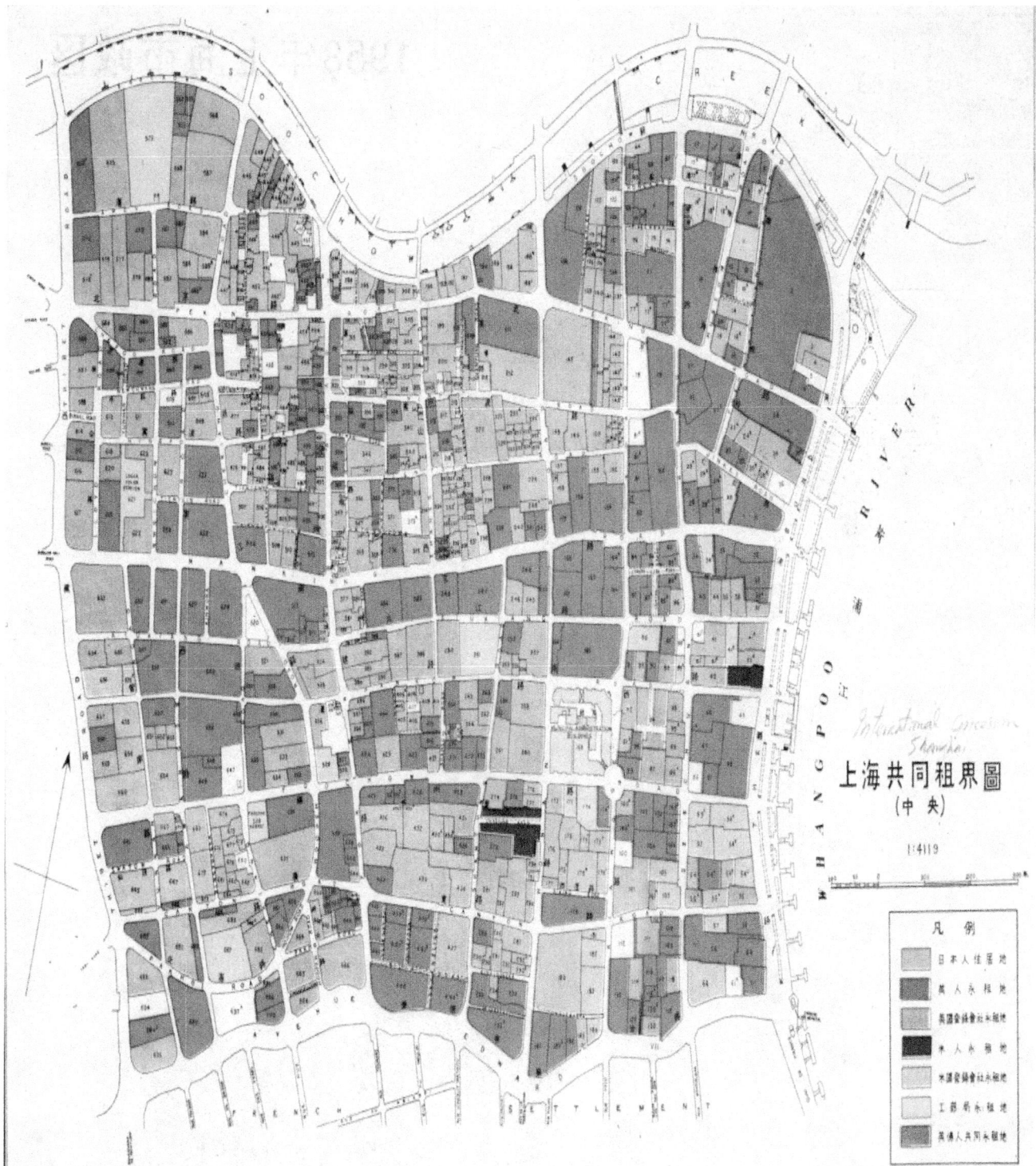

Shanghai 1941 Map

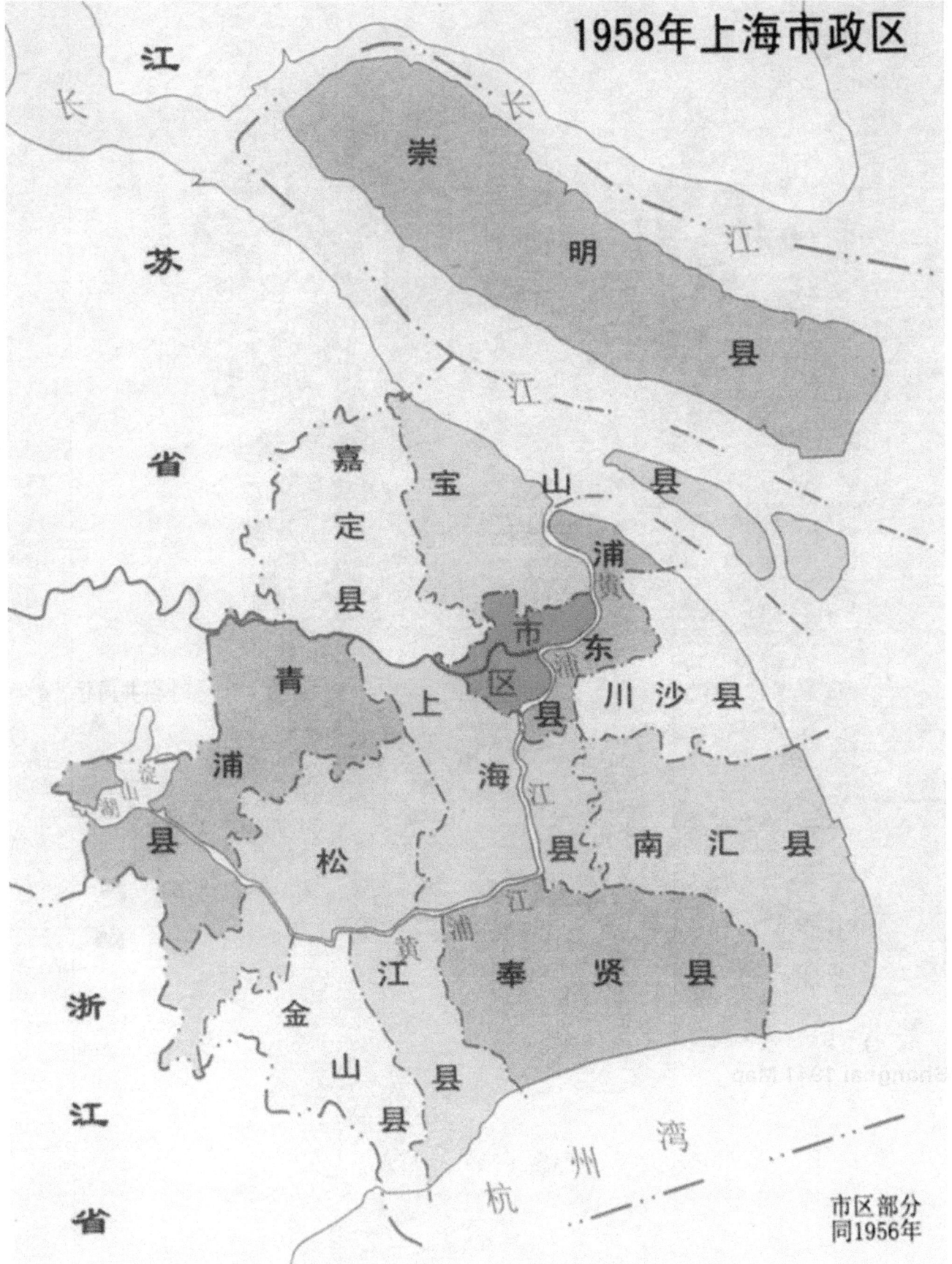

1958年上海市政区

江

苏

省

长

崇

明

县

长

江

江

嘉定县

宝

山

县

浦

市区

县

东

川沙县

青浦县

上

海

县

松

江

县

南汇县

金

山

县

奉贤县

黄

浦

江

浙

江

省

杭

州

湾

市区部分
同1956年

Shanghai 1958 Districts & Counties Map

1960年上海市政区

江

长

苏

省

崇

明

县

嘉
定
县

宝

山

县

浦

东

川沙县

青

浦

县

上

海

县

1

市
区

松

南汇县

金

山

县

黄
浦
江

奉 贤 县

浙

江

省

杭
州
湾

2

市区部分包括
黄浦区　静安区
南市区　普陀区
卢湾区　闸北区
徐汇区　虹口区
长宁区　杨浦区
1吴淞区
2闵行区　以下各图与此相同

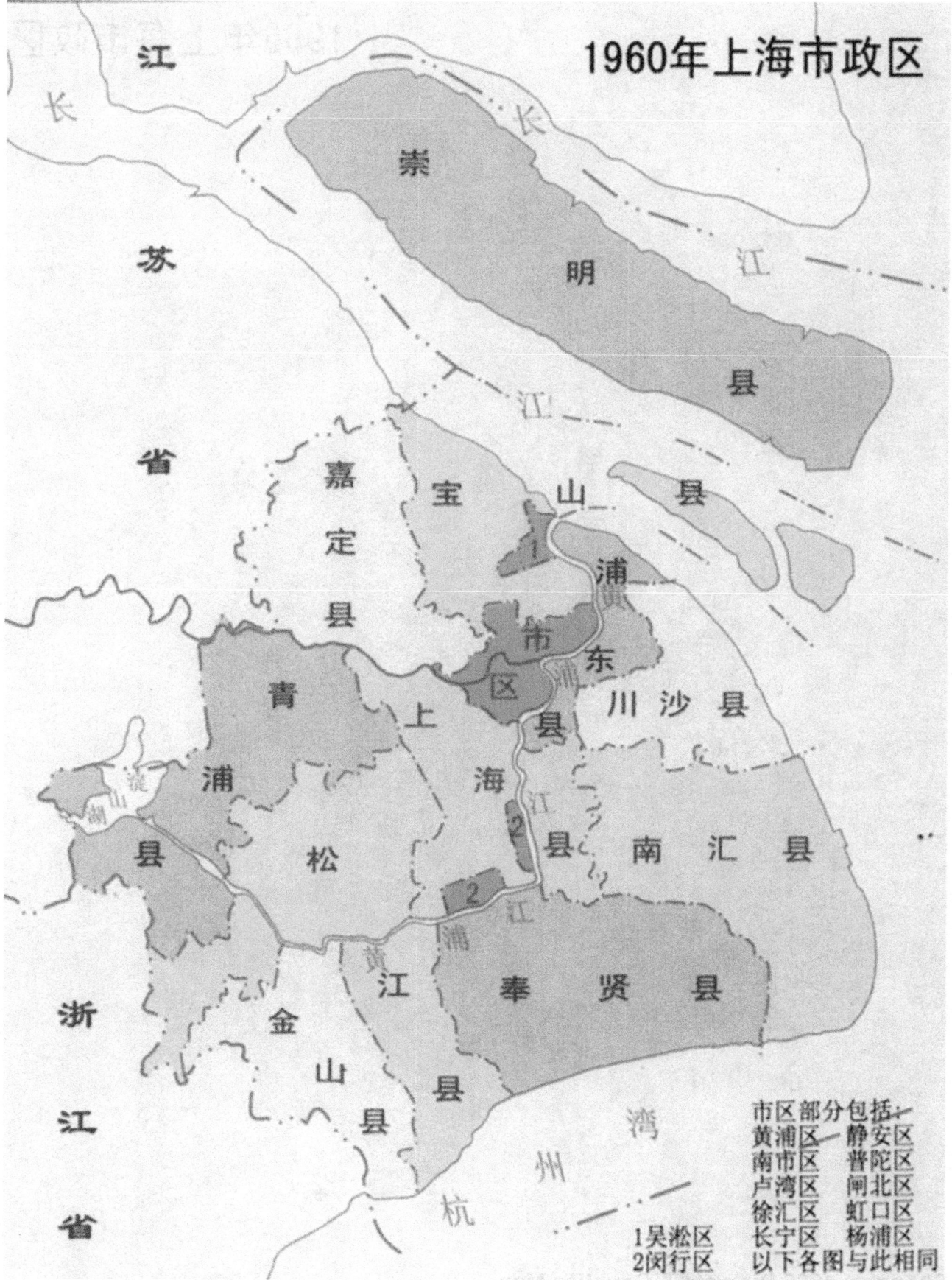

Shanghai 1960 Districts & Counties Map

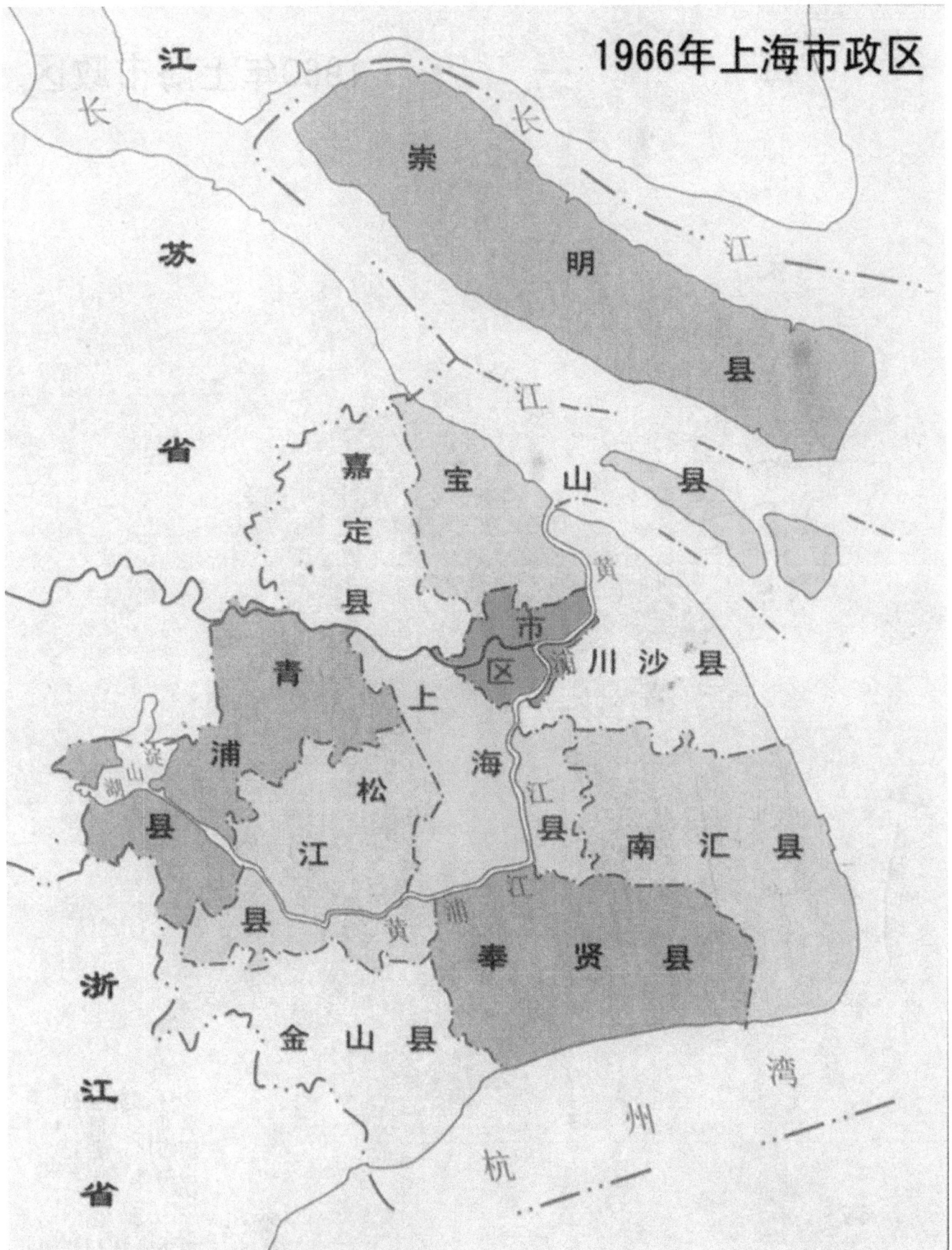

1966年上海市政区

江

长

苏

省

崇

明

长

县

江

江

嘉
定
县

宝

山

县

黄

青

浦

县

上

松

江

县

市
区

上

海

县

黄

浦

江

川沙县

江

南 汇 县

淀
山
湖

奉 贤 县

金 山 县

浙

江

省

杭

州

湾

Shanghai 1966 Districts & Counties Map

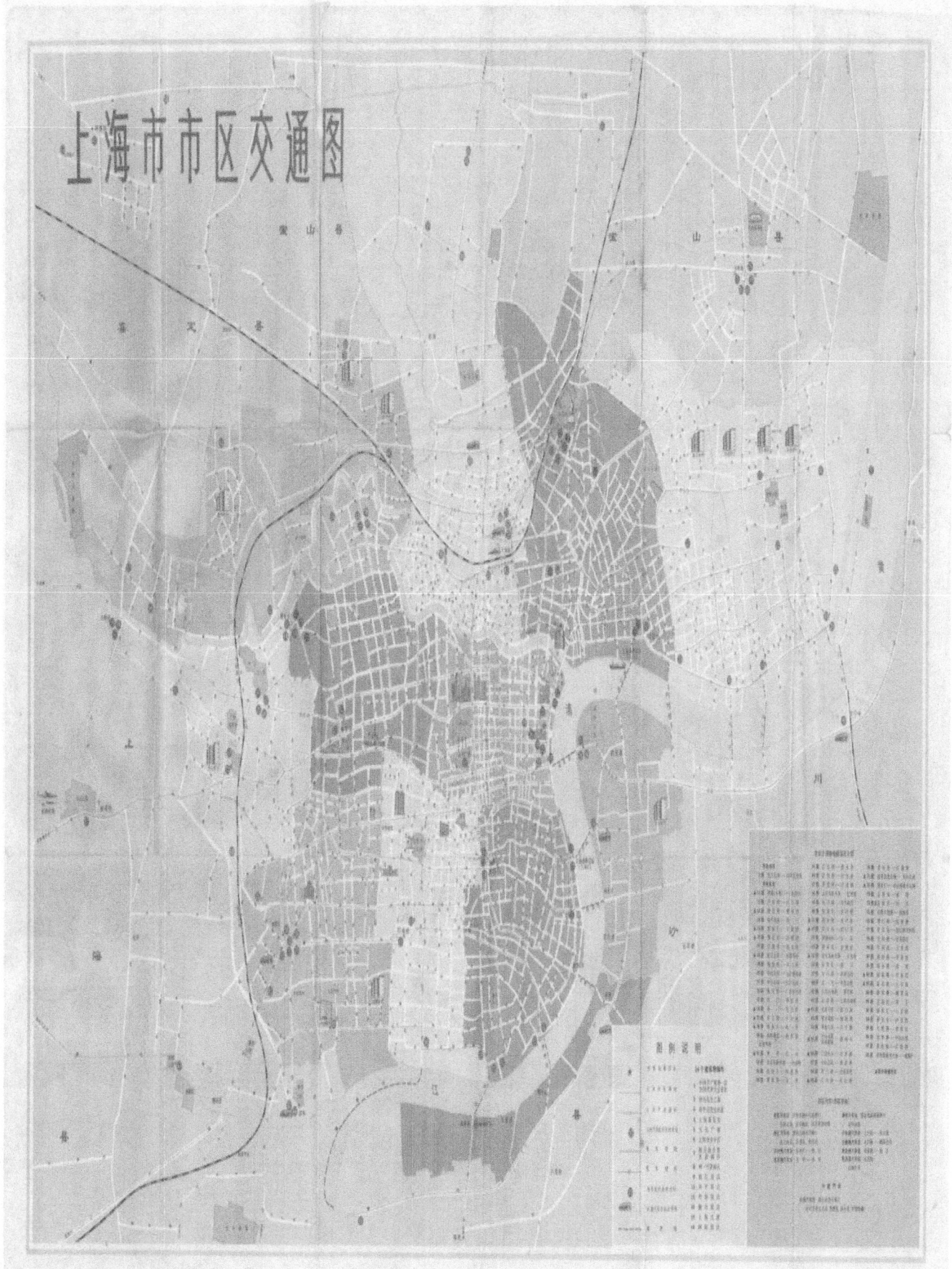

Shanghai 1973 Map

上海市市区交通图

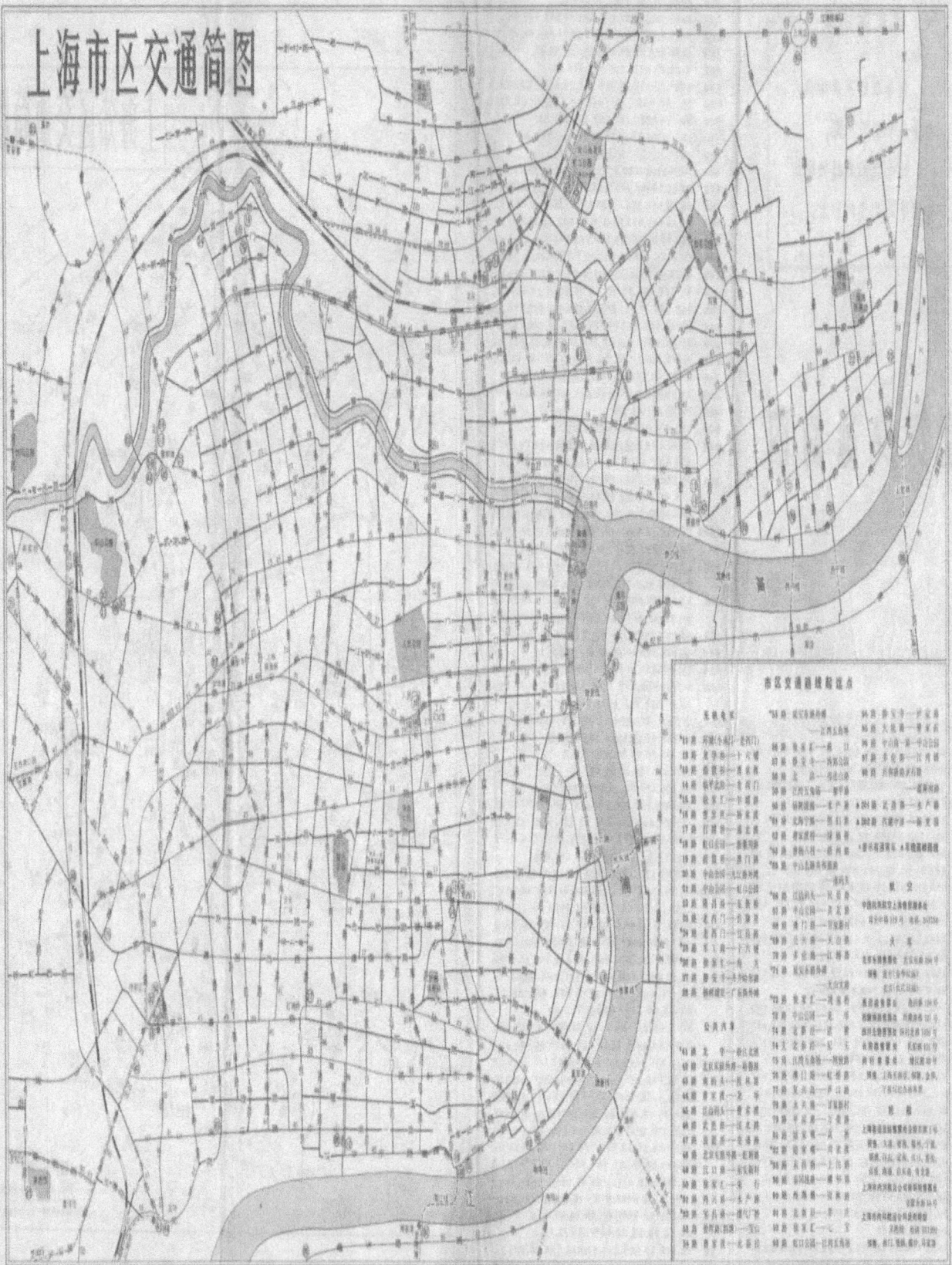

Shanghai 1976 Map

Shanghai 1980 Map

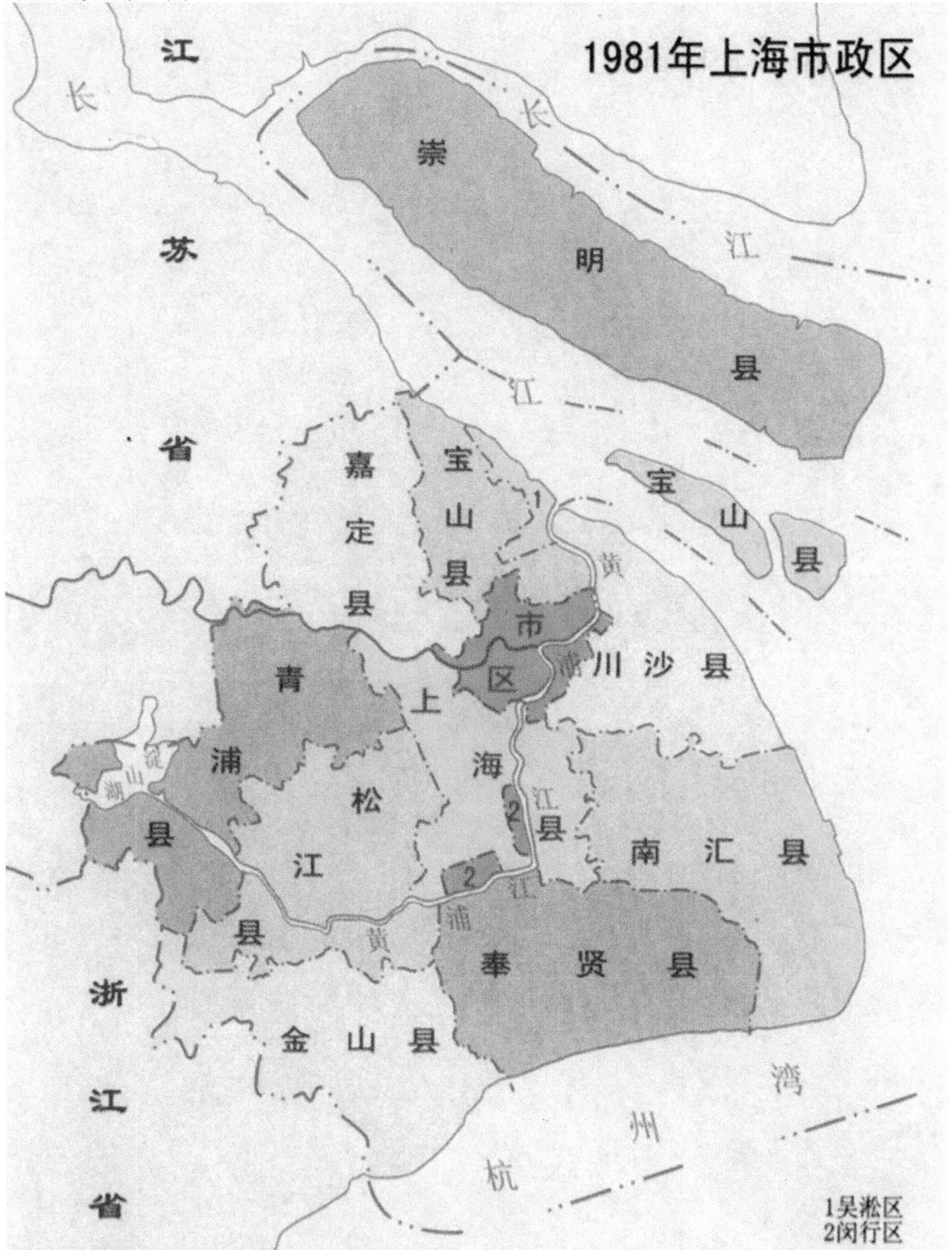

1981年上海市政区

长 江

江 苏 省

崇 明 县

长 江 江

嘉 定 县

宝 山 县

宝 山 县

黄 浦 江

市 区

川 沙 县

青 浦 县

上 海 县

松 江 县

1

2

江 县

2

南 汇 县

淀 山 湖

奉 贤 县

浙 江 省

金 山 县

黄 浦 江

杭 州 湾

1吴淞区
2闵行区

Shanghai 1981 Districts & Counties Map

460

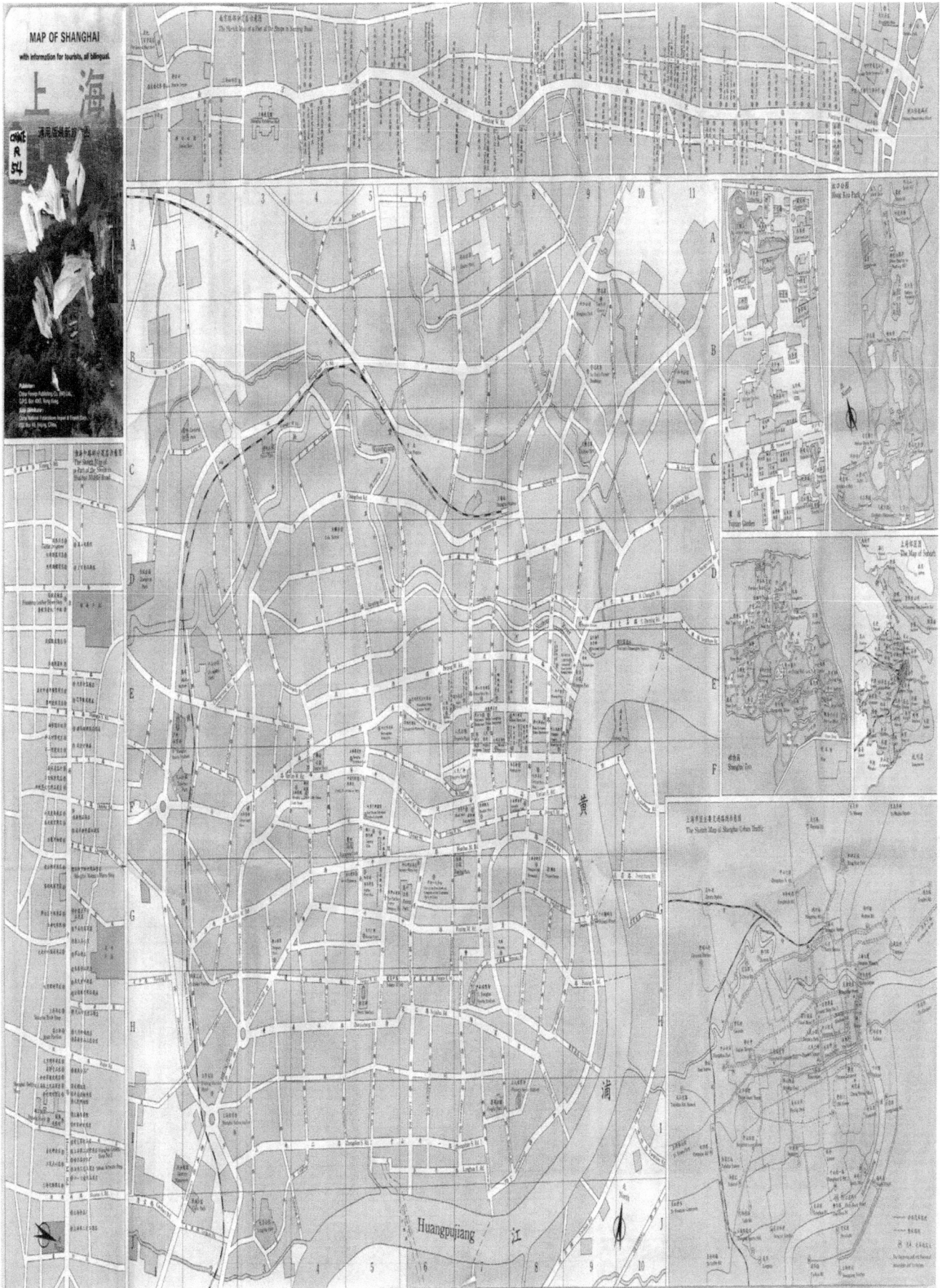

Shanghai 1985 Map

上海市区交通图

宝山

嘉定县

吴淞地区

上

闵行区

县

Shanghai 1992 Map

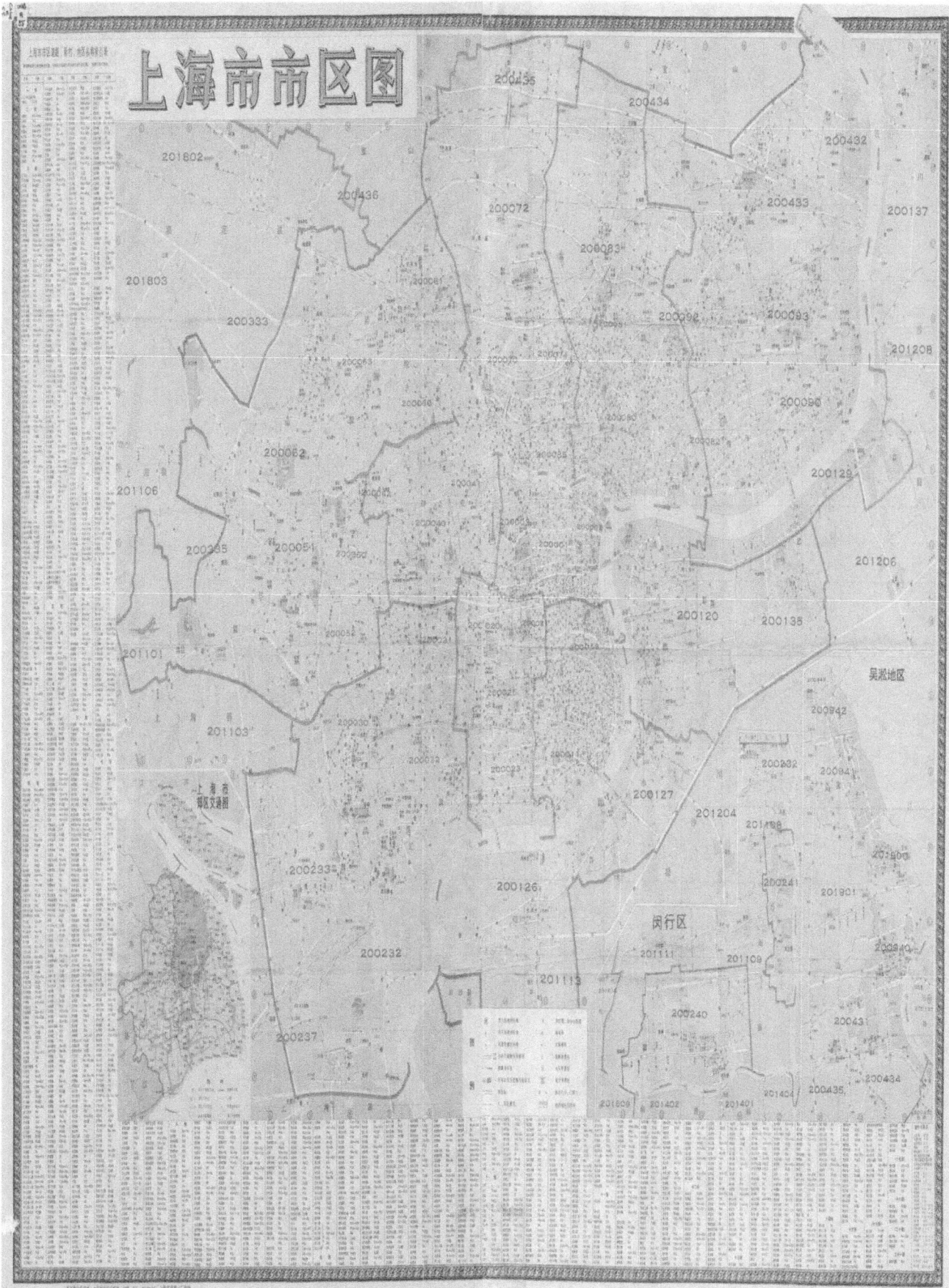

Shanghai 1992 Map

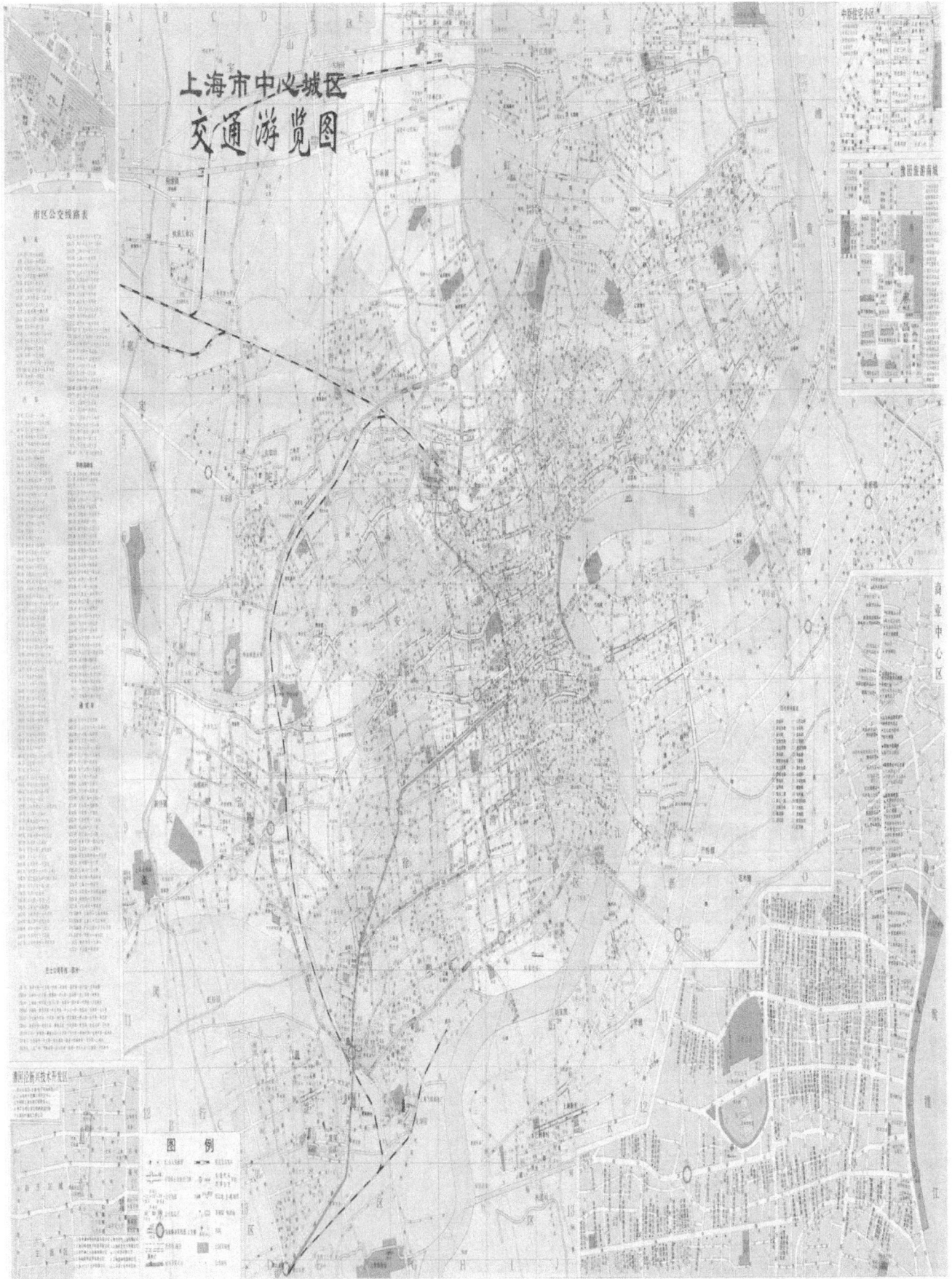

Shanghai 1996 Map

Made in the USA
Monee, IL
02 November 2024